Business Studies

Business Studies

DAVID NEEDHAM

Lecturer in Business Studies
Darlington College of Technology

ROBERT DRANSFIELD

Shell Research Fellow
Centre for Industrial Studies, Grantham

McGRAW-HILL BOOK COMPANY

London · New York · St Louis · San Francisco · Auckland
Bogota · Caracas · Hamburg · Lisbon · Madrid
Mexico · Milan · Montreal · New Delhi · Panama
Paris · San Juan · São Paulo · Singapore
Sydney · Tokyo · Toronto

Published by
McGRAW-HILL Book Company (UK) Limited
Shoppenhangers Road, Maidenhead, Berkshire, SL6 2QL, England
Telephone 0628 23432
Fax 0628 35895

British Library Cataloguing in Publication Data

Needham, David
 Business studies.
 1. Business studies
 I. Title   II. Dransfield, Robert
 658

 ISBN 0-07-707224-3

Library of Congress Cataloging-in-Publication Data

Needham David
Business studies / David Needham, Robert Dransfield.
    p.   cm.

 1. Business.   2. Industrial management.   I. Dransfield, Robert,
 II. Title.   HF5351.N39   1990   90-5893
 650—dc20   CIP

 ISBN 0-07-707224-3

 234 IP 9210

Typeset by Eta Services (Typesetters) Ltd, Beccles, Suffolk
and printed and bound in Malta by Interprint Limited

Contents

Introduction

Business Studies has been written to encourage you to engage actively in business investigations. We have used hundreds of case studies from the real world to give you a feel of how businesses operate in ever-changing circumstances, and to help you to develop problem-solving skills.

Many of the questions ask you to refer in your answers to businesses with which you are familiar. We would strongly recommend that part of your Business Studies 'A' level course is devoted to business placements, which give you the opportunity to experience business activities first hand.

Business investigation is concerned with finding out how businesses operate in a wide setting, i.e. a setting in which the business is only one among a number of groups and bodies with claims to scarce resources. Business investigation is therefore concerned with examining the alternative ways in which a community can allocate scarce resources, particularly focusing on the way in which business units operate. Investigating involves thinking about the questions you need to ask to gain information and to make sense of how things work in the world about you.

Two of the key features of the business world are that:

- business activities are interdependent;
- business operates in a dynamic environment, i.e. one that is constantly changing.

Thinking about business activity is rarely a simple process. You are required to weigh up different situations, to look at the causes and repercussions of changes, and to forecast the future implications of given activities. However, business investigation can be tremendously rewarding because it enables us to raise further questions, to take less for granted, and to build up a framework for analysing relationships concerning the business in its environment.

Each chapter is made up of text and a variety of activities including data response questions, essays, short answer questions and fieldwork suggestions.

Preface

This book has been designed to meet the need of many teachers and students for a comprehensive guide to business studies. Over the last few years we have frequently been asked to recommend such a book, and we have now got round to writing it. Our research has indicated a requirement for an extensive integrated text involving a large number of real case studies. A further requirement is the need for the text to be combined with related examination questions.

The text is an adaptation of materials that have proved popular with our own students. Their comments have been invaluable in helping to structure the final product.

Business studies is an area which is rapidly growing in popularity. It is a subject of great relevance in a period of dynamic change. As we move towards the twenty-first century, we are experiencing a new industrial revolution. New products are invented and old ones can be produced more cheaply. The pace of change is very rapid indeed. It is difficult to quantify with precision, but will clearly be as rapid as at any time since the Industrial Revolution. These are exciting times. It is important for students to be able to understand and critically evaluate the forces behind, and the implications of, these changes. Business studies is very much in at the leading edge.

David Needham
Robert Dransfield

Acknowledgements

We would like to thank:

Cheryl Deans and Sheila Sheehan for helping to process the manuscript.

The exam boards for allowing us to use questions from past papers: The AEB, The University of Oxford Delegacy of Local Examinations, and the University of Cambridge Local Examinations Syndicate.

Magazines and newspapers for furnishing many of the case studies: *Management Accounting*, *Your Business*, *The Economist*, *The Independent*, *Business*, *Grantham Journal*, *Marketing Week*, *Personnel Today*.

Business organizations for providing us with material: National Westminster Bank PLC, ICI, Shell UK, Concept Graphics, Clandrex Ltd, BP.

Other groups and individuals: Understanding Industry, Young Enterprise, HMSO, Department of Trade and Industry, Animal Rights Confederation, John Day, David Hodgson, Mike Kirton, Stuart Graham, Marilyn Elliott and Aubrey Nokes.

We would like to thank the teaching and library staff at Darlington College of Technology and, in particular, Rod Harris and Alistair Clelland. Also, Val Charles and Peter Fletcher for their sterling work in the field of Business and Industrial Education.

1

Background to business studies

What is a business organization?

A business organization is a decision-making unit that sets out to produce a product in the form of a good or service.

There are many views as to how businesses should operate and this gives rise to a wide range of types of business structure. The way in which a business is run will give some form of indication as to the philosophy behind its operation. One business may work on the basis of cooperative decision making and profit sharing, while another is centred around a single decision maker who takes all the profits after subtracting wages and other costs.

In this introductory chapter we have set out to introduce the background against which a business operates. Businesses operate within a framework of interlinking systems. Component parts of these systems interconnect and are dependent on each other in various situations. Relations within business life take many forms ranging from cooperation and sharing to competition and conflict. Businesses are concerned with the use of resources. These resources are limited and therefore there are alternative ways of using them. Different systems and structures exist for resolving the use of resources. The structure of modern economic society is in a continual state of change. Against this background a wide range of different types of business will exist each with its own individual objectives.

Ways of looking at business activity

There are a number of possible ways of exploring business activity which depend on your focus of interest. For example, some researchers may be interested in looking at the role of the individual within a business organization. *Interactionist theory*, for example, is concerned with exploring small-scale human relations and personal transactions within an organization (perhaps looking at the relationship between two or three people).

In contrast, other researchers may have a wider interest in the way that systems operate, as well as ways in which they interact. *Systems theory*, for example, can be employed either to isolate a particular system and study how it operates or to explore the interface between various sub-systems in a larger system. It is useful to be able to isolate a particular system, to explore how the system operates, to analyse and evaluate its operation and to assess performance. For example, it is possible to isolate the production system of a manufacturing company, to review its structure and performance. A key criterion for effective performance will be that the outputs, measured in money terms, are greater than the inputs.

Systems theory can also be used to explore the interrelationship between subsystems such as that between individual businesses within the overall system of the national economy, or between the various systems within a workplace, e.g. the production system and the information system. Systems theory can be used to explore changes in the total system as the relationship between its parts alters.

A number of systems come together in the wealth creation process (see Fig. 1.1).

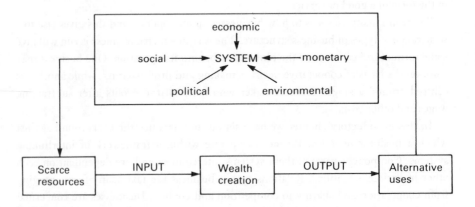

Figure 1.1 The interrelationship between systems in wealth creation.

A distinction can be made in theory between:

- the economic system;
- the social system;
- the monetary system;
- the political system;
- the environmental system.

In the real world, however, it is impossible to distinguish between these systems because of the way in which they interact with each other. Economic, social, monetary, political and environmental considerations cannot be separated in decisions involving both the long and the short period, the quality of life as well as the quantity of production. For example, in the short period it may appear to be beneficial to exploit natural resources as quickly as possible—in the long term the policy makes no sense. It may be cost effective to pump factory waste into our rivers, but by doing so we might spoil the environment in an irreversible way.

Economic system

The economic system is the organization of the economy to allocate scarce resources between alternative end products, and is examined in greater detail later in this chapter.

Social system

The social system is the fabric of ideas, attitudes and behaviour patterns that are involved in human relationships. Social systems can be viewed either on a macro level (i.e. studies of the structure and organization of large-scale systems such as national groupings) or on a micro level (i.e. studies of small-scale groupings such as members of a school class). Larger systems can be seen as being made up of various sub-systems, e.g. a department of teachers within a school, the school system as part of the educational system and so on. The meanings and attitudes which influence social behaviour are formed and influenced by a range of economic, political, religious and other factors.

Monetary system

The monetary system facilitates much of the economic activity that takes place within and between societies. Monetary activity is based around earning, spending, saving and borrowing. Money has been likened to the oil that lubricates the wheels of commerce. Monetary activity involves businesses in a web of relationships involving financial institutions (e.g. banks and building societies), creditors, debtors, customers and suppliers. Many of the attitudes which shape monetary behaviour are formed by economic, political and social considerations. For example people's attitudes to buying on credit have changed in the 1980s. There was a clear trend towards people borrowing and spending more and saving less during the decade.

Political system

The political system is in the form, organization and administration of a state or part of one. It is also the way in which relations with other states are regulated. Political changes have widescale repercussions for business affairs. Major national decision making in this country is carried out by Parliament. Parliament is the forum for the views of Members of Parliament who represent political parties. Parliament has also the powers to create new laws and to modify old ones. The power to create new laws is very much in the hands of the political party that forms the government at any time, subject to getting the majority of Members of Parliament to vote for its policies (new laws also need to be passed by the House of Lords). Decisions at a local level are made by local government where councils are made up of members of political groupings. Pressure groups also play a significant part in British politics in their attempts to influence decision-making processes. The ideas and beliefs that shape political decision making are inevitably tied up with economic, social environmental, religious and other considerations. Businesses operate against a backcloth of constantly changing rules. A change in any one of these rules can have widespread implications for business life. For example, you should consider who would be affected and how they would be affected in the following examples: the government's decision to extend public house opening hours; the government's decision to make it easier for retailers to sell spectacles; and the government's decision to introduce membership schemes at football clubs.

Environmental system

Ecology, or the environmental system, is the relationship between living things and their environment. Over the years a balance is created in the natural environment. However, rapid changes created by human development can threaten to upset this balance. For example, the Russians have toyed for a number of years with the idea of reversing the course of two of their major north flowing rivers so that they flow south. However, the policy decision has never come into effect because of the cost implications and because of environmental uncertainty over the destruction of plant and animal life as well as the unpredictable effect on climate as a result of a warming of the oceans. Other major environmental concerns have been about the creation of acid rain and the destruction of the earth's protective ozone layer. The survival and growth of industrial society require a careful balance between industrial and ecological systems. Major decisions concerning the environment require careful collaboration between individuals, businesses and governments on an international scale. The ecological system is very much a prey to the social, political and economic systems. For example, substantial social changes will be required to achieve a major reduction in emissions of reactive hydrocarbons from the very wide range of sources involved.

Conflict theory is an alternative way of looking at the role of organizations in society. Conflict theorists see society as being based on fundamental differences of interest. At any one time power will be vested in certain individuals, institutions and groups. These groups will develop mechanisms for reinforcing their power. The dominant ideology (belief system) of a society will tend to reflect the views and interests of the ruling class. However, within a society there will develop the seeds and manifestations of change. Those individuals and groups with less power and influence, and with a disproportionately small share of the good things that society offers, will seek change—they may seek a change in the rules, the distribution of income and wealth, and the prevailing dominant ideology. Society is thus primarily based on conflict. Conflict theorists will thus be concerned with observing, analysing and making people aware of these fundamental contradictions. For example, modern-day Marxists would regard giant corporations and multinational companies as powerful capitalist groupings which represent the interests of the ruling classes.

Consensus or conflict?

Societies consist of individuals, groups and organizations that are mutually inter-dependent. The economic system is built up of an unlimited number of individual decisions. Each decision will affect, and be affected by, many other individual decisions—decisions we all make every day. For example, when a British firm decides to import coal from Nigeria, this will create extra revenue for a Nigerian mining company. The mine might then decide to employ extra labour and buy new machinery. The extra miners taken on in Nigeria will then have more money which they might decide to spend in local shops. Some of the goods they buy will be made in Nigeria while others will be imports. These buying decisions will then have further effects on production decisions and so the process continues. At the same time the original decision of the British company to buy Nigerian coal also involved the decision *not* to purchase other forms of fuel. Alternative suppliers therefore lost a potential customer and this will have affected their decisions whether or not to take on labour, and whether or not to invest in new machinery.

In a society certain values will be shared by all (or nearly all) of the members of that society. Other values will be exclusive to particular groups within a society. For example, most people would share the belief that a prosperous society is a good thing. However, there would be considerable disagreement as to how prosperity should be achieved. There would even be disagreement as to what the word 'prosperity' means. The life of a society is therefore the tapestry based upon conflict and consensus. Some thinkers believe that conflict is the predominant feature. They see society as involving fundamental conflicts of interest between those groups that own the means of production (e.g. those with sizeable shareholdings in business), and other groups made up of individuals who are primarily wage employees. In contrast, other thinkers see society as being fundamentally based on consensus, in which individuals have a shared self-interest and a mutual aim of contributing to the growth of economic society.

In studying business life you will find that the issues of conflict and consensus are never far from the surface.

The pattern of the book

The aim of this book is to introduce an enquiry-based approach to business studies in a modern setting. The study of business life can only be done against a wider background of interdependence and interrelationships. In the modern world no individual or group can make decisions that are not affected by a wide range of outside factors. In the United Kingdom we are particularly aware of how other groups and individuals influence our everyday life. We are still very much a trading nation and as such are heavily dependent on the world market. When world prices rise for products such as oil, copper, other raw materials and foodstuffs we soon feel the effect and the same applies to a fall in prices. A favourite topic of conversation for people in this country is the weather, not far behind come subjects such as the exchange rate of the pound against other countries, the state of Britain's trade, and interest rates—all of which are heavily influenced by our relationships with the rest of the world.

Business life takes place against a wide setting and when we look at individual businesses we will have to focus them against the following:

- The international setting
- The national setting
- The local setting
- The influence of government
- The influence of competitors
- The influence of buyers
- The influence of suppliers
- The influence of the local community and environment
- Other influences

Needs and wants

Natural and man-made products are a basic requirement for human survival. At the base line of survival people require basic necessities including items of food, shelter and clothing. However, it would be impossible to devise a generally accepted definition of a absolute standard of level of provision of goods and services that would meet every individual's needs. Needs vary according to a person's age, physical environment, health and many other factors.

At different times it has been argued that the old need less than the young, the low-born less than the high-born, the mentally ill less than the sane, the healthy less than the sick, the clerk less than the coalminer and so on.

Perceptions of needs also seem to alter over time. For example, it is likely that many of the standards which are 'required' for survival by many modern Western citizens would have been regarded as extravagant luxuries in the not so distant past including: our current levels of heating in winter, the use of hot water, lighting, soap and the variety of foodstuffs.

A distinction is usually made between *needs* and *wants*. Our needs make up our survival kit while our wants are the desires we have for needs together with all our additional requirements. Most people strive for better conditions for themselves, their family, and frequently also their community, their nation and the whole world. People want better clothing, better living conditions, improved transport and many other products. Our wants are infinite. This is just as true for the relatively wealthy as it is for the poor.

In practice it is impossible to draw the line at which absolute needs are met. Different measures have been produced at different times to define minimum levels of well-being below which people can be said to be living in poverty. Such measures produce an absolute standard which can be called the 'poverty line'. For example, in January 1989 the city council in Manchester published a report which found that one-

Figure 1.2 Residents on some housing estates in Manchester are caught in a poverty trap caused principally by unemployment, but intensified by urban deprivation. (*Source of photograph*: David Rose, *The Independent*, 9 January 1989.)

third of Manchester's 17 000 households were living in poverty. The researchers defined poverty according to people's ability to buy 16 goods and services which are generally accepted as basic necessities of life. Those who were unable to afford three or more of these items, such as beds for everyone in the household, a warm water-proof coat, carpets in the living room and meat or fish every other day, were considered poor.

Another way of looking at poverty is to regard it in relative rather than absolute terms. A relative definition relates the living standards of the poor to the standards which dominate the society in which they live. For example, the poor might be defined as those whose incomes fall below, say, half the average income. Relative poverty is regarded to be a real problem in modern society in which people are all too aware of the lifestyle enjoyed by others and in which advertising puts on public display a range of commodities which it associates with 'modern lifestyles'. However, relative definitions of poverty are also riddled with problems. For example, to adopt a strictly relative definition of poverty is to imply that the poor in Bangladesh are no worse off than the poor in Britain, which is clearly absurd.

Ideally a definition of poverty should incorporate both relative and absolute concepts. However, no generally agreed definition has been found.

Scarce resources

In any society resources will be scarce relative to the number of uses to which they could be put. A resource is a means of support. A resource from the point of view of business studies can be regarded as any feature of our environment that helps to support our well-being.

There are two main types of resources:

1. Physical or natural resources—such as oil, climate, water, minerals, forests and fisheries.
2. Human resources—people and their various skills.

If we were to take stock of the world's existing bundle of resources we would find that there are severe limitations to its ability to meet our infinite wants.

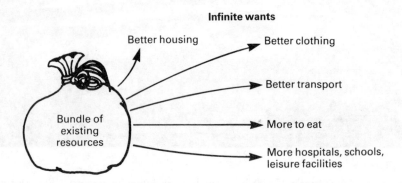

Figure 1.3 Our wants are infinite but the resources available to meet them are limited.

Scarce resources can be broken down into four key ingredients: land, labour, capital and enterprise. Land includes all natural resources; labour includes all physical and mental effort; capital includes machinery and other items that go into further production; and enterprise is the art of combining the other three factors in the production process. These four production resources are termed the factors of production.

Scarcity can be seen as resulting from the lack of availability in resources, from people's insatiable wants, or from a combination of the two (see Fig. 1.3). People have different views about how scarcity arises. Mahatma Gandhi said 'the earth has enough for every man's need but not for every man's greed'.

A society's strategies for using resources to produce finished products should consider long-term as well as short-term objectives. Some resources such as mineral reserves cannot be replaced. Once they are finished, new reserves cannot be created. At the same time certain activities such as the creation of acid rain have been shown to destroy parts of the environment. Acid rain is an unwanted result of the emission of fumes into the atmosphere in the production of energy and other manufacturing processes. The chemicals created by this process have helped to destroy important timber, recreation and scenic resources in Europe.

Opportunity cost

Businesses use up resources which are scarce. If society had all the land, labour, raw materials and other resources that it needed to make all the goods that people could possibly want, then we could produce goods without making sacrifices. However, resources are scarce and therefore when we produce an item we are preventing the resources which we use to make it from going to produce something else. This is a major problem for any society. The real cost of using resources for a particular purpose is the next best use to which they can be put.

We use the term opportunity cost to describe the next best alternative that is given up in carrying out any particular activity. When referring to opportunity cost we need to be clear about to whom these costs are related. For example, if a new road is built the costs of this activity will be quite different for the person whose house has to be knocked down to build the road compared with the person whose journey to work is shortened by the road or the firm that builds the road, and the taxpayer who contributes to financing the road.

Opportunity cost can be applied in all decision-making situations. The small child with only 20p to spend hesitates between a chocolate bar and a packet of sweets; the opportunity cost to the individual of the chocolate bar that is chosen is the packet of sweets that is sacrificed. The same idea applies to production. A farmer decides to plant rape seed rather than sugar beet; the opportunity cost of the rape is the sugar beet he might have grown instead. The opportunity cost of a country spending a high proportion of income on armaments is the lower standard of living that would be possible if resources were channelled instead into producing other types of goods.

Case Study—Alternative uses for scarce resources

Study the following extract.

> The swords, we are told, are being beaten into ploughshares. Seven weeks after Mikhail Gorbachev's historic address to the United Nations, announcing a cut of 500 000 men, or 10 per cent in the Soviet army, the Soviet Union claims to have embarked upon the transfer of spending from military to civilian purposes, without which economic perestroika will remain just the words of its leader's countless speeches.
>
> Over 200 military design offices are turning their hand to farm equipment. Between now and 1995, defence plants are supposed to supply 17.5 billion roubles (£17.5bn) of food processing goods to the civilian economy, even tin cans and machines to make ice cream. The military sector is already starting to produce fridges, television sets and vacuum cleaners.
>
> (*Source: The Independent*, January 1989)

Questions
1. What does the article suggest is the opportunity cost to the Soviet economy of producing the consumer goods indicated?
2. Who will benefit from this alternative use of scarce resources? In each case state how they will benefit.
3. Who will lose out from this change in the use of scarce resources? How will they lose out?

4.   Is it possible to evaluate whether the Soviety economy as a whole would be better off as a result of this change? What considerations would you have to bear in mind in attempting to answer this question?

Interdependence

Interdependence is one of the basic facts of business life. Business decision making is thus part of a complex system of dynamic interrelationships. This means that the internal structure and functioning of an enterprise and the environment in which it exists will be in a continual state of flux. Some changes may be almost imperceptible, such as a gradual build-up of sales orders, while others, such as the arrival of a new managing director or the creation of the single market in the European Community in 1992 with the new opportunities for international sales coupled with the threat of increased competition, can have a dramatic impact.

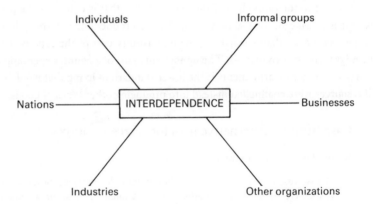

Figure 1.4 The web of interdependence.

An appreciation of the importance of interdependence is vital for effective business understanding (see Fig. 1.4). Enterprise involves not only the ability to come up with new ideas and to put them into practice, but also an awareness of changing business conditions, and the ability to respond with effective and positive measures in a changing climate.

The following examples illustrate some of the features of interdependence. The first example illustrates the interdependence between processes and employees in the production of chicken nuggets (see Fig. 1.5). The second example illustrates geographical interdependence in the production of a modern motor car (see Fig. 1.6).

Whole chickens arrive at the factory from the farms where the chickens have been reared. The chickens have already had their feathers plucked. In the factory the chickens are sliced into the required segments: drumsticks, wings and breasts. These segments will then either be frozen and stored for future use, or be passed along a conveyor belt to the mixing room where they will be prepared for their conversion to nuggets. The pieces of chicken will then be converted to individual nuggets. Each

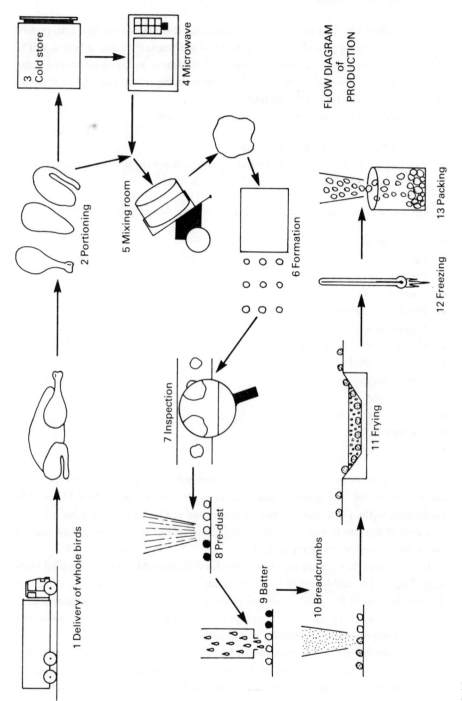

FLOW DIAGRAM of PRODUCTION

1 Delivery of whole birds

2 Portioning

3 Cold store

4 Microwave

5 Mixing room

6 Formation

7 Inspection

8 Pre-dust

9 Batter

10 Breadcrumbs

11 Frying

12 Freezing

13 Packing

Figure 1.5 Interdependent processes in producing chicken nuggets.

piece of chicken will then be inspected to check that it contains the correct proportion of meat before being passed to the next stage of the production line where it will be dusted with flour. Batter will then be added to the nuggets, followed by breadcrumbs. The nuggets will now pass along to the fryer before being frozen and packed ready for storage and final delivery to the retailer.

The production of chicken nuggets will have involved:

- The farmers who reared the chickens
- The nugget manufacturer who processed and transported the chicken bits
- The retailer who sells the goods to the manufacturers

The nugget manufacturer employs a range of specialist employees:

- Management
- Cleaners
- Packers
- Lorry drivers
- Process operatives
- Supervisors
- Quality control inspectors
- Secretarial staff
- Wages clerks
- Salespeople
- Electricians
- Canteen staff
- etc.

If we look at the construction of a modern technological product such as the motor car we can see the way that specialization takes place on an international level. The production of the Ford Sierra is now concentrated at Genk in Belgium but the construction of the component parts takes place throughout the European Community and in the United States (see Fig. 1.6).

Bringing together a range of components for final assembly requires detailed planning. The final assembler (in this case the plant at Genk) is very much dependent on the effectiveness of the production processes and delivery from the component suppliers. The jobs of thousands of employees and the satisfaction of end consumers depend on international cooperation and shared skills.

One of the major themes that you will be able to see running through this book is that of interdependence. This is particularly true in the area of business decision making. Some of the important decisions made by firms in the 1990s are likely to include:

- How will we be able to make sure that we can get an adequate supply of labour, when most other firms are competing for a dwindling number of school leavers?

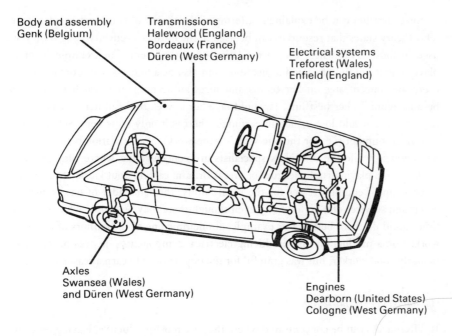

Body and assembly
Genk (Belgium)

Transmissions
Halewood (England)
Bordeaux (France)
Düren (West Germany)

Electrical systems
Treforest (Wales)
Enfield (England)

Axles
Swansea (Wales)
and Düren (West Germany)

Engines
Dearborn (United States)
Cologne (West Germany)

Figure 1.6 International interdependence in constructing a Ford Sierra.

- How can we make sure that we have the technology required to make us competitive in a rapidly changing market?
- How can we respond to changes in patterns of demand and supply as we open up frontiers in the European Community to freer trade?
- How can we react to variations in international prices for basic commodities, raw materials and fuels?
- How effective is our location in the light of the European Tunnel link?

The theory of specialization

Specialization is fundamental to modern industrial societies. It takes place at a number of levels:

- The division of labour
- Specialization of equipment
- Specialization by plant
- Specialization by firms
- Specialization by industry
- Specialization by region (including national specialization)

We have only to count up the large number of different workers, areas and types of plant and equipment that have contributed to the goods and services consumed every day by a typical family to realize how completely we depend on other people, on specialization, to satisfy our wants.

Specialization can be explained in terms of the theory of comparative advantage. This theory states that resources can be used in the most cost-effective way if they are used in those areas where they are relatively most efficient. For example, a tennis player might not only be good at her sport but also be a first-class accountant. However, she concentrates on her tennis and hires an accountant to do her bookwork because tennis is her best line. It would take her a week to do all her paperwork. In this time she would lose £5000 in earnings whereas it only costs her £800 a year to hire an accountant (i.e. for the one week's paperwork). Specialization benefits everyone because while the first-class specialists are concentrating where they are most talented, e.g. playing rugby league for Great Britain, carrying out kidney transplants, or designing wedding dresses for the royal family, the remainder of us can provide goods and services of a high quality even though there may be people who, given the time, could do them better. For example, at one time one of the authors of this book worked on a production line producing electrical components—he was never a particularly good worker, but was grateful for the opportunity to earn a reasonable wage.

Advantages of specialization

1. Resources can be concentrated where they are most productive, leaving other resources to concentrate elsewhere.
2. Factors of production become more effective if they concentrate on a set task. For example, the worker that specializes on the same task becomes faster and more accurate.
3. Specialization makes it possible for a larger output to be produced at lower unit costs.
4. Concentrations of specialists can lead to an increased sharing of skills and experience. This is as true for individuals as it is for the growth of a number of specialist companies in a particular region (who are able to pool resources to organize combined training courses for employees).
5. Specialization makes possible a higher standard of living. If individuals, groups and nations concentrate on their talents and trade openly then everyone should be better off. Surplus output can always be used to produce investment goods such as machinery which can lead to further increases in output.
6. Specialization means that one job can be done well rather than a number of jobs done badly.

Disadvantages of specialization

1. Specialization can lead to a boring lack of variety. If people repeat the same task over and over again they may find work has little meaning for them. If a particular region specializes in a narrow range of industries, choice of career and job opportunities may be felt by some to be too limited.
2. Specialization can present a problem when one stage of production is dependent

on the previous stage. If there are hold-ups and delays in the flow of production this can be very frustrating. It can also be very annoying if another specialist fails to deliver goods for the quality and price that you expect.

3. Narrow specialism can make it difficult for factors of production to respond to change. Markets are continually in a dynamic state of change. This means that old skills and old industries will sometimes have to give way to new ones. This may be difficult when an individual, a group of workers, or a whole region have become set in their ways.

4. Generalism is often more useful than narrow specialism. When flexibility is required—for example to ascertain quickly whether a business can meet a new order—it sometimes helps to have someone who can make a general audit of the various parts of the company to devise an overall strategy, rather than narrow specialists who are not prepared to look outside their own department.

Case Study—The division of labour in an eighteenth-century pin factory

Perhaps the most famous observation of the process of the division of labour was that done by Adam Smith in a pin factory and quoted in *The Wealth of Nations*.

> A workman not educated to this business (which the division of labour has rendered a distinct trade), nor acquainted with the use of the machinery employed in it (to the invention of which the same division of labour has probably given occasion), could scarce, perhaps, with his utmost industry, make one pin in a day, and certainly could not make twenty. But in the way in which this business is now carried on, not only the whole work in a peculiar trade, but it is divided into a number of branches, of which the greater part are likewise peculiar trades. One man draws out the wire, another straights it, a third cuts it, a fourth points it, a fifth grinds it at the top for receiving the head; to make the head requires two or three distinct operations; to put it on is a peculiar business, to whiten the pins is another; it is even a trade by itself to put them into the paper; and the important business of making a pin is, in this manner, divided into about eight distinct operations, which, in some manufactories, are all performed by distinct hands, though in others the same man will sometimes perform two or three of them. I have seen a small factory of this kind where ten men only were employed, and where some of them consequently performed two or three distinct operations. But though they were very poor, and therefore but indifferently accommodated with the necessary machinery, they could when they exerted themselves, make among them about twelve pounds of pins in a day. There are in a pound upwards of four thousand pins of middling size. Those ten persons, therefore, could make among them upwards of forty-eight thousand pins in a day. Each person, therefore, making a tenth part of forty-eight thousand pins, might be considered as making four thousand eight hundred pins a day. But if they had all wrought separately and independently, and without any of them having been educated to this particular business, they certainly could not each of them have made twenty, perhaps not one pin in a day; that is, certainly not the two hundred and fortieth,

perhaps not the four thousand eight hundredth part of what they are at present capable of performing, in consequence of a proper division and combination of their different operations.

(*Source*: Adam Smith, *The Wealth of Nations*.)

Questions

1. Why are pins produced in large quantities? (Give at least four different reasons.)
2. What factors prohibit small-scale pin manufacture?
3. Why is it easy to use a process of division of labour in pin manufacture?
4. What problems might arise as a result of the division of labour in pin manufacture?
5. Adam Smith explained that in some factories distinct operations would be performed by distinct hands while in other factories the same employee could carry out two or three operations. How would you account for this difference?
6. What modern industries operate in a similar fashion to Adam Smith's pin factories? Do these industries have anything in common?
7. Using your own personal observation of manufacturing plant employing a high level of specialization what advantages and disadvantages immediately come to light? How could the difficulties you have noted be overcome?

Money

Money is anything which is generally accepted as a means of making a payment in a given area at a given time. We hear for example of cowrie shells being used as currency on South Sea Islands, and of the use of cigarettes as a means of exchange in the trenches during the First World War.

Advantages of using money

1. It makes specialization possible. For example, there is no need for a vet to build her own house, grow her own food and make her own clothes. Instead she can concentrate on her practice because the money she earns can easily be exchanged for goods and services. In addition, she is able to save some of her money to make future purchases.
2. Money is often regarded as the most effective means of facilitating the process of satisfying consumer wants. Every consumer has his or her own set of preferences for goods and services. Using money as a measure of value makes it possible for thousands of different consumers to decide how they will best spend their disposable income.

3. Money makes it possible to create loans. Borrowers are able to use money to buy goods and services when they want them instead of having to save up to make a cash payment. Credit is particularly important to businesses and many business transactions are carried out on this basis.

Types of economic system

All societies must develop a system for dealing with three interrelated problems:

1. What will be produced?
2. How will it be produced?
3. For whom will it be produced?

We can illustrate the wide differences in possible systems by looking at two imaginary island communities which are dependent on fishing and farming.

We shall call these two communities Sealand and Skyland. In Sealand all decisions are made by a small group of chieftains. The chieftains decide who will do the fishing and who will do the farming. They decide how many hours are put into each activity and how equipment will be made (e.g. the fishing boats, and agricultural implements). They have also decided that everyone will receive an equal share of the produce, except for the chieftains who will have a double portion of everything.

In Skyland, there is no organizing group. Individuals are left to their own devices. They decide individually what to make and trade or store their surpluses. They decide how to produce their equipment, and how long to spend at particular activities. They consume the bulk of their own produce, except for what they can exchange.

Make a list of eight strengths and eight weaknesses of each of the economic systems described. Devise a third system which you would regard as preferable to those of Sealand and Skyland. In what ways do you think that your system is preferable? Why might other people disagree with you? What would be the reasoning behind their beliefs?

In the past the basic economic problems were solved by custom and tradition. For example, the way that crops were grown and shared out was decided by folk tradition. In many parts of the world traditional economies are giving way to three major systems:

1. The planned system
2. The free market system
3. The mixed system

Within these three basic models there will be a wide range of variations and differences.

Planned systems

Planning involves some form of official coordination of activities. Planning can take place at either a local or a centralized level. Planning authorities will be responsible in some way for the creation of targets, systems and procedures.

The process of organized planning is most commonly associated with countries in the Socialist bloc. It is worth examining some of the common features associated with socialist economies. However, it must be stressed that in recent years many socialist economies have experienced substantial phases of economic reform such as 'Perestroika' in the Soviet Union. Such changes have involved the relaxation of price controls, control from the centre and greater freedom to set up private enterprise.

In the customary division of the world into three parts—the West, the Socialist bloc and the Third World—the socialist countries (including the Soviet Union, Albania, Campuchea, North Korea, Cuba, Ethiopia, etc.) represent over one-third of the world's population and industrial output. Although there are wide differences in the economic organization of these socialist countries and their respective stages of development, there are also a number of important similarities:

1. The means of production are publicly owned. This takes the form of state, collective or cooperative ownership. Although the means of production are collectively owned, decisions about their use can be made by a variety of means—ranging from collective decision making, to decision making by a small committee of people.
2. Centralized planning and control of strategies to increase the quantity and/or quality of overall output.
3. The existence of a market for consumption goods (although consumers will not necessarily have the freedom to spend money in the pattern that they would freely choose) and for labour. A large proportion of consumer goods will be exchanged in the market, with wages being paid and transactions taking place using some form of money.
4. Prices for all goods sold by the state are decided by planning authorities. Prices will not be able to change spontaneously.
5. Nearly all decisions related to capital formation will be made and controlled by planning authorities. Capital formation is the production of goods and equipment which go into further production such as factory machinery.

The key feature of a planned economy is that planning committees are appointed to decide what will be produced, how it will be produced and how products will be distributed.

In a centrally planned system many of the decisions are made by a central planning organization. Smaller groups such as factories and other business units submit their plans to a local committee. The local plans are then fed back for approval at the centre. The central organization might then decide which resources will be made available to each local area, which in turn allocates resources to each factory, farm or other productive unit.

Productive units are often set production targets, and are then given a set quantity of resources and a time constraint to meet set targets.

Advantages of a planned economy

1. Effective long-term strategies can be developed taking into account the needs of the total system.
2. Planning can be carried out according to the collective needs and wants of each of the individual parts of a system.
3. Duplication of resources can be cut out.
4. Resources and products can be shared out more equitably according to the dominant value system prevailing in that society.
5. Planning decisions can be shaped into a consistent pattern.
6. The system can be shaped in such a way as to reflect the social and political wishes of a collective of people.

Disadvantages of a planned economy

1. Heavy handed planning and control may stifle individual enterprise.
2. The process of planning itself uses up scarce resources for administration and supervision.
3. The absence of the profit motive removes the spur to individual effort and enterprise. It is argued by some that people are more inclined to work harder and to make personal sacrifices if they can profit from doing so.
4. In command economies the process of communication between consumers and producers can become distorted so that the goods which are produced fall far short of consumer requirements. If planning decisions are made well in advance of consumption decisions, then by the time goods appear in the marketplace tastes and fashions may have changed.
5. In command economies where price controls are established unofficial black markets may develop leading to bribery and corruption.

The free market system

In a free market the decisions about what, how and for whom are made by consumers and producers; the government does not intervene. Consumers in effect 'vote' for a certain pattern of output by the way in which they distribute their spending between the alternatives on offer. How much they are prepared to pay is thus a reflection of the strength of consumer preferences. (Some people think that it does not always work quite like this; they think that producers often decide what they would like to make and then persuade consumers to follow their wishes through advertising.) If a product sells well firms will be inclined to produce it. The amount the producers offer for sale will depend on their production costs. The prices that they charge will thus reflect the relative scarcity of the various resources that they need in order to produce for the market. If a product sells well firms will be inclined to produce it, but if no one buys the product firms will stop making it, since under the market system firms will seek to make profits from the goods they sell. Producers are forced to pay attention to the wishes of consumers in order to survive.

The interests of consumers and producers conflict. Consumers want low prices while producers would like prices to be high. The market serves to strike a balance, with prices just settling at those levels that match the strength of consumer preferences with the scarcity of resources. When prices change this acts as a signal for the pattern of production and consumption to alter. For example, when a new book becomes popular, the publishers are able to push its price up and put more resources into producing more copies; while for a book which is going out of fashion, the publishers may be forced to lower its price, put fewer resources into its production and eventually take it out of circulation.

Advantages of the free market system

1. Production reflects the wishes of the consumer.
2. The system is flexible in the way that it responds to different conditions of demand and supply.
3. Individuals have greater freedom to make their own demand and supply decisions.
4. Scarce resources do not have to be wasted on administering and running (planning) the system.
5. It is argued that the free market will lead to larger, better quality outputs at lower unit costs.

Disadvantages of the free market system

1. The free market system does not guarantee everyone what many would regard to be the minimum acceptable standard of living in a healthy society. When it is freely operating, the price mechanism fails to provide a 'safety net' for citizens less able to compete, e.g. the sick and the elderly.
2. There are some goods which by their very nature include elements of what is known as 'non-excludability'. For example, all ships using a particular seaway benefit from its lighthouse; all citizens could be seen to benefit from a national system of defence. If we take the example of bridges in central London, it is immediately apparent why the price system would be ineffective as a means of provision. If people were made to pay to go over these bridges, the traffic system would rapidly snarl up. However, it is worth bearing in mind that when road traffic was less common many toll bridges were used in this country. Indeed, toll bridges are still operated in various parts of the country.
3. The free market can lead to great inequalities. Those with the means to purchase large quantities of goods can use large block votes of money to ensure that the goods and services they want are produced (hence taking away resources from other products). One way of looking at the opportunity cost to society of produ-

cing luxury goods (speedboats, expensive clothes, etc.) is to consider the inability of society to meet the needs of the less fortunate.

4. Resources may not be able to move as freely as a pure market theory would suggest. Human resources in particular may be resistant to move to new areas and away from their established roots. People may be reluctant to learn new skills which offer high pay packets if they feel that the job does not meet their needs for such factors as self-respect/pride in the job or the ability to work at their own pace.

5. Many buying decisions are made by consumers with imperfect knowledge of the market. Producers frequently change the details of their products including prices, shapes, sizes and packaging. This makes it very difficult for consumers to weigh up alternative purchases and many buying decisions may be based on impressions rather than hard evidence. For example a recent survey conducted by the authors revealed that out of a sample of 400 shoppers fewer than 10 per cent of them could remember the prices of five randomly selected commonly used items in their shopping basket.

6. In a free market many resources can be wasted through the high failure rate of new businesses. A lot of time and money are spent on setting up a new business. When a new business closes down after a few months many of its resources may end up as little more than scrap.

The mixed economy

In the real world no economy relies exclusively on the free market, nor can we find examples of purely planned economies. A mixed economy combines elements of both the free market and planning systems. Some decisions are made solely through the private sector while other decisions are made by the government. The United Kingdom is a good example of a mixed economy; some parts of industry are owned and

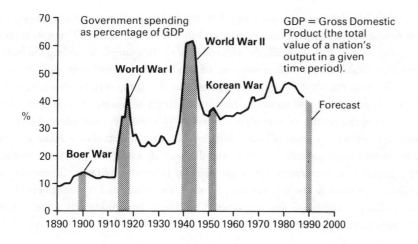

Figure 1.7 Changes in government spending as a percentage of national expenditure. (*Source*: HM Treasury.)

operated by the government but large chunks of the business world remain in private hands. The public sector is that part of the economy that is government owned. The private sector is that part of the economy that is owned by private citizens.

Throughout much of the twentieth century government spending in the United Kingdom has made up a significant percentage of all spending (see Fig. 1.7). However, it is noticeable that during the 1980s significant steps have been taken by the Conservative Government to reduce the relative size of government spending. A major aim of the government since coming into office in May 1979 has been the restoration of market forces throughout the economy.

In a mixed economy, one of the central issues of debate will be about the nature of the mix between private and public sectors.

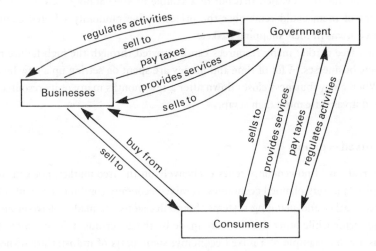

Figure 1.8 Links between businesses, consumers and government.

Figure 1.8 illustrates the ways in which the activities of government, consumers and businesses are inextricably intertwined in a mixed economy. The government regulates the activities of producers and consumers, for example by setting out health and safety standards for the production of goods and by stipulating legal requirements limiting the ways in which consumers can buy using hire purchase. Government produces goods and services which it sells direct to businesses and consumers, for example the selling of consultancy services to exporters, and the provision of goods and services by nationalized industries. The government also provides services to businesses and consumers such as the disposal of waste, the provision of street lighting and repairs to roads, which are paid for indirectly by taxes. Businesses sell goods and services to the government, to other businesses and to consumers. Businesses also pay local and national taxes. Consumers buy goods and services from government and from businesses.

Case Study—Altering an economic system

Study the article in Fig. 1.9.

China fears backlash from bankrupt firms

THE MAN in charge of implementing China's new bankruptcy law, which took effect this week, says the greatest challenge to the Communist Party is not overstretched business, but the potential backlash from sacked workers.

In an interview with *China Daily*, Zhang Yinjie, section chief in the Peking Economic Planning Commission, said: "What if the workers who have been fired throng around the government buildings, raising signs and chanting 'I want to work.. I am hungry. I want to eat.' This is a far more serious problem than a bankrupt factory in debt to the tune of three or five million yuan (£500,000 to £750,000)."

Bankruptcies are one of the most explosive issues in the party's faltering reform programme, which stresses that market forces are the key to increased production and seeks to break the Maoist principle of "the iron rice bowl", guaranteeing all state employees a job for life.

After the first bankruptcies were proclaimed in August 1986, when a factory in north-east China was closed, party officials repeatedly failed to agree on how to extend the bankruptcy principle. But Mr Zhang and his colleagues will have to implement the new law, despite their worries.

By Jonathan Mirsky

In Peking alone, he said, 30 of the 430 enterprises under the control of the municipal government were in debt. He is determined to let one or two go broke.

Unproductive enterprises present the Chinese leadership with a vast dilemma. According to the *Economic Daily*, 400,000 are in the red, and three-quarters of them should be closed. Thirty million workers in such firms have nothing to do. This year, the paper claimed, half of China's industrial profit will subsidise failing state-owned enterprises.

Mr Zhang favours successful firms taking over failing ones, although such mergers merely prolong overstaffing and low efficiency. But the deeper problem remains: the new bankruptcy law, says Mr Zhang, "catches most workers in state-owned enterprises mentally unprepared". They insist that it is often not their fault if a factory is unproductive.

What worries Mr Zhang and his colleagues is that bankruptcies are regarded in China as symbols of capitalist decay, and he admitted few firms would be closed. Those declared bankrupt, he said, would be used as a warning to debt-ridden enterprises.

Figure 1.9 Economic reform in China. (*Source*: *The Independent*, December 1988.)

Questions

1. What types of economic reform does this article indicate had been taking place in China?

2.   Why do you think that these reforms had been introduced?
3.   What drawbacks to these reforms are indicated in the article?
4.   In what ways does the article show that changes in the economic system require changes in cultural, political and social attitudes?

Production

The concern of production is to add value to things so that they become goods or services that people will want. Production includes a wide range of occupations including acting, playing professional tennis, selling ice cream, running a laundry, growing crops to sell, working as a buyer for a textile business, making heavy engineering parts, acting as a paid child minder and thousands more. Each of these occupations is concerned with adding a bit more value to something to turn it into the product that is finally purchased by a consumer who derives satisfaction from it.

It is important to stress this definition of production because some people mistakenly associate production just with manufacturing. In fact one of the most important trends in Britain in the twentieth century has been that of de-industrialization. While jobs in manufacturing have been disappearing, service industries like tourism, catering, finance, banking and leisure pursuits have boomed.

Figure 1.10 illustrates this change by comparing the breakdown of employment by industrial sector between June 1959 and June 1988. Manufacturing has been increasingly squeezed out to be increasingly replaced by service employment. We can also

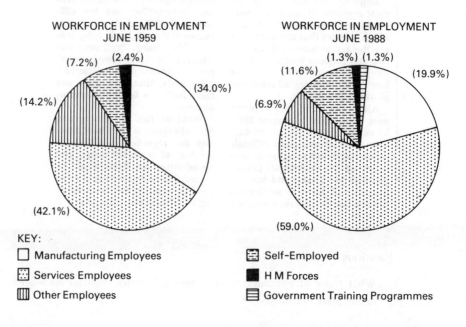

Figure 1.10 The changing composition of the working population between June 1959 and June 1988. (*Source*: Department of Employment.)

see a significant growth in self-government and this reflects the large increase in the number of small enterprises in the 1980s.

Figure 1.11 looks at the process of de-industrialization over a shorter period taking in the figures for changes between March and June 1988. Taking the year up to June 1988 as a whole, the industry divisions experiencing the biggest rise in employees were distribution, hotel catering, repairs; banking, finance and insurance; and other services.

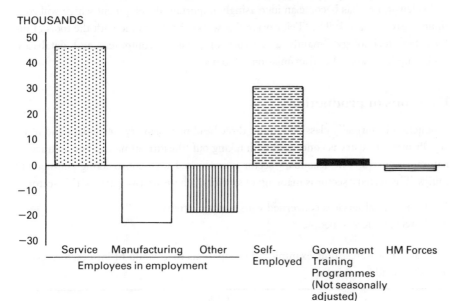

WORKFORCE IN EMPLOYMENT: GREAT BRITAIN
CHANGE MARCH 1988 — JUNE 1988 (Seasonally Adjusted)

Figure 1.11 Short-term changes in the occupational structure. (*Source*: Department of Employment.)

De-industrialization refers to the fall in the relative importance of the manufacturing sector, as measured by output, employment or capital expenditure. However, the process of squeezing out manufacturing has not been uniform. While many of the traditional manufacturing industries such as coal, steel and shipbuilding have declined, others have grown—particularly those using advanced technological systems including food processing, and the production of automated factory systems.

Much of the growth in jobs has been centred around particular localities which are sometimes referred to as 'growth poles'. Areas which were well known as growth areas in the late 1980s included the South East region, 'the M4 corridor' following the M4 from the Thames Valley through to South Wales, and the 'Cambridge Triangle' taking in boom towns such as Peterborough. A number of other smaller pockets of growth were dotted all over the United Kingdom and included towns like Telford and Harrogate. In Scotland, many jobs in the computer industry have been created around Stirling in an area now known as 'Silicon Glen'.

Commuting to work and home working have also become significant modern trends. It is now estimated that more than 10 000 workers commute to the South East each week. A report published by the Policy Studies Institute entitled Britain's New Industrial Gypsies says that weekly commuters, who come from as far north as Tyne and Wear, receive few time concessions from their bosses. This means that migrant workers have to start early on Monday and stay late on Friday and so have less time to relax over a shortened weekend. Commuters to the South East are often victims of redundancy in the North. Many workers find jobs in the South East, but retain their northern base to maintain their standard of living.

'Teleworking' has become an increasingly important development which will continue to grow in the 1990s. 'Teleworking' is working from home with the tools of information technology—mainly a network of personal computers and databases, backed up by fax or other transmissions systems.

Divisions of production

Production is normally classified under three headings: primary, secondary and tertiary. Primary industry is concerned with taking out 'the gifts of nature', i.e. extracting natural resources. The secondary sector is concerned with constructing and making things. The tertiary sector is made up of services. There are two parts of this sector:

1. Commercial services concerned with trading activity
2. Direct services to people

The table illustrates some examples of occupations that would fit into each category. You should add to this list.

| Primary | Secondary | Tertiary | |
		Commercial services	Direct services
Oil drilling	Oil refining	Petrol retailing	Hairdressing
Farming	Food processing	Food transportation	Police
Coal mining	Building work	Wholesaling	Chiropody
Forestry	Brewing	Business insurance	Cinema

Explanations of structural changes in the economy

The economy can be seen to be made up of a number of component parts or 'sectors'. Sectors may be defined widely to include groups of industries (e.g. the energy industries) or narrowly drawn to identify parts of industries (e.g. solar panel supply), depending on our purpose for making the definition.

In addition to the commonly used broad classification of primary, secondary and tertiary sectors, the following are also important. The *goods sector* is the primary and secondary sectors combined. The *production sector* (production industries) includes the secondary sector together with mining and quarrying from the primary sector. The term 'industry' is widely used to mean this sector, and an index (measure) of industrial production is drawn up on this basis.

Structural change refers to the changing relative significance of sectors within an economy (however sectors are defined). Structural change is a basic feature of the historical development of all societies. In advanced industrial societies structural change will need to be carried out at a rapid pace. In advanced industrial societies people taken as a whole will have more income to spend—this will lead to a change in patterns of demand. This is illustrated by the boom in demand in the 1980s in the United Kingdom for 'recreation, entertainment and educational services'. (However, within this overall sector, while there was an increase in demand for television and video goods, real spending on books actually fell.)

Structural changes are not only initiated by changes in the demand for goods; changes in supply can also have a significant impact. Changes in the conditions of supply, such as improvements in technology, mean that some existing goods can be produced cheaply, and that new varieties and variations of products come to the market. Improvements in the processes involved in producing goods help to lower unit costs and hence prices. For example the development of automated production lines and robotics in motor vehicle manufacture has helped to reduce the process costs of manufacture (for example by requiring less labour time per product) and has also added to the variety of gadgets and optional extras available in a motor car. Developments in information technology have created a whole new range of products such as video games and word processors.

Modern industrial societies such as the United Kingdom and the United States of America have been termed 'third wave societies'. 'First wave' societies mainly depend on agriculture. 'Second wave' societies see the transfer of domination to 'manufacture'. Finally, 'third wave' societies see a major switch in employment to service occupations.

In Fig. 1.10 we saw the switch of swathes of the labour force in this country from manufacturing to service between June 1959 and June 1988. There are a number of explanations that have been put forward to account for this change.

1. *Stage of maturity*   We have already seen that some analysts see the process of development of economies over time to go through a stage of primary concentration of employment into agriculture, followed by manufacturing and finally a domination by the service sector. The United Kingdom, as the world's oldest industrial nation, could reasonably be expected to be one of the most mature. With the growth of service sector employment, the labour force would transfer from manufacturing employment over a period of time.

2. *The effect of low wage competition*   Another explanation put forward to account for de-industrialization is that the prices of UK manufactures have been undercut by cheap foreign products from low wage economies. In particular we have

heard these arguments related to the textiles and electrical components industries. However, in low wage countries output per head is usually low, and it is often in markets where the United Kingdom competes with high wage economies that we have failed to be competitive.

3. *Crowding out*   An explanation for the decline of manufacturing that was particularly popular in the late 1970s and early 1980s was based on the notion that manufacturing was being crowded out by the non-market public sector (i.e. services such as health and education which are provided by the government free to end users). However, this argument has lost some of its early popularity as the percentage of total national expenditure allocated to the non-market public sector declined in the late 1980s.

4. *The high pound and high interest rates*   Some people argue that the high cost of borrowing money (interest rates) combined with a high relative price of the pound in 1979/80 (and more recently in 1988/89) had disastrous effects for British manufacturing industry.

    Most businesses have to borrow to carry them forward from the time when they buy in components, raw material and stocks until they are able to sell finished goods. High interest rates can create crippling short-term debts. A high value to the pound means that British goods become relatively more expensive than competing foreign products. It is argued that a policy of high interest rates and high exchange rates has helped to slim down Britain's manufacturing. Consumers have thus had to resort to buying imported manufactures which has seriously affected the balance of our payments with the rest of the world. (Details about why the government has raised interest rates and encouraged a high pound are given in Chapter 16.)

    In theory we would expect high interest rates to discourage borrowing. However, in the late 1980s government has found that even relatively high increases in interest have limited effects in the short run. Once people have developed the habit of borrowing it is difficult to damp down.

5. *The North Sea*   Some analysts regard the importance of North Sea oil to Britain as being a contributory cause to the decline of manufacturing. Because the United Kingdom is one of the few industrial economies to have been able to produce and export large quantities of oil, speculators have tended to see the British pound as a potentially strong currency. The buying of pounds gave the pound a relatively high value on international markets in the early 1980s. However, a relatively strong pound makes it more difficult to sell other items including manufactures on international markets.

Productivity

Until the middle of the 1980s, output per head in British manufacturing lagged well behind that of our international competitors. However, in recent years, a slimmed down manufacturing base has also proved to be a more productive one.

The aims of a business

In the next chapter we shall see that there are many different types of business. Some of these are in the hands of a few owners, some are owned by a large number of shareholders and others are owned by the government. What are the aims of a business organization? (This section should only be seen as a general introduction to this topic, a more detailed look at the implications of some of these aims is considered in the section of pricing strategies in Chapter 7.)

In the long run firms need to make a profit. People as a rule will only tie up their money in a business if they are satisfied with the return they get from it. This would suggest that profitability is a major business aim although it is not the only one. The principle of profit maximization is illustrated in Fig. 1.12. An entrepreneur has calculated the total cost of producing different outputs of a commodity and total revenues. Profit maximization will entail calculating the output which will achieve greatest total profit (i.e. the point Q on the quantity axis at which the difference between total revenue and total cost is greatest). However, in reality this process is a lot more complex than simply drawing a diagram. It will involve a thorough programme of research taking into account costings for different levels of output, the effects of charging different prices, calculations of potential sales and many other factors.

If we simply measure profit in money terms then it would appear to be logical to consider that the rational business will in the long term seek to maximize the difference between its total revenue and total cost. Accountants, for example, claim to be

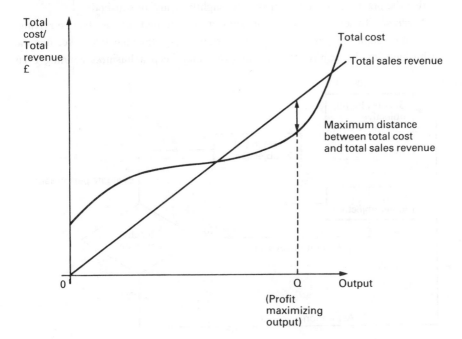

Figure 1.12 Profit maximization.

able to weigh up quickly the success of a business in terms of the financial profit—'the bottom line'. (You will see in Chapter 9 that financial profit is not a straightforward calculation—accountants can produce more than one set of figures.) However, when we observe and explore the way that large numbers of businesses operate, it immediately becomes clear that there are different views as to the nature of profit—for example an alternative perspective of the nature of profit is implicit in the belief of a number of influential business people that the contribution that their company can make to a thriving community is part of the profit equation.

Other motivations in the running of a business might include:

1. *Maximization of sales*   In some large companies the salaries earned by managers may depend on the size of the business. Thus their objective may be to make the business as large as possible. Controlling a large business concern might also give individuals satisfaction from the power at their command. Increased sales might also mean reduced sales for competitors, which in the long term can be seen as being consistent with a policy of profit maximization.

2. *Prestige*   For other people the image and name of a company may be very important. The company may spend a lot of money on public relations so that the company is well thought of. Again, this policy does not have to be inconsistent with that of long-term profit maximization.

   Projecting an image of quality can be seen as being important for the morale of shareholders, customers and employees. Shareholders and customers are likely to withdraw their support for a company when they feel that its practice and performance are sub-standard. The loyalty of employees will be tested if they feel that the practices of their company are 'slightly shady' or slipshod.

3. *Survival*   In some businesses, the aims of the firm may just be about surviving. An old-established company may, for instance, have the objective of keeping the business in the family. Proud employers may keep a business running even

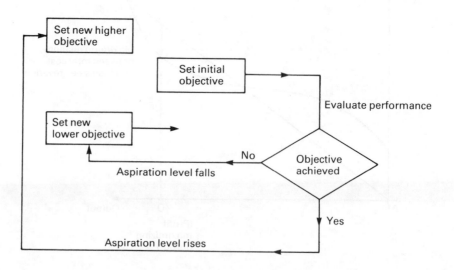

Figure 1.13 Management by objectives strategy. (*Source*: Needham, D. and R. Dransfield, *Business Studies in Practice*. McGraw-Hill, Maidenhead, 1988.)

though it is a loss-making position simply to protect its employees. League football clubs have been known to be subsidized, even though they are in a loss-making position, for years on end by entrepreneurs who have a strong loyalty to their town, to the club and to sentimental memories.

4. *As a hobby or interest*   Some people can afford to run a small business at a financial loss. There is enjoyment in running the thing for its own sake. This brings home the point that profit should not simply be measured in money terms. It is possible to argue that activities are profitable if they give people a feeling of worth and enjoyment.

5. *Satisficing*   Most of us at some time have had the word 'satisfactory' written on our school report or profile. This indicates that we managed to do enough to get by without making a great success of the task in hand. The theory of business 'satisficing' is that managers in given situations set minimum standards which they regard to be satisfactory rather than going all out for excellence. Managers may set satisfactory levels of: profit, sales, revenue, labour turnover and so on. The theory is not based on an assumption of complacency. Instead, it is based on the realization that managers in the real world will rarely have a sufficient quantity and quality of information to calculate accurately the profit maximizing output. They will therefore choose to set attainable targets given imperfect information.

Management by Objectives (MBO) is a commonly used business strategy which can be used to upgrade targets in the light of experience. It is a strategy which accommodates for adjustment of objectives (see Fig. 1.13).

At the initial starting point managers will set objectives, which can then be evaluated in the light of performance. If the objective is achieved, then aspiration levels can be raised, and new targets set at higher levels. Alternatively, if the objective is set at too high a level, then aspirations can be lowered and lower objectives established. (Satisficing is also dealt with in Chapter 7.)

In a study carried out by Shipley in 1981 (*Journal of Industrial Economics*), the author concluded that only 15.9 per cent of a sample of 728 UK firms could be regarded as 'true' profit maximizers. This conclusion was reached by cross-tabulating replies to two questions shown in the table. Shipley considered as true

	Percentage of all respondents
1. Does your firm try to achieve:	
a. Maximum profits	47.7
b. 'Satisfactory' profits?	52.3
2. Compared to your firm's other leading objectives, is the achievement of a target profit regarded as being:	
a. Of little importance	2.1
b. Fairly important	12.9
c. Very important	58.9
d. Of overriding importance?	26.1
(Those responding with both 1(a) and 2(d)	15.9

(*Source*: Adapted from Shipley, 1981.)

maximizers only those firms that claimed both to maximize profits and to regard profits to be of overriding importance. Of course, there are a number of criticisms that can be levelled at any form of statistical analysis of motivations. However, there would appear to be a clear case for arguing that profit is only part of a set of business objectives.

The objectives of business firms are clearly of central importance to a course in business studies. We suggest that students carry out an applied piece of research preferably by (a) talking to a small group of managers about their objectives, and (b) surveying a larger number of businesses.

6. *Coalitions in goal formation*   To take a managerial perspective of business objectives can be very narrow. Many business structures can be seen as being based on a coalition of interested groups. There are a number of internal groups within a business whose interests might be widely divergent—e.g. employees, managers and shareholders. At the same time external interests will include consumers, governments, pressure groups and other producers. It is inevitable that goal formation will involve a balance of interests. Establishing business objectives will therefore involve a compromise between interested parties whose interests may conflict—e.g. over the distribution of company earnings between shareholders and employees.

Short answer questions

1. What is the purpose of systems theory?
2. Distinguish between relative and absolute poverty.
3. What is meant by production?
4. Distinguish between needs and wants.
5. Define opportunity cost, giving
    (a) an example of opportunity cost to an individual;
    (b) an example of opportunity cost to society.
6. What is a resource? What types of resource are there?
7. Are resources scarce?
8. Give an example from the real world to illustrate interdependence (the example should incorporate areas of business activity).
9. Illustrate the principle of specialization by reference to:
    (a) division of labour;
    (b) specialization by process;
    (c) regional specialization.
10. If money did not exist, man would rapidly invent it. Explain this statement.
11. Explain how the what, how and for whom decisions are typically made in:
    (a) a free market economy;
    (b) a planned economy.

12. Explain how decisions are made in a mixed economy.
13. What is an industrial sector? For what purposes is the economy divided into sectors?
14. What is meant by the term de-industrialization?
15. Which sectors of the British economy have grown in recent years, and which sectors have declined?
16. What is meant by:
    (a) the primary sector;
    (b) the secondary sector;
    (c) the tertiary sector;
    (d) the goods sector;
    (e) the production sector?
17. Illustrate the profit maximizing point of a firm on a diagram showing total cost and total revenue. (Draw your revenue curve on the assumption that price does not vary with output.)
18. What is meant by the term 'satisficing'?
19. In what way can goal formation in a company be seen to be based on a coalition of interests?
20. What is meant by Management by Objectives?

Essays

1. Consider the opportunity cost of:
   (a) building the Euro-Tunnel;
   (b) purchasing a copy of this book;
   (c) spending more money on nurses' pay;
   (d) the research and development of a cure for AIDS.
2. Do the advantages of specialization always outweigh the disadvantages?
3. The economic problem is that of infinite human wants with only a limited basket of resources with which to fulfil them. Discuss this statement.
4. Why does the structure of industry change over time? Illustrate your answer by reference to an economy of your choice.
5. How would you account for the process of de-industrialization in the United Kingdom?
6. Compare and contrast free enterprise with planned economies.
7. Business life is based on conflicting interests. Discuss this statement.
8. The purpose of business is to make profits. Discuss this statement.
9. The price mechanism is the most effective way of allocating scarce resources. Discuss this statement.
10. What is the purpose of a business organization?

Data response questions

1 Forecast employment change by industry group UK

	Level 000's	Net change 000's		Growth % pa
	1987	1980–87	1987–95	1987–95
Agriculture	558	−58	−38	−0.9
Mining, etc.	207	−147	−34	−2.3
Utilities	291	−77	−22	−1.0
Metals, minerals, etc.	443	−213	−23	−0.7
Chemicals	345	−82	−17	−0.7
Engineering	2329	−980	−91	−0.5
of which				
Mechanical engineering	737	−290	−25	−0.5
Electrical engineering	567	−182	35	0.7
Motor vehicles	245	−191	0	0.0
Food, drink and tobacco	581	−164	−61	−1.4
Textiles and clothing	563	−180	−39	−0.9
Other manufacturing	1102	−99	5	0.1
Construction	1569	−40	201	1.5
Distribution, etc.	5268	253	414	1.0
of which				
Distribution	3972	75	97	0.3
Hotels and catering	1295	178	317	2.8
Transport and communication	1500	−85	18	0.2
Business services	2631	750	602	2.6
Miscellaneous services	2420	580	615	2.9
Manufacturing	5362	−1723	−230	−0.5
All industries above	19807	−552	1523	0.9
Health and education	3001	128	265	1.1
Public administration	2178	83	−66	−0.4

Note: Employment levels relate to annual average figures covering employees in employment and the self-employed.

Source: Institute for Employment Research.

The information above relates to recent trends in employment, and to predicted future trends.

(a) Which industry groups are experiencing clear changes in numbers employed? How would you account for these changes?

(b) Analyse and explain the changes in employment patterns in the primary, secondary and tertiary sectors of the economy.

(c) How is it possible to make predictions about future changes in employment structure?

(d) How can predictions be made about future employment trends, for example the growth of employment by industry group between 1987 and 1995?

2 Study the article in Fig. 1.14.

Recharging Russia's batteries

O. MIKHAILOV

PRAVDA'S "Repair Shop" had a group of visitors from Kiev with an unusual request. They came straight from the counter of Home Radio, a shop which is forever throwing all sorts of batteries on the market.

But is it? That's the point. This time (and we may safely add, many times before) there were no batteries in stock. Our visitors, ex-customers of Home Radio, were naturally annoyed and took the opportunity to exhibit their recently-acquired, but already silent transistor radios, portable tape-recorders and useless pocket-calculators.

● SHORTAGE

With our darkly muttering visitors still crowding around us, we telephoned the Ministry of Trade's Department for the Ukraine. They told us that every year shops in the Ukraine receive inadequate supplies of Krona, Uran and Yupiter batteries.

Inadequate? A mild word for an annual shortage of 60 million batteries! Shop assistants begin to complain that due to this lack, people are not buying transistor-operated equipment. Nobody wants to spend all their time running round shops in search of batteries.

Who is responsible for these drastic cuts? Customers reckon the Department of Trade is to blame: there has long been a dearth of batteries on the market.

The Department of Trade passes the buck to the Ministry of Electro-Technology. After all, the factories which systematically fail to manufacture adequate supplies of batteries, like the Yelets Factory of Batteries, the Klaipeda Dry-Cell Batteries Factory 'Sirius', and many others, come under this Ministry.

What's more, these shortages run into many millions of much-needed batteries. For their part, the factories explain their failure to meet demand by pointing to shortages of necessary materials.

The shortages of batteries for transistor-operated equipment are exacerbated by lack of proper coordination within trade departments. Millions of transistor radios, tape-recorders and other battery-operated articles often spend weeks sitting in storerooms and warehouses before being sent off to retail outlets.

During that time the elements deteriorate, so when they finally reach the customer there is not much life left in them. Sometimes they are no longer saleable merchandise. What a waste.

● ESSENTIAL

"It is the lack of coordination," complains L. Nikiforov, general manager of the Korolev factory in Kiev which manufactures Meridian transistor radios. "It is essential that regular supplies of batteries are ensured. Their production should be in conjunction with battery-operated equipment".

Thousands, even millions of people who have wasted their money buying expensive transistor-radios and tape-recorders which they can only use for a brief period, would like to ask the central Planning Office, the Ministry of Electro-Technology and the Ministry of Trade, when the problems of missing batteries will be solved.

Figure 1.14 Comments on 'coordination' in Russia. (*Source*: *Pravda*, English Language Edition, vol. 2, No. 4, 1988.)

(a) What is meant in the article by lack of coordination? Why is this seen to be a problem?

(b) What conditions would be required for coordination to be effective?

(c) In what ways might the process of coordination use up scarce resources?

(d) Using the example of batteries, explain how the price mechanism might help to deal with the problem of coordination.

(e) What problems might be introduced by introducing the price mechanisms in this situation?

3 The table on page 36 gives the total cost schedule for 'Pinebeds', a small business making wooden beds.

Costs of the Pinebeds Company

Output of beds per week	Total cost (£)
0	120
1	220
2	300
3	350
4	370
5	420
6	490
7	590
8	720

Assuming that the firm is able to sell any quantity of beds at a price of £80.

(a)   Draw a diagram to illustrate the total cost and total revenue of producing different quantities of output.

(b)   How much output should the firm produce in order to maximize profits? Give five reasons why it might set this objective.

(c)   How much output should the firm produce in order to maximize revenue without making a loss? Give five reasons why it might set this objective.

(d)   Assuming that the firm had originally set the management objective of producing five beds and selling them for a total revenue of £450, how might management react if it finds that customers are prepared to pay £200 per bed?

4   Study the article in Fig. 1.5.

4 million home-workers by 1995, CBI predicts

Peter Large
Technology Editor

FOUR MILLION people could be working from home by 1995, using personal computers and the phone line, the CBI forecast yesterday. That, it said, would be double today's total and represent around a sixth of the workforce.

John Banham, the CBI's director general, said home working would cut expensive invest-ment in office space; increase people's efficiency — not least through the removal of the strain of crowded rush-hour travel; and help to solve the UK's shortage of skilled people, because employees could more easily combine retraining with their work.

The TUC, which is concerned about employment rights in home-working, questioned the CBI's estimate of a current total of about 2 million. Department of Employment figures, it said, showed that 2 million could only be reached by including home-based people, such as area sales staff (400,000), and workers living on the job, such as hotel employees (750,000).

Nevertheless, a trend to hi-tech home-working, forecast by futurologists for more than 30 years, seems to have begun at last; and Britain was the pioneer.

F International, a company started in 1962 by Mrs Steve Shirley, has about 700 freelance computer programmers work-ing at home.

Mrs Shirley's aim was to cure the waste of talent among fam-ily-raising computer profession-als. Today, the workforce is still 90 per cent women. The arche-type is a graduate aged 38.

If the CBI's forecasts are right, Steve Shirley should soon be relieved of a chore: supply-ing information to world-wide academic research teams, all keen to demonstrate that F In-ternational's basis of highly-skilled, independent self-em-ployment is the work pattern of the future.

Figure 1.15 Home working a new phenomena? (*Source: The Guardian.*)

(a)   What is meant by 'home working'?

(b)   On what basis are the CBI figures for the current level of home workers based? On what grounds are these figures subject to dispute?

(c) What will be the principal benefits of home working to:
   (i)   individual home workers;
   (ii) British industry;
   (iii) society as a whole.
(d) What factors need to be taken into consideration in deciding whether 'home working' is a 'good thing'?

Suggested reading

Needham, D. and Dransfield, R., *Exploring Industry and Enterprise*. Cassell, 1989.
Sawyer, M. C., *The Economics of Industries and Firms*. Croom Helm, 1985.

2

Business organization in the private sector

Introduction

This chapter sets out to explore different types and forms of business organization in the private sector. Organization is required to turn ideas into activities which can be maintained over a period of time, and carried out effectively. All businesses start off from an original idea. This idea may be new or copied from somewhere else. If the original business idea is to be given shape and form to become a product which will be sold successfully over a long period, then it will need to be nurtured and developed by a business organization with clearly established aims. The organization must develop patterns and structures.

Most large companies started off as small companies, usually owned and run by one person. The idea for the business may have come from a chance invention, copying an idea that has worked somewhere else, spotting a gap in the market, or in many other ways. The starting point to this chapter is therefore the business idea, and the creation of a small business.

There are a number of ways of defining a 'small firm'. For example, a firm may be defined as small if it employs less than a certain number of people, if it operates from less than a certain number of plants, if its sales value is less than a certain figure, and in other ways.

In 1988 there were more than 1 million businesses in this country with annual sales figures of less than £100 000. There were a further 300 000 businesses with sales between £100 000 and £1 million per year. In percentage terms, 68 per cent of all businesses fell within this description of a smaller business, that is to say, with sales of less than £100 000.

The original business idea needs to be followed up by detailed business planning around which the business organization will be constructed.

There are a number of elements which combine to create the business organization (see Fig. 2.1). These elements are:

- The form of organization. Will it take the form of sole trader, partnership or something else?
- The infrastructure or pattern of authority within the organization.

- The superstructure or pattern of organizing employees into groups within the organization.

This chapter therefore follows through

Figure 2.1 Business ideas into practice.

Where do business ideas come from?

Most people at some time or another think about setting up an enterprise of their own. You will hear people say things like: 'Someone could make a fortune out of selling such and such' or 'If I had some money, I could make a business out of making this or that'.

Where does the idea to set up an enterprise come from? Some people copy ideas that they have seen somewhere else (such as selling flowers at a busy railway station). Other people spot a gap in the market—'Nobody round here runs a mobile disco service!' Others turn a hobby into a business—'I always enjoy making wooden toys!' These are just some of the many ways in which people come up with business ideas.

Developing a business idea

With very few exceptions, every big company began as a small company, often with just one or two enterprising individuals at its head.

William Morris began by mending bicycles in a back street garage in Oxford, and built up a major motor manufacturing company.

Michael Marks arrived in this country from Russia in the nineteenth century speaking very little English. He set up as a door-to-door hawker of buttons, needles, ribbons and other small items. He progressed to selling from market stalls setting up in partnership with Tom Spencer. Today Marks and Spencer is the best known brand name in the United Kingdom.

Anita Roddick set up her own small shop in the 1960s to sell her own preparations of cosmetics based on natural substances. Today the Body Shop can be found on most major high streets.

Developing a business idea usually requires a combination of careful planning, and good luck. It also requires careful attention to detail in a number of key areas including production, finance and marketing.

Case Study—Finding a gap in the market

Twenty-five-year-old Karan Bradley has set up her own business, Romantique, producing a range of lingerie. Perched on a stool among the clutter of sewing machines, ribbons, lace and cotton threads decorating the carpet, Karan told me of her ambitions.

'I am aiming at the designer market, but you have to have the bread-and-butter sales which means that you have to aim certain lines at the mass market in order to keep the cash flow.'

Karan also does bread-and-butter free lancing for a couple of companies in Lincoln and London when they need extra work. Up-market is the hardest part to break into.

'This is what is taking the time. I have to help to make the mass market lines when I'd like to be designing. I do have one person working for me at the moment and other people doing part time. There are various people I can call on if I need extra help.'

Karan studied contour fashion at Leicester Polytechnic, gained her BA honours in it and came to Grantham for a job with one of the main lingerie firms in the town. 'I am a bra designer really,' she told me.

'After three years I decided to start my own business. Janet Reger's is the sort of business I would like. I want to be known in my own right, not that I want my name in lights, but I do want to do my own thing. I just would rather be working for myself and while I am young enough to I have decided to start and see how things progress.'

'I want to be selling to the small boutique. Nationally really, not just in London. The ones I've spoken to seem quite interested.'

Garments are either made in polyester satin at the lower end of the market or in all natural materials, real silk with cotton lace, at the top. Her range of colours is limited at the moment. 'I cannot have anything too out of the ordinary because you have to consider all the trims. I'm sticking with basic blacks, creams and whites at the moment.'

Prices have got to be competitive. 'I have to sell a silk teddy for £20 to £25 to a shop to cover my overheads and make a small profit and the shop would have to add their mark-up,' I was told.

'What I'd like to be able to do is export and I think there is potential there. I think you will get a better price. I have already done some export work which I am told is very good in your first few months.'

'I think I have to go designer possibly with the Common Market in 1992. It is going to open the market and we are going to have a lot of cheap imports and are the big companies going to be able to compete? Are the people who are going to survive be the ones who can offer designer?' she asked.

(*Source: Grantham Journal*, 2 December 1988.)

Questions

1. What is Karan Bradley's business idea?
2. What advantages will Karan get from setting up in business?
3. What problems might she encounter from setting up in business?
4. What sorts of information would Karan require before setting up in business?
5. What evidence is given in the article that Karan had researched and planned her business before setting up.

6. What areas of planning could Karan have improved on (given the information in the extract)?
7. What factors will influence Karan's success or failure to sell goods?
8. Apart from the ability to sell goods, what other criteria could be applied to measure the success of Romantique over a period of time?
9. What markets is Romantique trying to sell into? What factors influence this choice of markets?
10. What information would you need to know in order to evaluate Karan's business idea?

Case Study—Gale that breathed life into timber

Figure 2.2 Destruction to construction: logs cut from a great oak that was dashed to the ground at Chartwell being marked by Tony Penrose. (*Source: The Independent.*)

On the night of the Great Gale in October 1987, Tony Penrose, a Sussex farmer and woodland owner, lay awake listening to the great trees around his house crashing and falling. A year on, the remains are guyed and roped together in the expectation that they will toughen up and continue to grow.

The gale had far greater effect on Mr Penrose and the timber business he runs at Chiddingly, in East Sussex's Great Weld. On Monday, 17 October, a year and a day later, he will be taking delivery of a Danish timber drier, part of his £1.4 million investment in a business which will handle every aspect of timber production, from soil to sawdust.

'We were doodling along before the gale, but it was the gale which really kick-started us,' he says. He used to employ four people. Today he has 21 on the staff.

Inside Mr Penrose's present timber yard is the workshop of Rod Wales, one of England's leading furniture-makers. He has worked with John Makepeace, who is largely credited with restoring confidence to modern furniture craftsmen, not least by commanding enormous prices for his work.

Neatly planked in the yard in the middle of the village, there lies one of the gale's victims—a great oak from Chartwell, Winston Churchill's home. Mr Penrose bought it and it is slowly drying, getting ready to be turned into furniture. Mr Wales plans to fashion from it a dining-room suite.

Mr Penrose deliberately bought wood from local landowners. He wanted to build up stock, and prices were easy after the gale. But he also wanted to build up a reputation with potential customers for his woodland enterprise. After the gale, overnight the woodyard was able to stock up with at least seven years' supply of timber. This has made it possible to think about expanding to a new larger timber yard.

Mr Wales and Mr Penrose represent the modern feeling that English woodlands should become a prime resource for the entire range of wood products. Mr Wales says that concern about the tropical rainforest makes it important to get indigenous wood production going again.

To that end, Mr Penrose has started work on a big new yard on the A22, just by the village. This will overcome the objections of some villagers that the roar of his present mill adds nothing to the amenity of their homes, and will also provide a site for his new drier.

The machine is designed to take an English tree and make it capable of withstanding the central heating of a modern house. No matter how long he had kept it in the open air, Mr Penrose's stock of Chartwell oak would have been unlikely to have achieved that state by itself.

(*Source*: *The Independent*.)

Questions

1. What is the core activity (central business line) around which Mr Penrose's business is based?
2. What factors have made it possible for the business to 'take off'?
3. Why is planning important to Mr Penrose's business?
4. What investment projects are being considered by Mr Penrose and why is investment important to the business?
5. What factors are likely to (a) constrain and (b) encourage the development of the business?
6. What measures could be used to chart the growth of the business (e.g. number of people employed)?
7. Does Mr Penrose have a good business idea? Explain your reasoning.
8. In what ways is Mr Penrose's business dependent on other industries and groups?

Business planning

An idea on its own does not create a business. What is required in addition is the ability to organize and plan. Businesses require inputs of time, information, raw materials, capital, labour, paperwork. These inputs need to be put together in an organized way. However, that is not the end of the story; in addition, a company needs to create a public image to market and sell its products, it needs to consider channels of distribution, packaging, display and many other details involved in getting goods to the final customer. All of this requires detailed planning.

A business plan is one of the key ingredients of any successful business, no matter how big or well established. If you want to start a business, it is vital. It helps you to anticipate problems and make arrangements to deal with them. It also gives essential information to the people whose support you need—particularly anyone lending you money.

Before setting out a business plan it is necessary to carry out some preliminary research to find out:

- whether people are prepared to buy the goods or service
- what competition exists
- what premises and equipment are required
- whether planning permission is necessary
- how much money/capital is needed
- the cost of borrowing money
- what grants and other forms of assistance are available

The contents of a business plan

A business plan should be clearly set out under the following headings:

1. *Contents page*   A contents page is useful in any kind of report that is more than two or three pages long.
2. *The owner*   This section should give some information about the owner (or owners) including their educational background and what they have done. It should also contain the names and addresses of two referees.
3. *The business*   This should first contain the name and address of the business and then go on to give a detailed description of the product or service being offered; how and where it will be produced; who is likely to buy it; and in what quantities.
4. *The market*   This section will describe the market research that has been carried out and what it has revealed. It should give details of prospective customers—how many there are, and how much they would be prepared to pay. It should also give details of the competition.
5. *Advertising and promotion*   This section should give information about how the business will be publicized to potential customers. It should give details of likely costs.
6. *Premises and equipment*   This section should show that the business has considered a range of locations, and then chosen the best site. It should also give

details of planning regulations (if appropriate). Costs of premises and the equipment needed should also be given.

7. *Business organization*   This should state whether the enterprise will take the form of sole trader, partnership, company or cooperative.

8. *Costings*   The business should give some indication of the cost of producing the product or service—and the prices it proposes to charge. It is then possible to make profit calculations.

9. *The finance*   This should give details of how the finance for the business is going to be raised. How much will come from savings? How much needs to be borrowed?

10. *Cash flow*   This should give all expected incomings and outgoings over the first year. Cash flow calculations are important, but at this stage can only be approximate.

11. *Expansion*   Finally, the business should give an indication of future plans. Does the business want to keep on producing a steady output or is a dramatic expansion possible? Does it intend to add to its product range? What kind of new competition is likely to emerge, and how will the business deal with it?

Business structures

Formally constituted bodies are set up to achieve particular *objectives*, and are called *organizations*. A business is an example of an organization and every business will need to have an *organizational structure*.

A business will need to adopt a basic *form of organization* from a range of alternatives which are commonly recognized. In the United Kingdom the most common forms are sole traders, partnerships and companies.

A business will also need to formulate an *internal structure* which is a pattern for command, communication and relationships within the organization.

The *prime objectives* of business organizations will be established by those with the highest level of authority within a concern. For example, the directors of a major company may establish a major objective of making their company into a market leader through offering a quality service.

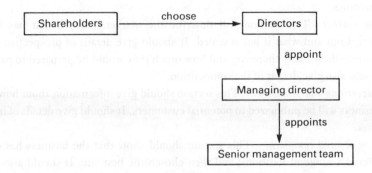

Figure 2.3 Company organization.

In order to attain this (or another) objective it will be necessary to establish a *pattern of responsibility* within the organization. Individuals within the organization will be given varying levels of *authority and responsibility*. At one extreme of the spectrum of responsibility you will find the managing director of a multinational oil company handling millions of pounds worth of business each day and at the other the petrol station forecourt attendant.

Individual members of an organization are *accountable* to the person or people that have given them responsibility. For example, in a company shareholders will choose directors to represent their interests, the directors will choose a managing director to run the company, the managing director will in turn choose managerial staff. Senior managers are accountable to the managing director, the managing director reports back to the board of directors, and the directors report back to shareholders (see Fig. 2.3).

What makes an effective organization?

There is no set pattern that helps an organization to be effective. Some organizations prosper because they are 'at the right place at the right time'; others because they are made up of the right blend of personalities. However, if an organization is going to be successful over a long period of time it will need to combine most of the following ingredients:

1. *Unity of purpose*　All parts of the organization should be working towards a common aim. If parts of the organization work in different directions this can be very confusing and bad for morale.
2. *Effective leadership*　Positions of authority and responsibility in an organization should be vested only in those who are capable of putting them into effect. Decisions can only be implemented if those in authority have the confidence and determination to see that they are carried out.
3. *Flexibility*　An organization should not be too rigid. It should be able to alter course quickly if things are not going right and be able to adapt to changing circumstances.
4. *Operational efficiency*　This means that the operations that a company carries out must be studied, and the results of this analysis used to ensure that things are done in the best way possible. At one level this will involve studying each operation and function separately to see that time is not wasted, costs are kept down, work is done accurately, etc., to ensure a smooth operation.

    At another level the whole functioning of the organization needs to be studied at a global level. It is important that the various parts of the organization work smoothly together and in the same direction (this is called overall efficiency).
5. *Interrelationships*　Each member of an organization needs to understand clearly his or her rights and obligations with regards to other members. Lines of authority and communications need to be clearly defined and acted upon.

The theory of organizations

There are a number of organizational theories that have been developed to help our understanding of the ways in which organizations operate. The major ones that the student might come across can be put under four main headings:

1. Bureaucratic theories
2. Systems theories
3. Interaction theories
4. Conflict theories

Bureaucratic theories

Max Weber (1846–1920) set out a model of how bureaucracy might operate, which has served as a starting point for the study of organizational society ever since.

Max Weber studied organizations at a time when large organizations were increasingly becoming important in industrial society. He argued that bureaucracies are the most functionally effective form of organization, although at times they operate in an 'inhuman way'.

Weber saw bureaucracies as representing the application of rational thought to practical problems in large industrial combines, in the civil service, and in other important organizations (e.g. schools, churches, government departments).

He set out a model of bureaucracy based on typical characteristics of such a form of organization:

1. A set of offices (official positions) for the purpose of carrying out given organizational tasks. These offices will be governed by a set of rules and procedures.
2. A hierarchical structure of offices.
3. Management based on office procedures, files, documents and office staff.
4. The appointment of trained officials to take on roles within the bureaucracy.

Today, various forms of bureaucracy have become the dominant form of administration in political and economic systems in advanced industrial societies. Bureaucracy is the most rational form of social organization and dominates the structure of many business organizations.

The advantages of bureaucratic organization are:

- The application of bureaucratic division of labour combined with new technologies has made possible massive increases in the production of goods and services.
- Bureaucracy usually helps to create a predictable pattern to work cycles. People know what they are supposed to do, how they are supposed to do it and the extent of their responsibilities. Production targets can be set and plans established to meet them.
- Bureaucracy is often seen as being a 'fair' method of organization. Officials are appointed on the basis of qualifications, and the organization will deal with indi-

viduals and groups with which it comes into contact on the basis of pre-determined rules and procedures. Provided that officials 'stick to the rules' there should be no possibility of giving 'preferential treatment'.

However, a number of criticisms have been levelled at bureaucracies:

- Bureaucracies are sometimes seen to be slow moving, unimaginative organizations because of the way they stick to rules and procedures. Decisions may be slowly arrived at because of the way that they have to be processed through the 'right channels'.
- Within a bureaucracy a displacement of goals might take place. Instead of bureaucrats focusing on the aims and purposes of the organization they might become wrapped up in procedures. For example, a business might set itself the target of making a profit. In order to achieve this it will need to carry out a certain amount of documentary paperwork. However, if officials become wrapped up in the paperwork and the procedures involved, insisting that orders are filled in using a certain method and processed by a certain department, they might try the patience of customers and suppliers, hence losing business and profits. In the extreme case, bureaucratic procedures follow the old adage: 'the patient died but the operation was a success'.
- Bureaucracies are sometimes seen to be inhuman structures which fail to account for the fact that many of their internal and external relationships are between people. Bureaucracies have a depersonalizing effect, concentrating on relationships that are remote, anonymous and confined to rigorously defined topics rather than face-to-face informal contacts.

Systems theories

Systems theories are used to study the operation of systems within organizations or the organization as a total system. Systems theory is helpful in contrasting different types of system.

A basic distinction is often made between mechanistic and organic forms of organization (see Fig. 2.4). An example of the mechanistic form of organization is the bureaucracy structure outlined above. In contrast, organic structures are less rule bound, have a less rigid division of labour, are less hierarchical and more open to the influence of informal relationships within the organization. There is more of an emphasis on teamwork and communication and decision making can be done laterally across a network. Teams can share power and responsibility. Figure 2.4 contrasts lines of communication and command in mechanistic and organic forms of organization.

Organic structures are most likely to occur in groups where there is a need to share common expertise and skills. Such a network may be found among high level technicians or research workers in the oil or chemical industries. Alternatively, it may be found in an advertising agency where one person's skill might be in drawing, another

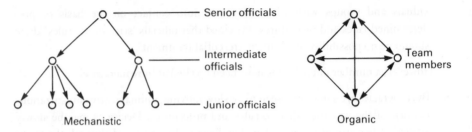

Figure 2.4 Mechanistic and organic organizational structures.

in design and layout, a third with producing slogans and captions and a fourth in finding the best media for getting a campaign across. In such a system individual members of an organization may feel that their individual needs are being met. There is more of an opportunity for them to make an original contribution to decision making and to feel that they are helping to shape organizational behaviour.

Organic approaches have also been successfully tried with manual workers. A frequently quoted example is that of Volvo's Kalmar plant where assembly work was broken down into 20 different functions. Each function is performed by a team of between 15 and 20 workers. The cars pass along from team to team on trolleys, allowing workers considerable freedom of movement. Teams work collaboratively, sharing work and ideas. They tackle problems together.

This process of organic team building is very important in a number of Japanese companies. For example, the tractor manufacturer Komatsu aims to create a group spirit in its workforce at its Greenfield site in Newcastle.

The company has tried to keep terms and conditions the same for everybody. Everyone wears the same uniform, exercises in the morning, starts and finishes at the same time, and uses the same sick pay and pension schemes. The aim behind this is to create a feeling of commonality and commitment. Groups of workers are organized in quality circles, with the joint responsibility for identifying problems and coming up with solutions.

Although mechanistic (bureaucratic) and organic systems are in some ways in competition with each other they often appear side by side in different parts of the same company. Bureaucracy is often best suited for the pursuit of clear goals in stable conditions, such as producing a standard product for a market in which demand is constant. Organic systems are most effective where conditions of demand, competition, production and other factors cannot be readily predicted.

Systems theory is also used to explore the ways in which different organizational structures respond to the types of changes outlined above. In a rapidly changing technological society it is likely that organizations will frequently need to change their structure.

Interaction theories

Interactionist theories are concerned with studying the human side of organizations and the way that individuals and groups interact with each other. Interactionists are concerned with exploring the meanings and values which individuals attach to life in organizations. Interactionist theory will scratch beneath the surface of organization charts, official rules and procedures to study real human relations. Interactionist studies of individuals in prisons, mental hospitals and other organizations have revealed that in order to understand how individual members of an organization (e.g. inmates) feel about their position it is often necessary to challenge official definitions of what is going on.

Conflict theories

Conflict theory is based on the premise that there is an underlying conflict of interest in society between classes or groups. In capitalist societies (e.g. the United Kingdom and the United States of America) there is a fundamental division between the owners of productive resources (e.g. factory owners, shareholders) and their employees.

Karl Marx (1818–83) and other conflict theorists believe that power is used by groups to further their own class interests. The basic power structure of society will be reflected in organizational structures. The purpose of most organizations is to organize the labour process.

At one level this sort of analysis can lead to broad views of the world economy. For example, Wallerstein suggests that economic and social analysis should concern itself with the *capitalist world economy* rather than a narrow focus on national societies. This view is based on the belief that the organization of capitalism is an international phenomenon.

Other studies of organizational conflict focus on relationships within industrial units. For example, the extreme fragmentation of the labour process in industrial and office work can be seen as one way of controlling the labour force because they are no longer able to grasp the production process as a whole. Conflict theory is thus concerned with developing an analysis of power relations within organizations and underlying conflicts of interest.

Forms of business organization

Before a business starts trading, a decision will have to be made about what legal form to take as this affects taxation and the accounting records that need to be kept.

Business organization structures in the private sector

There are various types of business organization and each of these types is subject to different kinds of control. The United Kingdom has a mixed economy and this means that, as well as many businesses being privately owned, many organizations are run by the State (see Fig. 2.5).

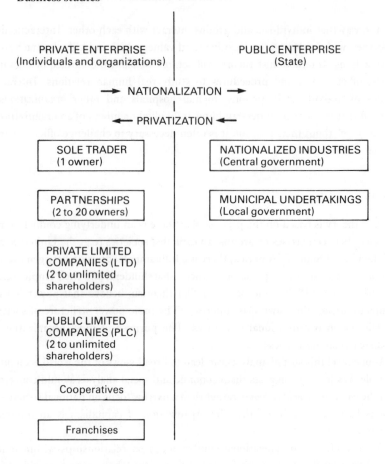

Figure 2.5 The different types of
private and public enterprise. (*Source*:
Needham, D. and R. Dransfield,
Business Studies in Practice. McGraw-
Hill, Maidenhead, 1988.)

The four main forms of business organization in the private sector are:

- Sole traders
- Partnerships
- Private companies
- Public companies

In addition, there are a number of other forms of business organization which are becoming increasingly popular, including cooperatives, franchise operations, and others.

The sole trader

Although there may be others employed by the sole trader, he or she will be personally responsible for the financial liabilities of the company. The individual setting up the business may borrow some or all of the capital required to set up and run the enterprise.

Many small businesses set up in the sole trader form. This is because until the operation becomes established it is difficult to generate enough profit to support more than one owner.

Common examples of businesses which have the sole trader form are sign writers, graphic designers, plumbers, decorators, mobile hairdressers, window cleaners, book keepers and chiropodists. Common features of these businesses are that they do not require a lot of capital, they can be done effectively by one person and they require flexibility (e.g. willingness to work long hours).

There are a number of advantages to setting up as a sole trader:

- There are no legal formalities to complete before commencing to trade.
- There are no legal requirements governing the layout of the accounts.
- Annual accounts do not have to be audited.
- Decisions can be made quickly.
- All profits belong to the sole owner.
- The owner has the freedom to run the business in his or her own way.

However, there are also a number of disadvantages:

- Capital is limited to the owner's savings, profits and the amount that he or she can borrow.
- The owner has sole responsibility for debts. If necessary the owner might have to sell personal possessions to meet business debts.
- The responsibility for a range of separate tasks rests on the shoulders of the owner, e.g. paperwork, tax returns, management, dealing with suppliers and customers.
- The success of the business will often depend on the willingness to work long hours.
- An unforeseen accident or illness may cripple the business at an important part of its development.

Case Study—The sole trader: Nursery Pieces

Marion Tate first became interested in producing wooden puzzles when she saw some for sale on a craft stall at a brass band concert. Marion has always been interested in art and making things. She felt she could produce a similar product herself.

Initially she began to produce puzzles as a hobby and these attracted a great deal of interest from friends. She decided to produce a collection for a craft fair and these proved to be 'a hit'. Marion then decided to invest £700 on an electric band saw and spent a lot of her spare time producing a collection of three main animal puzzle designs to sell at craft fairs.

At the time Marion was working as an administrator at a 'special school' and was able to learn a lot about the sorts of colours that appeal to children.

Marion's decision to set up in business in a serious way was in many ways influenced by her personal circumstances. As a single parent, she needed some means of securing a steady income, and yet be able to work flexible hours. Marion's daughter suffers from asthma and often has to take time off from school. This means that Marion is never sure when she will need to be at home to look after her daughter.

In 1987 Marion decided to set up in business as a sole trader under the name Nursery Pieces. Nursery Pieces is situated in a small workshop unit, from which Marion is able to carry out her manufacturing (sawing is a noisy process). Marion concentrates her time on three main lines of woodworking: wooden clocks, personalized name jigsaws, and a range of 30 different animal jigsaw pictures. Only a small part of Marion's time needs to be spent at the workshop because sales, packaging, accounting and other activities can all be done from home.

The business provides Marion with a modest living, and gives her the flexibility and freedom to combine home and work.

Running Nursery Pieces gives Marion a sense of achievement and satisfaction. Her time is her own (although she finds making puzzles addictive), she enjoys her work and feels that people respect her for what she does. People have also been known to remark that her work is better than that of many of the 'big name' firms.

Problems of running the business include the fact that when expenses are accounted for profits are very low. Nursery Pieces can sell as much as it makes, and for a substantial mark up. However, a lot of Marion's time is taken up in arranging to supply shops, keeping the books up to date, packing and posting items. Marion felt that the business could really take off if she employed a few members of production staff. However, it would take at least three months to train them and there would be no guarantee that they would stay with the business. There would also be a considerable risk in using Marion's house as security to raise a loan. At times Marion feels that she would like the security of a steady job. She finds that cash flow is always a problem. A minimum order of wood (which is her basic raw material) costs £300 but the shops who are her customers might take several months to pay her for supplies of puzzles.

Questions

1. Do you think that the sole trader form is a suitable type of business organization for Nursery Pieces? Explain your reasoning.
2. What would be the main benefits and drawbacks to Marion Tate from such a form of organization?
3. What do you think are Marion Tate's prime objectives in setting up in business? How far do you think she has been able to meet these objectives?

4. Give ten examples of businesses which might suitably operate as sole traders. Explain why in each case.

The ordinary partnership

There may be two or more partners in a partnership. A sole trader will often take on a partner when there is too much work to be done by a single person or when extra skills are required. Many partnerships take advantage of a division of labour based on specialist skills or on the division of time so that partners will work different shifts. Many professional businesses take the partnership form, e.g. doctors, accountants, vets and solicitors.

A partnership agreement is usually set out in a legal document called a Deed of Partnership which is witnessed by a solicitor. However, it is possible to set up a partnership without any legal formalities, as the provisions of the Partnership Act 1890 will be taken as the partnership agreement. This Act set out a detailed framework to govern the affairs of partners in cases where a Deed of Partnership is not drawn up. For example, one of the provisions of this Act is that if a partnership ends the partners will be equally responsible for debts.

A Deed of Partnership will cover such issues as:

- How much capital each partner will contribute.
- How profits and losses will be shared.
- Rules for admitting and expelling partners.
- Voting rights.
- Termination of the partnership.

A carefully worded and detailed Deed of Partnership will help to outline a clear working arrangement.

There are a number of advantages to setting up as a partnership:

- Partners can raise more capital by pooling their resources than they could do by operating as sole traders.
- Partners can share expertise and effort.
- Partners can arrange to cover for each other, e.g. for holidays and lunch breaks.
- Partners may be able to borrow more capital than if they sought individual loans.
- A partnership, like a sole trader, has the advantage of secrecy in that it is not obliged to publish its accounts or have them audited.

The disadvantages of the ordinary partnership form are that:

- Each partner is personally liable for all the firm's business debts.
- Disagreements can arise between partners about the amount of work that each is doing, and how work should be done.
- Partnerships can only raise limited amounts of capital when compared with businesses that are organized as companies.
- For most forms of ordinary partnership there is a legal maximum of 20 partners.

Limited liability

A legal protection known as limited liability exists to protect people who put money into a business but play no active part in running that business. Limited liability means that the maximum amount that a part owner of a limited business can lose is the sum he or she has invested in the business. Private possessions are safeguarded; it is only the participant's stake in the limited business that may be lost.

Limited partnerships

A limited partnership is one in which one or more of the partners has limited liability. A sleeping partner is one who provides capital but takes no part in the running of the business. There must always be at least one partner with unlimited liability. The greater the proportion of the firm's capital that is protected by limited liability, the bigger the risk that will be taken by those partners with unlimited liability. Limited partnerships are therefore fairly unusual. They might be found for example where a business owner has retired, passing on the day-to-day running of a business to a younger relative. The limited partnership also gives scope for an individual or company to invest in a partnership without having to run it.

Case Study—The partnership: 'Concept Graphics'

Mike Pawson and Sue Wakefield both worked in the publicity department for a printing company known as Lyne Printers, in Grantham. Mike had been the Studio Manager and Sue the Chief Designer. When Lyne Printers were taken over by a larger company the publicity department was closed down and Sue and Mike made redundant.

They then decided to set up their own business partnership called Concept Graphics. They knew that there was a demand for good quality art work and that most of their existing clients would use their services. The main problem was in finding premises because the rents and rates of most of the property in the town were too high. They were fortunate to find a small unit at the local Enterprise Agency and were offered a start-up grant by the local council.

In order to secure the grant and to obtain a loan from their bank they produced a business plan giving details of their expected costs and sales revenues.

Mike and Sue set out a Partnership Agreement which they had signed and witnessed by a solicitor. The Agreement set out that they would jointly share the profits and losses of the business, contribute equal time and effort, and other matters.

Mike and Sue feel that a partnership is the best form of business structure for them. Mike's skill is in producing detailed technical illustrations (such as engineering drawings), whereas Sue concentrates more on book illustrations and cartoons. They are able to share out the work, and discuss the best ways of doing jobs. They are able to take holidays, and if one of them is ill the other keeps the business open. If one of them has to leave the studio the other will be available to meet callers and take phone messages. In this way they are able to maintain the 'goodwill' of the business.

Being a small business there are many little tasks that they must do themselves. These include making the coffee, tidying up, doing the hoovering, the paperwork and the accounts. In the spirit of the partnership they choose to share these tasks.

Questions

1. Do you think that a partnership is a suitable form of business organization for Concept Graphics? Explain your reasoning.
2. What would be the main benefits and drawbacks to the two owners from such a form of organization?
3. Give six examples of businesses which might suitably operate as partnerships.
4. Choose two of these and explain in detail why a partnership might be a suitable form of organization for them.
5. If you were going to set up a doctor's partnership, what details would you think necessary to include in the Deed of Partnership?

Limited companies

Limited companies are the most common form of business organization. A limited company is a separate body in law from its shareholders and directors. The company may form contracts, sue and be sued on its own name. The shareholders are not liable for the company's debts except for the value of their shareholdings.

There are two types of limited companies: public companies, which have their shares traded on the main market of the Stock Exchange; and private companies, which impose some restrictions on the trading in their shares.

To set up a limited company it is necessary to go through a number of legal procedures in order to gain recognition. This mainly involves the presentation of various records and documents to the Registrar of Companies. These documents are open to scrutiny.

All limited companies must present a Memorandum of Association and Articles of Association in order to receive a Certificate of Incorporation (see Fig. 2.6).

The Memorandum spells out the nature of the company when viewed from the outside. Someone reading the Memorandum would be able to get a general idea of what the company is and the business with which it is concerned. The Memorandum sets out:

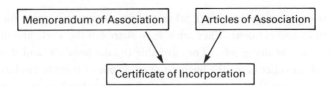

Figure 2.6 Documents required for corporate status.

- The name of the company.
- The registered address of the company.
- The objectives of the company, i.e. what types of activities it will engage in.
- The capital of the company.

Many companies will produce a fairly vague list of objectives in their Memorandum. This will give them the opportunity to alter their activities if market opportunities arise.

The Articles of Association set out the rules which govern the inside working of a company. They set out:

- The rights attached to the holding of the various types of shares offered by the company.
- The rules and procedures for issuing and transferring shares.
- The procedures and timing of company meetings.
- The details of how accounts will be kept and recorded.
- The powers and responsibilities of the directors.
- The details of how company officers will be appointed.

Once a private company has lodged and had these documents accepted it will be granted a Certificate of Incorporation and can start to trade. The Certificate of Incorporation sets up the company as a legal body in its own right. The company (not the individual shareholders) enters into contracts and can sue or be sued in a court of law.

A public company, however, must take further steps before being granted a Certificate of Trading. The Memorandum of a public company must state that the company is to be a public company, and it must abide by a legally set minimum figure for allotted share capital. Before a Trading Certificate is granted, shares allotted must be paid up to at least 25 per cent of their nominal value plus the whole of any premiums payable.

Private limited companies (Limited)

The owners of limited companies are called shareholders because they each own a part of the business. Private companies can have from two to an unlimited number of shareholders and companies can expand by raising finance from new shareholders. However, their shares are not quoted on the Stock Exchange and they are not allowed to advertise the sale of shares publicly. There is also a danger of issuing too many shares and thus having to divide the profits between large numbers of shareholders.

To warn creditors about the dangers of dealing with these companies, Limited appears after their name.

Public limited companies (PLC)

Public limited companies have the opportunity to become larger than the other forms of private business organization. They are allowed to raise capital through the medium of the Stock Exchange which quotes their share prices, and this creates a breadth of financial possibilities.

Only two persons are needed to form a public company and there is no stated maximum of shareholders. The process of becoming a public company is in many ways similar to that of a private company.

Once a public company has received a Certificate of Incorporation it will issue a Prospectus which is an advertisement or invitation to the public to buy shares in the company. Allotment of shares then takes place and the Registrar of Companies will issue a Trading Certificate. Contracts can then be entered into and share prices will be quoted on the Stock Market.

All limited companies must, each year, file with the Registrar of Companies a set of audited accounts. These will include a directors' report, auditors' report, profit and loss account, balance sheet, source and application of funds and an explanation of these accounts. It is also necessary to file an annual return giving details of the directors, shareholders and other information required by law. All this information will be kept on file at Companies House and is open to inspection by members of the public.

There are a number of advantages of forming a limited company:

- Shareholders have limited liability.
- It is easier to raise capital through share issues.
- It is often easier to raise finance from banks.
- It becomes possible to operate on a larger scale.
- It becomes possible to employ specialists.
- Suppliers feel more confident about trading with legally established bodies.
- Directors are not liable if they follow the rules.
- It is easy to expand.
- It is easier to pass the company down from one generation to another.
- The company name is protected by law.
- There are tax advantages associated with giving shares to employees.
- Company pension schemes can give bigger benefits than those available to the self-employed.
- Larger outputs can be produced at lower unit cost.

There are a number of disadvantages associated with becoming a limited company:

- Formation and running costs can be expensive.
- Decisions can be slow and 'red tape' can be a problem.
- Dis-economies of being too large.

- Employees and shareholders are distanced from one another.
- Affairs are public, e.g. audited accounts and annual returns.
- Affairs are tightly regulated under various Companies Acts.
- Heavy penalties are imposed if 'rules' are broken.

Case Study—The private company: 'Clandrex Limited'

In 1976 under the name of David B. Cleaning Services, a small business started providing a window and general cleaning service in a small Midlands town. Over the following years, as more companies contracted out their cleaning requirements to contract cleaners, this business expanded to meet the needs of the local community. It was and still is the largest window cleaning business in the town.

Contract cleaning is a very demanding business with long unsociable hours and expansion required obtaining contracts out of the immediate area. The nature of the business means that it is very labour intensive and management of a widely scattered labour force would create a great deal of work. It was therefore decided to target another sector of the cleaning market in order to expand.

A lot of experience had been gained in the use of cleaning chemicals, equipment and materials. It was felt that this knowledge could be put to good use in providing cleaning requirements to commerce and industry.

Every business needs some form of cleaning equipment every day of its life, whether it be an industrial chemical in a factory or a roll of toilet paper in an office with one staff member. Most businesses at some stage or another will also need advice on how to get something clean, from a stain on a carpet to cleaning up a stone building.

David B. Cleaning Services was a father and son partnership (David and Paul Bridle). In 1982 the two proprietors started a Sales Division. Working from home became impossible because of the quantity of materials they needed to store. They therefore bought a small industrial unit which also served as an office.

The owners felt that it would now be sensible to form a private limited company in which they would have a joint and equal shareholding. They felt that the provision of limited liability would be a valuable form of protection. It was quite possible that they would be dealing with a small number of major buyers. If a buyer failed to pay up this could cause serious cash flow problems and threaten the survival of the business.

With limited liability status shareholders only stand to lose at most their stake in the company. As a private company therefore the Bridles would have personal protection against market trends leading to a slump in demand for their products, or from bad debts. Furthermore, being able to put Limited after their name would give the business status. They had previously found that many larger companies were not prepared to deal with non-limited companies.

To become a private limited company you can either go to the trouble of carrying out all the necessary paperwork of registering as a company yourself or simply buy a ready-made company. There are a number of companies that make a living from setting up ready-to-run companies and then selling them off. These companies make out all the necessary documentation and registration including choosing a company name. David and Paul were able to cut out a lot of paperwork by simply buying a company which was ready to run under the name Clandrex Limited which was registered with the object of supplying cleaning materials.

Larger premises were obtained and the company was now employing five full-time members of staff and several part timers. The company was split into two divisions—'Contract Cleaning/Window Cleaning' and 'Sales'.

Today Clandrex is one of the biggest distributors of Numatic vacuum cleaners in the United Kingdom. Machines are shipped all over the country—to hospitals, factories, offices and even private individuals.

Clandrex still supplies a range of cleaning chemicals, hand cleaners and other janitorial products. Next to machines, the biggest line is paper products and cleaning cloths/wipers.

Questions

1. Do you think that a private limited company is a suitable form of business organization for Clandrex Limited? Explain your reasoning.
2. What would be the main benefits and drawbacks to David and Paul Bridle from such a form of organization?
3. Give five examples of businesses which might suitably operate as private limited companies.
4. Choose two of these and explain in detail why a private limited company might be a suitable form of organization for them.
5. What extra work is involved in setting up and running a limited company which does not exist for the sole trader and partnership forms?
6. What advantages and disadvantages might there be to allowing additional shareholders to become part owners of Clandrex Limited?

Major decision makers in a company

The board of directors is the major executive body in a company. It is given authority by, and makes decisions for, its shareholders.

The board of directors is essentially a committee. Normally, a board will be made up of executive and non-executive directors. Executive directors are those that hold positions within a company, whereas non-executive directors will be primarily engaged in their outside activities.

The executive directors will be involved in the day-to-day decision-making process of the business. They will be able to bring this expertise to board meetings. The accounts director, for example, will have first-hand experience of the company's figures and how they were achieved, and the marketing director will have been instrumental in steering marketing decisions.

Non-executive directors can bring to board meetings experience gained outside the company, perhaps from directing another company, academic experience, or experience of international trading relations.

It is only by ensuring a diverse blend of knowledge and skill on a board of directors that a company will benefit from a broad perspective of business trends. The boards of directors of major public companies are littered with the names of politicians, financiers and others with power and influence.

A board of directors will be responsible for:

- appointing senior managers including the managing director;
- deciding on how profits will be distributed;
- deciding on how to raise and spend capital;
- establishing the major policies of a company;
- ensuring that all legal requirements are complied with;
- ensuring that the company is successful.

The board of directors will select a chairperson with the responsibility for acting as a 'figurehead' for the company. He or she will be responsible for chairing all board meetings and for making major public policy statements.

The board of directors will appoint a managing director with the responsibility for managing and steering a company on a day-to-day basis. The duty of the managing director is to put into practice the decisions which are made at board meetings. As a board member the managing director will help to create policy but his or her primary function will be to make sure that policies are carried out.

The cooperative

Although cooperatives are still a very small part of the private sector economy, they have undergone a rapid growth in the 1980s. In 1980 there were only 300 recognized cooperatives. Two years later the numbers had expanded to 500 and in 1984 there were 900. By 1989 there were reckoned to be more than 2000 producing everything from shoes to bread and creating employment for around 20 000 people.

The basic idea behind cooperation is that people join together to make decisions jointly and to work and share together.

Cooperatives occur most frequently in three main areas of business activity:

- Production
- Retailing
- Marketing

Producers' cooperatives

These involve groups of people clubbing together to produce goods or services, e.g. a growers' cooperative producing vegetables, or a baby sitting cooperative.

A workers' cooperative is a commonly found type of producers' cooperative. In a workers' cooperative members will:

- share responsibility for the success or failure of the business;
- work together;
- take decisions together;
- share profits among the cooperators.

There are three basic forms of worker cooperatives:

1. Common ownership cooperatives are owned and controlled by the workers. Each has one share in the business, which costs £1 and carries one vote. The shares do not pay dividends and any profits are held in a bank or building society to pay overheads and wages. These cooperatives cannot be sold for personal gain.
2. Co-ownership cooperatives are owned by the workers through one share and one vote per worker. However, the shares are linked to the profits and losses, so the value of the shares can rise and fall. Any worker can take the value of those shares with him or her.
3. Community cooperatives are owned and controlled by the workers, by non-working community members and sometimes by local organizations. This is ideal for a business that brings together local traders and members of the community.

All producers' cooperatives adhere to the principle of one person, one vote when it comes to decision making. But some delegate day-to-day decisions to an appointed manager. Many cooperatives operate an equal pay policy with everyone receiving the same wages and conditions. A few do have pay differentials, but these are usually kept to a minimum.

Retail cooperatives

Nowadays, people tend to think of the Co-op as just another supermarket chain. This is not the case because Co-ops see themselves as having an important role in serving the community. The first Co-op was set up by a group of weavers in Toad Lane in Rochdale in 1844. At that time, workers were paid low wages partly made up of tokens which could only be exchanged in the company shop where prices were high.

Twenty-eight weavers, known as the Rochdale Pioneers, pooled money to buy foodstuffs at wholesale prices which were then sold cheaply to members. Profits were shared out among members in the form of a dividend, depending on how much each had bought. Since then Co-ops have spread and there are many retail Co-ops in Britain.

To become a shareholder in a Co-op you need only buy a £1 share and this entitles you to a vote at meetings to choose the president and other officers of the local Co-op society.

Cooperatives are organized on a regional basis. Over the years many of the smaller cooperatives have tended to be swallowed up by larger societies. The largest single retailing society is the CRS with its headquarters in Manchester. A small number of regional cooperatives give stamps to shoppers. These stamps can be collected and stuck in books which can be used in payment for goods. However, many Co-ops have stopped distributing their dividend in this way and simply use profits to improve their facilities and to make prices more competitive.

Some Co-ops don't just provide supermarket services; they also have their own bank, milk delivery service, funeral service and libraries and provide other benefits such as education courses for members.

In the latter part of the nineteenth century the Co-ops flourished and societies sprang up all over Britain. The Co-ops brought in some of the first supermarkets. However, in recent years the Co-ops have had to face very severe competition from multiples like Tesco. In retaliation many smaller cooperative societies have merged, and organizations like the CRS have established their own hypermarkets (CRS hypermarkets trade under the name Leo).

Marketing cooperatives

Marketing cooperatives are set up to buy, distribute, sell and promote various products. Distribution is often a problem when there are large numbers of small producers. A cooperative organization will help to advise producers about production methods, collect produce, store produce, grade and pack, promote and sell.

Marketing cooperatives are frequently found in developing countries where they play a major part in the distribution of agricultural products. Small farmers will have a small share in a marketing organization. The cooperative might hire advisers to suggest what sorts of products are best produced and by what methods. Cooperative members can then concentrate on production (to the specifications of the co-op) without having to worry about the storage, transport and selling of their produce.

In Zimbabwe, for example, the government has supported the development of cooperatives. Government encouragement and assistance has enabled cooperative unions to construct and make operational over 50 warehouses and more than 200 distribution centres. Rural farmers who belong to cooperatives are able to get credit from the Agricultural Finance Corporation to buy seeds and fertilizers. The loan does not have to be repaid until after the harvest when they take their grain to the Grain Marketing Board. Without the cooperative, finding credit would be difficult and the cost of seeds from private companies high. Farmers do not have to worry about the marketing process.

Franchising

Franchising is one of the most rapidly growing business forms in this country although we still lie well behind the United States where over half of all retail sales are made by franchise organizations. A franchise system operates on the basis that an entrepreneur (known as the franchisor) will have developed a particular business activity such as producing fast food, manufacturing ice cream, producing cosmetics, unblocking drains. The franchisor will then sell the right to trade under the business name to other individuals—franchisees. The franchisee will have the sole right to trade under that name in a particular locality. Examples include Thorntons, Pizza Hut, and Dayvilles American Ice Cream.

Once an agreement has been made to sell a franchise, the franchisee will normally make an initial payment to the franchisor and in return will receive help and advice in setting up the business. The franchisor will often supply equipment and stocks of materials. For example, in the fast food business cooking equipment might be supplied, menus, recipes, packaging and clothing.

Once the business is up and running it is up to the franchisee to make a success of it. However, the element of risk is reduced if the business has been proven to be a success elsewhere and expert help and assistance is provided. A major advantage for the franchisors is that they do not have to risk their own capital and will take a regular share in the profits of franchised outlets.

The main disadvantage to a franchisee is that while it is his or her own business, the franchisee will at times feel beholden to the franchisor (e.g. there might be an agreement that stocks have to be purchased from the franchisor) and a given share of the profits will have to be paid over. It might also be difficult to change methods from those recommended by the franchisor.

Case Study—The Bermudan Ice-cream franchise

Margaret Westlake had worked for a number of years in the restaurant of a large department store. She worked long hours and wages were on the low side. In September 1989 she saw an advertisement in a national newspaper inviting people to buy franchises for £30 000 from a franchising company called Bermudan Ice-cream.

Using her savings and a loan from the bank she was able to buy the franchise for Winchester. The franchisor provided her with a trade name and logo, help with the internal decoration, training in the manufacture of ice cream and customer relations, as well as items of equipment such as menus, refrigerators, cash tills, furniture and other assorted items. She was granted the monopoly of selling the range of ice cream products and using the Bermudan name within a 15 mile radius of Winchester.

In return Margaret had to hand over 7 per cent of her profits to Bermudan Ice-cream.

Margaret described the advantages of the connection in the following way. 'I feel that I am now doing something for myself. Work is my investment in my own future. The harder I work, the more money I take. At the same time I have the help and security of knowing that I am with a national name. They provide me with a lot of help and assistance, and only take a minimal amount of my earnings.'

Questions

1. Make a list of what you consider to be the advantages of such a business relationship to (a) Margaret and (b) the franchisor.
2. Make a list of what you consider to be the disadvantages of such a business relationship to (a) Margaret and (b) the franchisor.
3. What reasons would you put forward to explain the growth of franchising.
4. List six types of business that could suitably be organized as franchises. Choose one type and explain why you think it lends itself to franchising.
5. Why do you think that Margaret thinks franchising is a good thing? In what circumstances might her views be different?

Structures within organizations

Every organization will need to choose those structures which most effectively help it to put its ideas into practice. There are a number of alternatives, each of which will suit different circumstances.

In the typical sole proprietor or partnership form of organization, it will be relatively easy to formulate policies and then put them into practice. This is because only a few people are involved in the decision-making process and the coordination of decisions will not be unduly complicated once procedures for consultation and the passage of information have been established.

In a larger organization, however, the process becomes more complex. While one person or group will make a decision the responsibility for putting that decision into effect will frequently rest with another individual or group. An effective organization will need a well-structured network of communication. Decisions will be communicated in one direction and reports and feedback on progress will be communicated in the reverse direction. The structure within the organization will be based upon the

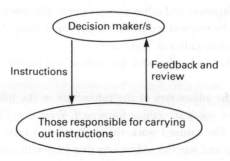

Figure 2.7 Coordinating the decision-making process.

need for effective coordination between those responsible for giving and receiving instructions (see Fig. 2.7).

Hierarchical and democratic structures

Some organizations are based on a distinct chain of command passing down from senior to junior officials. Decisions are made from the top and passed down. Such organizations are usually based on clearly defined procedures and roles within the organization. They tend to exist in situations which are fairly predictable (e.g. the civil service) and/or where it is necessary to be seen to be following carefully laid out rules (e.g. government departments, the police and armed forces).

Other organizations are based on a more democratic basis. Decisions are made as a result of a consultation process involving various members of an organization. Ideas will be discussed and thought through collectively. Democratic structures tend to be found in situations where it is felt to be important for all members of an organization to understand what they are doing, where decisions require individual initiative and where people need to work as a team.

A frequently quoted study of industrial structures is that carried out by Alvin Gouldner of a gypsum plant in the United States ('Patterns of Industrial Bureaucracy', 1954). The plant consisted of two parts: a gypsum mine and a factory making wallboards for which gypsum is an important ingredient. Gouldner found that there were significant differences in the ways in which the two units were structured. In the mine the hierarchy was less clearly defined, and the division of tasks and work areas was more loosely prescribed. Relationships between workers and supervisors were fairly informal and there was only a limited amount of reference to rules and procedures. For example, supervisors tended to issue general instructions leaving it to the miners to decide how a job should be done. Doing a job involved collaboration between workmates, and jobs were rotated, with all miners being capable of doing a variety of jobs from repairing machinery to operating the coal cutting machinery. Breaks were taken at irregular intervals. One miner summed up the situation, 'Down here we have no rules. We are our own bosses.'

In contrast, the factory was based far more on a hierarchical chain of command and on rules and procedures. There was a clear-cut division of labour, a set pattern to the working day, formal relationship between officials and a distinct chain of offices.

Gouldner explained the difference in organizational structures in the following way. Work in the mine was far less predictable than in the factory. The amount of gypsum which could be cut would vary widely between different areas of the mine and occurrences such as 'cave ins' could not be predicted. Miners needed to be able to make their own decisions 'on the spot', and to react quickly to changing circumstances. The problems they encountered did not follow a set pattern so that flexibility was important. In contrast the production of wallboards in the factory followed a clearly set pattern which could be organized into a tight schedule of production.

Case Study—A view of decision-making procedures in Britain and Japan

'British managers are brought up in a tradition of debate. Put ten British managers, especially senior managers, around a table and there will never be agreement.'

The British way is that all the arguments are discussed and then the boss says we will do it this way. Everybody falls in or resigns. Jones compares it with a skier heading for the jump. The decision-making process is very fast and it is very efficient provided nothing happens to throw the skier off course.

In Japan it is different. The Japanese culture builds in a desire for consensus. Japanese managers actively seek it out. The purpose of a meeting is to iron out the differences and thereby reach consensus. On the surface it is a much slower decision-making process, and frustrating for British managers. But once a decision is taken, putting it into action is much faster because everyone is behind it. It is more like passing through a maze. A Japanese team will have explored every avenue. Although the decision-making process is slower and more convoluted, once agreed the team understands all the options it rejected as well as the ones it is pursuing. Changing course is not a problem. It means all operational decisions can be taken much faster.

(*Source*: Alan Jones of Sony (UK) in *Personnel Today*.)

Questions

1. Do you think that the 'British way' or the 'Japanese way' as described above is more likely to require a hierarchical organizational structure? Explain your reasoning.
2. What are the main advantages and disadvantages of the 'British way' of management?
3. What are the main advantages and disadvantages of the 'Japanese way' of management?
4. In what circumstances would you expect (a) the 'British way', (b) the 'Japanese way' to be more effective? Explain your reasoning.
5. What alternatives to these two methods can you think of? Explain the good and bad points of each.

The infrastructure of an organization

The infrastructure is the pattern of authority (and hence the line of communication) *within an organization*.

An important distinction is made in organizational theory between line and staff authority.

Line organization

Line organization is the typical structure of a hierarchical body. There will be direct communication links between superiors and subordinates. Each member of the organization will have a clear understanding of the chain of command within the organization and to whom he or she is responsible. This type of structure can be very effective on account of its clarity. There are set rules and procedures which can be referred to. Figure 2.8 illustrates the way in which communication will flow down from top management in such an organization.

Line management is typically used to organize a firm's central activities such as the making and selling of products. In these areas there will be a clear hierarchical framework. Larger organizations will tend to have more rigid and bureaucratic structures than smaller ones. Although agreed and clear procedures will be necessary in such organizations, it will also be important to have an element of flexibility. Formal structures will frequently be subject to informal changes in the course of time as new situations arise.

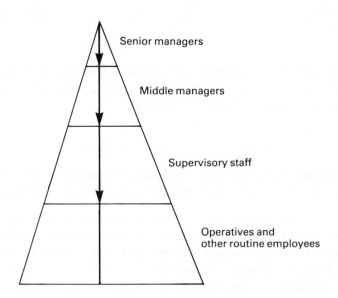

Senior managers

Middle managers

Supervisory staff

Operatives and
other routine employees

Figure 2.8 The downward flow of communication in line organization.

Staff organization

Most organizations combine a mixture of line and staff organization (see Fig. 2.9). Staff organization primarily services the various line departments of a company. Typical staff areas could include personnel, corporate affairs, data processing and office administration.

Staff departments typically cut across an organization providing a range of specialist services and consultancy skills. For example, any line department of a company might require specialist legal help from time to time, data to be processed, or help with recruiting new staff. Figure 2.9 illustrates the way in which various staff areas can be made available to all line departments within an organization. Staff areas thus

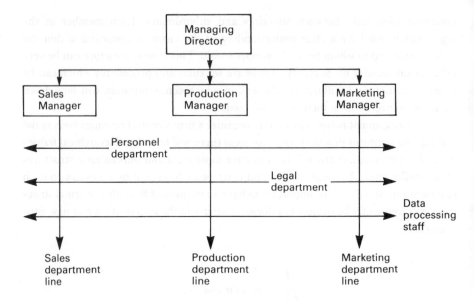

Figure 2.9 Combining line and staff organization.

play an important role 'through' an organization. However, a staff department itself might be organized on hierarchical lines. For example, the personnel department may have several tiers below the personnel manager.

Line and staff organization

Most medium and large business organizations will combine elements of line and staff organization. There will be a number of advantages to having this blend:

1. Line departments are able to concentrate on achieving the central objectives of a business, i.e. marketing, making and selling. At the same time they are complemented in the achievement of these objectives by specialist service departments. Line departments can thus concentrate on their core function without the clutter of organizing activities which are secondary to their main purpose.
2. Line managers only need to familiarize themselves with information related to their core activity.
3. Staff groupings can be called in to provide specialist information and advice in a number of key areas.

However, there will also be a number of disadvantages to combining the two areas:

1. A major disadvantage is that it can lead to confusion within an organization. There will be less clarity over departmental responsibility and lines of authority. 'Unity of command' is often regarded to be the mark of an effective organization. Where there is more than one centre of responsibility confusion can arise; one section can blame another for failure to carry out work effectively or for a breakdown in communication. Where department managers compete with each other

to secure high status work, or where they try to avoid less prestigious work, numerous problems can occur.

2. Many line managers rise to a particular position through many years of hard work. This is particularly true in production departments where it is not uncommon for managers to have worked their way up from the shop floor. In contrast, many staff managers are 'academics' with a university background. Line managers may resent staff managers' rapid rise to managerial status, while staff managers may regard themselves to be better than those who have worked their way up. Such clashes can be detrimental to the smooth running of an organization.

3. Line managers may resent having to listen to the opinions of staff managers who may have different priorities to their own. For example, a corporate affairs or personnel manager might try to push a company into employing more youth trainees in order to project a certain image for a company within the community. In contrast, a production manager may be more concerned with using older, more experienced labour.

In order to overcome difficulties which may arise from combining line and staff organization it is essential for an organization to devise a clear strategy to coordinate staff and line groupings. This strategy will involve setting out the goals of the organization and then deciding on the responsibilities of line and staff groupings. These responsibilities need then to be set out in a clear statement of company policy. Some companies even have an organization and methods department with the responsibility for clarifying such issues.

The superstructure of organizations

The superstructure of an organization is the way in which employees are grouped into various departments or sections. There are various ways of grouping employees depending on the needs and aims of an organization.

The main methods of grouping employees are by:

1. Function
2. Product
3. Process
4. Geographical area
5. Type of customer

We will also see later that a matrix structure can be used to combine grouping methods.

Grouping by function

This is probably the most important way of grouping employees in a company (see

Fig. 2.10). Functional organization means that a company is divided into broad sectors each with its own particular specialism or function, for example marketing, accounts or personnel. Every company will have its own way of structuring its functions.

However, there are a number of common functional areas which will be typical of many large companies. These functions are referred to in outline here, and dealt with in greater detail in specific chapters.

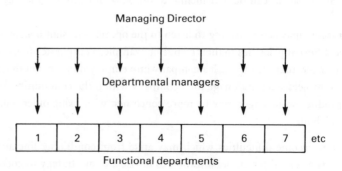

Figure 2.10 Grouping by function.

The company secretary and the legal department

By law it is necessary for every company to have a secretary. The company secretary is responsible for all the legal matters of the company. If paperwork is not done in the correct fashion, the company secretary could end up in court. He or she must fill in the documents that set up the company including the Memorandum and Articles of Association. The company secretary will also keep the share register which is a record of shareholders and any transfers in shareholdings that take place. The company secretary is regarded as a key link between the shareholders of a company and the directors. The secretary will handle correspondence to and from shareholders informing them of company meetings and other important matters. In some companies a registrar will be appointed as a subordinate to the company secretary with responsibility for keeping the share register.

In some companies the secretary might also have other areas of responsibility such as that of office manager. The company secretary will also offer specialist legal advice to other departments within a company.

The administration officer and administration department

Many large firms have a central office which is responsible for controlling the general paperwork of the firm. This department might handle the filing of materials, the company's mail, word processing and data handling facilities. The modern office is increasingly using computers and information technology.

In many companies each department will have its own clerical and support staff. However, it is common practice to have an office services manager with the responsibility for coordinating office services and offering expert advice to departmental managers.

The work of the office manager will include the following areas:

- To take responsibility for and to organize clerical training.
- To advise departments on office layout, office equipment, working practices, staff development.
- To coordinate the supply of office equipment and stationery.
- To study and analyse office practice within the company in order to develop an overall strategy for administration.
- To ensure the standardization of office practice, the layout of forms, invoices and other documents.
- To provide and maintain a communications system within a company including phones, mailing systems, computer hardware and other data processing facilities.
- To report to, and provide statistics for, the company board about the effectiveness of existing office practice.

The information and computing manager and department

In a modern company a large proportion of the staff may work directly with or have access to computer terminals. Information technology (IT) refers to the large and developing body of technologies and techniques by which information is obtained, processed and disseminated. The term therefore embraces computing, telecommunications and office developments.

These three areas, which were intially distinct, are now seen as having more and more in common. They are progressively merging and blending together, while at the same time expanding to play an ever-greater part in business activity.

The role of the information and computing function will be to promote effective exploitation of IT in a company and to provide the guidance, support and co-ordination necessary to accomplish this objective.

Information is vital to decision making in both commerce and industry. The quality of any decision depends on the relevance, accuracy and timeliness of the information available. The main task for the information manager will therefore be to identify the decision maker's information needs, to decide how best they can be met and to develop the systems for meeting them.

Very rapid improvements in computing technology are providing opportunities to support businesses in ways which were not dreamed of a few years ago. For example, a computer workstation on the desk of all management and professional staff, as well as many support staff, in many major companies seems likely by the early 1990s.

The chief accountant and the accounts office

The chief accountant is responsible for supervising the accounts department. The accounts section must keep a detailed record of all money paid in and out and present the final balance sheet, source and use of funds, profit and loss account, and other financial records at regular intervals. Modern accounts are stored on computer files and accounting procedures are greatly simplified by the use of computers.

Within the accounts department there will be two main subdivisions:

1. The financial accounting department is responsible for keeping records of financial events as they occur. Accounts need to be kept of all moneys paid to or by a company and records must be kept of all debtor and creditor transactions. The payment of wages will also require calculations involving deductions for national insurance, pensions and other factors.

    As well as keeping day-to-day records the financial accounting department will also be responsible for producing periodic records such as the annual accounts and figures for discussion at meetings of directors.

2. The management accounting department has the responsibility for nudging the company in certain directions based on its analysis of figures for the present and predictions for the future. Management accounts will break down figures, in order to extract information about a company's present performance and what sorts of improvements can be made in the future. Using systems of budgetary control it will set targets for achievement and limits for spending for the various parts of a business.

Within the accounts department other sub-functions (i.e. functions within functions) might include a cashier's department and a wages department. The cashier's department will be concerned with handling all cash transactions as well as cheque and other payments through a bank account. These records will be kept in a cash book or computerized system.

The wages department will be responsible for supervising the payroll, calculating and paying wages. The data for these calculations will be generated by the works department or other department responsible for recording the amount of work carried out by employees.

The production manager and production department

The production manager is responsible for making sure that raw materials are provided and made into finished goods effectively. He or she must make sure that work is carried out smoothly, and must supervise procedures for making work more efficient and more enjoyable.

In a manufacturing company the production function may be split into five main sub-functions.

1. The production and planning department will set standards and targets for each section of the production process. The quantity and quality of products coming off a production line will be closely monitored.

2. The purchasing department will be responsible for providing the materials, components and equipment required to keep the production process running smoothly.

3. The stores department will be responsible for stocking all the necessary tools, spares, raw materials and equipment required to service the manufacturing process.

4. The design and technical support department will be responsible for researching new products or modifications to existing ones. It will be responsible for estimating costs of producing in different quantities and by using different methods. It will be responsible for the design and trialling of new product processes and product types. It will be responsible for the development of prototypes through to the final product. The technical support department may also be responsible for work study and suggestions as to how working practices can be improved.

5. The works department will be concerned with the actual manufacture of a product. This will also encompass the maintenance of a production line and other necessary repairs. The works department may also have responsibility for quality control and inspection.

The marketing manager and the marketing department

The marketing function is responsible for identifying, anticipating and satisfying customer requirements profitably. Marketing and sales are sometimes combined in a single department, but there is an important distinction between the two. Marketing is concerned with getting the company to produce what the customer wants. Selling tries to get the customer to want what the company has. The marketing department then will primarily be concerned with investigating consumers' needs and wants. This will involve carrying out market research to find out who comprises a particular market, what they want, where they want it, how they like it and at what price. In a manufacturing company there will be very close cooperation between the marketing and the production planning departments. This is so that the wishes of consumers can be closely tied in with product development.

The sales manager and the sales department

The sales department is responsible for creating orders for goods or service. The size of the department will vary considerably as will the way in which it operates. Some companies will employ a large sales force operating in the field on a regional basis. Sales representatives will visit businesses and other customers in order to secure orders for products. Other firms will sell their product by means of some form of advertising or other publicity and will only employ a small sales force. The sales manager will work from a central office based location. Sales team meetings will be called from time to time to discuss strategy and to analyse performance.

The publicity manager and department

Publicity is closely allied to sales and marketing. The publicity department will be responsible for a number of areas which may include advertising, promotions and public relations.

The distribution manager and distribution department

Distribution departments will generally be responsible for control over warehousing and dispatch as well as transport. The distribution manager will be responsible for making sure that goods are sent out on time, that orders are made up accurately and that transport is regularly maintained. The distribution manager will also be responsible for ensuring the company employs the most cost-effective and reliable distribution channels.

The customer relations manager and customer relations department

The goodwill of customers can only be maintained by an effective policy of customer care. The customer relations department will be concerned with handling customer complaints and feeding back suggestions and problems to other functional areas.

The personnel manager and the personnel department

The personnel function has three principal areas of responsibility:

1. It is responsible for recruiting, training, developing and deploying the people in a business.
2. It is responsible for ensuring that their terms and conditions of employment are appropriate, competitive and properly administered.
3. It is responsible for employee relations policy.

The overall objective of the personnel department will be to provide a highly productive, quality workforce.

Personnel provides a specialist service which facilitates the smooth running of a business's core functions. Personnel officers will be responsible for or help with the interviewing of job candidates, the placement of job adverts, and the assessment of staff needs and requirements.

The labour relations manager and labour relations department

In addition to personnel officers some companies employ specialists in the labour relations field. These officers will be responsible for industrial relations and the monitoring of employees' perceptions of working conditions.

The health and safety officer

Every organization must pay close attention to health and safety regulations and laws. Large companies will frequently employ an in-house advisory service on health matters. A wide range of guidance notes and pamphlets will be available from this department on clinical matters such as diabetes, hypertension and alcoholism. In a similar way, guidelines will be produced on safety performance and the identification and correction of every unsafe act and condition before they can lead to accidents.

Community projects manager and the community projects department

A number of large companies in the United Kingdom work on the basis that their business can only be successful in a successful community. A community projects manager might be given the responsibility of running a department which handles a diversity of projects such as help to small businesses, an educational department, and environmental concern units.

There are a number of clear advantages to organizing on a functional basis:

● If groups of specialists are given control over specific work areas this will prevent wasteful duplication within an organization. Invoices can be processed in a particular department, orders won by another, and payment collected by a third. Provided clear guidelines are laid down as to who does what then organization members are clear about their responsibilities.
● Specialists are able to work in a pool of like-minded people.
● An organization is able to concentrate on its primary functions of production, marketing and finance.
● Because each part of the organization is pursuing its primary function it will contribute to the overall well-being of the total system.

Disadvantages to organizing on a functional basis are:

● Narrow specialism will restrict the abilities of individuals and departments to develop a global view of the total organization.
● Individuals cannot move easily between departments.
● Jealousies arise between divisions and departments may come to see themselves as having primary importance. Departments may come to block each other's initiatives.
● As organizations become bigger communication channels may become slower or distorted, particularly between upper and lower levels.
● Divisions may pull in opposite directions to one another. In many large organizations you will sometimes hear complaints such as 'this company is run by a bunch of accountants!' or 'not enough attention is being paid to selling the goods'.

Grouping by product

When a large organization produces a range of different products, it might find it convenient to create an organizational structure based on product lines. For example, a firm in the publishing industry might have a newspaper division, a magazine and periodicals division and a book publishing division. Each division will then contain a mixture of all the specialist ingredients required to enable it to work independently. A great advantage of this form of structure is that divisions can concentrate on their own market areas. It also becomes possible to assess the profitability and effectiveness of each sector. At the same time it is still possible to share expertise between divisions and to share combined services such as a combined transport fleet. By isolating the various parts of a business organization it becomes possible to cut out loss making divisions and to amalgamate divisions by merging them with similar divisions in other

Divisional structure of Northern Foods 1988

Dairy Group	Convenience Foods Group	Meat Group	Grocery Group
Northern Dairies	Park Cakes	Queens Drive	Fox's Biscuits
Dale Farm Dairies	Smith's Flour Mills	Hollands	Elkes Biscuits
Dale Farm Foods	Flecks	Trentham	Batchelors
N.F.T.	Jeffs	Binghams	
Turners Decorating	Dale Farm Dairy Products	Bowyers	
	Riverside Bakeries	Witney Foods	
	Savoury Foods	Mayhew Foods	
	Fenland Foods	Nottingham Poultry	
	Lenton	Plymouth	
	Parrs	Dorset Foods	
	Gunstone		

(*Source:* Northern Foods report to employees.)

companies. It also becomes possible to generate competition within a company and to create greater scope to create an internal promotion ladder. The table is an example of a divisional structure based on product lines.

Case Study—Nestlé grocery to link with Buitoni

Nestlé is merging its Buitoni pasta foods operation with the Nestlé grocery division in order to develop the range of products in the United Kingdom and Europe.

The move follows Nestlé's announcement last week that it is planning to sell its Princes and Trex food brands acquired as part of its Buitoni purchase earlier this year.

Alongside pasta products, Nestlé grocery division will now be responsible for the sales and marketing of Perugina Italian chocolate, Berni antipasto products, Olio Sasso olive oil and a range of charcuterie. However, a Nestlé spokesman claims that with access to all types of manufacturing techniques, future Buitoni products could span a wider range of foods.

Nestlé will also be increasing the advertising spend behind its Buitoni range.

Meanwhile, under the new arrangement, Buitoni's frozen food products will be handled by Nestlé's Findus division—a move which Nestlé has been planning for some time, while catering products will become the responsibility of the Nestlé Foodservice division.

(*Source*: *Marketing Week*, 4 November 1988)

Questions

1. What advantages would you expect Nestlé to have from operating a grocery division?

2. What advantages would you expect Nestlé to benefit from bringing Buitoni products into its grocery division?

3. Why might sales of Buitoni products (a) increase or (b) fall as a result of becoming part of Nestlé's grocery division?

4. For what reasons might Nestlé have disposed of Princes and Trex food brands?

5. What evidence is presented in the article that Nestlé operates a number of product divisions?

Grouping by process

Where a product requires a series of processes, departments will be set up to perform each process. To take the example of the publishing company, within each of the divisions departments are responsible for carrying out the various stages—for example the editing of copy, page layout and design, buying of print, etc. Figure 2.11 illustrates the way in which process departments might take the responsibility for each stage.

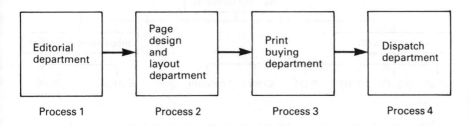

Process 1   Process 2   Process 3   Process 4

Figure 2.11 Grouping by process in a publishing company.

There are a number of clear advantages to organizing on a process basis:

- Grouping by process makes it possible to set up teams of similar minded specialists.
- It becomes easy to identify points in the production process at which things go well or badly.
- It is easy to introduce new technology at a given stage of production (i.e. a given process) and to familiarize the appropriate staff with new skills and working practices.

Disadvantages are as follows:

- Process production will only work effectively if there is a steady flow from one stage to another. If one process gets out of step by producing too much or too little, problems will occur as stocks pile up or run out. This situation might arise if, for example, one group of process workers goes on strike or has high absenteeism levels.

- Sections of employees become too specialized and fail to communicate effectively with other sections.
- It may become difficult to transfer employees from one process to another if divisions between processes are too rigid. Employees might prefer to stick with their existing work group and with skills that they are familiar with.

Grouping by geographical area

Many companies will have branches spread throughout the country and sometimes overseas. Multiple retailing companies are a good example. A company like Marks and Spencer will have shops on every major high street in the United Kingdom. Groups of shops will be organized into a regional division which will have overall supervision of such features as training of staff and distribution policy. Figure 2.12 illustrates a company with six domestic divisions and two overseas divisions.

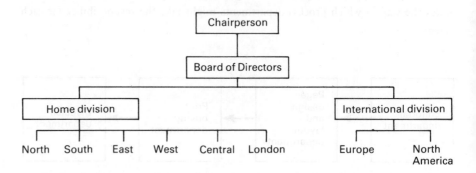

Figure 2.12 Grouping by geographical area.

There are a number of clear advantages to organizing on a geographical basis:

- Setting up distinct regional divisions makes it possible to respond quickly to local needs, issues and problems. The organization thus becomes more sensitive to customers, employees and other groups. At the same time it might be able to cut through a lot of red tape if the regional groups are allowed to make their own decisions.
- Setting up national and regional divisions makes it possible to tailor the operation of an organization to local conditions. Differences would include those of language, law and custom. Local knowledge is best gained by hiring local specialists.
- National governments will often look more kindly on multinational divisions which have a local head office and organization.

Disadvantages are:

- Having too many regional divisions can lead to wasteful duplication of facilities and roles. Too few divisions can lead to lack of coordination, gaps in communication and breakdowns.

- Having an extensive regional structure requires the creation of a series of management positions. It is not always easy to recruit personnel of the required calibre to fill these positions.
- Regional headquarters might take on a life of their own and start pulling in opposite directions to central policy makers.
- Although the local divisions will frequently have the best understanding of the situation 'on the ground' they might find themselves at loggerheads with central officials many thousands of miles away.

Grouping by type of customer

Organizations will often set up different structures to deal with different sets of customers. This is because they will often give some groups more time and attention than others. An obvious example would be in a hospital where casualty patients would require a different type of attention to those requiring a routine X-ray.

In a department store the restaurant department will operate in a different way and have different procedures to a department selling underwear. The furniture department will need to set out a process of documentation and make arrangements for delivery to customers which clearly contrasts with purchase procedures for toys.

Banks will usually have a counter for foreign currency transactions, a department dealing with enquiries, as well as the regular departments for dealing with private and business account holders (customers).

Many businesses will have different procedures for dealing with large and small customers. Separate departments might handle these accounts, using different types of paperwork, offering different rates of discount, and treating customers in different ways.

The advantages of organizing in a pattern based on having different sets of customers are:

- Different types of customers can be dealt with by separate departments.
- Customers will be more inclined to deal with a business with departments concentrating on their particular needs.
- It is easier to check on the performance of individual products.

Disadvantages are:

- Divisions may compete with each other for the use of company resources.
- The structure may be costly to set up and will only be cost effective if there is sufficient demand.
- More administration and accounting services will be required.

Matrix structure

So far we have looked at the internal organization of a business as if there will be a single pattern of organization. However, many large organizations will combine two or more patterns in a matrix structure, e.g. combining functional and geographical lines of command.

In a matrix structure each member of the organization will belong to two or more groups. This can be illustrated, as in Fig. 2.13 where groups of employees are organized into regions (e.g. north and south) as well as into functions (e.g. marketing or sales). In this example a particular group of workers will be accountable to both the northern manager and the marketing manager (i.e. Marketing Section A).

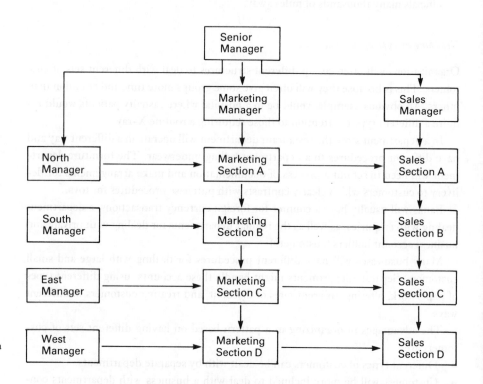

Figure 2.13 An example of part of a matrix structure.

Each member of the organization (below managerial level) will be accountable to two or more managers. Marketing, sales and other key functional managers will have a global responsibility for their function within the organization, while divisional managers have responsibility for these functions on a divisional basis.

Each divisional manager will be responsible for a specific project. In order to carry out this project, he or she will be able to call upon the full range of departments to collaborate in achieving project targets. Projects may be based on products, types of customer, geographical area or any other specific criterion. Inevitably a matrix structure can be complicated and needs to be clearly laid out if it is going to be understood.

There are a number of advantages to be gained from implementing a matrix structure:

● A matrix makes it possible to structure an organization in such a way as to focus on a number of aims at the same time, e.g. servicing different types of customers, servicing different regions, producing different types of products, etc.

- A matrix structure gives an organization extra flexibility to respond to new situations where there is an increase in demand for its resources.
- The system makes it possible to draw groups from specific departments in the required numbers.
- There can be cross-fertilization of ideas across departments, rather than departments just working internally.

Disadvantages are:

- A complex matrix structure may be difficult to understand, and employees can lose sight of the major organizational aims.
- This system will often require extra administrative resources, which can be costly in terms of time and money.
- Because the system establishes more than one chain of command, this can lead to power struggles, contradictory orders and general confusion.

A matrix structure can be very effective. However, it must be clearly laid out and clearly explained to all those involved.

The legal background to business

We look for security in the society in which we live. The legal system consists of rules, supported by courts of justice on behalf of the State, which provide an ordered environment. The rules determine how society is ordered and controlled. Governments are elected on the basis of support for their political philosophy and have the ability to change the framework of the legal system. Laws are therefore a product of the political process and may change in accordance with decisions made by the ruling party of the day.

In business we need laws to protect the majority against the practices of powerful bodies and individuals. For example, without rules governing employment protection, monopoly legislation (see Chapter 6), consumer protection and health and safety legislation, many would argue that our society would be an unsafe place in which to live. The legal system provides a framework governing a wide range of business activities and the ways in which they affect the providers of finance, employees, customers and society in general while at the same time this framework allows businesses to achieve their chosen objectives.

Broad areas of influence include:

1. *Laws relating to the constitution of businesses*   When people associate together to engage in a business or profession for profit they are deemed to be in a partnership under the Partnership Act of 1890. As a result each is separately liable for all of the debts of the business in which he or she engages. If these people incorporate and create a separate legal person who owns the business and is responsible

for paying debts and fulfilling contracts, they have then become members of a corporation running the business on their behalf. Successive Companies Acts control the establishment, performance and functions of companies. For example, to register a company the Registrar of Companies must receive both a Memorandum and Articles of Association. The Memorandum describes factors which affect the outside of the company such as features of the company's constitution and the objects it was incorporated to achieve. The Articles contain rules governing members' relationships with each other and with the company and which do not generally affect outsiders. Companies must have officers of three kinds: directors, a secretary and auditors. Directors of a company must present the annual accounts and a report to members, and members have the right to dismiss directors. The word 'limited' warns creditors that there is a limitation on the liability of members and it is an offence to use the word limited if the person(s) in business are not incorporated with limited liability.

2.   *Consumer protection*   Organizations provide goods and services for consumers in return for payment. The legal system enables transactions to take place and provides a mechanism for resolving disputes. Laws attempt to overcome the inequality in bargaining power between large organizations and relatively small consumers. The need for such laws exists because of events such as poor quality goods, misleading information, manufacturers' negligence, breach of contract, and consumer safety. Legislation concerning business activities includes the Fair Trading Act of 1973 which set up the Office of Fair Trading to keep a constant watch over monopolies and restrictive practices. In response, the Restrictive Practices Act of 1976 ensures that traders who restrict competition by making agreements with other traders must register their agreements with the Office of Fair Trading and the Competition Act of 1980 allows the Director General of Fair Trading to investigate businesses operating anti-competition policies restricting growth. Other areas of consumer protection refer to the poor quality of goods and services and to the provision of credit.

3.   *Contract law*   Contract law consists of legal rules governing the enforcement of obligations between individuals arising from voluntary agreements. By making contracts, companies can buy raw materials and sell finished goods in relative safety as long as each side gives something of value.

4.   *Law of torts*   The law of torts protects parties from each other's actions, particularly if a party suffers injury as a result of these actions, e.g. negligence.

5.   *Employment law*   Under the Employment Protection Act of 1978 employers are required to provide employees with the terms of their employment within 13 weeks of their employment commencing. Terms relate to holidays, pay, hours of work, job title, notice to terminate the contract and pensions. Of particular importance in recent years has been the Health and Safety at Work Act of 1974, designed to maintain and improve standards of health, safety and welfare at work.

6.   *The law of agency*   When organizations use outside specialists the relationship of

principal and agent is created. An agent is someone empowered to act on behalf of a principal in contractual relations with third parties. With this strong element of trust, clear legal guidelines are set to ensure the success of this relationship.

The potential list of areas covered by our legal system is almost endless. We could also mention the requirements of the legal system in relation to insurance, negotiable instruments, bankruptcy, data protection, financial services and the topical area of environmental law. With the prospect of considerable change in the near future when the 12 member states of the EEC come together in 'The Single Market' in 1992, businesses cannot ignore the implications for areas such as quality, safety and common standards.

Short answer questions

1. What are the key features of an 'organization'?
2. What are the most important ingredients of an *effective* organization?
3. What are the advantages and disadvantages of bureaucracies as organizational structures?
4. What is meant by systems theory? In what ways can systems vary between organizations?
5. What is meant by the private sector of the economy? Give examples of types of business organizations that would form part of the private sector.
6. What is meant by limited liability? What protection is provided by limited liability?
7. How is an ordinary partnership set up and run? What advantages are provided by partnership forms of business organization when compared with the sole trader form?
8. What steps need to be followed before a company can start to trade?
9. What advantages are available to public limited companies and not to private limited companies?
10. Who are the major decision makers in a company?
11. What is meant by franchising? What type of businesses are most suited to this form of organizational structure?
12. How does the *direction* of decision making vary between hierarchical and democratic structures?
13. What is meant by (a) line and (b) staff organization?
14. Illustrate how a company may group by function. Look at organograms (organizational charts) from actual companies. Which company appears to have the most effective organizational structure? Why?
15. Describe the role within a company of:
    (a) the marketing director;
    (b) the information and computing manager;

      (c) the company secretary;

      (d) the managing director.

16.   What is meant by grouping by process? Explain how this operates in a business with which you are familiar.

17.   Draw a diagram to illustrate how a company might use a matrix structure.

18.   What is meant by (a) contract law and (b) the law of torts?

19.   Why is a legal framework essential to the smooth running of a business?

20.   How does the law of agency operate?

Data response questions

1   Getting the right management for 1992

With human resource management now regarded as a central business issue, the impact of the single European market on the way managers are recruited, trained and developed is likely to be considerable.

British companies, including UK-based multinationals, are particularly affected. A survey last year by the journal *Multinational Employer* found that other European companies had management teams that were better prepared for post-1992 competition and that UK groups could lose out in the greater exchange of managerial talent that will result from a freer flow of labour.

Management practice in Europe has already been drawn closer together, well before 1992, by the steady stream of mergers and acquisitions generated by companies diversifying or expanding beyond domestic markets.

A *Financial Times* report in January 1988 highlighted no fewer than ten reports of inter-country mergers and acquisitions. According to the European Commission, the number of major mergers involving EC-based companies nearly tripled between 1983 and 1987 and this growth is expected to accelerate.

The result is that many companies are now undergoing a fundamental structural and cultural growth, and the changes involved have prompted a major reassessment of how managers at all levels of the organization are developed.

European experience has shown that the process of building management teams capable of operating in international markets has to start at several layers in an organization. It should include recruitment drives that are international in their scope, general management development schemes that provide international experience, team-building exercises that extend beyond national boundaries and the better use of employee communications and events to foster a truly international corporate culture.

One of the most impressive examples of a truly international recruitment drive is Olivetti's 'No Frontiers' training programme, which aims to fill a demand for more than 1000 systems support specialists by 1990.

The programme was formulated as an international exercise specifically in response to the increasingly international business of the company's clients. The third intake, for example, included 13 different nationalities in a group of 58. A careful assessment was made of global needs. A worldwide advertising campaign was run in English. All successful candidates were flown in to undergo the 'No Frontiers' training programme at the company's headquarters in Ivrea, Italy.

The programme is intensive. Close ties are formed. Candidates are encouraged to form a strong personal network, so that back at their jobs they can phone each other to talk over problems and help each other.

Olivetti recruits are all considered potential managerial material.

(a) What changes will be required in the organizational structure of British multinationals with the creation of the single market?

(b) What do you understand by 'cultural growth' in relation to business organization?

(c) Why is it important for the process of building management teams to take place at several organizational levels?

(d) What advantages do you expect Olivetti to benefit from as a result of its 'No Frontiers' policy?

(e) What will be the main costs and benefits to British companies of developing a more 'European' flavour to their organizational structures?

2 Setting up and running a small business

A group of sixth form students from the King's and Kesteven and Grantham Girls' schools set up their own company as a general studies exercise. The students set out to run the company for a year, using two hours of their time a week.

The first meeting of the students was concerned with brainstorming ideas for a company. Emphasis was placed on spotting a gap in the local market, copy an existing successful product, or developing a new innovatory product based upon existing skills within the group of 11 students.

A number of ideas were suggested including:

- A stationery stall.
- Buying and selling secondhand sports equipment.
- Making gingerbread (Grantham is famous for gingerbread).
- Production of neckscarves.
- Hiring out a piece of land to learner drivers.

At the end of the day the group decided to investigate further the possibility of making gingerbread on the basis of a skills audit, because costs would be low, and the risks appeared to be minimal.

Market research

Market research involved finding out how many could be sold in a week at different prices, where the products would sell best, who would make up the target audience, what form the product should take (i.e. size, packaging, etc.).

Product research

Product research involved finding out alternative ways of making the product. Grantham gingerbread is a distinct product compared with ordinary gingerbread. Bakers had to be consulted, ingredients purchased and trial runs carried out. The prototype products needed to be sampled as part of the initial market research.

Initial finance

The initial finance came from a £5 loan. However, because the gingerbreads were very cheap to produce, relative to the price determined by market research, the loan was paid back within a few weeks. The company was then able to finance its expenditure out of income.

Forming a company organization

It soon became apparent that a company structure was required if all the functions of the company were to be carried out effectively. The following organizational structure was therefore formulated on the basis of making gingerbreads:

Figure 2.14 Members of Concept, Caroline Tomkins and Matthew Hollingsworth producing truffles.

- *Managing Director*—overall supervision of other functions.
- *Accountant*—responsible for money forecasts, all moneys in and out and keeping detailed records.
- *Secretary*—responsible for handling all paperwork.
- *Purchasing Director*—responsible for purchasing and smooth flow of equipment and ingredients to production.
- *Production Director*—responsible for ensuring that products are made to agreed quality standards.
- *Marketing Director*—responsible for finding out consumer preferences.
- *Sales Director*—responsible for ensuring that products are sold.

Early problems

It soon became obvious that the company would be unable to meet demand for the product. The first production run ran out in two minutes and twelve seconds. Gingerbreads take too long to cook, and take up too much oven space to be produced in large batches given the oven space available to a school company.

Looking for an alternative product

Given that the company felt that it should continue to concentrate on its existing skill area it was decided to go for an alternative food product with greater value added potential which would not require oven space. A survey of alternative recipes came up with the idea of truffles (which simply require the heating up of chocolate for a few seconds). The truffles proved to be an important 'bread and butter' line for the company because they are always popular and it is almost impossible to make mistakes in manufacture.

Cash flow forecasting

One of the earliest stages in setting up the company was to prepare a cash flow forecast. This involved calculating the likely income and expenditure of the company over a three-month period. It was necessary to work out the total expenditure and revenue each week in order to forecast future problems, and to anticipate future profits. The cash flow forecast was only a rough and ready guide, but it indicated that if sales matched market research predictions then income would always exceed expenditure. Using the cash flow predictions it was possible to estimate total income, total expenditure, the break-even point of the company and profits.

The period of growth

Once the company had become established and had created a surplus of capital it was decided to use the capital to diversify into new lines. The basis for further expansion needed to be based on the company's existing practices, i.e.:

- Detailed product research
- Detailed market research
- Accurate record keeping
- Participative management

Research indicated the scope to establish two new products: presentation glass apples (Grantham is the birthplace of Isaac Newton)—the apples were bought at trade prices from a crystal manufacturer; and stationery—the stock being purchased from a wholesaler. Pricing for the new products was based on slightly undercutting competitors.

The company now chose a trading name, Concepts. (It may seem an unusual step to wait so long to choose a business name. However, it was decided to wait until the full range of products was established before taking this step.)

Concepts printed its own order forms, invoices and statements. It made sure that stock was kept at a level which could be sold within a month, so as not to be burdened with unsold product. The company went on to make a very good profit.

(a)   What types of background research did Concepts have to undertake before going into the production of gingerbread?

(b)   What key questions would they have needed to answer before committing themselves to production?

(c)   Why was it essential for Concepts to prepare a cash flow chart?

(d)   What alternative sources of finance could Concepts have used in setting up their business?

(e)   What elements of running Concepts as a business would you regard to be (i) realistic and (ii) unrealistic?

(f)   What problems did Concepts face which would be untypical of those faced by a small starter business?

(g)   What business ideas can you come up with for your own locality?

(h)   What steps would you need to take in creating a small school or college business?

3   Smalley Excavators Limited

Richard and Ann Smalley have built up Smalley Excavators into a business with a turnover of over £4 million.

Richard comes from a farming family and it was his familiarity with agriculture and farm machinery, coupled with mechanical engineering talent, that enabled him to find a profitable niche in the market for his specialized form of excavator. Always inventive by nature, he had trained as an agricultural engineer before gaining experience with hydraulics at Lucas and Massey Ferguson, developing and testing hydraulic pumps.

In 1960, Richard started his first company, making a mechanical ditcher that sold for £69. A year later, while he and Ann were on honeymoon, he designed the first of his excavators. It was an hydraulic, portable grave digger to which he later added wheels and 360 degrees slewing, making it into a walking excavator. The usual practice of using four strong men to dig a grave was excessively labour intensive, and the new product, launched in 1963 after a year's development, was an immediate success. He sold 50 all over the world in the first year.

Since then, he and Ann have always worked together. Today she is the Publicity Director with additional responsibility for equipment and transport purchasing. But 25 years ago she was a fully fledged working member of the production line, drilling holes and painting the finished units being turned out at the rate of four or five a week from their farm workshop. She was also sending out letters and typing invoices, preparing the publicity and chasing around agricultural shows and exhibitions to boost sales.

Richard's early ideas proved to be effective. He had put a cab on an engine on a chassis.

He knew that by pushing all the load down into the feet, all the weight was going into the bucket and imparting a very substantial tearout force. It was an elementary principle of commonsense engineering that was very effective and it is one that has been retained in his machines for a quarter of a century.

He continued developing two-wheeled excavators up to about 5 t weight. Ann says that up to the size of small conventional excavators, the customer is not really interested in saving money. She realized that when the purchaser of their first machine walked away saying 'I can throw away my spade. I have always been a navvy but now I have an excavator.' In the boom days of the 1960s, the capital outlay on such a machine would be written down on the first contract and the operators didn't have to worry about saving money.

When the Smalleys began looking to other possibilities, the Waterway Authorities of England provided the biggest stimulus as old canals began to be used as leisure facilities and maintenance was essential. The authorities provided the boats and Smalley mounted machines on them that could dredge and clear weed, working in shallow waterways under low, narrow bridges, unhindered by a counterweight tailswing.

At the same time the firm started making peat excavators and more grave diggers. It was the peat machines that led the firm into producing low ground pressure crawler machines which brought about the Smalley rubber band type of track.

To a large extent the Smalley success formula has been based on the flexibility of his designs. The units are all made from standard units produced by a variety of companies. These units can be mixed and matched to meet most customers' requirements without involving a lot of expensive specialized one-off production.

Another important ingredient in the formula is the belief in personal contact with customers. The company has now spread its business over about ten different markets, and diversification is the name of the game.

(a) Where did the original business idea come from?
(b) What would have been the main problems in developing the idea into a finished product?
(c) Could either Richard or Ann have run the business on their own?
(d) Describe the most important stages in the growth of the business.
(e) What were the key functional areas of the business?
(f) What have been the main reasons for the success of the business?
(g) What major problems can you possibly foresee for Smalley?

Suggested reading

Dransfield, R., *Business Studies Investigations*. Shell Education, 1989.
Dunkerley, D., *The Study of Organisations*. Routledge and Kegan Paul, 1972.
Handy, C. B., *Understanding Organisations*. Pelican, 1985.
Rose, M., *Industrial Behaviour: Theoretical Developments since Taylor*. Pelican, 1985.

3

Business organization in the public sector

The public sector of the economy is that part of it which is owned by the government.

Government and business in the wider economy

Michael Heseltine, writing about the Conservative Government in 1987, stated that, 'This government, like all its predecessors for at least the last fifty years, is up to its neck in the business life of this country, stimulating one enterprise here, stifling another there and interfering everywhere'.

The influence of government is a key variable in the dynamic business environment. Government policy invariably has an effect on business. This is as true for an increase in government expenditure as it is for a decrease, the creation of greater controls or the reduction in controls, support for a particular activity as for reduction in support for another. Government has the means to create widescale changes in the industrial climate. For example:

- An increase in interest rates can, and often does, reduce the general level of spending in the economy while at the same time making it difficult for enterprises that have borrowed to finance capital expenditure.
- When the government gives a contract to one firm rather than another, it can make the future of one firm more secure, and help to develop a competitive advantage through the profits resulting from the contract.
- A reduction in personal taxes may provide a greater incentive to individuals to work harder, leading to a general increase in productivity.
- The reduction of taxes on a product, e.g. lead free petrol, can change the structure of demand, leading to changes in the structure of supply.

All these and many other areas will have widespread repercussions for the ways in which businesses operate.

There are a number of reasons why the government plays such a prominent part in the economy:

1. Some goods and services are provided by the government because it is felt that all citizens are entitled to a share in the public provision of such items. For example,

most people in the United Kingdom believe that all children should have some form of health care and education.

2.   Some goods and services which everyone benefits from can only be produced by the government if they are going to be properly provided. An example of this is the police force.

3.   Some people believe that the government should try to reduce inequality. This might involve taxing some people at a higher rate than others and giving more benefits to those who are worse off. Of course, there are others who believe that inequality is not a bad thing because it gives people a motive to try and better themselves. They would argue that the government should remove any obstacles which prevent people from bettering themselves by working harder.

4.   The government might also try to make the economic system run more smoothly. For example, it passes laws against monopolies and to protect consumers and it takes measures against pollution and other antisocial practices.

A very important role played by the government is to set 'the rules of the game' within which business activity takes place. These rules are constantly changing and when they do some people will lose out and others benefit. It is important to bear in mind the following questions:

1.   Who makes the rules?
2.   Why do the rules change?
3.   How do they change?
4.   Who loses and benefits when they change?

Government activity in the general economy is dealt with in other sections of the book, and in particular in Chapter 16 which looks at the influence of the economy on organizations. This chapter therefore concentrates on those activities which are more directly controlled by the government.

Public enterprise

Public corporations

In the United Kingdom the government still owns a number of industries and businesses on behalf of the people. Most of these take the form of public corporations. However, in recent years there has been a sustained period of privatization of government enterprises.

A public corporation is set up by an Act of Parliament. In 1990, examples of public corporations include British Rail, British Coal, and the Bank of England. Once a public corporation has been set up, the government appoints a chairperson to be responsible for the day-to-day running of the industry.

There are a number of reasons why public corporations have been set up:

1.   To avoid wasteful duplication. In the nineteenth century, for example, there

were three railway lines between Leeds and Harrogate. This is wasteful competition. Imagine the problems caused by having three electricity companies operating in your street.

2. To set up and run services which might not be profitable. Would a private company supply post, electricity, gas and water to a small remote village if a lot of capital were needed to set up services which may not make a profit?

3. To gain the benefits of large-scale production. It may be more efficient to have one big firm producing lots of output than to have several smaller firms. When there is only one firm, the government as owner might be less inclined to charge high prices than a private firm.

4. To protect employment. The government might take into consideration the need to create and keep jobs rather than just considering financial profits.

5. To control industries which are important to the country such as coal, steel and the railways. The 'infrastructure' is the term used to describe the basic backbone of the economic system including the transport network, energy and water supplies. Some people argue that the government has an important responsibility for the supervision and maintenance of the infrastructure.

During the 1980s a number of public corporations were privatized and it is likely that this policy will continue in the early 1990s. Privatization involves turning the public corporations into companies owned by shareholders.

There are a number of reasons for doing this including the following:

1. Some people argue that state-run firms are not efficient because (a) they do not have any real competition and (b) they do not have the threat of going bankrupt as the government will always pay off their debts.

2. It is argued that in a modern society as many people as possible should have shares in businesses. The idea is that everyone—not just the very rich—should become shareholders and therefore people have been encouraged to buy in some cases just a few hundred pounds' worth of shares in enterprises like British Telecom and British Gas.

Other people argue against privatization. They argue that competition can be harmful in areas where standards need to be maintained such as the National Health Service. Competition can lead to 'cutting corners' and the deterioration of safety standards. There is also the strong argument that it is a nonsense to sell to the public shares in industries which are already owned by the people. Instead of an industry being owned by all citizens it becomes the property of shareholders.

When a public corporation is set up, an independent body is also formed to protect consumers' interests. Consumers can take their complaints to this body; for example, the Post Office Users' National Council will take up complaints made by users of the Post Office such as those about the late delivery of letters.

The government keeps the power to make major decisions about how public corporations should be run, such as the decision to close down large sections of the railway network and whether to build new power stations. However, the chairperson and

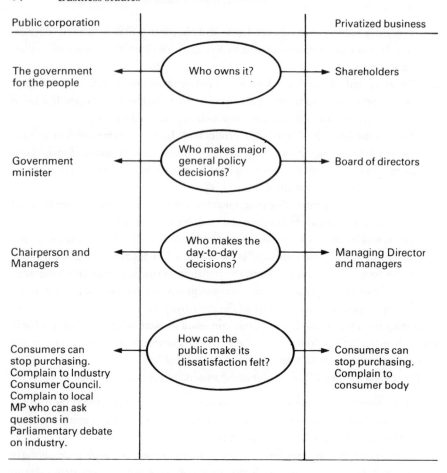

| Public corporation | | Privatized business |

Figure 3.1 Some comparisons of public corporations and privatized industries.

managers will decide on day-to-day issues such as wages and prices, timetables and industrial relations. The government does sometimes interfere even in these areas—leading to public argument and debate.

Whereas a limited company has to make an annual report to its shareholders, a public corporation must present its annual report to the appropriate government minister, who makes a verbal report to Parliament, and at this time Members of Parliament will make criticisms or voice support for the way the corporation is being run. A committee of MPs has the job of studying the running of each public corporation and of reporting on its operation. For example, there is a select committee of MPs acting as a watchdog over British Coal.

Figure 3.1 highlights some of the differences between public corporations and privatized industries.

Other central government enterprises

In addition to public corporations, the other two major areas of government control over economic activity occur where:

- an activity is run by a government department;
- an activity is run by a public company in which the government has a shareholding.

When an activity is run by a government department, a government minister will have overall charge for the department. The department is staffed and run by civil servants. A typical example of this would be the Customs and Excise Department which deals with the supervision and collection of some taxes.

The major criticisms of such a form of organization from the business point of view are that:

1. Decisions are made slowly because there are many links in the chain of command, usually wrapped up in rules and regulations.
2. The organization may appear to be inefficient because of lack of competition.
3. There is no external agency to protect the public's interest by checking on how the department runs. While in many cases there will be a mechanism for making complaints, it may be so complex as to be inaccessible to the ordinary person.

In recent years the government has reduced its shareholding in public companies as an extension of its policy of privatization.

Local government enterprises

In the United Kingdom certain services in local areas are supervised by locally elected councils. These councils usually run some forms of business organizations such as the municipal car parks, swimming baths, sports centres, bus services, lavatories, etc.

However, in the late 1980s council activities have also been the subject of the policy of privatization. Today many activities such as road cleaning and refuse disposal are contracted out to firms which put in the lowest tender for a particular job. Council officials simply monitor the effectiveness with which the work is done, and can refuse to continue a contract if work fails to meet the required standards.

Local councils receive money from two main sources: a grant given to them by central government, and a local tax. Local councils often subsidize loss-making activities such as local parks which provide benefit to the community.

Case Study—The public and the privatization of natural monopolies

Study the articles below which were written for the Free Speech column of *The Independent*. Each week *The Independent* invites national figures in a given area to debate openly on given issues. In these articles Norman Tebbit and John Smith argue over the issue of privatization of natural monopolies.

This week: What, if any, advantages does the public gain from the privatisation of natural monopolies like gas, water and electricity?

One thing is clear. The public is agin it. Whatever its views on British Petroleum, Aerospace, Steel, Airports, Authority and all, and despite the share bonanza that followed them, the great British public was and remains solidly opposed to privatising electricity, gas and water.

In an opinion poll by NOP in December 1986, 71 per cent of those polled wanted to keep these essential services in state hands; only 21 per cent were in favour of privatising them. This did not, of course, prevent more than five million people becoming shareholders in British Gas a week later, thereby acquiring shares worth £5.6bn at an opening price of 50p. (They were 183p yesterday.)

Two years later, in December 1988, public hostility to the selling of water and electricity remained. A Mori poll found 69 per cent opposed to privatising the electricity industry, and only 23 per cent in favour; while 75 per cent of those polled opposed the sale of water authorities, a mere 15 per cent were for it.

People evidently have strong feelings about water. Even more than gas and electricity, it is seen as a primal natural resource, and indignation is aroused by the thought of anyone claiming to 'own' what naturally springs (or falls, or droppeth as the gentle rain from heaven) and thus belongs to everyone, or no one. In spite of these polls, the water authorities sell-off is due in November this year, and the electricity industry will follow in spring 1990.

Privatised companies' shares outperform other sections of the market by some 5 per cent, according to Hoare Govett, the brokers, so the great British public is here displaying one of its periodic fits of selflessness. It is not usually against measures which make it richer. A successful applicant for the minimum tranche of shares from the flotations of British Airways, British Gas, British Telecom and BAA would have paid £1262.50 for them. Those shares were worth £1994.24 on Monday night, which means a profit of £731.74, or just under 60 per cent, on that original investment, without even including the dividend payments that investors would have received over the years. So what is the objection to privatising utilities?

The most obvious is that industries which have no competitors, since the product they supply is unique and essential, are in such a strong monopoly position that they should be operated purely in the public interest. Take electricity. You can cook by gas, if you prefer, or coal or even wood, if you have a nostalgic yen for an Aga; but it is exceptionally difficult to operate a shaver or washing machine by gas (though it *can* be done) and virtually impossible, nowadays, to light your home by gas. And although you can shave and launder clothes by hand, it is not really practical to light your home with candles. So you still need electricity when darkness falls.

The distribution (though not necessarily the generation) of electricity is a natural monopoly, and consumers are forced to pay whatever price the suppliers care to impose. Having no alternative supplier, they cannot withdraw their custom; and once the industry is privatised, why should their needs be rated above those of the electricity company's shareholders? This makes customers feel indignant and somehow cheated, just as they do if the electricity workers go on strike (*pace* Channel 4's *A Very British Coup*).

All these considerations apply even more clearly in the case of water. Water is an essential and irreplaceable commodity. (No, I don't know if anyone has ever bathed in Perrier, though I suppose they could if they were rich enough. Asses' milk has got *nothing to do with it*). Further concern has been expressed about the disposal of the various local water authorities' land and other assets, and the possible misuse of these amenities in pursuit of ever-higher profits for the lucky shareholders.

'The business of government,' Nigel Lawson famously said, 'is not the government of business.' Agreed. But the business of government *is*, above all, the happiness of the governed; and *they* have shown every sign of being unhappy with the privatisation of utilities. Is it sufficient answer to say that in that case they should buy shares and use them (a) to exercise a vote in the running of those industries and (b) to assuage their sorrows by making a healthy profit?

Angela Lambert
(Editor of the 'Free Speech' column in *The Independent*.)

When profit turns the lights off

by John Smith, Labour MP since 1970; former Minister at Department of Energy and Secretary of State for Trade; Opposition spokesman on Treasury and Economic Affairs since 1987.

It was John Baker who blew the gaff. The chief executive designate of National Power—the larger of the proposed duopoly of privatised generating companies—opined, in speech notes for a pep talk to his staff: 'The job is not about shouldering national responsibilities but about meeting contracts, improving profitability, seeking out opportunities but exploiting them only if it pays to do so.' He went on: 'Our task will not be to keep the lights on whatever the cost. It will probably pay us to ensure we never overstress our plant.' He later delivered a sanitised version of his speech, but nobody, I hope, was fooled by that. One should not, however, be hard on Mr Baker. He rendered a public service by revealing with startling clarity how a profit-driven company is most likely to approach a public service obligation. It is in business to make a profit. That is what its managers are paid to achieve. The animal will behave according to its nature when it is confronted with the questions raised—and answered—by Mr Baker.

I believe, therefore, that the onus of proof must rest on the privatisers to persuade the rest of us that to hand over industries (such as electricity and water) which are essential public services to profit-driven companies will not prejudice these very services in the way Mr Baker so graphically describes. I do not think they have done so—or indeed can.

The privatisers normally point to two influences which they claim will moderate the instinct for aggrandisement: the effect of competition and the power of statutory control. Competition, it is said, will put control in the hands of the consumers who, by having the power to reject the provision of a particular service by a particular company can oblige it to maintain quality of service or a reasonable price. It is hard to foresee such a process at work in either a privatised electricity or water industry. Such limited competition as is envisaged in electricity in England and Wales is between the two privatised generating companies into which the Central Electricity Generating Board is to be split—National Power and Power Gen (Big G and Little G)—one with 70 per cent of the action, the other with 30 per cent.

In assessing the competitive effect of this structure, Professor Colin Robinson and Allen Sykes, of Consolidated Gold Fields plc, told the Select Committee on Energy: 'Duopoly is generally an unsatisfactory market structure. There is a strong incentive to collude... Firms in duopoly tend not to compete on price in the hope of avoiding price wars.' They concluded: 'We would expect prices to be higher than under continued nationalisation.' Striking evidence from a non-leftwing source.

But it is worse than that. Electricity customers will not contract with the generating duopoly but with the privatised successors to the area boards, which will be monopolies. The consumer has no choice as to his electricity supplier.

Can we rely alternatively on statutory obligation for our protection? Hardly, in the case of generators, since they are to be relieved of the statutory obligation to supply presently imposed on the CEGB (Mr Baker's reference to 'keeping the lights on'). There is, of course, an obligation to supply to be imposed on the privatised area boards. But they can only supply what is generated. Removing the obligation to supply from the only entities capable of fulfilling it does seem an odd way of going about it.

In the case of water there is no question of competition. The only source of water for a consumer will be the particular privatised water company. It is intended to impose upon them standards of water quality as a necessary public protection. But these obligations may well be in conflict with the dynamic of the profit motive: with the result that either corners will be cut, or the standard will only be met by passing the costs on to the consumer by increasing prices. If any doubt exists about the primacy of the profit motive one need only refer to the memorandum from the Water Authorities' Association to a group of Conservative MPs (beguilingly known as 'The Friends of Water'). It argues that, if the privatised companies are to be managed 'successfully and profitably', they should not be open to prosecution or enforcement orders for environmental improvements.

No wonder that public opinion is so hostile to the privatisation of water. It is a precious national resource, crucial to the health and well being of the whole population. The public feeling that it should therefore be a matter of public stewardship, rather than private profit, is soundly based.

Such public concern it also evident in relation to nuclear power. Not only is nuclear power taken out of the limited competition of the duopoly: it looks as if the risks and costs of both the disposal of nuclear waste and the decommissioning of nuclear power stations are to remain with the taxpayer while the profits go to the shareholders. Again, there is a well-founded public belief that an industry so sharply affecting public health and safety should remain in public stewardship.

In the face of these powerful considerations, why is the Government so determined to proceed with these privatisations? I believe the answer is threefold. A dogmatic aversion to public ownership; the raising of funds to create a public sector financial surplus; and what a London Business School study described as 'a momentum behind privatisation independent of any economic benefits'. This momentum is further stimulated by the benefits conferred on the managers of privatised companies, the advisers to public flotations, and the initial shareholders. None of these can properly justify such a wholesale sacrifice of the public interest and the greatly increased prices for vital services described so aptly by the Confederation of British Industry as an 'inflationary own goal'.

The shareholder is the best watchdog

By Norman Tebbit, former chairman of the Tory Party; former Secretary of State for Employment and Trade and Industry; now director of Blue Arrow, British Telecom, and BET.

A managerial failure in the South West Water Authority last year caused thousands of people to be supplied with toxic drinking water. It was not an act motivated by, or caused by, greed for profits or as a result of striving for higher earnings per share. The authority is a public body responsible not through a board of greedy, unscrupulous directors to rapacious shareholders, but through worthy, public-spirited folk to the public they serve—in this case with poisoned water.

Had the water authorities been privatised before this particular affair—never mind the methodical fouling of the seas around Britain by sewage—the opponents of privatisation would be riding high on venom and sanctity.

The fact is that most accidents, such as the one in Cornwall, arise from weak management, flabby direction and in this case inadequate regulation of a monopoly. The latter is an inherent characteristic of public-sector monopolies. It encourages chronic lack of capital investment, misdirection of that which is made, consequent low or negative returns on capital and inadequate returns on the cost of labour too.

I was once the minister to whom the nationalised British Telecom, which is in part a public utility, was responsible. I am now a director of the privatised—that is, truly publicly owned company. As a government minister I had to receive BT's corporate plan. My officials, good able men, but not carrying executive responsibility, second-guessed the BT management. I had to third-guess them and then take the plan to the Treasury, where officials fourth-guessed us. The Chief Secretary to the Treasury then fifth-guessed us, with E Committee of the Cabinet, or the Star Chamber, ready with a sixth or seventh guess and the Cabinet a potentially eighth- or ninth-guesser. The process took months. Matters entirely extraneous to BT affected the outcome as well, such as the demands of other public-sector enterprises for capital investment or for subsidy to continue to produce poor-quality goods at prices too high to compete.

Eventually a plan for the year would be approved, sometimes after it had already commenced. The management was frequently not properly rewarded for fear that competitive pay for highly mobile professional managers might cause unrest amongst the generals, the Whitehall warriors, the nurses or the judges. The advantage they enjoyed was near-immunity from dismissal and an index-linked pension in retirement.

This Whitehall near-farce was not a characteristic of Margaret Thatcher's term in office—read Tony Benn's memoirs if you think that. It is an inherent feature of so-called public ownership, which is ownership by a tiny group of officials and politicians controlling the fortunes of businesses or whole industrial sectors.

Contrast the scene with British Telecom today. The company can plan and carry out its capital investment programme without Whitehall battles. So long as it retains the approval of its shareholders and bankers, capital is available and a five-year rolling plan can be executed. If the company needs key people it can recruit them—without reference to the pay of judges or generals.

Yes, of course, the company is driven by the need to reward its owners: the shareholders. But it can do that only by serving its customers. Where there is competition, the customers are protected by that. Where there is not, the Director General of the Office of Telecommunications is the surrogate for competition, and the protector of the consumer. Indeed, he is also there to ensure fair play between BT and its far smaller competitors.

Does the system work? Well, contrast postal and telecommunication services.

When the Post Office fails to meet its own targets for the deliveries of letters, Pounc (the Post Office Users' National Council) may well issue a rebuke—but that is about all. If BT fails to meet Professor Carsberg's (director of Oftel, BT's regulatory body) complaints on behalf of consumers it can suffer sanctions that really hurt, and those penalties fall on the shareholders. Pounc has no such powers and the Treasury would always oppose financial penalties, since it (or more correctly the taxpayers) would have to pay.

What is more, today the Secretary of State is no longer the sponsor of BT and has no conflict of interest in holding the ring between BT, its competitors and customers. And the Treasury, instead of financing the business, will in the current year receive more than £1.5bn in dividends, interest and tax whilst mainstream prices to users have been frozen.

Water and electricity are not different from other commodities because they are essentials of life. After all, food and clothing are far from inessential and no one in their right mind suggests that public ownership of food manufacturing, processing and distribution would give better consumer service than we receive in the street markets, small shops or supermarkets. The utilities are different because final customer supply (although not generation) are largely natural monopolies. Monopolies or neo-monopolies require regulation to protect consumers. Monopsonies (that is, a single or an unduly powerful buyer for the product of several sellers) require regulation to protect suppliers. The question is whether a regulator appointed by government is more likely to be effective in dealing with a dominant supplier owned and financed by that government or with a private-sector business whose shareholders want profits which the regulator can reduce if service is poor.

In short, where regulation is needed to protect consumers against monopoly or neo-monopoly, it is more effective against the private than the public sector, precisely because a private company maximises returns to its shareholders.

(*Source:* 'Public troubled over private water', Free Speech column, *The Independent*, 4 February 1989.)

Questions

1. What would you consider to be the eight key points made by Norman Tebbit in favour of privatization?
2. What would you consider to be the eight key points made by John Smith against privatization?
3. Who do you consider to be the main winners/losers from policies of privatizing natural monopolies?
4. Write an essay explaining how you would go about evaluating whether the privatization of natural monopolies is in the public interest or not.

Short answer questions

1. What is meant by (a) the public sector and (b) a public corporation?
2. List four existing public corporations and four that have recently been privatized.

3. What is meant by (a) nationalization and (b) privatization?
4. Why does the government interfere in the running of the economy?
5. Explain how a change in national government policy with which you are familiar has changed the environment within which businesses operate.
6. Describe three arguments which could be put forward for increased state control of industry, and three against.
7. What are the key features of a government department?
8. What is meant by a municipal enterprise?
9. What would be the main arguments in favour of privatizing swimming pools?
10. Should prisons be part of the public or the private sector?
11. How is a public corporation run? Who makes the decisions within the organization?
12. Is it necessary for some business organizations to always remain in the public sector?
13. How do people in 'out of the way places' benefit from the activities of public corporations? Is it fair for the rest of the community?
14. What incentives has the government offered to encourage small investors to become shareholders in privatized companies?
15. What control does the public have over the activities of privatized companies?
16. What major business criticisms can be levelled at government departments?
17. What is meant by 'a share-owning democracy'? What would be the major benefits of such a system?
18. What activities are carried out by local councils in your area? How effective are they?
19. Study the progress of a process of privatization. What are the main issues involved?
20. Find out how the level of state ownership of industry in the United Kingdom compares with that in other European Community countries. Is it possible to compare efficiency of the industrial structure by referring to the level of government control?

Suggested reading

Hurl, B., *Privatisation and the Public Sector* (Series, Studies in the UK Economy). Heinemann, 1988.

4

Decision makers and types of decision making

Economic society is a decision-making society. Decision-making is the central process of business activity.

In Chapters 2 and 3 we concentrated on types of business organization. We now go on to explore the types of decisions that will be made within such organizations.

Who are the decision makers?

We saw in the previous chapters that there is a wide variety of organizational structures and hence patterns of communication and decision making. In any organization

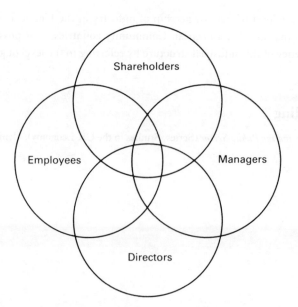

Figure 4.1 Decision makers within a company.

there will be several layers of decision making. In a rapidly changing technological society it is important that employees 'on the ground' should be able to tackle problems using their own initiative. This point can be illustrated by considering the labour market requirements of a major oil manufacturing company. In a large organization operating over a wide geographical area and producing in a variety of product markets, it will be essential for decisions to be made quickly by 'managers on the ground'. Decisions will require the 'sounding out' of opinions from a range of specialists and generalists from research analysts and computer programmers to maintenance operatives. The ability of individuals to make a contribution to the decision-making process depends very much on their ability to question existing viewpoints, to challenge the meaning of data and to ask a series of relevant questions.

Employees who do what is expected of them are frequently valued. However, organizations will operate most effectively and produce the best long-term results when employees are able to think for themselves and produce fresh insights into novel and changing situations. The petrol pump checkout operator is as much a *decision maker* as is the managing director of the company.

There are four main groups of decision makers within a company: shareholders, directors, managers and other employees. These categories are not exclusive. For example an employee might also be a shareholder (see Fig. 4.1).

Shareholders

Shareholders are part owners of a company and elect the board of directors. Shareholders have more influence in some companies than in others. For example, in late 1988 a group of shareholders in Newcastle United Football Club attempted to buy up the majority of the shares in the club in order to bring the policy of the club more into line with the wishes of paying spectators. In some companies shareholders feel remote from policy-making decisions. The law requires a meeting of shareholders once a year, but because the annual general meeting involves complex procedures such as the presentation of the accounts, few shareholders feel fully in control at such meetings. Other companies such as Shell UK arrange informal meetings of shareholders at conference centres, where the everyday business of the company is explained. Shareholders are given the opportunity to ask questions and to discuss matters of interest or concern with senior company officials at a buffet reception.

Directors

Directors represent the interests of shareholders. Executive directors play managerial roles within the company while non-executive directors add a breadth of experience to board meetings. Non-executive directors might also represent important shareholding interests, e.g. when a pension fund has a large shareholding in a company.

The role of the board is to make the important policy decisions and to make sure that they are carried out. The board will deal on its own with relationships with other companies, but take-overs and mergers may require the approval of the shareholders.

Managers

Some senior managers will also be members of the board of directors. Their responsibility will be to see that the decisions made by the board are put into effect. Managers that fail to meet the expected targets will frequently be replaced. Within management there will be a management structure with a line of authority.

Employees

All employees will have a part to play in everyday decision making. This may include the way that a work task is carried out, the way in which customers are treated and many other aspects of working life. Employees will normally report to a line manager.

Types of decision making

Most classifications of types of decisions are based upon the predictability of decisions. For example, Herbert Simon (1960) made an important distinction between programmed and non-programmed decisions.

Programmed decisions are straightforward, repetitive and routine, so that they can be dealt with by a formal pattern, e.g. the re-ordering of stock by a company.

Non-programmed decisions are novel, unstructured and consequential. There is no cut-and-dried method for handling situations which have not arisen before.

Simon thought that these two types of decisions were ends of a continuum, with all shades of grey lying in between.

Gilligan, Neale and Murray (1986), in their book *Business Decision Making* extend this analysis to identify three types of decisions which managers might encounter stemming from the degree of certainty or uncertainty associated with the outcome, together with the time period involved, the frequency with which decisions have to be made, the extent to which the subject is routine or non-routine, and the implications of the decision for the organization.

The three types of decisions that the authors identified were:

1. *Short-term operating control decisions*   These are decisions which have to be frequently made involving short-term, predictable operations. These would include the ordering of new stock, the design of a production schedule, or the preparation of a transport route for deliveries.
2. *Periodic control decisions*   These are made less frequently and are concerned with monitoring how effectively an organization is managing its resources. For example, this might include the review of pricing strategies for certain products, reviewing problems occurring in an on-going company budget, or the re-apprai-

sal of the way in which the sales force is being used. Such decisions are concerned with checking for and rectifying problems concerned with meeting company objectives.

3. *Strategic decisions*   These are major decisions involving overall strategy. They will often require a considerable use of judgement by the person responsible for making the decisions. This is because although such decisions will require a considerable amount of analysis, important pieces of information will frequently be missing and so risk will be involved. Such decisions might involve the development of a new product, investment in new plant, or the development of new marketing strategy.

Levels of decision making

The structure of the decision-making process needs to be based on the types of decisions that need to be made. The most obvious implication is that routine decisions are dealt with by routine procedures and that time and money are not wasted unnecessarily on them. There would be no point, for example, in senior managers spending large amounts of time on routine tasks which can be done by somebody else. By the same token, decisions requiring in-depth analysis and thought will require careful consideration. Organizations therefore need to develop procedures for decision making most suited to the nature of the environment in which they are operating.

Gilligan, Neale and Murray recommend that in broad terms:

> ...short-term operating and periodic control decisions should be made by junior and middle management who are involved in the day-to-day administration of the organisation, and not by the company's senior management. The task of senior management is to concentrate upon non-routine, non-recurring, strategic decisions in which there is a high degree of uncertainty regarding the outcome and for which, as a consequence, a far greater element of judgement and creativity is required. In those organisations in which senior management does become embroiled in the day-to-day, straightforward operating decisions, the effectiveness and motivation of lower levels of management is likely to suffer, whilst at the same time, because of the preoccupation with short-term decisions, less time is available for long-term issues, with the result that the managerial focus switches from long-range strategic development of the company to short-range control.
>
> Thus, insofar as it is possible to generalise, the primary concern of senior management should be with strategic decisions, whilst short-term operational decisions should be left in the hands of operating management. Middle management then acts as the meeting point between the two, taking as its focus the periodic control decisions.

An open systems decisions model

Many of the decisions that need to be made by individuals within organizations involve uncertainty. In a complex, dynamic society change is ever present. In such an environment it is helpful to develop an open systems approach to decision making. A closed systems approach would assume that organizations have clearly defined and unambiguous goals.

An open systems approach dispenses with the notion that the effects of decisions can readily be computed and calculated and instead works on the premise that at best information will be imperfect. An open systems model places emphasis on feedback, learning and adaptation together with the effects of this upon ends and means.

An open systems approach can be used to show how the decision-making process can be made more flexible. The system can then adjust to changing circumstances and to changing perceptions and understanding of the meaning of available information. Figure 4.2 illustrates one way in which an open systems model might operate.

The first stage will be to identify the objectives to be pursued. These objectives will rarely be clear-cut and will therefore be subject to review. Setting objectives therefore involves setting out courses of action that will be appropriate to the organization, and establishing measures for assessing their attainment.

The second stage in the decision cycle is to outline some of the courses of action that are available. These courses of action can be evaluated in various ways using available information. Evaluation processes will range from a hunch, to an inspired guess, to a highly researched piece of analysis and assessment. A marketing department in a firm, for example, might want to carry out a SWOT analysis of existing and/or potential products in order to identify strengths and weaknesses. A SWOT analysis is an analysis of the Strengths, Weaknesses, Opportunities and Threats of a product or a particular course of action.

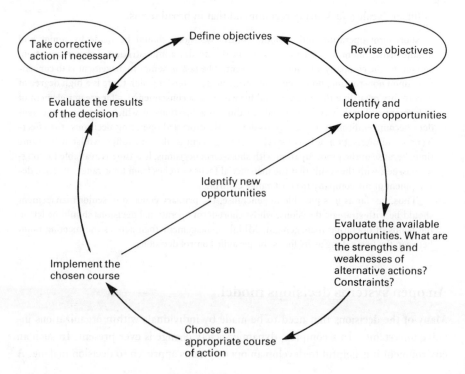

Figure 4.2 The decision cycle.

The next stage in the decision cycle involves comparing the likely results of alternative courses of action with the desired level of performance. At this stage you have already established your performance objectives. You should now be asking questions such as if we do X how close will we be to achieving our target?

Providing there is a match, the decision taker can then choose the most effective of the alternative courses of action that have been identified given the initial objectives.

If a firm's objective is to achieve some measure of guaranteed success it might choose a course of action that avoids risk. Alternatively, the firm might be prepared to take a risk if the objective is to gamble on high returns.

If the chosen course of action does not look likely to meet the required objectives the decision taker should then either reduce the target goal to manageable proportions or seek alternative courses of action to meet the target.

Once the groundwork has been covered and all aspects of potential decisions have been 'kicked around', a decision can then be made. The effects of the decision should be clearly monitored. Putting the decision into practice may immediately lead to the identification of new opportunities. For example, once the early space programme had been implemented researchers immediately became aware of fresh opportunities, e.g. the Space Shuttle. These new opportunities will help organizations to meet their objectives in new and different ways.

The results of decisions will need to be clearly appraised and evaluated to improve the decision-making process. Corrective action can be taken if necessary. The decision-making cycle is an on-going process. The open-ended nature of the process means that the quality of decisions should increase with time.

The open systems approach highlights the importance of evaluation to decision making. Results need to be continually fed back to decision makers so that they can re-appraise decisions in the light of an increasing quantity and quality of information. Feedback can lead to adjustment. A simple illustration of how this can have beneficial effects is in the training of young cricketers using computer programs which simulate their bowling action. Programs have been developed which will play back to a bowler a picture of his action in bowling a cricket ball. The young cricketer thus is provided with feedback on current performance enabling him to take corrective action, to appraise existing technique and to develop an understanding of new opportunities.

The human side of decision making

While a number of organization decisions can be programmed to follow set patterns (they can be made by reference to established procedures), there are many others that require an individual human input. Areas that spring to mind are consumer and personnel relations.

The human side of decision making is affected by factors influencing the individual decision maker and factors affecting group decision making.

In the modern business environment there are many factors which encourage the growth of group decision making:

1. The modern business environment is so complicated that effective decison making now requires groups of minds working together to tackle problems and think things through.

2. Participative management has become increasingly fashionable in business circles. The encouragement of a wider number of people within an organization to think of themselves as managers and to become involved in decision making means that a greater range of expertise can be drawn upon. At one time a large bank branch had just one person at the top—'the bank manager'. Now you will find that there are several 'managers'. For any company, and particularly ones with wide geographical spreads and a range of product types, decentralization is essential. Most decisions, especially tactical decisions, cannot be taken effectively at the centre which may be miles—or continents—away. They have to be taken immediately, on the spot, by people who know all the circumstances. There is often no time for referral back to central office. One way of achieving this sharing of responsibility is to remove layers from the chain of authority, so that each division head reports directly to the managing director rather than to one of several assistant managing directors—who themselves report to the top person. Another way is to create separate profit centres—sections of the overall business whose managers are given the responsibility and resources (and guidance where necessary) to run their own sections as their own business.

    In recent years this type of practice has become increasingly common in the public sector following on the success of decision-making operations in the private sector. Today, we see a national policy of local management of schools, where each school is responsible for its own finances, through group decision making within the school. Doctors are also to be responsible for managing their own budgets, as are hospitals and other units in the National Health Service.

3. In the nineteenth and early twentieth centuries it was not uncommon for businesses to be owned by one or a small number of owners who were also the decision makers. Nowadays it is far more common for businesses to be owned by shareholders who appoint a team of managers.

Factors influencing the way in which decisions are made

Decision making is influenced by a number of important factors.

The *personality* of the decision maker is a prime factor. Decisions are usually made by people. Even when decisions are made by machines, the machines will have first been programmed by human intelligence.

Decision making requires a number of skills. Some decisions require a particular type of skill—e.g. the ability to follow a set pattern of rules—other decisions require different skills—e.g. the ability to respond to novel and changing situations.

Some individuals may have the sorts of personalities which are suited to analysing and evaluating various options but are hopeless at implementing a decision. Others may have the strength to implement decisions, but are ineffective at evaluating the results. Some people will be cautious while others are rash. Different decisions require different types of decision makers. We have all heard comments such as 'He can never make up his mind', 'She comes up with ideas but never puts them into practice', 'He won't listen to advice and just ploughs ahead without admitting that he has got it wrong'. These are all criticisms of attitudes to decision making. Some decisions require caution, others require single mindedness, while others again require a combination.

The ability to make a decision and to put it into effect will depend on intelligence and confidence. Different individuals will have different abilities to cope with uncertainty. This will depend upon such factors as status which in turn will depend on things like age, sex, education and social class.

An individual's *perception* of a situation will also have a major influence on how decisions are made. Given the same set of stimuli, different individuals will select what they regard to be important. The way that individuals perceive a situation will depend on their previous experience and understanding. For example, when a Boeing 747 exploded in mid-air over the Scottish town of Lockerbie in December 1988 some of the residents thought that they were experiencing a major earthquake. This interpretation of events was on account of the wide media coverage of a catastrophic earthquake in Armenia the previous week which was still very much in the public imagination, and because they had no other way of explaining the widespread devastation. Other residents of the town who had been able to locate an explosion in the sky were immediately able to recognize that there had been an aircrash.

It has been suggested that there are four main ways in which perception influences the decision-making process:

1. Decision makers are sometimes influenced by factors that they are not conscious of at the time. For example, when interviewing a candidate for a job you may feel that you like or dislike a particular candidate without being able to explain why. A particular decision might 'feel right' for no apparent reason.

2. In making abstract decisions a decision maker might simply be influenced by emotional factors, e.g. you might take a particular decision because it appeals to you. The decision makes you feel good.

3. When it is not clear what the exact nature of the problem is you might make a decision on the basis of influences which are really irrelevant to the given issue. The novice gambler on horses doesn't always study the form card, he may select a horse on the basis of the horse's name, or the colours the jockey is wearing.

4. The comments and views of high status individuals may be given more attention than those of low status individuals. Status can be a key factor in influencing decision making in group meetings.

An individual's *attitude to risk* can have a bearing on decision making. Studies have indicated that people who are more intelligent are likely to study and analyse a situation in some depth before making a decision, whereas those with less intelligence are more inclined to 'hope for the best'. Individuals who worry about failure are less likely to take big risks.

An individual's *values* also influence the way in which he or she approaches decision making. Studies of managers indicate that there are two main sets of values that influence decision making:

1. The organization's goals, e.g. output maximization, profit maximization, etc.
2. Personal goals, e.g. security, promotion, a high income.

Different individuals will give different weightings to the relative importance of these two sets of goals. Some managers will be seen to be 'in it for themselves', others will be viewed as 'company people'. However, it is often difficult to make a clear distinction. Someone that appears to be 'a good company man' may in fact be a shrewd 'go getter'.

Decision making by groups

Many business decisions will be made by groups and managers will spend a high proportion of their time working directly or indirectly as members of a team. A group can loosely be defined as a collection of people with a common purpose who communicate with each other over a period of time. Key elements of this definition are:

*   Group members share a consensus of purpose.
*   There is interaction between group members.
*   There is a pattern of communication.

The definition also implies that there will be a system of rules and a group structure.

Group working

Whenever a group is required to make a decision there will be three strands involved in moving from the start of the decision-making process to the finish, i.e. the final decision. These strands are illustrated in Fig. 4.3.

Task

The task is the content of the work. For example, the task of a management meeting may be to decide on a location of a new factory, or the task of an interview may be to

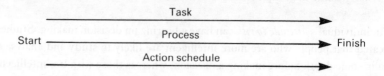

Figure 4.3 The 'strands' of decision making.

select the best candidate to take up a particular post. Thus, the task is the conversion of information and opinions from members into decisions or recommendations. In general terms this covers *what* has to be done and *why*. Most groups give a lot of attention to the *task*.

Action schedule

The action schedule is concerned with how a group will be organized to do a given task. The schedule will cover such questions as who will fill the necessary roles, how will progress be checked and monitored, how will it be made sure that the group keeps to the time schedule. It will also deal with the procedures of decision making, how to ensure that everyone gets a say, how conflict will be dealt with, etc. In general, the action schedule will cover the *where* and *how* of decision making. Most groups will give some attention to their action schedule.

For example, an action schedule for a meeting might set down when the meeting will take place, who will attend, who will run the meeting, how decisions would be voted on and other procedural matters.

Process

The process is the interaction which takes place between members of a group. It is about how people work together, their relationships and the feelings created by their behaviour within the group. It involves interpersonal skills such as listening to others and helping others to join in a discussion. It involves expressions of feelings and the giving and receiving of feedback. In general it covers *who* does what and *when*. Many groups pay little attention to *process*.

The three threads of group working are all important in group decision making. It will be obvious that a group which concentrates on its action schedule and its process entirely may have a wonderful time but is unlikely to achieve the task. It will not be long before morale will suffer and the group disintegrates. In contrast, concentration purely on the task is likely to lead to arguments about how things should be organized, and inattention to group members' thoughts and feelings will lead to mishandled resources and to misunderstandings.

Factors affecting group effectiveness

There are a number of important factors influencing the effectiveness of a group including the size of the group, the flow of communication within the group and the style of management.

The size of the group

There are a number of reasons why it is easier to make decisions within small (i.e.

groups of five or six people) rather than larger groups. The more people involved in the decision-making process, the more difficult it is to involve everyone, and the more difficult to get everyone to agree. As groups grow larger, the higher the level of dissatisfaction with the way the group operates. Individuals find it more difficult to identify with the group, and sub-groups start to form. In order to prevent a group from becoming fragmented, it is increasingly likely that a leader will need to take centralized control over decision making, as the size of the group grows.

Despite the disadvantages of large groups, there are also a number of clear advantages. A large group will be able to call upon a greater pool of skills, energy and resources. A further benefit is that if a wide number of members of an organization feel that they are involved in the decision-making process, they may be more willing to implement policies.

Communication within groups

The main factors influencing the flow of communication within a group are the formal organization of the group, the informal organization and the means of communication employed.

Research carried out by Bavelas (1948) suggested that there are four main types of communication network (Fig. 4.4). Both the wheel and the chain networks are typified by a centralization of the flow of information. Effective decision making thus depends to a great extent on those in key central positions and on the quality of the communications channels to them.

Bavelas and Leavitt saw these centralized forms as exhibiting the following characteristics:

- They were highly effective at making and carrying out straightforward, well structured, predictable activities.
- Levels of satisfaction for group members would be relatively low when compared with those for members of less centralized groups.
- They would help to strengthen the leadership position in such groups.
- A stable structure would rapidly emerge in the group.
- The group would become dependent on those with greatest access to relevant information.

In terms of our previous analysis, such a group structure lends itself to short-term operating control decisions.

In contrast, the circle type of network and the completely connected network lend themselves to a more decentralized form of decision making. Members of the group are mutually interdependent and share the decision-making process. The group is not so dependent on key individuals and levels of satisfaction are usually greater. Disadvantages are that because responsibility is shared, there might not be an effective mechanism for pushing decisions through. There may be a lot of talk about action

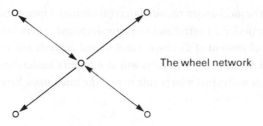

The wheel network

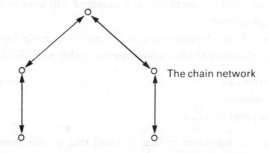

The chain network

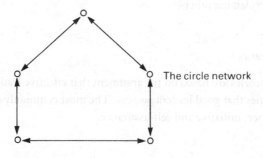

The circle network

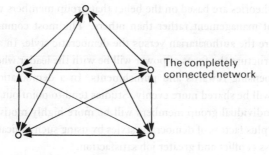

The completely connected network

Key:

○ group members

◄──► lines of communication

Figure 4.4 Types of communication network.

without the mechanism required to create action. Open networks may be more appropriate for periodic control and strategic decisions, where high quality decisions need a substantial amount of discussion and shared analysis and evaluation. However, long-term and major policy decisions will also require leadership, perhaps in the form of a prominent individual who is able to say 'the buck stops here'.

Style of management

The way in which an organization is managed will have an important effect on how well groups operate.

Studies of the characteristics of effective leadership have identified three main types of explanation of what influences the quality of leadership:

- Trait theories
- Style theories
- Contingency theories

However, it is important to bear in mind that no one theory has been effective in explaining all situations. Each theory is good at explaining a number of examples, but poor at explaining others.

Trait theories

These theories are based on the argument that effective leadership rests with particular qualities that good leaders possess. The most commonly quoted personal traits are intelligence, initiative and self-assurance.

Style theories

These theories are based on the belief that group members work harder given certain styles of management rather than others. The most commonly quoted contrasting styles are the authoritarian versus the democratic style. In an authoritarian management structure the focus of power will be with the leader who is primarily responsible for dispensing rewards and punishments. In a democratic management structure, power will be shared more evenly. Studies tend to point out that in democratic structures, individual group members will be more highly motivated. Such studies point out the plus factors of democratic styles by using such indicators as lower labour turnover, less conflict and greater job satisfaction.

However, it is important to point out that democratic styles are not always appropriate, e.g. in making a snap decision, or in dealing with an emergency. Furthermore, some people prefer working with a structure, they like to know what they are expected to do.

Contingency theories

Contingency theories set out to account for the range of variables which may be relevant in a particular situation, e.g. the task, the nature of the work group and the position of the leader in the group.

Such theories can produce valuable insights and clues about appropriate management techniques in given situations. For example, Fiedler (1967) suggested that the appropriateness of using an authoritarian or a democratic management style depends upon whether the situation facing management is 'favourable' or 'unfavourable'.

A favourable situation would exist in the following circumstances:

1.   The leader is popular and trusted by members of the group.
2.   The task is well defined.
3.   The power of the leader is high.

Fiedler felt that item 1 was the most significant. His findings led him to suggest that authoritarian approaches are most suitable in circumstances where:

- the task is well defined and the leader is strong and highly respected; or
- the task is ambiguous and the leader is not in a strong position relative to the group.

In the first case, decision making will be effective because subordinates will support a respected leader. In the second case, leadership must assert itself and clarifiy its aims for the organization, or go under.

In contrast, where a task is ambiguous and the leader is well respected, the leader can afford to draw on the whole expertise of the group while still retaining power and authority.

The '*best fit*' *approach* can be used as an extension to Fiedler's work. This approach is based on the assumption that managers need to take account of four factors if they are to operate effectively. These four factors are:

- The leader
- The subordinates
- The task
- The environment

The leader will have a given set of views about how things should be done and what is important.

The subordinates will have a given set of views about how they should be led and how things should be done. They will relate to tasks in different ways, and have varying levels of commitment to group tasks.

The task will vary in nature, complexity, time scale and importance.

The environment will vary according to the nature of the group, the position of the manager within the group, what the group or organization is trying to achieve, and the structure and technology of the organization.

The 'best fit' approach argues that there is no single best style of leadership. Different styles are appropriate to different circumstances. The best style in a given group will be the style that best matches up to the requirements of leader, subordinates and task.

The degree of fit can be measured on a scale running from tight to flexible. In Fig. 4.5 we have a leader whose preferred management style is relatively authoritarian, working with a group who feel happier with a more flexible style, on a task which is fairly ambiguous. Because of this lack of fit, problems and difficulties are likely to arise. In the real world it is likely that the three elements will move some way towards each other or the job will not get done.

The three factors are then placed along the scale.

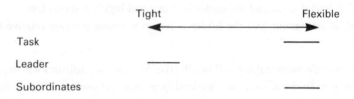

Figure 4.5 Illustration of degrees of fit in a fictional organization.

Working effectively in groups

Are groups more effective at making decisions than individuals?

The answer to this question depends on the context in which decisions need to be made. There are a number of important influences, including:

- the task in hand;
- the time available to make a decision;
- whether or not a range of views is required;
- the individuals involved;
- the effectiveness of the communication process;
- other factors (try to list them).

Generally speaking, the quality of decision making in a group is likely to be higher because of the quantity and quality of data that can be drawn on.

In any group situation individuals will take on formal or informal roles. In a formal situation group meetings may involve officials such as a chairperson, a time keeper and a secretary. In informal situations group members frequently play parts such as the person who tries to force a decision on a group, the opponent of new ideas, the peace maker and so on.

It has been suggested that the optimum group size is five people because:

- the odd number will prevent an impasse;
- the group is sufficiently large to avoid mistakes resulting from insufficient information, or the power of an individual with an entrenched view;
- the group is small enough to involve everyone.

Gilligan, Neale and Murray have identified the following features that should lead to effective group performance:

1. The structure of the group and the status of group members should be stable and well formed.
2. The groups should be large enough to fulfil the tasks, but not so large as to encourage the formation of sub-groups.
3. The group members should have the appropriate skills for the task.
4. The atmosphere should be informal and relaxed.
5. Objectives should be understood and accepted by group members.
6. Discussion should be encouraged and members be willing to listen to each other.
7. Decisions should be reached by consensus.
8. The leader of the group should not dominate, nor should there be evidence of a struggle for power.
9. The group should operate with mild or moderate levels of stress.
10. Disagreements should not be overridden. Instead, the reasons for disagreement should be examined and an attempt made to resolve them.
11. The allocation of tasks to members should be clear and accepted.
12. The group should act in a cohesive way.

Decision-making techniques

Decision making is rarely an easy process. The quality of information that is required to carry out a business decision can be immense and in a dynamic business environment the variables that require consideration will constantly change. For example, inquiries into the siting of nuclear waste dumps in this country have taken years to consider various alternatives and have often then been unable to make clear recommendations.

Business decision making typically involves weighing up alternative considerations and strategies and usually entails an element of risk. Examples of important decisions include:

- Where shall we site out plant?
- How shall we market our product?
- What are the most effective distribution channels?
- How shall we structure our company?
- How shall we produce our product?
- How can we use our stocks to best effect?

- How can we make our product 'environment friendly'?
- How can we implement a policy of equal opportunities?

The list is endless.

However, there are a number of decision-making techniques that can aid decision making, including:

- Cost–benefit analysis
- Decision trees
- Game theories
- Network analysis
- The minimax criterion

Cost–benefit analysis

Cost–benefit analysis is normally associated with the evaluation of large-scale government backed investment projects. The siting of an airport or the building of a new underground rail link are typical examples of where cost–benefit analysis will be used. However, cost–benefit analysis is a much more widely applicable technique than this. It could in fact be applied to appraise any policy decision, although it is not a magic solution that can solve problems with ease. Cost–benefit analysis is in essence an approach to decision making which sets out to organize all the relevant information facing the analyst in a manner structured to focus attention on the key issues and to encourage decision makers to face up to the real choices which might otherwise be lost in a mass of detail.

Cost–benefit analysis is concerned with quantifying the costs and benefits of particular projects in money terms in order to find out where the net advantages lie. For example, in carrying out an analysis of building a new training centre for unemployed workers, you would have to find out who would benefit and who would lose out. You would then have to make measurements in money terms. You would have to ask someone who would benefit how much he or she would be prepared to pay to see the project carried out. You would then have to ask someone who would lose out the minimum sum he or she would be prepared to accept as compensation for the project taking place. We then add up all the gains and all the losses. If the gains outweigh the losses the project passes the test. Cost–benefit techniques are dealt with further in Chapters 5 and 17.

Decision trees

Decision trees are so named because of the way in which they separate out into branches (outcomes) from an original stem (a decision). Decision trees are a technique for tracing through all the known outcomes of a particular decision in order to draw out the possible consequences. For example, the decision shown in Fig. 4.6 sets out to explore the possible consequences of a firm deciding to modify an existing product.

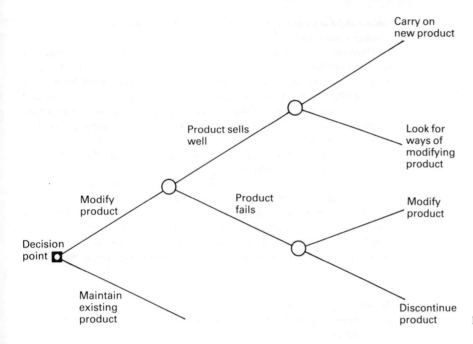

Figure 4.6 A simple decision tree.

Decision trees used in business will also set out to calculate the probability of each event (branch). The probability of each event is then multiplied by the expected profit or loss resulting from that outcome to arrive at an expected value.

The calculation of the probability of a predicted outcome very much depends on the information available to a decision maker and on the decision maker's interpretation of that information. It is therefore important for the decision maker to have available as much up-to-the-minute information as possible. A further problem is caused by the fact that the input at one stage of a decision tree depends on the output at the previous stage—if a calculation at one stage is poor, then the problem will be carried forward to the next stage.

Case Study—Setting out a decision tree

The following example will be used to illustrate the notation and basic layout of a tree diagram as well as the use of such a diagram to solve a decision-making problem.

The Cacus Chemical Company has recently developed a new product for which a substantial market is likely to exist in one year's time. Due to the highly unstable nature of this product, a new production process must be set up at a cost of £2.5 million to cope with the anticipated high temperature reactions. This process will take one year to develop, but it is estimated that there is only a 0.55 probability that it will provide adequate standards of safety.

In the light of this, the company are considering the additional development of a computerized control system (CCS) which will detect and warn against dangerous reaction conditions. Research on the CCS will take one year and cost £1 million and Cacus estimate that there is a 0.75 probability that the CCS can be developed successfully.

Development of the CCS can either begin immediately or be postponed for one year until the safety of the new process is known. If the CCS is developed immediately and the new process proves to have an adequate standard of safety, then the CCS will be unnecessary and the £1 million expenditure will have been wasted. On the other hand, if the CCS is postponed and the new process turns out to be unsafe, a subsequently successful development of the CCS will have delayed the product by one year. If neither the new process nor the CCS is successful, there is no way in which the product can be safely manufactured, and the project will have to be abandoned.

If sales of the new product can commence in one year's time, it has been estimated that the discounted profit would amount to a total of £10 million before any allowance is made for depreciation of the new process or the CCS. If the launch of the product is delayed by one year, however, the total return is expected to fall to £8.5 million due to the possibility of other manufacturers entering the market. For simplicity, you may ignore the effects of discounting on the expenditure on the CCS.

Required:
(a) Draw a decision tree to represent the various courses of action open to the company.   (7 marks)
(b) Which course of action would you recommend to the management of Cacus?   (5 marks)
(c) By how much would the probability of a successful new process development (currently estimated to be 0.55) have to change before you would alter your recommendation in (b)? Does the decision in question appear particularly sensitive to the value of this probability?   (8 marks)

                                                                      (20 marks)
                                                          (ACCA Level 2: Dec. 1986)

ANSWER
(a) The decision tree for this problem is shown in Fig. 4.7. In such a diagram each decision to be made is represented by a rectangle. For purposes of illustration one such rectangle in Fig. 4.7 is labelled 'Decision point'. Emanating from the decision point we have one line for each strategy that might be adopted.

The uncertainties in a decision tree are represented by circles. In Fig. 4.7 one of these circles is labelled 'Expected value point'. Emanating from each expected value point we have one line for each state of nature which might prevail, and marked on that line is the probability of the corresponding state of nature.

The diagram is drawn from left to right, taking account of every decision and uncertainty and showing the relationships between them. Eventually all the decisions and uncertainties will be accounted for and on the right-hand side of the diagram we shall have lines with nothing on the end. At the ends of each line we write the value of the outcome corresponding to the succession of decisions and states of nature which led to the point concerned.

(b) Solving the problem now involves working through the diagram from right to left. Against each expected value point we note the expected value

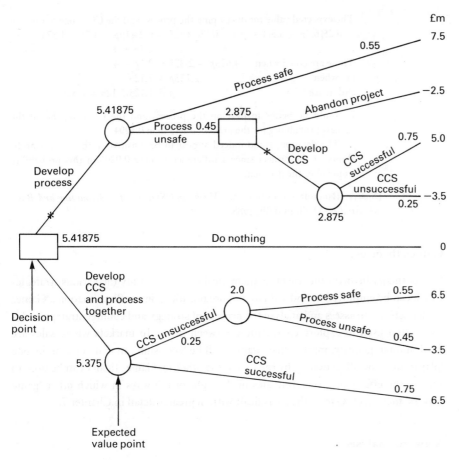

Figure 4.7 A decision tree for CCS. (*Source*: Bancroft, G. and O'Sullivan, G. *Maths and Statistics for Accounting and Business Studies*, Second Edition. MGraw-Hill, Maidenhead, 1988).

obtained using the probabilities on the lines emanating from that point and the values at the ends of those lines. Thus

$$0.75 \times 5 + 0.25 \times (-3.5) = 2.875$$
$$0.55 \times 6.5 + 0.45 \times (-3.5) = 2.0$$
$$0.25 \times 2 + 0.75 \times 6.5 = 5.375$$

Against each decision point we note the best expected value that can be obtained at the end of a line emanating from that decision point and we put an asterisk on the appropriate line.

Working through this process for the example we see that the figure of £5 418 750 emerges on the initial decision box, and the asterisks indicate that the best initial decision is to develop the process alone. If it then proves to be unsafe, develop the computerized control system at that stage.

(c) Let p be the process success probability at which the initial decisions to develop the process alone and to develop the process and the CCS together have equal expected values.

Then the expected value for developing the process alone is

$$7.5p + 2.875(1 - p) = 4.625p + 2.875$$

The expected value for developing the process and the CCS together is
$$0.25[6.5p - 3.5(1 - p)] + 0.75 \times 6.5 = 0.25(10p - 3.5) + 4.875$$
$$= 2.5p + 4$$
These are equal when $4.625p + 2.875 = 2.5p + 4$
i.e. when $2.125p = 1.125$
and hence $p = 1.125/2.125 = 0.5294$

It would be better to develop the process and the CCS together if the success probability for the process is less than 0.5294.

The decision would indeed appear to be sensitive to the success probability of the project since a difference of only 0.0206 in this probability would alter the decision.

(*Source:* Bancroft and O'Sullivan, *Maths and Statistics for Accounting and Business Studies.* McGraw-Hill, 1988.)

Games theories

Games theory involves the use of mathematical models to study the various strategies which can be employed by individuals and organizations in conflict situations. Games theory sets out to assess and analyse the process of strategy and counter strategy and is most often used to explore competition between firms. In markets where sales are fixed in total quantity, market share games will be 'zero sum', in that any gain by one 'player' must be offset exactly by the loss of the other(s). Games theory can be used to analyse the effects of given strategies in the light of the ways in which other 'game players' may react. Games theory is dealt with in greater detail in Chapter 7.

Network analysis

In carrying out business projects it is important to map out the sequence of events that is required to follow through the operation. Certain activities need to be carried out in a pre-determined sequence—for instance in building a house the walls would normally be assembled before the roof was put on, the layers of a sponge cake are made before the icing is put on, etc. These *events* take place in a *sequence* and can be linked in diagrammatic form in the way indicated in Fig. 4.8. Before B can be started A must be completed.

Figure 4.8 A sequence.

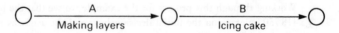

However, other activities do not have to take place in sequence, they can be carried out *simultaneously*. For example, the icing could be made at the same time as the cake is being cooked in the oven. This can be illustrated in Fig. 4.9 which shows that before you bake the cake and prepare the icing, you need to mix the ingredients—but the latter stages of production can be carried out simultaneously. Network analysis

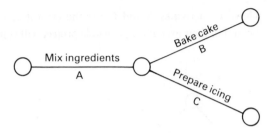

Figure 4.9 Simultaneous activities.

can be used to map out programmes of activities in such a way as to create the most effective planning.

Case Study

Set out a network diagram to indicate the performance of the following activities:

Activity	Relationship to other activities
A	Must be done first
B	Can only be started when A is finished
C	Can only be started when A is finished
D	Requires completion of B
E	Requires completion of C and D
F	Completes project and must await completion of all other activities

A further important ingredient of constructing a network is the element of time, which will be a crucial element in project planning. Time needs to be incorporated into the diagrams (see Fig. 4.10). It now becomes possible to

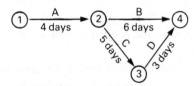

Figure 4.10 Introducing time to a decision tree.

calculate the minimum amount of time required to carry out a particular project. Those activities which take longest to complete in moving from one stage to the next in a project are described as 'critical' activities. The 'critical path' of a project is the line along which these activities follow. It is essential that these activities are done well and that they are given priority if the project is not to fall behind. This can be illustrated by a simple diagram (Fig. 4.11). Activities A and B can be carried out simultaneously, as can C and D.

However, activities A and C are the critical activities in that if they fall behind in their execution the whole project will suffer.

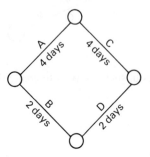

Figure 4.11 Establishing priorities.

The minimax criterion

The minimax criterion is a useful tool for risk limitation. Minimax involves providing decision makers with information about the worst possible results that could follow alternative courses of action.

Information technology as a decision-making tool

The American business author Peter Drucker sees the late twentieth century as being the dawning of the age of the information-based organization—the latest stage in the development of the modern corporation.

At the beginning of the century we saw the separation of management from the ownership of a company, as shareholders handed over responsibility for the running of a company to paid managers. This led to the growth of the command-and-control organization made of departments and divisions. Now we are entering a third period of change, with the development of information-based organizations of knowledge specialists.

In this third phase members of staff are freed from day-to-day administrative tasks by using computers as a tool. Computers bring a large section of employees closer to the work of management, departmental hierarchies are broken down, creating a much flatter organizational structure with the opportunity to develop more skills. Networking of computer systems gives people access to many disciplines. When a company uses a number of personal computers, it is possible that some of the information on one is useful to another user. Rather than continually swopping data using floppy disks, it is possible to connect the machines together using a local area network. This consists of a mixture of hardware and software which enables data to be transferred between the machines. Networking thus makes it possible for a range of experts to rapidly tap into each other's specialist skill areas while sitting at their own work-stations. Such employees no longer need to sit in the same building, and can quite easily work from home. No longer is knowledge compartmentalized, but instead becomes part of a pool of mutually shared information. Information technology saves time, cuts costs and makes companies more competitive. With new technology the new organization is born.

However, we are still a long way from the widespread development of information-based organizations which are democratically structured. Rather than restructuring job design many companies have tended to automate the existing organizational structure. Dramatic contrasts can be made between companies which have combined information technology with a more effective decision-making structure and others which have simply borrowed the new technology and retained their existing struc-ture.

This point is illustrated by the Management in the Nineties programme report (spring 1989) which includes a telling comparison of two organizations in the pen-sions business which were each responsible for managing an investment portfolio of £15 million. It showed how a new model business compared with an older style organization.

The traditionally run business is represented by the division of a bank employing 108 professional staff and 36 support staff. The newcomer, Battery March, a Boston-based financial investment management firm, handles a comparable business, but with 18 professional staff and 17 support staff.

From the outset, Battery March's founder operated on the principle that there was a better way of managing funds that would add value to the company's services. The operation was consciously organized to optimize the creative contribution of analysts and professionals with a strong emphasis on teamwork. It was a vision that depended on information technology.

Buying and selling stock directly, computer to computer, takes care of some routine clerical work. Technology is also used extensively to monitor stock and fund changes and to select best options and so on to enable staff to concentrate more on the creative aspects of the business. As a result, Battery March enjoys lower costs and a record for highly effective performance.

It is not just the younger companies like Battery March that are exploring the pos-sibilities for innovative organization. Rank Xerox, for example, has dared to ask why all white-collar workers need to work in a central office. The company is one of the trail blazers in the use of networkers, i.e. home-based specialist and professional workers contracted to the company but also working for other clients.

Computer-based simulations are important aids to decision-making. A computer simulation involves feeding in a range of relevant data to a program in order to simu-late a real situation. The program can then be used for training purposes or to assist with real decisions which can be as trivial as selecting winners in a horse race or as serious as trying to locate a fault in the operation of a rocket in a manned space launch.

Short answer questions

1. Identify one decision that would be made by each of the following members of a small company:
   (a) a shareholder
   (b) an employee
   (c) a director
   (d) a manager
2. Why are information systems important to decision-making processes? Give three examples of how an information system can help in decision making.
3. What is meant by middle management? What is the responsibility of middle management in a large company?
4. Study the decision-making process in a local company. Who are the decision-makers? How are decisions made? What is the structure of decision making?
5. Distinguish between task, process and action schedule in a decision making process.
6. Distinguish between programmed and non-programmed decisions. Give an example of each.
7. What is meant by a:
   (a) chain network
   (b) circle network
   (c) completely interconnected network
   Give an example of each from organizational situations with which you are familiar.
8. What is meant by cost–benefit analysis?
9. What is meant by a 'critical' decision?
10. Distinguish between 'open' and 'closed' systems.
11. Explain the various stages in a decision cycle.
12. What is meant by evaluation?
13. Draw a decision tree to illustrate a personal decision-making process with which you are faced in the near future.
14. What is a game theory?
15. To what use can the minimax criterion be put?
16. What are the main advantages and disadvantages of using decision trees in decision making?
17. How can participative management facilitate decision making?
18. What are the main advantages of the information-based organization?
19. What is meant by a local area network?
20. Give three examples of situations in which computer simulations can be used as tools in decision making.

Essays

1. Who are the decision makers in a company?

2. Discuss the view that an effective and 'happy' organization is one that gives responsibility to *all* its employees.
3. Organizations need to develop procedures for decision making most suited to the nature of the environment in which they are operating. Discuss.
4. What factors are likely to influence individual decision making?
5. How can large groups work effectively together?
6. Show how the decision-making network needs to be tailored to
   (a) the size of the group;
   (b) the nature of the decisions that need to be made.
7. How important is the 'leader' in the decision-making process?
8. What are the pre-requisites of effective group collaboration?
9. How can decision-making techniques facilitate the decision-making process?
10. Large modern organizations cannot survive without systems which are based on modern information technology. Discuss this view.

Data response questions

1   The network shown in Fig. 4.12 sets out the sequence of activities for a project to be carried out. (The numbers indicate the number of days required to complete an activity.)

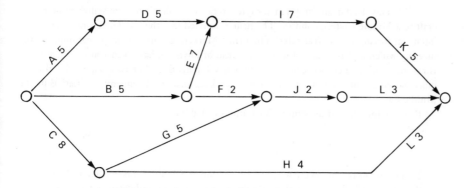

Figure 4.12 A sequence of activities.

(a) What is the critical path? What should be the total length of time required to complete the project?
(b) Which of the activities indicated is the most crucial, if the project is to be completed on time?
(c) Imagine that a project planner has come up with a new network of activities whereby I would precede J, and K would be incorporated with H to take eight days. Draw a new network.
(d) Explain how project management can help decision makers to plan new projects.

2   IOM is an international consulting group offering a wide range of management services to companies which operate on an international basis or which are extensively involved in importing and exporting, and it has established a sound reputation in these areas. The company is organised into a number of specialised divisions. These include economic intelligence, organisation and management development, computing and telecommunications, and technology and marketing. Because IOM has developed such a wide reputation it now receives commissions to undertake consultancy work from a very wide range of organisations. IOM has recently recruited a number of young graduates. One of them, who graduated from the London School of Economics five years ago and has three years of commercial experience, is now working in the Economic Intelligence Division.

Assume that you are this person, and that you are currently involved in the following three tasks which have been passed on to you by the Head of the Division.

Task 1

Your Division has been presented with an assignment from an international computing company requiring analysis of the economic situation in Malaysia. You have been asked to sketch, in outline, those areas of information which would provide a useful basis for assessing a country's economic performance. More specifically, the Head of Division, with his now familiar sense of urgency, asks you to give him a very brief draft of what he describes as 'a framework of analysis' which might be used as a basis for assessing a country's economy.

Produce this first draft.

Task 2

IOM is involved in advising a major UK aircraft manufacturing firm selling military aircraft to a Middle Eastern country. The firm is worried that the UK Government is clearly intent on forcing up interest rates. The firm's Marketing Director, in preparation for the meeting which he has arranged with your Head of Division, has asked you for a list of the **three** most adverse consequences of this policy for his firm. For each aspect, he also requires a simple illustration of how it will work against the Company's initiative in the Middle East.

Produce this list and the simple illustrations called for.

Task 3

In the light of recent experience, the Association of Scientific, Technical and Managerial Staffs has asked IOM to brief them on the possible reasons and motives for decisions by multi-national firms in the motoring industry, on the location of their manufacturing operations. Write brief preliminary notes on the reasons and motives which might obtain.

(*Source: Industrial Studies*, Oxford, 1986)

3   Study the following article and answer the questions.

Concern over risk to nuclear plants

An air crash such as the one at Lockerbie could cause even greater devastation than the Chernobyl disaster if the wreckage hit a nuclear power station, according to Dr Raymond Seymour, a scientific adviser with Somerset County Council, Nicholas Schoon writes.

Dr Seymour disputes this official estimate of the chance of an aircraft directly hitting a nuclear power station as being once every two million years. Dr Seymour, a radiation expert, says the risk is 10 times higher. He has been assessing the risks in evidence to be presented later this month to the public inquiry into plans for a third nuclear power station at Hinkley Point in Somerset.

Much of the wreckage of the Pan Am Boeing 747 came down within 10 miles of the BNFL reactor at Chapelcross. If the bomb had detonated about a minute earlier the debris would have landed around the reactor. 'The effect of such a disaster could be far worse than Chernobyl and the chances of it happening at Hinkley Point are unacceptable,' he said yesterday.

In his evidence, given on behalf of a consortium of 23 local authorities opposing the Hinkley C reactor, he says the main risk comes from jets from the Royal Navy airbase at Yeovilton which fly to a practice bombing range in the Bristol Channel.

A spokesman for the CEGB, which wants to build Hinkley C, said the risks of aircraft impact had been assessed for the Sizewell inquiry. Even in the extremely unlikely event of an aircaft crashing into the power station, there was only a one in ten chance of this causing a big release of radioactivity, and a one in two chance of this leading to a meltdown. Aircraft are not allowed within two miles horizontally of a nuclear power station or 2000 feet vertically.

(Source: The Independent, January 1990)

(a)   Why might mathematical techniques be useful in:
    (i)   making siting decisions for nuclear reactors;
    (ii)   calculating safety risks for nuclear reactors?

(b)   What do you think that Dr Seymour meant by 'the chances of it happening at Hinkley Point are unacceptable'?

(c)   Why do you think that Dr Seymour's calculations differ from the official estimates?

(d)   What criteria do you think should be applied to the siting of nuclear reactors? Explain your reasoning.

Suggested reading

Bavelas, A., *A Mathematical Model for Group Structure. Applied Anthropology*, Vol. 7. 1948.

Fatseas, V and Vag, T. *Quantitative Techniques for Managerial Decision Making*. Prentice-Hall, 1984.

Fiedler, F., *A Theory of Leadership Effectiveness*. McGraw-Hill, 1967.

Gilligan, C., Neale, B. and Murray, D., *Business Decision Making*. Philip Allan, 1983.

Kast, F. and Rosenzweig, J., *Organisation and Management: a systems and contingency approach*. McGraw-Hill, 1979.

Pascal, A. and Athos, A., *The Art of Japanese Management*. Penguin Business Library, 1986.

Simon, H., *The New Science of Management Decision*. Harper and Row, 1960.

5
Using statistical and quantitative techniques

The word statistics contains three fundamental elements. Firstly, it can be used as a 'blanket' to describe a set of figures. Secondly, it also enables a mass of information or data to be presented according to a particular pattern and, thirdly, it provides a method to interpret business data.

The very nature of the information a business has to deal with is often financial, involves figures and so is therefore quantitative. To understand figures, at any level, will clearly need some basic knowledge of statistics. Though decision making requires common sense, problem-solving skills and the ability to communicate, it will be enhanced by an ability to understand figures. No decision can lead to certain results. Though something is likely, it might not happen. Statistics enable guidelines to be as precise as possible in an area of uncertainty. They are essentially a form of communication and it could well be argued that in business numeracy plays as vital a role as literacy.

Information needs for simple problems

The first question any business will need to ask is what information do we need? Information will need to stem from the market and then cover as many aspects of business activities as possible. The more thorough and accurate the information, the more successful decision making is likely to be. Misleading information will result in poor decisions.

If someone says that a motor car is the best, he or she is making a *qualitative* comment about the vehicle. By looking at the specifications for the car and analysing details such as maximum power, torque, compression ratio and maximum speed in miles per hour, the *quantitative* details can be checked. Businesses are therefore concerned with gathering reliable quantitative information.

Before gathering information a number of important questions need to be asked:

1. What are the precise objectives of the exercise? It is important to consider the aims of the exercise to ensure that time is not spent upon collecting information which might not be needed.

2.   What units of measurement are you to use? If you are collecting information such as sales figures, will you need to analyse them in pounds, volume or both?

3.   What degree of accuracy do you require? By obtaining a greater degree of accuracy you will have to spend more upon gathering information. An investigation of a sample might be just as revealing.

4.   Is obtaining this information cost effective? The whole point of an exercise to collect information must be that it is worth while spending money to do so.

Each level of management will have different information needs.

Strategic level managers deal with policy decisions and matters concerning the future of the organization. They need carefully prepared and scientifically presented information not only from within the business but also from outside sources.

Tactical level managers tend to make decisions based upon strategic policy decisions. They will invariably be concerned with analysing issues within the organization and will often require information relating to a particular time period.

Organizational decision making will involve dealing with grass root problems associated with the day-to-day running of an organization. Though the information required need not be precise it must help to provide a solution to a practical problem.

Case Study—Information needs

Have you ever had that feeling that the information you are giving managers is not exactly what they want? Have you ever tried to find out what they do want? If you have then you may well have reached—or at least approached—a state of despair! For years, no matter what variations and improvements I made to the information I gave to managers, I just never seemed able to satisfy their exact needs. I even went through the stage of believing it was some kind of plot to make management accountants feel inadequate.

Then one day I discovered—some people might say stumbled on—a solution to the problem of defining management's information needs. My 'amazing' discovery was that information is the raw material of decision making and that, in order to know what information managers need, we have to know what decisions they take. This pretty obvious statement led to the development of a process which I have appropriately named 'decision information analysis'. This requires a careful analysis of the decisions that managers make and then, for each decision assessing the information needed.

(Source: Management Accounting.)

NB   Internal data comprise information extracted from within an organization whereas external data are found outside the business's immediate environment (see Fig. 5.1).

Collecting primary data

Primary data comprise information collected by the firm for its own purposes (see Chapter 7). These data are therefore specific to the firm's needs and collected solely for a particular purpose.

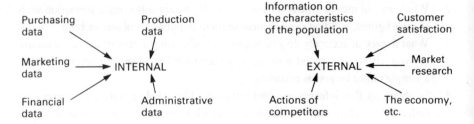

Figure 5.1 Internal and external data available to an organization.

In organizing the collection of information three important questions need to be put:

1.   Whom do you ask to get the information you require?
2.   What questions are you going to ask?
3.   What techniques do you use to obtain the right information?

In order to obtain information the ideal situation would be to interview every member of your target group. This could be both an extensive and costly task. By *sampling* you will be able to obtain conclusions by asking questions to a representative group reflective of a larger member of respondents. This can be done in a number of different ways.

Sampling

1.   *Random sampling*   With this technique every member of the target group has an equal chance of being selected.
2.   *Quota sampling*   Interviewers avoid the expense of having to find particular people and interview everyone up to a given number. In practice this can lead to bias and interviewers are told to fill their quota by breaking down their sample according to class, age, sex, etc.
3.   *Systematic sampling*   This is really a structured way of obtaining a random sample. For example, if a 5 per cent sample is required, then this can be done by interviewing every twentieth person on a list.
4.   *Cluster sampling*   With this technique the country is divided into areas and interviewers seek every person they can find who fits a particular description, e.g. retired men.

Case Study—Sampling

You have been asked to obtain information on behalf of a company with four factories in different parts of the country. The following is a breakdown of the company's employees by age and sex:

		Under 40	Over 40
Sutton Coldfield	M	111	140
	F	89	32
Hull	M	240	80
	F	120	115
Camberley	M	148	120
	F	175	180
Darlington	M	105	60
	F	125	60

You are required to construct a quota sample of 5 per cent of the workforce to reflect fully the location, age and sex. As the total workforce is 1900 you are therefore required to interview 95 employees and this is 1 in 20 of the total employees. You have to divide each number in the table by 20 and round to the nearest whole number.

		Under 40	Over 40
Sutton Coldfield	M	6	7
	F	4	2
Hull	M	12	4
	F	6	6
Camberley	M	7	6
	F	9	9
Darlington	M	5	3
	F	6	3
		55	40

If age and sex were no longer relevant to your survey you would combine the classes and interview:

19 in Sutton Coldfield
28 in Hull
31 in Camberley
17 in Darlington
95

The questionnaire

The design of the questionnaire is fundamental to the success of any survey. A badly constructed questionnaire can irritate the respondent and affect the quality of the input. It is important that the person answering the questions knows why he or she is being asked to do so and is happy to cooperate. A good questionnaire should obtain information you require and exclude anything that is unnecessary.

1. The questions should be simple, unambiguous and easy to understand. If they are not, they will lead to inaccurate and incomplete responses.

2. The questions should be short and yet still fully cover a given area of investigation. They should not ask for too much information.

3. Questions should be logically presented. If the questionnaire is confusing to follow and illogical in order, it will be difficult to complete and unclear in its purpose.

4. The questionnaire should not contain personal questions.

Designing a questionnaire requires considerable expertise. Questions should be brief, functional and provide the sort of information you need. The aim must be to obtain the maximum information possible with the greatest of ease. Testing questions on a pilot group is an essential step in questionnaire design as no matter how carefully you try to anticipate reactions, it is difficult to judge how interviewees will respond.

Case Study—Questionnaire

Prepare a questionnaire to identify reactions to a local issue. Test it and then comment upon ways it could have been 'improved'. A number of *techniques* can be used to obtain information:

1. *Direct observation*   This reduces the chances of dubious data being recorded and is considered to be the most accurate form of collecting data. Though it is useful in determining customer patterns and for scientific surveys it can be very expensive.

2. *Postal questionnaires*   This is often not a very satisfactory method of obtaining data as responses to requests for information are usually not very high and often contain bias.

3. *Telephone interviewing*   Though this is a relatively cheap method of collecting information, depending upon the nature of the survey, results can be biased as not everyone has a telephone.

4. *Interviewing*   Face-to-face contact often leads to more accurate and useful results being obtained. Sometimes it is possible to employ teams of interviewers who pool results.

Collecting secondary data

Firms would always prefer to collect primary data as data collected for a particular organization are likely to be better. However, cost, time and circumstances dictate that it is not always possible to do so and secondary data, which are collected elsewhere, have to be used (see Chapter 7). The problems associated with collecting secondary data are that the data might not present a complete picture: they could be out of date; there is little knowledge of how such data are collected; and the reasons for collection may not be known.

Sources of secondary data are numerous and wide ranging. All published statistics of any kind are a form of secondary data and clearly a reference library is a useful source for such information. Useful information may be picked up by looking at any of the following:

- Company reports
- *The Economist, Investors' Weekly*, and other useful business publications
- Newspapers and, in particular, the *Financial Times*
- Trade periodicals and professional magazines

Government statistics are often provided as a base for further analysis and are available from a number of sources:

1. *Central Statistical Office*   The CSO coordinates government statistics and is responsible for the *Monthly Digest of Statistics*, the *Annual Abstract of Statistics*, *Economic Trends* (monthly), *Financial Statistics* (monthly) and the annual *Blue Book on National Income and Expenditure*. (For example, the *Monthly Digest of Statistics* will include information on population, employment, social services, law and order, agriculture, information on various industries, entertainments and weather.)
2. *Department of Trade and Industry*   The DTI publishes *British Industry* which provides information about the volume of production in various industries as well as details of imports and exports.
3. *Department of Employment*   This department publishes a monthly gazette with details such as employment, unemployment, wage rates, overtime working, stoppages and retail prices.
4. *Bank of England Quarterly Bulletin*   This analyses a vast amount of data upon UK banks, the money supply, borrowing, monetary aggregates and economic indicators.
5. *Office of Population Censuses and Surveys*   They produce a publication called *Population Trends* as well as a published census.

The European Economic Community also has a Statistical Office which gathers statistics from member countries and publishes *Basic Statistics of the Community*. The United Nations publishes statistics upon the world economy.

Libraries provide an abundance of useful material to be used as a means of supplementing reports and ideas.

Presentation of data

Once statistical data have been obtained, they need to be broken down so that they can be presented in a way that emphasizes their significance. Information can be displayed in the form of a frequency distribution or table, a chart or as a graph. The nature of the data collected and the circumstances for which they are needed will determine the way in which they are presented.

Frequency distribution and tables

As data come in, the likelihood is that they will not be in any kind of order. By introducing an order we can begin to understand something of the values and concentrations of values that we have come across.

An *array* is a simple arrangement of figures into ascending or descending values. If the number of days' credit for 20 customers varied as shown below:

```
12   21   32   65   18   20   14   51   81   32
31   45   16   51   71   40   24   32   18   33
```

We could arrange this in ascending order:

```
12   14   16   18   18   20   21   24   31   32
32   32   33   40   45   51   51   65   71   81
```

Tally marks are a quick and useful method of counting totals by displaying them in the form of matchsticks. After every four marks the fifth crosses out the previous four so that totals can be easily counted. The average age of a company's employees could be presented in a table as:

Age range	Tally marks	Number of employees
Under 20	II	2
21–30	JHf JHf I	11
31–40	JHf JHf II	12
41–50	JHf III	8
51–60	JHf	5
Over 60	III	3
Total employees		41

By grouping ages in to bands as shown in the table we do not know the individual age of each employee but we do know the age ranges. Within each band some measurements of a variable appear more than once, and as the table records how many times a value occurs, it is a frequency distribution. As groups have been used it is a *grouped frequency distribution*.

Case Study

The following number of machine breakdowns have occurred each hour over a 40-hour week:

```
 8   15   43   12   51    2    4   19
 4   18   39   56   12   23   27   28
11    2    5   25   18   51   19   50
12    5    6   29   16   57   19   33
24   37   18    3   12    6   60   39
```

Construct a grouped frequency distribution from these data using (a) eight class intervals of equal width; and (b) class intervals of five.

After data have been broken down, they can be organized into a *table*. A table is just a matrix of rows and columns demonstrating the relationship between two variables. It summarizes information into a form that is clear and easy to read.

Case Study

Top ten corporate donors to charity in 1987

		UK declared voluntary donations ($£'000$)	Profit before tax ($£'000$)
1	British Petroleum	2 900	750 000
2	Hanson Trust	2 600	741 000
3	Trustee Savings Bank	1 929	275 500
4	Barclays Bank	1 863	339 000
5	ICI	1 800	1 312 000
6	Nat West	1 651	704 000
7	Marks and Spencer	1 640	501 700
8	BOC Group	1 261	263 200
9	Shell	1 250	657 000
10	Hewlett-Packard	1 070	12 967

Questions

1. What does this table show?
2. Mention the respective roles of
    (a) Hewlett-Packard
    (b) ICI
    (c) TSB
3. What sort of information, if added to this table, would provide a more interesting scenario?
4. Is a table an appropriate way of showing this information?

Charts

Charts are eyecatching and enable information to be presented in a form which can be readily understood. By using a chart, information may seem to be more meaningful.

A *pictogram* is a diagrammatic form of display which uses pictures instead of numbers. When using a pictogram, symbols must be simple and items represented by a symbol must be shown in a key (see Fig. 5.2).

Barker's Pet Shop

Sale of dogs

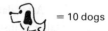 = 10 dogs

Figure 5.2 Using illustrative material to represent figures.

In a *pie chart* each slice represents a component's contribution to the total amount. The 360° of the circle is divided up in proportion to the figures obtained and, in order to draw the segments accurately, a protractor is necessary to mark off the degrees. The following method can be used to convert each relative proportion to degrees:

$$\frac{\text{Proportion}}{\text{Total}} \times 360°$$

A company's export figures are as follows:

Exports	Size (£m)
USA	5
Europe	3
Australia	4
Canada	2
Others	6
Total exports	20

$$\text{Exports to the USA} = \frac{5}{20} \times 360° = 90°$$

$$\text{Exports to Europe} = \frac{3}{20} \times 360° = 54°$$

$$\text{Exports to Australia} = \frac{4}{20} \times 360° = 72°$$

$$\text{Exports to Canada} = \frac{2}{20} \times 360° = 36°$$

$$\text{Exports to others} = \frac{6}{20} \times 360° = 108°$$

The pie chart can then be presented as shown in Fig. 5.3. Though pie charts provide a

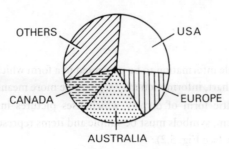

Figure 5.3 Illustrating export figures in a pie chart.

simple form of display, they only show limited information and it can be difficult to make accurate comparisons of segment sizes.

Case Study—Road accident casualties

The chart (Fig. 5.4) indicates road accident casualties by hour of the day in a typical year during the 1980s.

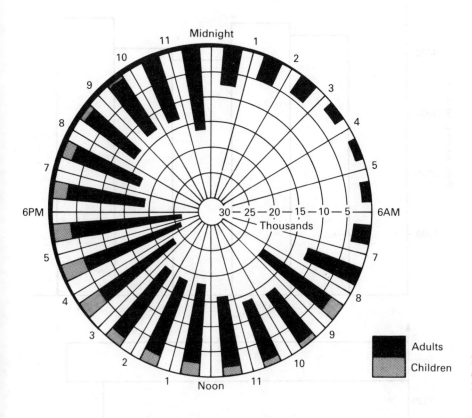

Figure 5.4 Chart illustrating road accident casualties. (*Source*: Department of Transport.)

Questions

1. In what ways is this chart (a) similar to and (b) different from a pie chart?
2. Explain briefly what the chart shows.

In *bar charts* the areas of comparison are represented by bars which can be drawn either vertically or horizontally. The length of the bar indicates the relative importance of the data.

Suppose a company's production figures over the last five years are as shown in the table.

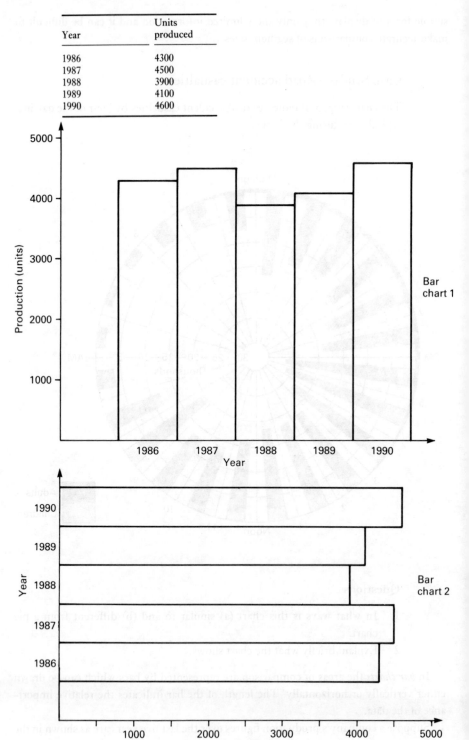

Year	Units produced
1986	4300
1987	4500
1988	3900
1989	4100
1990	4600

Figure 5.5 Two ways of illustrating a company's production figures in a bar chart.

Data could be shown in either of the ways depicted in Fig. 5.5

A *component bar chart* enables component areas to be subdivided. Individual component lengths represent *actual* figures (see Fig. 5.6). With *percentage component bar*

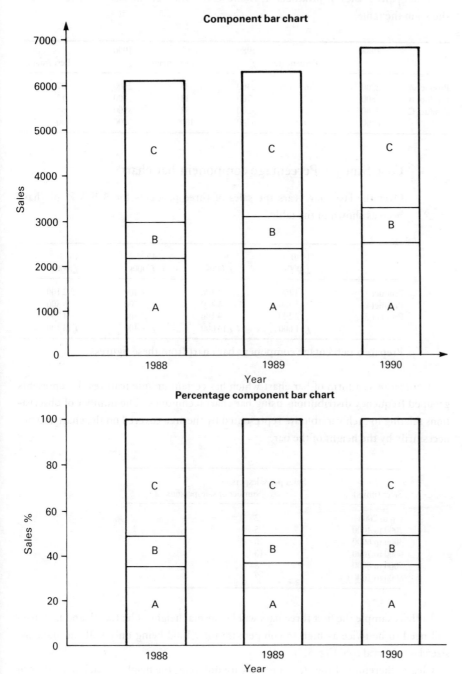

Figure 5.6 Examples of component bar charts.

charts individual component lengths represent the percentage each component forms of the overall total. All bars will therefore be at the full height of 100 per cent (see Fig. 5.6).

A company's sales of products A, B and C in value for the last three years are as shown in the table.

	1988 £	Percentage	1989 £	Percentage	1990 £	Percentage
Product A	2200	36	2400	38	2500	37
Product B	800	13	700	11	800	12
Product C	3100	51	3200	51	3500	51
	6100	100	6300	100	6800	100

Case Study—Percentage component bar chart

Over the last four years the sales of three products for A.S.A.P. plc have been as shown in the table.

	19–0 £'000s	19–1 £'000s	19–2 £'000s	19–3 £'000s
Product 1	4 100	4 500	4 400	2 100
Product 2	5 300	5 400	5 700	6 300
Product 3	2 200	4 100	4 300	4 700
	£11 600	£14 000	£14 400	£13 100

Prepare a percentage component bar chart from these figures.

A *histogram* is a form of bar chart which has certain unique features. It represents grouped frequency distributions using bar chart techniques. The number of observations relating to each variable are represented by the area covered on the chart and not necessarily by the height of the bar.

	Sales per salesperson
Sales (units)	Number of salespersons
Up to 2000	2
2000 to 4000	5
4000 to 6000	10
6000 to 7000	10
7000 to 8000	8
8000 to 10000	2

In this example the first three bars will be normal height. The fourth and fifth bars will need to be twice as high to compensate for £1000 being only half the standard size class interval (see Fig. 5.7).

Clearly therefore, if the class intervals are different, the height of each bar needs to

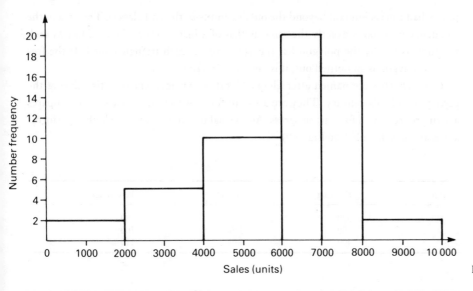

Figure 5.7 An example of a histogram.

be worked out. It is more than likely that the class intervals of each bar will be the same and that this procedure will not be necessary so that the histogram can be drawn straight from the frequency distribution. Histograms are a variation of a bar chart in which the area and not necessarily the height of the bar represents the frequency.

Whereas a histogram is a stepped graph, it might be desirable to show information in the form of a single curve. Such a curve is known as a *frequency polygon*. It is drawn by constructing a histogram, marking off the mid-point of the top of each rectangle and then joining the mid-points with straight lines (see Fig. 5.8).

The curve of a frequency polygon is extended at both ends so that it cuts the axis at

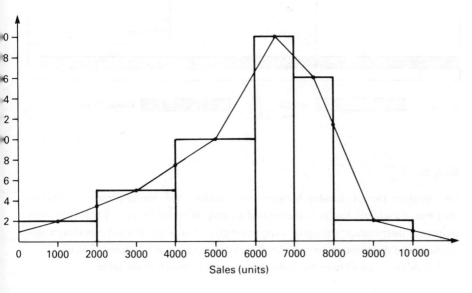

Figure 5.8 Frequency polygon and histogram.

points half a class interval beyond the outside limits of the end classes. The area of the frequency polygon is exactly the same as that of a histogram as the area lost as each rectangle is cut by the polygon has the same area as each triangle added. If the frequency polygon is smoothed out, it is known as a *frequency curve*.

Gantt charts were named after Henry Gantt, a management scientist, during the early years of this century. They are a useful form of bar/line chart which compares actual progress with forecast progress. As a visual tool they indicate whether performances are on schedule (see Fig. 5.9).

Month	Forecast	Actual	Percentage
1	300	240	80
2	350	350	100
3	400	440	110

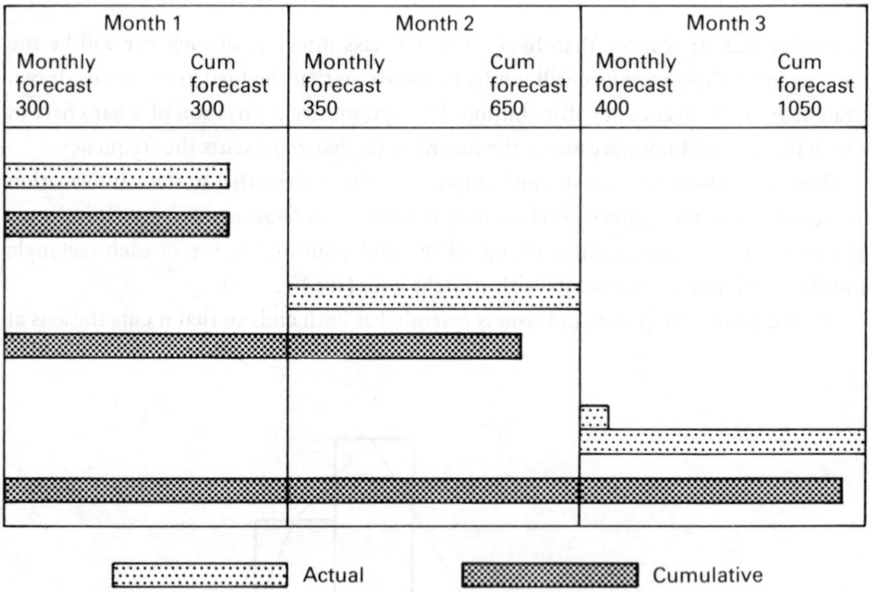

Figure 5.9 An example of a Gantt chart.

Graphs

Graphs show the relationship between two variables and can be presented either in the form of a straight line or in the form of a curve. Whereas frequency polygons show frequency distribution, the ogive is the name given to the curve when cumulative frequencies of a distribution are presented in the form of a graph (see Fig. 5.10).

A firm's sales totals over 40 weeks are achieved as shown in the table.

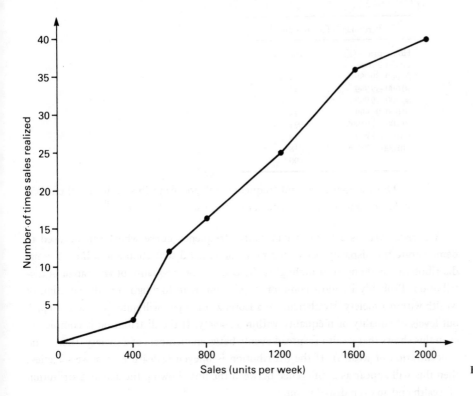

Figure 5.10 Example of an ogive.

Output (units)	Number of times sales realized	Cumulative frequency
0–400	3	3
401–800	9	3 + 9 = 12
801–1200	13	3 + 9 + 13 = 25
1201–1600	11	3 + 9 + 13 + 11 = 36
1601–2000	4	3 + 9 + 13 + 11 + 4 = 40
	40 weeks	

Any point on the graph will not directly relate sales achievements to output in the same way as an ordinary graph, but will indicate how many times the number of sales units or less was achieved.

Case Study—Building society

You work for a building society in Barnstable and have been asked by your employer to present the following information in a graphical form as part of an exploration of your branch's activities to a group of fifth formers in a local school.

Percentage of loans granted	
House prices (£)	Buyers
Under 20 000	3
20 000–39 999	7
40 000–59 999	11
60 000–79 999	13
80 000–99 999	14
100 000–119 999	21
120 000–139 999	13
140 000–159 999	18
	100

Draw a histogram and frequency polygon from this table and then construct a cumulative frequency table and use it to draw an ogive.

A *Lorenz curve* is a form of cumulative frequency curve which can be used to demonstrate the disparity between a range of actual distribution and a line of equal distribution. By doing so it highlights the equality or inequality of any range of distribution. Probably its most common application is to highlight the distribution of wealth within a society. By glancing at a Lorenz curve you will quickly be able to pick out levels of equality or inequality within a society. If the distribution is completely even this shows that wealth is spread evenly between members of a society (there is no concentration of wealth). If the distribution is uneven (a feature of most societies) then this will appear as a difference between the line showing the actual distribution of wealth and an even distribution.

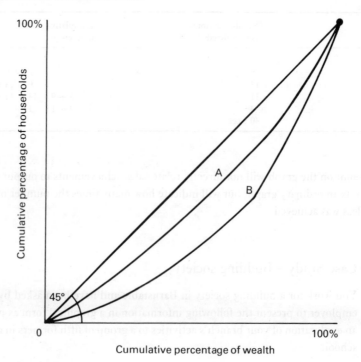

Figure 5.11 A Lorenz curve illustrating differences in the distribution of wealth in two countries.

In Fig. 5.11 we can quickly see that the distribution of wealth in Country A is a lot more even than in Country B.

It would be possible to draw a Lorenz curve to show the relationship between the size of the firm and the output of an industry. In this example the size of the firm is measured by the number of employees.

No. of employees	No. of firms	Output (tonnes)
Under 50	40	3 000
50–99	80	12 000
100–199	120	21 000
200–299	135	48 000
300 and over	25	36 000
	400	120 000

In order to construct a Lorenz curve, these figures need to be broken down further. The table below includes a column which calculates each figure as a percentage of its column total, as well as a column which includes the cumulative total percentages. The cumulative total percentages are the figures required to construct the curve (see Fig. 5.12).

No. of firms			Output (tonnes)		
No.	Percentage	Cumulative percentage	No.	Percentage	Cumulative percentage
40	10	10	3 000	2.5	2.5
80	20	30	12 000	10	12.5
120	30	60	21 000	17.5	30
135	34	94	48 000	40	70
25	6	100	36 000	30	100
400	100		120 000	100	100

If all firms were of equal size, then 25 per cent of output would have been produced by 25 per cent of the firms. The curve which would be expected to be obtained if all firms were of equal size is therefore the line of equal distribution. The extent to which a Lorenz curve deviates away from the line of equal distribution (Fig. 5.12) shows the degree of inequality. The Lorenz curve in the example shows that, as we would expect, larger firms generate more output. By looking at the curve at its furthest point from the equal distribution line, we can see that 60 per cent of firms control 30 per cent of output and so it is clearly not equally shared.

Case Study—Lorenz curve

A market research agency is undertaking a survey on behalf of a company concerned about falling sales in a town in Scotland. The company is particularly concerned about changes in the distribution of wealth caused by

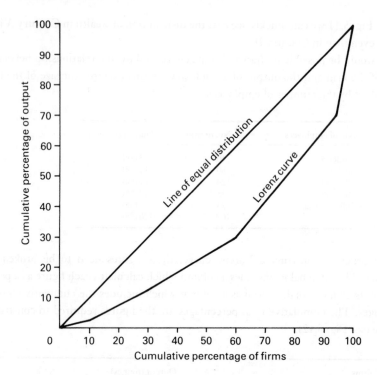

Figure 5.12 A Lorenz curve showing distribution of production between firms.

increasing unemployment and subsequent dependence upon benefits. After an extensive survey involving carefully worded questionnaires the agency has extracted the following figures relating to the spread of wealth in the area.

Wealth in £ per adult	No. of people	Total wealth
		£m
Under 10 000	1200	9.5
10 000–49 999	1500	52.5
50 000–99 999	1300	97.0
100 000–149 999	400	50.0
Over 150 000	100	20.0
	4500	229.0

Construct a Lorenz curve and comment upon the distribution shown by your graph.

Central tendency

We have looked at information needs for simple problems, the breaking down of data into frequency distributions and at how they can be represented diagrammatically. Having broken data down into a more manageable form we need to be able to draw useful information from them and a measure of central tendency provides one method of being able to do so.

Central tendency is a measure of middle values. We normally think of an average when we talk of middle values. An average, as we know it, is an arithmetic mean but two other measures of average or central tendency are the medium and mode.

A company's production levels over 50 days were as follows:

```
5  6  2  6  5  2  6  4  6  5
5  6  4  5  3  5  6  5  6  5
6  5  3  3  2  4  3  2  3  5
4  3  5  2  1  5  2  5  1  4
5  4  4  4  5  3  5  2  4  5
```

From these levels we can derive a frequency distribution:

Daily production levels (units)	Frequency	Level × frequency
1	2	2
2	7	14
3	7	21
4	10	40
5	16	80
6	8	48
	50	205

The mean is quite simply the total of a set of numbers, divided by a number of items. The mean of 6, 7, 14 and 5 would be:

$$\frac{6 + 7 + 14 + 5}{4} = \frac{32}{4} = 8$$

Arithmetic mean therefore $= \dfrac{\text{Sum of observations}}{\text{Number of observations}}$

In order to work out the mean of figures in the example we could either:

1. add up all of the daily production levels and divide the total by 50 (see table). This can be time consuming and prone to error; or
2. use the frequency distribution table. By multiplying the value or daily production level by the frequency (f) with which it occurs a similar total is achieved which can then be divided by the number of days (see table).

The arithmetic mean $= \dfrac{205}{50} = 4.1$ units per day.

Though the mean is the best known of the averages and we often hear about it and see it in our everyday circumstances, it can be distorted by a few extreme values and may also occasionally result in an impractical figure, e.g. 1.35 workers.

The arithmetic mean is often written as $\bar{x}$ and its formula shown as:

$$\bar{x} = \frac{\Sigma fx}{\Sigma f}$$

The *mode* refers to the value which occurs more frequently than any other. If the production level in units of four workers is 15, 12, 15 and 17, the mode will be 15 as it has occurred more than any other value. If two or more frequencies occur the same number of times, there is clearly more than one mode and the distribution is multi-modal. Where there is only one mode the distribution is unimodal. In the example below the daily production level of five units occurs with a frequency of 16 occasions and so is clearly the mode in a unimodal distribution.

Finding a mode in a grouped frequency distribution can only be approached with approximate mathematical accuracy.

The figures in the table relate to value and frequency:

	Value		Frequency
At least	Less than		
10	20		5
20	30		12
30	40		18
40	50		10
50	60		4

The mode is approximated by:

$$L + \left[\frac{(F - Fm - 1) \times c}{2F - Fm - 1 - Fm + 1} \right]$$

where L = lower limit of modal class
$Fm - 1$ = frequency of class below modal class
F = frequency of modal class
$Fm + 1$ = frequency of class above modal class
c = class interval

Our estimate of the mode would therefore be:

$$\text{Mode} = 30 + \left[\frac{(18 - 12) \times 10}{(2 \times 18) - 12 - 10} \right]$$

$$\text{Mode} = 30 + \left[\frac{(6 \times 10)}{(36 - 22)} \right]$$

Mode = 30 + 4.28
Mode = 34.28

As we have emphasized, when calculated this way the mode is only an estimated figure and so therefore is limited in use for further statistical processes.

The *median* is the middle number in a distribution or array of figures. When figures are arranged into either ascending or descending order, the median will be the one in the middle. For example, if data were ordered into an array containing 2, 7, 9, 12 and 15, 9 would be the one in the middle.

In our distribution of 50 days' production levels, we have an even number of figures. If we are calculating the median for a frequency distribution it is usual to accept the middle value as $\frac{n+1}{2}$ if the total frequency (n) is an odd number, and $\frac{n}{2}$ if the total frequency (n) is an even number. As we have 50 values the median will be $\frac{50}{2}$ and therefore the 25th number. The 25th number reflects a daily production level of 4 units in ascending order.

Even if data are incomplete the median can still be calculated. If you do not have information about lower or upper salaries but know how many employees you have, you can still find out the median item. Also, as the median only uses one value in a distribution it is not changed by distorted or extreme values.

Dispersion

Though averages are important in providing us with information about the middle of a distribution, they do not tell us how other figures in the distribution are spread. Information might reveal the same mean but the spread of some data might be tight while others might be well dispersed.

A *range* represents the difference between the highest and lowest values in a set of data. It is easy to find and provides information about a spread of figures.

Range = highest value − lowest value.

The problem with looking at a range is that it might be affected by one extreme value and provides no indication of the spread between values. The range for 4, 4, 4, 4, 4 and 20 000 is 4 to 20 000. This is misleading both in terms of values and the spread between the extremes. This disadvantage can be overcome and extreme values can be ignored by slicing away the top and bottom quarters and then by analysing what is left.

Whereas the median is the middle number of an array of figures and represents 50 per cent, a *quartile* represents a quarter or 25 per cent of a range. The lower or first quartile is the area below which 25 per cent of observations fall and the upper or fourth quartile is the value above which 25 per cent of observations fall.

The inter-quartile range = upper quartile − lower quartile

From this conclusions can be drawn about the middle 50 per cent of data analysed.

We can extract the lower quartile, median, upper quartile and inter-quartile range from the following array of 20 numbers:

$$4 \quad 5 \quad 8 \quad 9 \quad 15 \quad 18 \quad 20 \quad 22 \quad 24 \quad 29$$
$$32 \quad 35 \quad 37 \quad 40 \quad 44 \quad 44 \quad 48 \quad 52 \quad 58 \quad 60$$

The lower quartile will be the value below which 25 per cent of the numbers will fall and will therefore be 25 per cent of 20 and the fifth value of 15. Using $\frac{n}{2}$ the median will be $\frac{20}{2}$ giving us the tenth value. This is 29. The upper quartile will be the value above which 25 per cent of the numbers fall. As there are 20 values in the array it will be 75 per cent of 20 and the fifteenth value is 44. Whereas the range for this set of figures is 54 and extends from 4 to 60, the inter-quartile range will be the upper quartile of 44 less the lower quartile of 15 and will be 29.

Though the inter-quartile range or quartile deviation is easy to understand and is unaffected by extreme values it might not be precise enough for a large sample. In these instances it could be necessary to use *deciles* and *percentiles*. Deciles relate to various tenths of a distribution. From our example the first decile will be 10 per cent of 20 and the second value of 5; the second decile will be the fourth value of 9 and so on. Percentiles relate to hundredths of the way through a distribution. The 95th percentile of our values will be 95 per cent of 20 and the nineteenth value of 58.

A measure of dispersion which further analyses a group of values and makes use of all observations is that of the *mean deviations*. It simply measures the average deviation of all values in a distribution from the actual mean. It averages the differences between the actual values in a distribution and the mean while, at the same time, ignoring the negative signs of differences. For the figures 5, 6, 13, 20 and 26 the arithmetic mean ($\bar{x}$) is:

$$\bar{x} = \frac{5 + 6 + 13 + 20 + 26}{5} = \frac{70}{5} = 14$$

The differences from the arithmetic mean are:

$$5 - 14, 6 - 14, 13 - 14, 20 - 14 \text{ and } 26 - 14 \text{ and these are:}$$
$$-9, -8, -1, 6 \text{ and } 12$$

If we then ignore the negative signs we can find the mean deviation as follows:

$$\frac{9 + 8 + 1 + 6 + 12}{5} = \frac{36}{5} = 7.2$$

The mean deviation or average difference from the mean is therefore 7.2 and the more usual way of expressing this is as:

$$\text{Mean deviation} = \frac{\Sigma |x - \bar{x}|}{n}$$

$|x - \bar{x}|$ means the difference between the mean and the actual value but ignoring negative signs.

The major problem of all the methods of dispersion looked at so far is that they have limited uses in further analysing data. Having worked out a quartile or a decile you know more about a distribution but there are few further uses for this information. As the mean deviation ignores the plus and minus differences it also has limited uses for further statistical processing. This is not the case for the *variance* and *standard deviation* which have widespread use in statistical analysis and are considered the most important measures of dispersion.

Instead of ignoring the minuses in differences from the mean, the variance and standard deviation square the differences and this process instantly eliminates the negative signs. When the squared differences have been averaged, a variance is created and the square root of this variance provides the standard deviation. This can be seen more clearly from an example.

If the output over five days of a machine were 4, 5, 5, 7 and 9 units respectively, the arithmetic mean would be 6. The variance measures the extent of the dispersion around the mean by:

- calculating the difference between the number of units produced each day and the arithmetic mean. This is shown as $x - \bar{x}$;
- squaring the difference $(x - \bar{x})^2$;
- finding the average of the total of these squared differences. It is therefore shown as $\dfrac{\Sigma(x - \bar{x})^2}{n}$ where n is the number of values.

Outputs x	$x - x$	$(x - x)^2$
4	−2	4
5	−1	1
5	−1	1
7	1	1
9	3	9
	0	16

The variance would be $\dfrac{16}{5} = 3.2$ units.

The standard deviation is the square root of the variance. In our example it will be:

$$\sqrt{3.2} = 1.79 \text{ units}$$

Thus we have an arithmetic mean of 6 units, a variance of 3.2 and a standard deviation of 1.79 units. By taking into consideration frequency (f) and denoting standard deviation as s we can show its formula as follows:

$$s = \sqrt{\frac{\Sigma f(x - \bar{x})^2}{n}} \quad \text{or} \quad \sqrt{\frac{\Sigma f(x - \bar{x})^2}{\Sigma f}}$$

The following example takes into consideration frequency and has an arithmetic mean or $\bar{x}$ of 6.

Value x	Frequency f	$x - \bar{x}$	$(x - \bar{x})^2$	$f(x - \bar{x})^2$
4	4	-2	4	16
5	6	-1	1	6
6	9	0	0	0
7	8	1	1	8
8	3	2	4	12
	30			42

The standard deviation will be $\sqrt{1.4} = 1.18$.

Although it is sometimes difficult to understand the significance of the figure for standard deviation, it can be said that the greater the dispersion the larger the standard deviation. As all values in the distribution are taken into account it is a comprehensive measure of dispersion capable of being developed further.

Any frequency distribution may either be *symmetrical* or *skewed*. A symmetrical frequency curve will be divided into two equal halves so that the arithmetic mean,

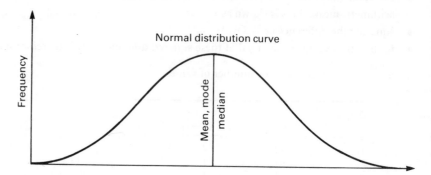

Figure 5.13 Normal distribution curve.

median and mode will have the same value. Such distributions create a normal curve with a symmetrical bell shape and represent a continuous variable in a frequency distribution (see Fig. 5.13).

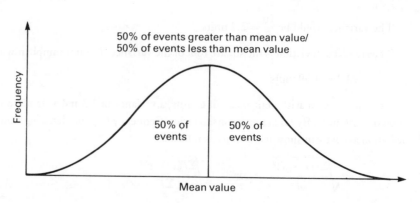

Figure 5.14 50 per cent of events greater than mean value/50 per cent of events less than mean value.

The normal distribution curve represents all possible outcomes and the frequency with which they will take place. As the curve is symmetrical 50 per cent of events will take place above the mean value and 50 per cent below the mean value (see Fig. 5.14). It therefore follows that this can be used with measurements that follow a normal pattern of distribution to find probabilities of certain events taking place.

Normal distribution tables can be used to find these probabilities as they measure the area from the mean to a fixed number of standard deviations away from the mean. Z is the letter which represents the number of standard deviations a value is above or below the mean. It is calculated by:

$$Z = \frac{x - m}{s}$$

Z = number of standard deviations above or below the mean
x = the value
m = the mean
s = the standard deviation

A frequency has a normal distribution, a mean of 50 and a standard deviation of 10. We can use this process to find what proportion of the total frequencies will be:

1. above 30
2. above 60
3. above 45
4. below 75

To calculate the proportion of frequencies *above* a value it must be remembered that:

(a) 50 per cent of the values are above the mean and so the proportion calculated as being between the mean and the value must be added to the 50 per cent. For (1) we can see that:

$$Z = \frac{50 - 30}{10} = \frac{20}{10} = 2 \text{ standard deviations}$$

By referring to the normal distribution tables the number of frequencies above 30 is therefore:

$$0.5 + 0.4772 = 0.9772 \text{ or } 97.72 \text{ per cent.}$$

The shaded area in Fig. 5.15 represents 97.72 per cent of the frequencies above the value of 30.

(b) If the value is above the mean the total proportion is 50 per cent minus the area between the value and the mean.

With (2) $Z = \dfrac{60 - 50}{10} = \dfrac{10}{10} = 1 \text{ standard deviation above the mean}$

Normal distribution tables

Z	0.00	0.01	0.02	0.03	0.04	0.05	0.06	0.07	0.08	0.09
0.0	0.0000	0.0040	0.0080	0.0120	0.0160	0.0199	0.0239	0.0279	0.0319	0.0359
0.1	0.0398	0.0438	0.0478	0.0517	0.0557	0.0596	0.0636	0.0675	0.0714	0.0753
0.2	0.0793	0.0832	0.0871	0.0910	0.0948	0.0987	0.1026	0.1064	0.1103	0.1141
0.3	0.1179	0.1217	0.1255	0.1293	0.1331	0.1368	0.1406	0.1443	0.1480	0.1517
0.4	0.1554	0.1591	0.1628	0.1664	0.1700	0.1736	0.1772	0.1808	0.1844	0.1879
0.5	0.1915	0.1950	0.1985	0.2019	0.2054	0.2088	0.2123	0.2157	0.2190	0.2224
0.6	0.2257	0.2291	0.2324	0.2357	0.2389	0.2422	0.2454	0.2486	0.2517	0.2549
0.7	0.2580	0.2611	0.2642	0.2673	0.2704	0.2734	0.2764	0.2794	0.2823	0.2852
0.8	0.2881	0.2910	0.2939	0.2967	0.2995	0.3023	0.3051	0.3078	0.3106	0.3133
0.9	0.3159	0.3186	0.3212	0.3238	0.3264	0.3289	0.3315	0.3340	0.3365	0.3389
1.0	0.3413	0.3438	0.3461	0.3485	0.3508	0.3531	0.3554	0.3577	0.3599	0.3621
1.1	0.3643	0.3665	0.3686	0.3708	0.3729	0.3749	0.3770	0.3790	0.3810	0.3830
1.2	0.3849	0.3869	0.3888	0.3907	0.3925	0.3944	0.3962	0.3980	0.3997	0.4015
1.3	0.4032	0.4049	0.4066	0.4082	0.4099	0.4115	0.4131	0.4147	0.4162	0.4177
1.4	0.4192	0.4207	0.4222	0.4236	0.4251	0.4265	0.4279	0.4292	0.4306	0.4319
1.5	0.4332	0.4345	0.4357	0.4370	0.4382	0.4394	0.4406	0.4418	0.4429	0.4441
1.6	0.4452	0.4463	0.4474	0.4484	0.4495	0.4505	0.4515	0.4525	0.4535	0.4545
1.7	0.4554	0.4564	0.4573	0.4582	0.4591	0.4599	0.4608	0.4616	0.4625	0.4633
1.8	0.4641	0.4649	0.4656	0.4664	0.4671	0.4678	0.4686	0.4693	0.4699	0.4706
1.9	0.4713	0.4719	0.4726	0.4732	0.4738	0.4744	0.4750	0.4756	0.4761	0.4767
2.0	0.4772	0.4778	0.4783	0.4788	0.4793	0.4798	0.4803	0.4808	0.4812	0.4817
2.1	0.4821	0.4826	0.4830	0.4834	0.4838	0.4842	0.4846	0.4850	0.4854	0.4857
2.2	0.4861	0.4864	0.4868	0.4871	0.4875	0.4878	0.4881	0.4884	0.4887	0.4890
2.3	0.4893	0.4896	0.4898	0.4901	0.4904	0.4906	0.4909	0.4911	0.4913	0.4916
2.4	0.4918	0.4920	0.4922	0.4925	0.4927	0.4929	0.4931	0.4932	0.4934	0.4936
2.5	0.4938	0.4940	0.4941	0.4943	0.4945	0.,4946	0.4948	0.4949	0.4951	0.4952
2.6	0.4953	0.4955	0.4956	0.4957	0.4959	0.4960	0.4961	0.4962	0.4963	0.4964
2.7	0.4965	0.4966	0.4967	0.4968	0.4969	0.4970	0.4971	0.4972	0.4973	0.4974
2.8	0.4974	0.4975	0.4976	0.4977	0.4977	0.4978	0.4979	0.4979	0.4980	0.4981
2.9	0.4981	0.4982	0.4982	0.4983	0.4984	0.4984	0.4985	0.4985	0.4986	0.4986
3.0	0.4987	0.4987	0.4987	0.4988	0.4988	0.4989	0.4989	0.4989	0.4990	0.4990

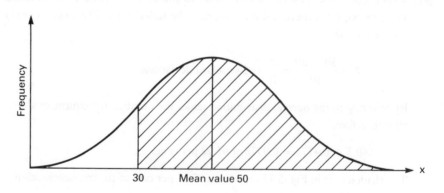

Figure 5.15 Frequencies above 30.

The number of frequencies above 60 is therefore

$$0.5 - 0.3413 = 0.1587 \text{ or } 15.87 \text{ per cent.}$$

The shaded area in Fig. 5.16 represents 15.87 per cent of the frequencies above the value of 60.

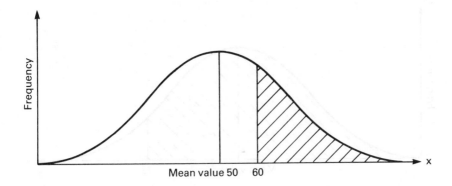

Figure 5.16 Frequencies above 60.

To calculate the proportion of frequencies *below* a certain value:

(a) If the value is below the mean the proportion is 50 per cent minus the area between the value and the mean.

With (3) $Z = \dfrac{50 - 45}{10} = \dfrac{5}{10} = 0.5$ standard deviations below the mean

The number of frequencies below 45 are therefore:

$0.5 - 0.1915 = 0.3085$ or 30.85 per cent.

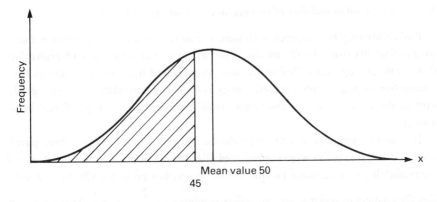

Figure 5.17 Frequencies below 45.

The shaded area in Fig. 5.17 represents 30.85 per cent of the frequencies below the value of 45.

(b) If the value is above the mean the proportion to be obtained is 50 per cent plus the area between the value and the mean.

With (4) $Z = \dfrac{75 - 50}{10} = \dfrac{25}{10} = 2.5$ standard deviations above the mean.

The number of frequencies below 75 are therefore:

$0.5 + 0.4938 = 0.9938$ or 99.38 per cent.

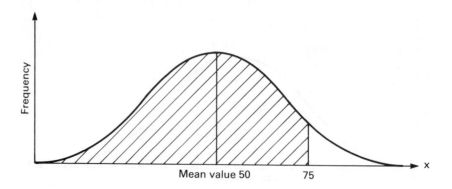

Figure 5.18 Frequencies below 75.

The shaded area in Fig. 5.18 represents 99.38 per cent of the frequencies below the value of 75.

The name *binomial* refers to an alternative method of analysing probability from a distribution and refers to any situation where there are two possible alternatives. You might change your car or you might not change your car. There are two possible courses of action. For any situation to fit the binomial pattern so that an experiment can take place it must:

1. be an either/or situation with only two possible outcomes;
2. consist of a number of trials denoted by n;
3. have a known probability of success on each trial denoted by p.

Probability may be measured with some certainty. If a die is rolled there is a one-sixth probability that a 4 will turn up. When a coin is tossed there is a 0.5 probability that it will turn up heads. Probability may be measured from past experiences from information such as weather records, analysis of machine breakdowns, faulty goods, working days lost, etc. It may also be estimated from surveys or a series of trials in the market.

If a sample contained five green products, two yellow products and three purple products and, if supplies were not replaced after having been taken, we can work out the probability of a customer picking out the two yellow products. On the first occasion the chances of picking out two yellow products are $\frac{2}{10}$ so $p = \frac{1}{5}$. As there is only one yellow left the chances of picking that out are one in nine with only nine products remaining. By multiplying the two probabilities together we can work out the chances of picking two yellow products out.

$$= \frac{1}{9} \times \frac{1}{5} = \frac{1}{45}$$

A knowledge of probabilities and using the binomial to model a problem enables management to predict more precisely the outcomes of future events.

Skewness is used to describe a non-symmetrical frequency distribution curve. A *positively skewed frequency distribution curve* will have a bias towards the left-hand side of a graph and will then have a long tail, sloping out to the right (see Fig. 5.19). With a positively skewed distribution the mode will have a lower value than the median and the mean will have a higher value than the median.

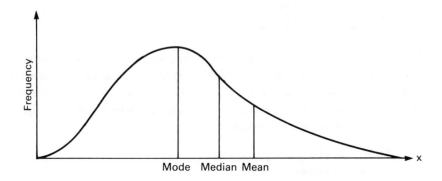

Figure 5.19 Positively skewed frequency distribution curve.

A negatively skewed frequency distribution curve will have a bias towards the right-hand side of the graph and will have a long tail sloping out towards the left (see Fig. 5.20). With a negatively skewed distribution the mode will have a higher value than the median and the mean will have a lower value than the median.

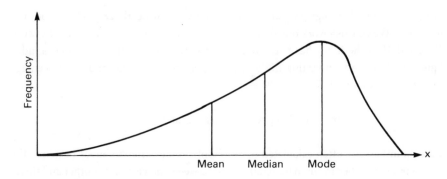

Figure 5.20 Negatively skewed frequency distribution curve.

Index numbers

It is sometimes difficult to make comparisons between sets of figures. Often the complexity, the relevance and the size of the units being measured can make direct comparisons meaningless. Instead of trying to make sense of complicated technical figures based upon a mass of information, it is sometimes better to strive for a single figure which shows a direct comparison between one time period and another. Index numbers provide the means to be able to do so by taking a typical year as a base and expressing figures for other years as a percentage of this. So if the sales figure for 19–0 was 100, and for 19–3 was 125, we would know that sales had increased by 25 per cent over the period.

An organization's sales figures might be presented as follows:

Year	Sales (000's)
19–0	458
19–1	535
19–2	573
19–3	584

It is usual to use 100 as a base as, in everyday life, we are used to making comparisons based upon percentages. In the example above we decide to use 19–0 as a base year against which all others are to be compared. The index for 19–0 is therefore 100. In order to work out the index for other years we must divide each year's sales figures by the base year and multiply this by 100.

$$\frac{\text{Figures for other years}}{\text{Base year's figures}} \times 100$$

For 19–1 this will be $\frac{535}{458} \times 100 = 116.81$

For 19–2 this will be $\frac{573}{458} \times 100 = 125.11$

For 19–3 this will be $\frac{584}{458} \times 100 = 127.51$

We can see from these figures that sales have increased by nearly 28 per cent from 19–0 to 19–3. We can also work out annual percentage increases from the index. Between 19–2 and 19–3 the index has risen by 2.4 points. By dividing this by the sales index figure for 19–2 and converting the result to a percentage we can find the percentage increase in sales for 19–3.

$$\frac{2.4}{125.11} \times 100 = 1.92 \text{ per cent increase in sales}$$

Index numbers are often calculated to represent a wide variety of areas or items. We use an index number to compare retail prices between one year and another and this is used as an indicator of domestic price inflation. Domestic prices cover a host of commodities and clearly more than one item is taken into consideration when putting this index together.

We can produce a hypothetical example for Country A where the four commodities included in the retail price index are bread, cheese, meat and vegetables.

Item	19–0	19–1
Bread	50p per loaf	55p per loaf
Cheese	130p per kg	125p per kg
Meat	160p per kg	180p per kg
Vegetables	40p per kg	50p per kg

Prices for bread, meat and vegetables have gone up but the price of cheese has fallen. We wish to produce a single index figure to reflect these changes but the table gives no indication of how important each item is to the cost of living and also tries to compare different units. This can be overcome by *weighting* each item in proportion to its relative importance. By selecting a weight the importance of each item and the units in which it appears are taken into consideration to produce a final figure which is directly comparable. This procedure for doing this is:

1. List all of the items with their prices.
2. Select appropriate weights.
3. Multiply prices by their weights.
4. Add the weighted prices together.
5. Produce an index by comparing the total weighted prices from the base year to the other year.

In our example we allocate a weight of 80 to bread, 50 to cheese, 30 to meat and 10 to vegetables.

Weighted cost of living index

		19–0		19–1	
Item	Weight	Price	Price × weight	Price	Price × weight
Bread	80	50	4 000	55	4 400
Cheese	50	130	6 500	125	6 250
Meat	30	160	4 800	180	5 400
Vegetables	10	40	400	50	500
			Total 15 700		Total 16 550

By using 19–0 as the base year and designating 100 to it we can see that:

$$\frac{16\,550}{15\,700} \times 100 = 105.41$$

Prices have risen during the year by 5.41 per cent.

Probably the best known of all UK official statistics is the Retail Price Index which is generally accepted as the official measure of price inflation. It measures inflation in real terms rather than must monetary terms and has considerable ramifications for pay negotiations and settlements.

Although indices are traditionally associated with prices they can also be used for a multitude of commercial purposes such as insurance, index-linked schemes, etc. Perhaps their greatest advantage is that they are easy to understand and provide a common scale to compare different types of information.

Case Study—Internal purchasing power of the pound

Internal purchasing power of the pound (based on RPI)

pence

	Year in which purchasing power was 100p														
	1973	1974	1975	1976	1977	1978	1979	1980	1981	1982	1983	1984	1985	1986	1987
1973	100	116	144	168	195	211	239	282	316	343	358	376	399	413	430
1974	86	100	124	145	168	182	206	243	272	295	309	324	344	356	370
1975	69	80	100	117	135	146	166	196	219	238	249	261	277	286	298
1976	60	69	86	100	116	125	142	168	188	204	213	224	238	246	256
1977	51	60	74	86	100	108	123	145	162	176	184	193	205	212	221
1978	47	55	68	80	92	100	113	134	150	163	170	178	189	196	204
1979	42	49	60	70	81	88	100	118	132	143	150	157	167	173	180
1980	35	41	51	60	69	75	85	100	112	122	127	133	142	146	152
1981	32	37	46	53	62	67	76	89	100	109	114	119	127	131	136
1982	29	34	42	49	57	62	70	82	92	100	105	110	116	120	125
1983	28	32	40	47	54	59	67	79	88	96	100	105	111	115	120
1984	27	31	38	45	52	56	64	75	84	91	95	100	106	110	114
1985	25	29	36	42	49	53	60	71	79	86	90	94	100	103	108
1986	24	28	35	41	47	51	58	68	76	83	87	91	97	100	104
1987	23	27	34	39	45	49	56	66	73	80	83	87	93	96	100

Note: To find the purchasing power of the pound in 1980, given that it was 100 pence in 1973, select the column headed 1973 and look at the 1980 row. The result is 35 pence.

These figures are calculated by taking the inverse ratio of the respective annual averages of the General Index of Retail Prices.

(*Source:* Central Statistical Office.)

Questions

1. Make a comparison between the purchasing power of the pound in 1973, 1980 and 1987.
2. Comment upon the differences between changes in the 1980s to changes in the 1970s.

Significance testing

Quite often when a hypothesis is made, a decision taken and then implemented, at a later stage a random sample fails to support the original hypothesis. The difference could be attributed either to mistakes in the original hypothesis or to elements of chance distorting the sample. Significance tests are necessary to test which of these two possibilities is more likely. If the difference is not properly explained as being due to chance it is said to be statistically significant.

The purpose of significance testing is therefore to check that a hypothesis is correct unless results exceed certain limits. If a hypothesis is rejected there is a possibility of a *Type I error*. A Type I error is the error of rejecting a hypothesis when it is in fact true. A sales manager might not be justified for admonishing staff for a sudden drop in sales. In the longer term the projected hypothesis on sales targets will be achieved but fluctuations will occasionally take place. On the other hand, a *Type II error* is the error of not rejecting a hypothesis when it is in fact false. With this error sales might continue to fall so that targets are not met and action is not taken to correct this when in fact the hypothesis should be rejected.

The *null hypothesis* is an assumption that there is no contradiction between expected results and actual results, and that if a difference occurs, it is due to chance. The object of a significance test is to see whether the null hypothesis should be rejected or not. A null hypothesis is always tested at a specific level of significance. A 5 per cent level of significance is often used and this creates a 95 per cent confidence level. If we expected 10 rejects from every sample of 100 objects and got 12, the null hypothesis would be that there would not be any significant difference between the 10 and 12 at a 5 per cent level of significance.

Data processing

Over recent years computers have proliferated in almost every business area so that, today, the role of the business statistician is significantly different. Whereas in the past statisticians were involved with manually compiling and presenting statistics, this role has largely been taken over by the computer which performs these types of calculations in a fraction of the time. Computers today are:

- substantially cheaper than they used to be;
- much faster than they were and capable of multitasking operations;
- able to store and manipulate vast quantities of data;
- capable of using a wider variety of packages.

Packages available to statisticians are either batch or interactive. Batch packages involve statistical information being entered as a complete task before the results are conveyed to the statistician for analysis. Interactive packages are more recent and involve information being entered as it is received so that, after each input, the computer updates its response. Statisticians can concentrate upon analysis rather than preparation while the tedium of the work is performed by computers which process and attractively present information in a fraction of the time taken previously.

Case Study—Video Show

Video Show is a graphics hardware device that inputs information from a floppy disk, controlled from either its own keypad or a separate infra-red handset, not dissimilar to a domestic TV. The user can input to the system via a wide range of graphics packages such as Harvard Business Graphics, Lotus Freelance or Lotus Graphic Writer, allowing either independent input of information or direct transfer from spreadsheets, such as Lotus 1–2–3.

With its own generic package, Picture It, the images are created by filling in a standard form on the screen. The required image is selected and the figures to be represented are typed in. The resultant graphics are then stored on a PC disk.

When the required number of images for the presentation have been created in this way, the disk is inserted in the Video Show unit and the presentation can commence.

(*Source: Management Accounting*)

Short answer questions

1. Distinguish between a qualitative statement and a quantitative statement.
2. Name two sources of external data.
3. By using an example explain how cluster sampling works.
4. Name four features of a good questionnaire.
5. Why are postal questionnaires often considered to be unsatisfactory?
6. Explain briefly why a company might wish to look at the *Monthly Digest of Statistics* published by the Central Statistical Office.
7. What is a grouped frequency distribution?
8. A business producing a range of products has total sales of £100 million in 1986. For its annual report it wishes to present this information in diagrammatic form. State one method that might be used.   (*Source:* AEB.)
9. Why might a Lorenz curve be useful?
10. Define two measures of central tendency.
11. What is meant by the terms
    (a) upper quartile?
    (b) lower quartile?
12. Make up an example to show how the mean deviation is calculated.
13. How does the formula for the variance differ from the formula for the standard deviation?
14. Name two features of a symmetrical frequency.
15. What types of probable statements can be made from a normal distribution?
16. Give two examples of a binomial problem.
17. Why will the mean have a higher value than the mode for a positively skewed frequency distribution curve?
18. Explain why many index numbers are weighted.
19. Distinguish between a Type I and a Type II error.
20. Explain the difference between a batch and an interactive package.

Essays

1. Explain the differences between the quality of information required for a company's
    (a) strategic needs
    (b) tactical needs
    (c) organizational needs
    What techniques would you employ to obtain information to satisfy each of these requirements?

2. Briefly describe four methods of presenting information and justify the suitability of each for reporting to:
   (a) directors
   (b) company employees
   (c) shareholders
3. Statistically presented information is often criticized for being open to misinterpretation. Discuss.
4. Make up an example to demonstrate each of the measures of central tendency and comment upon the usefulness of each.
5. What does a statistician mean by dispersion?
6. How does the standard deviation meet criticisms directed at the mean deviation? With reference to its formula state how the standard deviation is calculated. What would be the significance of an increase in the size of a standard deviation?
7. Discuss why probability is an essential ingredient in business planning.
8. Explain why probabilities can be extracted from a normal distribution and describe the process for doing so.
9. Why are index numbers considered to be a useful statistical tool? Explain the purpose of weighting.
10. Why is significance testing considered to be an important statistical technique?

Data response questions

1 The owner of a UK company selling coats, dresses and hats is considering expanding by setting up another shop in Europe.
   (a) What commercial information should the owner seek before making any decision? [4]
   (b) The pie charts [Fig. 5.21] are taken from the company's reports and accounts for 1986.

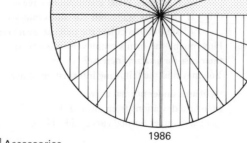

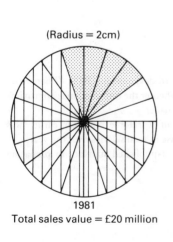

(Radius = 2cm)

1981
Total sales value = £20 million

(Radius = 3cm)

1986

Key ▨ Coats ▦ Dresses ☐ Accessories

Figure 5.21 Analysis of sales by product.

(i)   Discuss whether these pie charts satisfy the main principles one should always bear in mind when presenting data.   [4]

(ii) Show that the total sales in 1986 were £45 million.   [3]

(iii) Calculate the percentage increase in the sales value of accessories between 1981 and 1986.   [3]

(iv) If total sales continue to increase by the same average amount over the next three years as they did in the five years 1981–1986, and sales of dresses increase by 40% in total over the next three years, what angle of a pie chart for 1989 would represent the contribution to total sales by the dress department?   [4]

(c) The managers of the three departments each claim that their product is 'doing best'.

(i)   How could each manager use the above pie charts to support his claim? (You are not required to undertake any calculations to answer this question.)   [3]

(ii) Suggest an appropriate graphical method for displaying sales information. Give reasons for your answer.   [4]

(Source: Cambridge.)

2 (a) (i)   Three companies, A, B and C have roughly the same number of employees, and the distributions of their salaries have the same modes. The distributions for A and B are approximately normal but that for B has half the standard deviation of that for A. The distribution for C is positively skewed, but with the same range as that for A. Sketch the three distributions using the same axis for all three.

(ii) If you were an ambitious 'high-flyer', which company would you prefer to work for and why?

(b) The distribution of A's salaries is shown below:

Salary range (£)	No. of employees
7000– 7999	9
8000– 8999	33
9000– 9999	285
10000–10999	433
11000–11999	192
12000–12999	39
13000–13999	9
	1000

(i)   Estimate the median salary.

(ii) The mean salary is £10 500 and the standard deviation is £1000. (There is no need to confirm these values.) Determine whether the distribution is approximately normal. What assumptions have you made?

(iii) If the total wage bill for the same size of workforce one year earlier was £10 000 000 calculate the percentage increase in total salaries over the year.

(c) How might the firm's employees use government-published statistics in preparing their case for a salary increase?

You may find the following information of use:

% of area under normal curve
Standard deviations from mean 0–1 1–2 2–3
% of area under normal curve   34   14   2

(Source: Cambridge.)

3 (a) Why is 'weighting' necessary in constructing index numbers? Give a brief example.
   (b) Identify the limitations of a typical retail price index.
   (c) The following figures were provided by the Utopian Statistical Service for compiling a retail price index:

Item	Price relative (June 1988 Jan 1980 = 100)	Weights (1987 average)
Food	110.3	25
Fuel	122.1	20
Housing	141.3	25
Services	126.9	15
Clothing	130.8	5
Miscellaneous	118.2	10
		100

   (i)   Explain why the weights refer to a period other than the base period (January 1980).
   (ii) What is meant by the term 'price relative'?
   (iii) Calculate a weighted aggregate price index for June 1988.

   (d) A company calculates details of wage rates, material costs and factory overheads in index form, and in June 1988 these stood at 150, 60 and 130 respectively (January 1980 = 100). A particular product had the following cost structure in January 1980:

	£/unit
Labour	0.80
Materials	0.80
Factory overheads	0.40
	2.00

   (i)   Estimate the mean percentage increase in the costs of producing the product between January 1980 and June 1988.
   (ii) State any assumptions you have made.

(*Source:* Cambridge.)

4 Study Figs 5.22 and 5.23 before attempting the questions that follow. Figure 5.22 shows the total sales value of sports equipment by UK manufacturers for the period 1961–1977:
   (a) Sales at current prices.
   (b) Sales deflated by sports equipment price index.

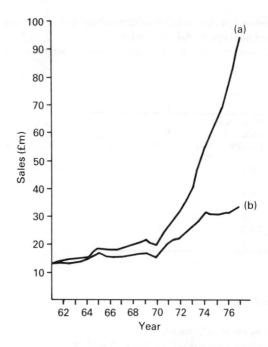

Figure 5.22 Total sales of sports
equipment by UK manufacturers for
the period 1961–77.

Figure 5.23 Exports and imports of
sports equipment. (*Source*: *Business
Monitor* PQ 4934.)

	Exports (£ thousand)	As proportion of total UK manufacturers' sales	Imports (£ thousand)	As proportion of total UK manufacturers' sales
1970	9 888	50.99	3 105	15.99
1971	13 562	48.47	4 285	15.31
1972	15 209	46.01	5 775	17.47
1973	20 393	48.76	8 981	21.47
1974	25 935	47.05	13 850	25.12
1975	32 184	50.42	18 168	28.46
1976	36 187	47.30	20 500	26.80

(a) Briefly explain why the two lines on the graph diverged between 1971 and 1977.

(b) On graph paper construct a bar chart to compare Exports and Imports for the years 1971, 1973 and 1975.

(c) (i) Calculate the relative increase in both Exports and Imports between the two years 1970 and 1976.

(ii) Identify **four** economic and social factors which might have led to these changes.

(Source: AEB)

5 (a) Using the figures given below calculate:
   (i) the range
   (ii) the mean
   (iii) the median

    (iv)   the lower quartile
     (v)   the upper quartile
    (vi)   the quartile deviation
   (vii)   the mean deviation
  (viii)   the standard deviation

5	12	24	23	4
16	17	7	35	21
43	19	42	27	60
18	21	47	20	55
2	44	18	19	5

(b)   Using examples explain what is meant by a measure of dispersion.

Suggested reading

Bancroft, G. and O'Sullivan, G., *Maths and Statistics for Accounting and Business Studies*. McGraw-Hill, 1988.

Clegg, F., *Simple Statistics*. Cambridge University Press, 1987.

Freund, J. and Perles, B., *Business Statistics*. Prentice-Hall, 1974.

Hanson, G. and Brown, G., *Starting Statistics*. Hulton, 1969.

6

The business in its environment

Entrepreneurs must try to achieve set organizational aims in the marketplace in competition with other business enterprises. Businesses will compete for scarce resources and to be able to sell products.

Business activity takes place against a background of many competing interests. These influences include:

1. Consumers
2. Suppliers
3. Other producers
4. Central government
5. Local government
6. Trade unions
7. Local residents

The effect of each of these influences is examined in other chapters but it is worth looking at them in combination here. We will look first at the influence of an individual business person.

Peter Thompson is a window cleaner. He works a set round of private houses and small business premises. He feels that his *consumers* remain loyal because of the quality service they receive. His prices vary from £3 to £6 for private houses. He charges £5 for shop fronts and from between £5 and £10 for other business premises. His customers tend to stick with him, so he regards his prices to be about right.

Peter's 'beat' covers an area around the town centre. He is able to carry his ladders, buckets and cleaning cloths around on his shoulder. Capital and material costs are very low. The ladder and bucket have lasted for over 20 years and water is free. The prices of detergents and cleaning cloths from *suppliers* do occasionally rise and in the long term this has had a slight effect in pushing prices up.

Peter must always keep 'one eye on the *competition*'. Window cleaners tend to have their own set patch of houses, but there is always a certain amount of 'poaching'. He needs to compete quite aggressively for the business of cleaning shop windows and he takes special care to do these well.

Peter Thompson must pay income tax to the *government*, the amount depending on his earnings. He has not registered to pay VAT because his turnover is not high enough.

Peter pays a local tax to the *council* for which he benefits from a wide number of services including well maintained pathways, and street lighting which is a great benefit in the darker months of the year.

Being self-employed means that Peter has no need to join a *trade union*.

Going about his work, he must pay careful attention to the people with whom the business comes into contact, and to organizations within the *wider community*. His ladders and equipment need to be positioned safely and he must avoid spilling water on to slippery pavements. Peter has taken out a public liability insurance policy to cover himself against accidents that he may be deemed responsible for and which involve members of the public.

The individual business enterprise can be seen to be at the centre of a set of local, national and international influences and constraints (see Fig. 6.1). In an interdependent world a small change in any one factor that makes up the business environment will send out ripples affecting a number of other factors. For example:

● An increase in local spending power might enable a firm to sell more products.

Figure 6.1 Influences on the business enterprise. (*Source*: Courtesy of Schools Industry Partnership.)

Larger sales might make modernization of plant worth while, making it possible for the firm to gain a competitive edge in national and international markets.

- A reduction in the number of local suppliers might force a firm to buy stocks from further afield, pushing up transport costs and reducing the enterprise's competitive edge.
- An increase in the local population might increase both the local demand for an enterprise's product and the availability of the required labour force. These factors would help to enhance the enterprise's competitive edge.
- National government decisions to tax profits may cut into the reserves being laid aside by a firm for modernization and expansion.

Consumers

A business needs to be constantly aware of the state of demand for its products. Business success depends on the ability of an enterprise to maintain a 'unique selling proposition' to which customers will respond. Businesses need to work constantly towards identifying and satisfying consumer needs. Consumers need to be convinced that products are worthy of purchase. Success will be based on thorough research of a wide range of consumer needs. This research will then have to be translated into products.

The ability of producers to satisfy consumers in a market economy based on pricing decisions depends on two interrelated sets of factors:

1. Factors influencing demand.
2. Factors influencing supply.

Factors influencing demand

Price

The demand for a product means that actual amount that will be bought at a given price. Common sense tells us that more of a product will be bought at a cheaper than at a higher price. For example, market research on the number of people who would use a new swimming pool produced the results shown in the table.

Price for adults	Demand to use the facility per week
£4	100
£3	150
£2	250
£1	800
75p	1200
50p	1400
40p	1500
30p	1600

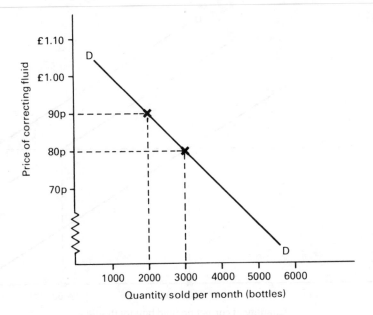

Figure 6.2 Demand for correcting fluid.

The demand for a product is commonly shown graphically by means of a demand curve. In the illustration (Fig. 6.2) a stationer has drawn out a demand curve for correcting fluid D–D. By reading off the graph you can see that by charging 90p per item, 2000 bottles will be sold in a month. By charging 80p per bottle, 3000 will be sold in a month.

An individual demand curve can be likened to a snapshot taken at a particular moment in time showing how much of a product would be bought at different prices. At that moment in time, price is seen to be the only variable that can be altered which will influence the quantity purchased.

Most demand curves drawn from real situations will have a shape which is more of a squiggle than a straight line. However, the common factor of nearly all demand curves is that they slope down to the right, indicating that – assuming conditions of demand remain the same – more units will be bought at a lower price than at a higher price. Therefore, in this book we will draw demand curves as if they are always straight lines.

Factors other than price

There are a number of factors which influence the demand for a product in addition to price. If one of these factors alters, the *conditions of demand* are said to have changed. These factors include tastes, income, population, the price of substitute products and the price of complementary products.

Changes in one or a combination of these factors will cause shifts in the demand curve. The demand curve can shift either in a leftward or in a rightward direction. A

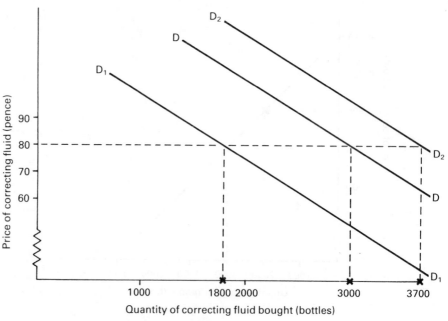

Figure 6.3 Shifts in the position of a demand curve.

D – D shows the original demand curve
$D_1 – D_1$ shows a shift to the left in demand
$D_2 – D_2$ shows a shift to the right in demand

shift to the left indicates that smaller quantities are wanted than before at given prices. A shift to the right indicates that larger quantities are wanted than before at given prices. These changes are illustrated in Fig. 6.3.

Figure 6.3 shows that in the original situation a quantity of 3000 would have been bought at 80p. When the conditions of demand move in favour of the product, more will be required at all prices so that, for example, at 80p perhaps 3700 bottles of correcting fluid would now be demanded. Alternatively, if the conditions of demand move against a product, less will be required at all prices so that for example at 80p perhaps only 1800 bottles of correcting fluid will now be demanded.

Factors which can cause these shifts in demand are outlined below.

Tastes

As time moves on, new products become more fashionable and popular while others go into decline. For example, the hot summer weather of 1989 provided an excellent climate for a fashion craze for Bermuda shorts. It would not be surprising if this craze were to be quickly dampened in the summers of the early 1990s. The effect on demand of tastes changing in favour of Bermudas was to push the demand curve for the product to the right. Many firms started producing Bermuda shorts, and many clothes shops sold them.

As time progresses other products lose popularity and the demand curve shifts to the left. For example, Citizens Band radios were very popular in the early 1980s. By the late 1980s demand had dropped considerably. A pronounced example of a rapid shift to the left in the demand curve for a product occurred in early December 1988 when the Junior Health Minister, Edwina Curry, pointed out a link between eggs and food poisoning. Overnight the demand for eggs crashed, huge stocks of eggs built up and some producers went out of business.

Population

Population statistics can be very helpful for forecasting changes in demand. Demographers (people who compile population statistics), frequently make predictions about future population trends based on existing statistics. Predictions based on the size of the population in particular age groups are particularly easy to chart, because once a child has been born, he or she will become steadily older.

Populations can be classified in a number of ways including age, sex, locality, race, educational background, and by the newspaper they read.

Demand forecasters will often analyse population statistics according to clusters of relevant factors, e.g. males in the 35–45-year-old age group living in Birmingham.

An increase in the relevant population will tend to move the demand curve for a product to the right. A decrease in the relevant population will tend to move the demand curve to the left.

Case Study

A unit trust company was considering producing a new savings scheme. It wanted to produce a savings package and target its marketing at a segment of the population that would be most likely to 'take up' a savings scheme. The information given in Fig. 6.4 was used to help make a decision.

Although the overall population is projected to increase at only 1.15 per cent over the next five years, there are considerable movements within this total figure.

There are four major age groups in which important changes are taking place:

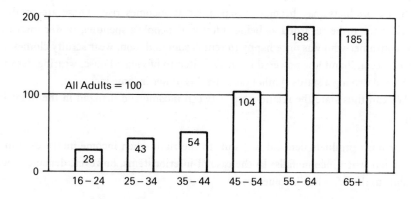

Figure 6.4 Savings by age group.

1. The 70 plus age group is set to increase by nearly *6 per cent* primarily as a result of longer life expectation.
2. 45–49-year-olds, a critical age group in unit trust purchasing, will expand by *nearly 19 per cent*. This section are the 'war babies', currently aged 40–45.
3. The 1960s 'baby-boomers' will move into their late twenties and early thirties, the latter sections increasing *by over 11 per cent* in the next five years.
4. As the 'baby-boomers' have their children another mini-boom will be created: 0–4-year-olds will increase *by 7 per cent* and the 0–9 section as a whole will enlarge by *4.8 per cent*—over four times the average population increase.

Task Use the above information to draw up a recommendation to the Board of the Unit Trust Company as to which sector of the population they should target their new savings scheme at. Explain your reasoning. You might also wish to include some details about how you would promote the scheme.

Income

The more money people have, the easier it is for them to buy products. The amount of income people have to spend on goods is known as their disposable income and is their pay minus taxes and other deductions.

Average incomes tend to rise over time and this will lead to a general increase in the level of demand for goods. The demand for individual items will, however, be related more to the changes in incomes earned by different groups such as teenagers (for teenage magazines and fashions), pensioners (for retirement homes, winter sun holidays) and others.

The demand for most products will rise as a result of an increase in incomes for the relevant population. This will lead to a shift in the demand curve to the right.

Rising incomes will tend to result from improving job opportunities, the increased use of cost-cutting technology and increases in demand for products.

Some products may become less popular as incomes rise. These are products which come to be regarded as being inferior as people's spending power increases. The consumer who was once happy to rent accommodation, wear scruffy clothes and drive a secondhand low powered car may switch to buying a house, wearing designer labels and driving a status symbol car when his or her income increases.

We can thus state the relationship between income and demand in the following way:

For most products demand will shift to the right when income increases, and to the left when income falls. In the case of inferior items, however, demand would shift to the left when incomes rise.

Inherited wealth

A number of studies have highlighted the level of inherited wealth that is coming the way of middle-aged households. Typical of these was a study by Morgan Grenfell in 1988 which pointed out that:

> ... about half the middle-aged households in the country will inherit property typically worth £35 000. ... As the proportion of elderly owner-occupiers rises, so will the proportion of middle-aged investors. By the end of the century property worth £9 billion (1986 prices) will be handed on each year. In south-east England granny will often leave her children a house worth £100 000.
>
> Most of the lucky legatees will be in their 40s or 50s. They will already have bought homes of their own, so they will sell their parents' home to a new generation of young house-buyers. Most of those who inherit their parents' home will have begun to plan for their own retirement.

The overall effect is that a sizeable number of middle-aged households inherit a considerable amount of wealth which is rapidly turned into spending power. An increase in inherited wealth in this way can have an important effect in raising the demand for products and thus shifting demand curves to the right.

The price of substitute products

The demand for products which have close substitutes will often be strongly influenced by the price of the substitutes. This would be the case, for example, with different brands of tinned fruit, or different brands of petrol because there are many different brand names from which to choose.

The demand curve for a product is likely to shift to the right if a substitute product rises in price. The demand curve for a product is likely to shift to the left if a substitute product falls in price. (Assuming that other factors influencing demand do not alter at the same time.)

The price of complementary products

Some products are used together so that the demand for one is linked to the price of another. An example of this might be a word processor and a floppy disk. If a particular make of word processor were to rise in price then users might switch new purchases to an alternative make. This would also reduce the demand for floppy disks which are compatible with the original brand of word processor.

Factors influencing supply

Price

The supply of a product is the amount that suppliers will wish to supply at a particular price. Common sense tells us that more of a product will be supplied at a higher than at a lower price. For example, a survey of tomato growers' intentions in a particular farming district revealed that the acreages shown in the table would be committed to tomato production at the prices indicated (bearing in mind that quantities produced would depend on the acreage planted, as well as weather conditions and other variables).

Price of tomatoes (market price per lb)	Quantity of land committed to tomato production (acres)
15p	800
20p	2 400
25p	4 400
30p	10 000
35p	14 000

The supply of a product can be shown graphically by means of a supply curve. In the illustration (Fig. 6.5) a newspaper manufacturer has plotted the numbers of copies of papers that the company would be prepared to supply per day at different prices. By reading off the graph you can see that at a price of 20p, 400 000 copies will be produced each day. At a price of 25p, 800 000 copies will be produced. The individual supplier (e.g. the newspaper manufacturer) will be prepared to purchase more capital and equipment and to employ more factors of production if he thinks that prices will be higher. The risk becomes more attractive and capital outlays (e.g. the cost of new equipment for an advanced printing process) can be recovered more quickly.

In the market as a whole (e.g. the market for national newspapers) more producers will be prepared to enter the market to supply at higher prices. More entrepreneurs will be prepared to risk capital, if returns promise to be higher, and even the less efficient producers will anticipate excess revenue over costs.

An individual supply curve can be likened to a snapshot taken at a particular moment in time, showing how much of a product would be supplied at different prices. At that moment in time, price is seen to be the only variable that can be altered which will influence the quantity supplied.

Most supply curves drawn from real situations will have a shape which is more of a squiggle than a straight line. However, the common factor of nearly all supply curves is that they slope to the right, indicating that—assuming conditions of supply remain

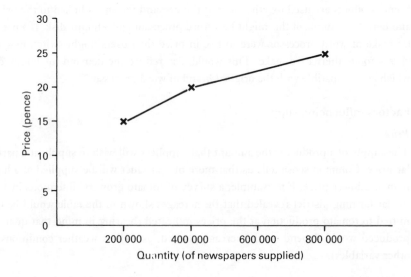

Figure 6.5 The supply curve of newspapers.

the same – more units will be supplied at a higher price than at a lower price. There-fore, in this book we will draw supply curves as if they are always straight lines.

Factors other than price

There are a number of factors which influence the supply of a product in addition to price influences. If one of these factors alters, the *conditions of supply* are said to have changed. These factors include the price of factors of production, the price of other commodities, technology, tastes of producers, etc.

Changes in one or a combination of these factors will cause shifts in the supply curve. The supply curve can shift in either a leftward or a rightward direction. A shift to the left indicates that smaller quantities will be supplied than before at given prices. A shift to the right indicates that larger quantities will be supplied than before at given prices. These changes are illustrated in Fig. 6.6.

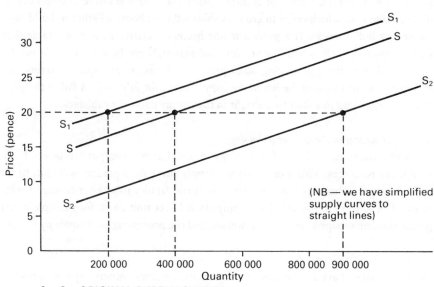

S – S = ORIGINAL SUPPLY CURVE
S_1 – S_1 = SHIFT TO LEFT IN SUPPLY CURVE
S_2 – S_2 = SHIFT TO RIGHT IN SUPPLY CURVE

Figure 6.6 Shifts in the supply curve for newspapers.

Figure 6.6 shows that in the original situation a quantity of 400 000 papers a day would have been supplied at 20p. When the conditions of supply move in favour of the product, more will be supplied at all prices, so that, for example, at 20p 900 000 newspapers will be supplied. Alternatively, if the conditions of supply move against a product, fewer will be supplied at all prices, so that at 20p, for example, perhaps only 200 000 newspapers will be supplied.

Factors which can cause these shifts in supply are outlined below.

The price of factors of production

Production is based on the combination of factor inputs in order to produce outputs.

If the cost of a factor input rises, then it will become more expensive to produce outputs. Factors of production will only be used in the long term if the value of their output is greater than their cost of hire. As factor prices rise, fewer factors will be used in production, and hence the supply of a product will fall.

For example, let us assume that an agricultural crop requires three main inputs — land, labour and chemical fertilizer. If the cost of one of these inputs (or a combination of them) were to rise, then farmers might cut back on the acreage committed to this particular crop.

Conversely when the price of factors of production falls, then supply conditions move in favour of increased production and supply is likely to shift to the right.

The price of other commodities

In a number of areas of production it is possible to switch production from less profitable to more profitable lines. For example, many arable farmers have a certain degree of discretion over which crops to grow. A shipyard can choose whether to build tugs, oil rigs, or bulk carriers. If a particular line becomes relatively more profitable then scarce resources such as equipment, time and materials can be switched into producing it and away from producing other products. A rise in the price of carrots may therefore lead to a shift to the left in the supply curve for cabbages. A fall in the price of carrots may lead to a shift to the right in the supply curve for cabbages.

Changes in the level of technology

An improvement in the level of technology means that more output can be produced with fewer resources. This means that the supply curve for a product will shift to the right. Modern technology based on computers and factory robots has enabled a wide range of producers to produce larger outputs at lower unit costs, for example in car production, newspapers, modern breweries, and the processing of cheques by banks.

The tastes of producers

Business owners have a wide range of objectives. To some owners expansion may be seen as a goal in itself. The firm might decide to produce more to gain a higher profile, to take a larger share of a market, or simply because the owner enjoys the cut and thrust of business life.

Other factors

One of the major factors influencing the supply of a number of goods and services is the weather. A number of services respond to changes in the weather, e.g. the appearance of umbrella sellers at the entrances to underground stations. The supply of agricultural products depends very much on changing weather conditions.

The formation of a market price

A market is a situation in which goods can be bought, sold or exchanged. The essential requirements are buyers, sellers, goods and money.

In the marketplace the forces of demand and supply will interact to create a market price. To illustrate this point we have drawn up a fictional daily demand and supply schedule for fish at a small fishing village. When the price of fish is high the owner of the only fishing boat will spend more time fishing than when prices are low. Consumers will want to purchase more fish at low than at high prices.

Table showing demand and supply in a daily fish market

Price of fish (pence)	Quantity demanded (fish)	Quantity supplied (fish)
35	800	350
40	700	400
45	600	450
50	500	500
55	400	550
60	300	600

This information can then be plotted on a graph, as shown in Fig. 6.7.

If you study the graph (Fig. 6.7), you can see that there is only one price at which the wishes of consumers and supplier coincide, i.e. 50p. At this price the quantity which will be bought and sold is 500.

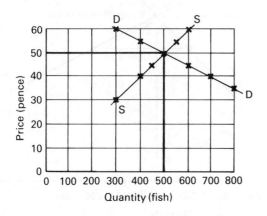

Figure 6.7 Graph showing demand and supply in a daily fish market.

We can see that the market provides a mechanism for automatically bringing the decisions of consumers and producers into line, even though the two groups have different motives. (The producer will want to sell at the highest price possible, and the consumer to purchase at the lowest price possible.)

We can see how the process of forming an equilibrium price comes about by considering two disequilibrium situations. If, for example, we consider the price of 60p we will see that at this price the owner of the fishing vessel would be prepared to work longer to supply 600 fish. However, at 60 pence, consumers would only be prepared to buy 300 fish—leaving a surplus stock of 300 fish which would go to waste. In this situation the owner of the fishing boat would lower prices and resort to working fewer hours.

Alternatively, if the price of fish was pitched at 40p, consumers would be prepared to buy 700. However, the owner of the fishing boat would only be prepared to work long enough to catch 400. There would now be a shortage of fish—stocks would rapidly sell out and customers would try to bid up the price. This would make it worth while for the owner of the fishing boat to work longer hours.

The net effect is that at prices above 50p, too much will be produced and so forces will interact to pull prices down to 50p. At prices below 50p, too little will be produced and so forces will interact to push prices up to 50p. At 50p prices are just right and there is no tendency to change (see Fig. 6.8). The above analysis is a simplification. In the real world markets do not always move smoothly towards equilibrium. Consumers and producers frequently lack important market information that would assist them to respond promptly to changes.

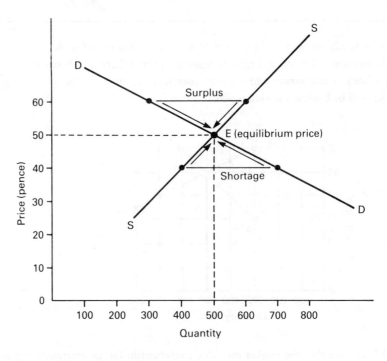

Figure 6.8 Creating the equilibrium price.

Shifts in demand and supply

So far we have analysed market price solely in terms of the relationship between price and demand and supply. This has been like taking a snapshot under the assumption that factors other than price do not alter.

However, in our earlier analysis we saw that there are a number of factors influencing demand, and a number of factors influencing supply. Markets are constantly in motion and combinations of factors will cause shifts in demand and supply.

For example, we can see that in Fig. 6.9(a) a shift to the right of the demand curve has increased the equilibrium price and equilibrium quantity in the market. A shift to the left of the demand curve has had the reverse effects.

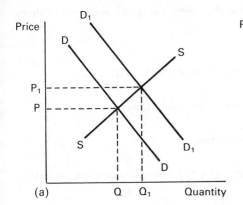

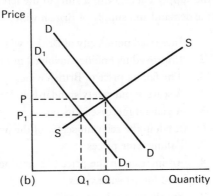

Figure 6.9(a) A shift to the right in demand.
Figure 6.9(b) A shift to the left in demand.

We can see that in Fig. 6.10(a) a shift to the right of the supply curve has decreased the equilibrium price and increased the equilibrium quantity. A shift to the left of the supply curve has increased the equilibrium price and decreased the equilibrium quantity. Real world situations will be complicated by the interaction of numerous demand and supply factors.

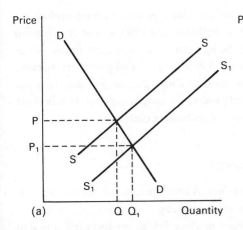

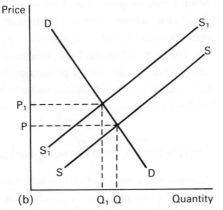

Figure 6.10(a) A shift to the right in supply.
Figure 6.10(b) A shift to the left in supply.

Review

Many students initially find it difficult to distinguish between factors causing *movements up or down* a demand or supply curve and factors causing *shifts to the left or right* of demand or supply curves.

The golden rule is that *movements along curves are solely caused by changes in the price of the item in question. Changes in factors other than price cause the whole curve to shift in position.*

State whether the following situations would lead to: (i) a movement up the demand curve; (ii) a movement down the demand curve; (iii) a shift to the right of the demand curve; (iv) a shift to the left of the demand curve; (v) a movement up the supply curve; (vi) a movement down the supply curve; (vii) a shift to the right of the supply curve; (viii) a shift to the left of the supply curve. All situations relate to the demand and supply of British wine.

1.   Increased popularity of British wine.
2.   Improved technology involved in British wine manufacture.
3.   The falling price of British wine.
4.   A scare about safety standards in British wine production.
5.   A general increase in incomes.
6.   A fall in the relevant sector of the population.
7.   Falling wine prices.
8.   An increase in the price of a product which is produced on land similar to that used for growing vines.
9.   Excellent weather for wine growing and harvesting.
10. Growing European consumption of beer at the expense of wine.
11. Removal of a government subsidy to wine producers.
12. A general reduction in all price levels.

Suppliers

Most firms are part of a chain of production. Many producers are therefore influenced by what goes on at the previous stage. In the late 1980s and early 1990s this is an important fact of life, particularly in the way that basic commodity prices such as those of fuels and metals have changed costs of production for all producers. Because fuel costs are a basic cost of production for most products, changes in their prices can lead to price rises and falls for thousands of products. Changes in prices, in turn, have an effect on wages and the standard of living of millions of citizens.

Competition from other producers

This is a major influence on business behaviour. A firm's prices and many other policies will be influenced by the level of competition it faces.

Direct competition exists when businesses produce similar products and appeal to the same group of people. Examples would include two firms manufacturing washing-up liquids, or two shops supplying children's clothes in the same stretch of high street.

Even when a business produces a unique product with no direct competition, it must still consider indirect competition. Consumers can choose to spend their money on one product rather than another quite different product—for instance, if it is too expensive to go to the cinema you might decide to go out for a pizza instead.

Firms compete with each other in many ways. Generally, competition is over product quality and performance. There can also be price competition, and in some product categories such as petrol and oil, free gifts are important.

For shops, the sharpest competitive edges are created by 'location', opening hours and the friendliness and efficiency of service. Companies also compete on the effectiveness of their advertising. If it were possible to have two identical but competitive products, the one whose benefits were more powerfully projected in the advertising would outsell the other.

In reality, the most critical competitive factors any company has to cope with are the knowledge, intelligence, experience, scepticism, and sometimes apathy, of the prospective customer. No company that wants to stay successful ever takes the customer for granted. We are now living in a 'consumer society', with a market that is educated, aware and prepared to give and withdraw its custom as it decides. Keeping ahead of the customer is the greatest challenge.

The degree of competition faced by an enterprise will constantly change. The extent of this competition will depend to a great extent on the willingness and ability of consumers to transfer their purchases to substitute products. This will depend on the answers to a cluster of interrelated questions including:

- Are substitutes available?
- Can consumers obtain them?
- Do consumers shop around?
- Do consumers know what is available?
- Can buyers switch to alternative sources of supply?
- Are the benefits of changing greater than the costs?

A number of market forms are commonly recognized which are defined according to a number of key ingredients that influence the level of competition (see Fig. 6.11).

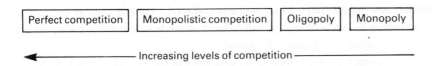

Figure 6.11 Degrees of competition.

A business that does not face direct competition is said to have a *monopoly*. It does not have outside pressure on it to compete. We must be careful, however, not to assume that monopolies are inefficient. Monopolies do not need to duplicate systems of administration, services, and other processes. They can also put a lot of money into product development and research in order to keep up a long-term competitive edge. In the real world there are unlikely to be many examples of pure monopolies because most manufactured goods can be copied. Some minerals are restricted to a few geographical areas—for example a large concentration of world gold reserves is found in the USSR and southern Africa.

Oligopoly exists when only a few producers or sellers dominate a market. Examples of products made and sold in markets with few firms are:

- National newspapers
- Petrol

- Breakfast cereal
- Beer
- Biscuits
- Chocolates and sweets
- Disposable nappies
- Washing powder
- Satellite television
- Contraceptives
- Petfood

There are no set rules as to the degree of competition that exists in such a market. Each producer will spend money on policies designed to create brand loyalty such as advertising and promotion. Each producer will attempt to differentiate his product from the others that are available. However, there is always a danger that open warfare with regards to pricing and other elements of competition will be to the disadvantage of all producers and sellers. The ability to make profits, and to plough profits into promotion, research and product development is seen as being of crucial importance. Such markets will therefore be typified by lulls and surges in the extent of competitive practice.

Oligopoly is in fact a concentrated form of monopolistic competition. *Monopolistic competition* exists where products or services are in some way differentiated from others. However, this differentiation can be eroded in the course of time because new firms have the freedom to enter the industry. Levels of profits in monopolistic markets will vary with the level of competition. The ability of firms to survive and prosper is in many ways dependent on their ability to keep innovating, to research and develop new product lines. Most products and services in this country are produced by monopolistic competitors, e.g. hairdressers, insurance companies, book publishing companies, retailers and grahic designers.

Perfect competition is a state which exists more in theory than in practice. In a perfectly competitive market there would be no differentiation of any sort—all products and prices would be identical. Consumers would have perfect knowledge of products, and there would be no sacrifice in buying from one outlet rather than another.

Although pure perfect competition does not exist there are still important lessons to be learnt from the model. Pure competition ensures that no excess profits can be made in the long run (producers and sellers just make enough to stay in business) and that prices, and hence costs, are kept to the minimum consistent with a given scale of operation.

Central government

The central authorities set up a legal framework within which businesses operate. As we shall see later, there is a wide range of laws that constrain the activities of businesses. The government establishes the rules of the game. An example of this is the way that the government has implemented anti-monopoly legislation to encourage competition between firms. For over 40 years the UK government has tried to prevent companies and traders from holding too large a share of the production or sale of a good or service. As a result, some mergers between companies have been stopped and the activities of a number of companies have been enquired into by a government committee. The Monopolies Commission is a body which has been set up to investigate cases involving monopoly situations referred to it by the government.

The main agency for carrying out government policy on competition is the Office of Fair Trading which was set up in 1973. Under the Fair Trading Act, the Director General of this office was given powers to keep commercial practices in the United Kingdom under scrutiny and to collect information about them in order to uncover monopoly situations and practices that restrict freedom of business, trade and contract. The Director General can refer cases of suspected monopoly or malpractice to the Monopolies and Mergers Commission for investigation.

In February, 1988, for example, the OFT discovered a web of glass supply cartels across the country when a West Midlands glass purchaser complained that he was 'tired of being ripped off'. (A cartel is a group of individual firms which make agreements to restrict competition.) The Director General assigned a team of three investigators to look into the industry. The team interviewed glass buyers and issued legal notices to companies suspected of operating cartels, compelling them to furnish details of agreements.

Among them was one from Pilkington, which revealed that its executives had clandestinely met with other glass suppliers to agree common price increases. Pilkington admitted to meeting several times with five other glass suppliers between 1978 and 1982. The purpose was 'to agree the same percentage increase to each company's gross price tariffs and to certain other items normally charged as extras in orders for double glazing units, such as for the drilling of holes in double glazing units'.

The document was one of a catalogue of admissions from seven UK glass suppliers, which referred to 12 different cartels and named a total of 60 different companies.

In its recommendations, the Monopolies and Mergers Commission in recent years has tended to consider whether the benefits of a monopoly situation outweigh the costs or not. Concentration has not been seen as being a bad thing in itself. More important has been the ability of new firms to enter an industry, and the way in which firms in concentrated markets have behaved. The 1980 Competition Act stressed that the Monopolies and Mergers Commission should be more concerned with the general competitive environment in an industry than with the level of concentration.

The government has powers to intervene in the case of takeovers of economic importance which raise public interest issues. Under the provisions of the 1973 Fair Trading Act, a merger where the gross assets taken over are at least £30 million or which involves the creation or enhancement of a market share of at least 25 per cent may be referred by the Secretary of State to the Monopolies and Mergers Commission. The Secretary of State for Trade and Industry has powers to prevent a merger or to impose conditions only if the Commission concludes that it would operate against the public interest.

The 1988 white paper 'DTI—the department for Enterprise' confirmed the government's policy that the main consideration in determining whether mergers should be referred to the Monopolies and Mergers Commission will be their potential effect on competition. Where competition is not affected, the government does not intervene as, for example, when the Secretary of State allowed the acquisition of Matthew Brown by Scottish and Newcastle Breweries. Competition policy is just one example of central government involvement in the creation of a business environment. Government activity is also writ large as we shall see later in its economic policy making, its purchases of goods and services, its business taxes and subsidies and a range of other interests and activities.

Local government

A small local business or a plant of a larger business must take into account local by-laws and rules. The local authorities are responsible for looking after the interests of local residents. Business activity is thus constrained by a wide range of local influences, including the protection of the local environment and planning-permission specifications. An example of this might be when a redevelopment project can only take place if it fits in with the style of the existing architecture.

Local government taxes local businesses, provides a range of services including litter collection, provides grants and other incentives, and carries out a number of policies which affect business activity.

Trade unions

These can be looked on as both an internal and an external influence on the business. The local branch of a trade union can be seen as part of a larger national movement. Bargaining may take place between a group of employers and trade-union representatives. Trade unions are dealt with in depth in Chapter 14.

Local residents

Local people may interact with a firm in a number of ways:

- as consumers;
- as workers
- as shareholders;
- as neighbours.

In each of these situations the firm will have to take account of their interests.

Business in an international setting

Business activity takes place against a background of world trade.

1. Many businesses based in the United Kingdom are owned by overseas share-holders or are offshoots of foreign companies.
2. Many UK firms buy raw materials and supplies from overseas.
3. Many UK firms face overseas competition.
4. Many UK firms sell their products or services overseas.
5. Many UK businesses have offshoots overseas and foreign companies have UK shareholders.

In recent years we have become particularly aware of the impact of the world market on business life in the United Kingdom. In particular, as we move into the 1990s we are made increasingly aware of the repercussions for business of the creation of the single market in the European Community in 1992.

Interdependence lies at the heart of all trading relationships. Changes in production or consumption patterns in one part of the world can have repercussions thousands of miles away. For example, a series of mishaps to the world's food supplies in 1988, starting with the great UK–Canadian drought and including crop failures in China, the Soviet Union, Australia and South America, left global cereal stocks at their lowest level, in relation to world needs, for 40 years. Any more such failures could lead (perhaps already have done so) to drastic food shortages. The pattern of change in demand and supply is shown in Fig. 6.12.

GRAIN STOCKS, PRODUCTION AND CONSUMPTION

Total in store (worldwide) millions of tonnes		
	ALL GRAINS	WHEAT
END OF 1986-87 MARKETING YEAR	457.4	175.2
1987-88	397.6	145.6
1988-89 (ESTIMATE)	286.5	115.3

Production and consumption (worldwide) millions of tonnes				
	ALL GRAINS		WHEAT	
	Production	Consumption	Production	Consumption
1986-87	1684.6	1657.4	530.2	523
1987-88	1604.5	1664.3	504.3	533.8
1988-89	1549.7	1660.8	503.2	533.5

Source: US Dept of Agriculture

Figure 6.12 Stock, production and consumption of wheat.

1992—The single market

What will be the effect on British business of the single market? Will it be a bonanza for British industry or a disaster? There are a number of conflicting views on this subject. (Detailed background information about the EC is given in Chapter 16.)

The opportunities

The European Commission (EC) has forecast that removing frontier barriers and the resulting increased competition should help bring down shop prices by 6 per cent to stimulate demand which will create 2 million jobs. Governments could act to boost the total to 5 million throughout Europe. Lord Young, Secretary of State for Trade and Industry (until summer 1989), with a major responsibility for preparing British business to meet the challenges of the single market, is on record saying 'Our vision in Europe very much mirrors our vision for Britain. The single market should be a dynamic entrepreneurial market, not one tied down in red tape. We are working to achieve that.'

The single market will present British business with the opportunity of selling to an open market of 320 million consumers. The following year (1993) will see the opening of the Channel Tunnel providing direct road and rail links to the Continent.

The problems

Not all observers see the creation of the single market, or at least the implementation of it, as necessarily being beneficial to Britain. For example a paper, prepared by Henry Neuburger, economic adviser to the shadow industry secretary in 1988, stated that Britain stands to lose more from the internal market than any other member country and projected nearly 200 000 job losses, mainly in the Midlands. It warned that the industries most likely to be hit would be motors, office machinery, footwear, carpets and electrical household goods.

In March 1989, Sir John Hoskyns, who at the time headed the Institute of Directors, launched a withering attack on EC bureaucracy, saying that the then existing plans for 1992 would result in a 'collectivized, protectionist, over-regulated Utopia'. While acknowledging that the single market offered great potential and that it was important for it to succeed, he said that the warning signs of failure were clearly visible and that 1992 had the makings of a fiasco. While business prepared for a Europe without frontiers, the single market project itself was going wrong because of shifting objectives, bad organization, wrong people, poor motivation, inadequate methods, weak management, personal politics and pilfering on a heroic scale.

The changes

Physical barriers to trade

Frontier safeguards like those on firearms, drugs, and plant and animal diseases will continue for security, social and health reasons. But restrictions on the legitimate movement of goods and people should be abolished, or greatly reduced.

European standards

National standards will be removed wherever possible to be replaced by Community ones. The barriers which national standards put in the way of trade will be removed by:

- setting levels of quality and safety which products must meet within the Community;
- agreeing common standards;
- agreeing to accept other member states' tests and certificates.

Community standards will now apply to nearly all products. This means that if British firms are going to sell their products in the Community they must get into line on standards.

Jobs

The European Community aims to establish a single internal market and to remove all barriers to the free movement of workers between member states. Its associated work on standards and qualifications has concentrated on the comparability of vocational training qualifications, and the recognition of 'higher education diplomas' and professional qualifications.

By enabling qualifications between member states to be readily compared, it is hoped that job seekers will find the process of job application easier — although the identification of qualifications across member states will not confer any guarantee of employment.

Public purchasing

Selling to governments and public bodies accounts for about 15 per cent of all goods produced in the Community.

The single market will mean that public bodies should buy on the basis of fair competition. In other words the UK government, for example, should buy the goods and services which it thinks gives best value for money rather than giving orders to British companies because they are British.

Open markets

In the past, information technology systems and telecommunications have been made to national standards. This has meant, for example, that a British system has not been able to be combined with a French one. These systems must now be able to be combined through a Community Standard.

Financial services

By 1992 there will be freedom for the movement of funds throughout the Community. This will mean, for example, that there will be no restrictions on a business raising funds in another EC country. There will also be free competition between Community institutions such as banks and insurance companies.

Transport services

By 1992 transport companies will be able to provide transport facilities in other Community countries without the necessity of permits or other restrictions. There will be more competition in the provision of shipping, aviation and road haulage.

Competition

Restrictive agreements and practices and the abuse of monopoly powers are already forbidden as they may affect trade between member states. The European Commission has the power to investigate suspected breaches of the rules: unfair practices can be stopped and fines imposed of up to 10 per cent of an undertaking's turnover.

Companies affected by such unfair competition can take action through the UK courts or complain to the European Commission.

Trade marks

Afte 1992 protection of trade marks should be given by one application to a central Community Trade Marks Office.

Short answer questions

1. List the external influences on the behaviour of a firm with which you are familiar. Give two examples of how these external influences have affected the behaviour of the business.
2. What is meant by the terms:
   (a) consumer
   (b) producer?
3. What factors are likely to influence the demand for a branded chocolate bar?
4. What factors may shift the demand curve for the commuter rail fair to the right?
5. What factors may shift the demand curve for a brand of washing powder to the left?
6. How can knowledge of likely demographic changes help producers to predict the future pattern of demand for a product? Illustrate your answer with an example taken from the real world.
7. Does the demand for consumer goods always increase with rising incomes? Explain your answer with examples.
8. Give three examples of pairs of goods that can be seen to:
   (a) complement each other;
   (b) act as substitutes for each other.
9. How will the demand curve for a product be likely to be affected as a result of:
   (a) a rise in price of a complementary good;
   (b) a fall in price of a substitute good;
   (c) a general fall in the relevant population?
10. Why does a typical supply curve slope upwards from left to right?
11. How are changes in the level of technology likely to affect the supply curve for a

processed food, e.g. canned peas? What other factors are likely to affect the position of the supply curve.

12. What is a monopoly? Give an example of a firm with a monopoly or near monopoly in the United Kingdom. Does being a monopoly affect the way in which they operate?

13. Are consumers likely to get a better service from a monopoly firm?

14. Define monopolistic competition.

15. Why is perfect competition unlikely to exist in the real world?

16. What is the role of the Director General of Fair Trading in competition policy?

17. In what ways can local authorities influence business activity?

18. Give an example of the way in which local business has to take account of your local community.

19. In what ways is 'interdependence' a basic feature of business life?

20. What will happen to 'national standards' for EC member states after 1992?

Essays

1. In what ways does business activity involve (a) competition for, and (b) co-operation in, the use of scarce resources?

2. Reconcile the following statements: 'A decrease in demand leads to a decrease in price.' 'A decrease in price leads to a rise in the quantity demanded.'

3. Explain how the demand for a particular product depends on a complex interdependence of factors.

4. How do the supply conditions for a product interact with demand to create a market price?

5. Markets which are dominated by a small number of firms will rarely be competitive. Discuss this statement.

6. How does the UK government seek to make markets more competitive?

7. 'Mergers reduce competition and must always be against the public interest.' Discuss this proposition.

8. Do the benefits to Britain of the single market outweigh the costs?

9. What major changes will be required for British businesses to succeed in the single market?

10. Supply is determined by price. Discuss.

Data response questions

1 Study the newspaper article in Fig. 6.13.

(a) What do you understand by 'funeral costs are soaring above the rate of inflation'?

(b) What evidence is supplied in the article that undertaking is increasingly being concentrated in the hands of a few firms?

Funeral prices soar and undertakers' attitudes attacked

By Kate Muir

FUNERAL COSTS are soaring above the rate of inflation, and the service provided by some undertakers is "grossly insensitive", according to a report published yesterday by the Office of Fair Trading.

Undertakers' bills have increased by 28 per cent more than inflation since 1975, and up to three-quarters of funeral directors had broken their code, which states that a price list and estimates should be provided.

But it was the insensitivity of some undertakers which angered respondents to the OFT survey, which was supplemented by the experiences of listeners to the Radio 4 programme *You and Yours*. One couple reported being handed their son's ashes in a plastic container wrapped in a brown paper bag, and then being asked to pay for them on the spot.

Another listener said his relative's body was undressed before the family left the room. More complained of high pressure selling and of staff being dressed inappropriately, smoking or laughing in the background.

Margaret Fairchild, of Peter-

borough, Cambridgeshire, said of her mother's funeral: "She'd been embalmed and she looked as if she'd been squeezed into a coffin that was too small. She had no hair showing, although she had lovely hair, and they hadn't bothered with any cosmetics. It was very upsetting taking leave of her like that. It was only afterwards I realised our local family firm had been taken over by a big chain."

Only 11 per cent of the 893 people surveyed who arranged funerals in March 1987 had been dissatisfied with some part of the service, but many complained of the cost, an average of £586, with charges of £800 to £900 quite common. Few people can bear to shop around; Trevor Dell, of New Haw, near Weybridge, Surrey, was an exception. His father asked him to find the cheapest possible funeral before he died.

"I was steeled by that to ring round about half a dozen undertakers, but they all quoted me similar prices of between £680 and £720 for the simplest funeral.

Then I got an estimate of £350 from a local firm which did a very satisfactory job."

Many small undertakers' businesses are being taken over by three expanding companies — Hodgson Holdings, Kenyon Securites and Great Southern — which between them have 18 per cent of the market. The Co-operative Wholesale Society has 20 per cent. Firms like Hodgson buy several family-run businesses, keeping their names and reputation but centralising all embalming, refrigeration, coffin and car supplies at one depot.

Howard Hodgson, director, whose business is now worth £40m, said: "It's the only way to make a profit on these small margins, and with the death rate staying static, the only way to expand is to acquire new businesses."

The report says that price lists should be available in every undertaker's and that staff should be trained to be more sensitive.It warns that if the National Association of Funeral Directors' Code is not adhered to, it will ask the Government to intervene.

Figure 6.13 Changes in the funeral market. (*Source: The Independent*, January 1989.)

(c) What are the advantages and disadvantages to the consumer of concentration of business in undertaking?

(d) What are the advantages and disadvantages of concentration to producers?

(e) Is it important for the Office of Fair Trading to become involved in take-overs in this industry?

2   Study the journal leader in Fig. 6.14.

(a) What potential costs and benefits does the Leader writer identify as resulting from the Channel Tunnel?

LEADER

Blight at the end of the Chunnel

It is doubtful whether any campaign, however professionally conducted, will wholly overcome the hostility of the good citizens of Kent (and Sussex) to the Chunnel rail link. After all, like the current Secretary of State for the DoE, we're all for progress, until it abuts on our own back gardens.

Still, with insensitive BR planners apparently using out-of-date maps and routing one possible high-speed link through a new housing estate, it was clear something had to be done. Probably, once Saatchi has sufficiently emphasised the nature of BR's financial compensation to unfortunate homeowners who will be displaced or environmentally "inconvenienced", the locals will accept the price of progress with the same resignation that greeted the M25's advent.

However, the problems surrounding the marketing of the rail link (long overdue if we compare BR with the French railway system) shrink to irrelevance beside those likely to face the Chunnel itself when (or if) it opens in 1993. No one (hopefully) would claim that the Eurotunnel scheme's 33-minute transit experience will be anything other than claustrophobic; it will certainly lack the "cruise" element of ferries and hovercraft. Pricing, given the phenomenal investment, will have to be competitive.

But great play can be made of frequency and duration. Until, that is, we come to the matter of Customs. Mrs Thatcher's determination to stamp out drug smuggling and other forms of cross-border criminality in the deregulated world of 1992 may be laudable, but the price of bureaucracy is time-wastage; given the 15-minute frequency of the trains, and the traditionally long-winded airport-style checks planned for the Waterloo terminus, it is hard to take at face value BR and Eurotunnel's assertion that Customs hold-ups will be "unlikely to add significantly to journey times".   ☐

Figure 6.14 Changes resulting from the Chunnel. (*Source: Marketing Week*, January 1989.)

(b) Why are some people likely to have strong views about the building of the Tunnel?

(c) Why is it important for British Rail to take account of these views?

(d) What will be the advantages and disadvantages of government regulation of the new Channel Tunnel?

(e) How could British Rail go about securing maximum public support for the Tunnel project, and its accompanying rail link?

3   Study the journal article in Fig. 6.15.

Cinema boom to stay, say exhibitors

Cinema exhibitors are predicting a continued boom in 1989, despite the imminent arrival of satellite television.

According to Rank Screen Advertising, cinema admissions for 1988 were 78 million, the highest figure for seven years, which represents a 46 per cent increase over the past five years.

Rank sales director Peter Howard-Williams says that advertising is buoyant and that there is less need to "hard sell" the medium. He has little space to sell for the rest of the year.

"I think there are a number of reasons for the revival of cinema," he says. "Cinemas are now nice places to visit. They are comfortable and the product is much better than it was a few years ago.

"Whatever people say, TV really isn't that exciting, no matter how many episodes of Minder are shown."

He adds that cinema attracts a growing number of young, up-market consumers.

The main concern for cinema now is the advent of satellite film channels, but Howard-Williams says it will be the video industry that suffers.

"My understanding is that these films will be shown on satellite channels several months after their theatrical release. Look at the US which has had satellite for years — the cinema is thriving." □

Figure 6.15 Cinema boom. (*Source*: *Marketing Week*, January 1989.)

(a) What factors are likely to influence the demand for cinema seats?

(b) What factors are likely to influence the supply of cinema seats?

(c) What competition does the cinema face, and how is this likely to affect the way it operates, including service and price?

(d) What other external influences affect the ways in which cinemas operate?

Suggested reading

Barback, R., *The Firm and its Environment*. Philip Allan, 1984.
Donnelly, G., *The Firm in Society*. Longman, 1981.

7

Marketing

In setting out to study the marketing function of business organizations it is important to make a distinction between marketing and marketing services:

Marketing involves developing a strategy to coordinate and plan ways of identifying, anticipating and satisfying consumer demand in such a way as to make profits. It is this strategic planning process that lies at the heart of marketing.

Marketing services are the tools and tactics used by the marketing department. The marketing department will set out to identify the most appropriate marketing services to employ to make profits. These marketing services will include advertising, public relations, trade and consumer promotions, point-of-sale material, editorial, publicity and sales literature.

The role of marketing in the firm

The marketing department will initiate research and development to assess and meet customer needs and wants. In doing so it must coordinate the production and distribution of goods and services and make sure that activities are organized in such a way as to sell items profitably.

Marketing is therefore a complex process involving the coordination of a range of related activities. Market research is necessary to find out the wants and needs of consumers. Product research must be coupled with market research to ensure that product development follows the wishes of consumers. Research into patterns of distribution must guarantee that goods and services get to the right place at the right time.

The marketing mix

The marketing mix is often referred to as the '4 Ps', i.e. product, price, place and promotion. To meet customers' needs a business must develop *products* to satisfy them, charge the right *price*, get the goods to the right *place* (making sure the product is available when needed), and it must make the existence of the product known through *promotion* (see Fig. 7.1).

The marketing mix

Figure 7.1 Ingredients of the marketing mix.

Products

People buy goods and services for a wide variety of reasons. There are many characteristics of a product that can influence the decision to buy. Some of the most important features of a product are:

1. *Function*   When you buy a new car what will you want it to do? Will you want it to look good, to accelerate quickly, or to last a long while? The function of a car might be radically different for a taxi driver than for someone looking for a vehicle for recreation purposes.
2. *Appearance*   For a number of products the way they look is as important as what they do. This is as true for birthday cards and furniture as it is for clothing and jewellery.
3. *Status*   Consumers often associate certain products with a particular lifestyle. Advertisers often use this form of association to create an image for a product. Status symbols include items such as cars, jewellery, clothes, and consumer durables such as washing machines and fridge freezers.

Price

The price that a firm charges is quite clearly an important determinant of the volume of sales made. However, it would be wrong to assume that firms will set prices purely with the aim of maximizing profits or sales. The pricing policy that a business employs will vary with time and circumstances. For example, it is often the case that firms will launch a new product for a lower price than the one they intend to charge when the product becomes established.

A firm's pricing decision might also be aimed at finding a particular niche in the market. For example, if it wants to sell at the top end of the market it will charge a high price; at the bottom a low price, and so on.

Place

Roughly one-fifth of the cost of a product is spent getting it to the customer. Of course, the actual figure varies widely from product to product but generally distribution is a very important element in the marketing mix. Distribution is a key feature in the trading process—i.e. getting the right product to the right place at the right time.

Promotion

The cost of promoting or advertising goods and services can represent a sizeable proportion of the overall cost. However, through successful promotion a firm can increase its sales so that advertising and other costs are spread over a larger output. By selling more goods firms can lower their selling prices, raise profits, or both.

Case Study—Making a profit from Perrier water

This case study highlights the way in which the elements of marketing (as reflected in costs for advertising and distribution) are combined with the elements of production (as reflected in production costs) to produce profits for retailers, manufacturers and bodies such as restaurants. The marketing process can only be judged to be successful if it leads to profits.

The market for bottled water is rapidly expanding in this country. In just one week in July 1987, Perrier sold 4 million bottles. The market for bottled water is estimated to be worth £200 million in the United Kingdom by 1990. Perrier is a great profit maker for high class restaurants, who charge up to £2 per bottle in return for putting it in the fridge.

Perrier is the Hoover of fizzy waters, thanks to imaginative marketing and an extension of lines to include lime and lemon flavours. The restaurant

Figure 7.2 Why a bottle of water costs 50p.

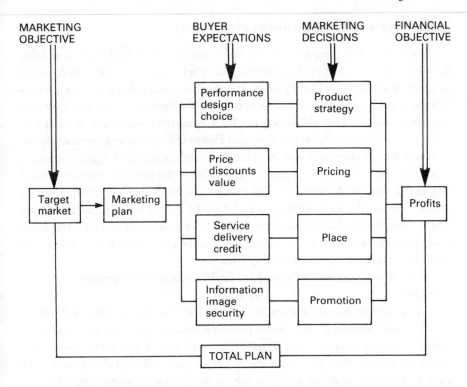

MARKETING OBJECTIVE | BUYER EXPECTATIONS | MARKETING DECISIONS | FINANCIAL OBJECTIVE

Performance design choice — Product strategy

Price discounts value — Pricing

Target market → Marketing plan

Service delivery credit — Place

Profits

Information image security — Promotion

TOTAL PLAN

Figure 7.3 Effective marketing.

mark-up is a mouth-watering 300 per cent. In other words, restaurants can purchase Perrier for 50p and sell it for 200p.

In order to achieve successful profitability Perrier must produce a product that consumers want, at a price which they feel is value for money, by means of an effective distribution channel and promoted in an appealing way. Figure 7.2 illustrates the combination of production and marketing costs that lead to a 2.5p profit for Perrier from selling a 50p bottle.

Figure 7.3 illustrates the importance of developing a marketing plan to ensure that financial objectives are met. An effective marketing plan will involve finding out the expectations of buyers and translating them into marketing decisions. Perrier water has been a successful product because market research in this country revealed that there was scope for an upmarket alternative to tap water and existing mineral waters. People were prepared to pay a relatively high price for a product which could portray an exclusive image. Perrier needed to be readily available from shops and other outlets as well as in restaurants.

In the markets for other goods and services the expectations of buyers will be radically different. The task of marketing will be to find out what these buyer expectations are and then to translate them into effective marketing decisions to ensure profits.

Marketing as a total business philosophy

A number of modern companies see the major function of the total business as being that of satisfying the desires of customers. The belief is that unless they can do so in a competitive world they will not survive. It is therefore essential to match the production and development of goods and services with the identification and anticipation of customers' desires. This philosophy has for a number of years been important to major Japanese companies such as Sony and Honda and is becoming increasingly important in British companies such as Marks and Spencer and Shell. Quality is seen as a total ingredient that will be found in every aspect of the company from the original idea and design to the final sale. For example, at Shell staff attitudes on service stations are regarded to be a critical element of the quality mix. Special courses are held for everyone including managers, cashiers, forecourt staff and cleaners. Little things like looking quickly at the credit card and calling the customer by name are just small elements of what is called 'Quality Care'.

The *marketing orientation* of a company can be contrasted with *production* and *sales orientations*.

A *production orientated* company works with the view that products will tend to find their own markets if they can be produced cheaply and to a good standard of quality. Such companies spend a relatively small time investigating consumers' wishes. As a result, they will often come to grief because although their products are good in a technical sense they do not match the benefits the consumers require.

A *sales orientated* company works with the view that success depends on effective advertising, selling and promotion rather than on a real difference between the product you are selling and those offered by competitors. This philosophy will come to grief if consumers shop around and see through the selling strategy.

The real distinction between a marketing and a sales orientation is that 'selling tries to get the customer to want what the company has; marketing on the other hand tries to get the company to produce what the customer wants'.

While on the surface these distinctions may appear to be somewhat theoretical, in the real world they are all too common. This is particularly true in small growing companies. Also large companies, with a proven track record, may fail to adjust effectively to changes in rivals' production, selling and marketing techniques. A company might find that it is failing to meet the targets it sets because of neglecting one or more of these areas.

Case Studies

Read the following extracts and answer the questions that follow them.

Case 1

Edward Sanson has recently moved his carpentry business from the East

End of London to a small unit in Peterborough. In London Edward had been able to sell as much furniture as he could produce working from a small side street workshop in an area renowned as a centre for the carpentry business. However, Edward had found operating costs to be a real problem. The rent and rates he had to pay for his premises were high and because of competition from larger scale furniture manufacturers Edward had only been able to make a low margin of profit on sales.

Moving to Peterborough meant that Edward was able to reduce drastically his overhead costs and at the same time take on a larger unit. The unit was one of a number housing a range of different types of business set on an industrial estate four miles from central Peterborough. Edward was able to build up quickly a large stock of furniture and to store it in his unit. Unfortunately, however, he found that stocks began to cramp his working space and that his order book was very low.

Questions

1. What problems can you identify in Edward Sanson's business strategy?
2. What solutions would you employ to deal with this problem?
3. From first hand observation of local businesses try to identify enterprises that tend to have production, marketing, or sales orientations. What steps could their owners take to remedy these problems?

Case 2

Study the article in Fig. 7.4 overleaf.

Questions

1. What weaknesses in business strategy does the article in Fig. 7.4 highlight amongst British companies?
2. Make a list of at least eight ways of dealing with these problems?
3. Why do you think that Marks and Spencer come out particularly well from this survey?
4. Try to arrange a visit from a speaker from Marks and Spencer to discuss the marketing and quality policies of the company.

Case 3—The yacht builder

Yacht builders who paid £50 000 or more for a sleek, French-made fibreglass boat from the Bénéteau yards were horrified when blisters appeared on the hull. The boats, from a class called Firsts, almost sank Bénéteau, which

Customer service gets low rating

MARKS AND SPENCER is the only UK company to emerge with a strong reputation for high standards of customer service in a survey published this week by management consultants Ernst & Whinney.

Of 154 senior managers in 151 companies in the retail, financial services, travel and public service sectors, 30 per cent cited Marks and Spencer for its high customer service standards. But almost 25 per cent of the managers interviewed were unable to name any company that they respected for having high standards in customer service.

The survey paints a gloomy picture of the attention paid to customer service by UK companies.

For example, although 75 per cent of managers highlighted the importance of staff quality to customer service, only 56 per cent cited understanding customers' requirements and just 8 per cent thought motivation at manager level was important.

Although 98 per cent of managers said they had introduced training courses to promote customer service, in most cases the courses were only available to staff with everyday contact with customers.

Only 35 per cent of senior managers interviewed said they had thought about devising a strategy

By Sarah Barclay
Business Reporter

for customer care within their organisations.

About 19 per cent of senior managers said they were given customer training less than once a year, compared with the 23 per cent of junior managers and 40 per cent of shop staff that have weekly training sessions.

According to Dick Randell, a consultant with Ernst & Whinney: "We know that the most successful programmes are those which involve all levels of staff and are implemented at the top management level and include a clear mission statement on customer service."

Another area highlighted by the survey was the reluctance of customers to complain about poor service. According to research carried out in the UK and US, only 10 per cent of people bother to register a complaint. Instead, they tend to take their custom elsewhere.

This casts doubt on the value of organisations' own feedback on customer service. Although 75 per cent of those interviewed said they monitored customer satisfaction, the monitoring process was usually based on the level of customer complaints.

Figure 7.4 The importance of customer service. (*Source: The Independent*, 9 August 1988.)

had risen from nowhere to become the world's leading seller of sailing yachts.

Demands for compensation—plus the disastrous commercial effect of rumours sweeping European, American and Pacific marinas—plunged the firm into a loss-making position in 1987.

Questions

1. What major problem can you identify in Bénéteau's business strategy?
2. What solutions would you employ to deal with this problem:
    (a) in the short term;
    (b) in the long term?

The life cycle of a product

Markets are in a constant state of change. Over a period of time tastes and fashions will alter and the technology used to produce goods and services will move on. As a result there will always be the demand for new products and old lines will become redundant.

The life of a product is the period over which it appeals to customers. We can all think of examples of goods that everyone wanted at one time but now have gone out of fashion. Obvious examples being certain clothes and hairstyles.

The sales performance of any product rises from nothing when the product is introduced to the market, reaches a peak and then declines to nothing again (see Fig. 7.5). A good example of products that have had short lifespans in recent years have been some makes of home computers. These products were originally ahead of their time and were able to achieve high sales. However, with the development of competition, they lost popularity until they were no longer saleable.

The life cycle can be further broken down into distinct stages. Sales grow slowly at the introduction stage when a product is new on the market and there is only a limited awareness of its existence. Sales then grow rapidly during the period of growth. It is now that competitors enter the market and promote their own products. This will reduce the rate of growth of sales. This period is known as maturity and it is at this

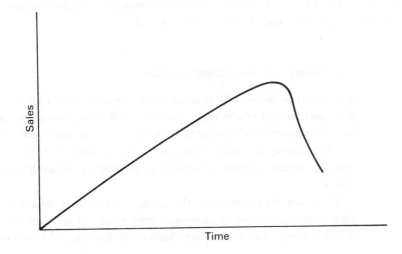

Figure 7.5 The product life cycle.

time that the market becomes saturated as there are too many firms competing for customers. Firms will compete in a variety of ways and some will drop out of the market. The product market finally declines and the existing product becomes unprofitable (see Fig. 7.6).

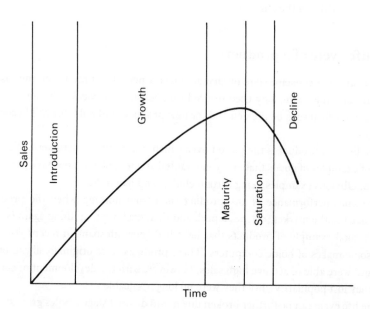

Figure 7.6 A more detailed breakdown of the product life cycle.

The life cycle of some products may last for hundreds of years while for others it may be a few months. If a firm wants to prolong the life cycle of its own distinct brand of product it is essential to invest well in the development of the product and the promotion of it. This may mean that a lot of work is put into the product before it is launched. Once the product is on the market it may be necessary periodically to inject new life into it. This can be done in several ways including: product improvement, extending the product range, improved promotion, etc.

Case Study—Relaunching a product

It is important periodically to re-assess the presentation of a product. It is likely that many products never reach their full sales potential because of lack of consumer knowledge, or from a failure to present the required image.

The following case study highlights the way in which MIM Britannia, a financial services company, managed to successfully relaunch a savings scheme.

MIM Britannia introduced the savings scheme at a time when the government was trying to encourage more people to save and invest in British industry. The government effectively changed the rules covering the taxation of savings, allowing tax-free profits, provided certain simple rules are followed (e.g. the maximum that can be invested is £45 per month). The new saving scheme that the government was encouraging was called a Personal Equity Plan.

In 1986 MIM Britannia launched its personal equity plan by producing a 14-page booklet. The text was detailed but required a lot of reading. It was designed primarily to appeal to the readers of quality newspapers such as the *Financial Times*, the *Guardian* and *The Independent*.

The MIM Britannia scheme was received with a certain amount of interest particularly from higher income earners. However, the marketing department took a fresh look at the product and felt that it could do a lot better. After all, the scheme only required a relatively modest amount of savings.

It was decided to retarget the project at anyone who could save between £25 and £45 a month. This would involve promoting the scheme to a wide audience. The product was now given the brand name Taxaxe and publicized in a short pull out leaflet designed for easy reading (see Fig. 7.7). The scheme was now promoted simply as a savings scheme and the term Personal Equity Plan was rarely used.

The leaflet read:

> Like most people, you probably have something special you want to save for. Retirement perhaps, or to give your children a start in life, or just to have a large sum of money to spend and enjoy.
>
> Regular savings schemes are an ideal way to build up a lump sum. And monthly contributions don't make a big hole in your pocket.
>
> With most savings schemes, however, the profits you make are subject to tax.

BUT TAXAXE IS TAX-FREE

The opening to the new leaflet was radically different from the previous one which had read 'In the 1986 Budget, the Chancellor of the Exchequer announced a new scheme, Personal Equity Plans, to encourage the British public to take a greater interest in the country's leading companies, by actually investing in those companies' shares.'

The relaunch of the MIM Britannia, Personal Equity Plan, under the name Taxaxe was a resounding success. It was relaunched in November 1988 and rapidly gained media interest from papers as diverse as the *Sun* and the *Financial Times*. All the major papers featured stories about Taxaxe. In November 1988 three times more people joined the Taxaxe scheme than in the previous two and a half years. The product was the same, it was the marketing that was different.

During the life cycle of a product the ingredients of the marketing mix will be used in different ways at different times. For example the *product* may need to be changed and modified to keep it up with or ahead of the times. The *pricing* policy may alter

TAXAXE – TAX FREE – FROM MIM BRITANNIA

Now you can save from £25 to £200 a month – without paying a penny in tax on your profits

Beat the taxman! MAKE MORE
TAX FREE PROFITS on your regular savings

JUST LOOK WHAT THESE NEW TAX FREE BENEFITS WOULD HAVE MEANT TO YOUR MONTHLY SAVINGS OVER THE LAST 15 YEARS:

	BUILDING SOCIETY	BEST INSURANCE POLICY	TAXAXE
£50 a month	£17,584	£33,576	£55,384
£100 a month	£35,168	£67,152	£110,768
£200 a month	£73,336	£134,304	£221,530

Of course, past performance is no guarantee of future success as unit trust prices can fluctuate and investors may not get back the amount they have invested.

NO TAX TO PAY!

Quite simply, with TAXAXE, you can AVOID PAYING TAX on the profits from your regular monthly savings by taking advantage of a Personal Equity Plan (PEP) linked to a unit trust.

You can save for any period you like to build real personal wealth from a modest monthly outlay – and you have access to your money at any time.

ACT NOW

It's easy to beat the taxman, and enjoy TAX FREE GROWTH on your savings. There's just one simple Application Form. We'll do the rest.

For full details, just complete and return the coupon below or consult your financial adviser or:

Call us FREE on
0800 010 333
Lines are open 9 a.m. – 6 p.m. weekdays, 9 a.m. – 1 p.m. weekends.

To: MIM LIMITED, FREEPOST, 11 DEVONSHIRE SQUARE, LONDON EC2B 2TT.

Please send me details of how I can build up my savings with TAXAXE. I understand my enquiry places me under no obligation and no salesman will call.

NAME

ADDRESS

POSTCODE

POST TODAY.
NO STAMP NEEDED. WI 06/89   MIM BRITANNIA

Your plan is managed by MIM Limited and invests directly into the MIM Britannia Income and Growth Trust - a unit trust with a long history of successful growth. All figures to 1/4/89, insurance from Planned Savings, building society from Micropal. Taxaxe figures are offer to bid gross income re-invested. MIM Limited is a member of IMRO.

Figure 7.7 A press advert for TaxAxe.

with the level of the competition. This will be particularly true when firms are struggling to gain a leading market share or when the market is declining. The *place* might
alter with consumer preferences and as patterns of distribution alter. The style of *promotion* will also alter. At first it will be necessary to create an awareness of the product
whereas at later stages it may be better to point out the advantages of the product over
its competitors (see Fig. 7.8).

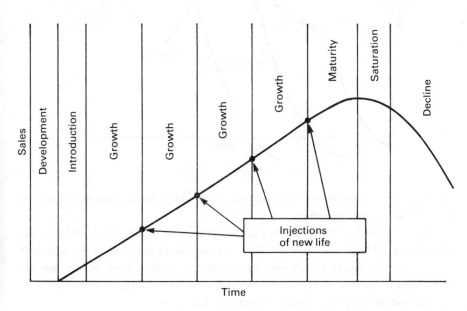

Figure 7.8 Injecting new life into a
product.

Product portfolios

Many large companies will produce a range of products each with its own life cycle.
These companies will diversify their interests so that as old products go into decline

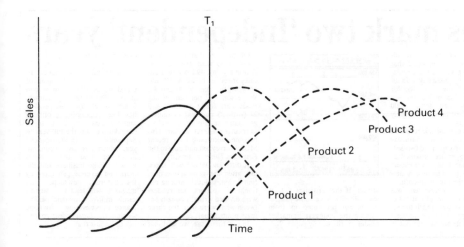

Figure 7.9 A portfolio of products at
different stages in their life cycles.

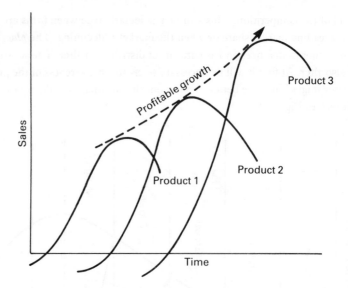

Figure 7.10 Planning for profitable growth.

new lines will come on stream. The collection of products that a company produces is known as its product portfolio.

In Fig. 7.9 the line T_1 represents a particular moment of time. Product 1 is in decline, Product 2 on saturation and Product 4 is just about to come on to the market. If the company is going to benefit from continuous growth then it will need to arrange its product portfolio in a well-timed way. This will be best achieved by creation at regular intervals of appealing new products (see Fig. 7.10).

Case Study—The introduction of a new product to the market

Figure 7.11 The life cycle of *The Independent*. (*Source: The Independent, 7 October 1988.*)

Read the newspaper article in Fig. 7.11 before answering the questions.

Record sales mark two 'Independent' years

TWO YEARS ago today *The Independent* was born. Although the launch was widely judged a success (if only because new media ventures have a habit of being catastrophes), there was widespread scepticism as to whether we could survive with apparently slim resources and when the existence of a "gap" in the quality newspaper market was difficult to demonstrate.

The conventional wisdom deemed that the best we could hope for was to be taken over by some reasonably benevolent proprietor when the money, sooner rather than later, ran out. *The Independent* might continue, but its independence would be in name only. With some luck and the support of our readers and advertisers we have escaped that fate. Having reached a circulation low of 257,000 a day in January last year, the circulation for September 1988 hit 395,000 — a new record and some 8,000 above our best previous monthly figure.

With the enthusiastic response of readers to our new Saturday offering — an expanded two-section newspaper accompanied by a colour magazine — we expect to be able to announce a new record for the present month.

When *The Independent* was launched a number of critics believed that we were much too serious to appeal to the younger readers whom we had set out to

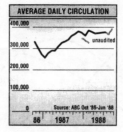

attract. If that criticism did, at least initially, have some justice, it has not prevented us from gaining the youngest upmarket reader profile of any paper.

Of the more than one million people who read *The Independent* every day, 49.1 per cent are categorised as being ABC1 and between the ages of 20 and 45. While some 22 per cent of our readers are aged between 15 and 24 (with 25 per cent of undergraduates describing themselves as regular readers), we have also become, according to a recent MORI survey, second only to the *Financial Times* in the City.

A different MORI poll, taken just after the general election, found that, uniquely among national newspapers, our readers were divided virtually equally between what were then the three main political parties.

In our first issue, we said that only through becoming a profitable newspaper could we remain an independent newspaper. In April we re-financed, ahead of schedule, the £9m worth of loan stock raised to fund the launch. Since March *The Independent* has been operating profitably and we expect to be close to "break-even" for the full year to September 1988. In the financial year which has just begun, we anticipate that the natural growth of the business and the increased revenue generated by the Saturday newspaper and magazine will lead to a significantly improved financial performance, thus ensuring — we hope — that *The Independent* continues to be just that.

Questions

1. In what ways does the sales pattern for *The Independent* (up to October 1988) differ from the classic pattern for the life cycle of a product?
2. How would you account for these differences?
3. Look at examples of national newspapers in order to compare and contrast different styles of design, presentation, content and other features. What would you regard to be the key features that differentiate *The Independent* from other newspapers?
4. What would you regard to be the advantages and disadvantages of this differentiation?
5. What does the article tell us about *The Independent*'s target market?
6. What does the article tell us about the actual readership of *The Independent*?
7. Why do you think that the title '*The Independent*' was selected for the newspaper?
8. How do you think that the features you identified in Question 3 as differentiating *The Independent* from other newspapers will help to sell the paper?
9. What other major source of revenue will the paper have taken in as well as sales to readers? In what ways will the paper market itself to try to maximize this revenue?
10. Why do you think that in September 1988 *The Independent* launched a new Saturday offering—'an expanded two-section newspaper accompanied by a colour magazine'?
11. How does this case study fit in with the theory you have just explored? What does theory tell us that the paper should do next?

Translating products into benefits

When customers contemplate buying products they will weigh them up in terms of the potential benefits to be gained. For example, someone who wants to buy a car may weigh up the benefits in terms of image, speed, safety, reliability and many other factors.

It is important to understand what benefits are being sought in order to develop a marketing mix that appeals to customers.

There are four basic varieties of benefits that customers seek:

1. *Standard benefits*   Standard benefits would include all the benefits of a particular product to a customer. For a petrol station, for example, these might include self-service, free gifts, easy access, free air and water supplies.
2. *Company benefits*   These would be the benefits resulting from a particular relationship between a customer and a supplier. A garage, for example, may offer customers who have bought cars there a preferential servicing arrangement.

3. *Differential benefits*   These are the benefits of a particular product relative to rival products.
4. *Personal benefits*   These are benefits seen purely by the purchasers. For example, they may like the salesperson.

It is important to make customers aware of all these benefits when marketing a product. The marketing department will need to clarify all the specific benefits of a particular product, the benefits of an association with their particular company, and the benefits of the product relative to alternatives.

Pricing strategies

Businesses will have different pricing policies depending on what their objectives are at the time. The notes below look at the relationship between different types of pricing policy and business objectives. A more in-depth analysis of possible pricing strategies is given on pages 221–230.

1. *Maximizing profits*   A key assumption of many business theories is that profit maximization is the most important pricing target. While it is true that unless businesses can make profits in the long run their futures will be uncertain, studies of actual business behaviour reveal a wide range of alternative strategies to short-term profit maximization.
2. *Cost-plus pricing*   Some firms set a target of how much profit they would like to make over what their costs are, e.g. costs + 10 per cent. The firm would then work out the expected costs and add 10 per cent for profits.
3. *Competitive pricing*   Pricing decisions might be based on what competitors charge.
4. *Maximizing sales*   Some firms may be more interested in increasing sales in order to take a large share of the market than in maximizing profits.
5. *'Satisficing'*   H. A. Simon put forward the view that businesses might want to 'satisfice', that is to achieve given targets for market share and profits from sales which may not maximize profits but would instead inflate boardroom egos. This can arise when the managers of a company are clearly different from the owners. Providing that the managers can produce sufficient profits to keep the shareholders satisfied, then a proportion of profits can be diverted to provide more perks for managers and larger departments. 'Satisficing' policies are most likely to be associated with industries where there is only a limited degree of competition. 'Satisficing' strategies are fairly common in many organizations ranging from schools to oil companies. Managers will readily produce long lists of achievements which do not always relate to a profit margin at the bottom line. In large organizations it is often difficult to relate activities to financial statistics and managers with the ability to make a lot of noise can give the impression of being effective.
6. *Other short-term pricing objectives*   In the short term a business may also have

other pricing policies. For example, it may sell new promotional items at a low price to introduce them to the market. A firm might also adopt a low price policy in order to destroy the market share of rivals, or to prevent new firms from entering the market. A firm might also set a price that will give them a particular position in the market, i.e. as a positioning decision. For example, a high price might be selected by a firm that wanted to project an 'upmarket' image.

Factors affecting pricing decisions

There are a number of important factors to consider before arriving at a pricing decision.

Costs

Many enterprises relate price to cost in the following way. They first calculate fixed costs such as rent, interest repayments and salaries. To these they will add variable costs. These are costs which increase with the level of output (see Chapter 10 and Fig. 7.12).

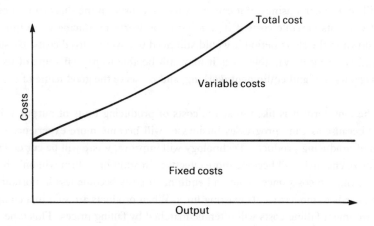

Figure 7.12 Components of total cost.

A break-even chart can be set out to show the relationship between costs, profits and revenues at different levels of output. Using this information an enterprise can then establish a revenue target. The revenue target will coincide with a given level of output. The revenue target will establish the price charged per unit. In Fig. 7.13 the revenue line crosses the fixed cost line at A. At this point the business would be just covering its fixed costs. As output increases the revenue line rises to the point B at which total revenue covers total cost (comprising fixed and variable costs).

Above point B (i.e. to the right of it) the firm moves into a profit position. Point X represents the chosen target revenue and the line XY is the profit margin.

The amount of sales that the firm makes will depend among other things on the

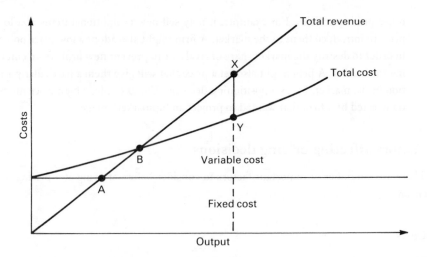

Figure 7.13 Establishing a revenue target from a break-even chart.

price charged. If prices are too low the revenue line would be less steep and revenues might not cover costs, or profit margins may be too low. If prices are too high then the revenue line could be very short.

Pricing policies are therefore crucial to the success of a business. In the long run a firm will continue in business if it can cover its total costs. In the short run it needs to at least cover its variable costs if it is going to be worth producing an output. If it closed down in the short period it would still need to cover its fixed costs. By staying open and covering its variable costs it may still be able to pay off some of its fixed costs, keep its staff and equipment working, and preserve the good name of the business.

In the long term it is likely that the costs of producing units of output will fall. This is because as time progresses businesses will become more experienced in all aspects of producing products. Technology will improve, waste will be cut down and distributive channels will become more effective. In addition, a firm will only have to pay its setting up costs once. Tool and equipment costs become less important until the firm needs to modernize its existing lines. When products are sold in a competitive environment falling costs will often be matched by falling prices. This type of relationship, illustrated in Fig. 7.14, can be related to a wide range of products including personal computers, television sets, package holidays, etc.

Price sensitivity

A measure known as elasticity of demand is used to calculate the way in which the quantity demanded of a product will alter as price changes. Some products are highly sensitive to price changes so that demand is said to be elastic. For example, the demand for a product with many competitors such as a brand of washing powder is likely to be highly elastic. In contrast a good with a little competition such as a distinctive luxury motor car may face an inelastic demand curve over a range of prices.

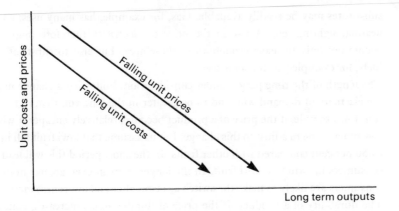

Figure 7.14 Falling costs and falling prices.

There are a number of factors influencing elasticity including the following:

1. Whether a good is a necessity or a luxury. Necessities by definition will be needed by purchasers. These would include basic items of food, shelter and clothing. When the price of a necessity increases consumers will be reluctant to reduce their purchases. In contrast it is easier to give up or postpone the purchase of a luxury item. Of course, with the passage of time individuals' perceptions of what is a necessity or a luxury will alter. Today, for example, many people regard central heating in winter to be a necessity in colder climates. If consumers perceive an item to be necessary they will continue to purchase more or less the same quantity as the price increases. For example, the demand for petrol is seen to be highly inelastic over a considerable price range.

2. There may be many or just a few substitutes for a product. Goods and services offered by a number of competitors tend to be faced by elastic demand conditions. Examples would include brands of fish fingers, tabloid newspapers, and various tinned groceries. Inelastic demand would be most likely to occur where there is little competition, e.g. the only service station on a long stretch of motorway.

3. A variable proportion of household income may be spent on an individual product. If only a small proportion of a household's income is spent on a product then demand is more likely to be inelastic. The reason for this is that if a household only spends a very small fraction of its income on an item, e.g. salt, shoe polish, mustard, then a rise in the price of the item will hardly be felt. However, in contrast, items which comprise a sizeable proportion of expenditure, e.g. bread, meat, electricity, etc., will have a more dramatic impact when their prices change. The items comprising small fractions of income will tend to have inelastic demand curves over a particular price range whereas items making up large fractions of income will tend to greater elasticity.

4. A product may have a large or a small number of different uses. If a product has many uses there will be many different markets in which price changes can exert their effect. There is therefore a greater possibility that in some of the markets

substitutes may be readily available. Gas, for example, has many uses: cooking, heating, lighting, etc. A rise in the price of electricity therefore might cause people not only to make economies in these areas but also to substitute other fuels, for example gas, for some uses.

5. The length of the time period under consideration. Following a change in price, the elasticity of demand will tend to be greater in the long run than in the short run. For example, if the price of a product becomes relatively cheaper it will take consumers time to adjust to this change. Let us assume that kiwi fruit fall in price by 50 per cent compared with other fruits. In the short period this will lead some consumers to switch to kiwi fruit. In the longer term an even greater number of consumers are likely to make the switch as tastes alter and awareness increases.

6. The durability of a product. If the price of durable items increases, consumers are likely to try and spin out the lifespan of that product. This applies to a whole host of consumer durables and factory machinery. For example, you might make your existing car last one year longer before trading it in. This is impossible with non-durable items such as cream cakes, eggs and bread.

Consumers' responses to price changes are an important ingredient of price determination. Businesses have more scope for charging high prices in markets where consumers are insensitive to price increases (inelastic demand).

In Fig. 7.15 a firm has a choice of charging a high price, A, or a lower price, B. The demand curve for the product is relatively steep indicating an inelastic demand for the product. The total revenue accruing to the firm is calculated by the formula:

$$\text{Total revenue} = \text{Quantity sold} \times \text{Price}$$

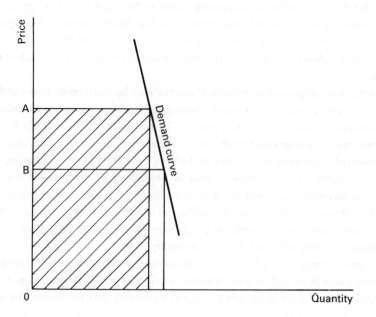

Figure 7.15 Comparing revenues at different prices (demand inelastic).

The shaded area represents total revenue at price A. Quite clearly this is larger than the rectangle under price B, so the firm will gain most revenue from charging the higher price.

In contrast, if consumers are sensitive to price changes then firms might adopt a low price strategy. In Fig. 7.16 the demand curve is relatively flat and the firm gains greatest revenue from charging price B rather than price A. (The reader should note, however, that costs are an important factor in determining price and output. If the extra costs of expanding output exceed extra revenues it may pay to produce a smaller output even when demand is elastic.)

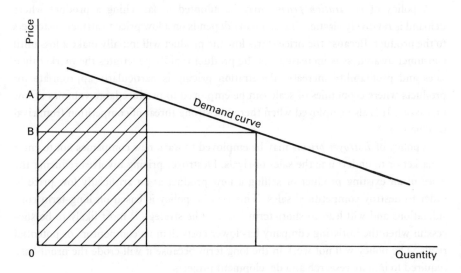

Figure 7.16 Comparing revenues at different prices (demand elastic).

Price elasticity is measured by dividing the percentage increase or decrease in the quantity demanded (or sales) resulting from a change in price by the percentage change in price.

$$\text{Price elasticity of demand} = \frac{\text{Per cent change in quantity demanded of A}}{\text{Per cent change in price of A}}$$

'Elastic' markets are those where the change in quantity demanded is a higher percentage than the change in price. Conversely 'inelastic' markets are those where the change in quantity demanded is a lower percentage than the change in price.

The problem is that in the real world it is very difficult to apply theory to the making of price decisions. For one thing firms rarely possess the empirical data (i.e. realistic figures showing how much would be demanded at different prices) required to construct actual demand or revenue curves for their products, and are often unable to distinguish costs sufficiently clearly to construct cost curves. Secondly, the goals which firms set themselves are rarely ones which are easy to build into theories such as 'profit maximization'.

A policy of *skimming pricing* may be adopted in launching a new product where demand is relatively inelastic because there are few competitors in the market and consumers have little knowledge of the product. Using this policy firms will set a high price in order to capitalize on the fact that there are people prepared to pay a high price for the new product. Once the first segment of consumers is saturated the manufacturer will lower prices in order to tap fresh segments of the market. The process continues until a large section of the total market is catered for. By operating in this way the business removed the risk of underpricing a product. This might also be a good strategy to employ when manufacturers are unsure of the elasticity of demand for their product.

A policy of *penetration pricing* may be adopted in launching a product where demand is relatively elastic. The company depends on a low price to attract customers to the product. Because the price starts low the product will initially make a loss until consumer awareness is increased. As the product rapidly penetrates the market then sales and profitability increase. Penetration pricing is particularly appropriate for products where economies of scale can be employed to produce large volumes at low unit costs. It is also employed when there is a strong threat of competition from rival products.

A policy of *destroyer pricing* may be employed to warn new companies not to enter a market or to undermine the sales of rivals. Destroyer pricing involves reducing the price of an existing product or selling a new product at an artificially low price in order to destroy competitors' sales. This type of policy is based on long-term considerations and will lead to short-term losses. The strategy is most likely to be successful when the initiating company has lower costs than its competitors or potential rivals. The policy will not work in the long term because it will erode the profit base required to initiate research and development projects.

A policy of *promotional pricing* may be used from time to time to inject fresh life into an existing product or interest in a new product. Again, it is a short-term policy because as we have seen it will not match long-term revenue targets.

Customers' perception of price

Customers generally have views about what constitutes value for money. If prices are too high they might consider that they are not getting value for money. If prices are too low they will begin to question the quality and value of a product. (There is the story of the very expensive fur coat that was reduced to £20 in a department store window. Nobody bought the coat because they thought that there must be something wrong with it.)

Figure 7.17 shows that the product costs A to produce. The business cannot sell the product for less than B without quality being questioned. Competing products are selling for prices between C and D, and the maximum chargeable price would be E.

If the product is not very exciting the business will need to pitch its price between

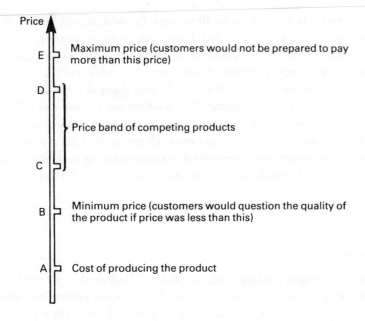

Price

E ⊐ Maximum price (customers would not be prepared to pay more than this price)

D ⊐

↦ Price band of competing products

C ⊐

B ⊐ Minimum price (customers would question the quality of the product if price was less than this)

A ⊐ Cost of producing the product

Figure 7.17 Price bands.

B and D. If, however, the product is a market leader and has some novel features then it can pitch the price between C and E.

Competition

The nature and extent of competition is often an important influence on price. If a product is faced by *direct* competition then it will compete against other highly similar products in the marketplace. This will often constrain pricing decisions so that price setting will need to be kept closely in line with rivals' actions. In contrast, when a product is faced by *indirect competition* (i.e. competition with products in different sectors of the market) then there will be more scope to vary price. This opens up the possibility for a number of strategies. For example, a firm might choose a high price strategy to give a product a 'quality' feel. In contrast, it might charge a low price so that consumers see the product as a 'bargain'.

Because price is only one factor that gives a product a competitive edge, it is not always necessary to charge the lowest price in the market. For example, Shell stresses the point that price is considerably less important than other factors. The annual report for 1987, for example, stated that: 'The Company's marketing strategy is based on establishing a differentiation between Shell and its competitors through quality in its facilities, products and services.' This policy is based on the belief that customers are most interested in performance and reliability—'You can be sure of Shell!'

Although there are only a relatively small number of companies operating in the petrol sales market there is intense competition. Price competition frequently does occur in this sector although it frequently proves to be self-defeating (for example if all producers were to lower prices by 10 per cent, the total increase in the volume of sales would inevitably be much smaller). Competing petrol companies have therefore more commonly resorted to non-price competition which includes opening hours, the offer of free gifts, a range of services offered, and various other features.

Price competition depends very much on the availability of substitute brands and products. In situations where producers have no direct competition they will have far more power to fix prices than in areas where there are many competitors. However, the number of firms in a market is a very poor indicator of the level of price competition. Some of the fiercest price competition in recent years has been in markets with only a few firms such as tabloid newspaper production, petrol sales and supermarket chains.

Product range

A number of companies produce a range of products. Each product is geared to a particular sector of the market. This is particularly true in car production where it is common practice to refer to 'middle of the range models' and 'the top end of the market'. A manufacturer will either aim to cater for as many sectors of the market as possible or for a specific market segment. When the former strategy is applied careful consideration will have to be given to the product range. When new products are introduced, the price of existing products will set boundaries on the price that can be set. It would not be wise to compete against yourself by producing two models in the same price range.

The art of 'positioning' is to identify distinct segments of a particular market, to identify the requirements of consumers in these segments, and to create an image for your products that will sell them in the required segments.

Distribution

The cost of distribution will be another important consideration in setting prices, particularly when producers use outside transport, wholesaling and retailing services. Each of these services will want to take its own profit margins and these need to be considered in terms of the price strategy.

Until 1967 manufacturers were able to control the prices at which their goods were resold. The 1967 Resale Price Maintenance Act stopped this practice. This means that the retail price of items can vary considerably. The implication for producers is that if retail outlets compete extensively with each other, then inefficient units will be forced out of the market. This could lead to producers being faced with fewer sales outlets.

Some producers own their selling outlets in order to control distribution and pricing. Examples include breweries, shoe manufacturers and some bakers.

Making a pricing decision

There are two main pricing decisions:

1. Setting a price for a completely new product.
2. Setting a price for an existing product.

The only time a firm genuinely has complete freedom in setting prices is before it has committed itself to developing and marketing a new product. Once the product has left the drawing board a whole host of factors will influence the pricing decision.

Pricing decisions are influenced by a wide range of factors, some of which are internal and others external to the business.

Internal influences on price include:

1. The objectives of the business (e.g. profit maximization, satisficing, etc.).
2. The pattern of direct and indirect costs.
3. Existing prices of similar and other products produced internally by the company.
4. Existing ideas about price setting in the company.
5. The firm's knowledge of the market.
6. Pressures from feedback from salespeople and other members of the organization.
7. Levels of research and development and the pace of new product development.

External influences on price include:

1. The strength and behaviour of competitors.
2. The attitudes and influences of other groups involved in the chain of production and distribution (e.g. what size margin do distributors want and how much power do they have?).
3. Pressure from suppliers of raw materials and components used in the product.
4. Elasticity of demand for the product.
5. Motivations of customers.
6. Existing and anticipated government policies.
7. General conditions in different markets.

Because there are so many variables involved in pricing decisions and because information available to a firm at any one time will be imperfect it will be necessary to select certain 'critical' factors to help make pricing decisions.

We have already seen that there are several approaches to pricing. We can now look in greater detail at four main strategies:

- Cost-plus pricing
- Contribution pricing
- Competitive pricing
- Customer-value pricing

Cost-plus pricing

Information about costs is often easier to collect than is information about other variables such as likely revenues. Firms will often therefore choose to make pricing decisions based on adding a margin to unit cost. (The unit cost is the average cost of each item produced, e.g. if a firm produces 1000 units at a total cost of £2000 the unit cost will be £2.) Talk to many small business owners and they will tell you that they cost out each hour worked and then add a margin for profits.

The process of cost-plus pricing can best be illustrated in relation to large firms where economies of scale can be spread over a sizeable output. As we have seen, large firms are often characterized by flat bottomed average cost curves. Average cost is therefore constant over a large range of output. It is therefore a relatively simple calculation to add a fixed margin, e.g. 10 per cent to average cost. The firm is therefore able to select an output to produce and to set a price that will be 10 per cent higher than unit costs of production (see Fig. 7.18).

The dangers of applying this pricing method are that if the price is too high sales may fall a lot short of expectations and if the price is set too low then potential revenue is sacrificed.

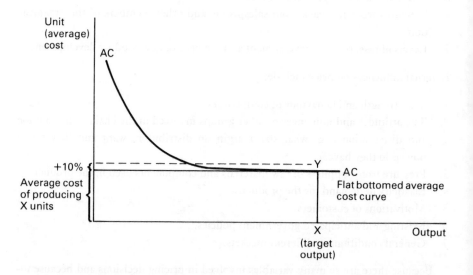

Figure 7.18 Cost-plus pricing.

If a firm applies average cost pricing too rigidly this can cause problems in the marketplace. If demand is lower than expected, for example, average costs may be slightly higher (bearing in mind that although we talk about flat-bottomed curves they will inevitably have a slight downward slope). In this situation the company accountant may press for price increases. This will make it even more difficult to make sales.

Conversely, if demand is higher than expected, average costs may fall slightly, demanding a price reduction. This may lead to a loss of potential revenue.

Contribution pricing

Contribution pricing involves separating out the different products that make up a company's portfolio, in order to charge individual prices appropriate to a product's share in total costs.

As we have already seen (page 213) two broad categories of costs can be identified:

1. Direct costs that vary directly with the level of output.
2. Indirect costs that have to be paid irrespective of the level of output.

Contribution is the sum remaining after the direct costs of producing individual products have been subtracted from revenues.

When the contributions of all the individual products that a firm produces have been added together this should more than cover the firm's indirect costs.

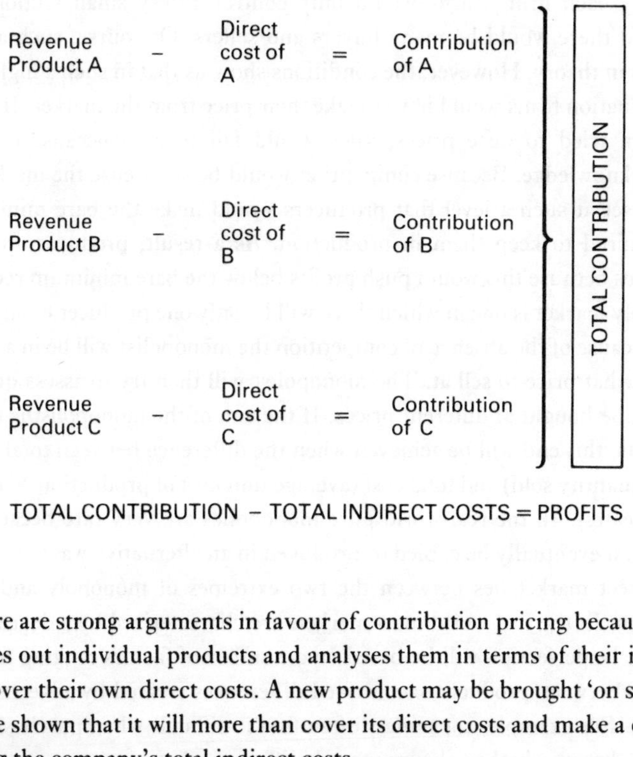

TOTAL CONTRIBUTION − TOTAL INDIRECT COSTS = PROFITS

Figure 7.19 Contribution pricing.

There are strong arguments in favour of contribution pricing because of the way it separates out individual products and analyses them in terms of their individual ability to cover their own direct costs. A new product may be brought 'on stream' because it can be shown that it will more than cover its direct costs and make a contribution to covering the company's total indirect costs.

In contrast, if we analysed individual products in terms of the relationship between total revenue and total cost for the products, calculations might show a loss. For example, if two products used the same distribution facilities, it would not make sense to expect both products to cover their own distribution costs individually. Contribution pricing enables a more rational analysis of individual products. Prices can be set in relation to each product's own direct costs (see Fig. 7.19).

Competitive pricing

An important 'critical factor' in forming price decisions may be that of competition. A firm may feel that it needs to tie its own price strategy to that prevailing in the market.

This may mean that there are frequent price changes in highly competitive markets. Alternatively, some form of price leadership may prevail whereby a market leader tends to establish other prices for other, often smaller, companies. In more established markets set prices may come to dominate and the firms that constitute the market may be reluctant to 'rock the boat'.

An individual firm might try to insulate itself against price sensitivity for its product by differentiating it from rivals. Markets are sometimes classified according to the level of competition that applies:

1. A perfect market would consist of firms producing identical products. Consumers would have perfect knowledge of the market, being aware of the prices charged by each firm. Firms would only control a very small section of the market and there would be many buyers and sellers. Of course, such a market only exists in theory. However, the conditions show us that in such a highly competitive situation firms would have to take their price from the market. If an individual firm tried to raise prices, sales would fall to zero because of perfect consumer knowledge. Because competition would be so intense the market price would be set at such a level that producers would make the bare minimum of profit required to keep them in production. As a result, producers could not lower prices because this would push profits below the bare minimum required.

2. A monopoly market is one in which there will be only one producer or supplier of a good. Because of the absence of competition the monopolist will be in a position to choose what price to sell at. The monopolist will then try to assess quantities which will be bought at different prices. If the aim of the monopolist is to maximize profits, this end will be achieved when the difference between total revenue (price × quantity sold) and total cost (average unit cost of production × quantity sold) is greatest. In the real world pure monopolies are very rare because most products can eventually be copied or produced in an alternative way.

3. An imperfect market lies between the two extremes of monopoly and perfect competition. In the real world most markets are characterized by a degree of imperfection. Imperfection will be based on a number of factors ranging from real differences between products to contrived differences created by advertising and promotion. For example, consumers often find it difficult when purchasing soap powder to know whether the supposed difference between one powder and another is really an elaborate hoax by the advertiser or not. Imperfection is also caused by imperfect knowledge on the part of consumers about a host of details that would enable them to make detailed comparisons of products.

    The widespread existence of imperfect markets makes it possible for firms to benefit from degrees of inelasticity for their products over critical price ranges.

    In many imperfect markets it is possible for firms to make more than the required minimum of profit, at least in the short term. In the long term new firms will be attracted into the market and excess profits will be competed away.

The most important type of imperfect market is oligopoly. This is the name given to a market dominated by a small number of large firms. For example, banking in England until recently was dominated by the 'Big Four' (Barclays, Midland, Lloyds and National Westminster). Of course, this has changed with the growth of competition from other high street financial services organizations such as Abbey National. The car and petrol markets are dominated by a handful of large producers.

An enterprise's policy in an oligopoly market depends on how it thinks its competitors will react to its decisions. The outcome of the firm's policy depends on other firms' reactions. When one firm cuts its price others may feel obliged to follow suit. When it raises price, it needs to consider whether or not others will follow. The danger of such price warfare often leads to price agreements between competing oligopolists. Price leadership may be vested in a dominant firm.

The demand curve for competing oligopolists' goods is said to be 'kinked' (see Fig. 7.20). If they raise prices demand will be elastic because consumers will switch to rival products. If they lower prices demand will be inelastic because competitors will follow suit. Revenue is therefore lost by moving away from the prevailing market price.

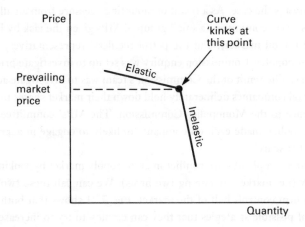

Figure 7.20 A kinked demand curve.

However, in the real world oligopoly markets are frequently highly competitive. Individual oligopolists apply a mix of non-price and price competition strategies to gain a long-term advantage in particular markets. Large conglomerates (i.e. large companies producing a range of often quite different products) are able to channel excess profits from markets in which they have near-monopoly positions to other markets where they are fighting for an increased share of sales.

The 'theory of games' is sometimes used to try and explain the behaviour of firms in oligopoly markets. A 'game' situation is said to exist when there are a number of players (firms) with a conflict of interests and limited rewards to be shared out between them. For individual players to make decisions they will need to be aware of how others will respond and what effect this will have on the eventual outcome. This situation will arise because oligopoly markets are based on uncertainty and inter-dependence.

The theory of games sets out two possible scenarios:

Scenario 1   Pure conflict. This is likely to exist when the gain made by one firm will directly lead to losses by others. This will remove the incentive for firms to co-operate.

Scenario 2   A mixture of conflict and cooperation. This is most likely to exist if firms can benefit by increasing total market share through cooperation. However, con-flict might arise because individual firms attempt to gain for themselves the biggest share of the increased total market.

These scenarios can and frequently do exist in the real world. Oligopolists will normally be engaged in activities directed towards protecting and increasing their market share. Periods of outright conflict are interspersed with periods of co-operation. A major incentive for cooperation is that all firms stand to gain from the continued prominence of their main product lines. A good example of cooperation and conflict is in the oil market. Although the oil giants can at times be fiercely com-petitive this is not always the case. As a result of mounting pressure from an all party House of Commons select committee (a small group of MPs given the task by Parlia-ment to investigate the oil market), and the petrol retailers' representatives, in the autumn of 1988 a Monopolies Commission enquiry was set up to investigate price fix-ing in the oil industry. The remit of the Commission's team was to investigate accusa-tions that the major oil companies deliberately hold down their market shares to avoid an automatic reference to the Monopolies Commission. The MPs' committee in its report said that this policy made each oil company 'unlikely to engage in aggressive pricing to increase that share'.

Let us consider an example of pure conflict in an oligopoly market by looking at a situation of duopoly (i.e. market containing two firms). We can call these two firms Shell and BP. Each firm controls half of the market. Fig. 7.21 shows that both firms have a wide range of possible strategies that they can employ to try to increase their market share. Each firm will hope that its strategy will increase consumer preference for its particular brand.

As with a game of chess, the moves of each player will affect the other's situation. Between them they satisfy the total market for petrol. Any increase in the market share of one will result in a reduction in the market share of the other. The total market is a constant sum. The game the two firms play is thus called a constant sum game.

Let us now assume that Shell and BP have narrowed down the effective strategies that they can employ to increase market share. Shell is considering four possible strat-

COMPETITIVE OPTIONS AVAILABLE
IN A DUOPOLY PETROL MARKET
(What are the best strategies?)

lighter hoses?

lead free?

attendant service?

more grades of petrol?

free car wash?

cheaper petrol?

better logo?

better locations?

easier forecourt entry?

what else?

Figure 7.21

egies to gain the largest possible market share. It is, however, aware that it is impossible to disguise its strategy from BP.

The four possible strategies are:

1. To offer free gifts with petrol.
2. To spend more on advertising.
3. To cut petrol prices.
4. To open new petrol stations.

The table below shows the percentage of the market that Shell would expect to control after the implementation of each strategy. A further dimension is added to the table because BP can respond to Shell's chosen decision in four different ways. For example, if Shell cuts petrol prices, BP could respond by a reactive strategy, e.g. by opening new petrol stations. For each of Shell's potential strategies there will be four

Percentage market share for Shell as a result of applying different strategies

	BP strategies			
	Free gifts	More advertising	Price cuts	New petrol stations
Shell strategies				
Free gifts	60	50	45	60
More advertising	70	60	50	55
Price cuts	75	60	55	65
New petrol stations	60	40	45	50

possible outcomes. (It is important to remember that this model is only a simplification of the real world in which there is a range of possible strategies, and degrees to which they can be applied.)

Reading the table. If, for example, Shell offers free gifts and BP responds by opening new outlets then Shell's market share will reach 60 per cent. If BP had responded instead by cutting prices then Shell's share would have fallen to 45 per cent.

It is likely that Shell will expect BP to respond in those ways that will minimize the effectiveness of Shell's own initiative (what is sometimes referred to as damage limitation policies). For example, if Shell offers free gifts it would expect the response—price cuts. The expected response to increased advertising, and price cuts would also be—price cuts. The response to opening new petrol stations would be increased advertising. Because Shell expects BP to respond to each of its strategies in the way that will have the worst effects for Shell, then Shell will concentrate its attention on those figures underlined in the table. The effects for these *worst responses* (for Shell) are called row *minima*.

If Shell wants to make the most of situations in which it can predict BP's reactions to its own policies it will carry out policies which produce maximum gains from dynamic situations. These 'best possible' policies are referred to as the *maximin*. The maximin will be the highest figure from the row minima. Shell will therefore resort to the strategy of price cutting which will give it 55 per cent of the market. This is because by price cutting in this situation it will gain whatever BP does. Of course, the table only applies to a given moment in time. Changing circumstances will lead to changing figures, e.g. if Shell improves its advertising performance then this will give it an increased advantage in the advertising column.

The theory outlined above simplifies the real world in many ways. In the real world there will usually be several oligopolists, many different game strategies, and variations in which strategies can be practised.

However, the theory does give us a useful insight into the way that oligopolists' strategies are interdependent and the way in which they have to think out how their rivals will react to their actions. Large corporations keep an eagle eye on the policies of rivals, and constantly discuss and evaluate ways in which competitors will react to their strategies. Elements of game theory in oil companies include many factors: prices, location of petrol stations, range of services offered, availability of lead-free petrol, greenness of the company's image, the design of the logo, customer care policy and many other details.

From time to time oligopolists are suspected of collusion. In many countries formal and informal price fixing and other forms of restrictive practice are illegal. However, from time to time price-fixing agreements between groups of firms do come to light.

Pricing according to customer valuation

If this strategy could be employed then it would be a very effective way of maximizing revenue. As we have already seen, a customer's valuation of a product is influenced by price. Certain price bands are acceptable to consumers and prices need to be set within this range.

Different consumers will have different valuations of products. As a result it is inevitable that a number of consumers will reap considerable consumer surpluses. It would be impractical to charge different prices according to individual valuations of products.

Price is also determined by bargaining strength and large-scale buyers and sellers can exert enormous pressure on weaker parties.

Case Study—Pricing policy

The information given in Fig. 7.22 was produced in a booklet called *Starting Your Own Business*. Read the information provided before answering the questions.

One of the crucial problems you have is to find the right price. It's full of pitfalls—what seems like common sense may not be the best thing to do. Try this two-step process:

Step 1

If your business is going to provide a service, calculate your service charge on a weekly, daily or even hourly basis, e.g. weekly service charge: all the costs of running a business divided by 46 (the number of weeks in a year, less an allowance for holidays and sickness time).

This calculation will show you the amount that the business has to charge out weekly in order to cover its costs, i.e. breakeven.

If you divide this figure by the number of working days in a week you will have calculated the daily charge, and this figure divided by the number of *working hours* in a day gives you the true hourly rate for the business, i.e. the amount per hour the business will have to charge to breakeven. Don't forget to review your calculations regularly, taking into account how well the business is doing.

Your business however may be involved in manufacturing, in which case you will need to calculate the unit cost of the product. In a one product firm, this will be calculated as follows:

Unit cost of product: all your fixed costs and all your variable costs (e.g. raw materials and sub-contract labour) divided by the number of units made in the period.

In this calculation, you will need to make an assumption about how many units your business can make *and sell* in any one period. The resulting calculation will show you the amount the business needs to charge for each unit to cover its costs, i.e. breakeven, *assuming that the business sells the expected number of units*.

Step 2

The price you set

You'll always need a *mark-up* on your basic cost. That's your profit—you need it

Figure 7.22 Advice on pricing policies for small businesses. (*Source*: Barclays Bank Information and Advisory Services.)

to help your business grow and prosper. The ideal price is the highest that the largest number of customers will pay. One guideline to use is 'the going rate'—what your competitors charge for similar things. Or you could simply add a figure to your costs, say 50%. Bear in mind:

● People will pay more for better quality and better service.
● Low prices can make customers suspect low quality and poor service.
● Economies of scale cost a lot of money—you have to spend more to achieve them.
● If your price is too low, you have to work harder to get the same amount of return. Selling one expensive thing once in a while can be better than dozens of cheap things all the time.

Remember:

The most important rule of pricing is—never undercharge.

When you are small, think small. Don't get seduced by economies of scale, especially if you have to spend everything you have and borrow up to the hilt to do it. Charge more, it's dangerous to risk everything being cheap.

Figure 7.22 (*concluded*)

Questions

1. In terms of the pricing theories that you have just examined what type of pricing policy is being recommended by the article?
2. What advantages and disadvantages can you point out in such a policy?
3. What alternative policies could you suggest?
4. Would they be more (or less) effective than the ones suggested?

Place

As we have seen, the main objective of a firm's distribution policy is to make sure that products are where they are wanted at the right time. This will involve a network of distribution often involving intermediaries linked by a communications system.

The total cost of distribution should be kept as low as possible in relation to output. The real cost of distribution is made up of all distribution-related costs including the obvious ones of transport and warehousing.

The process of distribution is not just concerned with physically moving goods from manufacturers to consumers. Distribution policy is also concerned with: choosing from available channels; whether to use one channel or several; whether to sell direct to consumers or to go through intermediaries; how much spending to allocate to distribution; and how much financial involvement to make in the existing channels.

Successful development of sales might require quite a large involvement by the manufacturer in the process of distribution. Close contact with intermediaries might enable manufacturers to promote best the image they would like to convey.

Intermediaries such as wholesalers, transport companies and retailers may be more effective than the manufacturer at providing goods in the right place for consumers

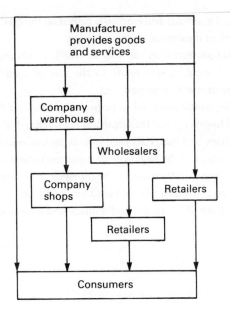

Figure 7.23 Some of the many channels for distribution.

(see Fig. 7.23). They will expect a reward for their services, the margin being the difference between the price at which they take on products and the price for which they sell them. The profits for distribution will frequently need to be shared between several intermediaries and this all adds to the end price.

The total cost of distribution is made of five main ingredients:

1. Facilities
2. Inventory
3. Transport
4. Communications
5. Unitization

Decisions about facilities include how to locate warehouses most effectively, the size of warehouses and how many to have. The more warehouses a company has the higher will be its overheads and numbers of staff employed. However, this will need to be traded off against a reduction in transport costs.

Decisions about inventories include how much stock to hold and which items to stock up on. The higher the level of inventories the greater will be the costs of insurance, deteriorating stock and theft. However, this will need to be traded off against the ability of the well-stocked company to meet and hence keep orders.

Decisions about transport relate to the type of transport to be adopted, whether to own or lease vehicles, how to plan delivery most effectively and other matters. Once again, trade-offs need to be made in relation to speed, reliability, effectiveness in different weather conditions, etc.

Decisions about communications relate to communications systems employed, procedures for processing documents and emphasis placed on the quality of service. A good communications system is essential in any company.

Decisions about unitization relate to the way in which goods are packaged and assembled for handling. Considerations relate to the size of loads, reductions in breakages, reductions in manpower employed, etc.

Raw sugar, for example, would not need to be packaged and could be transported in bulk by lorry or ship. However, once the sugar has been refined, decisions need to be made about the size, shape and materials used in making individual bags of sugar. Decisions about the unitization of the bags will be based on factors such as strength and cost of materials. The bags will then need to be transported in larger units such as boxes. Decisions about size and shape will be based on such factors as ease of handling and storage, minimization of breakages and damage and a number of other considerations.

Channels of distribution

The channel of distribution is the route which products follow from the manufacturer to the consumer. Market research will often reveal channels of distribution used by competitors.

Modern commerce involves thousands of different channels and methods of distribution including newspapers, mail order, computer link-ups, television, as well as more traditional routes.

The traditional way of distributing goods from a manufacturer to a market is through a small number of wholesalers who then sell the goods to a large number of retailers.

In this way a wholesaler is a go-between who buys in bulk from manufacturers and breaks the bulk down into small units for retailers. Wholesalers often provide a variety of services which benefit both manufacturers and retailers, such as warehousing, credit, transport and packaging. However, the existence of wholesalers adds to the selling price and wholesalers cannot be expected to concentrate on any one manufacturer's goods.

If a manufacturer sells to a retailer directly it can exert firmer control over its sales and the manufacturer and retailer can work together on sales promotion schemes. Selling direct to retailers involves a larger salesforce and increased transport charges when sending smaller consignments. If circumstances allow, it can be possible for manufacturers to sell directly to consumers, particularly if the product is a high-cost one and has a good reputation within the market.

Retailers are in direct contact with consumers and are therefore often in the best position to understand individual consumers' desires. An efficient system of retailing is essential if the types of commodities made by producers are to relate closely to consumers' desires. A retailer is the outlet through which goods are sold to the consumers and may exist in a variety of different forms.

Promotion

Promotion is the business of communicating with customers. *Impersonal communications* are things like advertising, point-of-sale displays, promotions and public relations. *Personal communications* are direct face-to-face meetings, for example between a seller and a customer.

Impersonal communications

When you publicize an item you are advertising it. There are all sorts of ways of publicizing a product and the method you use to advertise must reflect the product you are selling and the money you can spare to carry out the campaign.

A business can either organize its own advertising or arrange for an advertising agency to do the work for it. Whatever arrangement is made, it is important to decide who your target audience is going to be.

The target market

The marketplace for products is divided into segments. For example, if we take the rail transport market we can see that there are two main segments—the carriage of passengers, and the carriage of freight. However, these segments can then be further subdivided. There are many different types of passengers: commuters, pensioners, students, holidaymakers, day trippers, shoppers and many more. There are many different types of freight: liquids, mail, urgent deliveries, livestock, perishables and many more. The company's capabilities must be geared towards the different requirements of each of these segments. Marketing strategies need to differentiate between the different segments. This relates to a whole range of marketing features including product, price, promotion and place. For example, British Rail might put on a special London Week-End Break for pensioners from Southampton in the autumn at a discount price. The trip could be advertised by direct mail to old people's homes in the city. In fact British Rail employs a wide range of marketing techniques and divides its market into hundreds of segments to each of which it offers a different price structure. By recognizing the characteristics of each segment British Rail is best able to meet customers' specialized needs at an acceptable price.

Consumer markets are commonly divided up into broad sub-groups on the basis of a number of criteria such as age, class, income, geographical location, type of house and sex. The most common grouping used is that of occupation, which is regarded to be a reflection of income and other factors.

A classification that is commonly used divides consumers into classes, A, B, C1, C2, D and E and is regarded to be a general indicator of spending power.

Any classification will inevitably be flawed by simplification. The assumption underpinning social classification is that you are grouping together people with similar backgrounds, lifestyles and tastes. Quite clearly there will be fundamental differences even between people living next door to each other or sharing the same

Class	Occupational grouping	Percentage of population in each class
A	Higher managerial, administrative and professional, e.g. lawyers, architects and doctors	3.1
B	Intermediate managerial, administrative and professional, e.g. shopkeepers, farmers and teachers	13.4
C1	Supervisory and clerical, and junior managerial administrative and professional, e.g. office administrators and bank clerks	22.3
C2	Skilled manual, e.g. electricians and miners	31.2
D	Semi-skilled and unskilled manual, e.g. bus conductors and farm workers	19.1
E	Casual labourers, state pensioners and the unemployed	10.9

occupation. However, when you lump broad categories of people together meaningful differences in consumer behaviour do become noticeable.

Regional differences will also be significant in making marketing decisions. Important statistics from the regions will include population and earnings (see tables).

Table illustrating the regional differences in population in the United Kingdom

	Population (000s) 1986
United Kingdom	56 763
North	3 080
Yorkshire and Humberside	4 899
East Midlands	3 920
East Anglia	1 992
South East	17 265
South West	4 543
West Midlands	5 181
North West	6 374
England	47 255
Wales	2 821
Scotland	5 121
Northern Ireland	1 567

The market analyst would examine the above information to quantify the total population in particular areas. This might, for example, be related to costs of distribution by looking at the area to be covered. Further information which may be of interest might be a contrast with previous years. For example, although the population of East Anglia is less than that in the North, the population in East Anglia had risen by 27 000 since 1985 whereas in the North it had fallen by 6000.

This sort of information gives marketeers a breakdown of spending power by location and further possibilities of analysis by sex. Where particular products are geared towards particular spending levels this sort of information can be very useful.

Other significant data for marketing decisions will be gleaned from studies of the age structure of the population and predicted changes in numbers in each category.

Table illustrating average gross weekly earnings (full time) (£)

	April 1986	
	Male	Female
United Kingdom	207.0	137.0
North	192.7	128.1
Yorkshire and Humberside	193.2	126.4
East Midlands	190.9	125.7
East Anglia	195.1	128.6
South East	232.8	153.8
South West	193.1	128.8
West Midlands	193.9	126.7
North West	198.4	130.7
England	209.0	138.6
Wales	190.5	127.1
Scotland	201.3	129.8
Northern Ireland	182.2	128.1

Numbers of people comprising households are also of interest. Today there are far more single-person households, and households consisting of a number of single sharers. Consumption patterns do in some ways reflect household composition.

Marketeers will often split total markets into segments based on a number of variables. For example, one segment of the market may be made up of Social Class 1 males in the 25–44-year-old age group.

Industrial markets

So far we have been concentrating on consumer goods markets. A number of producers, however, are far more interested in industrial goods markets where goods range from heavy items of capital such as oil drilling platforms to the nuts and bolts of the engineering trade.

Industrial purchases tend to involve a more detailed critical analysis of the relative merits of alternative products than do household consumer purchases (although there is a wide range of situations in which the reverse can be true). Industrial purchases will also frequently involve a team of decision makers, so that, for example, a range of technicians, accountants, buyers and other staff might inspect a plant producing industrial goods before placing an order with a firm. Industrial purchases often also involve bulk orders and quotations may be sought from several suppliers.

The industrial market can be split up into a wide number of sectors dependent on a wide range of classification systems. Classification may be on the basis of size, sales, share of the market, nature of raw materials, nature of product and many other classifications.

One commonly used classification is that of the Standard Industrial Classification which is found in government statistics. There are ten major divisions each of which can be further subdivided.

The Standard Industrial Classification

Industry division

0	Agriculture, Forestry and Fishing
1	Energy
2	Extraction
3	Metal Manufacturing
4	Other Manufacturing
5	Construction
6	Distribution, Hotels and Catering
7	Transport
8	Banking, Finance
9	Other Services

The government market

The government is the largest single purchaser in the United Kingdom. Government purchasing decisions are made by a range of officials and departments. Government expenditure is dealt with in detail in Chapter 16. Features of government spending decisions include: the involvement of a range of experts; consideration of a range of alternative products; quotations and tendering; bulk purchases and discounts; and very large orders.

Customers have different needs and wants: some buy more than others, some want high quality products, some want the lowest price, of fast delivery and so on. However, some customers are better than others. *Pareto's Law* states that 20 per cent of the customers in any given market are responsible for 80 per cent of the sales. The implication is that a sensible marketing strategy should focus on the 20 per cent of 'best' customers. In order to find out what your customers are actually like it is important to do market research to find out more about your customers' attributes. Market research will also reveal the best channels of communication to reach specific categories. One section of your customers may be reached via newspapers like *The Times*, other by the *Sun*. Posters and TV advertisements can be angled at one section or another.

Case Study—Selling British Gas shares

The advert in Fig. 7.24 was part of the most successful advertising campaigns ever launched in the United Kingdom. The aim of the campaign was to encourage people who would not normally think of buying shares to do so. It was therefore felt necessary to use advertising techniques and media which would not normally be used for selling shares, e.g. the tabloid press and adverts during prime time television. The campaign started with a gradual build-up of television adverts introducing the idea of gas as a major British industry. It then developed into a jokey campaign in which members of the public were invited to find a fictitious character called Sid and tell him

UP AGAINST TIME by Jeanne Willis and Trevor Melvin

Figure 7.24 Advertisement for British Gas shares.

to buy British Gas shares. The notion of finding Sid captured the public imagination. The campaign was run in the tabloids, and on the sides of bus shelters—anywhere where it would catch the attention of the citizen on the street.

Questions

1. What was the target market for the advertising campaign for British Gas shares?
2. In what ways would this market segment be different from that traditionally associated with share buying?
3. What sort of advertising and promotion strategy would be required to successfully reach this segment?
4. What problems would be encountered in trying to reach this segment of the market?
5. Why do you think that the British Gas campaign proved to be such a success?
6. Choose a particular advertising class and explain what methods you would use to promote a particular product to this class.
7. How would your promotional methods vary if you were promoting
   (a) the same product to a different class?
   (b) a different product to the same class?

Choosing marketing strategies

Undifferentiated marketing, whereby a single marketing mix is offered to the total market, is unlikely to be successful because, as we have seen, markets are made up of different types of buyers with different wants and needs (see Fig. 7.25).

Differentiated marketing is the strategy of attacking the market by tailoring separate

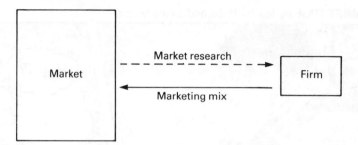

Figure 7.25 Undifferentiated
marketing.

products and marketing strategies to different sectors of the market (see Fig. 7.26). Different marketing mixes will be involved for each sector of the market. For example, the car market might be divided into an economy segment (buyers looking for a cheap form of car transportation), a luxury segment, a sporting-orientated segment, etc. The marketeer needs to develop different strategies for each segment.

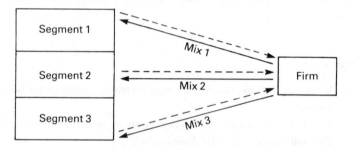

Figure 7.26 Differentiated marketing.

Concentrated marketing is often the best strategy for the smaller firm. This involves choosing to compete in one segment and developing the most effective mix for this sub-market (see Fig. 7.27). Jaguar, for example, concentrates on the luxury segment of the car market.

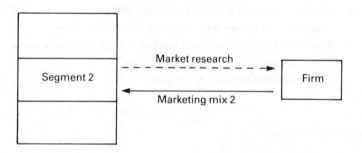

Figure 7.27 Concentrated marketing.

Although companies will try to select and dominate certain market segments they will find that rivals are engaged in similar strategies. As we have seen, companies will therefore try to create a differential advantage over rivals. In a market where no firm has a differential advantage consumers will choose on the basis of price, and competition will push profits down towards zero. As a result modern businesses will try to establish 'quasi-monopolies'—whereby customers recognize the uniqueness of their product and are unlikely to switch to rivals on account of minor price changes.

The *positioning strategy* of a business relates to selecting a market segment and creating a differential advantage over rivals in that area. Thus Porsche is positioned in the prestige section of the car market with a differential advantage based on technical performance. Mothercare store is positioned to serve mothers with young children with a differential advantage based on breadth of merchandise assortment for that target segment.

Once a company is clear about the nature of the segments of a market it needs to decide which segments to concentrate on and how best to win a large share of sales available in particular segments.

A useful marketing tool is the SWOT analysis. This involves looking at the Strengths, Weaknesses, Opportunities and Threats to product lines. SWOT analysis helps the marketing department to appreciate what is good about particular products and what needs to be improved.

Henry Ford is reputed to have centred his business strategy on the principle that consumers could have any car they wanted, provided it was a black model T Ford. However, today Ford, like most of the other major motor giants, separates its market out and pitches its promotion and sales drives to the needs and wants of the customers that make up these segments.

Advertising

Most people understand advertising to be sellers publicizing their goods to customers. In fact, any type of publicity is advertising. In the United Kingdom, the body that spends most money on advertising is the detergents giant Unilever. In second position is the government which has all sorts of messages to put over to the public— advice on joining a government training scheme, publicity about AIDS prevention measures, health warnings and many other messages. The government rarely tries to sell things to people. More often it sets out to inform them about their rights. This passing on of information is a very important part of advertising.

Most adverts, however, are not just there to inform the public—you do not see a soap powder advert that simply gives information about the powder. The advert goes further and contains a persuasive message. Most firms that try to sell goods will use persuasive advertising. A major aim of persuasive soap powder advertising will be to support customer loyalty to the brand.

A persuasive selling message is one that promises to the people to whom it is addressed a desirable and believable benefit. There are many different types of advert that can be used to persuade, including the following:

- Adverts showing a famous personality using the product, e.g. Daley Thompson and Lucozade.

- Adverts comparing one product with other products.
- Adverts using sex appeal.

Many firms aim to develop strong brand images for their products. A brand is the name of a company's product, such as 'Frosties', 'Marathon' and 'Fairy Liquid'. If consumers can be led to associate a brand name with a product then a firm will be in a better position to make large sales and to attract loyalty to the brand. The creation of a good brand image depends on developing a good marketing mixture including producing quality products at competitive prices coupled with attractive advertising.

Effective advertising

For advertising to be successful it must contain a number of ingredients including the following:

1.   It must reach the right audience.
2.   It must be attractive and appealing to the reader or viewer.
3.   It must cost little in relation to the extra sales made.

1.   *Reach the right audience*   Advertising needs to be geared towards the right target audience. This will involve selecting appropriate media and particular areas of the media. For example, if you want to reach Advertising Class B you will need to research the media slots which are most likely to reach Class B.

Test marketing may be employed to gauge the reception a sample of the population gives to a selected product. For example, when a new biscuit is being prepared for a market 'launch', members of the public may be tested to find out what they think of various possible presentations of the product. For example, several different alternative coloured labels may be designed for the product. A selected audience of consumers might then be asked to watch a TV screen while the labels are flashed in front of them. They will then be asked to fill in a questionnaire saying which labels they remember and which they liked best.

Market research thus makes possible the design and preparation of adverts and other promotional techniques that will have maximum impact. The remainder of the recipe for success depends on the flair with which the advertising campaign is constructed and projected.

Advertising expenditure is wasted if it reaches the wrong households.

An interesting recent development has been the growth of firms that specialize in supplying mailing lists. For instance, the 'Wish-Wash' company wants to send leaflets directly to houses advertising their new dishwashers. However, research has revealed that only higher income families invest heavily in new dishwashers. The company therefore purchases from a mailing list company a list of all the names and addresses of people in the area who live in the more expensive grades of housing. The mailing list company will have compiled its list by gathering names from the electoral register of people who live in particular streets.

2.   *Attractive and appealing advertising*   Firms will either have their own advertising department or will employ an advertising agency. Sometimes the firm selling the goods will have a big say in what goes into the advert, and other times the advertising agency will decide entirely how the advertising should be done.

Sometimes the advertising agency will hire another specialist firm to come up with a name for a product. Market research will be carried out to find out what potential customers want.

3.   *A good advertising campaign should be cheap in relation to the extra sales made*   The extra sales made as a result of an advertising campaign should bring in far more money than the cost of advertising. As a result adverts will only be effective if consumers respond to the selling message.

Sometimes when a new product is being marketed it will be given a trial run in a selected area of the country. Usually this will be in a particular ITV region. For example, a crisp manufacturer launches a new star-shaped crisp. Initially the crisp will be advertised in a television region where the costs of advertising time are low. If the crisp then proves to be popular in the pilot region it will be launched on a national basis. By carrying out a cheap pilot scheme, huge sums of money will not be lost if the product flops.

Case Study—Planning an advertisement

A recent survey (October 1988) carried out by the executive selection division of the accountants Price Waterhouse throws some light on what makes an effective job advertisement. It found that 65 per cent of a sample of more than 1000 business executives regularly read appointments advertisements, whether or not they are looking for a job; 41 per cent read job advertisements twice a week.

The position of an advertisement on the page was held to be unimportant by 90 per cent of those surveyed. The size of the advertisement seems of relatively minor importance: 63 per cent of respondents looked at smaller advertisements as well as large ones. And what caught their eye was little influenced by the inclusion of pictures and diagrams—84 per cent said that these did not matter.

There was a strong reaction against composite advertisements—those in which more than one job is advertised by the same recruiter: 60 per cent of the sample disliked them. Among those aged 45 and upwards—which presumably means those whose jobs are more senior—the negative response was 70 per cent. The general opinion was that a serious recruiter would use an individual advert.

One of the clearest lessons to emerge, though, is that of the weight of information contained in an advert counts for more than the way it is presented. That begins with the headline: 98 per cent of respondents liked to be able to identify the job from this right away and were not attracted to 'cryptic openings' (gimmicky openings which are unclear). They preferred texts that gave a full job description, however long, that were clear on specifics, and that avoided mentioning too many unquantifiable personal attributes. The key ingredients in order of preference were: job title, salary, nature of business activity, location, name of employer, advertisement heading, the standing of the recruitment agency handling the assignment, and graphical presentation.

To the 91 per cent of people who did the survey, stating the salary was vital. Only about 40 per cent attached the same importance to full description of fringe benefits; 64 per cent said they would probably not reply to an advertisement that did not state a salary.

Questions

1. In the light of the Price Waterhouse survey design a job advertisement to appear in a national newspaper for a European Sales Manager with a salary of £35,000 + bonus, car and benefits. Make up the rest of the details of the advertisement yourself.
2. Look through the jobs page of a newspaper. Select two which you think are effective and two which you think are ineffective. Explain your reasoning to the rest of your group.
3. Rewrite one of the adverts which you felt to be ineffective.
4. How might different styles of job advertisements be effective or ineffective in different circumstances?
5. Why might the features that make up a good advertisement for a job be radically different from those that make a good advert for a consumer product? Explain your answer with examples.

Control over advertising in Britain
Advertisers cannot say anything they like when preparing an advert.

1. They must keep within the law. For instance, the Trades Description Act lays down that goods put up for sale must be as they are described (e.g. a waterproof watch must be waterproof).
2. The advertising industry has its own code of practice which advertisers must obey.

The British code of advertising practice   This is a voluntary agreement by firms in the advertising industry to keep their adverts within certain standards. For instance, when advertising slimming products like slimming pills and biscuits, the advertiser must say that these should be taken in addition to a balanced diet. In other words, the advertiser should not suggest that a person can slim simply by eating slimming biscuits—this would obviously be dangerous to health. The British Code of Advertising Practice covers newspapers, magazines, cinema adverts, leaflets, brochures, posters and commercials on video tape, but not TV and radio adverts.

Advertising Standards Authority (ASA)   The ASA is responsible for supervising the British Code of Advertising Practice except for Independent Television. You might have seen an advert which appears in newspapers and magazines part of which looks like Fig. 7.28. The advert goes on to say that if you have any complaints about adverts in the paper you should write to the ASA, which will take up your complaint. Of course, some of the complaints received by the ASA are frivolous like the man who complained that he had poured Heineken on his pot plant and it had died.

However, if the ASA feels that an advert is indecent or untrue it will ask the advertising agency that produced the advert to change it.

The advertising agency will then change the advert because it knows the ASA can ask the media to stop printing adverts by that agency.

Figure 7.28 Advert for the Advertising Standards Authority.

The Independent Broadcasting Authority (IBA)   The IBA controls radio and television advertising. Examples of some of the rules involved are that products which appear in a programme cannot be shown in advertisements immediately before or after the programme and that newsreaders cannot appear in adverts.

Personal communications

Personal communications should not be underestimated as a marketing tool. Personal communication involves building up a network of contacts through some means of direct approach.

Most large organizations have their own public relations staff. The public relations department will be concerned with creating and sustaining an image of a company. This will cover a variety of areas including press relations, and the way in which staff are trained to deal with members of the public.

The most important rule to bear in mind when dealing with the media is that they are working for their own readers, viewers, listeners or subscribers. It is therefore important to be well prepared so as not to be caught off balance by a difficult question. It is also important to think carefully about the type of impression which you want to put over and about what your audience would like to hear. Messages which are direct and straightforward and those that are couched in simple language and presented with confidence are often best understood.

Exhibitions and displays are another useful marketing tool. Exhibitions offer direct contact with customers, distributors, wholesalers and retailers, as well as providing the benefit of media coverage. Media coverage varies widely depending on whether the exhibition has local (e.g. a craft show) or national (e.g. The Ideal Home Exhibition) significance. Exhibitions will often help to create new contacts who then go on to become firm customers at a later date.

The disadvantages are that exhibitions are relatively costly and the space occupied by a stand is just one of a number of expenses. Additional expenses are staff time, the cost of travel, subsistence and accommodation, the preparation of the stand and sales literature.

Field personnel are another form of personal communication. Salespeople, demonstrators and merchandisers can be effective in projecting a company's message to a target audience. They can be used in many ways—to offer samples, or coupons, to show how a product works, to give information and answer questions, or just to ask people if they would like to buy the product.

Direct mail can be used to reach specified target individuals and firms. The key to effective direct mail is the quality of the mailing list. Thorough updating of the names on a list is vital, especially if the message is to be personally addressed.

Few people today write letters as a matter of personal choice. Most people use the telephone. Since many promotional techniques require the public to respond in some way, it is natural to choose the means of response that they normally prefer. Double glazing firms are a prime example of a group that tends to use the direct phone call as a means of gaining a sales lead (i.e. an introduction to a more formal interview with a customer). However, with frequent exposure to telephone selling householders have become increasingly more skilled at putting off telephone salespeople.

Marketing Case Study—Promoting Economy 7 for East Midlands Electricity

Setting the scene

In the 1970s East Midlands Electricity had been faced with a downward trend in electricity sales.

Like any other industry having to achieve acceptable financial results

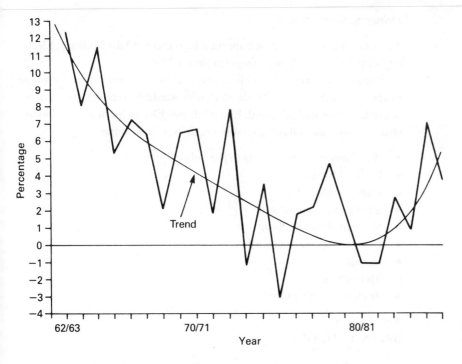

Figure 7.29 Percentage changes in wool sales.

when faced with rising costs and falling sales, the electricity supply industry had three main interacting options:

1. Increased prices.
2. Cutting costs internally.
3. Improving the sales position.

In order to reverse the trend, since 1980 East Midlands Electricity has used aggressive marketing to sell products that use electricity (see Fig. 7.29).

One of East Midland Electricity's main strategies for improving sales has been through advertising to develop a strong image of East Midlands Electricity—particularly through the projection of a well known 'Strapline'.

The strapline

A strapline is a short saying that identifies a company without mentioning the organization by name. It uses association in a similar way to a logo, and is a powerful element in marketing. (Can you identify the following straplines? 'I know a man who can.' 'Schhh!' 'Vorsprung durch Technik.' 'Gotta Lotta bottle.' 'Soft, strong and very, very long.')

'The Team You Can Trust' was chosen by East Midlands Electricity to convey an image of a trustworthy, credible organization. One that could suggest a group of people working together to provide excellent standards of service.

Delivering the strapline

The strapline was to form an important ingredient of East Midlands Electricity's aggressive marketing campaign for the 1980s.

Someone was needed to deliver the strapline and convey the corporate image for which East Midlands Electricity would be remembered. A range of products also had to be sold. East Midlands Electricity needed to choose a character with the following qualities to deliver its strapline:

- Well known and frequently in the public eye.
- Disliked by few.
- Plenty of character.
- Strong local connection.
- Successful but not flashy.
- Convincing and trustworthy.
- Honest
- Memorable
- Associated with a team.

The choice was:
BRIAN CLOUGH.

How Brian Clough was used in the promotion

Brian Clough was used as the central character in all East Midland Electricity's promotions including television, newspaper, leaflets, posters, direct mailing and many other forms of advertising.

Brian Clough was used to deliver the main message by giving information on prices, information about products, and finally to deliver the strapline 'The team you can trust'.

The ultimate objective was to build 'awareness' of East Midlands Electricity as the team you can trust, to encourage customers to make purchases. Clough gave East Midlands Electricity a trustworthy, down-to-earth approach to get the message across.

Task

For this activity you will need to promote Economy 7 to new home owners who may not even know what Economy 7 is.

Economy 7 is a method of purchasing electricity at a cheap rate, storing it and then using it later for your household central heating needs. Economy 7 is a cheap night time rate that is available for seven hours between midnight and 7 o'clock.

It is free to convert to this system and just involves a meter change (about two hours' work).

Questions

1. Choose a personality to advertise Economy 7 to a young (18–24) audience moving into new homes. Explain why you have chosen that individual.
2. Write a TV advertisement with a storyboard using the personality you have chosen. (A storyboard is a set of drawings with captions mapping out the sequence of an advert.)
3. Decide during which programmes you would show your advertisement and why.
4. Write a press advertisement headline (people look at the average press advertisement for four seconds before deciding whether to read further).
5. Which national papers would you use for your press advertisement and why?

Market research

Whatever kind of business you hope to establish, you should research carefully a wide range of aspects related to the potential market.

Market research involves collecting, recording and making sense of all the available information which will help a business unit to understand its market.

Market research sets out to answer the following questions:

- *Who* makes up the target audience?
- *What* do they want?
- *When* do they need it?
- *Where* does it sell best?
- *How* can it be taken to them?
- *Why* do they want/need it?

Market research helps firms to plan ahead rather than to guess ahead.

In business, demand is always changing and therefore it is essential to know how things are changing. Market research requires a special form of skill and therefore market research companies are often employed because they have the necessary experience and also because market research takes up a lot of time.

Market research can be used to find out information in a wide number of areas including the following:

1. *General* This would include up-to-date statistics about the size and nature of the market—the age, sex, income level, geographical distribution, social status and other features of customers; the share of the market controlled by different companies in the industry, what trends, laws and other changes are likely to change in the industry in the future.
2. *Sales* This would include information about sales and sales methods. Are the

salespeople as effective as they should be? Are the best possible sales methods being used?

3. *Product*   What do customers think of the product? Who buys it and why? The product itself and its packaging will be tested. The market researchers will also investigate competition.

4. *Advertising*   How effective are the advertising and public relations? Is there scope for improvement?

Methods used in market research

The investigative approach used by a market researcher lays down some useful guidelines for any piece of fieldwork.

Data gathering

Basically, this involves collecting as much information as possible about the market, usually before any further steps are taken. It relies on desk research and field research. Data are divided into primary and secondary categories. Primary data are collected in the field. Secondary data are gathered from all the material that is at present available on the subject, and is always studied first when doing desk research.

Desk research

This method involves the search for secondary data, whether published or unpublished. A good place to begin is with a company's records of items such as production, sales, marketing, finance and other data. Other sources of secondary data are government publications (e.g. *The Annual Abstract of Statistics*), trade journals (e.g. *Farmers' Weekly, Packaging Monthly*), materials produced by business groups, and information that is made available by commercial research organizations such as Gallup.

Field research

This method involves the search for primary information.

Sampling/sample surveys

This is the most common way to gather field data. It involves taking a census of a small sector of the population which represents all of a particular group, e.g. married working women in Bristol aged 30–45 are taken to represent all urban, married working women in the United Kingdom. *Convenience sampling* is taking information from any group which happens to be handy—walking down a high street for example. *Judgement sampling* is slightly more refined: the interviewer would select high street respondents on the basis of whether or not they appear to belong to a particular segment of the population—say, middle-class business people. *Quota sampling* deals with specific types of respondents—working-class male Asian youths aged 14–19, for example.

Questionnaires

This is the most popular method of extracting information from people. They are usually conducted by post, telephone or in person. Questionnaires are easy to administer and easy for respondents to deal with. They simplify the analysis of results, and can provide surprisingly detailed information. However, they are easy to 'cheat' on and a market research agency will ensure that 'control questions' have been built in to check that the questionnaire has been filled in in a suitable fashion.

Postal questionnaires: These are easy to administer but unfortunately they yield a poor response. They are rarely used on their own: more often they are used to support a programme of telephone or personal interviews. Benefits include relatively low cost, no interviewer bias, and reaching people who are otherwise inaccessible. Disadvantages are the 'hidden' costs—paper, envelopes, printing, postage, clerical and researcher time, design and collation of the results—are all expensive.

Telephone interviews: These are ideal when specific information is required quickly. However, for consumer research it is biased because it is limited to households who have telephones. The benefits are that it is easy to set up and the response is quick. The disadvantages are that a trained tele-interviewer is necessary, it is not possible to get a spread of the total population, and the interview can come to a quick end by someone putting down the receiver.

Personal interviews: In a structured interview, the interviewer has to follow a set pattern of questions and responses (e.g. ticking boxes). In semistructured interviews the order and wording of the questions are laid out in an interview guide but the response is open ended, and the interviewee is allowed to reply in his or her own words. Unstructured interviews are what they sound like—certain topics are covered in a relaxed fashion. The benefits of personal interviews are that by using trained interviewers, one is able to get a high percentage of usable interviews. It is the most popular and widely used form of gathering information. The disadvantages are the high cost and difficulty of getting trained interviewers. This method also takes a long time and semistructured and unstructured interviews are difficult to analyse for hard facts.

The theory of sampling

If a sample is chosen by correct methods, every member of the relevant population will have an equal probability of being selected. There will be no bias in the selection so that the results remain unknown and uncalculated.

At the heart of the theory of sampling is the concept of standard error. There are many ways of selecting samples from a very large population. Imagine that a very large number of different samples of a given size are selected. What would we expect the variation to be in any estimate derived from the samples? For example, let us suppose that we want to find out the proportion of all adults who are men. We know that it should be about half. The different samples will not give exactly the same estimate, but we would expect most of them to give roughly the right estimate—otherwise sampling would be of little value.

In fact we know from sampling theory that the estimates given by a large number of samples fit into a standard pattern, called the normal distribution, a bell-shaped curve in which most of the sample estimates bunch together around the centre while some tail off in either direction, above and below the central estimate. It is possible to calculate how sample estimates form themselves into a normal distribution, by calculating the standard error; two-thirds of all the estimates would be within plus or minus one standard error of the average (central) estimate, 95 per cent within two and 99 per cent within three standard errors (see Fig. 7.30). Thus we know, by calculation based on sampling theory, the probability that the true proportion for the population lies within a certain range of the estimate given by our one sample.

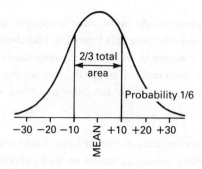

Figure 7.30 A normal distribution curve.

Sampling theory is dealt with at length in Chapter 5. When carrying out market research it will usually be necessary to limit the cost of the research. Therefore two important modifications are often made to limit the size of the sample:

- Clustering
- Stratification

A cluster is a sample made up of individuals with a common characteristic. The existence of this characteristic simplifies the process of collecting data about the sample. A common form of clustering is based on geographical location. Samples are taken in stages. A sample is first selected from geographical areas (e.g. polling districts or census enumeration districts). Inevitably the clustering technique will slightly increase the standard error of a sample, but the error can be calculated and is a small price to pay for the benefits of cost-effective survey work. Samples can be chosen so that interviewees all live in a small radius.

Stratification involves deciding on what common characteristics will produce a representative sample. If your sample is going to represent a typical selection of individuals in a total population, it will be necessary to classify the common characteristics of the total group. Individuals will then be interviewed who match these characteristics.

Whatever form of sampling you select can be classified also under the headings random, and non-random. In random, or probability sampling, the interviewer has no choice and will have to contact specific individuals, e.g. every fiftieth person on the electoral register. We have already considered various non-random sampling techniques.

Uses of market research

There are a number of major uses for market research including the following:

1. To find out the nature of a problem—exploratory research.
2. To describe and explain what is happening—descriptive research.
3. To uncover possible reasons for what is happening—explanatory research.
4. To predict what might happen—predictive research.

Exploratory research might involve an investigation of primary and secondary data in order to find out what is going wrong. This may involve interviewing the relevant personnel and asking them to explain their perceptions of the problem.

Descriptive research is simply concerned with identifying what is happening and identifying trends. For example, it may simply be involved with describing sales figures in a particular market over a period of time or describing changes in the age structure of the population.

Explanatory research will try to explain trends, sequences and other phenomena. It might involve looking at alternative hypotheses to uncover the assumptions on which they are based.

Predictive research is concerned with forecasting and other techniques used to look into the future.

Types of market research project

Project	What is involved
Attitude surveys	Carrying out research to find out how people feel about particular products
Awareness tests	Carrying out research to find out whether people are aware of the existence of particular products and how informed they are
Product testing	Carrying out research to find out the reactions of samples of people to various products, wrappings for products, and other features of product presentation
Repeat awareness studies	Monitoring products at particular intervals to check on the public's on-going perception of the product
Test marketing	Trialling products in a specific area before making an introduction to the total market

Questions

Short answer questions

1. Give two reasons why a company may sell, for a limited period, part of its product range at a loss. *(Source: AEB.)*

2. Give two examples of non-price competition. *(Source: AEB.)*

3. What is the purpose of the Advertising Standards Authority? *(Source: AEB.)*

4. How does the Government attempt to prevent misleading advertising? *(Source: AEB.)*

5. Give three reasons, which are within the control of the firm, for a loss in market share. *(Source: AEB.)*

6. What is meant by 'undifferentiated marketing'?

7. What is meant by the 'life cycle of a product'?

8. Why are changes in the structure of the population of interest to producers? *(Source: Cambridge.)*

9. What might be the objectives of a local newspaper publisher introducing a free paper in addition to their existing publication? *(Source: Cambridge.)*

10. What is meant by a policy of penetration pricing?

11. How might the manufacturer of a new chocolate bar decide to market the product? *(Source: Cambridge.)*

12. Explain how primary and secondary sources can be utilized to construct market research.

13. A furniture manufacturer is concerned about a reduction in sales of its existing product range. What action should it take? *(Source: AEB.)*

14. How might different pricing strategies be appropriate for different firms depending on:
    (a) availability of data;
    (b) levels of competition in the market;
    (c) size of firm?

15. Analyse the role of the marketing department in a large organization.

16. Discuss the elements beyond a firm's immediate control which may influence its marketing decisions. *(Source: AEB.)*

17. The manufacturer of a new breakfast cereal wants to find out the attitudes to this new innovative product. How would you go about devising:
    (a) a random sample;
    (b) a non-random sample?

18. What do you consider to be the main differences between marketing to the consumer market and to the industrial market?

19. What criteria would you employ for segmenting the following markets:
    (a) Motor cars?
    (b) Newspapers?
    (c) Industrial machinery?

20. 'Cost-based pricing is the easiest to apply.' Discuss this statement.

Essays

1. How important is market research to the marketing and production strategies of a business?
2. Why might a firm wish to:
   (a) change the position of a product in a particular market;
   (b) relaunch an existing product?
   Explain your answer by using actual examples.
3. Describe the statistical techniques that can be used in market research.
4. Why does the emphasis on different elements of the marketing mix vary between products?
5. Are costs the most important determinant of price?
6. How can a knowledge of price elasticity help a business to make pricing decisions?
7. Why is it essential to have a clear picture of your target market?
8. Describe the part played by the marketing function in business.
9. A good product does not require marketing! Do you agree with this statement?
10. Marketing is a dynamic function. Discuss.

Data response questions

1   Figure 7.31 shows positioning in the market for daily newspapers in early 1990. Each of the newspapers is located in terms of the age and social class of its typical reader.

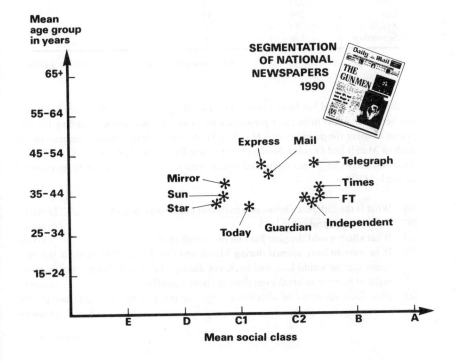

Figure 7.31 Position in the market for daily newspapers in early 1990.

(a)   Can you identify three main segments in the market structure?
(b)   Can you spot any obvious market gaps?
(c)   What information about a potential market should a newspaper publisher try to discover before deciding on whether to publish a new paper?
(d)   The diagram indicates that socio–economic groups and age are important dimensions of segmentation. What others can you identify?
(e)   Most periodicals have to serve two markets, the reader and the advertiser. Can a newspaper effectively cater for these two markets? Explain with examples.
(f)   Why do you think that there are no *daily* newspapers targeted at:
    (i)   The 54 + age group.
    (ii)   The 24 and under age group.
    (iii)   Social class E.

(*Source:* Cambridge.)

2   The cost accounts for the Suntrap Hotel for the period 1 January 1985 to 31 December 1985 are shown below:

	Total number of room/nights let	Revenue per room per night (£)	Variable cost per room/per night (£)
April	160	8	6
May	180	10	6
June	220	12	7
July	280	15	8
August	340	15	8
September	170	10	6

Total annual semi variable and fixed costs are: £1440.

In the past the hotel has had a season of six months per annum from 1 April to 30 September. In an effort to increase profits, the proprietor is considering extending his 1987 season to cover the period from 1 March to 31 October. Market research suggests that in each of March and October he can expect to sell 100 room nights at £7. Variable costs are estimated to be £6 per night, and annual semi variable and fixed costs are expected to rise by £100.

(a)   What is the difference between a fixed cost and a variable cost?   (*4 marks*)
(b)   Calculate the profits for 1985.   (*10 marks*)
(c)   What affect would the plan have on his overall profits?   (*2 marks*)
(d)   If he were to have opened during March and October in 1985, what is the minimum that he would have had to charge during March and October per room per night, if he were to break even **during those months**?   (*6 marks*)
(e)   Give **four** examples of alternative ways for the proprietor to increase profits.   (*8 marks*)

(*Source:* AEB.)

3   Read the attached extract of the marketing of the Cadbury Wispa and answer
    the questions which follow.

Marketing the Cadbury Wispa

The gigantic brands in the 'pure' chocolate
market had, without exception, origins dat-
ing back to before the Second World War.
5 Cadbury's Dairy Milk was launched in 1905
and has sold prodigiously ever since. Some
twenty years later Cadbury launched Flake,
which was discovered as a by-product of
manufacturing milk chocolate.

10 These two products set the pace in the
market for eighty years. There have been
many attempts to launch a product to stand
alongside CDM and Flake. None succeeded
until the late 1970's when Cadbury started a
15 secret R & D project.

It was found that the latest technology
applied to chocolate manufacturing could
confer a different texture and new eating
characteristics on the classic milk chocolate
20 product.

All the pre-launch research suggested that
the product was a winner. However, as
years of bitter experience have taught many
manufacturers in this market, having a
product that the public likes is not always 25
enough. The complete marketing package is
just as critical.

Nothing new under the sun

This was the attitude of most consumers to
chocolate products. They simply didn't 30
believe you could produce anything new.
Reversing this belief was the problem facing
the Young and Rubicam advertising agency
when Cadbury brought them the product
now named 'Wispa', in 1980.   35

In October 1983 the product was launched
... Cadbury spent heavily on Television
Advertising ... and on a massive poster
campaign. Wispa is now the third largest
brand in the total confectionery market and 40
11 weeks after launch spontaneous awareness among consumers reached 73%.
Whichever way you look at it the product is
a superb technical and marketing accom-
plishment, unique in a fiercely competitive 45
market.

(Adapted from a Cadbury advertisement, *The Economist*, March 1986.)

(a)   Give three examples of what would be included in 'the complete marketing package'.
      (line 26)   (*3 marks*)
(b)   The initial launch may well have been accompanied by special pricing deals. What
      factors might the company have taken into consideration when setting the long term
      price?   (*5 marks*)
(c)   Cadbury now have three major confectionery products instead of two. What advant-
      ages does this give the company?   (*3 marks*)
(d)   Outline the factors that the company might take into consideration, before embarking
      upon a European launch of the product.   (*9 marks*)

(*Source:* AEB)

4   Study the journal article in Fig. 7.32 and answer the questions that follow it.

Almay tries men's skin care range

Almay, the leading UK hypo-allergenic cosmetics company has launched what it claimed is the first middle-market skin care range for men.

The new range, aimed at young ABC1 men is being launched through a press campaign by Lovell and Rupert Curtis Advertising.

Almay, an independent UK-distributed sister of its US namesake, is convinced this is the next major opportunity in the male cosmetic market.

"Nicholas Laboratory, which handles Almay here, has a flexible arrangement with the US allowing it to develop and launch new products off its own back," explains Lovell and Rupert Curtis' deputy managing director, Brian Hargreaves.

"There is just so much opportunity in the UK market as opposed to the US which is far more conservative," says Hargreaves.

"It is the first hypo-allergenic middle-market range for men. In the past such ranges ended to be by more up-market groups like Clinique and the men's perfume houses which tried to launch aftershave balms but not much more," he says.

The only similar ranges on the market are own-label products through Body Shop and Marks & Spencer, but neither is claimed to be hypo-allergenic.

The Almay range incorporates a moisturiser, cleanser, aftershave soother and a foaming shaving gel. All are distributed exclusively through larger Boots branches.   □

Figure 7.32 Marketing men's skin care cosmetics. (*Source*: *Marketing Week*, September 1989.)

(a) What do you understand by the terms:
   (i)   middle market;
   (ii) ABC1 men;
   (iii) launch new products.

(b) What background work would Almay have had to do before launching the product?

(c) What does the success or failure of the product depend on?

(d) How has Almay tried to increase the chances of success?

(e) What evidence is given in the article that the Almay range may be successful?

(f) Why is distribution important to the range of products?

Suggested reading

Chisnall, P., *Marketing—A behavioural analysis*. McGraw-Hill, 1985.

Chisnall, P., *Marketing Research*. McGraw-Hill, 1986.

Lancaster, G. and Massingham, L., *Essentials of Marketing*. McGraw-Hill, 1988.

Oakes, B., *Running a Good Business*. Shell Education, 1990.

8

Production

The extent to which private organizations are successful in selling their products depends on their ability to satisfy the wishes of consumers. The market might be satisfied either through the provision of a physical product or through the provision of a service. Because productive activities add value to goods and services, they create wealth.

It is possible to classify production under three headings:

1. *Primary production* This is the earliest stage in the production process and is concerned with extracting the gifts of nature. Examples of primary activity would include tree felling, fishing and agriculture.
2. *Secondary production* This is the second stage in the production process. It involves processes that transform raw materials from the primary stage into finished or part-finished products, either through constructing or manufacturing.
3. *Tertiary production* This includes the productive activities of the service sector of the economy. It comprises commercial services which facilitate business activity, such as banking and insurance, as well as direct services, which are of benefit directly to members of the community, e.g. police, teachers and nurses.

Production includes occupations from all three sectors so that, for example, a rugby league player can be just as productive as a factory superintendent. This is because all service industries have a 'production function' which serves the same purpose as the 'production function' of manufacturing industry. All industries and all occupations are concerned with adding some value to a product or service so that consumer satisfaction can be created. This feature of industrial society is of major importance and is illustrated by the following examples:

1. Forecasting college courses for the forthcoming year is similar to the production manager's assessment of capacity for the forthcoming period.
2. Organizing the flow of production is similar to producing a bus timetable.
3. All organizations, whatever their nature, aim to get the most from their labour force.

Organizations therefore depend upon the management abilities of their production or operations team to carry out the production function which performs activities necessary to satisfy the needs of the customer. Many would argue that this function is the most difficult to understand and carry out. Production often employs the largest amount of capital, assets, labour and other factors and it is important that a company has a proven strategy for dealing with problems as and when they arise. The aims of such a strategy would invariably be to:

- minimize costs;
- maximize quality;
- satisfy the requirements of customers;
- maximize the use of plant; and
- minimize the inventory.

Clearly, supervising production involves the use of a diversity of skills to control a vast volume of resources in a variety of areas which are all interdependent.

We can try to break down the function into the five broad areas shown in Fig. 8.1, though in practice there will be considerable overlap.

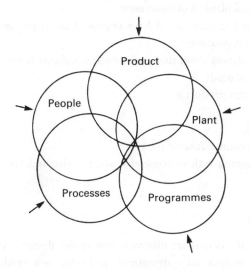

Figure 8.1 The five broad areas of production.

The product

In an ideal world a customer's needs would be spotlighted by marketeers who would then communicate this information to product developers. Too often in the past, marketing information was ignored and products were developed because production costs appeared to be low. Scant regard was paid to the demands of the market. Instead of looking at appearance, performance, quality, safety and durability, producers concentrated their efforts upon what they considered to be an efficient use of materials, skills and processes so that their profit margins could be maximized. Their approach was clearly product led rather than market led. Products *should* be designed to appeal to buyers while at the same time lending themselves to manufacture in a cost-effective way.

Case Study—Product led or market led

Examine an electrical product that you have bought in the last three years and that you use at least once a week (e.g. hair drier, stereo).

Questions

1. List five features of this product that you feel would appeal to consumers and would encourage them to buy it.
2. How would you rate the product (relative to similar products and in terms of value for money) in the following areas:
   (a) appearance;
   (b) special features;
   (c) safety;
   (d) durability and planned obsolescence.
3. What qualities and features could have improved the appearance and performance of this product?
4. What features or details about this product might indicate to you that it has been mass produced?
5. Do you feel that this product is:
   (a) market led;
   (b) product led;
   (c) an effective combination of the two.
6. Discuss your response with someone else who has also undertaken this exercise.

Research and development

A *new* design is one in which the details are different from earlier designs. The responsibility of management is to seek out systematically and select new products as well as to create the sort of working atmospheres that will encourage the creation of new ideas. The opportunity, or sometimes the necessity, to progress may occur in a number of ways:

1. *A chance idea* This might be based upon a technical report, a discussion with colleagues or simply an invention from an original thought. For example, Nick Munro the winner of the Shell Livewire competition (a business competition for young people) in 1988 came up with the original idea for an egg cup design purely by chance. One day he was simply playing around with an old bedspring when he noticed it was the ideal shape for an egg holder. Using the original design and some new materials he had stumbled across a winner!

2. *To fill a gap in a commercial range*   The existing range may have a number of gaps which need to be filled and a new product may enable the firm to provide a more comprehensive selection. For example, textbook publishers will try to develop a portfolio of textbooks. A publisher with established GCSE textbooks in business studies and economics may seek to extend the range with 'A' level books.

3. *To use idle resources*   Organizations will look to maximize the use of their resources. Unoccupied plant, unused machinery and idle cash reserves need to be put to work. By producing a new product, the firm might be able to mobilize its excess capacity. For example, a magazine publisher may only need to use its printing press for a few days in the month to produce a particular magazine. The plant could be used more effectively by producing additional titles or taking on smaller jobs for paying customers.

4. *To spread the risk through product diversification*   If a range of products is too narrow it can present a real danger, particularly in a rapidly changing market. This is particularly true in the production of fashion items such as clothes, where demand for styles may be for a few short months.

5. *To gain prestige*   Producing a good quality 'flagship' commodity may improve the image of an existing range. For example, Concorde acts as a 'flagship' for British Airways.

There are a number of stages which can be identified in the preparation of a launch of a new product (see Fig. 8.2). As new products and ideas go through successive stages, unsuccessful ones are eliminated.

Testing a concept will involve trying to make sure that the product on the drawing board will succeed in the marketplace. This will involve asking questions such as:

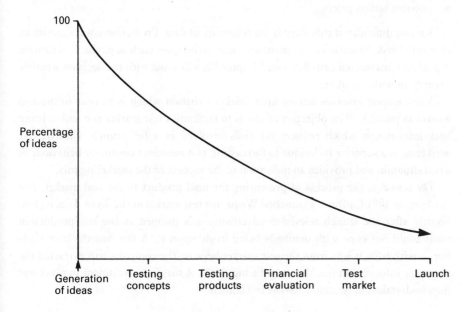

Figure 8.2 Stages in launching a new product.

- What benefits does this product offer compared to the competition?
- What appeals to the consumer?
- Does the product meet the needs of the market?
- How can the idea be improved upon?
- How long will there be a demand for the product?

Testing the product will involve developing a prototype and then trying to see if it matches consumer needs. The objective at this stage will be to understand the problems by looking at such areas as:

- quality, performance and safety;
- ensuring that the product works efficiently;
- ensuring that it is aesthetically sound and that the psychological effect of its appearance is pleasing to consumers;
- the ability to produce it economically;
- planned obsolescence so that the product will need replacing after a given period of time;
- the ingredients of the marketing mix (see Chapter 7).

In certain cases it may be worth while for a company to apply for a patent, which is a legal protection, giving the exclusive right to produce and sell a given item.

Financial evaluation of a new product's potential is essential to assess whether or not it will ultimately generate profits. In order to apply investment appraisal techniques the company will need to make accurate predictions of:

- sales;
- the investment required;
- the costs of manufacturing and marketing;
- possible selling prices.

A major difficulty at this stage is the reliability of data. Prediction always carries an element of risk. Standard investment appraisal techniques such as payback, return on capital and discounted cash flow (see Chapter 10) will assist with the decision whether to carry on with a project.

A *test market* involves setting up a market situation which is as near to the real market as possible. The objective of this is to facilitate a test market run and to bring back information which reduces the risks involved in a full launch. Clearly, test marketing is a superior technique to forecasting as it measures consumer behaviour in a real situation and provides an indication of the success of the marketing mix.

The launch is the process of presenting the final product to the real market. For example, in 1981 Cadbury's launched Wispa in a test market in the Tyne Tees region. Shortly after the launch television advertising was stopped as the test production plant could not cope with demands being made upon it. A few months later Cadbury's withdrew Wispa from the test market because the company had extracted the necessary information (i.e. that it had a big 'hit'!). A massive investment in plant was then undertaken in readiness for the full launch.

When a Japanese manufacturer wants to find out about changing consumer tastes and fashions, it will sometimes open a shop or restaurant where new product and service ideas can be tested and where the consumer responses can be monitored.

Called 'antenna shops' because they are used both to 'broadcast' ideas from the manufacturer and to 'receive' ideas from consumers, they are concentrated in the fashionable districts of Tokyo and a few other major cities.

For Nissui, Japan's largest fishery company, the problem was that fish was becoming unfashionable among young Japanese, many of whom thought it smelly and unappealing.

To counteract this trend, Nissui developed new fish products for modern tastes such as frozen tempura and fresh frozen oysters. Spicy red chilli peppers were added to liven up canned fish and ranges of fish *hors d'oeuvre* garnished with mustard relishes were launched.

To taste-test its new ranges and to explore how the Japanese could be wooed back, the company opened up a number of antenna restaurants, flying in fresh fish from around the world to try and start new fashions.

Computer aided design (CAD)

The purpose of computer aided engineering is to use computers to solve engineering problems. Design engineers, particularly in high technology industries, have used computers to model designs mathematically and to solve design problems for many years. Using computers has made possible the creation of sophisticated graphics with considerable savings in time and effort.

Computer aided design refers to the application of a computer to solve design problems. A CAD system will consist of a computer, a workstation and a graphics board with a magnetic pen which enables the operator to touch symbols and select options so that a design can be made up. This technique can be used to draw the following:

- two-dimensional engineering drawings;
- design layouts;
- three-dimensional views and models;
- electronic printed circuit board design layouts;
- architectural drawings.

CAD has completely transformed the role of the designer. Companies now need to use CAD to remain competitive and to minimize their costs. Developments in artificial intelligence, mathematical modelling, and other areas represent fundamental changes in the ways in which the needs of consumers can be noticed, catered for and ultimately satisfied.

Value analysis

The objective of value analysis is to satisfy the customer as economically as possible.

Design, manufacturing and distribution techniques and methods will be examined in order to cut out any unnecessary expenditure.

For example, if designers were left free to operate without cost control guidelines, they would undoubtedly produce components of a higher quality than those required for a specific task. This could be costly, fail to satisfy the manufacturer's objectives and would not be seen as value for money by the purchaser.

A value analysis team will be made up of experienced personnel with the specialist knowledge to be able to contribute to cost-cutting decisions. Such a team might include, for example:

- a designer—for knowledge of the product;
- a member of the sales team—for knowledge of the market;
- a production engineer—for knowledge of processes;
- a member of the work study staff—for experience of efficient working procedures;
- an accountant—for the ability to analyse costs;
- a buyer—for specialist knowledge of sources of supply.

Each of these members would try to ensure that the new product provides the customer with real value for money.

Product life cycle

Constant changes in the marketplace will determine the success or failure of a product. In the same way that marketing managers are interested in changing tastes and fashions and their impact upon a product's sales performance, designers will wish to base their plans upon what they expect a product's lifespan to be. Life cycles for different products might vary considerably in length. Designers must keep in touch so that the right product can be put forward, tested and developed at precisely the right time. As Chapter 7 points out, careful timing of a portfolio is essential.

The plant

In order to manufacture the product or to provide a service some sort of plant or base is necessary. Often the plant accounts for the larger proportion of a company's fixed assets and could involve a massive capital injection. The location, size, capacity, design, layout, performance of equipment and safety of the plant are all of fundamental importance to the production manager.

The location of the factory

The location of the factory will undoubtedly have a major effect upon its performance. The problems of location are long term, and clearly decisions taken today have implications for tomorrow. For many smaller businesses, the problem is not so much one of location but one of finding a site. An owner who lives in a specific area may not

want to set up a business away from his immediate locality. The local area may provide the entire market for a small local business such as that of a plumber, electrician or fast food seller. In contrast, large companies may have the world as their market and numerous factors taken together are capable of influencing any decision that is taken.

Whatever the type of business, the aim will be to locate in an area where the difference between benefits and costs is maximized. Important considerations will be those of minimizing unit costs and maximizing outputs from given quantities of resources.

Some of the important factors influencing the choice of location are:

1. *Transport* In situations where raw materials or finished goods are bulky, the importance of transport costs are more significant. If the output of an industry is more expensive to transport than its input, it is a *bulk-increasing industry*, and is more likely to locate near to the *market* (see Fig. 8.3). For example, many of the platforms and other bulky equipment used in North Sea exploration are likely to be built and assembled on the North Sea coast both for financial reasons and because of the difficulty of overland transport.

On the other hand, if the raw materials are bulky, expensive to transport and the industry is a *bulk-decreasing industry* it would be beneficial to locate near to *raw materials* (see Fig. 8.3). For example, the steel industry tends to locate near to sources of coal, iron ore and limestone.

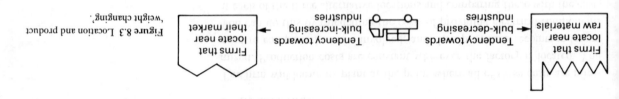

Figure 8.3 Location and product 'weight changing'.

In practice, decisions are not as clear-cut as theory would indicate. Markets tend to be spread out and raw materials tend to come from a number of suppliers. The type of industry, the spread of the market, the availability of raw materials and their influences upon the costs of transport all have to be weighed against each other.

Case Study—High Tech Operations Limited

High Tech Operations Limited is a firm in the electrical components industry which is in the process of reviewing its present location at site D (see Fig. 8.4). *A, B and C are three possible alternative locations for an electrical components factory.*

The management at High Tech understands the need to take many

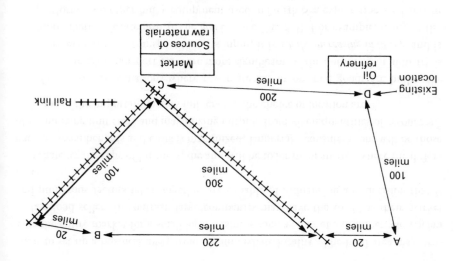

Figure 8.4 Alternative locations for an electrical components firm.

factors into consideration when deciding upon the most appropriate location. These factors include:

- The cost of transporting finished goods to the market.
- The cost of transporting raw materials and oil supplies to the plant.
- Grants and other inducements available from the government.
- Labour costs.
- Removal costs.

The firm will locate its plant at the point where all of these costs are minimized. Production costs are constant wherever the factory is located. You need to compare the costs involved, and then provide a recommendation. You can do this by calculating the costs of providing electrical components at each of the three alternative locations and comparing these with the costs of staying at the existing location.

The preferred location will be the one with the lowest cost. The market for components exists at location C and locations A and B are eligible for government grants.

For each 1000 electrical components:

- Transporting oil is £2 per mile by road and 50p per mile by rail.
- Transporting raw materials from C is £4 per mile by road and 70p per mile by rail.
- Labour costs are £1300 at A, £1400 at B, £1300 at C and £1500 at D.
- Transporting finished goods to the market at C is £5 per mile by road and £1 per mile by rail.
- Removal costs would be spread over 10 years and would be £1000 per 1000 units per annum.
- Government grants reduce costs by 20 per cent.

Work out the costs by copying out and filling in the table.

	A	B	C	D
	£	£	£	£
Oil transport costs				
Raw material transport costs				
Labour costs				
Finished goods transport costs				
Removal costs				
Effects of government grants				
Total cost per 1000 units				

Questions

1. Find the lowest cost location.
2. Production is forecast at 492 000 units for next year. How much would moving to the lowest cost location save in the first 12 months?
3. What additional information do you think would help the firm in making a locational decision?
4. What factors are likely to alter, which could upset the calculations you have made?

2. *Integration with group companies* A large company will want to locate a factory where its work can be integrated with the work of other companies in the same group. The ease with which it can integrate will influence its location.

3. *Labour/housing* Labour and skills are more readily available in some areas than in others. Providing labour with incentives to move can be expensive and has had little success. There are also a number of problems associated with housing costs. House prices in some parts of the South East and in other areas discourage the movement of workers from other areas. These factors inhibit the mobility of labour, so that many firms will find that it is easier to move work to the workers rather than to try and encourage workers to move to the work.

4. *Amenities* There are five standard amenities to be considered: gas, electricity, water, disposal of waste and drainage. For example, certain industries use considerable reserves of water such as for food preparation, metal plating, and paper production. Their use of water could exert considerable pressures upon a local system. In the same way, the disposal of waste can be an expensive business and an assessment must be made of these requirements, as underestimating the cost of amenities can be costly and problematic.

5. *Land* Land costs will vary from area to area and some organizations will need a larger square footage than others. In certain circumstances the geology of the area needs to be looked at, e.g. whether the land can support heavy weights. The climate may affect the manufacturing process. For example, the Mars confectionary company occasionally has to shut down its Mars Bar production line in a very

hot summer—it would not be wise for the company to produce the product in a very hot country. Local regulations may affect certain types of activity and these need to be checked. It would be unwise to build a factory that used up all the land available on a given site with no room available for expansion. A large employer will need to provide parking space, investigate public transport facilities, etc.

6. *Regional advantages*   Locating in an area which contains similar businesses, suppliers and markets may be a considerable advantage. Local research facilities, technical college expertise and commercial expertise may be of use.

7. *Safety requirements*   Certain types of industry may be considered to be a danger or a nuisance to their local environment, e.g. nuclear power stations, munitions factories and some chemical works. Locating certain plants away from high-density population levels is considered desirable.

8. *Communications*   Accessibility of ports, airports and motorways has become an increasingly important factor over recent years. A developing infrastructure will encourage industry to move to a region. Recent examples of towns that have boomed partly as a result of motorway and rail connections have been North-ampton and Telford while the whole of the M4 corridor between Wales and London has felt the effect of improved communications. A large number of major companies have found it necessary to locate head offices in the South East and yet their production units operate elsewhere!

9. *Government influences*   High levels of unemployment in certain areas which are disproportionate to levels in other parts of the country were undoubtedly a prominent feature of the 1980s and are likely to be so in the 1990s. The decline of many heavy industries upon which certain areas were dependent has reaped cata-strophic consequences. The North/South divide has become a disputed and fre-quently discussed topic of conversation. Governments look towards balanced growth and, in order to overcome hardships, provide packages of incentives to encourage firms to move to areas of particular hardship.

Wherever a factory locates there will be certain limiting factors to the choice of site. For example, a chemical plant needs to be near vast sources of water, a large engineering workshop will need to be close to its labour force, and an ice cream seller needs to be close to customers. Choosing a site means taking a number of relevant factors into consideration and attempting to weigh them up in relation to each other. Sometimes a ranking technique which gives appropriate weights to relevant factors can be helpful. Factors affecting location are assigned weights relative to their importance and each location is examined and ranked in terms of each factor. When ranks have been multiplied by the weighting factor and the scores totalled, the desirability of loca-tions can be compared. An example of such comparison is illustrated in Fig. 8.5.

In the example in Fig. 8.5 the rank attached to the relative importance of each locational factor for each location appears in the top left-hand corner of each cell and the rank multiplied by the weight appears underneath the diagonal. Location D is shown as the most desirable location using this method.

Factor	Weight	Possible Location A		Possible Location B		Possible Location C		Possible Location D	
		A		B		C		D	
Transport	7	1	7	2	14	2	14	4	28
Integration with group	2	4	8	3	6	1	2	2	4
Amenities	4	1	4	4	16	6	24	1	4
Land	2	1	2	2	4	1	2	5	10
Regional advantages	3	2	6	3	9	1	3	5	15
Communications	6	2	12	3	18	2	12	1	6
Government grants	2	6	12	1	2	1	2	3	6
Totals			51		69		59		73

Figure 8.5 Possible factory location by rank and weight.

The size of the factory

Firms will often generate operational benefits if they produce goods in large volumes. Whereas bridges and submarines will never be mass produced, the vast majority of everyday consumer goods can be. The scale or size of production is usually measured by the number of units produced over a period of time. If the scale of production increases, average unit costs over most production ranges are likely to fall because the firm will benefit from *economies of scale* (the advantages it gains from becoming larger). All businesses will aim for the scale of production which suits their line of work best and this will be achieved when unit costs are at their lowest for the output produced. Beyond this point a firm will start to find that inefficiencies push average costs up and *diseconomies of scale* account for this (i.e. the disadvantages of growing too large).

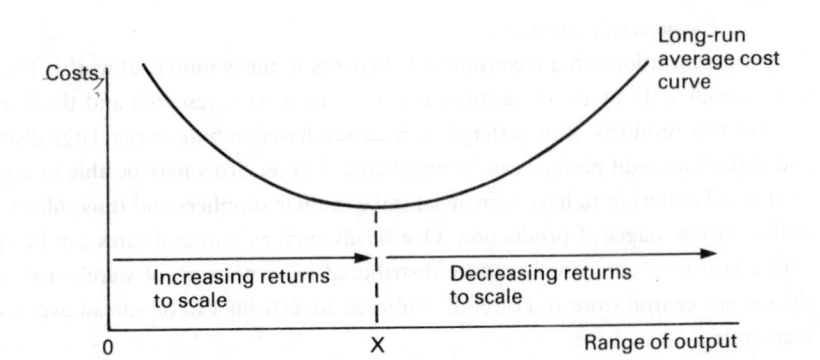

Figure 8.6 Returns to scale.

If output increases faster than the rate of inputs, average unit costs will be falling and a firm is said to be benefiting from increasing returns to scale. Beyond the point at which average unit costs are at their lowest the increase in output will be less than the increase in input, so that average unit costs are pushed up and the firm is suffering from decreasing returns to scale (see Fig. 8.6).

If, as the firm becomes larger, it manages to organize its production more efficiently, it is benefiting from *internal* economies of scale. If that firm is a member of an industry which is growing, benefits will be felt outside the individual firms, i.e. by all the firms in an industry and are known as *external* economies of scale.

Internal economies

Technical economies

Large organizations use techniques and equipment which cannot be adopted by small-scale producers. For example, a firm might have four machines each producing 1000 units per week at a unit cost of £2; as the firm becomes larger these could be replaced by one machine which produces 5000 units per week at the lower unit cost of £1.75. If small firms tried to use such specialized machinery, costs would be excessive and the machines might become obsolete before the end of their physical life. (Economic lifespan of machines may be shorter than their physical life because demand for the goods produced by the machines will diminish before the machine wears out.) An essential by-product of higher-tech operations is that processes are simplified and standardized so that cost reductions can be made in other areas, e.g. labour.

Labour and managerial economies

In larger organizations highly skilled workers can be employed in jobs which fully utilize their specialized skills whereas in a small business unit they might have to be a 'Jack of all trades'. This element of division of labour therefore avoids the time-wasting element caused by the constant need to switch from one type of job to another. In the same way a larger firm can also employ a number of highly specialized members of its management team such as accountants, marketing managers, personnel managers, etc., in the hope that the improved quality of work and decisions made by this more qualified workforce will reduce overall unit costs.

Commercial economies

Larger organizations obtain considerable benefits in the commercial world. They can gain considerably by devoting more resources to market research and the development of new products. Raw materials can be purchased in bulk so that large discounts and extended credit periods can be negotiated. Larger firms may be able to organize their retail outlets or to have a financial stake in their suppliers and thus collect profit at the various stages of production. Overheads such as rent and rates can be spread over a larger output. Goods can be distributed via a network of warehouses rather than at one central store and carefully targeted advertising can be spread over a wider marketplace.

Financial economies

As larger companies tend to present a more secure investment they find it easier to raise finance. For example, during the early 1980s, in a period of recession when businesses often required periods of extended credit, many large companies were kept afloat by securing bank loans whereas smaller organizations with similar problems were often treated less favourably. Larger firms are in a better position to negotiate loans at preferential interest rates. A further financial advantage to large firms is their ability to raise capital by issuing new shares on the Stock Exchange.

Risk-bearing economies

As well as having a financial stake in suppliers and outlets, a larger firm may have the opportunity to diversify by investing in a variety of new operations in order to spread risks. By spending more on research and development and producing a wider product range, a business covers itself against any loss of business in certain areas.

External economies

In many industries the reduction of average unit costs and the benefits of internal economies of scale will depend upon the ability of a company to increase the length of production runs, introduce mass production and standardization techniques and increase the output capacity of the industry as a whole. This could lead to the following external economies of scale:

Concentration

A concentration of special benefits builds up as firms within an industry concentrate in a particular locality. These benefits of concentration may include: a skilled workforce, the development of the reputation of an area for high quality work, local college courses tailored to the needs of a particular industry, and better social amenities.

Information

Larger industries often set up information services designed to benefit producers such as the Motor Industry Research Association.

Disintegration

Firms producing components or supplying specialist machinery might well be attracted to areas of specialized industries as well as where there are firms able to help with maintenance and processes.

Case Study—Summers Shoes

You are trying to describe to a friend the benefits of economies of scale. Use the table to justify the points you make. Explain why you prefer to work for a

The number of machines used to produce shoes per hour

Hourly output (in pairs)	Number of machines	Machines per pair per hour
200	33	0.165
400	41	0.102
600	47	0.078
800	53	0.066
1000	58	0.058
2000	102	0.051

large organization like Summers Shoes rather than for a small-scale producer. Alternatively, explain why you may prefer to work for a small-scale producer.

Organizations can obtain the benefits of economies of scale through a gradual build-up of their business through acquiring assets, developing products and/or expanding sales. *Organic growth* of this kind, however, is often a slow business. A quicker and more dynamic form of growth is through mergers or take-overs which involve the *integration* of a number of business units under a single umbrella organization.

As well as enjoying the benefits of being larger the new organization will have a larger market share, will probably be more competitive in export markets and, depending on the type of merger, could be in a position to control raw material supplies or the sales of the finished product. A *horizontal merger* takes place when two firms producing goods of a similar type at the same stage of production join together. A *vertical merger* takes place when two firms producing goods of a similar type at different stages of production join together. *Backward* vertical integration would involve the take-over of a supplier and *forward* vertical integration would involve joining with a firm at a later stage of production. Figure 8.7 illustrates the way in which a car manufacturer may integrate horizontally and vertically.

It is common practice today for firms in industries which are only loosely con-

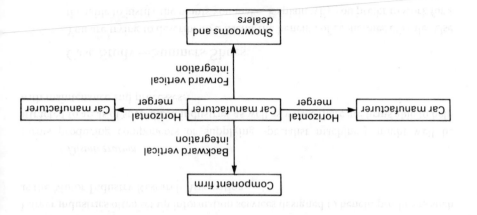

Figure 8.7 Forms of integration.

nected to join together in order to maximize risk-bearing economies. For example, a firm producing toothpaste may join with a soap manufacturer in order to benefit from similar channels of distribution. A firm producing a product which is going out of fashion, e.g. record players, may choose to join with a company producing a completely unconnected product which is becoming popular, e.g. compact disc players.

Case Study—Mergers

Study the financial pages of newspapers and professional business magazines and make a list of some of the recent mergers of larger companies. Find out about the main trading activities of the companies involved and comment on whether the mergers were horizontal, vertical or lateral. What motivations would you expect to lie behind the merger?

You will often find that businesses will be prepared to reply to a letter that you send seeking information about why a particular merger has taken place. Do not be afraid to write. In this way you will uncover some excellent first hand data.

Mergers can sometimes lead to an undesirable level of competition (i.e. too little competition) or the optimum size of a business could easily be exceeded. Large organizations are considerably more difficult to manage and these inefficiencies are known as *diseconomies of scale*. These include:

1. *Human relations* Larger numbers of workers are always more difficult to organize. It can be difficult to communicate information and instructions which need to be passed down long chains of command reduce the personal contact between senior staff and shop floor workers. This can lead to a low level of morale, lack of motivation and ultimately industrial relations problems. Larger firms tend to be involved in more industrial disputes than smaller firms.

2. *Decisions and coordination* The sheer scale of production may limit the management's ability to respond to change and make good decisions. With a large hierarchy, both the quality of the information reaching the decision maker and the quality of the instructions passed on could be affected. Difficulties arising from discussions could involve considerable paperwork and many meetings. It is difficult for such organizations to provide a personal interest in satisfying customer requirements.

3. *External diseconomies* In recent years many consumers have become more discerning both about the quality of products and the activities of companies. Public displeasure can turn to action such as consumer boycotts and this can affect output. Many consumers feel concerned about the number of additives in food and are not prepared to purchase those goods which do not meet up to their requirements. Some large stores refuse to stock South African goods and the campaign for real ale caused brewing combines to alter radically their production policies in the 1970s.

Not only is the existence of small business units necessary because of diseconomies of scale, they also obtain many separate and vital economic advantages. They can operate in competitive markets, take risks and have the flexibility to respond quickly. Small firms often specialize and so contribute towards division of labour within the wider productive process. Relations with both employers and customers tend to be good and, though specialists are not employed on a full-time basis, consultants can be called in.

Clearly some industries will suit larger scale organization better than others. A firm needs to look carefully at the effects of size upon its cost structure before deciding upon the most appropriate scale for its productive unit.

There may be little scope for economies of scale because of limited demand. The small corner shop, for example, may cater for a limited local demand, or the product may be highly specialized as in the case of the market for 'customized' motor bikes.

Government policy also plays a part in encouraging smaller businesses, for example, the Department of Employment runs over 200 schemes to help small businesses. In the late 1980s the Conservative Government introduced a number of regulations designed to chip away the whole field of government regulation to keep down the number and cost of requirements including: tax changes, some easing of planning controls, VAT changes to help small businesses, much wider choice of opening hours for some 100 000 pubs, bars and clubs, and the deregulation of new residential lettings by private landlords.

Design and layout of plant and equipment

The design of a plant and the positioning of equipment should enable it to function efficiently. Though designing the layout is normally a work study problem, it needs to be carried out with specialist engineers who are concerned with factors such as the structure of the plant, power availability, maintenance requirements, and so on.

Plant layout tends to follow a number of basic designs:

1.   With *product or line layout* plant is laid out according to the requirements of the product in a line of production. Products 'flow' from one machine or stage to

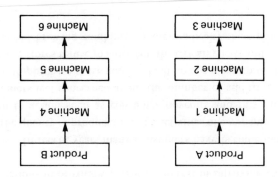

Figure 8.8 Product layout.

another. Control is simplified as paper work, material handling and inspection procedures are reduced (for example, see Fig. 8.8).

2. With a *function or process layout* all operations of the same type are performed in the same area, e.g. spot welding may be in one location, riveting in another, stapling in another, etc. It is rather like the provision of a typing pool or central-ized photocopying in a large institution. Though this system is flexible, consider-able pre-production planning is necessary to ensure that machines are neither overloaded nor idle (see Fig. 8.9).

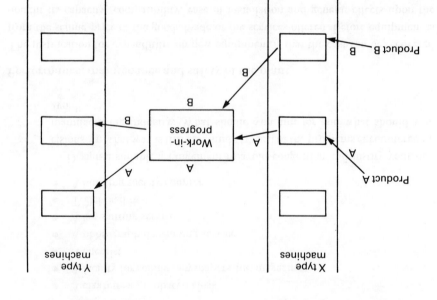

Figure 8.9 Process layout.

3. With *layout by fixed position* operations are performed with the material or part-finished good returning to a fixed location after each process (see Fig. 8.10). Whatever techniques are used in setting up a layout the aim must be to maximize

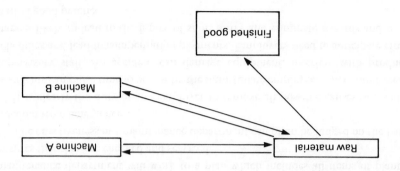

Figure 8.10 Fixed position layout.

flexibility and the ease of coordination so that process time and costs will be minimized.

Case Study—The supermarket

You have been given the responsibility of planning the entrance layout of a large hypermarket and have been asked to draw up a chart suggesting locations for the following:

- A bay of trolleys
- A cigarette and tobacco kiosk
- A facility for selling newspapers and magazines
- A chemist
- A photograph developing service
- A key cutting service
- Toilet facilities
- A building society counter

Design a suitable arrangement to avoid congestion and justify your decisions. In what way is this case study typical of the problems encountered in manufacturing industry? What should you aim for and what should you avoid?

Performance, maintenance and safety of the plant

The justification for expenditure on new equipment is that the cost can be recovered from the selling price of the goods made or the services offered. Before equipment is bought its capacity, compatibility, ease of installation and general effects upon the existing organization are carefully evaluated so that the standard economic appraisal techniques such as payback, return on capital and DCF can be accurately considered. Maintenance of plant and equipment is essential for the efficient operation of any factory, to ensure that valuable production time is not lost. Though operators look after machines and keep them clean, maintenance is carried out as a specialist service to production. A typical maintenance department will include a cross-section of specialist technicians such as electricians, plumbers, millwrights and others. Each maintenance department will work to a plan which includes all items of plant and ensures that they are checked and serviced.

The effectiveness of a maintenance department can often be judged on the basis of freedom from emergencies.

It is clearly the duty of any employer to remove all possible causes of accidents. Accidents can cause time to be lost by the unfortunate employee, other employees and supervisory staff. An accident can damage equipment, interfere with production schedules and lead to compensation payments. Employers need to anticipate circumstances likely to lead to the injury of staff, to try and eliminate hazards and to train staff in good practice.

The process

There are three main types of process: job, batch and flow production. The operation of each type of production will depend upon the stage of a company's development, the nature of the work and the conditions necessary for working. Many factories start on a job production basis and, as they develop and become larger, move to batch production and finish up with flow production. It is, however, rare to find any one factory where only one type of production is carried out. Certain items tend to be produced individually under job production conditions, others in batches, and others in a flow.

Job production

Job or 'make complete' production is the manufacture of single individual items by either one operative or teams of operatives, e.g. the Humber Bridge or a frigate for the navy. It is possible for a number of identical units to be produced in parallel under job production, e.g. several frigates of a similar type. Smaller projects can also be seen as a form of job production, e.g. hand knitting a sweater, writing a book, rewiring a house, etc. Job production is unique in the fact that the project is considered to be a single operation which requires the complete attention of the operative before he or she passes on to the next job.

The benefits of job production are:

1. The job is a unique product which exactly matches the requirements of the customer, often from the very early as the design stage. It will therefore tend to be specific to a customer's order and not in anticipation of a sale. For example, someone doing a customized spray paint job on a motorcycle will first discuss with a customer the sort of design he would like. A detailed sketch would then be produced on a piece of paper. Once the sketch has been approved the back of the sketch will be chalked over and traced on to the relevant piece of the motorbike. The background work is then sprayed on with an airbrush before the fine detail is painted on. The finished work is then inspected by the customer who will pay for a unique product.

2. As the work is concentrated on a specific unit, supervision and inspection of work are relatively simple.

3. Specifications for the job can change during the course of production depending upon the customer's inspection to meet his or her changing needs. For example, when a printing firm is asked to produce a catalogue for a grocery chain it is relatively simple to change the prices of some of the goods listed in the catalogue.

4. Working on a single unit job, coping with a variety of tasks and being part of a small team working towards the same aim would provide employees with a greater level of satisfaction. For example, a football team would treat each new match as a specific job, with particular tactics to be employed, plans for marking key opponents, etc.

There are however a number of problems:

1. Labour, plant and machinery need to be versatile in order to adjust to a range of relatively specialized tasks associated with the same job. Trying to provide the right type of tools, equipment and labour to cope with such a range of specialized operations may be expensive. For example, if you want someone to produce photocopies for you of a document there is a range of outlets you can go to, e.g. the local library, and small bookshops. However, if you want colour photocopies you will find it difficult to find a supplier. The main reason is because demand for this service is relatively low given existing prices (1989). Few suppliers are prepared to invest in expensive colour photocopiers given the limited demand for jobs that require such a facility.

2. Because job production is unique, costing is based upon uncertain predictions of future costs and not upon the experience of past events. The builder who agrees to put up a village hall for a given price may find that the unforeseen difficulties of the job eat into profits.

3. Unit costs tend to be high. For example there will be fewer economies such as bulk purchasing and the division of labour.

Batch production

The term batch refers to a specific group of components which go through a production process together. As one batch finishes, the next one starts.

For example, on Monday Machine A produces a type 1 engine part, on Tuesday it produces a type 2 engine part, on Wednesday a type 3 engine part, and so on. All engine parts will then go forward to the final assembly of different categories of engine parts.

Batches are continually processed through each machine before moving on to the next operation. This method is sometimes referred to as 'intermittent' production as different job types are held as work-in-progress between the various stages of production.

The benefits of batch production are:

1. It is particularly suitable for a wide range of nearly similar goods which can use the same machinery on different settings.
2. It economizes upon the range of machinery needed and reduces the need for a flexible workforce.
3. Units can respond quickly to customer orders by moving buffer stocks of work-in-progress or partly completed products through the final production stages.
4. It makes possible economies of scale in techniques of production, bulk purchasing and areas of organization.
5. It makes costing easy and provides a better information service for management.

Problems associated with batch production include:

1. The considerable organizational difficulties associated with batch production, e.g. sequencing batches from one job to another to avoid building up excessive or idle stocks of work-in-progress is difficult in terms of routeing and scheduling.
2. The time lag between an initial investment in material and its eventual transfer into cash upon the sale of a product.
3. The time spent by staff upon problems of paperwork, stock control and effective plant utilization.
4. The need for part of a batch to be held waiting until the rest is completed before moving on to another stage.

Flow production

Batch production is described as 'intermittent' production and is characterized by irregularity. If the rest period in batch production disappeared it would then become flow production. Flow production is therefore a continuous process of parts passing on from one stage to another until completion. Units are worked upon in each operation and then passed straight on to the next work stage without waiting for the batch to be completed. To make sure that the production line can work smoothly each operation must be of equal length and there should be no movements or leakages from the line, i.e. hold-ups to work-in-progress.

For flow production to be successful there needs to be a continuity of demand. If demand varied this would lead to a constant overstocking of finished goods (or periodic shortages if the flow is kept at a low level). Apart from minor differences, all flow products need to be standardized as flow lines cannot deal with variations in the product.

Achieving a smooth flow of production requires considerable pre-production planning to ensure that raw materials are purchased and delivered on time, that sufficient labour is employed, that inspection procedures fit in with the process and that all operations take the required time.

For example, we will assume that a production level of 800 units per hour is required and there are three stages in the process requiring the use of Machine A for Stage 1, which can process 200 units per hour; Machine B for Stage 2, which can process 100 units per hour; and Machine C for Stage 3, which can process 400 units per hour. How can a balanced production flow be established (see Fig. 8.11)?

Case Study—Town traffic

Carefully consider the traffic situation within your local town or city. Try to identify roads or traffic areas that are processed by:

- batch
- flow

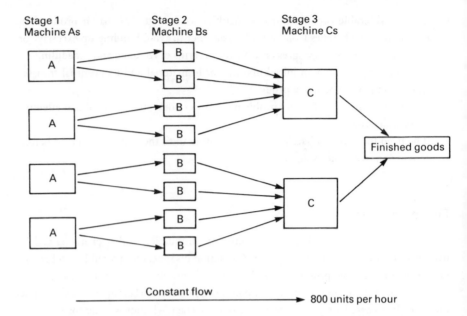

Figure 8.11 Flows in production.

Questions

1. What factors influence the ways in which traffic is processed?
2. How could particular situations be improved?

The benefits of flow production are:

1. Labour costs will tend to be reduced as comprehensive planning and often investment will generate economies in both the type and numbers of those employed.
2. Deviations in the line can be quickly spotted through inspection.
3. As there is no rest between operations, work-in-progress levels can be kept low.
4. The need for storage space is minimal as there is no waiting period between processes.
5. The physical handling of items is reduced.
6. Investments in raw materials are more quickly converted into sales.
7. As material and line requirements are easy to assess, weaknesses are highlighted and control is more effective.

There are, however, a number of problems:

1. It is sometimes difficult to balance the output of one stage with the input of another, and operations may function at different speeds.
2. Flow production requires constant work study.
3. Providing a workforce with diverse skills to cater for circumstances such as cover for absence may be difficult and excessive and regular absences may have far-reaching effects.

4. Parts and raw materials need to arrive on time.
5. Maintenance must be preventative to ensure that emergencies do not cause the flow to stop.
6. If demand falters overstocking may take place.

Simplification, standardization and specialization

Production variety is inevitable within all industrial units. While variety is clearly sometimes desirable, increases in variety are bound to add organizational problems. For example, an increase in the number of component types will require more space in the stores. Control of variety is essential in reducing storage space, the number of production runs, types of machines, production aids and in making production control easier (see Fig. 8.12). As firms move towards specialization, opportunities increase for *mass production*. Mass production is the production of goods on a large scale and can be applied to job, batch or flow production. It will usually follow that the greater the volume of mass production, the greater the benefits of economies of scale as the firm moves towards its lowest unit cost size. It is often assumed that mass production will affect quality. However, this is rarely the case. With mass production, quality will be more uniform and will not depend upon the scale of production but upon the skill of the managers.

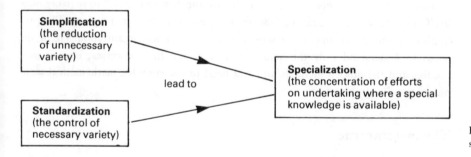

Figure 8.12 Simplification, standardization and specialization.

CADCAM and CIM

Over recent years considerable developments in technology have taken place in production industries. As well as Computer Aided Design, developments have also taken place in machine tools and many are now controlled numerically (Numerical Control—NC) or controlled numerically by a computer (Computer Numerical Control—CNC). Other developments have taken place in robotics. CADCAM (Computer Aided Design/Computer Aided Manufacturing) exists where data from the CAD system is used to drive machines and has therefore become involved in manufacturing processes.

A more recent development in this process is called Computer Integrated Manufacturing (CIM). This process goes further as not only is the product designed on a

CAD system but it also orders materials, drives CNC machine tools and his its own control system which provides data for purchasing, accounts, sales and other functions.

The production planning and control department

All organizations will make plans which are designed to fulfil their corporate function. These plans will differ according to:

- the levels of operation; and
- the time period.

Much of production planning and control will be concerned with the company's plans for the future and will need to be carefully coordinated with marketing policy, for example on areas such as product life cycles.

Looking at the near future, however, production planning and control will look at immediate concerns such as:

- How do we meet that order?
- How close is the job to completion?
- Can it be completed on time?
- Do we need to use more labour?

In order to try and cope with these problems, the department will have to organize itself in such a way as to gain the most from its materials, labour and plant. The production controller has one of the most difficult jobs in any organization. He or she needs to understand fully the organization of production processes, costing procedures and the office's methods and will need to use complex mathematical techniques to solve problems.

The programme

Programming is essentially concerned with timetabling the vast resources used by the production department. Much of its success will depend upon the abilities of the production planning and control department, whose staff will set dates and timetables for the delivery of finished products and will allocate production services accordingly. Delivery timetables will generate further timetables for areas such as purchasing, stock control and quality control.

Purchasing

Procuring materials is a key management function for any type of business. The importance of its role can be considered when one considers that an average manufacturing company spends about half of its income upon supplies of raw materials and services.

The purchasing department will aim to provide the company with a steady flow of materials and services while, at the same time, ensuring the continuity of supplies. It will aim to obtain the best value for money and will try to provide the best service for a low cost. The use of value analysis often makes it possible for considerable savings to be made, though a particular danger is that quality could be sacrificed to cost considerations. A successful purchasing department will keep costs down, produce a fast stock turnover, reduce obsolescence, ensure continuity of supply and reduce lead times (the interval between the realization of a need and its ultimate fulfilment upon delivery).

Stock control

In an ideal world where businesses know demand well in advance and where suppliers always meet delivery dates, there would be little need for stocks. In practice, demands vary and suppliers are often late and so stocks act as a protection against unpredictable events.

Businesses hold stocks in a variety of forms:

- Raw materials
- Work-in-progress
- Finished goods
- Consumables
- Plant and machinery spares

The aim of any stock control system is to provide stocks which cater for uncertainties but which are at minimum levels and so ensure that costs are kept low while, at the same time, not affecting the service to customers.

Clearly, balancing stocks at the right levels is of fundamental importance to the business. The keeping of low stocks or excessively high stocks can have harmful effects. High stocks will represent money lying idle when it could be put to better use, whereas low stocks could result in not being able to take on and meet orders. The table illustrates the disadvantages of having the 'wrong' stock levels:

Problems of low stocks	Problems of high stocks
1. It may be difficult to satisfy consumer demands.	1. There is an increased risk of a stock item becoming obsolete.
2. It can lead to a loss of business.	2. The risk of stock losses is increased.
3. It can lead to a loss of goodwill.	3. The costs of storage are high.
4. Ordering needs to be frequent and handling costs are higher.	4. Stocks can tie up a company's working capital.

Buffer stocks can be built up as a preventative measure against running out of stocks due to unexpected variations in demand. A minimum level will be set, below which it will be hoped that stocks will not fall though this may depend upon the lead time between placing an order and its receipt.

Figure 8.13 illustrates an ideal situation in which stock never falls below the set minimum stock level or goes above the set maximum stock level. Stocks will be replenished just at the point at which the minimum stock level is about to be breached. (It is worth noting that in the example, should the replacement stock not arrive on time the firm will at least be tided over by the buffer stock.) In reality, delivery times, reorder quantities and rates of usage will vary and either a continuous or periodic review system will monitor and control the levels.

At regular intervals stock is counted and accurately recorded so that trading results can be calculated. The physical counting of stock can be time consuming and it is inevitable that inaccuracies creep in. After stock is counted it is checked against records so that discrepancies can be investigated.

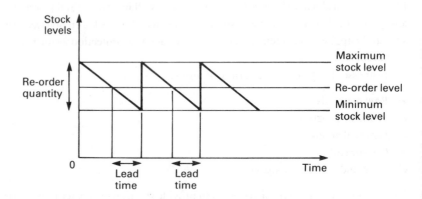

Figure 8.13 Managing stock levels.

Case Study—Computers in distribution

We have seen an enormous number of changes take place in distribution networks in recent years. The value of consumer goods distributed to the market has increased, retailing and distribution organizations have grown in average size and there has been a net decline in the number of wholesale and retail outlets. New technology has facilitated these changes by making the process more efficient and enabling better methods of selling to take place. The computer can deal with thousands of details in a systematic manner. With broad product ranges and continually changing lines the distributor needs to be continually updated with information such as:

- What stock is moving
- What stock is not moving
- Different brands
- Past sales
- Present sales
- Other information

Complex information systems make it possible for management to be given the quality of information managers need so that they have the flexibility to become involved with broader aspects of the firm's organization.

Questions

1. What is a distribution network?
2. How has new technology helped changes to take place in distribution?
3. Explain why information technology has particular importance for the area of stocks.
4. In what ways are the benefits of information technology carried through to the consumer?

Quality control

Those of us who enjoy listening to music would undoubtedly prefer to listen to the best possible system though, unfortunately, few of us can afford to do so. In the same way, many times when we purchase consumables we are aware that better models of particular items exist, but we are prepared to forfeit quality in the interest of saving money. Clearly, quality, reliability and cost should be seen as interrelated and often competing threads of production and consumption decisions.

Quality relates to the individual characteristics of each product or service which enable it to satisfy customers. The basic objective of any control system is to satisfy the customer as cheaply as possible with a product that can be delivered on time. Though quality control was seen in the past as a form of inspection department, it is seen today as a system which tries to coordinate groups in an organization to improve quality at a cost-effective level (see Fig. 8.14). In doing so they will look at:

- *Design quality*—the degree to which features within a design satisfy customers.
- *Product manufacture quality*—the success of a manufacturing process in matching design specifications.
- *Product quality*—the degree to which the finished good or service satisfies the wishes of customers.

There are five essential stages in the quality process:

1. Setting the quality required by the customer.

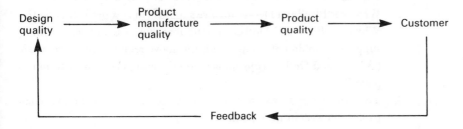

Figure 8.14 Ensuring quality control.

2. Planning to achieve the required quality, e.g. by selecting the right materials, costs of prevention such as maintenance, shop floor quality control, the training of operators and other measures.
3. Monitoring the manufacturing process.
4. Correcting any problems such as scrap.
5. Providing long-term planning.

The essential requirement of any system is a feedback so that deviations can be picked up quickly and at their source so that faults can be corrected.

Case Study—Quality control at Black and Decker

Study the information (Fig. 8.15) which is produced by Black and Decker for suppliers of Black and Decker equipment.

Preventative Quality Control

If the supply of poor quality is to be prevented then the procedures previously referred to must be enhanced by a joint Black & Decker/Supplier programme which:

- Involves suppliers at the earliest possible stage in new product design. Black & Decker is committed to listening constructively to supplier comments and expects suppliers to take this first step to avoid future quality problems.

- Will use all existing techniques and develop new ones to ensure that any new design of component when produced will consistently meet the requirements as specified — quality, supply, price.

- Requires the suppliers to submit samples of a new part only after a representative number of components have been measured (where appropriate using three dimensional equipment) and a process capability study has been completed.

- Requires the supplier, once in production, to use techniques to provide parts with a continuously improving level of uniformity. If 100% automatic process control is not feasible then Statistical Process Control will be the most appropriate technique and it is expected that all suppliers will introduce SPC as quickly as possible. Black & Decker is committed to the provision of all possible assistance.

Business will cease with all suppliers who do not comply with the above requirements after a reasonable period.

Figure 8.15 Information on quality control at Black and Decker.

Questions

1. Explain what is meant by the term Preventative Quality Control.
2. Why does Black and Decker involve suppliers in new product design?
3. Why does Black and Decker indicate that 'business will cease with all suppliers who do not comply with the above requirements'? How will (a) Black and Decker, (b) suppliers, (c) the customer, benefit from this policy?
4. To what extent do you feel that quality control is an issue that companies will wish to air in public?

Today quality is seen as part of the total business process covering every aspect of an organization's activities. The belief is that quality should concern everybody from the most junior member of staff to the most senior member of the management team.

The people

The success of the production process depends upon people. Just as with other resources, the abilities of any labour force will vary and will depend upon such elements as training, background and experience. Management will always be looking to obtain the most from employees and yet, at the same time, will want to nurture employees as a valuable resource. As the bulk of this resource will be employed in the production process, senior production staff need to be involved with policy decisions involving employees who fall within their responsibility. Not only are work study techniques important but also personnel administration concerning areas such as employment, industrial relations, staff welfare and so on.

Work study

Work study is an area which over the years has been linked with terms such as time and motion study, organization and methods, work measurement and so forth. Its primary concern is to analyse efficiency in order to maximize the use of resources. By looking at activities and the ways in which they are carried out by human and material resources, it tries to ensure that the techniques used are creating the maximum possible benefits for the company. Its objectives are:

1. To reduce costs by establishing the most cost-effective ways of doing manual work.
2. To standardize such methods.
3. To establish a time pattern.
4. To install such methods as standard working practices.

Work study therefore not only consists of a form of method study but also a form of measurement.

The *method study* will involve an examination of both existing and proposed methods of undertaking a job, in order to do the job more easily as a way of reducing costs. *Work measurement* is the establishment of techniques to time workers so that jobs can be carried out with a defined level of performance for the purpose of creating worker incentives, motivation and predictions of future performance.

The stages in a method study are given in Fig. 8.16.

Work measurement uses time study as a technique for recording the times and rates of a specified job carried out under tested conditions. The stages involved are shown in Fig. 8.17.

An essential feature of work study is the understanding of ergonomics. *Ergonomics* is the study of behaviour in the working environment. It looks at the relationship of

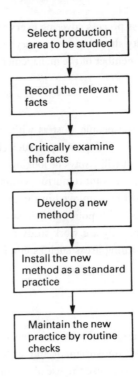

Figure 8.16 Stages of a method study.

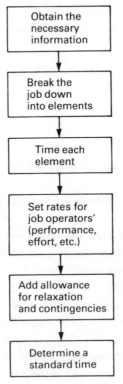

Figure 8.17 Stages of a time study.

workers to machines and tries to understand how these relationships can affect performance. For example, in the working environment it will be concerned with such questions as:

- Is it too hot/cold?
- Are noise levels too high?
- How will lighting arrangements affect operatives?

In the relationship of operator to machine it will look at issues such as:

- Are all machine performance indicators visible to the operator?
- Is the operator likely to be given too much information to handle effectively?
- Are all the controls within easy reach?
- Are seats provided?
- Are seats of the right dimensions?

In some ways ergonomics works in the opposite direction to work study in that it argues that workplaces should be designed around the capabilities of the operator. Although this field is a complex one because it involves the analysis of human behaviour, it is very important because its purpose is to produce a better, safer and more amiable working environment so that performances can be optimized.

Human relations

The practice of work study can make its practitioners unpopular because of its associations with controversial areas such as bonus payments, incentives, redeployment and redundancy. Success in handling such an exercise will clearly depend upon the abilities of management and the extent of the trust between management and workforce. Some organizations run appreciation courses to bring out the benefits of work study so as to counter misunderstandings. In doing so they try to illustrate how work study benefits the organization as a whole and so will benefit employees. In this way it can be used as an incentive for motivation. For example it could be shown that:

- using piece-work employees are paid a set amount for each unit produced, althouth there will also usually be a guaranteed minimum level;
- using measured day work, workers are guaranteed a weekly wage if a certain level of performance is achieved, but if performances are not achieved, rates are reviewed.

Other areas of policy concerning human relations have fundamental importance for production including conditions at work, safety, education and training. These topics are covered in Chapter 12.

Short answer questions

1. Explain the ways in which primary, secondary and tertiary production are:
   (a) different;
   (b) similar.
2. List three aims of a production strategy.
3. Name the 5 Ps of production.
4. List two appraisal techniques used for the financial evaluation of new products.
5. Explain the importance of value analysis.
6. Give two factors which limit the mobility of labour.   (*Source:* AEB.)
7. Explain the difference between internal and external economies of scale.
8. Distinguish between organic growth and integration.
9. Distinguish between vertical and horizontal expansion.   (*Source:* AEB.)
10. Explain what is meant by a process layout.
11. Name three differences between
    (a) job production;
    (b) batch production; and
    (c) flow production.
12. Explain why simplification and standardization lead to specialization.
13. What is meant by the term mass production?
14. Describe what is meant by CADCAM.
15. Name three day-to-day problems faced by a production controller.
16. What are the benefits of an efficient purchasing department?
17. Give four reasons why a manufacturing company might choose to hold stocks of raw materials.   (*Source:* AEB.)
18. What is the objective of a quality control department?
19. Distinguish between method study and work measurement.
20. Give one advantage and one disadvantage to a manufacturing firm for the introduction of an incentive bonus scheme.   (*Source:* AEB.)

Essays

1. (a) Why are changes in the structure of the population of interest to producers?
   (b) In what ways will these changes be viewed by:
      (i) builders of old people's residences;
      (ii) manufacturers of school uniforms?
   (c) Distinguish between the production system which might be used in producing (i) white shirts and (ii) school ties.   (*Source:* Cambridge.)
2. Discuss how systems of wage payments may sometimes conflict with quality standards.   (*Source:* Cambridge.)
3. (a) Do entrepreneurs always aim to minimize average costs when deciding on a location for a new factory?

(b)   Identify other factors which might influence the decision and explain difficulties which are likely to rise in reaching such a decision.

(Source: Cambridge)

4.   (a)   Differentiate between work measurement and method study.

(b)   What do you consider to be the main problems likely to be caused by the
introduction of a work study unit to a manufacturing firm?

(c)   Discuss the usefulness of data collected by the work study team and suggest to whom it should be made available.   *(Source:* Cambridge.)

5.   To what extent is the availability of such facilities as good restaurants, schools
and golf-courses a more important locational factor for modern Hi-tech industry than any of the conventional factors?   *(Source:* AEB.)

6.   How far do the marketing and production functions have to compromise their
objectives in order to accommodate each other?   *(Source:* AEB.)

7.   It has been asserted that management is the process of getting things done
through people. How can managers improve the productivity of their manpower without additional expenditure on capital equipment?   *(Source:* Oxford.)

8.   'Fitting the person to the job' or 'fitting the job to the person' are two of the
major approaches employed by the ergonomist. What are the main concerns of
the ergonomist in ensuring that a working environment is conducive to efficient
manufacturing?   *(Source:* Oxford.)

9.   Discuss the considerations which influence a firm in deciding between growth
by internal or external expansion.

Present a reasoned case for the criteria you feel the Government should use
in deciding whether or not some merger is against the public interest.

(Source: Oxford.)

10.   The nature of any company is influenced by:

(a)   the nature of the product;

(b)   the manufacturing process;

(c)   the market forces in its field.

What criteria is a manufacturer likely to take account of, in reconciling the different priorities arising from each of these areas?   *(Source:* Oxford.)

Data response questions

1   The following passage is adapted from Buy-outs and British Industry. Read it
carefully and answer the questions that follow.

The buy-out of companies by their management has been one of the more important changes in the UK commercial and industrial scene in recent years: a development which was taken one step further in 1982 with the staff buy-out of the National
Freight Corporation. This experience can be seen in the wider context of change
within industry which has shown an increasing tendency to emphasize smaller scale,
more autonomous units of control. In many respects we are seeing a reaction to the

increased concentration which took place through the merger activities of the 1960s and 1970s.

In general the view is that big has been disappointing, and that much of the problem can be accounted for through either the diseconomies of managerial control, or more pertinently, the effects of an increased divorce between ownership and control. The management buy-out has primarily been seen in terms of a remarriage of ownership and control. The resultant companies have had a substantial portion of the equity owned by a small management group.

(Source: Adapted from *Lloyds Bank Review*, October 1982.)

(a) What do you understand by the expression 'buy-out' in line 1?

(b) The extract argues that 'big has been disappointing' as a result of either 'diseconomies of managerial control' or 'increased divorce between ownership and control'. Elaborate on each of these arguments.

(c) Describe three examples of the problems which the new owners may face following a buy-out.

2 Micro Tech plc is a progressive and very profitable UK engineering company producing high technology equipment for the aerospace industry. Its biggest customer is the military which takes over 80%, by value, of Micro Tech's products.

An important factor in the firm's success is its ability to modify quickly its standard products and to meet a customer's special needs. It can do this by virtue of a very competent design department well-equipped with up-to-date computer-aided design (CAD) facilities.

The company employs over 500 skilled and well-trained personnel in the manufacturing processes in which it is engaged. Labour turnover is very active and there are plenty of alternative employment opportunities for Micro Tech's employees. Replacement and recruitment are a headache to the company, and the performance of the personnel department is beginning to assume a position of key importance in the company's operations. The company is facing growing competition from a number of American firms and there is evidence of Government support for these companies. At the same time there has been a change of UK Government and the new Chancellor is clearly concerned to make savings and cut back on government expenditure. This is bound to affect the economic environment in which Micro Tech is operating.

Increased overseas competition and the new UK Government's expected austerity measures were the main subjects of Micro Tech's last Board Meeting. The Board decided that the company must diversify its range of products and extend its market opportunities. Such a policy would involve the company in a significant re-equipment programme and there is considerable doubt concerning the company's capacity to finance such an investment programme from within its own resources.

(i) As Micro Tech's Personnel Manager, how would you set about tackling the company's labour turnover and recruitment problems?

(ii) Identify the characteristics of the CAD which make the facilities so important for the particular needs of Micro Tech.

(iii) What are the main mechanisms available to the UK Government to shape the environment within which companies such as Micro Tech operate?

(iv) What financial alternatives are available to the Board which might facilitate a capital investment programme and allow Micro Tech to diversify its range of products?

On what basis might Micro Tech choose among these alternatives? Make your assumptions clear.

(Source: Oxford.)

3   Rowntree gets a taste for success.

The Rowntree revolution started at the top and nobody knows for certain where it will end.

For the chairman, Kenneth Dixon, it meant a fundamental but quantifiable change in the last 12 months of his 32 years with the company he joined as a marketing assistant. For the GMB (General Workers' Union) site convenor, George Tuthill, who joined Rowntree two years after Mr Dixon, the evidence of change has yet to emerge.

Both work in York, headquarters of the international Rowntree empire until last June [1988] when the Swiss food and confectionery giant, Nestlé won control in its first hostile takeover bid. That began on 13 April with a 'dawn raid' by Nestlé's compatriots, Suchard. It was the day George Tuthill started his new job as convenor.

Since then 'I have never worked so hard in my life but we haven't seen any sort of change. I think a lot of people still think they work for Rowntree, even now.' He represents 3500 people on the 134 acre site where a change of wind direction can alter its flavour from Polo mint to KitKat chocolate.

Mr Dixon, who retires in August, has become the leading architect in amalgamating Rowntree and Nestlé, drafting global planning through an innovative strategy group based in York.

Within that group, he said, confectionery had been given special prominence. High on the agenda would be 'new opportunities for exploration', examining areas with marketing potential like Latin America, where a toehold of food sales would become base camp for a potential overall expansion.

Both Rowntree and Nestlé are enthusiastic about company compatibility. Both plan long term, and the Nestlé predominantly 'solid chocolate' range complements the Rowntree range of 'count line', more mixed chocolates and biscuit-based products.

Rowntree employs about 33 000, producing Scots Clan in Eire, Escargots in France, Oddfellows in Australia and Suckers in South Africa—among other things. About 15 000 work in Britain where leading brands include KitKat, Polo, Smarties and Yorkie, and where Easter egg production starts before Christmas.

Nestlé has enjoyed a British presence almost as long as Rowntree, although it dwarfs its new British acquisition. Nestlé, with a turnover of about £1.4 billion is roughly ten times larger.

In 1988 Rowntree achieved record production figures. For example, the new Kit-Kat production line at York runs 120 hours a week with three-shift continuous working with just 45 employees supervising the production of 2000 bars a minute when all 12 lines are working.

Factory deputy general manager, Malcolm Jackson, said expectations of change had proved unfounded. 'The workforce is looking for something to happen and not finding it happening.'

In his cramped union office, just round the corner from the snooker room, George Tuthill hopes for job security and investment of £100 million in the next three to five years. 'Rowntree didn't have that sort of money.'

(Source: Adapted from the *Guardian*, January 1989.)

(a)   In what ways would you expect production processes and styles to be similar at Nestlé and Rowntree? What factors would have given rise to this compatibility?

(b)   What factors are likely to have given rise to this particular take-over bid?

(c)   Give an example of an economy of scale mentioned in the article. Explain the benefits which would arise from such an economy. From what further economies of scale does the combined group stand to benefit?

(d)   What do you think is meant in the article by 'a change of wind direction can alter its flavour from Polo mint to KitKat chocolate'? What does this tell us about the production line at York?

(e)   What evidence is given in the article that forward planning is a key ingredient of chocolate manufacture?

4   You are to design a simple assembly line in a group of four to produce the model shown in Fig. 8.18.

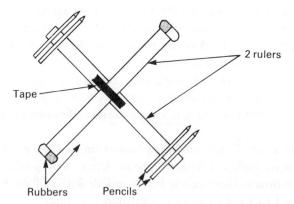

Figure 8.18 Product design layout.

(a)   Carefully consider a workplace layout for the operation.

(b)   Have a dummy production run lasting five minutes.

(c)   Describe how you could improve the location of equipment.

(d)   Compete in a 10-minute production run with another group and discuss your results.

(e)   Comment on areas such as quality, method study, work measurement and ergonomics.

5   Compare two items with which you are familiar which attempt to serve the same
function for the user or customer. Show for each how cost, quality and reliability are
related. Suggested items are:

(a)   A small car versus a luxury car.
(b)   A stereo record system versus a compact disc player.
(c)   A biro versus a high quality pen.

Suggested reading

Bittel, L., *Business in Action*. McGraw-Hill, 1980.
Leonard, R. and Clews, G., *Technology and Production*. Philip Allan, 1985.
Lockyer, G., *Factory and Production Management*. Pitman, 1974.

9

An introduction to the accounting process

We saw in Chapter 1 that businesses will have a number of major objectives. Whatever its prime objective a business must always keep one eye on its financial position. For many businesses a primary target will be to maximize financial returns on investments in the long term. All businesses will be keen to minimize the effects of financial losses.

Entrepreneurs need compensation for taking business risks. They need a return on their investments to justify the time and effort of running or at least contributing to an enterprise.

Profit arises when there is an excess of income over expenditure (if expenditure is larger than income, then the business will be making a loss). A pre-requisite of an effective financial system is this creation of profit.

Accounting acts as an information system by processing business data so that interested parties can be provided with the means to understand how well or badly a business is performing.

For example, the advert (Fig. 9.1) was placed by United Biscuits in a number of newspapers. It is a summary of the company's performance in 1987 in the form of financial highlights. This sort of presentation enables a wide number of interested parties to appreciate the performance of the business. This information was recorded, collated, analysed and presented by the accounting function at United Biscuits.

Business data is an input for the accounting system. The output is valuable financial information (see Fig. 9.2). The financial information can then be fed to those who require such information for decision-making and record-keeping purposes.

For example, *managers* need information in order to manage the business efficiently and constantly to improve their decision-making capabilities. *Shareholders* need to assess the performances of managers and need to know how much profit or income they can take from the business. *Suppliers* need to know about the company's ability to pay its debts and *customers* wish to ensure that their supplies are secure. Any *provider of finance* for the business (bank/debenture holder, etc.) will need to know about the company's ability to make repayments. The *Department of Inland Revenue* needs information about profitability in order to make an accurate tax assessment. *Employees* have a right to know how well a company is performing and how secure

EXCELLENT RESULTS.

1987 has been an excellent year with sales at a record £1,955m. All major sectors of our business have played their part in this success story.

1987 FINANCIAL HIGHLIGHTS

Trading profit	£157.6m	+ 14%
Pre-tax profit	£147m	+ 17%
Earnings per share	23.9p	+ 18%
Dividends per share	11p	+ 16%
Pre-tax profit margin to sales	up from 6.5% to 7.5%	
Return on investment	increased from 22% to 23%	
Cash flow from operations	over £200m	

■ **DIVIDENDS** to shareholders – £46m.

■ **'DIVIDENDS'** to employees in our profit-sharing scheme – £1.2m.

■ **'DIVIDENDS'** to the communities in which we trade – £1.4m.

PROSPECTS FOR 1988 ARE EXCELLENT.

UB United Biscuits

United Biscuits (Holdings) plc, Grant House, Syon Lane, Isleworth, Middlesex, TW7 5NN.
For a copy of the Annual Report, to be published in April, please write to Jean Ferguson at the above address.

Figure 9.1 Financial results at United Biscuit in 1988.

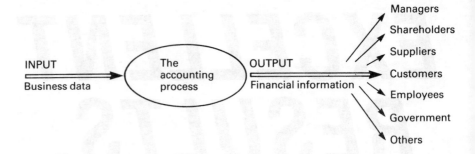

Figure 9.2 The importance of the accounting process.

their futures are. *Financial advisers and brokers* need to know about company performances so that they can advise clients accurately.

Accounts are in many ways similar to story books and the story-lines are extracted from various parts of the business.

The process of accounting can be divided into two broad areas:

1. *Financial accounting*   Accounts from this area are primarily concerned with the accuracy of the record-keeping process. They will ensure that a firm's accounts bear a 'true and fair' view of a business's activities and that they comply with the provisions of the Companies Acts. Financial accountants provide statements called *final accounts* which are handed to shareholders who will then know how well the directors or 'stewards' have performed on their behalf. From final accounts ratios and other figures can be extracted which can provide fairly precise indicators of a company's performance. The knowledge of these would enable managers and directors to improve the quality of their decisions. The professional association representing financial accounts or 'auditors' is the Institute of Chartered Accountants.

2. *Management accounting*   Though financial accounting is of importance it deals with the past and views the firm as a whole. Management accounting tries to guide a business in a particular direction so that it can achieve its objectives. This will involve controlling events within the business using financial information either as and when these events occur or based upon predictions of the future. It also attempts to influence all activities by treating all the various business activities and processes as separate entities. Fundamental to the success of any management accounting system is the process of planning based upon budgets and their subsequent relationship with real events. Through costing activities business operations can be monitored to ensure their successful operation and then accounting can be used to measure what has happened and how the various areas of operation have performed. The professional association closely linked with management accounting is the Chartered Institute of Management Accountants.

If a number of accountants were presented with the same data and asked to prepare the accounts of an organization, they might well produce different sets of accounts. This happens because estimates have to be made about future events which involve an element of opinion and guesswork. For example, in calculating the figure for depreciation, estimates have to be made of the useful life of an asset. Different accountants will make different estimates.

In the 1960s the accounting profession came under pressure to impose standard procedures upon its members to avoid inconsistencies between companies and to improve the quality and usefulness of financial statements.

An example of varying practices occurred in 1967 when AEI was taken over by GEC. AEI had forecast a profit for that year of £10 million but when the figures were published they showed a loss of £4.5 million. At the time it was argued that such diversity of practice brought the accountancy profession into disrepute. Financial accountants try to ensure that a company's accounts bear a 'true and fair' view of business activities. The question is, however, can they do this? In recent years many questionable practices have come to light in accounting statements and often frauds have failed to be discovered by the audit. Auditors are often considered to be private investigators using detective-like methods to probe the inner depths of a company's affairs. In practice they are accountants, often dealing with totals reflecting millions of financial transactions from a myriad of operations. Trying to find a fraud can be almost impossible.

The 1970s saw the introduction of a number of accounting standards. In 1970 the first Statement of Standard Accounting Practice (SSAP) was introduced and such standards have limited the ability of accountants to use diverse accounting procedures. SSAPs are created by the Accounting Standards Committee which is a subcommittee of the Consultative Committee of Accounting Bodies which links the six major accounting bodies. Members of the professional bodies are expected to observe accounting standards while undertaking responsibilities in connection with financial statements.

For example the second Statement of Standard Accounting Practice refers to the four fundamental concepts that should underlie financial accounts (see Fig. 9.3).

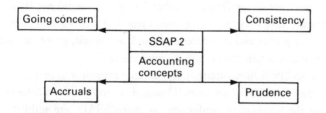

Figure 9.3 The fundamental concepts of accounting practice.

Case Study—Custom cars

Jane Anderton has carried out her life-long ambition and has set up a business which makes custom cars. At the end of her first year:

1.   Jane valued partly finished vehicles at cost on the balance sheet and not

at their disposal value because she believes that they are more valuable to the business in the future and she therefore assumes that the business will be a going concern.

2. As a result of an advertising campaign carried out this year, which is likely to benefit the business over the next five years, some of the costs are carried forward and matched to future years.

3. Jane is consistent in her approach to profit and always assumes that profit is made as soon as a car has been delivered.

4. Although Jane's stationery stock is worth £200 she does not show it in the balance sheet, as it is to be used in the near future and she wants to be prudent.

Jane's case illustrates how accounts can be set out to give a 'true and fair' presentation of an enterprise's financial position.

The *going concern concept* assumes that the business will persist with its business activities in the foreseeable future. This means that the accountant will not assume a desire to cut back on business operations or an intention to liquidate. The significance of this concept is that goods should not be valued at their break-up value but at their net book value based upon the estimation of the cost of the depreciation provision.

The *accruals or matching concept* recognizes that revenues and costs are incurred when their liability is taken on and not as money is received or paid. Thus at the end of a trading period all transactions relating to that period will appear in the accounts whether payments have been made or not. Revenues and profits earned in that period are 'matched' with the costs and expenses associated with these business activities.

The *consistency concept* indicates that the accounting treatment of similar items should be consistently applied within each accounting period and from one period to the next. For example, later in this chapter we refer to the various ways in which stocks can be valued using methods such as LIFO, FIFO and cumulative weighted average cost. This concept indicates that once a business has selected its stock valuation method, it should stick to it.

The *concept of prudence or conservatism* is that businesses should not lay claim to profits unless they are sure that they have been earned. Accountants will therefore tend to underestimate profits and overstate losses and, as a result, profits are only included in accounts if it is certain that they have been made.

The purpose of SSAPs is to ensure that accountants provide a 'true and fair' presentation of a company's financial position. Though it is impossible to achieve absolute uniformity in the accounting profession, as more SSAPs are published, the accounting process gains greater credibility.

The recording process and its influence upon final accounts

The recording of business transactions provides accounting information. Records of transactions are taken by book-keepers who initially record transactions in day books,

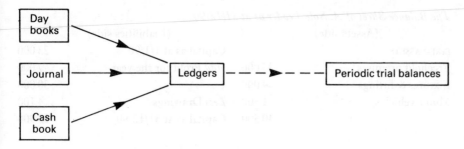

Figure 9.4 Stages in the recording process.

the journal or a cash book before transferring them to a series of ledgers (see Fig. 9.4).

Auditors will require information from these books in order to draw up final accounts at regular intervals. These final accounts can be used to assess performance. Information is taken from the ledger and compiled in the form of a list of balances called the *trial balance*. The use of information technology in business has meant that today integrated software packages contain the books of first entry and these are linked to a system which updates all records whenever a transaction takes place.

In this chapter we are concerned with the implications of recorded entries for the final accounts. The double-entry system is the backbone of accounting providing information for ledgers and then the final accounts.

The double-entry system assumes that all entries into an accounting system reflect a process of exchange. It takes into consideration the fact that every transaction involves two parts and both of these are recorded in the books of account. For example, if we buy equipment for cash, we lose cash but gain equipment. We must therefore record both the loss in cash and the gain in equipment. In the ledger two records are made for each transaction and, as we will see, the dual element in this process is carried through to the final accounts.

Final accounts are made up of the following four elements:

1. A balance sheet
2. A trading account
3. A profit and loss account
4. An appropriation account

A *balance sheet* is a picture of what a firm owns and owes on a particular date. We will first look at how a balance sheet appears in a horizontal format and then show how business transactions have a dual effect upon it. A horizontal balance has two sides—an assets side and a liabilities side. In the table we have set out a fictional balance sheet for A. Sole Trader.

The balance sheet is a clear statement of liabilities, assets, and the capital of a business at a particular moment in time (normally the end of an accounting period). As you can see, a horizontal balance sheet is divided into two halves with assets shown on one side and capital and liabilities on the other. The accounting process ensures that

The Balance Sheet of A. Sole Trader as at 31/12/90

(Assets side)			(Liabilities side)		
FIXED ASSETS			Capital as at 1/1/90		23 000
Freehold premises		35 000	*Add* Profit for the year		7 000
Fixtures & fittings		4 000			30 000
Motor vehicles		1 500	*Less* Drawings		4 100
		40 500	Capital as at 31/12/90		25 900
CURRENT ASSETS			LONG-TERM LIABILITIES		
Stock of goods	4 000		Loan		20 000
Debtors	1 500				
Prepayments	500		CURRENT LIABILITIES		
Bank	1 000		Creditors	1500	
Cash	400	7 400	Accrued costs	500	2 000
		£47 900			£47 900

the total value of one half will equal the total value of the other half. The following equation always applies to balance sheets:

$$CAPITAL + LIABILITIES = ASSETS$$

We can now look at each part of the balance sheet in more detail.

In business accounts we always treat the business owner (or owners in the case of partnerships and companies) as a separate legal entity to the business itself. The capital provided by the owner/s is therefore deemed to be owed by the business to the owners. The balance sheet therefore keeps an updated record of the amount owed by the business to the owner/s.

During a year's trading the owner's capital will be increased by inflows of *profits* and decreased by outflows of *drawings* (moneys/assets taken out of the business for personal use). Having taken these into consideration a new capital figure will exist at the end of the year.

Other liabilities are classified as being current liabilities or long-term liabilities depending on their duration.

Current liabilities are debts of the business which need to be paid in a fairly short period of time (normally within the year). Creditors are normally suppliers of goods on trade credit for which the business has been invoiced but has not yet provided payment. Accrued charges are outstanding bills, often for expenses, at the end of an accounting period, which have not yet been paid. They must be included in the accounts as they are a debt, often for a service which has been provided, e.g. gas or electricity. Other short-term current liabilities could include a bank overdraft, short-term loans and any taxation which is owed to the Department of Inland Revenue. A *long-term liability* is sometimes called a deferred liability as it is not due for payment until some time in the future. By convention this means longer than one year in a set of accounts. Examples would include long-term loans, e.g. bank loan, a mortgage (loan secured against a freehold property) and debentures. Debentures are sometimes issued by companies at fixed rates of interest which have to be repaid on a specific date in the future. Those who hold debentures are therefore lenders of money.

Assets are items which are *owned* by a business and money and other items *owed* to the business. The asset side of the balance sheet will normally be set out in what is called an inverse order of liquidity. This means that items which are difficult to convert to cash quickly and are therefore illiquid, appear at the top of the list of assets. By looking down the order you can gauge the ease with which successive assets can be converted to cash until you come to the most liquid asset of all, cash.

A useful way of classifying assets is to use two classes:

1. Fixed assets
   (a) tangible fixed assets;
   (b) intangible fixed assets;
   (c) investments (long term).
2. Current assets

The simple distinction is that all *fixed assets* must have a lifespan of more than one year. (Therefore current assets will have a lifespan of less than one year.) A *tangible fixed asset* is one which can be touched and seen, e.g. machinery, building, vehicles and so on. An *intangible fixed asset* is one which does not have a physical existence and therefore cannot be touched. For example, the 'goodwill' of a business is an intangible fixed asset. Over a period of time a business builds up a clientele and a reputation. This is a very real asset of an enterprise. For example, over the years Shell has built up a considerable international reputation—'You can be sure of Shell'. Years of trading have given the company millions of regular customers and considerable prestige in the community.

The 'goodwill' of the company will only normally appear in the books if businesses are being taken over or transferred to new owners. The 'goodwill' will have to be included in the purchase price. It is then depreciated over its useful economic life. (It is interesting to note that an increasing number of companies have recently begun to include 'goodwill' in their balance sheets. The reason behind this has been to fend off take-overs from companies who take over others for bargain prices because 'goodwill' has not been fully accounted for.)

Investments are also counted as fixed assets. A company might invest in the shares of another company or purchase debentures. These are investments which are usually made with a view to retaining the assets for more than 12 months.

Fixed assets might be held for a number of years but they will eventually wear out. The accounts of a business try to recognize this gradual erosion of value and depreciation is written off against profits so that the value of fixed assets should be at their net book value after depreciation has been accounted for.

Current assets are sometimes called circulating assets because the form they take is constantly changing. A business will hold stocks of finished goods in readiness to satisfy the demands of the market. When a credit transaction takes place stocks will be reduced and the company will incur debtors. Debtors will have bought goods on credit and therefore owe the company money. After a reasonable credit period, payment will be expected. After this inflow payments will be made on further stocks. Thus the firm has a cash cycle (see Fig. 9.5).

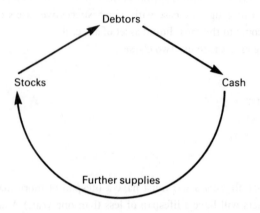

Figure 9.5 The cash cycle.

Current assets might include short-term investments and, though these may be in the form of stocks and shares in other businesses, it would be intended to sell them in the near future. It could also include prepayments. These are sums paid for goods or services which have not yet been received, e.g. rates in advance.

NB   Stocks are normally valued at cost based upon the particular system used (LIFO, FIFO, etc.). However, if the net realizable value of stocks is less than their cost, stocks will be valued at NRV rather than the cost (see page 319).

We can now try to understand the implications of the double-entry system for the balance sheet. Assume that A. Box sets up a business on 1 January by putting £25 000 into a business bank account. The business would then owe A. Box the amount he had invested but, at the same time, will have received £25 000. The asset side of the balance sheet will have increased as the liability side.

The Balance Sheet of A. Box as at 1 January

	£		£
Bank	25 000	Capital	25 000
	£25 000		£25 000

On 2 January the business purchases a motor vehicle for £5000 by cheque. This transaction involves a transfer from one asset to another.

The Balance Sheet of A. Box as at 2 January

	£		£
Motor vehicles	5 000	Capital	25 000
Bank	20 000		
	£25 000		£25 000

On 3 January the business purchases stocks for resale for £15 000 on credit. Therefore liabilities increase as creditors are incurred and assets increase as stocks are now owned.

The Balance Sheet of A. Box as at 3 January

	£		£
Motor vehicles	5 000	Capital	25 000
Stocks	15 000	Creditors	15 000
Bank	20 000		
	£40 000		£40 000

On 4 January stocks valued at £10 000 are sold for £13 000 on credit. Clearly there is a profit element here. Stocks will decrease by the value sold (not by the sale price) so that assets reduce by £10 000 but debtors will now have been created and so assets will increase by £13 000. The profit element of £3000 made upon the sale of the stock items will be added to capital and as a result liabilities will also rise.

The Balance Sheet of A. Box as at 4 January

	£		£
Motor vehicles	5 000	Capital	25 000
Stocks	5 000	*Add* Profits	3 000
Debtors	13 000	Creditors	15 000
Bank	20 000		
	£43 000		£43 000

On 5 January A. Box's business pays the creditors off and the debtors all pay up. Both liabilities and assets will decrease when the creditors are paid. One asset disappears and another increases when the debtors pay up.

The Balance Sheet of A. Box as at 5 January

	£		£
Motor vehicles	5 000	Capital	28 000
Stocks	5 000		
Bank $\left(\begin{array}{l} 20\,000 \\ 15\,000\,(-) \\ 13\,000\,(+) \end{array} \right) =$	18 000		
	£28 000		£28 000

On 6 January, A. Box's business pays expenses of rent, rates and electricity totalling £100 by cheque. As we will see in the profit and loss account, business expenses are deducted from the gross profit to leave the final or net profit. In this example, expenses will be treated as a negative item and carried forward from the profit and loss account by reducing capital by £1000 and bank by £1000.

The Balance Sheet of A. Box as at 6 January

	£		£
Motor vehicles	5 000	Capital	27 000
Stocks	5 000		
Bank	17 000		
	£27 000		£27 000

We could continue this process and record many more transactions. It is important for you to appreciate that all business transactions affect the balance sheet in some way or another. Because of the double-entry system transactions will influence both sides of a horizontal balance.

Though it is common practice to use horizontal balance sheets for demonstration purposes, the majority of businesses today present their balance sheets in vertical form. Vertical balance sheets are often thought to be easier to interpret so that working capital and net current assets figures, for example, can be identified at a glance.

The trading account, profit and loss account and appropriation account are, more often than not, linked together in a profitability statement which compares a company's income with outgoings over an accounting period. If a balance sheet is a snapshot these accounts are like a video which has recorded how the business has performed over a period of time.

The *trading account* shows the gross profit made over an accounting period. Gross profit is the difference between the value of sales and the cost of purchases or the production costs of manufactured goods.

$$\text{SALES} - \text{COST OF SALES} = \text{GROSS PROFIT}$$

Cost of sales is found by applying the following:

$$\text{OPENING STOCKS} + \text{COST OF PURCHASES}$$
$$- \text{CLOSING STOCKS} = \text{COST OF SALES}$$

(In a manufacturing company the cost of purchases is the cost of production.) The opening stock is effectively a purchase as it will be sold in the current trading period but the closing stock must be deducted from purchases as it will be sold next year.

The *profit and loss account* shows the net profit of the business.

$$\text{GROSS PROFIT} + \text{INCOME FROM SOURCES OTHER THAN SALES}$$
$$- \text{BUSINESS EXPENSES} = \text{NET PROFIT}$$

Income from sources other than sales might include any rents received, commissions received, discounts received, profits on the sale of assets, etc. A full list of business

Boxed Clever Limited Balance Sheet as at 31/12/90 (Illustration of a vertical balance)

FIXED ASSETS AT NET BOOK VALUE	£	£	£
Freehold premises			45 000
Machinery			6 000
Fixtures and fittings			3 000
Motor vehicles			5 000
			59 000
CURRENT ASSETS			
Stocks		14 000	
Debtors		3 000	
Prepayments		500	
Cash		100	
		17 600	
Less CURRENT LIABILITIES			
Bank overdraft	1 300		
Creditors	1 200		
Accrued costs	100		
Taxation payable	1 000	3 600	
Net current assets			14 000
Assets employed			£73 000
Financed by:			
Share capital			
Ordinary shares			20 000
Preference shares			20 000
			40 000
Reserves			15 000
			55 000
LONG-TERM LIABILITIES			
Debentures			18 000
Capital employed			£73 000

NB   Current liabilities are deducted from current assets in order to achieve the net current assets or working capital. Under the Companies Act 1985, many limited companies are now obliged to show long-term liabilities in the top section of the balance sheet where they are deducted from the assets employed.

expenses would be too comprehensive to mention. However, some of the more important ones would be salaries of staff and directors, travelling costs, marketing costs, discounts to customers, electricity, rates, bad debts (debts written of as bad if a debtor has failed to make a payment, interest payment, etc.).

The *appropriation account* is the section of the profit and loss account where profit is shared between the owners. In this section the Inland Revenue will require its statutory levy in the form of corporation tax on a company's profits. Also in this section companies set aside funds for reserves. Reserves are either set up as capital reserves from the balance sheet or as revenue reserves from the appropriation account. Revenue reserves represent tied up retained profits which are unlikely to be distributed. Retained profits generally increase from year to year as most companies do not distribute all of their profits as dividends. A full appropriation account would include:

NET PROFIT − CORPORATION TAX = PROFIT AFTER TAXATION
          − DIVIDENDS TO SHAREHOLDERS
          − ANY TRANSFER TO A RESERVE
          + BALANCE OF PROFIT FOR THE PREVIOUS YEAR

Transfer the final balance to the balance sheet. Remember the four stages:

1. Tax
2. Dividends
3. Reserves
4. Last year's balance

We can now look at a complete profit and loss account and see how these four stages are combined.

Makemore Limited—Profit and loss account for the year ending 31/12/90

	£'000s	£'000s	£'000s
Sales			2300
Less Cost of sales			
Opening stock		150	
Purchases		1700	
		1850	
Less Closing stock		200	
			1650
Gross profit			650
Add Profit on disposal of plant			50
			700
Less Overheads			
Wages and salaries		250	
Sundry expenses		105	
Light and heat		5	
Depreciation—buildings	12		
—plant	8	20	
Debenture interest		4	
Bad debts		2	
Advertising and distribution		4	
			390
Net profit			310
Less Corporation tax			108
Profit after taxation			202
Less Dividends—Preference shares		18	
—Ordinary		20	38
			164
Less Transfer to general reserve			64
			100
Add Retained profit brought forward			40
Retained profit carried forward			140

The interpretation of accounts

Under the Companies Acts all limited liability companies are required to file copies of their accounts with their annual return to the Registrar of Companies. The Acts specify the information which should be contained in the balance sheet and profit and loss accounts and indicate that these accounts must give a true and fair view of the affairs of the company for the period concerned. Additional information is required with the accounts and this includes:

1. Details of subsidiaries.
2. Group accounts if there is a group of companies.
3. A directors' report which has to contain certain information.
4. An auditor's report.

Shareholders and debenture holders receive copies of these accounts and notice of the company's general meetings.

A company's accounts are useful sources of information upon the condition of that business. Final accounts can be carefully analysed, often by using ratios, to make comparisons between one year and another. Earlier in this chapter we mentioned a number of people who need to know accounting information. It is important that these groups fully understand the feedback they gain from a company's final accounts. A company's accounts can be analysed to look at:

- Profitability
- Liquidity
- Asset usage
- Capital structure

We are going to look at each of these areas and the usefulness of the information which it is possible to extract.

Profitability

The profitability of a company could be assessed on the basis of the profits the company is making on sales and on the general profitability of the investment made in the company.

Gross profit to sales

$$\frac{\text{Gross profit}}{\text{Sales}} \times 100$$

This will indicate the percentage gross profit made on sales. It is sometimes called profit percentage. Changes in this percentage might reflect increases in the cost of raw materials, stock losses, changes in pricing policy, etc.

Net profit to sales

$$\frac{\text{Net profit}}{\text{Sales}} \times 100$$

This indicates how much final profit is made as a percentage of sales. If the gross profit percentage is consistent, any changes in net profit percentage could indicate an increase in overheads as a proportion of sales and a need to make economies.

Return on capital employed (ROCE)

$$\frac{\text{Net profit}}{\text{Capital employed}} \times 100$$

This is the amount of profit made as a result of the capital employed in the business. Capital in this instance would be the resources invested by shareholders, reserves and debentures. This is an important figure because it relates profits to the size of the business.

Return on equity capital

$$\frac{\text{Profit after tax and preference dividend}}{\text{Ordinary share capital and reserves}}$$

Reserves are surpluses of profits retained in the business and owned by the ordinary or equity investors. Their return would be the profit left after tax and preference dividends and its relationship to their size of investment.

Earnings per share

$$\frac{\text{Profits after payment of tax and preference dividends}}{\text{Number of ordinary shares}}$$

This indicates the amount that each share is earning. It provides the ordinary shareholder with information about the earning capacity of each share.

Price/earnings (P/E) ratio

$$\frac{\text{Market price per share}}{\text{Earnings per share (EPS)}}$$

This is a comparison of the current market value of a share with the earnings per share. These ratios vary from company to company and industry to industry. Companies with a higher status tend to have higher market prices and higher P/E ratios. Retail stores tend to have ratio averages of about 10 whereas property companies have averages in the region of 35. From this it is possible to estimate how long it would take the earnings from an investment to pay back that investment.

Dividend yield

$$\frac{\text{Dividend per share}}{\text{Market price per share}} \times 100$$

This relates the shareholders' dividends to the market price of the shares. If the percentage yield is poor the investor might consider alternative uses for the investment. This might depend on interest rates, the future prospects of the company, changes in the prices of shares and other factors.

Liquidity

This refers to the ability of a firm to convert its short-term or current assets to cash to cover payments as and when they arise. Stocks are the least liquid of the current assets because they must first be sold (probably on credit) and the customer provided with a credit period. As a result there is a time lapse before stocks are converted to cash. It is the responsibility of the company to ensure that it can meet debts likely to arise in the near future. Current liabilities are items which have to be paid for in the short period.

Current or working capital ratio

> This is the ratio of current assets to current liabilities

Clearly some current assets are more liquid than others and the time factor involved in transferring them to cash is something an experienced manager should be able to estimate. A prudent ratio is sometimes said to be 2 : 1. This might not necessarily be the case if stocks form the bulk of the value of the current assets. Companies have to be aware that bank overdrafts are repayable on demand and that figures extracted from a balance sheet might reflect the position of the current assets and liabilities at that time but not over the whole year. In practice most businesses operate with a slightly lower ratio than 2 : 1.

Acid-test ratio/quick ratio/liquidity ratio

> This is the ratio of current assets *less* stocks to current liabilities

This ratio assesses how well a business can meet its current liabilities without stocks. It ignores stocks because they are the least liquid current asset. A prudent quick ratio is 1 : 1 though some businesses operate with a lower quick ratio of 0.5 : 1.

Debt collection period

> This is calculated by the formula $\dfrac{\text{Debtors}}{\text{Average daily sales}}$

It may be possible to improve liquidity by reducing the debt collection period. Customers who are late in paying their debts are receiving free finance for their businesses. This ratio indicates the average number of days of credit received by customers before they provide a payment.

NB   Average days' sales are calculated by dividing sales by 365. The normally accepted level of debt period is about 60 days.

Period of credit taken from suppliers

This is calculated by the formula $\dfrac{\text{Creditors}}{\text{Average daily purchases}}$

Just as liquidity can be analysed by looking at the debt collection period, it could also be beneficial to look at the average period of credit taken from suppliers.

Case Study—Cavity Contractors Limited

The final accounts of Cavity Contractors at the end of its first two years' trading are illustrated below. The company is concerned about whether liquidity has improved during its second year.

Profit and Loss Accounts

	Year 1 £	Year 2 £
Sales	18 500	18 900
Less Cost of sales	11 200	10 100
	7 300	8 800
Less Overheads	5 000	5 200
Net profit	2 300	3 600
Less Dividends	300	400
	2 000	3 200
Add Retained profit brought forward	—	2 000
Retained profit carried forward	2 000	5 200

Balance Sheets

	Year 1 £	Year 1 £	Year 2 £	Year 2 £
FIXED ASSETS		14 100		16 000
CURRENT ASSETS				
Stocks	2 500		3 000	
Debtors	2 100		3 500	
Bank	400		200	
	5 000		6 700	
Less CURRENT LIABILITIES				
Creditors	2 000		2 400	
Net current assets		3 000		4 300
		17 100		20 300
Financed by:				
Ordinary shares		15 100		15 100
Reserves		2 000		5 200
		17 100		20 300

Cavity Contractors Limited		Liquidity ratios	
		Year 1	Year 2
1.	Current ratio	2.5	2.8
2.	Quick ratio	1.25	1.5
3.	Debt collection period	41 days	68 days
4.	Period of credit taken from suppliers	65 days	86 days

(NB   Purchases taken as cost of sales figure)

Increases in both the company's current and quick ratios have improved the company's liquidity during the year. A deterioration has taken place in the debt collection period as the number of days' credit allowed to customers has increased from 41 to 68. Cavity Contractors is also now taking longer to pay suppliers and this has increased from 65 to 86 days.

Asset usage

Asset usage ratios make it possible to assess the efficiency of certain areas of business activity. For example, use of these ratios assists in the analysis of stock turnover and enables comparisons with other industries and previous periods to be made. They are also useful tools in analysing the efficiency of asset handling.

Stock turnover

This can be calculated by using the formula:

$$\frac{\text{Cost of sales}}{\text{Average stock}}$$

$$\text{NB}\quad \text{Average stock} = \frac{\text{Opening stock} + \text{Closing stock}}{2}$$

Stock turnover is the average length of time an item of stock is held in stores before it is used or sold. The adequacy of this ratio depends upon the type of industry a particular business is in. For example, a greengrocer would expect a much higher stock turnover than a furniture business. Many firms today hold smaller stock levels than in the past. They operate a 'just in time' philosophy (i.e. keeping just enough stock to meet current demand) and consequently have a higher stock turnover.

Asset utilization

This is calculated by the formula $\dfrac{\text{Sales}}{\text{Fixed assets}}$

This ratio indicates how effectively fixed assets are being used to generate sales. It is really an efficiency ratio designed to show how well managers are using fixed assets to generate sales. The level of the ratio will depend upon the type of business concerned.

Capital structure

Companies are financed by share capital, loans and several other sources. The return on these investments is in the form of dividends or interest payments. Both investors and suppliers of loan finance will wish to ensure that their incomes are maintained and that the future of their moneys looks secure.

Gearing

This is calculated by:

$$\frac{\text{Prior charge capital (long-term loans and preference shares)}}{\text{Equity (ordinary shares plus reserves)}}$$

Gearing makes a direct comparison between the long-term capital in a business provided by ordinary shareholders with that provided in the form of long-term loans and preference shares. Using the above formula we can say that a company is:

- low geared if the gearing is less than 100 per cent;
- high geared if the gearing is more than 100 per cent.

If a high geared company wishes to raise extra finance it may find it difficult to raise a loan. Lenders like to see shareholders provide a large proportion of a company's capital. Shareholders might prefer a company to be low geared because if it took on further loans, it would mean that the profit allocation would be reduced because of the necessity to make interest payments. The advantage of using debt capital is that interest rates are fixed, loans do not carry voting rights, interest payments attract tax relief and the reward to debt holders is generally lower than that required by shareholders. Gearing levels vary from firm to firm and from country to country. If a company has a stable background, higher gearing would be safer.

Interest cover

This is calculated by: $\dfrac{\text{Profit before interest and tax}}{\text{Interest paid in the year}}$

This refers to the risk of gearing. If the ratio is less than 1 a company has not earned enough to cover interest charges. A ratio of 3 would provide the minimum level of safety required.

Case Study—Lopex PLC

During the latter part of 1988 Lopex reported another half year of record results together with an increase in its interim dividend. Increased trading activity and successful acquisitions have contributed to results and this has demonstrated the benefits the Group is receiving from developing its range

Interim results

	Unaudited 6 months ended 30 June		
	1988	1987	
	£'000s	£'000s	
Turnover	73 209	65 577	+8.3%
Gross revenue	21 030	17 775	+18.3%
Profit before tax	2 750	2 034	+35.2%
Profit after tax and minority interests	1 425	1 003	+42.1%
Earnings per share	9.26p	7.32p	+26.5%
Dividend per share	2.4p	2.0p	+20.0%

of communication services. The Board has expressed confidence about the full year's trading results.

Questions

1. Why might gross revenue have increased by a greater percentage than turnover?
2. Comment briefly on the strength of these figures.
3. Explain the difference between earnings per share and dividend per share.
4. Identify four groups of people who would want to know this information.

Dangers of using ratios

There are a number of dangers of using ratios. It is difficult to make comparisons between the accounts of two firms in the same industry. They may vary so considerably in size and structure that these comparisons become unrealistic. For example, they may have different techniques of asset valuation. Ratios can be criticized for over-simplifying business activity. They can often cloud events with generalizations so that any conclusions become unrealistic. There are many positive factors within businesses which are completely ignored by an analysis of final accounts, e.g. good quality staff, good location, etc. Another problem with accounting statements is comparisons made with the past. These comparisons might easily be distorted by inflation and, in the same way, it is often unwise to use this year's accounts to predict business activity next year.

Funds flow statements

The profit and loss account provides information which matches sales with costs and a balance sheet is a static statement showing a business's position. Neither of these shows how a business obtains and uses its funds.

It would be useful for a business to know how profits have been allocated, why its bank balance has changed, etc. In 1975 the tenth Statement of Standard Accounting Practice was issued which requires all businesses with a turnover of £25 000 or more per annum to provide a statement to fill this gap as part of their final accounts. A *funds flow statement* is a further analysis of the position of a company because it shows where a business obtains its funds and then how these funds have been used. It will indicate how profit has contributed to funds and whether a business is generating sufficient funds to meet needs.

Funds flow statements are prepared through a process of comparison. If the balance sheets of a company are listed alongside each other for two successive years, then clearly the changes can be seen. Differences between the two years are then listed and grouped together either as sources or as applications of funds. Sources of funds might include:

- Profits
- New loans
- Share issues
- Profits on sale of assets, etc.

Applications of funds might include:

- Purchase of fixed assets
- Tax paid
- Dividends paid
- Loans repaid, etc.

The example below shows how an increase in stocks has been financed:

B. Nice Balance Sheets	£ 31/12/89	£ 31/12/90	£ Comparison
Premises	3 000	3 000	0
Stocks	8 000	10 000	+ 2000
Bank	3 000	3 000	0
	£14 000	£16 000	
Capital	14 000	14 000	0
Creditors		2 000	+ 2000
	£14 000	£16 000	

Clearly this increase in stocks has been financed through the credit provided by suppliers and this can be shown in the form of a statement.

B. Nice Funds Flow Statement from 31/12/89 to 31/12/90

	£
Sources of funds—creditors	2000
Applications of funds—increasing stocks	2000

The more modern way of presenting a funds flow statement is to have a section which analyses any working capital changes. The reason for this is to enable managers to exert a firmer grip upon working capital levels. The change in working capital between the two balance sheets will equal the difference between the sources and applications of funds.

T. Chest Co. Limited Balance Sheets	£ 31/12/89	£ 31/12/90	£ Comparison
Fixed assets	450	550	+100
Long-term investments	500	450	−50
Current assets − Current liabilities	150	200	+50
	£1100	£1200	
Capital	360	400	+40
Profits	300	500	+200
Loans	440	300	−140
	£1100	£1200	

T. Chest Co. Limited Funds Flow Statement from 31/12/89 to 31/12/90

Sources of funds		
Capital	40	
Profits	200	
Sale of investments	50	290
Applications of funds		
Fixed assets	100	
Loan repayment	140	240
Increase in working capital		50

Accounting policies

Irrespective of the limitations placed upon auditors by the Statements of Standard Accounting Practice they are still able to provide an individual approach to the preparation of a set of final accounts. It is therefore usual for companies to attach a note of the accounting policies they use. Three elements normally mentioned in these statements are policies on:

1. inflation accounting;
2. stock valuation;
3. depreciation.

As items portrayed in final accounts might vary according to accounting policies in these three areas, it becomes evident why these statements are made.

Inflation accounting

Under the section entitled 'Accounting policies', which appeared in a recent Annual Report for ICI, it began with, 'The accounts have been prepared under the historical cost convention and in accordance with the Companies Act 1985'. The term 'historical cost' indicates that ICI records assets taken into the business at entry cost and then these are reduced in 'book value' over each period through depreciation. Many would argue that this method:

- bases measurements on actual costs;
- is easy to understand by accountants and users;
- relates to documentary evidence, e.g. invoices;
- is the system recognized for tax assessment, etc.

However, there are a number of criticisms which can be levelled at the historic cost valuation method. The major criticism of the method is that it can severely under-value assets during periods of inflation. Over a number of years this would mean that it would be difficult to compare financial statements. In an inflationary period profits can be over-stated, and they would not include adequate provision for the replacement of fixed assets at higher prices. The analysis of a company's performance would be distorted. The company would find itself paying excess dividends or making over-generous pay settlements. The accounting profession has taken measures to overcome these problems. Various techniques have been applied in recent years to minimize these difficulties including:

- Current Purchasing Power (CPP)
- Current Cost Accounting (CCA)

SSAPs have been introduced and then withdrawn for both techniques. For example, in June 1985 SSAP 16, entitled Current Cost Accounting, was suspended because many companies did not comply to it and so now neither technique has a mandatory status.

Current purchasing power was a system which translated the amounts extracted from historical accounts into inflation-adjusted units calculated by reference to price indices. (A price index is a measure of average prices, see Chapter 5.) Because this system used as its base historical cost figures it retained many of the advantages of the historical cost method.

Under this system company assets would be given values which reflected how much the original expenditure on them would be worth at current prices. However, this is clearly an unrealistic calculation because price indices cover average baskets of goods—the price of individual items may vary widely from the average.

Current cost accounting involves making four adjustments to historic cost figures in order to counteract the distortions of inflation.

1. *Cost of sales adjustment*   The opening and closing stock should be restated at the average price for the year.
2. *Depreciation adjustment*   Fixed assets should be revalued in terms of the price index so that they reflect their current cost of replacement.
3. *Monetary working capital adjustment*   Average figures for current assets and current liabilities should be calculated for the year in terms of a price index. For

example, you should calculate the average annual figure for debtors and creditors.

4. *The gearing adjustment*   Companies gain by borrowing in times of inflation and therefore an adjustment needs to be made to account for the benefits of borrowing.

The problem of presenting accounting information and accounting for inflation is still in its early days. Inflation levels have varied throughout the 1980s. Early in the decade inflation levels were relatively high, before falling to under 3 per cent in the mid-1980s. In 1989 they had risen again almost to double figures. Accounting for inflation is clearly a problem, particularly in periods of high inflation.

Stock valuation

Controlling everyday stocks is nearly always a headache. A business has to balance the danger of running out of stock with that of overstocking. Business activities are continuous, but accounting statements must be drawn up on a particular date. Stock-taking therefore has to take place in such a way that:

1. the quantity of stock held on the balance sheet date is verified;
2. a monetary amount can then be allocated to each stock unit.

Stock valuation has a direct influence upon profits:

	£ High valuation	£	£ Low valuation	£
Sales		5000		5000
Less Cost of sales				
Opening stock	2000		2000	
Add Purchases	4000		4000	
	6000		6000	
Less Closing stock	5000		3000	
		1000		3000
		£4000		£2000

Including a higher stock valuation in the accounts has an obvious implication for the profit declared as higher stock valuations will lead to higher profits (see table).

The prudence concept rules out the use of selling prices in stock valuation as profits should only be recognized when they are actually made and after the goods are sold. SSAP 9 indicates that stocks should be valued at either their cost or at their net realizable value—whichever is lower. Net realizable value is the selling price of stocks *less* the costs incurred in getting them ready for sale and selling them.

Stock item	£ Cost	£ NRV	£ Lower of cost/NRV
No. 1	15	17	15
No. 2	21	18	18
	£36	£35	£33

It would be wrong to state stocks at £36 (column 1) in the balance sheet as the cost total would be ignoring a loss on item No. 2. The prudent valuation would be £33 which values item No. 2 at the lower of cost or NRV.

A major problem of stock valuation is allocating the purchase cost. A business will continually purchase items, and newer items will often be mixed with older items in a bin. Accountants are not concerned with physically identifying older items so that they are always used first. However, they are concerned with developing a pricing technique which allocates a cost to each component in the stores.

Three of the principal methods of stock valuation are:

1.   FIFO (first in, first out).
2.   LIFO (last in, first out).
3.   Cumulative weighted average cost (AvCo).

We will look at each of these methods in turn and relate them to the following 1990 transactions:

January—Balance 100 units at cost of £2.90 each
February—Received 100 units at £3.00 each
March—Issues 80 units
April—Received 70 units at £3.80 each
May—Issues 50 units, etc.

The *FIFO or first in, first out* method of stock valuation, as the name implies, makes the assumption that stocks are issued in the order in which they were delivered so that the stocks which have been held longest will be assumed to be issued first. This means that issues are priced at the cost of the earlier stocks while the stock remaining will be priced at a level nearer the replacement cost. FIFO provides a slightly higher valuation than some of the other methods we illustrate.

Date 1990	Receipt and price	Issue and price	Running stock valuation (£)	
Jan	Balance		100 at 2.90	= 290
			100 units	290
Feb	100 at £3.00		100 at 2.90	= 290
			100 at 3.00	= 300
			200 units	590
Mar		80 at £2.90	20 at 2.90	= 58
			100 at 3.00	= 300
			120 units	358
Apr	70 at £3.80		20 at 2.90	= 58
			100 at 3.00	= 300
			70 at 3.80	= 266
			190 units	624
May		20 at £2.90	70 at 3.00	= 210
		30 at £3.00	70 at 3.80	= 266
			140 units	476

The final valuation using FIFO is 140 units at £476.

The *LIFO or last in, first out* method of stock valuation assumes that recent deliveries are issued before the earlier ones. This means that stock issued is close to the replacement price while remaining stock is kept at the older and probably lower price. The tendency with this method is to undervalue stocks in comparison to current market values.

Date 1990	Receipt and price	Issue and price	Running stock valuation (£)
Jan		Balance	100 at 2.90 = 290 100 units 290
Feb	100 at £3.00		100 at 2.90 = 290 100 at 3.00 = 300 200 units 590
Mar		80 at £3.00	100 at 2.90 = 290 20 at 3.00 = 60 120 units 350
Apr	70 at £3.80		100 at 2.90 = 290 20 at 3.00 = 60 70 at 3.80 = 266 190 units 616
May		50 at £3.80	100 at 2.90 = 290 20 at 3.00 = 60 20 at 3.80 = 76 140 units 426

The final valuation using LIFO is 140 units at £426.

With *cumulative weighted average pricing* (*AvCo*) every time a new consignment arrives the average cost of stock is calculated. Each unit is assumed to have been purchased at the average price of all the components. The average unit cost of stock is a weighted average price and is calculated in the following way:

$$\frac{\text{Existing stock value} + \text{Value of latest purchase}}{\text{Number of units then in stock}}$$

Date	Receipts	Issues	Weighted average unit cost (£)	Number of stock units	Running stock valuation (£)
Jan		Balance	2.90	100	290.00
Feb	100 at £3.00		2.95	200	590.00
Mar		80	2.95	120	354.00
Apr	70 at £3.80		3.26	190	619.40
May		50	3.26	140	456.40

The final valuation using AvCo is 140 units at £456.40 (between FIFO and LIFO).

The recent ICI report comments on stock valuation by saying that, 'Finished goods are stated at the lower of cost or net realizable value, raw materials and other stocks at the lower of cost or replacement price; the first in, first out or an average method of valuation is used.

Depreciation

Fixed assets are acquired in order to earn profits. Though their lives are not limited to a single accounting period they will not last for ever. Most companies have expectations about the lifetime of their assets. They will wish to show a true asset value in the balance sheet and charge the cost of its declining value to the profit and loss account.

SSAP 12 defines depreciation as 'the measure of the wearing out, consumption or other reduction in the useful economic life of a fixed asset, whether arising from use, time or obsolescence through technological or market changes'.

There are a number of different methods of depreciation and of these the most common are:

1. The straight-line method.
2. The reducing balance method.
3. The machine hour method.
4. The sum of the digits method.

The most frequently used method is the *straight-line or equal instalment method* which charges an equal amount of depreciation to each accounting period for the life of an asset. The instalment is calculated by:

$$\frac{\text{Cost of asset} - \text{Residual value}}{\text{Expected useful life of asset}}$$

For example, a machine expected to last five years costs £20 000 after which its residual value will be £5000.

$$\text{Depreciation charge} = \frac{£20\,000 - £5000}{5 \text{ years}} = £3000$$

	Year 1 (£)	Year 2 (£)	Year 3 (£)	Year 4 (£)	Year 5 (£)
Cost	20 000	20 000	20 000	20 000	20 000
Accumulated depreciation	3 000	6 000	9 000	12 000	15 000
Net book value	17 000	14 000	11 000	8 000	5 000

The *reducing balance method* calculates the depreciation charge as a fixed percentage of net book value from the previous accounting period. This method allocates higher depreciation costs to the earlier years of asset. It can be argued that this system is more realistic as it caters for the increased expense of repairs and running costs as machinery becomes older.

For example, a machine is purchased by a business for £20 000 and its expected useful life is three years. The business anticipates a residual value of £4320 and thus wishes to depreciate it at 40 per cent.

		Accumulated depreciation
(£)	(£)	
Machine at cost	20 000	
Depreciation Year 1	8 000	8 000
Net book value	12 000	
Depreciation Year 2	4 800	12 800
Net book value	7 200	
Depreciation Year 3	2 880	15 680
Residual value	£4 320	

The *machine hour method* relates depreciation to use rather than time and therefore depreciation is calculated on the basis of the number of hours a machine has been worked. The depreciation charge per hour is calculated by:

$$\frac{\text{Cost of asset} - \text{Residual value}}{\text{Estimated life of asset in machine hours}}$$

For example, a machine is purchased for £34 000 with an estimated useful life of 10 000 machine hours and a residual value of £4000. The rate of depreciation per machine hour would be:

$$\frac{34\,000 - 4000}{10\,000} = £3 \text{ per machine hour}$$

Therefore, if the machine was used for 2000 hours in Year 1, 3000 hours in Year 2, 1000 hours in Year 3, depreciation would be charged in the following way:

	Depreciation charge (£)	Accumulated depreciation (£)	Cost of asset (£)	Net book value (£)
Year 1. 2000 × £3	6000	6 000	34 000	28 000
Year 2. 3000 × £3	9000	15 000	34 000	19 000
Year 3. 1000 × £3	3000	18 000	34 000	16 000

The *sum of the digits method* is similar to the reducing balance method in that higher levels of depreciation are charged in earlier years. However, it uses digits rather than percentages as a simplified way of working out the depreciation charge.

Digits are allocated in a descending order to each year of the life of an asset and a charge is worked out for each digit used.

For example, a machine is purchased for £15 000 and is expected to last for three years after which it will be sold for £3000.

Year 1	3 digits
Year 2	2 digits
Year 3	1 digit

Sum of the digits =   6

A weighted charge is then calculated as follows:

$$\frac{\text{Cost of asset} - \text{Residual value}}{\text{Sum of the digits}}$$

$$\frac{15\,000 - 3000}{6} = £2000 \text{ per digit}$$

	Digits	Depreciation charge (£)	Accumulated depreciation (£)
Year 1	3 × 2000	6000	6 000
Year 2	2 × 2000	4000	10 000
Year 3	1 × 2000	2000	12 000

Depreciation is treated as an expense and, for each period, it will be charged to the profit and loss account. The accumulated depreciation is added together to form a provision for depreciation which is then deducted from the cost price of the fixed asset it represents in the balance sheet.

Conclusion

The emphasis in this chapter has been towards providing the reader with an understanding of the process of financial accounting. It should enable the reader to answer questions like:

- What is accounting?
- Why does it exist?
- Are accounts necessary?
- What do accounting statements mean?
- How do stock levels and inflation affect accounts?

This chapter has been geared to providing the reader with an understanding of the format, presentation and meaning of a set of final accounts and the standards applicable to these areas.

Short answer questions

1. Name three groups of people interested in financial information about a company.
2. List the differences between the respective roles of financial and managerial accountants.
3. What are Statements of Standard Accounting Practice?
4. Describe two concepts which underlie financial accounts.
5. Use an example to describe the process of double-entry book-keeping.
6. State three items which might appear as current liabilities in the balance sheet of a company.   (*Source:* AEB.)
7. What is meant by the term 'goodwill'?
8. Name two ways in which a company might appropriate its profits.
                                                                (*Source:* AEB.)
9. The directors of a company recommend a dividend on their £1 ordinary shares of 8 per cent. How much would a company pay to an investor holding 100 shares, if the current market price was £1.20 each?   (*Source:* AEB.)
10. Explain the meaning of the expression 'A highly geared company'.
                                                                (*Source:* AEB.)
11. Sales at cost divided by average stock.
    (a) What is the name of this ratio?
    (b) What information does it provide?   (*Source:* AEB.)
12. Name two dangers of using ratio analysis.
13. Why is a funds flow statement a useful further analysis of the position of a company?
14. Name two advantages of keeping accounts under the historical cost convention.
15. Briefly explain what is meant by current purchasing power.
16. Using a numerical example show the influence of stock valuations on profits.
17. What is meant by 'the lower of cost or net realizable value'?
18. Explain the differences between FIFO and LIFO.
19. What is the residual value of an asset?
20. Choose one technique of depreciation and explain how it works.

Essays

1. SSAP 2 refers to accounting concepts. Explain why you feel that
   (a) SSAPs are necessary;
   (b) accounting concepts should be followed.
2. Company financial statements, including profit and loss accounts, balance sheets and statements of sources and applications of funds, are used by a variety of individuals and institutions for a variety of purposes. Required: Specify six different types of uses of financial statements and explain in each case the aspects of performance or position in which they are interested.
                                                                (*Source:* ACCA.)

3. (a) State three items which might appear as current liabilities in the balance sheet of a company.

   (b) Define the terms 'Dividend per share' and 'Earnings per share' and explain the difference between them.   (*Source:* AEB.)

4. To what extent would Ratio Analysis enable you to draw meaningful conclusions about the performance of different public companies?   (*Source:* AEB.)

5. State the reasons why companies prepare financial statements and accounts. Comment on their usefulness.   (*Source:* AEB.)

6. Explain how funds flow statements operate. Why are funds flow statements a useful further analysis of a company's position?

7. Is inflation accounting necessary? Comment on the differences between current purchasing power and current cost accounting.

8. Explain what is meant by the valuation of stocks at the lower of cost or net realizable value. How does this relate to the consistency concept?

9. 'Accurate calculation of depreciation is essential.' Discuss.

10. Outline the differences between each of the techniques for calculating depreciation.

Data response questions

1   Look carefully at the following list of balances of B. Williams, a sole trader, taken on 31/12/90: Freehold premises £81 000, fixtures and fittings £2300, profit for the year £4400, mortgage £18 000, stocks £5300, machinery £1100, debtors £1400, creditors £300, bank overdraft £6200, cash £400, drawings £5800, capital £68 400.
Prepare a balance sheet in
(a)   a horizontal format; and
(b)   a vertical format.
Comment on the performance of B. Williams's business.

2   Show by using successive balance sheets (i.e. draw up a new balance sheet after each transaction) the effects of the following transactions:
(a)   Start the business up with £55 000 in cash.
(b)   Buy property for £24 200 by using cash.
(c)   Buy stock on credit for £14 800.
(d)   Pay overheads by using cash £1700.
(e)   Sell stock costing £9000 on credit for £15 000.
(f)   Pay creditors the amount due.
(g)   Debtors settled.

3   A business started trading in a particular line of merchandise using capital placed in the business's bank account. The transactions that took place are listed below—none is a credit transaction. Takings are always banked immediately and suppliers paid by cheque.

Purchases		Sales	
Quantity (number)	Price per unit (£)	Quantity (number)	Price per unit (£)
1300	1.00	700	1.80
1100	1.05	800	1.85
700	1.10	1100	1.90
900	1.15	600	1.95
800	1.20	500	2.00
1200	1.25	300	2.05

At the same time the trader incurred expenses of £2150. Prepare separately, using both FIFO and LIFO methods of stock valuation:

(a)   a statement of the cost of sales for the period;

(b)   a balance sheet at the end of the period.

4   The summarized balance sheets of Cumbrian Food Processors Limited at the end of consecutive financial years were as show below:

Summarized Balance Sheets as at 31 July

1990				1991	
£000	£000			£000	£000
		FIXED ASSETS (at written down values)			
32		Premises		35	
105		Plant and equipment		170	
31	168	Motor vehicles		75	280
		CURRENT ASSETS			
64		Stock		173	
48		Debtors		55	
48		Bank		18	
160				246	
		Less CURRENT LIABILITIES			
73		Creditors		141	
22		Proposed dividends		32	
95				173	
	65	Working capital			73
	233	Net assets employed			353
		Financed by:			
200		Ordinary share capital		200	
33	233	Reserves		53	253
		Shareholders' funds			
		Loan capital: 7% debentures			100
	233				353

Calculate for each of the two years, the following:

(a)   Current assets/Current liabilities

(b)   Quick assets/Current liabilities

(c)   Gearing ratio

(d)   A funds flow statement

Make brief comments upon the figures you calculate and mention some possible reasons for the differences between the years.

5   The following table shows details of the movements in the stock level of a product which is purchased for resale:

Date	Purchases (units) (£)	Purchase price per unit (£)	Issues (units) (£)	Balance (units) (£)
1986				
1 June balance	—	—	—	300
8 August	200	8.00	—	500
15 September	—	—	500	—
17 September	500	8.25	—	500
1987				
5 January	—	—	100	400
8 January	—	—	200	200
16 March	200	8.75	—	400
31 May	—	—	200	200

(a)   Explain the meaning of the following terms:
   (i)   FIFO
   (ii)   LIFO.
(b)   Using the available information, calculate the value of the closing stock on 31 May 1987:
   (i)   if the method of valuation is FIFO;
   (ii)   if the method of valuation is LIFO.

(*Source:* adapted from AEB.)

6   Fisher's Furniture Ltd is a small furniture retailer whose accounts for the year ending 30 April are given below.

	£		£	£
Shareholders' Funds		*Fixed Assets*		
Share capital	100,000	Land & Buildings		120,000
Reserves	30,000	Van	12,500	
		Depreciation	(2,500)	10,000
Long term liabilities				
Loans	60,000	*Current Assets*		
		Stock		85,000
Current Assets		Debtors		8,000
Creditors	24,000	Cash		3,500
Provision for tax	12,500			
	226,500			226.500

(*a*)   Explain what you understand by the following terms which appear in the balance sheet above:
   (i)   Shareholders' Funds
   (ii)   Long term liabilities.   [4]

(*b*)   During the year ending 30th April 1987, the following transactions took place.

£240,000 of goods were bought.
£300,000 of goods were sold. These were originally bought by Fisher's for £195,000.

£220,000 was paid to suppliers.

£7,500 was paid on average each month to cover wages, the running expenses of the shop and van, and interest on the loan.

£12,500 was paid for last year's tax.

£2,500 allowance was made for depreciation on the van.

All profits are retained within the firm and tax is chargeable on them at the rate of 50%. Debtors have risen by £2,000.

(i)   Calculate the profit made for the year ending 30th April 1987 and the cash in hand at this date. [6]

(ii) Draw up a balance sheet for the year ending 30th April 1987. [5]

(c) Explain how the following assets which appear in the balance sheet have been valued and identify alternative methods that could have been used.

(i)   The van (which was purchased on 1st May 1985 and was expected to have a five year life). [3]

(ii) Stock. [4]

(d) What else is legally required (other than the balance sheet and profit and loss account) to appear in all published accounts? [3]

(*Source:* University of Cambridge, Local Examinations Syndicate.)

Suggested reading

Ashton, R., *UK Financial Accounting Standards*. Woodhead-Faulkner, 1983.

Black, G., *Accounting Standards*. Longman, 1987.

Farmer, E., *Accounting for Inflation*. Gee and Co., 1980.

Farmer, E., *Understanding and Interpreting Company Reports and Accounts*. Van Nostrand Reinhold, 1983.

Whitehead, G., *Success in Principles of Accounting*. John Murray, 1980.

10

Finance and decision making

In business the provision and successful management of finance is vital. Investors have to make sacrifices if they want to see their interests expand and develop. Savers and borrowers of funds come together in the market for finance. The forces of demand and supply guide the operation of financial markets and the price paid for using money is called the interest rate. Prices frequently change in this market. For example, if the demand for funds increases and the supply remains unchanged then interest rates are likely to rise. Conversely, if the demand for loan capital is low in comparison with the availability of funds, interest rates are likely to fall.

Governments often have a strong influence on financial markets. They can use their position as borrowers to influence interest rates by increasing or decreasing their own demand for finance. The government may push up (or pull down) interest rates to further its economic policies. For example, in 1988 and 1989 the Conservative Government increased rates to soak up demand and stop the economy from overheating.

The market for finance is a complex arrangement involving banks, unit trust companies, stockbrokers, investment and venture capital companies, pension funds, assurance companies and many more.

Each of these institutions acts as an intermediary accepting savings and channelling them to businesses through short-term money markets or long-term capital markets. Savers have a wide range of investment possibilities and each of these bears a different degree of risk. One person may opt for risk capital in the form of company shares where the return is the dividend earned by each share, while another may place funds with a bank which passes them on to businesses as loans or overdrafts. A company's financial possibilities are not just limited to the availability of loans or the expansion of share capital. Retained profits are a major source of funds for many organizations while others work hard to maximize their benefits from trade credit.

Sources of finance

Decisions about a company's source of finance will determine the financial structure of that organization (see Fig. 10.1). Though short-term finance is more expensive, it is

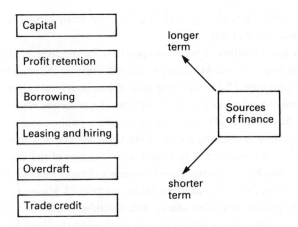

Figure 10.1 Sources of finance.

also more flexible and this benefit would offset the lower cost of long-term funds which might not be fully employed due to fluctuations in business activity. Many companies expand by using short-term finance and then replace it with long-term finance through a funding operation. Funding raises long-term funds to pay off the short-term finance so that further short-term finance is then available to help the business to expand again. In a similar vein, in Chapter 9 we looked at how gearing compares long-term capital provided by shares with that of loans and showed how this reflected both the degree of risk and the allocation of profits.

Capital

A sole trader is easy to set up and is the most common form of business ownership. Though they have considerable flexibility, most of their finance often comes from personal sources and additional sums can be difficult to raise. They often look to expand by taking in partners and thus increase the business capital. Partnerships provide further opportunities for expansion and are particularly suitable for the professions, but limitations exist upon the number of partners and this further restricts capital-raising opportunities. In order to achieve the benefits of limited liability and extend the capital-raising opportunities, many partnerships opt for corporate status with the issue of shares. The company comprises a group of people who unite together to form a separate legal entity. This legal personality provides the company with perpetual succession and continuity. As we have seen, companies can be either private or public. A private limited company is one which restricts the rights of members to transfer their shares and limits the ability of the public to subscribe for its shares. Membership of the Unlisted Securities Market (USM) is often seen as a half-way stage between a small company and a fully listed company on the Stock Exchange. The USM was created in 1980 by the Stock Exchange and has enabled many smaller companies to become public and raise money for expansion before progressing to a full Stock Exchange listing. A fully listed public limited company on the

Stock Exchange has almost limitless opportunities to raise fresh capital from the market as long as it abides by its rules.

A public company has a number of methods open to it for the issue of shares. It can create a *public issue by prospectus*. An issuing house will organize the issue by compiling a prospectus, accompanied by an advertisement and an invitation to buy shares. This can be an expensive method and up to 7 per cent of the money raised by the issue can go to meet the costs. An *offer for sale* exists where a public company issues shares directly to an issuing house which then offers them for sale at a fixed price. This is also an expensive method and is best used when the size of the issue is too small to need a public issue by prospectus. A *rights issue* is a cheaper method whereby existing shareholders are made an offer at an advantageous price. A *placing* avoids the expense of going to the market by placing shares with a number of investors through an intermediary. Since this method avoids the market mechanism the Stock Exchange keeps a close eye on these transactions. An *offer by tender* is sometimes used. With this method an offer is made to the public but the company states a minimum price below which shares will not be offered. Buyers then have to indicate the price they are willing to offer for the shares.

Most capital is normally in the form of *ordinary shares*. An ordinary share is a fixed unit of ownership and gives the holder the opportunity to share in the profits or losses. Most ordinary shares carry voting rights at shareholders' meetings. Shareholders elect the board and can sanction the level of dividends proposed. Authorized capital is the maximum amount of share capital a company is empowered by its shareholders to issue. Issued capital is the nominal amount of share capital issued to shareholders. Another class of shares is sometimes called '*founders' shares*. These are issued to members of the family which built the business and they sometimes carry enhanced voting rights so that a small group of people can maintain control of a family business. A less flexible class of share is that of *preference shares*. Owners of these shares are not, strictly speaking, owners of the company and their exact rights will be found in the company articles of association. Holders of these shares have preferential rights to receive dividends if profits exist and, in the event of a company winding up, will receive the face value of their shares before the ordinary shareholders are paid. Dividends on preference shares are limited to a fixed percentage of the par value. Some companies issue *cumulative preference shares* and this avoids the difficulty of having to pay preference shareholders if profits are too small. The holder of a cumulative preference share will receive arrears of dividends accumulated from the past in later years. With *redeemable preference shares* the company can buy back the shares from the shareholders. Redemption can be made from profits or reserves or it may be financed by a fresh issue of shares.

The benefits of using risk capital rather than an alternative source of finance are:

1. If the business has had a bad year the company is under no legal obligation to shareholders.

2. Unlike loans whereby the principal has to be returned at the end of a period on a contracted date, the company does not have to pay the share capital back.

3. Interest on loan capital is an overhead which reduces profits whereas share capital does not create overheads.

The dangers of using risk capital are:

1. It can be expensive to issue shares.

2. Companies have to undergo the rigorous financial requirements of the Stock Exchange to be listed and then demands for shares would be subject to the uncertainties of the marketplace.

3. The creation of more shareholders may dilute the influence of the founders of the company and their ability to make decisions.

Case Study—Virgin goes private

Share ownership assumed a lavish flavour when the Virgin Group went public in 1986 at a price of 140p per share. However, shareholders were disappointed, because although share prices reached a peak of 177p, they slumped to a low of 83p and throughout 1988 they remained below the purchase price. Mr Branson blamed the falling value of the group's shares on the City's low opinion of their worth. Virgin seems to have been a victim of City short-termism. Institutions expected them to produce good short-term results and not to take risks which could affect confidence or profits. Both Mr Branson's style of management and the nature of the Virgin Group's operations were high risk and not viewed favourably. Virgin had been planning a £50 million rights issue as the crash hit in October 1987 and this affected its expansion plans. Many felt that Branson and the stock market were incompatible and that he did not fulfil his obligations to shareholders.

In October 1988 Richard Branson made a £248 million offer to slash the losses of the Virgin Group's 40 000 small shareholders. Glowtrack was formed to buy out the group's minority shareholders before re-forming Virgin the private company. The deal was struck at 140p per share—the same price at which Virgin went public two years previously. Branson will need to maintain the group's performance to pay back the £128 million of debt used to finance the buy-out.

Questions

1. In what ways did the emergence of the Virgin Group PLC as a fully quoted company of the stock market
    (a) advantage the company;
    (b) disadvantage the company?

2. Why has Richard Branson decided to convert the group back to a private company?

3. Why is it now more important than ever that the Virgin Group maintains its performance?

4. Explain the meaning of the following terms:
   (a) Public company
   (b) Private company
   (c) Short-termism
   (d) October stock market crash
   (e) Rights issue
   (f) Obligations to shareholders

5. How might Richard Branson have financed the buy-out?

Profit retention

The most important sources of capital for British industry are profits which have been ploughed back into the business (see Fig. 10.2). Initially, profits are subject to corporation tax and a proportion is payable to the Department of Inland Revenue. Then a proportion is paid to shareholders as dividends. The board of directors recommends how much profit should be allocated to dividends. The board needs to satisfy shareholders and, at the same time, ensure that sufficient funds are available for reinvestment.

Directors do not want shareholders to express dissatisfaction at the annual general meeting or to sell their shares and thus cause share prices to fall so that the undervaluation leaves the company subject to a take-over bid. The profits retained in the business are shown in the balance sheet as reserves. The funds represented by these reserves are spread among the assets.

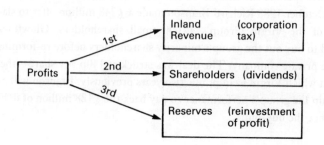

Figure 10.2 Order of profit allocation.

Borrowing

Many businesses need considerable financial help, particularly in their infancy. In order to obtain this they prepare a business plan with a cash flow forecast so that they can represent their needs to financial backers. By analysing their reserves and overheads it can be seen whether both the loan repayments and the interest can be afforded. If payments are not sustained the lender could take legal action in order to recover both the principal and the outstanding interest.

Loans which carry a higher risk tend to carry higher interest rates, e.g. longer term loans have higher interest rates and smaller companies tend to have to pay higher interest rates. Financial institutions involved in lending activities try to provide a package of lending facilities to match the needs of the borrower.

A *debenture* is an acknowledgement of a debt made to a company for a fixed rate of interest and which specifies the terms of repayment at the end of a period. It is therefore a long-term loan which is transferable on the Stock Exchange. A debenture holder is not a company member but a creditor. This means that interest payments are an expense to the company and are allowable against profits for corporation tax purposes. Thus it can often be cheaper to finance a company with debentures rather than issue shares. Though holding debentures is much less risky than holding ordinary shares their value on the marketplace will vary with interest rates. A debenture which pays a 10 per cent rate of interest will be worth 10/8 or 1.25 per cent of its face value when interest rates are 8 per cent. If interest rates rise to 15 per cent it would only be worth 10/15 or 0.66 of its face value. Thus if interest rates rise the value of the loan falls and vice versa.

Though loans often come from a variety of sources the main source is the *banks*. Repayments are usually credited to a separate loan account in equal monthly instalments and these have a fixed rate of interest.

There is a variety of schemes offered by centrally coordinated organizations, e.g. companies might be eligible for loans under *The Government Small Firms Loan Guarantee Scheme* whereby loans of up to £75 000 can be made for two to seven years to most types of small business. *The Rural Development Commission* aims to help small businesses in rural areas. *The European Coal and Steel Community Global Loan Scheme* encourages the creation of new jobs in coal or steel closure areas, etc.

Lenders will always look to minimize the risks of loan finance. When providing finance for a limited company, it is conceivable that the lender will demand a *personal guarantee* of repayment from the main shareholder. This effectively removes that shareholder's limited liability and puts him or her in a similar position to a partner or a sole trader. Lenders frequently ask for *security* or *collateral* against a loan. In this way assets are secured and, if the business starts to flounder, the lender will have priority over other creditors on the receipts from the sale of these secured assets to repay the loan, e.g. a commercial mortgage enables business of all types to acquire freehold and leasehold premises and provides the lender with a good title upon default. It is possible for lenders to insist upon *covenants* or *conditions* to restrict the activities of businesses being lent money, e.g. these might limit their ability to sell assets or determine their levels of gearing etc.

The more usual sources of loans are from:

- High street banks, e.g. National Westminster, Barclays, etc.
- The merchant banks who provide specialist business and financial services.
- Suppliers of venture capital such as Investors in Industry. In 1975 the Industrial

and Commercial Finance Corporation and the Finance Corporation for Industry were merged and were later named Investors in Industry. Their purpose is to provide venture capital for projects unlikely to provide a profitable return in the near future.

- Public funds through various government departments and development agencies.
- Insurance companies, pension funds, building societies, etc.

The benefits of using loan capital are:

1. In relation to raising funds through share issue, it is cheap.
2. Inflation will benefit the borrower because the value of the interest payment will diminish. The loan and the interest will be worth less in real terms.
3. Interest payments are a company expense and appear in the profit and loss account before corporation tax is assessed.

The dangers of using loan capital are:

1. Any loan charge must be paid irrespective of the business performance.
2. A highly geared company would reduce its ability to allocate profits to shareholders.
3. Excessive loan capital may affect a business's flexibility. Repayments will have to be met at certain times and these dates might not match incomes from sales. Covenants, guarantees, etc., could affect decision making.

Leasing and hiring

Major banks have links with *finance houses* which provide a variety of schemes enabling customers to receive goods and make payments over time. Goods on hire-purchase remain the property of the finance company until the customer has made all of the payments, whereas other credit purchasing schemes enable the goods to belong to the customer from the first payment.

Another way in which a company can gain the use of an asset without having to pay for it is through leasing. The lessee will use the asset and make regular payments to the lessor who owns it. An operating lease is for a small amount and a capital or finance lease is for a large item over an extended period. As the asset does not belong to the lessee it will not appear in the balance sheet. The procedure for leasing is for a company to choose the equipment it requires and this is purchased by the leasing company. A contract determines the rent payable and the conditions, e.g. options to purchase, maintenance agreements, etc.

The benefits of leasing are:

1. It enables a business to have complete use of an asset without having to use risk or loan capital to finance it.
2. Leasing payments are an expense and are charged to the profit and loss account before tax is assessed.

3. Leasing enables businesses to change their equipment frequently and keep up to date with modern technology.
4. Tax allowances can be claimed by the lessor and be filtered through to the lessee in lower lease payments.

Though leasing enables the lessee to manage expenditure more easily, the lessee does not own the equipment. If income falters lease payments may impose a considerable burden upon a business and loans cannot be secured upon assets which are leased!

Overdraft

An overdraft is the most frequently used form of short-term bank finance and is used to ease cash flow problems. Arrangements are made between the customer and the bank to include an agreed limit beyond which the customer will not draw. Interest is calculated on the level of the overdraft on a daily basis. Often a bank will make a special charge for arranging an overdraft and committing the bank's money whether the withdrawal facilities are used or not. After an agreed period the bank looks at the account and makes a decision whether to revise or reinstate the limit.

Whereas the account of a personal customer will show a regular input of income per month and a regular pattern of expenditure (see Fig. 10.3(a)), this does not happen with a business customer who is dependent upon debtors paying their bills. As a result of these fluctuations it is easy to understand why business customers often slip into an overdraft situation (see Fig. 10.3(b)) and need this flexible form of short-term finance.

In order to overcome this problem a bank might offer the business the use of its *factoring* service. Trade debts can be tied up for periods extending beyond three months. A factoring company offers an immediate payment against these debtors

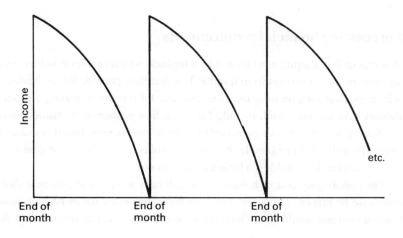

Figure 10.3(a) Personal account.

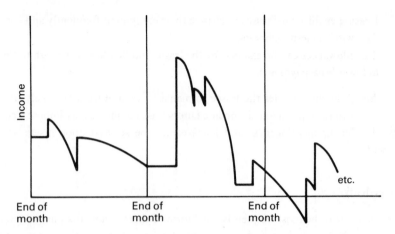

Figure 10.3(b) Business account.

(normally 80 per cent) and the rest when the debt is paid. In this way the firm improves its liquidity with immediate funds and ensures that its assets are not tied up in debtors. The factoring company takes away the burden of running the sales ledger and the problem of collecting payments. It charges interest on the sum advanced as well as administration charges.

Trade credit

A useful form of credit for all businesses is the trade credit advanced by suppliers. This is often governed by the type of industry and by the relationship between the purchaser and supplier. Though no rate of interest is attached to trade credit, cash discounts are forfeited if payments are not promptly met.

Businesses which try to maximize the benefits of trade credit might cause their reputations to suffer.

Forecasting financial requirements

Whereas cash is a liquid asset owned by a business which enables it to buy goods and services, profit is a surplus from trading. It is therefore possible for the business to be selling goods at a higher price than they cost and for them to be making a profit but, if debtors have not been paid, it could have cash flow problems. A business must look carefully at its flow of cash to ensure that the use of its most liquid resource is economically utilized. For example, if a business holds too much cash, it could be sacrificing profits and if it holds too little it could run out.

The opportunity cost of holding too much cash would be the interest that could otherwise be earned. If interest rates are high businesses are sacrificing income by holding cash and would like to hold the lowest possible cash balances so that they can earn interest from the rest. In times of inflation businesses will wish to hold larger levels of cash to finance the increasing price of transactions.

Case Study—Ark Geophysics Limited

For a number of years Richard Gleave, Kitty Hall and Andy McGrandle worked for companies involved in the processing and interpretation of geophysical software. Though they enjoyed the benefits of being involved in a high-tech industry they felt that they were earning money for others and wanted to make a more individual contribution to their work so that it would be more challenging, creative and stimulating. They clearly needed to satisfy a number of essential questions.

- Where could they obtain business premises?
- What were their financial needs?
- What equipment would they need?
- Would there be enough work?
- What about the competition? . . . and so on.

In order to answer these and many other questions, Richard, Kitty and Andy carefully researched their ideas and put together a *sensitivity analysis* to indicate the levels of risk they might face. They looked at their predicted sales, costs and overheads. They also looked at the capital expenditure necessary before trading began. From their analysis the indicators pointed towards the viability of their ideas. They drew up projections of cash flow and these were included in their business plan. The plan was taken to a number of banks and they were suprised that they were getting different offers from each. The National Westminster Bank provided them with their package which included a loan and leasing facilities from Lombard North Central. Ark Geophysics Limited officially started trading on 1 January 1986.

They found that their predicted cash flow closely matched their actual cash flow though revenues had come in in a slightly different order to that expected. Today Ark is a successful private limited company whose reputation is widespread in the geophysics industry.

Questions

1. Why did Richard, Kitty and Andy carry out a sensitivity analysis?
2. Would this analysis answer all of their questions and how would the answers from this analysis relate to the risks?
3. In what ways might the packages offered by banks vary?
4. Why is a predicted cash flow required as part of a business plan.

5. Think carefully of a business idea you may have. Draw up a sensitivity analysis to assess the risks. Provide a hypothetical forecast cash flow for your business idea. (Use the layout shown later in the chapter to help you.)

Cash flow

Looking carefully at the availability of liquid funds is essential to the smooth running of any company. With cash planning or budgeting the accountant will forecast the flows of cash into and out of the company's bank account so that any excess payments over receipts can be highlighted and then action can be taken to overcome this short-fall, e.g. overdraft facilities can be arranged well in advance so that funds are available when required.

In order to prepare a cash budget the accountant needs to know what receipts and payments are likely to take place in the future and the dates when they will happen. It is important to find the length of lead time between incurring an expense and paying for it as well as the time lag between making a sale and collecting from debtors. The art of successful cash budgeting is to be able to calculate accurately receipts and ex-penditures, e.g. goods might be bought in January and used in May. These goods could then be sold in May and the money received in August. This clearly refers to the principle of the cash cycle shown in the previous chapter.

Example

A cash budget for the six months ended 31 December 1990 can be drafted from the information below:

1. Cash balance on 1 July 1990 £4500.
2. Sales at £15 per unit and cash is received three months *after* the sale.
    Sale of units

	1990										1991	
	Mar	Apr	May	Jun	Jul	Aug	Sept	Oct	Nov	Dec	Jan	Feb
	60	60	75	90	55	140	130	150	150	160	170	150

3. Production in units is:

	1990										1991	
	Mar	Apr	May	Jun	Jul	Aug	Sept	Oct	Nov	Dec	Jan	Feb
	40	50	80	70	80	130	130	150	145	160	170	160

4. Raw materials cost £4 per unit and these are paid for two months *before* being used for production.
5. Direct labour £5 per unit paid in the same month as the unit produced.
6. Other variable expenses are £4 per unit—50 per cent of the cost is paid in the same month as production while the other 50 per cent is paid for in the month *after* production.

7.   Fixed expenses of £50 are paid monthly.

Receipts

					£
July	60	(April)	× 15 =		900
August	75	(May)	× 15 =		1125
September	90	(June)	× 15 =		1350
October	55	(July)	× 15 =		825
November	140	(Aug.)	× 15 =		2100
December	130	(Sept.)	× 15 =		1950

Payments

July

					£
Raw materials	130	(Sept.)	×	4 =	520
Direct labour	80	(July)	×	5 =	400
Variable expenses:	80	(July)	×	2 =	160
	70	(June)	×	2 =	140
Fixed expenses				=	50
					£1270

August

					£
Raw materials	150	(Oct.)	×	4 =	600
Direct labour	130	(Aug.)	×	5 =	650
Variable expenses:	130	(Aug.)	×	2 =	260
	80	(July)	×	2 =	160
Fixed expenses				=	50
					£1720

September

					£
Raw materials	145	(Nov.)	×	4 =	580
Direct labour	130	(Sept.)	×	5 =	650
Variable expenses:	130	(Sept.)	×	2 =	260
	130	(Aug.)	×	2 =	260
Fixed expenses				=	50
					£1800

October

					£
Raw materials	160	(Dec.)	×	4 =	640
Direct labour	150	(Oct.)	×	5 =	750
Variable expenses:	150	(Oct.)	×	2 =	300
	130	(Sept.)	×	2 =	260
Fixed expenses				=	50
					£2000

November

					£
Raw materials	170	(June)	×	4 =	680
Direct labour	145	(Nov.)	×	5 =	725
Variable expenses:	145	(Nov.)	×	2 =	290
	150	(Oct.)	×	2 =	300
Fixed expenses				=	50
					£2045

December

					£
Raw materials	160	(Feb.)	×	4 =	640
Direct labour	160	(Dec.)	×	5 =	800
Variable expenses:	160	(Dec.)	×	2 =	320
	145	(Nov.)	×	2 =	290
Fixed expenses				=	50
					£2100

Cash budget

	July	Aug.	Sept.	Oct.	Nov.	Dec.
	£	£	£	£	£	£
Cash balance	4500	4130	3535	3085	1910	1965
Add Receipts	900	1125	1350	825	2100	1950
	5400	5255	4885	3910	4010	3915
Less Payments	1270	1720	1800	2000	2045	2100
Balance carried forward	4130	3535	3085	1910	1965	1815

The cash budget has indicated that although the cash balance will fall over the six months from £4500 to £1815, no overdraft facilities will be required.

Managing working capital

Working capital is the difference between current assets and current liabilities. Current assets are either in the form of cash or soon to lead to cash, and current liabilities will soon have to be paid for with cash. In the previous chapter we indicated that a prudent ratio of current assets to current liabilities is considered to be 2 : 1 though most businesses operate with a slightly lower ratio than this. It is now more commonly thought that a satisfactory working capital ratio will depend upon the company concerned, the type of business operation, stock levels and other factors.

Working capital is often considered to be the portion of capital which 'oils the wheels' of business. Funds employed in fixed assets are concerned with producing goods and services. Working capital provides stocks from which the fixed assets may produce. It allows the salesforce to offer trade credit and create debtors. Firms with insufficient working capital are in a financial straitjacket. They lack the funds to buy stocks, and to produce and create debtors. In these circumstances providers of finance may well call a meeting of creditors and appoint a liquidator. Clearly, a business must always have adequate short-term funds to ensure the continuation of its activities.

The operating cycle expresses the connection between working capital and movements of cash. It can measure the period of time between:

- the purchase of raw materials and the receipt of cash from debtors;
- the time cash is paid out for raw materials and the time cash is received from sales (see Fig. 10.4).

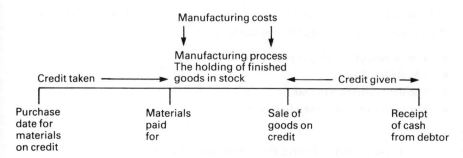

Figure 10.4 Managing the credit cycle.

Example

A firm buys raw materials on two months' credit, holds them in stock for half a month before issuing them to a production department from which they come as finished goods. These are held on average for one and a half months before sale. Debtors take three months to pay. The cash cycle would be:

	Months
Raw materials credit from suppliers	(2)
Turnover of stock of raw materials	0.5
Turnover of stock of finished goods	1.5
Debtors' payment period	3.0
Cash cycle	3.0 months

Not only does this cycle show the time ingredient it also shows that income from debtors should be more than enough to cover any manufacturing costs and overheads encountered.

The dangers of insufficient working capital are clear to see:

1. A company with limited working capital will not be able to buy in bulk and could lose the opportunity to gain trade discounts.
2. Cash discounts will be lost as the business will avoid paying creditors until the last possible opportunity.
3. It will become more difficult to offer extensive credit facilities to customers. By shortening the credit period, customers may well go to alternative suppliers.

4. The company is unable to innovate. Limited finances will hinder its ability to develop new products or improve production techniques.
5. A company's financial reputation as a good payer may be lost.
6. Creditors may well take action. As capital becomes squeezed a company will be forced to finance its activities by overdrafts and trade credit. A point could well be reached where its future is dependent upon the actions of creditors.
7. Overtrading can take place. This would involve financing a large volume of production with inadequate working capital often from short-term loans. This can lead to a complete imbalance of the working capital ratio.

Ratio analysis enables a check to be made upon a company's liquidity. Those ratios of particular use in assessing working capital are:

- The current or working capital ratio.
- The acid-test ratio.
- The debt collection period.
- The period of credit taken from suppliers.

Case Study—Dinsdale Electronics Limited

Dinsdale's Managing Director is constantly worried about the company's cash flow position and its effects upon decision making and innovation. Though profits have been fair, the company's market share has been falling.

$$Current\ ratio = 0.8$$
$$Quick\ ratio = 0.5$$
$$Debt\ collection\ period = 73\ days$$
$$Period\ of\ credit\ from\ suppliers = 45\ days$$

Many transactions are being financed with readily available overdrafts at a cost of 12 per cent p.a.

Questions

1. What sort of problems could Dinsdale's MD be experiencing?
2. Advise Dinsdale's MD on how to improve the working capital position.
3. It can be said that profits are not as important as cash flow when companies are trying to retain their market share. How valid is a statement of this kind?

Accountants are constantly reviewing a company's asset structure to ensure that resources are utilized efficiently and, dependent upon their review, it might be necessary to increase working capital. This might take place in a number of ways:

1. Reducing the period between the time cash is paid out for raw materials and the time cash is received from sales will provide funds for regeneration. Though the

improved efficiency of cash cycle will help working capital, it might be unpopular with creditors.

2. Fixed assets such as land and buildings might not be fully utilized or space might be used for unprofitable purposes. Space could be rented, sold or house a more profitable operation so that cash flow could be improved. Businesses might wish to improve cash flow by selling assets and leasing them back, though this can commit them to heavy leasing fees.

3. A company could review its stock levels to see if these could be the subject of economy measures. If the stock of raw materials is divided by the average weekly issue, the number of week's raw materials held in stock can be calculated. Some companies attempt to maximize liquidity by using the 'just in time' philosophy of holding the minimum possible stocks. Though they might save upon expenses associated with running a store and looking after stocks, they might lose out upon trade discounts and be susceptible to inconsistent supplies.

4. Many companies employ a credit controller to economize on debtors. A credit controller will vet new customers and set a credit limit, ensure that credit limits are not exceeded and also encourage debtors to pay. Credit controllers are often caught in a conflict with the sales department, whose staff wish them to extend credit limits, and the accounts department, which want debtors to pay quickly and so increase the working capital.

5. As we have seen, cash budgeting can be used as an important control mechanism to predict the effect of future transactions on the cash balance of a company. Cash budgeting can help a company to take actions to ensure that cash is available when required.

6. A number of short-term solutions are available to increase working capital. Companies might extend their overdraft or bring in a factoring company. It might be possible to delay the payment of bills, though this obviously displeases creditors.

Accountants will ensure that the solution adopted uses the capital employed more efficiently.

Investment decisions and the appraisal of capital

Investment involves the immediate risk of funds in the hope of securing returns later. There are often more investment proposals than the necessary finance to back them. Organizations need to decide upon the best way to invest money in a way which will maximize their returns. Entrepreneurs use their creative and imaginative skills to look for investment opportunities. In the early stages they will gather information in order to appraise the alternatives. When decisions involve non-financial aspects this can be difficult, for example, the image of the business. The decision-making process will be primarily concerned with weighing up the benefits against the costs. Once the decision has been made projects are put into action and their results are monitored.

The primary objective of any investment decision is to obtain a return on the investment which is greater than the initial outlay of capital. Three criteria determining that outlay will be the sum invested, its returns, and the length of time the project is expected to last.

We will look at:

1. Average rate of return method.
2. Payback method.
3. Discounted cash flow—net present value.
4. Discounted cash flow—internal rate of return.

Average rate of return method

Many express profitability as a rate of return on an investment. The average rate of return can be calculated as long as the net profits for the life of the investment and the book value are known. It is generally considered to be a quick and convenient guide for assessing the profitability of alternative projects. It is calculated by dividing the average annual profit by the initial investment. For example, if we had two projects we could select an alternative as shown in the table.

	Project A £	Project B £
Initial cost	− 10 000	− 20 000
Year 1 cash receipts	+ 4 000	+ 9 000
Year 2 cash receipts	+ 5 000	+ 9 000
Year 3 cash receipts	+ 5 000	+ 12 000
Year 4 cash receipts	+ 4 000	+ 10 000
Total cash receipts	+ 18 000	+ 40 000
Profit over four years	+ 8 000	+ 20 000
Average annual profit	+ 2 000	+ 5 000
Initial investment	10 000	20 000
	20 per cent	25 per cent

The average rate of return can be criticized as it is based upon book values and fails to take heed of changing price levels. Its process also fails to consider the timings of cash receipts.

Payback method

The purpose of this method is to establish how quickly the investment cost can be repaid. The shorter the payback period the better the project. For example, using this method, if we had two investment possibilities which both cost £15 000, we could select an alternative as shown in the table.

Project A repays the initial cost by the end of Year 4, whereas Project B does not repay until the end of Year 5.

	Project A £	Project B £
Initial cost	−15 000	−15 000
Year 1 cash receipts	+ 3 000	+ 1 000
Year 2 cash receipts	+ 3 000	+ 3 000
Year 3 cash receipts	+ 4 000	+ 3 000
Year 4 cash receipts	+ 5 000	+ 3 000
Year 5 cash receipts	+ 3 000	+ 5 000

Using the payback method we would choose Project A. The essential feature of the payback form of capital appraisal is that it takes timing into consideration and the early return of funds could be of primary importance to firms with liquidity problems. For businesses in a high-tech industry, where capital equipment is constantly being changed, it can provide a rough guide to the extent of a risk.

The main criticism of the payback method is that it does not take into account cash flows (see table).

	Project A £	Project B £
Initial cost	−15 000	−15 000
Year 1 cash receipts	+ 5 000	+ 1 000
Year 2 cash receipts	+ 5 000	+ 2 000
Year 3 cash receipts	+ 5 000	+12 000

The payback method does not differentiate between Project A and Project B because both methods pay back in three years. In the same way this method ignores cash receipts expected after the payback period. No attention is placed upon subsequent years. It does not therefore take into account the profitability of the two alternatives.

Not only does the payback method fail to account for the timing of cash flows, it also fails to relate the value of future returns with immediate investments. In money terms an investment made today should have a higher value in the future because, if it was invested, it would yield some sort of return. Discounted cash flow relates the expected value of future cash receipts and expenditures to a common date.

DCF—net present value

This is a method of weighing up investment decisions which leans heavily on the theory of opportunity cost. Before management commits a company to an investment decision, the benefits of which will be reaped over a number of years, the real value of future returns will need to be re-assessed. Because the value of money alters with time, it is helpful to look at future flows of money in terms of their present value.

Interest payments compensate for:

1. The cost of time (i.e. not having money available now).
2. The cost of inflation (price rises erode the real value of money).
3. The risk of investment.

The interest rate gives a guide to the future value of investment. Alternatively, the current value of investment can be compared with what it was worth in the past.

If an investor has £1000 in a bank account where it is earning 10 per cent interest, the balance will stand at £1100 at the end of the first year. By compounding this annually, at the end of:

> Year 2 it will be worth £1210 (£1100 + £110)
> Year 3 it will be worth £1331 (£1210 + £121), etc.

At the end of this time the investor can say that £1331 was worth £1000 three years ago.

This can be shown the other way round, e.g. what would £1000 now have been worth three years ago at a 10 per cent rate of interest?

$$\frac{£1000}{£1331} \times £1000 = £751.3$$

2 years ago?

$$\frac{£1000}{£1210} \times £1000 = £826.4$$

1 year ago?

$$\frac{£1000}{£1100} \times £1000 = £909.1$$

Thus assuming a constant rate of interest of 10 per cent, £1000 now was worth £751.30 three years ago, and will be worth £1331 in three years' time. Thus, the time element has been taken into account. DCF tables are available and these relate rates of interest to a period of time in years.

DCF tables from 1 per cent to 10 per cent over six years—per cent rate of discount

Future years	1	2	3	4	5	6	7	8	9	10
1	0.990	0.980	0.971	0.962	0.952	0.943	0.935	0.926	0.917	0.909
2	0.980	0.961	0.943	0.925	0.907	0.890	0.873	0.857	0.842	0.826
3	0.971	0.942	0.915	0.889	0.864	0.840	0.816	0.794	0.772	0.751
4	0.961	0.924	0.888	0.855	0.823	0.792	0.763	0.735	0.708	0.683
5	0.951	0.906	0.863	0.822	0.784	0.747	0.713	0.681	0.650	0.621
6	0.942	0.888	0.837	0.790	0.746	0.705	0.666	0.630	0.596	0.564

For example, look at the following net surplus returns for two projects which have an initial capital investment of £200 000:

	Project A £	Project B £
Earnings Year 1	100 000	80 000
Earnings Year 2	110 000	100 000
Earnings Year 3	100 000	100 000
Earnings Year 4	80 000	100 000
Earnings Year 5	20 000	30 000
Total return	410 000	410 000

Discounted cash flow at a rate of interest of 10 per cent

	Project A			Project B	
Year	Earnings £	NPV* £	Discount factor	Earnings £	NPV* £
0		200 000			200 000
1	100 000	90 000	0.909	80 000	72 720
2	110 000	90 860	0.826	100 000	82 600
3	100 000	75 100	0.751	100 000	75 100
4	80 000	54 640	0.683	100 000	68 300
5	20 000	12 420	0.621	30 000	18 630
		£323 920			£317 350

* NPV = Net Present Value.

Clearly, Project A is the project to opt for as, at today's value, returns will be higher. If net present value comes out at less than the original investment, it is not worth considering the project at all.

The clear advantage of the net present value method is that it takes into account the time element of money and is also easy to calculate. The dangers of depending upon it are that both interest rates and cash flows are subject to uncertainty.

Case Study—Sutton Coldfield Engineering PLC

Sutton Coldfield Engineering PLC is considering two alternative projects to develop its profitability. Until recently the company has always appraised projects on the basis that any investment should pay back within four years. After extensive discussions at board level it has been decided to use a DCF method of project appraisal (net present value) with a target rate of return of 10 per cent.

Project A   Setting up a production line to fully automate the productive process. This will cost £120 000 and provide a saving of £30 000 each year for the first six years.

Project B   Spending £100 00 on a prolonged advertising campaign. Evidence suggests that this will increase net revenues by:

	£
Year 1	20 000
Year 2	30 000
Year 3	30 000
Year 4	40 000
Year 5	10 000
Year 6	10 000

Both projects are to be evaluated using both the payback and DCF (net present value) methods.

Project A   Payback

As the initial investment is £120 000 and the annual saving is £30 000 it will be paid back in four years. This only just meets the criterion that the payback period should be reached within four years.

Project A   DCF (net present value)

Year	Earnings £	DCF (NPV) £	Discount factor
0	120 000		
1	30 000	27 270	0.909
2	30 000	24 780	0.826
3	30 000	22 530	0.751
4	30 000	20 490	0.683
5	30 000	18 630	0.621
6	30 000	16 920	0.564
		£130 620	

Clearly, the returns are greater than the initial investment and the project can be recommended as it provides a net present value of + £10 620.

Project B   Payback

The initial investment of £100 000 can be paid back in three and a half years and this is an improvement on the payback period for Project A. The returns are again greater than the investment and provide a net present value of + £4660.

We are now left with a problem. Project B is clearly preferable under the payback method because it pays back in three and a half years in comparison to Project A's four years. Project A brings in a net present value of + £10 620 whereas Project B brings in a net present value of + £4660.

Project B   DCF (net present value)

Year	Earnings £	DCF (NPV) £	Discount factor
0	100 000		
1	20 000	18 180	0.909
2	30 000	24 780	0.826
3	30 000	22 530	0.751
4	40 000	27 320	0.683
5	10 000	6 210	0.621
6	10 000	5 640	0.564
		£104 660	

Whereas Project B has been favoured by the payback method because it has a better cash flow earlier in its life, it could be argued that taking into account real values by using DCF, Project A would be more profitable.

DCF—internal rate of return

This method aims to find out the average return of an investment throughout its life-span. This 'internal rate of return' is then compared to the criteria for the project to see if it is worth while. This method is therefore concerned with percentage returns on investment, *not* with cash figures.

$$
\begin{array}{ll}
& \text{Project} \\
\text{Year 0} & -20\,000 \\
\text{Year 1} & +\ 8\,000 \\
\text{Year 2} & +\ 5\,000 \\
\text{Year 3} & +\ 5\,000 \\
\text{Year 4} & +\ \underline{5\,000} \\
& \overline{\underline{23\,000}}
\end{array}
$$

We try to find the internal rate of return by trial and error.
At 10 per cent it would be:

$$
\begin{array}{rl}
-\,20\,000 + 8\,000 \times 0.909 = & 7\,272 \\
+\,5\,000 \times 0.826 = & 4\,130 \\
+\,5\,000 \times 0.751 = & 3\,755 \\
+\,5\,000 \times 0.683 = & \underline{3\,415} \\
+ & \underline{18\,572}
\end{array}
$$

$$
-\,20\,000 + 18\,572 = \underline{-\,1428}
$$

The return is clearly not 10 per cent and so we need to try a lower rate.

At 6 per cent it would be:

$$
\begin{aligned}
- 20\,000 + 8\,000 \times 0.943 &= 7\,544 \\
+ 5\,000 \times 0.890 &= 4\,450 \\
+ 5\,000 \times 0.840 &= 4\,200 \\
+ 5\,000 \times 0.792 &= \underline{3\,960} \\
&+ 20\,154 \\
- 20\,000 + 20\,154 &= \underline{+154}
\end{aligned}
$$

We have shown that the internal rate of return lies between 6 per cent and 10 per cent.

To obtain the internal rate of return we:

1. take the lower rate (6)
2. add the difference between the two interest rates (4)
3. multiply by the difference at the lower rate ($+154$)
4. divide this by the total difference between the two rates (1582)

$$6 + \frac{(4 \times 154)}{1582} = 6.39 \text{ per cent}$$

As long as the firm can borrow money at a lower rate than 6.39 per cent, it will find the project worth while. The internal rate of return does not aim to obtain a cash figure but seeks a percentage rate, so that returns can be expressed as a percentage of investment cost.

Cost–benefit analysis

By their very nature, investment decisions not only affect the well-being of a particular organization, but also have implications for the community in which the company is based. Our analysis of investment decisions and capital appraisal only considered the benefits created for a particular organization. Cost–benefit analysis takes the process further and considers the wider and longer term social implications of investment proposals.

Commercial enterprise is about the creation of wealth. It provides employment and incomes for a variety of groups and, in doing so, improves living standards. Its *private costs* are the costs to the enterprise from engaging in a particular activity, e.g. building and running a factory. Its *private benefits* would be the income derived from engaging in this new activity, e.g. the revenue from the new factory. This organization will have created *social benefits* within the community such as jobs, sports grounds, etc. However, there are some bad effects. These are the *social costs* such as pollution, dereliction, noise, etc. External costs going beyond the management of the internal affairs of the firm are sometimes known as spillover effects or externalities.

Cost–benefit techniques developed after the war to help to analyse complex investment decisions in a developing industrial nation. They take into account a balance of both social and financial criteria in order to aid decision making. For example, the benefits of building a supermarket would be employment, improved facilities, rates for the local authority, etc., whereas the costs would be traffic congestion, effects on other businesses, etc. These benefits and costs would have to be considered by the local authorities.

Cost–benefit analysis attempts to look objectively at all of the aspects of a decision-making process and to express those values in monetary terms so that some level of measurement can take place. Costs and benefits are therefore given a common unit of account for each year of the project's expected life. The net social benefit is obtained by subtracting a particular year's social cost from the same year's social benefit.

Cost–benefit analysis aims to measure not just the quantifiable private costs and benefits of an investment decision but also the surplus of social benefit over social cost. It must therefore be a more complete analysis as it measures costs and benefits to members of the community. Techniques are more appropriate when a large investment takes place which has significant spillover effects.

Case Study—Northfield Tannery Limited

Northfield Tannery is in the process of acquiring a site which could be developed to provide a new factory at Wolverditch. The company is hoping to develop a compact new unit and then, over a five-year period, move all of its operations over from Bridgemoor. Though residents in Wolverditch are unhappy about the prospect of increased traffic noise and water pollution, they concede that the moving of the tannery to the town and the subsequent creation of jobs would provide a number of benefits. Alternative uses for the land could be as a new supermarket, though the town already has three, or as a multi-storey car park. Local fishermen have lobbied councillors over the possible effects on the local river. Conservationists in the town argue that residents' needs could best be served by a park or a municipal golf course.

Questions

1. Identify the
   (a) private costs;
   (b) private benefits;
   (c) social costs;
   (d) social benefits of building a tannery in Wolverditch.
2. Explain why social considerations are thought to be important.
3. Should chartered accountants involve themselves in social accounting?

Short answer questions

1. Why are interest rates known as the cost of using money?
2. Give an example of the use of funding.

3. Explain the workings of a cumulative preference share.
4. Name two dangers of using risk capital.
5. Name two ways in which a company might appropriate its profits.

(*Source:* AEB.)

6. What is an undervaluation?
7. How does a debenture work?
8. Give two reasons why a business may sell a debt to a factor.   (*Source:* AEB.)
9. What percentage of its face value will a debenture be worth when the rate of interest is 12 per cent?
10. What does the Rural Development Commission aim to provide?
11. Explain what is meant by a personal guarantee.
12. What is meant by the term 'venture capital'?
13. A company wishes to install a new machine. Give four methods of financing the purchase.   (*Source:* AEB.)
14. Name two benefits of leasing.
15. Why will businesses wish to hold cash in times of inflation?
16. Briefly explain why working capital 'oils the wheels' of business.
17. Name two dangers of insufficient working capital.
18. Name two disadvantages of the payback method of capital appraisal.
19. In your own words, explain the meaning of the term 'discounted cash flow'.
20. Distinguish between social costs and private costs.

Essays

1. What are the quantitative techniques of investment appraisal? Assess the extent to which they should be used by firms to plan future capital investment.

(*Source:* AEB.)

2. The following is an extract from the balance sheet of a public limited company.

	£
Ordinary shares	
Authorized 800,000 at £1 each	800,000
Issued and fully paid 700,000 at £1 each	700,000
Long-term borrowing	
Debentures 10 per cent (2010)	300,000
Capital employed	£1,000,000

The company now wishes to raise an additional £500 000 to finance the development of a new product. Assess the implications of the relevant alternative sources of finance.   (*Source:* AEB.)

3. How is it possible for a profitable firm to run out of cash, or for a cash-rich firm to be unprofitable?

4. Consider the view that a firm's growth imposes so many strains, of both an internal and external nature, that ultimate failure is inevitable.   (*Source:* AEB.)

5. Discuss the considerations which influence a firm in deciding between growth by internal or external expansion.   (*Source:* Oxford.)

6. (a) What do you understand by the term 'gearing', and how might it be measured?

    (b) How might a finance house use gearing ratios when considering an application from a medium-sized manufacturing company for a loan of £5 000 000 for expansion purposes?

    (c) What alternative sources of funds might the firm examine?

                                                                 (*Source:* Cambridge.)

7. Compare the benefits of using risk capital with the benefits of using loan capital.

8. Leasing is a way a company can gain the use of an asset without having to buy it. Why has leasing become an increasingly popular way of acquiring fixed assets?

9. Cash budgeting is an important technique for forecasting a company's financial needs and will influence the management of working capital. Discuss.

10. Explain how the following terms refer to investment appraisal:

    (a) Payback

    (b) DCF

    (c) Cost–benefit

Data response questions

1   Delta Machine Tools Limited is a well established light engineering company involved in the manufacture of specialist parts for the motor industry. It is listed on the Stock Exchange. A large proportion of its products are manufactured for the more expensive type of motor car such as Mercedes, BMW and Volvo and involves exporting to Germany and Scandinavia.

The company uses fairly traditional machinery, produces its product parts in medium size batches, and assembles the final products. It operates at 90% average capacity. Peaks are coped with by overtime in the evenings and weekends. The work-force is 30% skilled and 70% semi-skilled. Trade-union membership is 100% and is split between 2 craft unions and one general worker union.

A number of new products have been developed to the tested prototype stage and the commercial prospects for them are good. It is estimated that in 5 years these products will account for 30% of the company's sales. The effect will be to broaden the company's product range and the market for existing products will not be affected.

The development work was not cheap and the company faces a serious cash flow problem over the next 2–3 years while bringing the new products into production.

The Managing Director has decided to raise the finance to deal with the situation as follows:

Increase product prices	20%
Bank borrowing	40%
Internal savings mainly through labour lay-offs	40%

1. (a) Evaluate the Managing Director's solutions.

    (b) Suggest, giving reasons, other means whereby management might solve its cash flow problem.

                                                                    (*Source:* Oxford.)

2   J. Sinclair has approached you for some advice. He has inherited £5000 and intends to start his own business. He has arranged an overdraft limit of £12 000 with his bank manager and this is to last for the first six months of trading, starting on 1 January 1990.

His forecasts for the first six months trading are:

(a)   Receipts from sales:

Jan.	Feb.	Mar.	Apr.	May	June
4500	8300	10 100	11 000	10 200	10 100

(b)   Payment for supplies:

Jan.	Feb.	Mar.	Apr.	May	June
4000	12 100	13 200	14 100	8100	7500

(c)   His drawings are to be £500 per calendar month.

Draw up the cash budget showing balances for the six months to 30 June 1990. Offer Mr Sinclair any advice you feel to be relevant.

3   Draw up a cash budget for N. Long from the following information for the six months from 1 January 1990 to 30 June 1990.

(a)   Opening cash/bank balance 1 January £2250
(b)   Sales at £14 per unit. Debtors will pay 2 months after they have bought goods.

1989

Nov.	Dec.	Jan.	Feb.	Mar.	Apr.	May	Jun.	Jul.	Aug.
105	110	110	115	120	125	130	140	140	150

(c)   Production (units):

Nov.	Dec.	Jan.	Feb.	Mar.	Apr.	May	Jun.	Jul.	Aug.
90	95	120	120	125	125	130	130	135	140

(d)   Raw materials used in the production process cost £5 per unit and these are paid for two months after being used in the production process.
(e)   Direct labour of £3 per unit is paid in the same month as production.
(f)   Other variable expenses are £2 per unit with 50 per cent of the cost paid in the same month as production while the other 50 per cent is paid for in the month after production.
(g)   Fixed expenses of £100 are paid monthly.

4   A company issues 300 000 10 per cent preference shares with a nominal value of £1 and 300 000 ordinary shares with a nominal value of 25p. The directors agree to retain profits of 25 per cent of that left over after preference dividend has been paid. Calculate ordinary dividend, preference dividend and retained profit if profits are:

(a)   £40 000
(b)   £60 000
(c)   £120 000

5   Obtain an annual report of a company and look at the statement of sources and applications of funds. Distinguish between debt capital and loan capital and list:

(a) short-term sources of finance

(b) long-term sources of finance

6 Look at the following data on two investment projects:

	Project A £	Project B £
Initial capital expenditure	60 000	60 000
Profits Year 1	20 000	15 000
Profits Year 2	20 000	20 000
Profits Year 3	18 000	20 000
Profits Year 4	20 000	23 000

(a) The cost of capital is 10 per cent.

(b) Use the table for percentage rate of discount from earlier in the chapter.

  (i) Calculate the payback period, the net present value and the internal rate of return for each project.

  (ii) Comment on the merits of each of these methods.

  (iii) Explain which project you would recommend.

Suggested reading

Hines, T., *Foundation Accounting*. Checkmate Arnold, 1987.
Jennings, A., *Financial Accounting Manual*. DPP, 1984.

11

The management of costs

Managers are always interested in information which comes from the accounting system. All accounting information, whether it comes from published accounts or from changes in production costs, will be of use. Management accountants try to guide their organization in a particular direction in order to achieve objectives. This will involve:

1. creating short-term, medium-term and long-term plans;
2. controlling the organization's activities;
3. deciding between alternative strategies;
4. appraising performance at strategic departmental and operational levels.

Management accounting therefore involves getting data and processing them so that decisions to control operations can be more efficient (see Fig. 11.1).

Cost accounting and the knowledge of costing techniques provide important sources of data for management accountants. They will use their knowledge of costs to predict future events. In doing so they will try to anticipate changes in taxation, interest rates, actions of competitors and markets, etc. They will also look at past events and information from these records in order to guide future decision making.

Over the past 20 years the nature of industry has changed dramatically. Information technology has revolutionized the ways in which information is being provided.

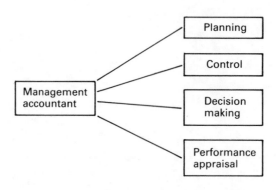

Figure 11.1 The role of the management accountant.

Managers have to be adaptable to changing disciplines so that they can provide the right information when required. In order to do so they are constantly aware of new concepts, principles and techniques designed to help them to meet their objectives.

Costs

Nearly all business activities involve some sort of cost. A good knowledge of costs and their influences is fundamental in assessing the profitability of alternatives as profits are only a reflection of income over these costs. Costs from the past and which have already been incurred should provide a guide to costs in the future. They have to be critically examined, discussed and often adjusted to be of use to the accountant for predicting future profitability. At a later stage accountants will make informed comparisons between actual events and standards which have been set.

There are a number of ways in which costs can be classified and these include:

1. *Fixed costs*   These are costs which do not increase as total output increases. Fixed costs do not change over a range of output even though output within that range will vary (see Fig. 11.2). For example, if a factory has the capacity to do so it might increase its production from 10 000 to 15 000 units. Its overheads such as rent, rates and heating bills will still be the same as they had to be paid when the factory was producing only 10 000 units.

    Economists say that fixed costs are costs which do not vary with output in a given period but, that in the longer term, they will vary, e.g. if the company needed to increase its production of units further it might have to build another factory, buy new machines and incur new overheads.

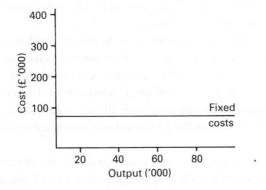

Figure 11.2 Fixed costs.

Average fixed costs will represent the percentage of total fixed costs incurred by each product. As output rises the level of average fixed costs will fall. It is found by dividing total fixed cost by output. For example, if fixed costs are £100 000 and output is 2000 units, average fixed costs will be £50 per unit. If production increases to 4000 units, average fixed costs will fall to £25 per unit.

2. *Variable costs* Variable costs are costs which increase as output increases because then more of these factors need to be employed as input to increase output (see Fig. 11.3). For example, if you produce more you may need more raw materials, more production line workers, more power, etc.

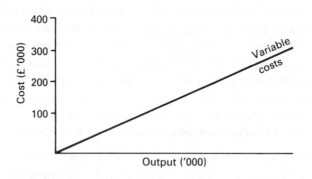

Figure 11.3 Variable costs.

Average variable costs will represent the average level of variable cost attributable to each item of output. It is found by dividing total variable costs by output. There is a strong argument that average variable costs rise when capacity goes beyond a certain level as this will lead to breakdowns, inefficiencies, overcrowding, managerial problems, etc.

3. *Semi-variable costs* The distinction between fixed and variable costs is not always easy to make. Some expenses may be considered to be semi-variable. If output increases this will put pressures upon costs which are relatively fixed. The telephone bill might go up as more calls are now made. Electricity usage in the office may go up as staff put in more overtime, etc.

4. *Direct costs (prime costs)* These are costs which can be directly attributed to the product whose costs are being assessed, e.g. it might be possible to say that 10 per cent of a particular product cost is the direct labour cost of producing it, 15 per cent might be the cost of its direct materials, etc. It tends to be easier to identify variable costs with direct costs as they vary more directly with output. Fixed costs are more difficult to allocate to the production cost of particular commodities.

5. *Indirect costs* These costs cannot be identified with the production of particular commodities. They will probably include costs attributable to all departments, e.g. costs of cleaning, salespersons' salaries, management salaries, etc. Though indirect costs tend to be more fixed than direct costs, e.g. rent, rates and overheads, some can vary considerably, e.g. factory power.

6. *Marginal costs* In economics the marginal cost is the extra cost of producing one more unit of output, e.g. the marginal cost of producing the 100th unit of output is the extra cost of manufacturing the 100th unit after having already

made 99. It is therefore the total cost (total fixed cost + total variable cost) of making the first 100 minus the total cost of making 99.

An accountant's definition of marginal cost is different to that of the economist. Accountants recognize the problems of trying to allocate indirect costs and only therefore allocate direct costs to a product. Indirect costs are left unallocated but not ignored. As we will see later, there must be a sufficient income to cover them and provide a surplus for profits.

7. *Average costs*   Average costs are quite simply the total cost divided by the total quantity produced. The relationship of the marginal concept to the average concept can be shown in this example:

> If a farmer normally receives £100 for each of his lambs when he takes them to an auction mart, revenue of £110 per lamb will push his average up and £90 per lamb will push his average down. Therefore the marginal return will affect his average return as at the top price the average will increase and, at the bottom price, the average will decrease.

In a similar way, if average costs are rising, marginal costs will be above average costs and when average costs are falling the marginal costs will be below them.

With a small output marginal costs per unit tend to be high, but in the long run as output increases costs fall due to economies of scale or the advantages of being large, e.g. discounts for bulk, preferential interest rates, etc.

As firms move beyond an ideal size they develop diseconomies of scale and incur disadvantages of being too large, e.g. poor morale, long chains of command, etc. At this point marginal costs will start to rise.

Budgetary control

Budgetary control is the technique of looking at a business's future in order to anticipate what is going to happen and then trying to make it happen. It is considered to be a system of responsibility accounting because it puts an onus upon budgeted areas to perform in a way that has been outlined for them. Its success will depend upon the quality of the information provided.

Businesses which do not budget have their accounts audited annually and they might be pleased or upset when presented with their final accounts. This technique is uncertain and undisciplined. In order to compete more efficiently it is not feasible that management should wait until the results of an audit to understand how they have performed. Budgeting enables them to develop an understanding of how they are likely to perform in the future. They can cover almost every aspect of business activity, e.g. production, cash, overheads, labour, purchases, debtors, creditors, etc. Information drawn from these budgets can then be used to forecast the final accounts for the end of the following year.

We all budget to a greater or lesser extent. Our short term budget might be how we are going to survive next week and do all of the things that we want to do. Our slightly longer term budget might involve being able to afford Christmas presents in December. Our longest term budget could involve the planning necessary to afford the car tax, MOT and motor insurance which all fall at the same time, next August. In the same way businesses try to dig deep into the future. Though a detailed budget is only prepared for the year ahead, it can be part of a five-year plan. The problem is that, the deeper one digs into the future, the more difficult it is to be accurate.

Companies often appoint a budget controller whose job is to coordinate budgetary activities. The budgeting team will consist of representatives from various areas of activity within the company. This team should be involved in every stage of the following process (see also Fig. 11.4):

1. *Consider objectives*   All decisions should enable a firm to work towards achieving its objectives, e.g. profit maximizing, improving product quality, increasing output, etc.
2. *Provide information*   Managers often look at figures from the past so that budgets are based upon the results of the previous year. Zero-based budgeting is a technique which starts each year afresh so the performance of the whole organization is re-appraised. A clear knowledge of the likely performance of the industry in general, the political and economic climate is likely to help.
3. *Make decisions*   Forward planning and coordination of departmental activities will inevitably present a need to take decisions, e.g. the amount to be spent on advertising, whether to put off the purchase of capital equipment, etc.
4. *Prepare budgets*   Detailed budgets are then prepared for all of the necessary areas of business activity.
5. *Prepare a master budget*   Various budgets can be linked together to product a master budget which will show a forecast set of final accounts.

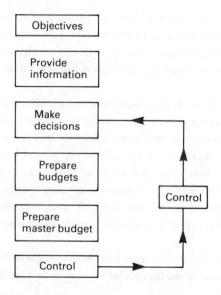

Figure 11.4 The budgetary process.

6. *Control* Even though a plan is outlined in the form of a budget, this does not necessarily mean that it will take place. Managers try to use budgets as a guide to achieve certain results. If there is a difference between actual performance and budgeted performance at the end of a year, action can be taken. Variance analysis is used to analyse the difference between the two. Feedback from variance analysis can affect decision making in subsequent years.

The benefits of a budgetary system are:

1. Every year the business is reviewed and this gives members of departments a better understanding of the working of the organization as a whole. Often by participating in the budgetary process they feel their experience is contributing to policy decisions. The process also provides targets and highlights areas of concern.
2. Budgeting increases cooperation between departments and lowers departmental barriers. In this way members of one department can become aware of the difficulties facing another department.
3. By being involved in the budgetary process non-accountants become aware of the importance of costs. Increasing awareness will probably encourage them to work hard to meet budgeted targets.
4. Budgeting will encourage those who participate in the exercise to think more about profitability and their role in helping the company to reach its objectives.

There are however some inherent dangers; particularly if the budgetary system is rigid. These could be:

1. If actual results are considerably different from the budgeted targets, the budget can lose its significance as a means of control. Whereas a *fixed budget* is unable to adapt to changes, a *flexible budget* will recognize changes in the behaviour of its variables and can be amended each control period in line with changing activities.
2, Following a budget too rigidly can restrict a business's activities, e.g. if the budget for entertainment has been exceeded and visiting customers are not treated to the usual hospitality, orders may be lost. On the other hand, if a manager realizes towards the end of the year that the department has underspent, it is quite possible that he could go on a spending spree.
3. If senior management decides to impose its budget upon departments or middle managers, they are likely to pay little attention to it and make no effort to ensure it succeeds.

The main objective of budgetary control is for management to survey the future and for managers to control their destiny. By doing this they can develop an insight into areas of concern and take action to avoid any problems.

Preparing budgets

In the last chapter we prepared a cash budget so that we could forecast cash flow over a period of time. We will now look at an exercise which looks at all of the budgets necessary to produce a master budget or a forecasted set of final accounts, e.g. at the end of Altron Limited's second year of operations, its balance sheet looked like this:

Altron Limited Balance Sheet as at 30th April 1990

	£	£	£ Net book value
FIXED ASSETS			
Premises			90 000
Plant and machinery			105 000
Office equipment			9 000
Motor vehicles			50 000
			254 000
CURRENT ASSETS			
Stocks: finished goods			
(2000 units)		30 000	
Raw materials		2 000	
Debtors		87 000	
Bank		4 000	
		123 000	
Less CURRENT LIABILITIES			
Creditors for fixed expenses	3 000		
Creditors for raw materials			
(March 28 500 and April 25 500)	54 000	57 000	
Net current assets			66 000
Assets employed			320 000
Financed by:			
Share capital			
Ordinary shares			250 000
Preference shares			50 000
Reserves			20 000
Capital employed			320 000

The company accountant of Altron Limited, Andrew Baxter, has been asked to set up a budgetary system to forecast the next six months' activities. As budgetary controller he has met representatives from various departments and discussed details at length before putting together budgetary estimates. Their plans for the period of six months ending 31.10.90 are as follows:

1. After lengthy consultations a sales price of £15.00 per unit has been agreed. By carefully analysing the market the sales figures are expected to be:

	May	June	July	Aug.	Sept.	Oct.
Number of units	6500	7750	8000	8200	8550	9000

All of the sales are on credit and debtors usually pay their outstanding balances one month after they have bought the goods.

2. In order to satisfy production requirements it has been agreed that purchases of raw materials will be:

	May	June	July	Aug.	Sept.	Oct.
	£23 700	£24 300	£24 500	£27 500	£28 250	£24 750

All raw materials are bought on credit and the creditors for raw materials will be paid two months after purchase.

3. It has been decided that production will be 8000 units per month for May to August and 9000 units per month for September and October.

4. Production costs will be (per unit):

	£
Direct materials	3.00
Direct labour	4.00
Variable overheads	6.00
	13.00

Direct labour and the variable overheads will be paid for in the same month as the units are produced.

5. Fixed expenses average £3000 per month and these are always paid one month in arrears.

Andrew Baxter intends to produce:

(a) A raw materials budget showing figures for each month.
(b) A production budget showing figures for each month (units).
(c) A production cost budget showing figures for each month.
(d) A statement showing total debtors and creditors at the end of October.
(e) A cash budget.
(f) A forecast operating statement (trading and profit, and loss account) for the six months ended 31.10.90.
(g) A forecast balance sheet as at 31.10.90.

The first deals with his *sales forecast* by multiplying the selling price of £15.00 by the number of units for each month.

In May the value of sales is expected to be £97 500, June £116 250, July £120 000, August £123 000, September £128 250 and October £135 000. The total sales figure for the six months is £720 000. Debtors pay one month after having bought the goods so the debtors from the balance sheet in April will pay in May; May debtors will pay in June, etc. When Andrew produces his cash budget these will be entered as receipts.

The *raw materials budget* ensures that there is always an availability of resources

Raw Materials Budget

	May £	June £	July £	Aug. £	Sept. £	Oct. £
Opening stock	2 000	1 700	2 000	2 500	6 000	7 250
Add Purchases	23 700	24 300	24 500	27 500	28 250	24 750
	25 700	26 000	26 500	30 000	34 250	32 000
Less Materials used in production	24 000	24 000	24 000	24 000	27 000	27 000
= Closing stock of raw materials	1 700	2 000	2 500	6 000	7 250	5 000

*Production is 8000 units from May to August and 9000 units in September and October. Production costs for raw or direct materials are £3 per unit. Production will therefore use up £24 000 of materials from May to August and £27 000 of materials in September and October.

moving on to production and that levels do not dwindle or run out. Decisions about minimum stock levels will have been taken beforehand. The raw materials budget involves adding purchases to the opening stocks of raw materials for each month and then deducting those used in production each month.

It must be remembered that creditors for raw materials are paid two months after purchase. This means that those for March (see Balance Sheet) will be paid in May, those from April in June, etc. In the cash budget these will be payments.

There is clearly a close link between the *production budget* and sales. Closing stocks of finished goods are also an important issue and the directors of Altron Limited will need to ensure that they can respond readily to increasing orders if this becomes necessary. The production budget is normally produced in units. The opening stock of finished goods is added to the anticipated production levels for each month and then the monthly sales are deducted.

Production Budget (in units)

	May	June	July	Aug.	Sept.	Oct.
Opening stock of finished goods	2 000	3 500	3 750	3 750	3 550	4 000
Add Production	8 000	8 000	8 000	8 000	9 000	9 000
	10 000	11 500	11 750	11 750	12 550	13 000
Less Sales	6 500	7 750	8 000	8 200	8 550	9 000
= Closing stock of finished goods	3 500	3 750	3 750	3 550	4 000	4 000

The closing stock of finished goods is therefore 4000 units. As stocks are valued at cost price the value of the closing stock of finished goods to be transferred to the balance sheet will be:

$$4000 \text{ units} \times £13 \text{ production cost} = £52\,000$$

The *production cost budget* supplies the costs of production on a month-by-month basis and produces the total cost of goods completed which can then be transferred to the trading section of the forecast operating statement. It involves multiplying the unit production costs of direct materials, direct labour and direct overheads by the number of units produced month by month.

Production Cost Budget

	8000 units per month				9000 units p.m.		
	May £	June £	July £	Aug. £	Sept. £	Oct. £	Total £
Materials cost	24 000	24 000	24 000	24 000	27 000	27 000	150 000
Labour cost	32 000	32 000	32 000	32 000	36 000	36 000	200 000
Overhead cost (variable)	48 000	48 000	48 000	48 000	54 000	54 000	300 000
	104 000	104 000	104 000	104 000	117 000	117 000	650 000

Andrew now works out the *debtors'* figure for the end of October. As debtors pay their outstanding balances one month after they have bought goods, the debtors' figure for the end of October will be the sales figure for September of £128 250. He knows that *creditors* for raw materials are paid two months after purchase. The creditors' figure will therefore be made up of September's and October's purchases of raw materials of £28 250 and £24 750, totalling £53 000.

Andrew now has sufficient information to work out the *cash budget*.

Receipts	£
May (April's debtors)	87 000
June (May's debtors)	97 500
July, etc.	116 250
August	120 000
September	123 000
October	128 250

Payments		
May		£
Raw materials (March)	=	28 500
Direct labour 8000 × 4	=	32 000
Variable overheads 8000 × 6	=	48 000
Fixed expenses	=	3 000
		£111 500

June		£
Raw materials (April)	=	25 500
Direct labour 8000 × 4	=	32 000
Variable overheads 8000 × 6	=	48 000
Fixed expenses	=	3 000
		£108 500

July		£
Raw materials (May)	=	23 700
Direct labour 8000 × 4	=	32 000
Variable overheads 8000 × 6	=	48 000
Fixed expenses	=	3 000
		£106 700

August		£
Raw materials (June)	=	24 300
Direct labour 8000 × 4	=	32 000
Variable overheads 8000 × 6	=	48 000
Fixed expenses		3 000
		£107 300

September		£
Raw materials (July)		24 500
Direct labour 9000 × 4	=	36 000
Variable overheads 9000 × 6	=	54 000
Fixed expenses	=	3 000
		£117 500

October   £

Raw materials (August)   =   27 500

Direct labour 9000 × 4   =   36 000

Variable overheads 9000 × 6   =   54 000

Fixed expenses   =   3 000

                                                                £120 500

Cash Budget

	May £	June £	July £	Aug. £	Sept. £	Oct. £
CASH BALANCE	4 000	(20 500)	(31 500)	(21 950)	(9 250)	(3 750)
Add Receipts	87 000	97 500	116 250	120 000	123 000	128 250
	91 000	77 000	84 750	98 050	113 750	124 500
Less Payments	111 500	108 500	106 700	107 300	117 500	120 500
Balance carried forward	(20 500)	(31 500)	(21 950)	(9 250)	(3 750)	4 000

Now that all of the sectional budgets have been completed Andrew is in a position to provide a *Master Budget* in the form of a forecast operating statement and a forecast balance sheet.

MASTER BUDGET

Altron Limited
Forecast Operating Statement for the six months ended 31/10/90

	£	£
Sales		720 000
Less Cost of sales		
Opening stock of finished goods	30 000	
Add Cost of goods supplied	650 000	
	680 000	
Less Closing stock of finished goods	52 000	628 000
Gross profit		92 000
Less Overheads		
Fixed expenses		18 000
Net profit		74 000

NB   For the purpose of this example we have assumed no taxation and no payment of dividends.

Information from the sectional budgets and the master budget can now be fed back to departments. The budgetary system has coordinated the revenue and expenditure areas and organized them into an overall plan.

Case Study—Widget Supply Limited

You have recently been appointed to the board of Widget Supply Limited, a company based in Hessle near Hull which has successfully supplied widgets to light engineering companies for the past 30 years.

The present Managing Director is only 42 and has recently succeeded his

The Forecast Balance Sheet of Altron Limited as at 31/10/90

	£	£	Net book value £
FIXED ASSETS			
Premises			90 000
Plant and machinery			105 000
Office equipment			9 000
Motor vehicles			50 000
			254 000
CURRENT ASSETS			
Stocks: finished goods			
(4000 units)		52 000	
Raw materials		5 000	
Debtors		135 000	
Bank		4 000	
		196 000	
Less CURRENT LIABILITIES			
Creditors for fixed expenses	3 000		
Creditors for raw materials			
(Sept. 28 250 + Oct. 24 750)	53 000	56 000	
Net current assets			140 000
Assets employed			394 000
Financed by:			
Share capital:			
Ordinary shares			250 000
Preference shares			50 000
Reserves (20 000 + retained profit)			94 000
Capital employed			£394 000

father who held the position over many years. In the past the only financial information available to management has been half-yearly profit and loss accounts and balance sheets. These have always been presented on traditional lines. In your role as company accountant you feel that management could improve decision making with an improved control structure and you suggest that budgeting will go a long way to providing the solution.

Questions

1. What steps would you take to initiate a budgetary system?
2. What problems are you likely to encounter and how might these problems be overcome?
3. Which budget statements would you suggest?
4. How will information be displayed in these statements?
5. How will this information improve the quality of decisions?

Variance analysis

As the budget period gets under way departmental coordinators will follow its progress and by exerting close control over their areas, try to ensure its success.

They could break the year down into monthly accounting periods so that, as the year progresses, they can compare actual figures with budgeted figures and analyse the difference or variance.

If actual figures are more than budgeted figures this will be:

- an adverse expenditure variance;
- a favourable sales variance.

If actual figures are less than budgeted figures this will be:

- a favourable expenditure variance;
- an adverse sales variance.

Variance analysis detects problems and enables managers to take prompt action to try to improve efficiency and profitability. For example, there could be a sudden upturn in the raw materials budget. This might be due to:

- increased wastage;
- inefficiency by operators;
- materials damaged in transit;
- inefficient buying;
- increasing raw material costs, etc.

The list is inexhaustive. The variance has indicated a problem. Managers would use their experience to find the cause.

Case Study—Beatties Wool Limited

The following report was extracted from a production department at Beatties:

Cost Variance Report

	Actual £	Budget £	Variance £
Direct labour	12 000	12 000	0
Indirect labour			
Clerical	450	400	+50
Supervision	1 200	1 200	0
Overtime	300	100	+200
Repairs and maintenance	500	200	+300
Power	700	1 000	−300
Total budget	15 150	14 900	+250

Department—Dyes Month June

(actual) Production — 40 000 units
(budgeted) Production — 38 000 units
Production variance + 2 000 units

Questions

1. Comment briefly on the budget variance report.
2. In what ways does a report of this kind support management control?
3. Why might a report be an investigative tool?
4. What would have happened to variances if the actual produced was 50 per cent greater than expected?

If variations persist and actual and budgeted figures differ dramatically, the budget will lose its relevance, unless flexible budgets have taken into account these variations.

Standard costing is a system of costing that can only take place where a system of budgetary control exists and works hand in hand with such a system. It provides a method of assessing efficiency by having an advance estimate of costs and providing a comparison between actual costs and this standard cost. Variance analysis enables differences to be highlighted and presented in a tabular form so that management can see from this breakdown why standard and actual costs have differed. Investigations reveal the causes of the variations.

Costing

Whereas the financial accountant analyses historic costs in order to produce financial statements, the management accountant will try to obtain information which will help current decisions to be made and plans to be established. Two major areas of concern for any manufacturing company are:

1. the cost of manufacturing each product and
2. the cost of running each department.

For example, the management accountant will want to know which products are profitable and which are not. He or she will also wish to know which departments are uneconomic and too expensive to run. Savings might be made if certain departmental activities were contracted out. Costing provides information enabling decisions of this magnitude to be taken.

Establishing *cost centres* enables costs to be attributed to a particular product or a particular department. It is a convenient unit from which accounting information can be extracted. However, there are sometimes problems. Allocating direct costs such as raw materials is relatively easy but how do you allocate canteen costs, maintenance costs, insurance, etc. Apportionment of costs needs to be carefully considered.

There are two contrasting costing methods determining the ways in which a product's cost is prepared.

Absorption costing

This method incorporates full costs into a product's manufacture. All costs are absorbed into the cost of a product. The absorption unit cost is calculated by dividing total costs (both fixed and variable) by the total production in order to obtain a unit cost. In order to price the product, a profit percentage is added to the cost to obtain a selling price.

For example, Safe Products Limited manufactures one particular type of cooker guard. Over a particular year it intends to manufacture and sell 20 000 units. It looks for a 20 per cent profit on sales and its fixed costs are £40 000 and variable costs are £80 000.

The absorption unit cost is found by adding together fixed and variable costs to calculate total cost.

	£
Fixed cost	40 000
Variable cost	80 000
Total cost =	£120 000

This is then divided by the number produced in order to obtain the unit cost.

$$\frac{120\,000}{20\,000} = £6 \text{ per unit}$$

The profit is to be 20 per cent on sales. This means that £6 will reflect 80 per cent of the selling price. In order to find this we multiply:

$$£6.00 \text{ by } \frac{100}{80} \text{ or } \frac{10}{8} = £7.50$$

The selling price necessary to obtain a 20 per cent profit on sales from costs of £6.00 is £7.50.

Marginal costing

Marginal costing takes into account all of the problems involved in allocating fixed costs. Only the variable costs are allocated to each product. The difference between the variable costs and the selling price is known as the contribution. By manufacturing and selling enough units to produce a total contribution in excess of fixed overheads, a company will make a profit.

In the case of Safe Products Limited, assuming a similar selling price of £7.50 the contribution will be the selling price of £7.50 less the variable costs of £4.00 to provide a contribution of £3.50.

(The variable cost per unit is found by dividing the total variable costs by the total number of units.)

$$\frac{\text{Total variable costs}}{\text{Total number of units}} = \frac{£80\,000}{£20\,000} = £4.00$$

The company will aim to generate sufficient £3.50s from each product sold to pay off fixed overheads and then provide a surplus.

At 20 000 units	Absorption costing £	Marginal costing £
Sales (£7.50 × 20 000)	150 000	150 000
Less Absorption cost (20 000 × 6)	120 000	
Less Marginal cost (20 000 × 4)		80 000
Contribution		70 000
Less Fixed cost		40 000
Net Profit	£30 000	£30 000

Using both costing methods if production increased to 30 000 units:

At 30 000 units	Absorption costing £	Marginal costing £
Sales (£7.50 × 30 000)	225 000	225 000
Less Absorption cost (30 000 × 6)	180 000	
Less Marginal cost (30 000 × 4)		120 000
Contribution		105 000
Less Fixed cost		40 000
Net Profit	£45 000	£65 000

With absorption costing the unit cost of fixed expenses at this level of production is not £40 000 at a unit cost of £2.00 (£40 000 divided by 20 000 units) but £40 000 divided by 30 000 units or £1.33. Absorption costing has therefore overstated the overhead if production goes beyond an anticipated level.

Marginal costing and the principle of costing the variable cost and providing a contribution to cover fixed costs is taken further in break–even analysis.

Break-even analysis

Breaking even is the unique point at which a business makes no profit and no loss. If sales are beyond the break-even point profits are made and, if they are below the break-even point, losses are made. In marginal costing it is the point at which the contribution equals the fixed costs.

To calculate the break-even point:

1. Calculate the unit contribution (selling price less variable costs).
2. Divide the fixed overhead costs by unit contribution.

For Safe Products Limited:

$$\frac{\text{Fixed overhead costs}}{\text{Contribution per unit}} = \frac{£40\,000}{£3.50} = 11\,429 \text{ units (to nearest unit)}$$

The sales value can be calculated by multiplying the 11 429 by the selling price.

$$11\,429 \text{ units} \times £7.50 = \underline{£85\,717.50}$$

Safe Products Limited has covered costs and has broken even with a sales value of £85 717.50. Anything in excess of this will provide it with profits.

If Safe Products Limited has a profit target, this technique can be used to calculate the number of units which need to be sold and the value of sales to achieve that target.

For example, if Safe Products Limited aims for £20 000 profit, by adding this £20 000 to the fixed costs, and dividing by the contribution, the number of units will be found which need to be sold to meet this target.

$$\frac{£40\,000 \text{ (fixed costs)} + £20\,000 \text{ (profit target)}}{£3.50 \text{ (contribution)}}$$

= 17 143 units (to nearest unit) need to be sold to achieve that target with a sales value of $17\,143 \times £7.50 = \underline{£128\,572.50}$.

Information such as this could be obtained quickly from a graphical representation of marginal costing techniques in the form of a *break-even chart*.

The break-even chart will show the position at which a business will break even and the extent to which it makes profits or losses at various levels of activity.

A break-even chart (see Fig. 11.5) is constructed by:

1. Labelling the horizontal axis for units of production and sales.
2. Labelling the vertical axis to represent the value of sales and costs.
3. Putting on fixed costs. Fixed costs will remain at the same level over all levels of production and will be plotted by a straight line parallel to the horizontal axis.
4. Variable costs shown rising from where the fixed cost line touches the vertical axis. The variable cost line will therefore also represent total costs. It is plotted by calculating total costs at two or three random levels of production.
5. Sales are plotted by taking two or three random levels of turnover and will rise from the intersection of the two axes.

The break-even point will be where the total cost and sales lines intersect. The area to the left of the break-even point represents losses and to the right of the break-even point represents profits.

Safe Products Limited

	5000 units £	10 000 units £	20 000 units £
Variable cost = £4 per unit	20 000	40 000	80 000
Fixed costs	40 000	40 000	40 000
Total cost	60 000	80 000	120 000
Sales = £7.50 per unit	37 500	75 000	150 000

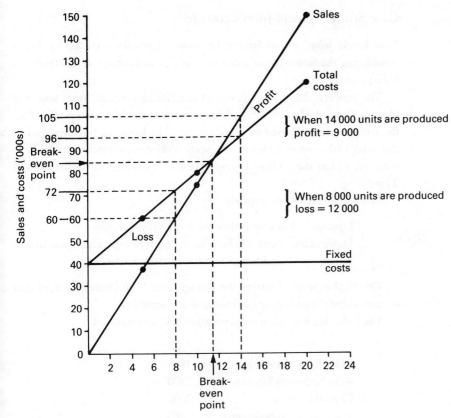

Figure 11.5 Break-even chart.

The chart graphically shows the break-even point of 11 429 units with a sales 'revenue' of £87 717.50. If sales are at 14 000 units, we can see that profit (the difference between sales and total costs) is at:

Contribution 14 000 × £3.50	= £49 000
Less Fixed costs	£40 000
Net profit	£9 000

This is known as the *margin of safety*.
If sales are at 8000 units:

Contribution 8000 × £3.50	= £28 000
Less Fixed costs	£40 000
Net loss	£12 000

The break-even chart is a simple visual tool enabling managers to anticipate the effects of changes in production and sales upon the profitability of a business. It emphasizes the importance of earning revenue to make profits and particularly helps those who are unused to interpreting accounting information.

Case Study—Uncle John's cottage

Your Uncle John, a local farmer, has come to you for some advice. He is considering the future use of a recently vacated tied cottage on his farm as a holiday cottage.

The property has been allowed to deteriorate over the years and it is obvious that considerable internal improvements would be necessary before the cottage could be used as a holiday let. The house is, however, full of character with extensive views over North Yorkshire, extending to the Pennines on a clear day. There is easy access to Teesside, Northallerton and Thirsk.

The accommodation comprises:

Upstairs—3 double bedrooms, large bathroom/toilet.
Downstairs—large kitchen/diner, large lounge with open hearth and french window into the garden.

The legal aspects of letting the cottage have been cleared, and all that remains is for the cottage to be renovated and furnished.

The following quotation for renovation has been received:

	£
Complete redecoration	1895
Refit bathroom/kitchen	2800
Central heating	2200
Wash basins in bedrooms	200

The quotation has been supplied by Pennine Rose Builders, a fairly large local firm with a reputation for doing work of a reasonable quality.

Your uncle decides to fit the cottage out with basic items of reasonable quality and durable furniture. These are:

	£
Furniture and fittings	3000
Kitchen equipment and household items	750

The finance for the renovation and for the purchase of furnishings and fittings is obtained by means of a five-year bank loan with a fixed annual interest rate of 10 per cent payable each calendar month, and based upon the original sum. The loan principal is to be paid in five annual instalments.

Your uncle anticipates the following fixed and variable costs:

Fixed

- Annual loan repayment
- Annual interest on loan
- Rates £215 per half year

- Water rates £80 per half year
- Insurance £150 per annum
- Electricity £17.50 per quarter

Variable

- Cleaner for £3 per hour/5 hours per week
- Electricity and heating £5 per week

The suggested scale of charges is as follows:

> April to September £170 per week
> October to March £110 per week

How many weeks would it take for Uncle John to break even in:

- the summer season;
- the winter season?

If variable costs and rental prices both increase by 10 per cent in the second year, what would the new break-even points be? (Your answer should be supported by the appropriate break-even charts.)

The latter part of the case study shows the effects on profit of changing selling prices, e.g. Safe Products Limited might want to reduce the selling price to £7.00 and its market information indicates that it expects to sell 10 per cent more at this price. It is hoped that this will improve profitability.

1. At 14 000 units and a price of £7.50, profits are £9000.
2. If the price falls to £7.00, the company expects to sell 10 per cent more at this price.

Sales will therefore be 15 400 × £7.00	=	£107 800
Less Variable costs 15 400 × £4.00	=	£61 600
Contribution	=	£46 200
Less Fixed costs	=	£40 000
Net profit	=	£6 200

Clearly, dropping the price by 50p to gain the 10 per cent extra sales this would generate, would not increase profitability.

Limitations on the use of break-even analysis
Marginal costing is often considered to present an over-simplification of business behaviour. It reduces business to an equation: how to generate enough contribution to cover fixed costs and provide a surplus for profit. Its limitations are:

1. It can be argued that, in reality, fixed costs are likely to change at different activity levels and that a stepped fixed cost line would be a more accurate representation.

2. The business might be restricted by a limiting factor restricting its ability to break even or meet a profit target such as lack of space, shortage of labour, shortage of orders, etc.
3. Variable costs and sales are unlikely to be linear. Discounts, special contracts and overtime payments mean that the total cost line should really be a curve.
4. Break–even charts depict short–term relationships and forecasts and are therefore unrealistic where the time scale covers several years.
5. Break–even analysis is dependent upon the accuracy of forecasts made about costs and revenues. Changes in the market and in the cost of raw materials could affect the success of the technique.

The usefulness of accounting in supporting decision making

An essential function of management is to take decisions and decisions have to be taken whenever there are alternative courses of action. The main problem of any accounting system is that information reflects data from the past and present and only

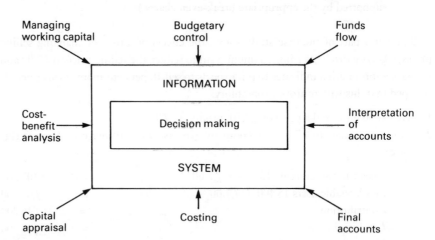

Figure 11.6 Accounting as a decision-making system.

enables predictions to be made about the future. Time pressures can often be imposed upon managers which constrain their ability to collate sufficient information. It might also be possible to extract information from the accounting system that is unmanageably large. The problems can be numerous. Many decisions will not only require information from within the system but careful consideration will be needed of:

● taxation
● current state of the economy
● market value of shares if listed
● market

- goodwill and corporate reputation
- industrial relations, etc.

Clearly nothing can be forecasted with absolute certainty. No matter what research takes place and however competent the accounting team, business involves taking risks.

Though accounting information has reduced the unpredictability, it will never eliminate it and there will always be a need for human judgement.

Short answer questions

1. Explain why fixed costs become less significant over a larger output.
2. Give two examples of variable costs.
3. State an example of a semi-variable cost and explain why such a cost might be semi-variable.
4. Why are fixed costs more difficult to allocate to departmental or product costs?
5. What is the significance of marginal costing for the accountant and how does the accountant's definition differ from that made by an economist?
6. Explain the relationship between average cost and marginal cost.
7. Why do businesses budget?
8. Name two dangers of a budgetary system.
9. Why would a budgetary controller need to estimate when debtors pay?
10. What is the purpose of a raw materials budget and what is its connection with the production budget?
11. What makes up a master budget?
12. Explain what is meant by the term 'adverse expenditure variance'.
13. Name two types of decisions influenced by costing.
14. What is a cost centre?
15. Define what is meant by absorption costing.
16. What is the significance of the term 'contribution'?
17. What happens if sales are lower than the break-even point?
18. How is the break-even point calculated?
19. Name two criticisms of break-even analysis.
20. What three factors external to an accounting system might affect the quality of decision making?

Essays

1. Describe the purpose of management accounting. Why is experience an essential requirement in a management team?
2. Describe how and why different types of costs vary with output.
3. Explain the objective of budgetary planning and control systems. Outline the duties of a budget committee.

4. What are the dangers of a rigid budgetary system? What implications might variance analysis have for a management team?

5. Make a comparison between marginal and absorption costing. Using an example show which system caters best for changes in sales volume.

6. Explain briefly how to draw up a break-even chart and point out its usefulness. In what ways can break-even analysis be considered superficial?

7. As a production manager for a firm which manufactures clogs you have been asked to make a presentation to a group of staff next week and you decide to use a break-even chart to represent profitability graphically. You obtain the following figures:

    (a) Variable costs are £5 per unit.
    (b) Clogs are to be sold at £7.50 each.
    (c) Fixed overheads are £140 000 per annum.
    (d) Sales are expected to be 60 000 units.

    Write out a speech explaining your technique. Draw a chart to show how great a profit or loss you are likely to be making.

    You would like to show the group effects of a drop in price on the market. If you drop the price to £7.00, there will be no increase in variable costs per unit or overall fixed costs and your marketing team have told you that orders would increase by 28 000 units. Show how this would affect your profitability.

8. Explain why break-even analysis is an important management tool. What are the dangers of relying too heavily upon this technique?

9. Costing provides management with information as to the right course of management action. Discuss.

10. In the light of advances in the development of management information systems, why are many decisions made under conditions of inadequate information?

Data response questions

1   (a) Define the concept of marginal cost.

    (b) A hospital X-ray department has a machine which cost £250 000 five years ago, when it still had an expected life of ten years. It costs £2,500 a year to maintain and, in addition, a new special part costing £6,600 is needed, on average, every eighteen months. The life of this part is directly related to the number of investigations carried out by the machine, which averages 400 per year. In order to reduce film costs the X-ray department is considering the purchase of a camera at a cost of £35,000 to replace the existing X-ray film unit. This camera will cost £200 per year to maintain and is estimated to have a residual value of £2,000 in five years' time. The direct costs per investigation under both systems are given in the table.

        (i)   On the assumption that the X-ray film unit is in use, calculate the marginal cost of an investigation both during the day and as a night time emergency.

        (ii) What additional costs should be included if you were calculating the total cost of an investigation in order to charge the patient.

    (c) (i)   Show that the annual cash flow can be reduced by £10,000 per year if the camera is bought.

	Machine with X-ray film unit	Machine with camera
Film costs:		
Average number of pictures	35	50
Fixed costs	—	£1
Cost per picture	£1	10p
Drugs	£5	£5
Minor equipment	£30	£30
Contrast injections (@ £14 per bottle)	2 bottles	2 bottles—75% of the time
		3 bottles—25% of the time
Labour (@ £5 per hour)		
Day	Not applicable as it can be regarded as a fixed cost	
Night	2 hours	2 hours

(ii) Calculate the payback period for the purchase of the camera.

(iii) If the camera is bought, the present value of the change in cash flow over the next five years is £4,000 using a discount rate of 10%. You are required to undertake the same calculation using a discount rate of 16%.

(d) (i) Discuss the relative merits of the methods of investment appraisal used in (c) (ii) and (c) (iii). On numerical grounds, would you recommend that the camera ought to be bought?

(ii) What other factors should be taken into consideration before a final decision is made?

Present value of £1 in future is given below at various rates:

	10%	12%	14%	16%
One year hence	0.91	0.89	0.88	0.86
Two years hence	0.83	0.80	0.77	0.74
Three years hence	0.75	0.71	0.68	0.64
Four years hence	0.68	0.64	0.59	0.55
Five years hence	0.62	0.57	0.52	0.48

(*Source:* Cambridge.)

2 The cost accounts for the Suntrap Hotel for the period 1 January 1985 to 31 December 1985 are shown below:

	Total number of rooms/nights let	Revenue per room per night (£)	Variable cost per room/per night (£)
April	160	8	6
May	180	10	6
June	220	12	7
July	280	15	8
August	340	15	8
September	170	10	6

Total annual semi-variable and fixed costs are: £1440.

In the past the hotel has had a season of six months per annum from 1 April to 30 September. In an effort to increase profits, the proprietor is considering extending his 1987 season to cover the period from 1 March to 31 October. Market research suggests that in each of March and October he can expect to sell 100 room nights at £7. Variable costs are estimated to be £6 per night, and annual semi-variable and fixed costs are expected to rise by £100.

(a)   What is the difference between a fixed cost and a variable cost?
(b)   Calculate the profits for 1985.
(c)   What effect would the plan have on his overall profits?
(d)   If he were to have opened during March and October in 1985, what is the minimum that he would have had to charge during March and October per room per night, if he were to break even *during those months?*
(e)   Give *four* examples of alternative ways for the proprietor to increase profits.

(*Source:* AEB.)

3   The following information relates to a company which produces a single product.

Direct labour per unit	£11
Direct materials per unit	£6
Variable overheads per unit	£3
Fixed costs	£200,000
Selling price per unit	£30

(a)   Explain the term 'break even'.
(b)   Using these figures, produce a chart to show the minimum number of units which must be sold for the company to break even.
(c)   Market research has indicated potential sales for the coming period of 30,000 units at the current price, or 37,500 units if the selling price were lowered to £28 per unit. Which strategy would you advise the company to adopt and why?
(d)   Outline the factors which *any* business should take into consideration before using break-even analysis as a basis for decision making.

(*Source:* AEB.)

4   Peter Bean intends to open up a shop on 1 January 1991 into which he is to invest £80 000 as capital which is to be placed into a business bank account. His plans are:

(a)   On January 1991 he will buy premises for £45 000, shop fittings for £4000 and a motor van for £6000.
(b)   He will employ a sales assistant who will receive a salary of £500, payable at the end of each month.
(c)   The following goods are to be bought:

	Jan.	Feb.	Mar.	April	May	June
(units)	450	500	550	550	800	800

(d)   Units will cost £15 from January to March inclusive and £19 from April to July. Suppliers are to be paid in the month of supply.
(e)   Sales are anticipated as follows:

	Jan.	Feb.	Mar.	April	May	June
(units)	400	450	500	500	720	750

(f)   Units are sold for £30 each. One half of sales are to be for cash and the other half on credit. Customers are expected to pay the month after they have bought the goods.

(g)   Peter is to take £900 per month as drawings.

(h)   Fixed expenses are estimated at £600 per month.

(i)   Stock at the end of June is to be valued on a FIFO basis.

Prepare:

(i)   A cash budget showing the balance at the end of each month.

(ii)   A budgeted profit or operating statement for the six months.

(iii) A budgeted balance sheet as at 30.6.91.

(iv)   Comment upon the performance of the business.

5   The accountant at Beaver Brothers wishes to review overtime costs and attempt to cut this expense back as far as possible. Forecast orders over the next six months are:

	Units
Jan.	700
Feb.	450
Mar.	550
April	600
May	700
June	650

Stocks of finished goods on 1 January are at 50 units and they must not fall below this level.

Normal manufacturing production is at 500 units and overtime can increase this by 200 units. Each month contains four calendar weeks. If all extra units over and above the normal production levels are to be manufactured as early as possible, when can overtime be stopped? Support your answer with a production budget in units.

Suggested reading

Batty, J., *Cost and Management Accounting for Students*. Heinemann, 1978.

Hitchen, W. and Lucey, T., *Practice and Revision Costing*. DPP, 1983.

Houlton, M., *An Introduction to Cost and Management Accounting*. Heinemann, 1979.

12

Recruitment and the role of personnel

From the personnel point of view, the purpose of recruitment is to buy in and retain the best available human resources to meet a company's needs. It is therefore important to be clear about:

- What the job entails
- What sorts of qualities are required to do the job
- What incentives are required to attract and motivate specific employees

There are a number of stages which can be used to define and set out the nature of particular jobs:

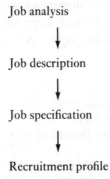

Job analysis

↓

Job description

↓

Job specification

↓

Recruitment profile

Figure 12.1 Stages in preparing for recruitment.

(However, the student should note that this pattern is most likely to relate to the creation of new jobs rather than recruitment to fill existing jobs.)

Job analysis

Job analysis is the process of examining jobs in order to identify the key requirements of each job. A number of important questions need to be explored:

- What tasks need to be performed?
- What skills and qualities are required to perform these tasks?
- How can these skills be acquired?

Job analysis is used in order to:

1. Choose employees either from the ranks of your existing staff (redeployment) or from the recruitment of new staff.
2. Set out the training requirements of a particular job.
3. Provide information which will help in decision making about the type of equipment and materials to be employed with the job.
4. Identify and profile the experiences of employees in their work tasks (information which can be used as evidence for staff development and promotion).
5. Identify areas of risk and danger at work.
6. Help in setting rates of pay for job tasks.

Job analysis can be carried out by direct observation of employees at work, by finding out information from interviewing job holders, or by referring to documents such as training manuals. Information can be gleaned directly from the person carrying out a task and/or from their supervisory staff.

Some large organizations specifically employ 'job analysts'. In most companies, however, job analysis is expected to be part of the general skills of a training or personnel officer.

Three different areas of job analysis can be identified:

1. *Task analysis*   This involves the study of a particular task aimed at achieving a particular objective or end product. For example, a particular employee may have the task of ensuring that all the assemblers in an electronics factory are supplied with a steady flow of components.
2. *Activity analysis*   This is the study of the elements involved in a given task. For example, one of the activities involved in circulating components in the electronics factory may be taking them down from the shelves in the stock room.

    Activities can be subdivided into physical (e.g. lifting, sorting, etc.) and mental (e.g. exercising judgement).
3. *Skills analysis*   This is the study of the ability to carry out a given task effectively. A wide range of skills may be identified such as the ability to work in groups, the ability to work independently, the ability to perform manual operations, the ability to make calculations, the ability to communicate, the ability to follow written instructions and many more.

Case Study—Carrying out a skills audit and involving your employees

In 1989 management and trade unions at Rowntree Mackintosh set up a joint skills audit of the company's 850 workers. The skills audit was set up to look at:

*   employees' existing skill levels
*   employees' needs
*   new technology

One of the main aims of the exercise was to prepare for multi-skilling within the company. (Multi-skilling means that employees are trained to perform in a range of skill areas.) Rowntree's believe that multi-skilling (and other new initiatives) is most likely to be successful when employees have an involvement.

The audit relates to several Rowntree sites at York, Halifax, Newcastle upon Tyne and Norwich.

The scheme has involved the engineering union (AEU), the manufacturing union (MSF), the electricians' union (EETPU), and the building union (UCATT).

Questions

1. What do you understand by the term 'multi-skilling'?
2. What are the potential benefits and drawbacks of multi-skilling for a confectionery manufacturer?
3. What is a skills audit?
4. How do you think that carrying out a skills audit will help Rowntree to introduce multi-skilling?
5. Why do you think that the skills audit has involved a joint initiative between management and trade unions?
6. What are the potential benefits and drawbacks of a joint initiative?

Job analysis is not an easy task. There are a number of major difficulties to be overcome. It can be a very slow process, and the outside observer will not always be fully aware of what is going on. This is particularly true of jobs which require *both* mental and physical skills because it is difficult to appreciate what is going on in the mind of the skilled operative. Individuals will often develop styles of work which suit their own particular aptitudes and which may not be appropriate to another employee. When a person is asked to describe a particular job, he or she may miss out important steps which have come to be taken for granted.

Job description

A job description will set out how a particular employee will fit into the organization. It will therefore need to set out:

- The title of the job.
- To whom the employee is responsible.
- For whom the employee is responsible.
- A simple description of the role and duties of the employee within the organization.

A job description could be used as a job indicator for applicants for a job. Alternatively, it could be used as a guideline for an employee and/or his or her line manager as to his or her role and responsibility within the organization (it is not, however, a contract of employment).

Job specification

A job specification goes beyond a mere description—in addition, it highlights the mental and physical attributes required of the job holder. For example, a job specification for a trainee manager's post in a retail store included the following:

> Managers at all levels would be expected to show responsibility. The company is looking for people who are tough and talented. They should have a flair for business, know how to sell, and to work in a team.

Job analysis, description, and specification can provide useful information to a business in addition to serving as recruitment instruments. For example, staff appraisal is a means of monitoring staff performance and is a feature of promotion in modern companies. In some companies, for example, employees and their immediate line managers discuss personal goals and targets for the coming time period (e.g. the next six months). The appraisal will then involve a review of performance during the previous six months, and setting new targets. Job details can serve as a useful basis for establishing dialogue and targets. Job descriptions can be used as reference points for arbitrating in disputes as to 'who does what' in a business. Job analysis can serve as a useful tool for establishing performance standards.

Job requisition (recruitment profiles)

The person responsible for interviewing and recruiting is not always the person with specialist knowledge of the job in question. For example, the personnel department may be given the responsibility of recruiting staff for all the functional areas within a company. Personnel will therefore ask for a recruitment profile giving the nature of the skills required, the type of person sought and a description of the job. The job requisition will therefore provide the specialist knowledge required to recruit the appropriate individuals. Job requisitions are also used to give an advertising agency more information to create recruitment advertisements, and also by specialist recruitment companies. (A business might employ a specialist recruitment firm to carry out a national recruitment campaign.)

Case Study

Study the journal article in Fig. 12.2 before answering the questions that follow it.

ELECTRONICS GIANT ON THE HUNT FOR TECHNICAL STAFF

Sony seeks specialist skills for Welsh plant

An intensive recruitment drive will accompany electronics giant, Sony's £36m investment at its plant in Bridgend, South Wales.

Sony's industrial relations executive, Alun Jones, said that a tough, hectic two months lie ahead for the five-strong recruitment team.

The company plans to have 300 extra engineers and managers working at Bridgend by May next year. Staff recruited need six to 12 months' training in Japan and the US to acquire the necessary technical skills for Sony's new technology.

Specialist high-tech skills are vital to Sony's ambitious expansion plans. Before the investment was finalised, Sony carried out detailed research to make sure it could recruit people with the necessary skills from the area.

But the search promises to be difficult. Jones pointed out

Sony: investing £36m

that there is a worldwide shortage of electronic and engineering staff as every industry relies on them.

Sony's investment will expand its 1,500 workforce by one-fifth and it hopes to recruit an initial 34 who will be partly responsible for the recruitment of lower level staff.

No campaign budget has

been set by Sony management and bosses are still assessing the best recruitment channels. They are looking at university and polytechnic research laboratories throughout Europe. They are targetting regions such as the West Midlands, Manchester, Southampton and Glasgow, where they suspect there are significant numbers of the people they need. It wants staff who are highly qualified in state-of-the-art automated manufacturing and surface-coating technology.

Sony recognises that these skills are unusual as its recent campaign for similar people only attracted 30 responses. The company may be forced to train up lower level people if it cannot find enough people with at least two years' experience.

The Welsh Development Agency welcomed Sony's expansion.

Figure 12.2 Job analysis at Sony. (*Source*: *Personnel Today*, February/March 1989.)

Questions

1. How might Sony have had to carry out job analysis in preparing plans to recruit 300 extra engineers and managers at Bridgend?

2. Lay out a job description for an imaginary new job at the Bridgend plant.

3. How would a job specification differ from the description you have just done?

4. What problems does the article suggest Sony is likely to have in its recruitment drive?

5. What suggestions would you put forward for dealing with these problems?

6. Why do you think that the Welsh Development Agency has welcomed Sony's expansion?

The challenge of the 1990s

A pressing problem for most companies as we move into the 1990s is that of recruiting employees in sufficient numbers and with the required skills. The Department of Employment's White Paper, Training for Employment (1989) warned: '1990 seems likely to bring radical change to the industrial economy. In looking to the future, three areas of change have profound implications for employment and training:

● the number of people who are available for work;
● the structure of employment;
● the nature of available jobs.'

It is perhaps the first of these predicted changes that could have the most serious implications for the recruitment sector. The White Paper says that while in the decade up to 1986 the population of working age in Britain grew by almost 2 million, between 1986 and 1990 that figure will have slowed to fewer than 500 000.

On top of that the White Paper predicts 'the number of 16 to 19-year-olds in the population is projected to fall substantially from a peak of 3.7 million in 1983 to less than 2.6 million in 1994'. In simple terms the number of young people available for jobs will fall dramatically. The Manpower Services Commission says those figures clearly show that fundamental changes will have to be made in the way companies develop their workforces. Businesses which today make older workers with older skills redundant in favour of new blood with new skills will be forced by the shortage to retrain. This presents a major challenge to the whole concept of recruitment.

Avenues for recruitment

Recruiting individuals to fill particular posts within a business can be done either internally by recruitment within the firm, or externally by recruiting people from outside.

Internal recruitment

The advantages of recruiting from within are:

1. Considerable savings can be made. Individuals with inside knowledge of how a business operates will need shorter periods of training and time for 'fitting in'.
2. The organization is unlikely to be greatly 'disrupted' by someone who is used to working with others in the organization.
3. Internal promotion acts as an incentive to all staff to work harder within the organization.

4. From the firm's point of view, the strengths and weaknesses of an insider will have been assessed. There is always a risk attached to employing an outsider who may only be a success 'on paper'.

The disadvantages of recruiting from within are that:

1. You will have to replace the person who has been promoted.
2. An insider may be less likely to make the essential criticisms required to get the company working more effectively.
3. Promotion of one person in a company may upset someone else.

External recruitment

In the United Kingdom, the most common way of finding a job is by directly contacting a firm or place of employment. Sometimes people apply for a job as a result of a personal contact such as a relative already working for a firm.

Recruiting through newspaper and magazine advertisements

Newspaper advertisements are an obvious place to scout for jobs. A good newspaper advertisement gives a substantial amount of information. Personnel managers place adverts in the most suitable medium. Jobs demanding limited skills can often be advertised locally, whereas jobs requiring specialist skills need to be advertised in specialist media. Adverts for marketing specialists, for example, may be placed in *Marketing Week* or in the recruitment section of the *Sunday Times*.

When recruiting labour the personnel manager will therefore do the following:

1. Target the recruiting campaign at the most suitable audience.
2. Advertise in the most cost-effective way (for example, the cheapest method possible to get to the right sort of people).

To ensure that a newspaper gets the right response it will be necessary to make at least some of the following points clear:

-   Where the job is.
-   How much the job pays.
-   What qualifications are required to do the job.
-   What the job involves.
-   What fringe benefits are available.
-   How to go about applying for the job.

The personnel manager will then sift through the applications. He or she will look for applications that show that the candidate has the required qualities.

Job centres

The Department of Employment is responsible for the running of job centres which can be found in a prominent position in major towns. The job centres run window displays of jobs, and people seeking work are encouraged to come in and look at the cards with details of job vacancies which are on open display. The job centre staff will arrange appointments for job hunters to meet personnel staff at the relevant form for an interview.

Private employment agencies

There is a wide range of private employment agencies, which help business to recruit staff. Fields in which these agencies are particularly common are secretarial work, high technology areas, nursing and casual work. A business looking for staff will approach an agency, which will supply workers who are interviewed either by the agency or by the business. The agency will take a commission on the salary of the worker. In the case of secretarial staff, wages may often be paid by the employing firm to the agency which will then pay the worker.

Case Study—Recruitment for a new Tesco superstore in Dover

The Tesco success story began during the Second World War when young Jack Cohen began trading from a barrow in Hackney, East London. By 1950, Cohen was the first to open supermarkets which he had seen in the United States.

Decades later, Tesco is among the top retailers, with an annual turnover of £4.5 billion. Competition is tough and recruitment has to be highly co-ordinated. More than 100 superstores have opened in the past ten years and Tesco now employs 72 000 staff.

Pat Lennon, Tesco's retail personnel director, explains that opening a

---

SUPERSTORE FEATURES

☐ Petrol station.
☐ Instore bakery.
☐ Market stalls, one of Tesco's innovations.
☐ Health and beauty sections with special lighting.
☐ Toy section.
☐ Special trolleys for disabled people.
☐ Checkouts with electronic points of sale (EPOS).
☐ Possible introduction of crêches.

Figure 12.3 Features of the new Tesco superstore.

superstore varies considerably from area to area: 'Every time we open a store, it is a one-off recruitment exercise which needs to be localized with in-depth research into potential customers and employees.'

The most recent recruitment exercise was that at Dover's new superstore which opened at the end of June 1988 (see Fig. 12.3). Tesco had to recruit 470 staff, from check-out operators to departmental supervisors.

The recruitment schedule began 12 months before the store opened (see Fig. 12.4). Staff managers and store managers were recruited internally and initial research was carried out into the area by Tesco. Three months later, Tesco met with advertising agency Charles Barker to discuss the campaign.

Charles Barker's research department then looked at potential competi-tors for staff at Dover's superstore. Salaries in the area were examined along with the available transport, housing and job centres. Research was carried out into the type of people likely to work in the store and the percentage of unemployed.

Meanwhile, Charles Barker's media department was looking at local media, including daily and weekly newspapers and local radio. Tesco advert-ises in local press rather than in national newspapers for recruiting its retail staff.

After about three weeks of collecting the necessary data, the agency put together a package for Tesco which included a suggested budget. This was presented to one of Tesco's six regional personnel managers. After a series of internal advertisements, the Dover campaign was launched.

Tesco always sets up a recruitment office either in offices above the local shopping centre or at the job centre. Job centres are not used often because, although free, they are rarely large enough. In Dover a terraced house in the middle of the town was used. The centre was kitted out in red with colour posters and red arrows.

The budget for the recruitment campaign was set at about £35 000 and slightly less was spent. Out of 470 staff, only 30 vacancies were left. The first advertisement did not specify job vacancies but invited people to go along to the centre. Tesco attracted about 200 applicants before even opening the re-cruitment centre.

Charles Barker designed four advertisements for the Dover campaign which appeared in the main local newspapers.

The campaign used mono (black and white) advertisements with occa-sional (spot) red. White space was used creatively with crisp outlines so as to show up on the busy newspaper pages. Tesco's personnel department wanted straightforward advertisements. It felt that the benefits and the sal-ary were the key ingredients.

Tesco's advertising campaign emphasized that the Dover superstore would be opening for 12 Sundays until 18 September. This meant an extra day's work for staff and was popular with applicants.

RECRUITMENT SCHEDULE

Countdown 12 months before store opens.
1.   Recruit senior management.
2.   Initial research into area.
3.   Advertising agency researches media and area.
4.   Advertising agency presents campaign package.
5.   Recruitment centre opens.
6.   Advertisements for supervisory staff appear.
7.   Advertisements for general staff go out.
8.   Store opens.

Figure 12.4 Stages in preparing for recruitment at Tesco.

Supervisory and skilled vacancies were advertised 19 weeks before the store opened and general vacancies were advertised 13 weeks before.

Charles Barker monitored the budget weekly, and reported to Tesco. Tesco's Dover campaign received good response but if it had not, the agency would have been able to draw on ideas in the original package. A contingency plan would have been put into effect immediately, perhaps with radio commercials or leaflet drops.

(*Source:* Adapted from *Personnel Today*.)

Questions

1.   Why was it necessary for Tesco to carry out research before opening up its Dover store? (A detailed answer is required to this question.)
2.   Why do you think that Tesco hired an agency to carry out the research work rather than doing it itself?
3.   From the evidence given in the article would you consider the research and subsequent recruitment exercise to have been effective?
4.   What do you think would be the major problems faced by Tesco in the recruitment exercise? What measures could have been taken to counteract these problems?
5.   If you were going to open up a new superstore in your local town, what are the key labour recruitment questions you would need to answer? List 15 questions.

The work of the personnel department

Personnel is a key function in all but the very smallest business units. Traditionally, personnel is associated with the 'employment procession' of recruitment, selection, induction, training, transfers and termination of employment (see Fig. 12.5). However, a modern personnel department will also take responsibility for the administration of disciplinary procedures, for the supervision of 'appraisal' processes, for workplace bargaining with unions, developing and supervising payment systems for employees, supervising health and safety, equal opportunities, and many other areas related to employment. In some companies employing as many as 100 workers a lone personnel manager will be found 'working himself to the bone'. In contrast, in some larger modern companies you will find personnel departments made up of a range of specialists housed in an extensive suite of offices.

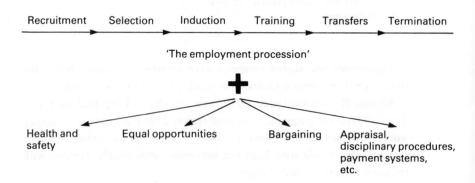

Figure 12.5 The employment procession.

Recruitment and selection

We have already dealt at length with recruitment earlier in the chapter. Recruitment will involve job analysis, description and specification. Selection will involve procedures to identify the most appropriate candidates to fill posts. An effective selection procedure will therefore take into consideration the following:

- Keeping the costs of selection down.
- Making sure that the skills and qualities being sought have been identified, and developing a process for identifying them in candidates.
- Making sure that the candidates selected, will want the job, and will stay with the company.

Keeping the costs of selection down will involve such factors as holding the interviews in a location which is accessible to the interviewing panel, and to those being interviewed. The interviewing panel must have available to them all the necessary documentation, such as application forms available to study before the interviews take place. A short list must be made up of suitable candidates, so that the interviews do not have to take place a second time, with new job advertisements being placed.

The skills required should have been identified through the process of job analysis, description and specification. It is important then to identify ways of testing whether candidates meet these requirements. One way of doing this is to study an applicant's application form and to interview him or her. Some employers go further and give applicants aptitude tests, putting them through a number of 'real' situations to see how they cope with given business situations.

To gauge whether applicants will stay with the company, it is important to ask them about their future intentions, and to familiarize them with the working environment into which they will be placed. There is no point in attracting a first class candidate only to find that he or she does not like your working conditions.

It is important to monitor the selection process continually to see how effective it is. Ratios can be a useful method of appraising the selection process. These may include:

● Number of interviews : Number of offers made

The most effective ratios would involve the minimization of interviews relative to offers made that fill the posts as required.

● Number starting work : Number of suitable employees

If a high number of workers that are offered employment prove to be unsuitable there will be something clearly wrong with the interviewing procedure.

Induction and training

This is another major area of the personnel function. New workers in a firm are usually given an induction programme in which they meet other workers and are shown the skills they must learn. Generally the first few days at work will simply involve observation, with an experienced worker showing the 'new hand' the ropes. Many large firms will have a detailed training scheme which is done on an 'in-house' basis. This is particularly true of larger public companies such as banks and insurance companies. In conjunction with this, staff may be encouraged to attend college courses to learn new skills and get new qualifications. Training thus takes place in the following ways:

1. On the job—learning skills through experience at work.
2. Off the job—learning through attending courses.

Promotion within a firm depends on acquiring qualifications to do a more advanced job. In banking, for instance, staff will be expected to pass banking examinations. At the same time, a candidate for promotion must show a flair for the job. It is the responsibility of the training department within a business to make sure that staff with the right skills are coming up through the firm or being recruited from outside.

As well as sending staff to local colleges and universities, the firm may use a government-run training centre. These are run by the Training Commission and provide specialist training in centres all over the country.

The business might also contribute to a national training scheme such as the Youth Training Scheme whereby the government subsidizes the firm to employ and train school leavers.

Case Study—Management training at 'Do It All'

W. H. Smith has designed a performance-related training package for assistant managers at their 'Do It All' stores. Performance-related training concentrates on the first six months after a new assistant manager has been appointed. The aim of the training package is to monitor and test the assistant manager's understanding of his or her role and to test understanding and skills in the job.

The assistant manager's job consists of everything from ordering the stock to making sure it is presented well. They are responsible for training staff, interviewing and have to follow the company's systems.

The trainers have broken every element of the job into testable parts. Within six months of being appointed, the assistant manager will attend a one-week assessment at the W. H. Smith college. Management On First Assessment (MOFA) tests all systems of work and skills against criteria which have been laid down.

To establish the criteria a number of experienced assistant managers were put through the same tests to produce benchmarks. Only when new assistant managers reach those benchmarks can they be said to be relatively competent in all criteria.

On completion of MOFA, each assistant store manager is interviewed by tutors, and 'Do It All' managers. The assistant manager's performance in each of the areas is discussed at length, particularly under-performing ones, which will then be reflected in further training.

To meet the needs of further training, a variety of training responses have been devised by the W. H. Smith college. In some cases, suitable courses in specific skill areas like interviewing are available at the college, whereas other managers may simply need to reread the operations manual.

Most managers will use open learning packages to study topics like budgets, target setting and security.

Alongside such training methods, the assistant store manager will be supported throughout the programme by his or her store manager, who will have received notification of those training needs identified by MOFA. Consequently, the store manager can ensure that the trainee gets whatever extra practice is required.

Questions

1. In what ways does an assistant manager's training at 'Do It All' involve:
   (a) on the job training;
   (b) off the job training?
2. How does 'Do It All' diagnose weaknesses in an assistant manager's performance? How does it assist these managers to improve their performance?

3. What would you consider to be the main costs and benefits to 'Do It All' of the training package?

4. What would you consider to be the main costs and benefits of the scheme to assistant managers?

5. How could W. H. Smith go about evaluating the effectiveness of the scheme?

Transfers and termination of employment

Personnel will have a responsibility for negotiating the smooth transfer of employees between departments. This may be necessary if employees are not able to 'get on', or if it is felt necessary to give an employee a 'change'.

Termination of employment may be as a result of a number of factors including retirement, dismissal and redundancy. When employees retire after a long period of service to a business, they will need some form of recognition for their service. Companies such as the John Lewis Partnership keep in regular contact with retired employees, and arrange regular reunions.

The procedure for dismissal must follow strict legal guidelines. When a new worker is taken on he or she must be given a written contract of employment within 13 weeks of starting the job.

Under the Contract of Employment Act 1972, the written contract must include the following:

1. Title of the job.
2. Date the job starts.
3. Hours of work.
4. Rate and method of pay.
5. Holiday arrangements.
6. Period of notice that must be given.
7. Pension-scheme arrangements.
8. Rights concerning trade unions.
9. The organization's discipline rules.

The personnel manager will agree a date with the employee for work to start and the contract becomes binding from this date.

Over the years an elaborate system for the dismissal of staff has developed as a result of the large number of cases that have been before industrial tribunals or other courts. The heart of the matter lies in the difference between what is termed fair dismissal and what the court regards to be unfair dismissal.

The period of notice that an employee must be given when being laid off is stated in the contract of employment which is a legal document.

'Fair dismissal' can take place in cases where grounds can be shown such as:

1. Wilful destruction of company property.
2. Sexual or racial harassment.

3. Continuous bad timekeeping.
4. A negligent attitude at work.
5. Inability to do the job.
6. Sleeping on the job.

In some cases, e.g. bad timekeeping, employees would normally receive written warnings and suspensions before dismissal.

'Unfair' dismissal would include:

1. *Pregnancy* You can only be sacked if you are unable to do your job properly, e.g. a shelf stacker.
2. *Race* A worker cannot be sacked on the grounds of race.
3. *Homosexuality* If a worker is a homosexual there is no reason why he or she should be sacked unless it can be proved that it affects his or her standard of work.
4. *Union membership* An employer cannot sack a worker for belonging to a trade union.
5. *Criminal record* If an employer does not find out about an employee's criminal record until some time after employing him or her, the employer cannot sack the worker on these grounds unless it was a very relevant crime, e.g. a cashier who has a record of stealing the petty cash.

Redundancy occurs when a business of firm closes down, when part of a business closes down, or when particular types of workers are no longer required. It will usually be the responsibility of personnel to supervise and administer the redundancy procedures.

Health and safety

The personnel department will also normally be concerned with health and safety at work. There are thousands of pages of legal regulations covering health and safety at work. Some firms employ a specialist health and safety department. Unions are also particularly concerned with this issue. The three main laws concerned with health and safety are described in Fig. 12.6.

Equal opportunities

Business has a legal obligation to provide equal opportunities at work. In addition, many enlightened employers provide their own codes of conduct which go beyond the bare essentials of statutory obligations. For example, Littlewoods has produced its own code of practice. Littlewoods Equal Opportunities Code of Practice is a 21-page booklet covering policy on recruitment and its advertising, selection processes, training, career development, job satisfaction, terms and conditions, part-time employment, responsibilities of managers and supervisors, ethnic minorities and religious

The Factories Act 1961

This Act covers most businesses that use mechanical machinery and therefore includes a wide range of premises, including garages, printing works, building sites and engineering establishments. Some of the important provisions of this Act are as follows.

1. Adequate toilet and washing facilities must be provided.
2. The inside of buildings must be properly heated and ventilated.
3. Floors, stairs and passageways·must be free from obstructions such as boxes and furniture.
4. Floors must not have slippery surfaces.
5. Machinery such as presses must have fenced screens to prevent serious injury.
6. Fire escapes must be provided and kept in good order. Fire doors should not be locked or obstructed.

The Offices, Shops and Railways Premises Act 1963

This is particularly important in relation to office and shop conditions.

1. Temperatures must not fall below 16°C (60.8°F) in places where people work for any length of time.
2. There must be adequate supplies of fresh or purified air.
3. Toilet and washing facilities must be adequate for the number of employees and kept in a clean state. There must be running hot and cold water with soap and clean towels.
4. Suitable lighting must be provided wherever people walk or work.
5. The minimum amount of space for each person is 12 square metres of floor area.

The Health and Safety at Work Act 1974

This Act establishes a responsibility of both employers and employees to provide safe conditions at work. The *employer's duty* is to ensure as far as is reasonably practical, the 'health, safety and welfare at work of all employees'. The *employee's duty* is to take reasonable care to ensure both his or her own safety and the safety of others who may be affected by what he or she does or does not do.

Employers or employees who do not abide by these rules can be punished in a court of law.

An example of an area covered by the Act is protective guards for cutting machines such as food-slicing machines and industrial presses. Accidents occur if the guards are faulty or if they are removed.

The Act also lays down training standards for workers in potentially hazardous occupations.

Generally the workplace must be designed in such a way as to minimize the risk of accidents.

This Act is backed up by a Health and Safety Executive which includes representatives of employers, employees and local authorities. Health and safety inspectors are appointed with responsibility for making sure that the law is being observed.

Not only must the safety officer be aware of general laws but there are also specific laws and codes relating to specific industries. For example, there are laws relating to workers in mines, the explosives industry, and textiles. On top of this, many industries establish their own safety regulations, often in conjunction with trade unions. A firm's personnel officer will normally attend conferences and refresher courses on safety as a regular feature of his or her work.

Figure 12.6 Legislation governing health and safety at work. (*Source*: Needham, D. and Dransfield, R. *Business Studies in Practice*. McGraw-Hill, Maidenhead 1988.)

beliefs and employees with domestic responsibilities. It states that no job applicant or employee should receive less favourable treatment on grounds of gender, marital status, social class, colour, race, ethnic origin, creed or disability or be disadvantaged by conditions or requirements which cannot be shown to be relevant to performance.

The company's aspirations, at least as far as employees are concerned, are backed up by an equal opportunities internal appeals procedure to be 'invoked in cases of alleged sexual or racial harassment'. Where this process fails to resolve a problem the employee can then use the company's formal grievance procedure.

The administration and implementation of equal opportunities policies often rests with personnel.

Bargaining

Bargaining over wages and conditions at work at a plant or office level is usually the responsibility of personnel. During a typical week the personnel manager may meet representatives from all of the major unions involved in a business to discuss conditions and working practices.

Appraisal

The supervision and implementation of a business's appraisal policy often rests with the personnel department. The purpose of an appraisal interview is to appraise a person's performance over a given period of time against targets which have been set in order to:

- assess performance, recognize achievements, build on strengths and identify weaknesses;
- identify areas of improvement, ways of overcoming weaknesses and the resulting needs for further training; and
- discuss potential and future development.

Other functions of personnel

Additionally, personnel may take under its umbrella the design and conduct of disciplinary procedures, and the organization of the payment system for wages and salaries.

Personnel will additionally have a welfare function. This will involve the provision of social facilities and activities, lighting, heating and ventilation, canteen facilities, Christmas activities, complaints at work and many other related areas.

Short answer questions

1. What key questions need to be answered in job analysis?

2. Explain the terms:
   (a) task analysis;
   (b) activity analysis;
   (c) skills analysis.
3. Carry out a skills audit of the members of your class. What problems would you have if you wanted to set up a cake manufacturing company using the members of your class?
4. Write a job description for a job with which you are familiar.
5. What is a job specification? Write out a job specification for a business studies teacher.
6. What is the purpose of a job requisition?
7. What are the advantages and disadvantages of internal recruitment?
8. What is the purpose of a job centre?
9. What is meant by staff 'appraisal'?
10. Describe the stages in the 'employment procession'.
11. What is the difference between 'on the job', and 'off the job' training?
12. What details are normally included in a contract of employment?
13. Give three examples of 'fair' and three examples of 'unfair' dismissal.
14. Give a simple definition of redundancy.
15. What details should be included in an 'equal opportunities' code of practice?
16. What arguments would you put forward for having a specialist health and safety department in a large company?
17. What do you think would be the best method of recruiting part-time secretarial staff for a large company in London?
18. Why is it important to make job applicants aware of the conditions in which they will be working?
19. How can ratios be used to monitor the effectiveness of a selection process?
20. What do you understand by the term 'job induction'?

Essays

1. Personnel is the most vital of all company functions because it deals with the human resource. Discuss this statement.
2. Why is it important for a business to devise an effective equal opportunities policy?
3. What are the most important stages involved in recruiting and selecting skilled managers?
4. Why is a detailed knowledge of health and safety regulations important to business?
5. What are the most important steps in interviewing candidates for a job?
6. 'The best method of recruitment is not always the cheapest!' Discuss this view.
7. In what situations should a company employ the services of recruitment agencies?

8. How can personnel help and support the other functions of a company? Illustrate your answer with examples.

9. What are the essential qualities of a 'good' personnel manager?

10. All management posts require an understanding of 'personnel'. Discuss this statement.

Data response questions

1   Study the pie chart (Fig. 12.7) which indicates ways in which people who are unemployed look for work.

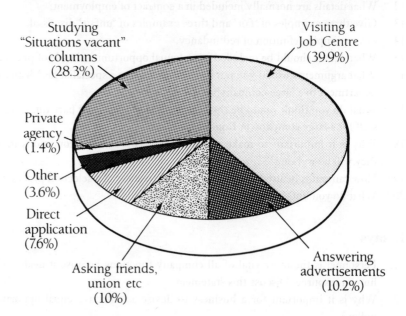

Figure 12.7 How the unemployed look for work. (*Source*: 1987 Labour Force Survey.)

(a) What does the chart indicate are the most common ways for unemployed people to seek work?

(b) What information would you like to know in order to check the accuracy of the figures?

(c) In what ways would the pie chart differ from one that showed how school leavers (at 16) look for work?

(d) How might the knowledge of the information contained in the pie chart in Fig. 12.7 be of use to an employer?

2 Study the journal article in Fig. 12.8 and answer the questions that follow it.

Lack of staff now a nationwide problem

Recruitment difficulties are spreading throughout the UK, says a fourth-quarter skills survey from the Association of British Chambers of Commerce.

Two-thirds of manufacturing companies and more than a half of service firms are now experiencing problems recruiting staff. And while shortages of skilled manual staff show signs of fading, the shortage of clerical and unskilled labour has become more acute.

Of the 65 per cent of manufacturers suffering from the shrinking staff supply, those in the Thames Valley have come out worst, with 75 per cent of employers reporting difficulties. In the West Midlands, 73 per cent of firms are severely affected. And in Merseyside and London the figure is 70 per cent.

Of the 12 UK regions and 3,000 companies surveyed, the lowest percentage of manufacturers staff with recruitment difficulties was 53 per cent.

Director-general of the ABCC, Ron Taylor, said: "Recruitment difficulties are no longer the preserve of certain regions; they are now a severe problem throughout the UK. For the business community, training is seen as the key priority."

AREA RECRUITMENT DIFFICULTIES		
REGION	**MFC**	**SERVICE**
Bucks	75%	69%
W. Midlands	73%	49%
London	70%	57%
Merseyside	70%	55%
Wales	65%	60%

Figure 12.8 Recent recruitment difficulties in the United Kingdom. (*Source: Personnel Today*, 21 February 1989.)

(a) What would you regard to be the underlying causes of the recruitment difficulties identified in the article?

(b) Which areas are identified as being worst 'hit'? What difficulties are likely to be faced in these areas? Why do you think that particular problems have arisen in these areas?

(c)   What recruitment strategies would you suggest for individual firms to deal with these difficulties?

(d)   What will be the likely consequences of failing to recruit employees with the required skills?

(e)   Why do you think that there are more difficulties in manufacturing than for services?

3   Study the journal article in Fig. 12.9.

Driving the job message home

Job description and salary are the most important items to be included in an advertisement for the motor trade. Job description was the most important to 25 per cent of survey respondents and salary to 22 per cent. Other significant factors are job title (13 per cent), location (11 per cent) and employers name (11 per cent).

The *Motor Trader* Employment Survey looks at how, when and why staff in the motor trade move jobs. It covers senior management and skilled jobs.

Over two-thirds of staff in the sector look at job advertisements even when they are not actively looking for a job.

According to the survey, the local press is the main information source. It is used by 44 per cent of staff looking for a job. It was used by 32 per cent when they were last looking for a job. The trade press follows in second place, used by 17 per cent of staff in this sector when they last looked for a job.

But the trade press and local papers are almost equally popular as the best source in which to look for a job.

Less than half of the respondents, 43 per cent were willing to move home for a new job. But distance was of little consequence. Of those prepared to move, 62 per cent would move more than 200 miles.

Of those prepared to move 28 per cent would move to the South West. The South East and East Anglia follow in popularity.

Figure 12.9 Features of a 'good' job advertisement. (*Source*: Personnel Today, September 1989.)

(a)   What does the article indicate are the best methods of placing job advertisements for senior managers and skilled employees in the motor trade?

(b) What features do members of the motor trade particularly look for in job advertisements?

(c) Design a job advertisement for a car sales manager. Study existing adverts for reference. How is your advertisement more effective than existing ones?

Suggested reading

Barber, D., *The Practice of Personnel Management*. IPM, 1982.

Cumming, M., *Personnel Management*. Heinemann, 1983.

13

The experience of working life

The experience of working life is a complex mix involving:

- The individual
- The group
- The nature of work
- The organization of the business.

For the *individual* the experience of work is a highly personal one. The creation of 'personality' is a complex process resulting from elements of heredity and environment. It should not be looked at in a simplistic way. For the purposes of business studies at 'A' level you will need to be aware that every individual will have his or her own needs and requirements, and these will need to be considered within the constraints of organizational needs. Research into stress at work consistently finds that the way individuals are treated is the main feature of their job satisfaction.

Work is about feeling valued as well as about receiving a pay packet. As the American writer Studs Terkel suggests in his book *Working*: 'It is about a search, too, for daily meaning as well as daily bread, for recognition as well as for cash, for astonishment rather than torpor; in short, for a sort of life rather than a Monday-through-Friday sort of dying.'

Many people spend considerable amounts of their working lives operating in *groups*. They will interact with others in formal and in informal settings. Formal groups are those that are set up for a particular purpose, with a set pattern of operation, with set targets and goals. Individuals will have set roles and positions within a formal group, e.g. works manager, supervisor, etc.

Informal groups exist on a casual basis involving loose arrangements. People frequently engage in informal relations at work with the people they work with. The quality of these relationships will influence an individual's attitude to work.

The *nature of the work* will be an important determinant of the quality of working life. However, there is no simple pattern of 'good' and 'bad' jobs, 'dull' and 'rewarding' ones. An individual's evaluation of a job will be influenced by other factors such as personality, and preferred group style.

The pattern of *organization of the business* and the style of management and leadership is important in influencing the experience of work. Rank Xerox, for example, believes that it is important to praise and recognize individuals within the organization.

A recognition programme has been introduced in the personnel department at Xerox. It is called 'You Deserve an X Today' (X being a positive letter at Xerox). Anyone in the department, whether an executive or not, can give an X certificate (redeemable for 25 dollars) to anyone for 'excellent support, excellent attendance, extra work or excellent cooperation'.

This means that any member of the organization can reward another colleague for a quality contribution.

Human needs and work

People have a wide range of attitudes to work. Many people see work simply as a means of earning money. Others find that work is tremendously rewarding. Attitudes to work often depend on how much opportunity individuals are given to express their skills and talents. Some work is alienating because people are treated like part of the machinery. They are expected to do very boring and repetitive work, without any responsibility. Some work is fulfilling because individuals are given a lot of freedom, and the opportunity to be creative.

Conditions of work are also important. Some modern workplaces are air conditioned, brightly decorated and there is a pleasant working atmosphere. Other workplaces are stifling in summer and freezing in winter, premises are decrepit and personal relationships are discouraged. Pay can be used as an incentive to encourage people to work harder, but it cannot help them to enjoy their work.

The following is a list of some of the things different people might look for in a job:

1. A good rate of pay.
2. Good opportunities for promotion.
3. Long breaks and holidays.
4. Prestige.
5. The opportunity to combine work and family life.
6. Job security.
7. Friendship with workmates.
8. Opportunities to be creative.
9. A degree of independence.
10. Responsibility.

Generally, satisfaction will be greatest for individuals who have the greatest freedom to choose a job and this will be those who have had the opportunity to acquire the most widely accepted range of qualifications and skills. Most jobs have some disadvantages but workers will enjoy work if these disadvantages can be minimized.

The ingredients of a 'good job'

It would be very difficult to find the 'commonly accepted' ingredients of a good job. One person likes the freedom to work when and how he wants, another only feels secure when there is someone there telling him what to do. One person likes variety and change, another wants a good steady job. There is an infinite number of variations on this theme.

Job satisfaction is a complex mix including:

- The individual employee
- The job
- The business
- The rewards
- The working environment

Individual employees bring their attitudes into the workplace, their attitudes are also shaped by the workplace. Some employees come to work looking for a challenge and excitement and place little emphasis on monetary rewards. Other employees might see employment as a means to enjoying a good life outside of the workplace so that they are not too bothered about the nature of the work provided that the pay is high.

The social researchers Goldthorpe and Lockwood studied workers in three firms which used a range of different technologies in production. Their sample of 250 men included assembly line workers at the Vauxhall Car Company, machine operators, machine setters and skilled maintenance workers at the Skefko Ball Bearing Company and process workers and skilled maintenance workers at Laporte Chemicals. Goldthorpe and Lockwood found that skilled workers had a greater level of enjoyment in the work they did than the routine machinists and assemblers. However, they also found that the level of technology made very little difference to employees' attitudes to work and to behaviour. In particular, they found that all workers had what they defined as an 'instrumental approach' to work. Work was seen as a means (an instrument) to earn high wages to enjoy life outside the workplace. Work was seen therefore as a means to an end to be able to buy a bigger range of consumer goods and to enjoy leisure. Goldthorpe and Lockwood felt that these attitudes to work resulted from the employees' attitudes which were formed outside of the workplace.

The nature of the job will inevitably influence the employee's perception of the pleasure involved. At one end of the spectrum will be the job which involves endless repetition of a simple and tedious operation, where there are only a few seconds to perform the task before it has to be repeated. Employees will get little sense of achievement from producing a very small part of an end product which they may never see. There may be very little time for conversation with workmates because of noise and the urgency to perform the next operation.

At the other extreme there will be jobs involving personal involvement and individual contributions to production methods. These jobs may require high levels of training and expertise and give the employee prestige as well as meaning to their working lives.

Dorothy Wedderburn and Rosemary Crompton investigated work attitudes at a large chemical plant in North East England which they called 'Seagrass'. They found that 'different attitudes and behaviour *within* the work situation could be manifested by different groups of workers largely in response to the differences in the prevailing technologies and control systems'. For example, the process workers in the plant (which was mainly automated) found their jobs interesting, and felt that they had enough freedom to try out their own ideas and sufficient freedom to organize their own work tasks. In contrast, the workers in the machine shop felt that their work was boring and gave them little freedom to organize their own work situations. Attitudes produced by the job situation tended to be reflected in attitudes to supervisors. Workers who found their jobs interesting and enjoyable tended to have a favourable view of their supervisors while the employees who found work boring tended to resent supervision.

Wedderburn and Crompton, while finding that within the work situation attitudes were influenced by technology, went on to conclude that workers still had an instrumental general attitude to work itself. For example, in the assessment of their jobs, the Seagrass workers listed four major considerations—'the level of pay, the security of the job, the good welfare benefits and the good working conditions'. 'Job interest' was regarded to be relatively less important.

The nature of the business organization is also of importance. Some business organizations try to create an atmosphere of employee involvement. For example, Toshiba UK holds a daily five-minute communication meeting between workers and management. Organizations which directly involve employees in decision making help to foster a feeling of shared involvement in the success or failure of the enterprise. Some organizations such as cooperatives deliberately set out to share the decision-making process. In contrast, large companies based on hierarchical procedures can foster feelings of alienation.

The way that employment is rewarded also helps to determine attitudes. Some methods of payment such as piece rate (where employees are paid according to the number of items produced) can add to a feeling of alienation (e.g. workers rushing to produce given targets in order to increase pay). In the past ten years there has been a dramatic rise in the number of British companies introducing incentive schemes to motivate staff. The range of incentives offered by companies is diverse. They cover school fees, pensions, executive cars, private telephones, merit awards, life assurance, bonus and profit-sharing schemes.

The working environment covers a range of factors including lighting, heating and ventilation, the state of furnishing and equipment, recreation facilities and many other details. For example, recent reports have pointed out some of the dangers of the high-tech office. Reports indicate that typists and computer operators nationwide are suffering from increasing problems caused by repetitive strain injury (RSI). Fast keyboard work can lead to overuse of muscles making it impossible to sleep, work or do ordinary household tasks.

Individual needs

What do people need to give them a general feeling of well-being? If you asked this question to a number of individuals they would come up with a wide number of differing answers. For example, in a recent article for *The Independent* newspaper Koo Stark (a former girlfriend of Prince Andrew) wrote that: 'In my view, privacy is as necessary to human happiness as eating or sleeping. If you are deprived of your privacy you cannot eat or sleep and you become ill. You cannot breathe, you distrust every flicker of light in case it is the glint of a long lens. You are deprived of a basic human need.'

Not only do our perceptions of needs vary from one individual to another, but they also vary over time and in different circumstances. Abraham Maslow (1970) suggested that although it is difficult, if not impossible, to analyse individual needs, it is possible to develop a hierarchical picture of needs which can be split up into five broad categories (see Fig. 13.1).

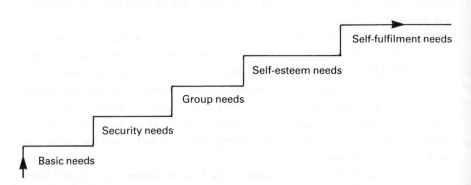

Figure 13.1 Abraham Maslow's hierarchy of needs.

Basic needs are for reasonable standards of food, shelter and clothing and those other items which are required to be the norm to meet the needs of the body and for physical survival. This base level of need will be typically met in modern industrial society by the exchange of labour for a wage packet or salary.

Security needs are also concerned with physical survival. In the context of the workplace these needs could include physical safety, security of employment, adequate rest periods, pension and sick schemes, and protection from arbitrary actions.

Group needs are concerned with an individual's need for love and affection. Within groups there are always some people who are strong enough and happy to keep apart; however, the majority of people want to feel that they belong to a group. In small and medium sized organizations (up to 200 people) it is relatively easy to give each member of the group a feeling of belonging. However, in large organizations individuals can lose their group identity becoming just another number, a face in the crowd. As we shall see later in this chapter, there are ways of dealing with this problem, by putting groups of workers into smaller work units with a common productive interest.

Self-esteem needs are based on an individual's desire for self-respect and the respect of others. Employees have a need to be recognized as individuals of some importance, to receive praise for their work, and to have their efforts noticed.

Maslow placed self-fulfilment at the top of his hierarchy of needs. Self-fulfilment is concerned with full personal development and individual creativity. In order to meet these needs it is important for individuals to be able to use their talents and abilities fully.

Maslow argued that an individual's first need is to have his or her lower level needs met. However, it is also important for higher level needs to be met if individuals are not to experience frustration. Frustrated employees are likely to develop either a 'couldn't care less approach' or to become antagonistic to working life. Maslow felt that in modern industrial settings lower level needs tend to be met. However, if employees are to feel a greater commitment to work, and to become more effective employees, then it is also necessary to meet their higher level needs. Self-fulfilment at work creates the 'complete' employee, the person that enjoys work and feels a direct involvement in it.

The research work of Herzberg in many ways complements the findings of Maslow. Herzberg argues that different factors in the work situation act in different ways to motivate people to work well or badly. Herzberg drew a distinction between what he called 'hygiene' factors (which potentially could act as 'dissatisfiers') and motivating factors or 'satisfiers'.

Herzberg set out nine 'dissatisfiers' ('hygiene factors'):

1. Company policy and administration.
2. Pay.
3. Working conditions.
4. Relationships between different levels in the hierarchy.
5. Relationships at the same level in the hierarchy.
6. Management and supervisory practices.
7. Unfair treatment.
8. Feelings of inadequacy.
9. Impossibility of growth and development.

Herzberg suggested that if these factors did not reach an acceptable standard, this would possibly lead to dissatisfaction, which could be expressed by absenteeism, poor levels of output, resistance to change, obstruction and other negative work practices.

In contrast, Herzberg pointed to five factors that could motivate. These he referred to as 'satisfiers', as they can increase the motivation to work better and harder:

1. Recognition of effort and performance.
2. The nature of the job itself—does it provide the employee with the appropriate degree of challenge?
3. Sense of achievement.
4. Responsibility.
5. The opportunity for promotion and improvement.

On the basis of his research, Herzberg went on to suggest that jobs could be given more meaning if they incorporated elements of responsibility, a more creative use of abilities and opportunities for a sense of achievement.

An alternative way of looking at motivation is presented in Vroom's expectancy theory. This theory states that the key ingredients in motivation are:

- an individual's wants; and
- his or her estimation of the likelihood of meeting these wants.

An individual's wants at work may include promotion, a high salary, a particular job, a company car, etc. Vroom used the measure 'valency' to describe the level of a particular want which can be placed on a scale of high to low. However, if high valency for a particular target is going to act as a motivator, the individual concerned must believe that the target is attainable. For motivation to be high it is essential that employees feel that they can have their wants met at work. For example, an individual who wants to work up to the position of running a company car, or managing a department at work must believe that this goal will be met in the course of time. The implications of the theory are that working life should offer opportunities for the wants of employees to be met, and at the same time provide clear evidence that these targets are attainable.

Vroom sets out a diagram to show that valence and expectancy are the two key ingredients in motivation. The × sign indicates the multiplier effect created by the interaction of valence and expectancy.

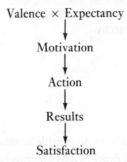

Valence × Expectancy
↓
Motivation
↓
Action
↓
Results
↓
Satisfaction

Theories related to motivation are all based on assumptions about the underlying nature of people. Schein has classified these assumptions under three main headings:

1. *Socio-economic drive*   This involves the assumption that people are driven by material urges. Satisfaction can be created by meeting these basic needs in the workplace.
2. *Social drive*   This involves the assumption that people have a basic need to feel part of a group, and to be accepted.
3. *Complex drive*   This involves a much broader perspective of motivation. People are driven by a host of different factors which change over time and in different circumstances. Simplistic explanations of motivation should be avoided.

Over the years many different approaches to work organization have been employed. Frederick Taylor, writing at the beginning of the century, spelt out the principles of scientific management. According to Taylor, there is 'one best way' of carrying out any work task. It is the job of management to find out this method by using scientific principles. For example, various tools should be tested to find the most effective for a particular job, rest periods of different lengths and frequency should be tried to discover the relationship between rest and productivity, the various movements involved in a task should be studied to find the least time consuming and tiring. Scientific managers would experiment with the various components of work tasks to produce the best methods. Employees would then be carefully matched with work tasks according to aptitudes. Instructions set down by management for the performance of tasks should then be followed to the letter. The workforce and the machinery could thus be seen as one and the same. It would then be possible to provide incentives, usually in the form of a high wage, to encourage employees to identify with scientific procedures. Employers would be able to maximize profits, and employees to maximize wages. Taylor's work is based heavily on the assumption that high wages are the key motivator.

Taylor's scientific management approach can be contrasted with the human relations school of thought. Elton Mayo and a team of researchers from the Harvard Business School carried out a series of experiments from 1927 to 1932 at the Western Electric Company in Chicago. Initially, Mayo had taken on board some of the assumptions of the scientific management school believing that physical conditions in the working environment, the aptitudes of workers and financial incentives were the key ingredients in motivation. Mayo had experimented with different levels of heating, lighting, lengths and frequencies of rest periods and other variables. However, the results of the experiments were inconclusive. For example, they were surprised to find that wide variations in the level of lighting had little or no effect on output. During the course of the experiments Mayo found that the productivity of the group studied kept climbing irrespective of various changes. Mayo came to the conclusion that as a result of the experiment, a great deal of attention had been given to the group and members of the group had come to feel much closer ties with each other. Mayo felt that this was the important factor and his work led to an appreciation of the importance of the informal group in industry.

The Hawthorne studies moved the emphasis from the individual worker to the worker as a member of a social group. Mayo suggested that managers should establish and maintain a sense of group purpose in industry. A famous example of this is the Volvo car assembly plant where the traditional assembly line has been scrapped and teams of workers build virtually the whole car. Not only do the workers build up a sense of group solidarity but also they are able to identify with the production process from start to finish.

Within an organization, it is management's role to ensure that objectives are delegated and communicated clearly from the highest management level through the management chain, ensuring that each manager within the chain knows clearly his or her individual role and objective.

To do this effectively requires shared values and the commitment of the whole organization. Thomas Peters's and Robert Waterman's model, the seven Ss for business success as delineated in their book *In Search of Excellence*, highlights this need (see also Fig. 13.2). Shared values are at the heart of a successful operation. Without them, things can start to disintegrate.

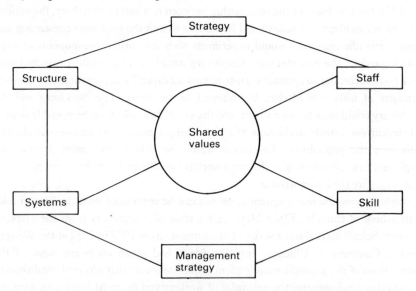

Figure 13.2 The seven Ss of success.

Case Study—Highlighting a lack of shared values at BCL Cellophane

A shrinking market and growing competition prompted BCL Cellophane in Bridgewater to review its culture.

Managing director Ken Vickers says: 'Cellophane manufacture is a complex chemical process, but it is a very traditional business.' He admits it had a conventional approach to management. 'It was very much a top down, blame-culture,' he says. The company, a division of Courtaulds Yarns, recognised it had to change or it would be out of business within five years.

Its problems stemmed not from marketing and distribution but from inadequacies in its manufacturing. Management concluded that the route to increasing productivity lay in improving teamwork, breaking down the mistrust between management and workforce and developing a common approach to solving the problems.

It invited the Coverdale Organisation to initiate a training programme to tackle the problem under its business results scheme. The scheme means paying for the training is directly linked to the improvement in the performance of the business as a result of the training.

The Coverdale approach is geared to developing teamwork concentrating on using training techniques to explore the effects particular behaviour has on working in teams. It also established a common approach to tackling problems, planning ahead and seeing plans through.

The programme began with an initial diagnosis of the company's problems. Specific, measurable, project aims were set. These were then cascaded down to precise targets even at individual shift level [see Fig. 13.3]. A monitoring process was set up next to log and measure progress, and the training programme began.

The factory management had identified the target. It wanted to reduce factory waste from 17.45 per cent to 15 per cent by March.

This translated down to specific goals within the company.

Managing director Vickers explains that it was important that any training exercise should be more 'than just a quick fix'. 'We had to make a permanent change to the culture and attitudes; to the way we were running the organisation. We wanted to weave into the fabric of the business,' he says.

Vickers explains that the market for Cellophane has grown very tough, declining at a rate of 12 per cent a year. There are nine companies all vying for larger shares of this smaller market. Survival depends on more efficient manufacturing.

According to Vickers, the company suffered because there were no shared values, and very little contact between sales and the shop floor. One of the key changes brought in by Coverdale was taking people of all disciplines and training them together. 'The shopfloor began to see that sales people were human and had problems too,' explains Vickers. But the most important aspect was behavioural changes. 'You do not change attitudes unless you change the behaviour of management,' he says.

So training began at the top and the re-setting of precise goals began there too. 'Managers were struggling because they did not have direction, they did not have the vision,' explains Vickers.

Coverdale's training programme was tightly linked to changes in the structure of BCL and driven by top management. In parallel, and in part through the training, improvements were being made to the internal organisation.

'We had to flatten the management structure,' explains Vickers. 'There were eight or nine levels of management. But the company management had recognised that productivity depended on sharing responsibility for production with the workforce, if it could not trust its workforce then it could not succeed. One of the important ways of developing that was through common training, which taught common methods.'

A mark of the success of the project was that barely a year into the programme there was a major programme of redundancy at the Bridgewater plant. Forty per cent of the workforce had to be made redundant and yet production had still to be pushed up even higher.

Efforts were made to do this as quickly as possible and without disruption. The company found other jobs for all those who wanted them. At the same time the relentless drive to push up production carried on and it lifted output from 25 to 35 tonnes per man per year. Part of the reason for this was, explains Vickers, 'the atmosphere that emerged. People were no longer resistant to change, they were seeking it.'

Coverdale is still working with BCL. 'It takes longer than you think,' insists Vickers. But it is important to him that the training be seen right through to the point at which he is satisfied it is changing the roots of the business.

Get it right first, he suggests, and then bolting on to other kinds of training, or making changes becomes easier because the base is solid.

(*Source:* Helena Sturridge, *Personnel Today*, 1988.)

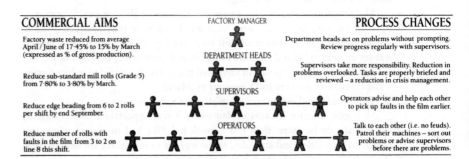

Figure 13.3 Changing behaviour in the manufacturing plant was achieved by addressing very specific problems and setting clearly identified goals.

Questions

1. What circumstances led BCL Cellophane to review its culture?
2. What evidence is given in the article that before the review, there was a lack of shared values at BCL Cellophane?
3. What weaknesses in company organizational structure existed before the review?
4. What changes in training procedures were introduced by Coverdale?
5. In what ways can the commercial aims of BCL Cellophane and process changes be seen to go hand in hand?
6. Why was it felt to be essential to change management attitudes?

Non-monetary techniques of motivating employees

There are a number of possible ways of motivating workers apart from pay. These usually involve an increase in one or all of the following:

- The variety of work
- Responsibility
- Recognition
- Sense of working as a team

Job enrichment involves giving employees an increase in responsibility and/or recognition. The aim of job enrichment is to make employees feel that their contribution has been upgraded so that it is more highly appreciated. Ways of doing this vary from an employee being given a new title, to an extension of the perks associated with a particular job.

Job enlargement involves giving employees a greater range of responsibilities. An employee who feels that a job is going 'stale' and as a result is losing interest in it may feel rejuvenated when asked to take on additional tasks. For example, an employee who has been used to handling routine mail and answering telephone calls may gain fresh motivation if asked to take on the additional responsibility of meeting clients and taking them out to dinner as part of the public relations function.

Employee participation in decision making can be a great motivator. The flattened organogram in which decisions can be made at all levels of an organization helps employees to feel important and valued for their contribution to the decision-making process. Effective employee participation goes beyond the factory floor suggestion box to actually giving a wider number of people the responsibility for making decisions. The flattening out of the organizational chart has particularly become possible in organizations that employ modern information systems so that communication links are better and information is more readily available.

Quality circles will be particularly important motivators in the 1990s. Although quality circles are a fairly recent arrival on the British industrial scene they have proved to be a very popular innovation. By the end of 1985 there were estimated to be between 400 and 500 quality circles operating in British manufacturing companies and between 30 and 40 in services. Quality circles in Britain are typically made up of small groups of seven to eight people who voluntarily meet on a regular basis to identify, investigate, analyse and resolve quality-related matters or other work-related arrangements using problem-solving techniques. Members tend to be from the same work area or do similar work.

Quality circles are about participation, teamwork, job satisfaction, self-esteem and organizational commitment as well as resolving work- and quality-related problems. Quality circles have been particularly effective in Japanese industry and have been a cornerstone in creating group loyalty coupled with high productivity.

However, there have been reservations about the introduction of quality circles in this country, because in many cases they have not worked because support has not been maintained from the top. For quality circles to be effective, the culture of an organization has got to be based on participation. Quality circles are not effective in autocratic environments. Circle members quickly become frustrated when their suggestions are ignored.

Case Study—Changing employment relations in British Rail

British Rail seems to have been chugging along the same line for some time. But according to the new director of personnel development, Steven Colloff, a dramatic culture change is about to take place, with customer service right at the top of the list of priorities.

Staff training is to be improved, better communications are planned with staff, a performance review is to be brought in for supervisors. Promotion at all levels is to be speeded up.

The first step in the culture change was taken with an attitude survey, the results of which have just become available. A random sample of 7000 staff was invited to fill in a questionnaire on what they thought about BR's customers, communication within the company, training, career development and job satisfaction. All the points being raised by staff are being considered.

'The name of the game is to move BR towards a more enterprising customer-orientated and result-based culture,' says Colloff.

Colloff was encouraged by the high level of response to the survey; about 40 per cent returned the questionnaire. Most of the respondents said they believe their job to be worth while and like working for the railway.

'There is a built-in loyalty to BR. We don't have the same problem some companies have of convincing staff their job is worth while. But we do need to make sure staff are getting the promotion and recognition they deserve,' says Colloff.

A new post has been created, the employment development manager responsible for identifying the potential in employees.

Although railway employees like working for BR and most want to stay in the company, the survey highlights a belief among staff that their capabilities are not being fully utilised. Eighty per cent said promotion should be decided on merit rather than length of service. And 85 per cent wanted more opportunities to be selected and trained for better paid jobs.

'Promotion will be more related to performance instead of staff waiting years to fill a dead man's shoes. We particularly need to improve the opportunities for high-performing employees. We must bring in young managers and rapidly give them responsibility instead of waiting until they are past peak performance. To do this, we must identify potential early on.'

Colloff has urgent plans to improve training in supervisory and management skills. A 'leadership 500' programme for BR's top managers is being set up, the first of which will be delivered at the end of November. The group will look at how to achieve quality management and how to identify the key values laid down at a recent top level conference. These values include making the customer number one and involving employees to a larger extent.

From the programme will come action policies which, says Colloff, will have to be incorporated into the whole infrastructure of the company. 'I believe the greatest mistake a company can make is to make changes from bottom to top. All that happens is that you get all these motivated employees knocking on managers' doors with ideas that then get rejected,' says Colloff.

Colloff has also introduced performance reviews for supervisors. When asked whether staff take notice of such a scheme when no financial incentives were offered, Colloff says: 'Our staff are more interested in basic rates of pay rather than performance related pay, so long as they are recognised for their capabilities.'

The survey, however, reveals that employees in operations and engineering find their present payment system offers very little incentive to do a better job.

Colloff explains that supervisors' and managers' attitudes need to be changed: 'We are trying to inculcate more of a 'can do' attitude into our managers. There is vast scope for introducing the new culture of tell me the problem and I'll do something about it instead of tell me the problem and I'll tell you why I can't do anything about it.'

To bring about the culture change, Colloff says smaller identified units are needed rather than remote bureaucracy.

Colloff says that he aims to make performance review non-threatening and creative, claiming that it is a process that should not produce conflict if carried out properly. Most workers, according to the survey, feel that their bosses are slow to praise or criticise their performance.

In fact, a large majority of staff say their management do not make any real effort to communicate with them. Only 30 per cent have a boss who holds a regular meeting to keep the staff informed. Employees want to know more about the outlook for their own area of function, including investment plans and actions to improve quality or service. *Railnews* was rated much more than managers as a good source of information.

A majority of staff do not feel that the top management's direction is right for BR or that management understands the problems faced by staff at work. Staff perceived their boss's priority to be doing the job properly and keeping costs down. Customer service is seen as the last thing on the boss's agenda.

But the staff themselves believe that customers' views are important and 50 per cent think that their jobs have an impact on the quality of service to customers. Customer relations training appears to be helping.

(*Source: Personnel Today*, November 1988.)

Questions

1. What do you understand by the term 'culture change'?
2. Why do you think that British Rail felt that it needed a culture change?
3. Why do you think that British Rail got such a high response from the questionnaires it sent out to its employees? Do you think that the results from the questionnaire would be likely to be representative of all British Rail staff?
4. Why has British Rail employed an Employment Development Manager? Do you think that this is a 'good' idea?
5. Do you think that the notion of promotion related to performance is likely to serve as a good motivator? What drawbacks can you see to such a scheme?
6. How does British Rail hope to change 'the whole infrastructure of the company'? Evaluate its policies for making these changes.
7. What suggestions would you put forward to British Rail to help improve employee motivation?

Work and pay

Pay can be seen as a way of 'compensating' or 'rewarding' employees for work done. There are many different types of jobs and there are many reasons why people receive different levels of payment.

Wages and salaries

Many organizations draw a distinction between those employees who are paid in the form of wages and those who receive a salary.

There are a number of differences between wages and salaries including:

1. Wages are normally expressed as an hourly rate, whereas salaries are expressed as an annual figure.
2. Wages are normally paid a week in arrears (i.e. the wage you earned at the end of one week would be for the previous week's work), whereas salaries are paid at the end of the month.
3. Salaries are normally paid on the basis of an annual rate divided by 12. A salary would thus be expressed in terms of an annual figure. Wages are calculated in several different ways including piece, and time rates (see below).
4. In many organizations the package of benefits available to an employee would be different for salaried than for wage employees.
5. Salaries are typically paid automatically into an employee's bank account by credit transfer. Wages will either be paid in cash or by credit transfer.

Fees

Fees represent an alternative system of payment to wages and salaries. In the United Kingdom today they are becoming increasingly commonly used as employees are hired indirectly to carry out a service contract for a business. The fee is paid as a 'reward' for work done but the employee is not taken directly on to the firm's payroll. A fee may be paid for a short-term contract, e.g. to a photographer helping to make a film about a company, or on a longer term basis, e.g. regular fees to a financial consultant. Fees may be paid on the basis of the time worked, on the quantity of output produced, on the basis of completing a particular contract, or some other means.

The objectives of systems of payment

Payment systems are usually arrived at as a result of a process of collective bargaining. In setting out the objectives of such a system we therefore need to explore the aims and purposes of both management and trade unions.

The objectives of management

1. The pay system needs to be effective in recruiting the right quantity and quality of labour.
2. The pay system needs to be effective in retaining labour over the required level of time. It is expensive to have to keep placing new recruitment adverts with the media, and to keep having to train new employees.
3. The system of payment needs to be effective in keeping unit labour costs as low

as possible. The unit labour cost is the proportion of output cost that can be attributed to labour. Keeping labour costs low is one of the key ingredients to being competitive in local, national and international markets.

4. The payment system can also be seen as one of the key ingredients in motivation. Careful thought needs to be applied to structuring payment systems in a way that encourages motivation and performance.

5. Payment systems can also be aimed at maximizing output per unit of factor of production employed—i.e. to maximize productivity.

6. Payment systems can be designed in such a way as to combine effectively with fringe benefits.

The objectives of trade unions

1. Trade unions may seek to secure a payment system that maximizes the growth of their members' real earnings.

2. Trade unions may seek to ensure that the system of payment is combined with working practices that best suit their members' needs—including considerations of fatigue, boredom, safety and other matters.

3. Unions will seek to balance wage considerations with those of hours worked, breaks and holidays.

4. Unions may seek to gain the best long-term benefits for their members, which may be tied in with notions of competitiveness.

5. Unions will seek to prevent payment systems which are unpopular with their members, e.g. systems based on unattainable bonus targets.

Clearly, different groups within an organization will have different perceptions of what makes an effective system of payment. What works in one company or one type of production will clearly be inappropriate in another. What is needed is a system that creates the 'best fit', given the type of company, types of employees, technologies used, time available for production, state of the market and other relevant factors.

Calculating pay

The amount paid for a normal working week is referred to as a 'basic' wage or salary. Many employees receive other benefits in addition to their basic wage, in either a money or a non-money form. The main ways of calculating pay are outlined below. Sometimes elements of these methods are combined.

Flat rate

This is a set rate of weekly or monthly pay, based on a set number of hours. This system is easy to calculate and administer but it does not provide an incentive to work harder.

Time rate

Under this scheme, the worker receives a set rate per hour. Any hours worked above a set number are paid at an 'overtime' rate.

Piece rate

This system is sometimes used in the textile and electronics industries among others. Payment is made for each item produced which meets a given quality standard. The advantage of such a scheme is that it encourages effort. However, it is not suitable for jobs which require time and care. Also, the output of many jobs such as service occupations is impossible to measure.

Bonus

A bonus is paid as an additional encouragement to employees. It can be paid out of additional profits earned by the employer as a result of the employee's effort and hard work. Bonuses may also be used as an incentive to workers at times when they might be inclined to slacken effort, eg. at Christmas and summer holiday times.

Commission

This is a payment made as a percentage of the sales a salesperson has made.

Profit-related pay

In 1987 the Conservative Government introduced a scheme to try and encourage employers to introduce profit-related pay. The government hoped to encourage employers to stop granting across the board pay increases, in the belief that wage rises can only be financed through increased productivity and profits. The PRP scheme allows employees limited tax relief if part of their take-home pay is linked to profits.

Employees covered by the scheme get tax relief on 50 per cent of their profit-related earnings up to a ceiling of £3000 per annum (1988 figures). To qualify for the cash they must have at least 5 per cent of their earnings tied to company profitability. Companies involved with PRP include household names such as Nationwide Anglia Building Society and Gallaher.

Performance-related pay

Performance-related pay involves relating all or part of the pay package to employee performance at work. For example, Komatsu, which makes plant machinery at Birtley near Newcastle upon Tyne, offer a 6 per cent bonus as an incentive, based on the results of individuals' performance reviews.

Running an effective payroll department

The wage bill in most companies constitutes a sizeable chunk of total overhead costs. The effective control of the cash necessary for the payment of wages is the payroll manager's most important task.

The size of a company, together with the frequency of payment to employees, determines the position of a wages department. To be effective it is vital that the payroll manager is seen as part of the middle management structure, and in some companies as part of the senior management team.

A host of tasks face the payroll manager.

Security

The most inefficient method of payment is payment in cash. It is time consuming and it is a security risk to every individual who uses the system. In those companies where cash payment continues, the payroll and personnel managers must try to convert the employees to direct payment into the bank or building society of their choice.

Payroll managers must pay close attention to the security and confidentiality of payroll details. These include not just details of salaries and wages, but also the deduction and payment of court orders.

Training

Training staff in modern methods of payrolling is essential. Important areas for training might include controlling the conversion from manual systems to computer systems, and assisting in the design and the implementation of any changes.

Communication

Lines of communication with other departments must be effective, particularly with personnel, if it is separate, and with accounts and production control. Wages departments generate the payroll based upon information supplied by others, usually personnel, the Inland Revenue, the Department of Health and Social Security or managerial staff.

Sick pay

Payroll departments must apply strictly the rules and regulations regarding statutory sick pay (SSP) and statutory maternity pay (SMP). (SSP are payments made if a worker is sick on normal working days; SMP applies in a similar way to maternity.) Both these articles of legislation are complicated and difficult to operate. These laws make it essential for the reconciliation of records maintained by the wages and personnel departments to be carried out on a regular basis.

Deductions

The payroll department must ensure that pay as you earn (PAYE) and national insurance contributions are deducted from pay. Such deductions must be passed on to the collector of taxes by the middle of the following month.

Accounting

The payroll department must supply the accounts department with the details of payments, deductions and net pay for them to be entered in the books of accounts, and to complete a bank reconciliation.

Benefits

An increasing burden on the payroll manager is the annual disclosure, to the Inland Revenue, of perks which have been provided by the company to certain employees. These include company cars and fuel, beneficial loans, free medical treatment and free holidays. By law these must be disclosed to the Inland Revenue to enable the inspector of taxes to determine the tax due on such benefits.

Computerization of wages

In large firms, much of the work on wages is done by computers. This involves the calculation of wages, the printing of wage slips and the production of payment instructions to the bank. Data relating to the time an employee works are picked up by computer from magnetic tape, enabling the continuous recording of wages. Computers are able to handle a lot of work quickly and accurately.

One danger of using computers to calculate and record wages is the risk of losing information if something should happen to the wages program or disk. Therefore, firms will normally keep at least two 'back-up' copies of a disk which will be continually updated.

Women at work

The Equal Pay Act 1970 aimed to eliminate discrimination on grounds of sex in relation to pay, overtime, piecework rates and holiday entitlements. The Act gave all employees the right to equal treatment to that given to an employee of the opposite sex in the same employment who is doing the same or 'broadly similar' work. This Act was amended in 1984 to include equal pay for work of equal value.

The Sex Discrimination Act 1975 made sex discrimination unlawful in employment training and related matters. This Act was updated in 1986 to remove restrictions on women's hours of work which had prevented them from taking on manufacturing jobs involving shift or night work.

The main problems for women as a group at work have been low pay and a concentration in low-paid occupations. Economic expansion in the United Kingdom from the 1950s onwards created more and more jobs for women. There has been a growth particularly in the proportion of married women at work, so that over half now work.

Women have been finding work in hard times because of the nature of the work they do, i.e. part-time work. Between 1979 and 1987 women's employment in Western Europe rose by 7 per cent while men's has fallen by 2 per cent.

Women have taken on the part-time jobs which are available. In Belgium, Denmark, West Germany and the United Kingdom, women do over 80 per cent of all part-time jobs. The growing service industries are the main employers of part-time workers. Part-time workers are especially low paid, but this is not the only reason for women's generally low pay. Another factor is that men's earnings are boosted by shiftwork, overtime and productivity deals. Such payments make up a quarter of men's earnings and only one-seventh of women's. The 1986 amendment to the Sex Discrimination Act may help with this.

Major problems for women are that they tend to work in industries where unions are weak and because of family commitments they are unable to work overtime. Women are concentrated in a very narrow range of occupations. Catering, cleaning, hairdressing, bar work and other services occupy over half of all women manual workers, and office work employs a large proportion of non-manual workers. The 1984 amendment to the Equal Pay Act, which allows for job evaluation to see if work is of equal value, is seen as an important change.

The effect of the passing of the Equal Pay Act and the Sex Discrimination Act was to raise women's pay to 75 per cent of men's; however, by 1984 it had fallen back to 59 per cent of men's earnings in non-manual work and 61.5 per cent in manual work.

A feature of the United Kingdom in recent years is that women now have more qualifications, which should lead to advancement in earnings. Women with better qualifications are choosing from a wider range of careers. Women now own a quarter of all American small businesses. The women graduates of the 1960s went into a small number of occupations, often teaching. The graduates of the 1970s are branching into medicine, law, banking and insurance among other areas. In the United Kingdom 47 per cent of medical school graduates are now women. Between the mid-1970s and the mid-1980s the proportion of women members in the Chartered Insurance Institute rose from 4 per cent to 14 per cent, and the proportion of women solicitors from 6 per cent to 17 per cent.

It is the fastest growing industries that are taking most women into their senior ranks, e.g. the information industry (including public relations, computer services and the press), financial services, tourism and design. The parts of the economy where women are rarest—upper and middle management in medium-sized and larger companies, especially in manufacturing—are generally those now entering into relative decline.

Ethnic minorities at work

The Race Relations Act 1976 makes it unlawful to discriminate against a person, directly or indirectly, in the field of employment.

Direct discrimination consists of treating a person, on racial grounds, less favourably than others are or would be treated in the same or similar circumstances.

Segregating a person from others on racial grounds constitutes less favourable treatment.

Indirect discrimination consists of applying a requirement or condition which, although applied equally to persons of all racial groups, is such that a considerably smaller proportion of a particular racial group can comply with it and it cannot be shown to be justifiable on other than racial grounds. Possible examples are:

● A rule about clothing or uniforms which disproportionately disadvantages a racial group and cannot be justified.
● An employer who requires higher language standards than are needed for safe and effective performance of the job.

The Commission for Racial Equality has produced a code of practice for the elimination of racial discrimination and the promotion of equality of opportunity in employment. This code aims to give practical guidance which will help employers, trade unions, employment agencies and employees to understand not only the provisions of the Race Relations Act and their implications, but also how best they can implement policies to eliminate racial discrimination and to enhance equality of opportunity. This code covers a variety of areas including recruitment, training and appraisal.

Ethnic minority groups tend to be concentrated in a range of relatively low-paid occupations compared to the national average picture. In 1987, 27 per cent of men from ethnic minorities were in hotels, catering and repairs compared with 16 per cent for whites. The proportions of Pakistani/Bangladeshi men were especially high in this sector, while 20 per cent of Indian men were employed in retail distribution.

Ethnic minorities were also fairly strongly represented in transport and communications, health services, and some manufacturing industries, while there were relatively few ethnic men in construction or agriculture.

The female workforce as a whole was concentrated into relatively few industries. Ethnic minority women were more likely than others to be in education or banking services. Over half of employed West Indian women were in 'other services', one-quarter of the total being in health services. Women of Asian or 'other' origins were more concentrated in the distribution, hotels and catering sectors.

Job sharing

Job sharing has become an increasingly important part of modern business life. It is likely to become increasingly more important as employers face recruitment difficulties in the 1990s.

A survey of 37 organizations offering job-sharing schemes carried out by Industrial Relations Services (an independent research organization) in 1989 showed that the majority found the advantages of job sharing outweighed the problems.

The main advantages cited by employers were as follows:

1. Being able to retain skilled employees.
2. Easing recruitment problems.
3. Opening up career paths for women with children.
4. Increased flexibility of cover for peak periods, holidays and sickness.
5. High motivation among sharers.

The survey said that the high motivation is perhaps due to sharers wishing to prove that the arrangements work. The sharers were able to combine a wider level of experience and ability in a job, bounce ideas off each other and develop different aspects of the work.

Working fewer hours, job sharers tended to bring more enthusiasm to the job, according to personnel managers. They start their part of the week or day fresher, when a full timer might be winding down.

Disadvantages mentioned by employers included the possibility of extra recruitment and administration expenses, worries about the lack of continuity, and concern that they might be left with half a job to fill.

Sharers used log books, special desk filing systems, telephoning and overlap periods to keep in touch. Concern about being left with a half a job does not appear to have been borne out in practice, the survey said.

Short answer questions

1. What are the most important factors influencing how an individual feels about his or her work?
2. Why does 'job satisfaction' vary from one individual to another?
3. Describe Maslow's hierarchy of needs.
4. In what ways can large organizations be 'alienating'?
5. Draw a distinction between 'dissatisfiers' and 'satisfiers' in a working environment with which you are familiar. (Perhaps a workplace where you have had a part-time job.)
6. Outline Vroom's expectancy theory.
7. What are the assumptions on which most theories of motivation are based?
8. List the seven Ss of business success. Why do shared values need to lie at the heart of a successful business?
9. Explain how a process of (a) job enrichment, (b) job enlargement could be used to improve a job with which you are familiar. What would be the main costs to the company implementing the scheme? What would be the main benefits (a) to the company, (b) to the employee? Would it be worth while?
10. What is a quality circle? How could it improve employee motivation?

11. What is the difference between a wage and a salary?
12. What are fees? (As a form of reward.)
13. What would be the main advantages and disadvantages of piece-rate payment in a factory making bridal wear?
14. What additional rewards might a factory operative earn on top of basic pay?
15. Why might the government want to encourage profit-related pay schemes?
16. Is performance-related pay a fair method of payment?
17. What was the main purpose of the Equal Pay Act? Has it been effective?
18. What are the main types of work carried out by women? What are the main features of these types of work?
19. What were the main provisions of the Race Relations Act 1976 in the field of employment?
20. What is meant by (a) direct discrimination, (b) indirect discrimination?

Essays

1. What are the essential human needs that must be met if work is to be carried out willingly?
2. What is the relationsip between technology and job satisfaction?
3. What do you understand by 'pleasant working conditions'? How can management create such conditions?
4. 'Scientific management' is the best way to get results from the human resource. Discuss this statement.
5. What methods other than pay are available to motivate employees?
6. Why is it important to define your objectives when drawing up a payment structure?
7. Outline the main responsibilities of a payroll manager. How does the payroll department need to relate to other functions?
8. What are the main problems encountered by women at work? How can these difficulties be reduced or removed?
9. The prospects for women at work are better than those for men in the 1990s. Discuss.
10. How important is the human resource to effective production?

Data response questions

1   The Government White Paper, Employment for the 1990s, December 1988, made the following points about pay.

Many approaches to pay bargaining 'beloved of trade unions and employers alike' will have to change if Britain is to secure the labour-market flexibility essential to future employment growth.

It said that such concepts as the going rate for a job, comparability of earnings between groups, and cost of living increases were all outmoded because they take no account of performance, the ability of employers to pay, or staff recruitment and retention.

The White Paper pointed to encouraging signs of changes in employment practice throughout the economy, with multi-employer bargaining breaking up in several sectors.

The White Paper said that the decisive change will come about when employers generally—not just a minority—have consciously worked out their strategies for pay that take full account of the realities of the product and labour markets in which they operate.

The White Paper said that earnings increases were much higher than in competitor countries. Further, although productivity improvements had restricted the rise in labour costs, this should not lead to complacency.

The White Paper indicated that pay arrangements in the 1990s should reflect a greater responsiveness to a variety of factors specific to individual companies. These include: local labour market conditions, changes in product markets and technology, differences in performance, merit and skills; continuing profitability of an enterprise; and international competitiveness.

(a)   Why might employers and trade unions take account of: the going rate for the job; comparability of earnings between groups; and cost of living increases in pay bargaining? Are these concepts important?

(b)   On what basis is the White Paper arguing for changing the criteria on which bargaining takes place? Would this change be justified?

(c)   What new criteria does the White Paper recommend for pay bargaining? Try to justify each of these criteria. What problems will be encountered in changing the criteria?

(d)   What criteria do you think would be most appropriate for making pay change decisions? Justify your criteria.

2   Study the newspaper article in Fig. 13.4 overleaf and answer the questions that follow it.

3   The 100 best companies to work for:

After two years' meticulous research, financial writer Bob Reynolds put together a guide to the modern British workplace in his book *The 100 Best Companies to work for in the UK*. Bob Reynolds listed his best five companies as Hallmark Cards, Nissan, United Biscuits, Glaxo and Mars.

The following extracts are made up of short interviews with an employee at Hallmark Cards and an employee at Nissan.

Employee: Moira MacKechnie, aged 50.
Job: Compensation and Benefits Manager, Europe.
History: Joined the company 12 years ago as a secretary and was quickly promoted into management.

Poor promotion prospects for women in Post Office

By Barrie Clement
Labour Editor

THE POST Office has come under fire for discriminating against blacks and women, and its management concedes that there are "disturbing" results from an ethnic monitoring exercise in Royal Mail Letters.

The Equal Opportunities Commission has also pointed to serious discrimination against female employees. There were, for instance, no promotion outlets beyond secretarial and typing grades for clerical staff, mostly women, belonging to the National Communications Union.

The pressure on the Post Office results partly from the commission's new policy of concentrating its resources on alleviating long-term labour shortages.

An internal report effectively concedes that many of the Post Office's practices are potentially unlawful and that there is considerable room to improve matters

for "under-represented groups, particularly ethnic minorities women and disabled people".

The report, circulated to managers and unions, admits that the Post Office experiences damaging wastage rates among women with "high potential".

Jenny Fosdal, national officer for the NCU, said that the Post Office was a predominantly white, male-dominated organisation. There was a limited number of people from minority ethnic groups, even in basic grades, and "very limited" numbers of women and blacks in management.

Ethnic monitoring procedures, conducted in 1988-87, found that some regions employed a particularly small number of blacks. The worst was Liverpool with only

0.67 per cent. The Post Office also failed to meet its 3 per cent target in respect of disabled employees, Ms Fosdal told the union's journal.

She welcomed the equal opportunities "action list" since drawn up by the Post Office, but added that initiatives at local level were also needed.

The internal report warned that action was needed urgently because of the tightening labour market, in particular the projected 23 per cent reduction in 16-to 19-year-olds by 1995.

This was coupled with a forecast growth in letter traffic. "This means that Royal Mail Letters needs to pay urgent attention to tapping all possible resources."

The Post Office confirmed that it was studying a letter from the Equal Opportunities Commission commenting on a "small" number of promotional procedures.

Figure 13.4 Promotion prospects for women at the Post Office. (*Source: The Independent*, December, 1988.)

(a)   What is an ethnic monitoring procedure?

(b)   What did the Post Office's ethnic monitoring exercise reveal? How would you account for these results?

(c)   Why do you think that the Post Office described these results as 'disturbing'?

(d)   How has the Post Office reacted to the findings of the exercise?

(e)   What policy recommendations would you put to the Post Office?

I joined Hallmark in my late thirties when my three children were all capable of looking after themselves. I never wanted a career but Hallmark offered me the chance to get involved. I became secretary to the European Managing Director and after six months I was asked to set up a personnel department at Henley.

I am now responsible for reviewing reward packages. As a manager I get free private health insurance for myself and my family, and I drive a company Ford Sapphire Ghia. There is a non-contributory pension scheme for all, and there is no separate directors' dining room. Everyone gets the same holiday entitlement—from MD to junior salesman.

Also, anyone who has been here a year gets an extra day off on their birthday. Until recently, they all received a large card signed by everybody but now the company is so big that's proved unmanageable.

I was the first secretary to move into management. Although Hallmark is a great place for women to work—an increasing number are in senior management positions—there is no bias towards us. It is more a case of everyone being treated equally. All 'Hallmarkers' are on first-name terms and there is an open-door management policy. When we moved into this building three-and-a-half years ago many of us were involved in its design and planning. All of us who helped were given a plaque recording our contribution.

Every year we have a staff dinner and dance which is free to staff while their guests pay a nominal sum. And if you want to study, the company will pay half the cost and if the course leads to a qualification then they pay all costs.

But, perhaps most importantly, if you have a problem or a crisis at home then the company is absolutely wonderful. Just after I joined I had a phone call to say my youngest son had been knocked over by a bus. They sent me straight home and told me not to come back until I was ready. If you are loyal to the company you can expect every consideration and support back.

Employee: Grahame Fyfe, 28.
Job: Team leader, manufacturing staff.
History: Joined Nissan almost three years ago and was trained in Japan.
Salary: £10 532–12 169 (on shifts)

I've been in the motor trade ever since I left school at 16 but never in manufacturing. I joined Nissan in March 1986, when 32 of us started on the same day. I was one of the first to be trained in Japan.

I've already progressed to being a team leader, responsible for 10 men, and the next step is supervisor. If I felt I was going to be stuck at one level for the rest of my life, I would look elsewhere. But I know there's a chance to get on here.

The benefits are incredible compared to garage work. It's more secure, there's a private health scheme, there's a pension, it's clean and it's much better paid! It's a totally different environment from one where you're lying out in the open on your back most of the day.

The lads here are very happy, and few people leave. We're especially pleased with our latest pay increase. Negotiations happen every two years through the Company Council, a body elected by the employees.

It definitely feels like working in a team, because everybody realises that we all rely on each other. If you've got a few people who want to go absent it destroys the team and people can't have their holidays and you can't rotate people.

The management are very approachable. There's never a problem and they work with you. On the shop floor you're as likely to see a manager standing behind you as you are one of your mates. They're really interested in what's going on.

This is the best place I've ever worked in. If I'm standing in the pub people will come up and ask if I can get them application forms. When people read in the papers about the benefits at Nissan they can't believe it.

(*Source:* Reynolds, R., *One Hundred Best Companies to Work for in the UK*. Collins, 1989.)

(a) What features of employment at Hallmark and Nissan, which are mentioned in the extracts, are likely to create motivation in employees?

(b) Why do you think that these companies are able to offer such favourable conditions?

(c) In what ways do good human relations at work help firms to be more competitive?

(d) Which practices highlighted in the extracts could be adopted by other British companies?

(e) Is it possible for all companies to implement the sorts of practices highlighted by the Hallmark and Nissan cases?

Suggested reading

Brown, J., *The Social Psychology of Industry*. Pelican, 1980.
Goodman, J., *Employment Relations in Industrial Society*. Philip Allan, 1984.
Reynolds, R., *One Hundred Best Companies to Work for in the UK*. Collins, 1989.

14

Trade unions

What is a trade union?

Trade unions are made up of groups of employees who have joined together in an organization to further their common interests. These employees may have in common a skill, a trade, an industry, an employer or an occupation. Trade unions are formed, financed and run by their members and a number of unions have existed for over a century.

Trade unions in a changing environment

Like other organizations in the business world trade unions have had to accommodate to a rapidly changing industrial environment. In the last decade of the twentieth century unions are having to adapt to survive.

Some of the important changes in the trade unions' environment include:

1. The development of new jobs and skills necessitating greater flexibility of working practices and attitudes.
2. The growing importance of women in the working population.
3. The growth of part-time jobs.
4. The growth of the service sector of the economy at the expense of manufacturing.
5. The hiving off of non-core service functions by large businesses to smaller organizations.
6. The growing affluence of many employees.

These changes have demanded widescale changes in union practice. In the late 1970s there were 12 million trade union members. By the late 1980s the number had dropped to 9 million. With prodding from the Trades Union Council unions have begun to develop new strategies for attracting members and updating their image.

Responding to a changing environment

Today the trade union movement is facing the challenge of a rapidly changing world of work. Many of the old jobs are disappearing to be replaced by ones requiring new

433

skills and working practices. Increasingly employers are seeking 'single union deals' with only one union operating in an industrial unit. The dominance of the blue-collar workers (i.e. manual operatives) has been whittled away by the decline of manufacturing and the rise of white-collar services (i.e. people who usually work with paper and pen). With 52 per cent of the population now women, the number of male unionists is falling consistently. A growth in skilled jobs has led to more people being considered in the ABC1 social group. Increased incomes have enabled more people to buy their own homes and shares. All these factors have helped to change people's attitudes to trade unions, and have led to changes in the relative size and importance of various trade union groups.

An indication of these dramatic changes was illustrated in a recent report from the Henley Centre for Forecasting which quoted the following example. The Centre predicted that by the end of the 1990s there will be over 700 000 electronics engineers in Britain. More than half will be women. Salaries for this group of workers will be on average 30 per cent higher than those for similar workers in the late 1980s, for working a maximum 35 hours a week. They will have the money to enjoy seven weeks' holiday a year, at least one of which will be spent abroad. When they are at home, each family will have the use of two cars. Unemployment will not be much of a worry and they are unlikely to want to become members of a traditional trade union. They will be attracted not by ideas of solidarity and collective action but pensions, investment advice and fitness clubs.

Throughout the 1960s and 1970s the numbers of employees who were members of trade unions had continued to grow. However, during the 1980s when the pace of new technology in industry greatly increased this trend was reversed.

Unions have not been seen as a natural part of some of the key growth industries and services. In response, a number of trade unions have become increasingly 'image' conscious and have adopted modern marketing techniques such as advertising and opinion research to influence public opinion. For example, the General, Municipal, Boilermakers and Allied Trades Union spent £35 000 on hiring the Jenkins design group, which had worked for W. H. Smith and Next, to help improve its image. A number of changes were made including shortening the initials of the union to the 'GMB' and replacing its motto from 'Unity is Strength' to the softer 'Working Together'. Other unions including the Transport and General Workers Union followed the GMB's lead. The T & G launched a 'Link-Up' recruitment exercise to recruit part-timers, women and ethnic groups. The campaign started with a large rally at Wembley costing half a million pounds. Recruitment adverts were placed on radio and coordinated literature and videos were produced to show the benefits of membership.

Unions are also realizing that they have to provide better services. The Electricians' Union led the way with a range of services and benefits, including free legal advice and attractive insurance and pension schemes.

Another way in which trade unions have responded to a changing environment is by merger. Most of the major trade unions have been involved in merger discussions during the late 1980s (e.g. the Amalgamated Engineering Union with the Electrical, Electronic, Telecommunications and Plumbing Union, and the National Union of Public Employees with the National Association of Local Government Officers). At the root of the merger talks was the loss of members and sharply lower income, coupled with what were regarded as changes in the law regarding trade unions in an anti-union way, all of which magnified the appeal of the economies of scale to be gained from merger. The result of mergers was to create at least five mega-unions with memberships of over three-quarters of a million. Large unions have more resources, enabling them to offer more benefits and services.

Trade unions have also adapted to a rapidly changing economic environment by allowing and encouraging more flexible working practices. A report published by ACAS in 1987 revealed that Britain now has a more flexible workforce and decades of demarcation between skilled and unskilled workers are being swept away. The survey painted a picture of rapid change in the way the country is working, particularly manufacturing companies where there is a growing tendency for production workers to do routine maintenance, normally the preserve of skilled craft workers.

Growing use of new technologies also means that the demarcation lines between manual, technical and clerical workers are fast disappearing. More people work flexitime, part time and companies are increasingly turning to contract or temporary staff rather than hiring full-time employees. The ACAS report confirmed the growing move away from big payrolls to companies employing fewer people directly and relying on contractors or part-time employees to carry out 'peripheral' work.

A further important development in trade union practice has been in the willingness to strike 'single union deals' with companies. Britain has tended to have a more complicated union structure than some of its major competitors at a plant level. It is not unknown for a UK car plant to have ten or more separate unions individually negotiating with management. Deals regarding pay and conditions will be struck at different times of the year and management will have to negotiate with separate groups of employee representatives. This process can waste a lot of time and effort and lead to continual instability. Increasingly, unions are coming to accept the principle of having a single union operating within a plant.

Trade unions have also been active in creating better opportunities for women at work. Amid warnings of an increasing shortfall in teenage labour, market forces look set to bolster women's position at work as employers compete to recruit and retain their labour.

Industrial relations

Industrial relations are concerned with communication between the representatives of employers and the representatives of employees. Successful industrial relations involve striking a balance of interests. From the employer's point of view, industrial relations is about having the right to manage—the ability to plan for the future so that a company can continue to be a success, to make profits for its shareholders and to keep its employees motivated.

From the employee's point of view, industrial relations is about securing the best possible living standards for trade union members.

Day-to-day industrial relations

On a daily basis the main industrial relations bargaining usually takes place between the personnel department and a shop stewards' committee. Normally they would meet regularly once a week and thrash out issues such as the following:

1. Pay
2. Bonuses
3. The working environment
4. Disputes
5. Work schedules
6. Grievances
7. Health and safety at work
8. Hours
9. Production targets

Major industrial-relations issues

As well as local bargaining which is concerned with small-scale industrial relations, larger issues may be thrashed out on an industry-wide scale. Wages for state employees, for example, are normally agreed upon at an annual pay award. The parties involved will normally be the central executive of a union and employers' leaders.

Union structure

This varies in different industries but a typical form is shown in Fig. 14.1.

Groups of workers are members of a branch. They choose branch officials to represent them. The branches also choose representatives to represent them at a regional committee. Regional groups then choose representatives to go to an annual conference. The annual conference makes decisions relating to the industry and chooses a full-time body of officials known as the national executive. The top official in the union is the president.

A good example of union industrial structure is in the National Union of Mineworkers. The local branch is based on the colliery, the unit of operation in mining, and the branch personnel deal with the day-to-day problems, disputes, grievances and many minor issues that can arise. Shop stewards as such are not found in the mining industry and the branch is based on the pit and includes in its membership all

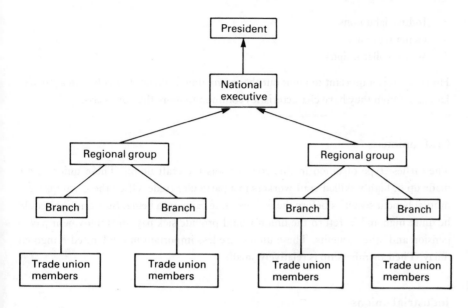

Figure 14.1 A typical union structure.

manual and craft grades; the branch officers undertake the duties allotted to shop stewards in other industries. (Factories in many trades are traditionally divided into 'shops', e.g. the cutting shop, the sewing shop, etc. Each shop chooses at least one steward to represent it in the workplace. The leading shop steward in the workplace is called the convenor, and is responsible for calling together and organizing meetings of stewards.) There is a single line of communication from the branch up through the area coalfield office to the national centre, and similarly from centre to branch.

Unofficial union structure

While much union activity takes place on a day-to-day basis through the official union structure as described above, we should not ignore unofficial union activity.

Unofficial action takes place when members carry out actions not approved by the union. Examples of this might be when local stewards call out workers in a lightning strike. In fact, in the United Kingdom, most industrial action is unofficial but only short lived. This was particularly true in the late 1970s in industries like car manufacture, in which shop stewards had a lot of local influence. Union funds cannot be used for unofficial action, because it is not officially approved. Unofficial action will generally take place if local unionists feel that the national union is out of touch with their feelings or if they want to take prompt action.

Types of trade union

Trade unions are typically organized into four main categories:

1.   Craft unions

2.   Industrial unions
3.   General unions
4.   White-collar unions

However, it is important to point out that many unions do not fit easily into a particular class. Often they have characteristics common to more than one class.

Craft unions

The earliest type of union in this country was the craft union. These unions were made up of highly skilled craft workers in a particular trade. Often these groups were mutual benefit societies before the welfare state came into being. Subscriptions could be quite high and in return the union would provide sick pay, unemployment pay, a pension and other benefits. These unions are less important in the United Kingdom today. Their membership is relatively small.

Industrial unions

Industrial unionism is common in many European countries, notably West Germany. The economy is divided up into industrial sectors, and workers in each sector belong to the industrial union for that sector. The National Union of Mineworkers at one time was often quoted as an example of an industrial union. However, in 1985, a rival union, the Union of Democratic Mineworkers, was formed and, on top of this, there are smaller unions such as the pit deputies' union, NACODS. In many areas of industry, there is a tendency for new 'super unions' to take in groups of workers from several industries.

   The advantage of an industrial union is that it caters for all workers in an industry whatever their job. Negotiation with employers is greatly simplified and all workers are united in their efforts.

General unions

These are some of the largest unions in the United Kingdom. They recruit workers from several industries. They include semi-skilled and unskilled workers. A particular advantage of this form of union is that it gives strength to workers who have little power on their own. It gives them the opportunity to belong to a well-funded and organized body.

   An example of the formation of a general union occurred in 1988 with the creation of what was then Britain's third largest union: the white-collar and supervisors' union ASTMS and the manufacturing union TASS joined together to form the Manufacturing Science and Finance Union (MSF). The leaders of the two merging unions put forward their case in the following way: 'We can now tackle even more effectively the problems our members face ... our objective is to work for a well rewarded, well trained, and highly skilled membership throughout the whole range of industries and services covered by MSF.'

White-collar unions

White-collar workers are those employees who carry out non-manual work. The term 'white collar' is used to distinguish them from 'blue-collar' employees who carry out manual operations and would traditionally be associated with blue overalls. Examples of white-collar employees would be office workers, and bank clerks. White-collar unions have seen the biggest increase in membership in the late twentieth century. As more people have become involved in office and administrative work, and as these groups have become more prepared to join unions, their ranks have swelled. Examples of white-collar unions include the teachers' unions such as the National Union of Teachers and the civil servants union the Civil and Public Servants Association.

Forms of union action

Unionists have a number of types of action available to them to put pressure on employers. A distinction needs to be made between individual and unorganized actions on the part of workers against management, and organized or group sanctions against employers. In unorganized conflict employees will respond in individual ways using strategies which seem right at the time, with little planning. Organized conflict, in contrast, is far more likely to form part of a conscious strategy to change the situation which is seen as the cause of discontent.

Unorganized industrial action can take the form of high labour turnover, bad timekeeping, and high levels of absenteeism. It may also occur in the form of slackness by individuals, poor working, deliberate time wasting and similar practices. Other evidence of discontent will be revealed in complaints, friction, ignoring the rules and apathy.

There are a number of forms of more organized industrial action:

1. *Picketing*   Primary picketing is legal. This involves members of a union who are on strike standing outside a firm's entrance and trying to persuade other workers not to cross the picket line.

    Secondary picketing is not legal, and involves workers from one firm trying to dissuade workers at a firm not involved with the strike from going to work. Secondary picketing takes place when unionists try to spread the impact of their action.

2. *Withdrawal of goodwill*   This involves workers becoming obstructive about things which need cooperation.

3. *Go slow*   Workers take their time over the work they are doing.

4. *Work to rule*   Workers stick strictly to the book of rules relating to their particular job in order to reduce efficiency. For instance, railway workers may check that every carriage door is firmly closed at each station.
5. *Ban on overtime*   Workers refuse to work more than the hours laid out in their contract of employment.
6. *Official strike*   Workers cease work with the authority of the union.
7. *Unofficial strike*   A group of workers cease work without the official approval of the union.
8. *Sit-in*   Occasionally the workers occupy a factory. Similarly, if a factory has been threatened with closure, the workers may remain at work operating a work-in whereby they refuse to leave the premises.
9. *Blacking*   This occurs when members of a firm refuse to handle particular materials or work with particular machinery.

Forms of employer action

Employers and management can use a number of sanctions against employees. These may take the form of either uncoordinated and individual actions or organized and collective actions. Uncoordinated, individual actions may include close supervision of working activity, tight works discipline, discriminatory employment practice against certain employees, lay-offs, demotions, and the unofficial speeding up of work processes of job tasks. Organized and collective sanctions include the withdrawal of overtime, mass suspensions, changing of work standards without negotiation, lock-outs, the closing down of enterprises, and the removal of workplace equipment.

The Trades Union Congress (TUC)

This is the annual meeting of the trade union movement. All the major trade unions are members of the TUC and send a number of delegates to the conference depending on the size of the membership. The annual congress takes place in September every year at seaside resorts like Scarborough and Blackpool where there is a lot of hotel space after the holiday season is finished and where large conference halls are available. The conference lasts for a week and during this time a number of motions and issues are debated.

The TUC appoints full-time officials including a president and vice-president, and it has its own substantial headquarters offices. The TUC is an important organization because it reflects the general feelings of the trade union movement. It is particularly active in the field of negotiation in industrial disputes. It offers advice and assistance to unions with problems and tries to iron out difficulties that arise between unions. It acts as a pressure group trying to influence government and employers on a wide range of issues.

The annual congress covers a wide range of issues. It is a false conception to assume that the TUC is simply concerned with wages. The congress will discuss matters as different as education, the health service, privatization, AIDS and the environment.

The TUC despite its importance is often regarded to have very little power. Individual unions are not bound by its decisions and the only threat it can use is to expel a union from membership.

Professional associations

Many workers belong to a professional association. These are organizations that do many of the same things as trade unions but are not registered as trade unions. They tend to cover better-paid white-collar workers. An example is the British Medical Association which is the body that negotiates on behalf of doctors. Professional associations also try to establish standards for members and to insist on a high level of competence for membership.

Employers' organizations

Like trade unions, employers' organizations fulfil a wide range of functions but the main one is collective bargaining. Faced by large and powerful trade unions small employers would be at a disadvantage if they had to stand alone. An employers' association may bargain on behalf of all firms in an industry. Other functions of employers' organizations include the following:

1. Pooling ideas and funds for industrial research.
2. Collectively setting up training centres.
3. Discussing common interests such as the threat of foreign competition.
4. Providing a collective voice to raise industry-wide problems with government and other bodies.

The Confederation of British Industry (CBI)

Britain's mouthpiece for the business community is the CBI. It exists primarily to voice the views of its members to ensure that governments of whatever political complexion—and society as a whole—understand both the needs of British business and the contribution it makes to the well-being of the nation.

The CBI is acknowledged to be Britain's business voice and, as such, is widely consulted by government, the civil service and the media. But it is not solely concerned with major national issues—an important part of its task is to represent business interests at local level, too. It is also directly involved in providing essential information and research services for its members.

CBI members come from every sector of UK business and include:

1. More than 250 000 public and private companies—half of them smaller firms with fewer than 200 employees—and most of the nationalized industries.

2.   More than 200 trade associations, employer organizations and commercial associations.

The organization

The main elements of the organization are:
1.   The CBI's ruling Council chaired by the CBI President, which sets policy.
2.   Some 30 Standing Committees, 13 Regional Councils and a smaller Firms Council contributing to policy making.
3.   The CBI permanent staff, headed by the Director General, based at Centre Point, in the UK regions, and at the CBI's own Brussels Office.
4.   National Conference and the President's Committee advising on major issues and overall CBI strategy.

Who belongs to the CBI?

Membership of the CBI is corporate—organizations and companies are members, not the individuals nominated to represent them. Well over 10 million people are employed by companies associated with the CBI, either directly or indirectly through trade organizations or chambers of commerce.

CBI membership is extensive and almost exactly matches the profile of business in the United Kingdom—from manufacturing to retailing, agriculture to construction, computers to finance, transport to consultancy.

The President

The President is the CBI's chief office bearer. Elected by the CBI membership, he or she normally serves for two years. The President chairs the monthly CBI Council meeting and the annual National Conference. The President will also lead delegations to see government Ministers.

The Director General

The Director General is the CBI's chief executive. He or she will be appointed by the President of the day with the approval of CBI Council and regularly puts across the business view on radio and TV and in the press. The Director General heads the permanent staff who carry out the bulk of the day-to-day running of the CBI, preparing policy and negotiating with Ministers and their civil servants.

Whom does the CBI seek to influence?

The short answer is anyone who, in turn, can influence how business performs—at Westminster, in Whitehall and the UK regions, around Europe and beyond, within the trade union movement, and the general public.

Westminster and Whitehall

The well-publicized meetings the CBI has with Ministers and as a member of 'Neddy'—the National Economic Development Council—indicate the central part the CBI plays in national affairs, but they are only a small part of its work.

The CBI seeks to influence government policy making at an early stage in its development. The CBI seeks to be continually aware of the thinking of Ministers, the research arms of political parties, back-bench MPs and civil servants to ensure its views are put forward at the best possible opportunity. It is a lobbying process that continues as government policy is published and bills pass through Parliament.

In the regions

The CBI has 13 regional offices which seek to influence local decision-making procedures.

Europe and '1992'

The CBI has played a prominent part in influencing the process of completing the single European market. CBI experts have followed Community developments for many years. The CBI is consulted by the European Commission as the voice of British industry. The CBI is permanently represented in Brussels, where it opened an office even before Britain joined the Community.

Trade unions

Although the CBI and TUC may put forward opposing views on a number of issues, a constructive working relationship is maintained both directly and through joint membership of such national bodies as Neddy, ACAS and the Health and Safety Commission.

The public

As part of the process of explaining business needs and concerns, CBI policies and views need to be put to the public at large as well as to official bodies.

Who decides CBI policy?

CBI policy is decided by CBI members—firms large and small throughout the country.

CBI policy work has two aspects. In the long term, the aim is to make a constructive contribution to attitudes and forward thinking on issues affecting business. In the short term, the CBI has to be equipped to react quickly and positively to any proposals by government, or others, which have a bearing on industry and commerce.

More than 2500 people are involved in the CBI policy-making process.

Governing body

The CBI's governing body is its Council, chaired by the President. Proposals must be approved by the Council before they can become official CBI policy. The Council membership is made up of leading national officials as well as representatives of employer, trade and commercial organizations, the public sector, the 13 CBI Regional Councils and people drawn from member companies of all sizes and activity.

The CBI's Standing Committees cover every aspect of business life and are responsible for most of the detailed work on policy making.

The government and industrial relations

Government has passed laws on a wide range of issues relating to industrial relations, which are dealt with in greater detail in other parts of the book. The main areas include the following:

- Health and safety at work
- Discrimination
- Training
- Employment of the disabled
- Employment of young workers
- Dismissal and redundancy
- Pay
- Industrial action
- Restriction in the workplace

The Advisory, Conciliation and Arbitration Service (ACAS)

This body was set up by the government in 1974, in order to improve industrial relations. ACAS is managed by a council of nine members—three chosen by the TUC, three chosen by the CBI and three who are independent.

In an industrial dispute in which there is deadlock, the parties might ask ACAS to help. Sometimes the parties might allow ACAS to look at the issue and come up with a solution that is 'binding'. At other times, ACAS might simply be asked to make recommendations.

Conciliation is the process of trying to get each side calmly to appreciate the other's point of view.

Arbitration is the process through which parties in a dispute allow a third party to come to a decision.

The media and public tend to view ACAS as ambulance chasers and firemen in situations of conflict. Although this sort of emergency repair work is a critical part of the work of ACAS it is only a small part of the overall workload. ACAS deals with around 25 new collective disputes a week (1988 figures). Nine out of ten disputes involving ACAS are settled before industrial action is taken.

The greater part of the work of ACAS involves individual grievances. In 1986 ACAS had to deal with over 51 000 cases of individual arbitration. Individual disputes involve a variety of cases including unfair dismissal and sex discrimination applications.

ACAS has a legal obligation to try and resolve individual grievances before they reach industrial tribunals. Most individual cases will be resolved either through conciliation or because the complaint is dropped.

The rest of ACAS's resources are dedicated to advisory work involving both unions and employers. In 1986 ACAS took part in 924 surveys, projects, joint working parties and training activities. It also made 9000 advisory visits.

ACAS works with employers and trade unions to help in the reform of pay systems, to put in new job evaluation procedures and to deal with questions of high absenteeism and labour turnover.

Short answer questions

1. What is a trade union?
2. What changes have taken place in the number of trade union members in the last ten years?
3. Illustrate the official union structure of a union. You should set out the structure of a typical union, or of a union for which you are able to gather the necessary information.
4. What is the difference between official and unofficial union action? Under what circumstances are union members likely to take unofficial action?
5. What are the main strengths and weaknesses of industrial unions?
6. What advantages are likely to result from the growth of a general union?
7. Why have white-collar unions accounted for the fastest growth in numbers of members?
8. What is the purpose of picketing? Under what circumstances is it illegal?
9. Explain the following types of union action:
   (a) work to rule;
   (b) go slow;
   (c) overtime ban.
10. What is the purpose of the Trades Union Congress?
11. In what ways is the CBI the mouthpiece of the business community?
12. Describe the role of (a) the President, (b) the Director General of the CBI.
13. What role has the CBI played in influencing the process of the completion of the single Community market?
14. What is meant by (a) arbitration, (b) conciliation?
15. Why is the government keen to promote harmonious industrial relations?
16. What do you understand by the term 'free collective bargaining'?

17. What are the advantages to an employer of having a single union operating in a workplace?

18. What is the role of a shop steward in an industrial workplace?

19. What is a professional association?

20. What are the five major trade unions in the United Kingdom? Who do they represent?

Essays

1. Do the interests of managers and trade unionists always conflict?

2. Trade unions are no longer required in modern industrial society. Discuss this statement.

3. The greatest challenge to trade unions today is to recruit members. Discuss.

4. What measures can trade unions employ to get employers to create a pleasant working environment?

5. How important are: (a) the TUC, (b) the CBI to Britain's industrial performance in the 1990s?

Data response questions

1 Study the journal article in Fig. 14.2 and answer the questions that follow it.

British Rail insists on individual deals

Figure 14.2 Pay scheme alternatives at British Rail. (*Source: Personnel Today*, 1988.)

British Rail (BR) middle managers will not receive a pay increase this year unless they agree to individually-based performance related pay schemes.

The final offer made to the 9,000 managers is a 6.09 per cent salary increase and a three per cent lump sum. They also have to agree to individual contracts. If they do not, they will remain in the current system until the next pay review in January 1989.

Managers have been given until 1 August to decide. BR has stopped negotiations with the two management unions, the Transport Salaried Staffs' Association (TSSA) and the British Transport Officers' Guild (BTOG). BR regards its offer as final.

Both the BTOG and the TSSA have told members to postpone action until further notification but current ballots are to establish members' views and not whether to take industrial action.

"British Rail is not only seeking to circumvent the current machinery of negotiations but to avoid the democratic process through which staff can collectively bargain," said Alan Jones, negotiations officer for the BTOG.

But a British Rail spokesman said that "present arrangements are just not appropriate to business challenges".

(a) What do you understand by 'individually-based performance related pay schemes'?

(b) (i) What would be the advantages to managers of accepting such a scheme?

    (ii) What would be the disadvantages?

(c) (i) What would be the advantages to British Rail of implementing such a scheme?

    (ii) What would be the disadvantages?

(d) What are the two trade unions mentioned in the article? Into what categories would you place these unions?

(e) What do you think the views of the unions regarding British Rail's actions were likely to have been?

(f) Why do you think that the unions concerned balloted their members?

2   Study the journal article in Fig. 14.3 and answer the questions that follow it.

EFFECTS OF DUNDEE ROW

Foreigners may shun UK

The row over a single-union deal at Ford has dealt a blow to Britain's chances of attracting investment from foreign companies.

"Most foreign companies wanting to set up in the UK are only prepared to unionise using single-union deals. What has happened at Dundee would be a major factor in them taking their business elsewhere, or having non-union plants," said Bill Jordan, president of the engineering union AEU, which negotiated a single-union deal with Ford Motor Company for the Scottish electronics plant.

Ford withdrew its commitment to build a £40-million plant in Dundee because of problems in introducing a single-union deal. "We did not expect when we signed a single-union deal it would prove so difficult to achieve," said Ford's electrical and electronic division general manager Frank Macher.

"We're very worried about the situation, and lay the blame at the door of the unions," said Robert Joy, employment research executive for the Institute of Directors (IOD).

"They don't seem to com-

prehend the international nature of this. The government's policy relies heavily on private investment, which we support, and this dispute could damage it," he added.

The Scottish Development Agency (SDA) is concerned that this will rebound on the Scottish electronics industry. A spokesman identified Ford as a market leader to which foreign companies may pay special attention. Its decision could affect others. It would certainly do no good for for Britain's reputation abroad, especially in the United States, he said (Jordan interview — page 18).

Figure 14.3 Single union deal failure at Dundee. (*Source: Personnel Today,* December, 1988.)

(a) What is a single union deal?

(b) Why do you think that Ford sought a single union deal for its proposed site at Dundee?

(c) Why do you think that Ford was not prepared to set up at Dundee when a single union deal could not be secured?

(d) What were the costs to Dundee of failing to get the Ford deal?

(e)   Who might be considered to have benefited from Ford not setting up at Dundee?

3   Study the journal article in Fig. 14.4 and answer the questions that follow it.

Bifu row flares at insurance centre

Members of the banking and finance union Bifu have voted for industrial action at insurance giants Eagle Star in Cheltenham following a row over union recognition and working conditions.

Earlier this year, the company derecognised Bifu in preference to Eagle Star's staff association, the ESSU. Employees in the firm's data processing section voted with a clear majority on three points of action against Eagle Star.

An overtime ban, extending to call-out, and a refusal to accept altered working conditions and standard working times are conditions of the planned industrial action. Central to the vote, is the demand for Eagle Star to recognise the Bifu which is claiming the majority of staff in the computer group.

Eagle Star's executive director Ian Dunbar is adamant that the company will not deal with Bifu. "Our position has been clear from the outset, we've chosen to recognise one union here and ESSU represents the majority of staff," said Dunbar. He conceded that the ESSU was not recognised in the computer department because of its low membership there.

"The data processing area is making the running here," said a Bifu spokesman. The recognition dispute may extend to clerical staff, although the EESU is better represented outside that department.

"Obviously we are hoping that the company will talk," said the Bifu spokesman. "We have always had a high representation at Eagle Star."

Figure 14.4 An example of a dispute in the insurance industry. (*Source: Personnel Today*, November, 1988.)

(a)   What do you understand by the term derecognition? Why do you think that Eagle Star in Cheltenham derecognized the banking and finance union?

(b)   Do you think that Eagle Star was justified in its action?

(c)   What problems are Eagle Star likely to encounter as a result of the derecognition?

(d)   What courses of action are open to Bifu? Evaluate the likely effectiveness of different courses of action.

Suggested reading

Crouch, C., *The Politics of Industrial Relations*. Fontana, 1979.
Jenkins, C. and Sherman, B., *White Collar Unionism: The Rebellious Salariat*. Routledge and
    Kegan Paul, 1979.

15

Communication

Communication is the passing on of ideas and information. In business we need good, clear communications. The contact may be between people, organizations or places and can be in a number of forms such as speech, writing, data communication, actions and gestures.

We all have to communicate. To communicate well requires not only the development of the basic skills of speaking, listening, reading and writing, but also an awareness and an understanding of the subject, the audience and the environment.

Successful communication requires not only that information should be transmitted, but that it should be fully received and understood. Listening and reading skills are therefore just as important as speaking and writing skills.

Communications problems arise when one of the following is the case:

1. The language used is not fully understood.
2. The receiver is not able or prepared to listen to the message.
3. The means of passing the message is poor.
4. There are too many steps in the communication of the message.
5. The message is poorly set out or ambiguous.

What other barriers to communication would you add to the above list?

The passage of information can be seen as a flow from the sender to the receiver (see Fig. 15.1).

The basic communication skills

The four basic communication skills are listening, speaking, reading and writing. However, perhaps in a modern technological society we could add a fifth skill—using information technology.

The table shows the order in which the four basic communication skills are learned, the degree to which they are used and the extent to which they are taught. Listening is the communication skill that is used most but taught least.

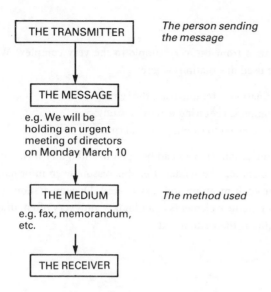

THE TRANSMITTER — *The person sending the message*

THE MESSAGE

e.g. We will be holding an urgent meeting of directors on Monday March 10

THE MEDIUM — *The method used*

e.g. fax, memorandum, etc.

THE RECEIVER

Figure 15.1 The flow of information from sender to receiver.

	Listening	Speaking	Reading	Writing
Learned	1st	2nd	3rd	4th
Used	Most (45%)	Next most (30%)	Next least (16%)	Least (9%)
Taught	Least	Next least	Next most	Most

(*Source:* Engineering Careers Information Service.)

Speaking and listening

In most businesses, the most frequently used method of communication is speech. Speech takes place between people in direct contact with each other and providing that the listener is being attentive, ambiguity in discussion can be removed by questioning. Questioning is a very important process because it can clarify meanings and points of view.

For speech to be an effective means of communication it is important that individuals are aware of:

- their own role as communicators;
- the receptiveness of the listener;
- the listener's own knowledge of the subject.

We tend to assume that listening is an easy skill. However, people tend to forget very quickly what they have heard. Listening involves: (a) the process of physically hearing a message; (b) the interpretation of the message; (c) the evaluation, when decisions are made on how to use the information; (d) the reaction to the message. It is therefore hardly surprising that many verbal messages are quickly forgotten, misunderstood or not followed up. As a result it is particularly important that after a meeting involving a lot of verbal discussion, conclusions, recommendations and plans for further action are written down.

Writing

Written communication varies from the very simple to the very complex. Written communications tend to be used in situations where:

- the receiver of the information is remote from the sender;
- information is highly complex, requiring extensive study;
- information needs to be referred to over a period of time.

The written word in some circumstances can be open to ambiguity if the receiver is not immediately able to question the sender. For this reason, even informal notes need to be accurate, clear in their meaning and easy to read. Documentation systems are widely used in industry to reduce elements of ambiguity and, very often, drawings and sketches are used to support the written text.

Reading

Some forms of written communication are more easily read than others. The target audience and the nature of the information are important factors in deciding how to present data.

Businesses present written information in a variety of forms from formal reports, memos and drawings, which usually follow a prescribed pattern, to informal notes and sketches.

Memos

The word 'memorandum' derives from the Latin *memorare* which means a 'thing to be remembered'. Today memos have a wider business use than just memory aids and have become the most frequently used form of written communication within a business. They are used to communicate information, instructions and enquiries and are the internal equivalents of letters.

As they are internal there are one or two minor differences. An organization's name does not normally appear on a memo for internal use. It is not necessary to have a salutation or complimentary ending. Memos should be kept as short as possible and deal only with one item. They will often be distributed to a number of people. Most organizations will provide memo pads of headed message forms.

The style of memoranda may often vary considerably. Instructions from senior management will probably be written in relatively impersonal language, whereas a quickly scribbled message to a close colleague may be written in conversational English. It will therefore be necessary to be more cautious about writing letters up the ladder, rather than down. It is important to take account of people's sensitivities and the position you hold.

```
MEMO
To: All Staff
From: CB & WS
Date: 25.06.90

Safety Reports

Please refer to the section on 'Safety Procedures'
on pages 81 to 84 of the Staff Handbook. Please
refer also to the copy of the letter showing how to
fill in a safety report.

Reports are to be dated June 1990.

Reports are to be signed by the member of the staff
with the appropriate initials and surname: eg
C. H. Clarke.

1st July—Reports to Section Head.
10th July—Reports to Department Head.
17th July—Reports to Safety Inspector.
```

Letters

Often the only direct communication that people have with a company is through the business letter. A good business letter will help a customer or client, yet at the same time benefit your organization and create goodwill. Letters are the most frequently used form of external business communication and provide a written record which can be used to send almost any type of information. Their greatest benefit is their reasonable cost.

Business letters are usually typed on headed A4 or A5 paper. Fully blocked layout is the most common form of display.

Letters should be presented in a logical sequence and be written in a style that lacks ambiguity. They should be concise and yet not leave out recent information. A good letter will be written in the style most appropriate for the recipient and will enable it to have the greatest impact. (See the letter on page 454.)

Reports

The prospect of having to write a report often fills people with trepidation. This is probably because reports are a less common form of communication than writing letters or memos. A report is simply a written communication from someone who has

```
                                    Bulltup PLC
                                    Auction Mart Lane
                                    HAWES
                                    North Yorkshire
                                    DL14 STR



Our Ref JS/PR

3rd May 1990

Mr R Field
12 Horse Lane
REETH
North Yorkshire
DL12 3SN

Dear Mr Field

INFORMATION REGARDING 1992

Thank you for passing on to me the two videos
'Europe Open for Business' and '1992—What's That?'

As a gesture of our appreciation I enclose two
stand tickets for the race meeting at Catterick.

If you come into possession of any more information
or resources we would certainly be interested in
borrowing them.

Yours sincerely,

M. Norman
Marketing Manager
```

collected and studied some facts to a person who has asked for the report because he or she needs it for a particular purpose. The report will probably form the basis for some sort of decision.

Reports may be used as follows:

1. To supply information for legal purposes, e.g. as a result of an incident, accident, or to be presented to shareholders.
2. To present the results of some research and to recommend some form of action.
3. To assess the possibility of changes in a company's policy.

A well-written report will be concise and will not contain anything the reader does not need to know. It should be clear and logically arranged but, at the same time, should not exclude anything that the reader needs. Reports may be written either as short informal reports or as formal reports set out according to a particular pattern.

Informal reports

These might be written on a report form or on a memo. They will contain:

1. Title
2. Introduction
3. Body of report (complete with findings)
4. Recommendations
5. Action required

Formal reports

A more usual structure of a long formal report will look like this:

1. Title page (name of organization, name and post of writer, subject)
2. Table of contents/index
3. Terms of reference (explaining the reason for the report)
4. Procedure (how the task was completed)
5. Findings
6. Conclusion (summary of findings)
7. Recommendations
8. Signature of writer and date

In preparing a report considerations have to be made over aspects such as language style, circulation list, presentation of cover and binding and confidentiality.

Notices

Notices are another common form of business communication and will need to be placed in prominent places.

Drawings/maps/charts

Drawings, maps and charts often need to be very detailed and accurate because they are going to form the basis of particular stages of productive activity. They need to be neatly produced, correctly dimensioned and provide good references to supporting data.

Minutes of meetings

Minutes of a meeting will need to be presented in a clear and unambiguous way. They will require concise sentence construction with accurate spelling, punctuation and layout. (See extract for Midtown Junior Chamber of Commerce, page 456.)

```
┌─────────────────────────────────────────────────────┐
│          Midtown Junior Chamber of Commerce          │
│                      Minutes                         │
│ of the meeting of members of the Junior Chamber      │
│ held at 7.30 p.m. on Thursday 10th July, 1990 at     │
│ the Angel and Royal.                                 │
│                                                      │
│ Present K. Thompson (Chair)                          │
│         P. Bridle                                    │
│         H. O'Neill                                   │
│         M. Khan                                      │
│         E. Obeng                                     │
│         D. Lee                                       │
│                                                      │
│ 1.  Apologies for absence                            │
│     Received from B. Cribb, I. Cottee and T. Wells.  │
│                                                      │
│ 2.  Minutes of previous meeting                      │
│     The minutes of the previous meeting held on      │
│     Thursday 12th June, 1990, were accepted as an    │
│     accurate record of the meeting.                  │
│ 3.  Sponsored walk                                   │
│     . . . etc.                                       │
└─────────────────────────────────────────────────────┘
```

Processing information

Presenting information in such a way that your message is clear and easy to read is never a simple process. The transmitter of a message will try to present material which he or she understands in a way in which recipients will also understand. However, it is unlikely that material can be transmitted from one person's understanding to the understanding of another person *intact*. The current belief is that knowledge has to be *reconstructed* as it passes from one person to another. What an individual already knows and understands controls how he or she interprets, processes and even stores new information. Since individuals' backgrounds differ and their store of knowledge and understanding varies, so will their development of new understandings differ. We can illustrate this point by a few simple examples. A motorist who is also a supporter of Aberdeen FC could pass a sign for Pitrodie (a village in Angus) and easily read it as Pittodrie (the home of his or her football team). A set of numbers would mean little to most people, but might indicate a telephone number to others or even a birthday date.

It is not surprising therefore that misunderstandings frequently take place in the communication of information. You will have experienced times in your life when you have said something and it has been taken 'the wrong way'. The clear lessons to be learnt from the problems of constructing meanings are:

1. When communicating information you should give the recipient as much possible opportunity to 'kick around' the idea and to ask questions.
2. When receiving information you should not always take it at what you presume is its face value—try to find out more about what is being communicated to you by asking questions.

Using information systems

Today, people use phrases such as 'the information society', or 'the wired society' to refer to the way in which the revolution in information technology is transforming our lives. This is nowhere more true than in the business environment.

A modern business system can be seen as consisting of three sub-systems. The management sub-system is concerned with all the people and activities involved in planning, controlling and decision making. The operations sub-system is concerned with all the activities, material flows and people directly involved with performing the primary function of the organization, e.g. manufacturing operations. The information sub-system is made up of the people, machines, ideas and activities that are concerned with gathering and processing data in order to meet the formal requirements of an organization for information. This may include for example the way in which information is collected, stored, handled, exchanged and utilized for accounting purposes, monitoring stocks, and a range of other interrelated functions.

Information systems are based on the use of data. Data can be handled in simple ways such as recording transactions by quill in a ledger. However, in modern business organizations the computer has become the most important tool for producing information from data. A number of standard operations are required to produce information from data—these operations can be applied to any form of information system.

- *Capturing data* involves recording data generated by an event or occurrence, e.g. capturing data from invoices, sales slips, meters, counters, etc.
- *Verifying data* refers to checking that data have been recorded/captured accurately, e.g. checking that an instrument is working correctly, or cross-checking someone else's recording procedures.
- *Classifying data* involves putting different types of data into appropriate sections. For example, the sales of a company could be sorted into the different departments that made the sales.
- *Sorting data* is the placing of data elements into a specified order. For example, an inventory file could be sorted into money value order, or into code number order, etc.
- *Summarizing data* can be used to aggregate data. One way this can be done is to total up various figures, e.g. sales figures, or to draw up balancing figures for a balance sheet. Alternatively, it could be used to reduce data logically to a common form, e.g. by producing a list of all employees that were working on the night shift on a particular day.

- *Calculating using data* involves computing various figures in a mathematical sense, e.g. by adding, subtracting, dividing. For example, wages of employees can be calculated by multiplying hours worked by the wage rate and then subtracting necessary deductions.
- *Storing data* will involve transferring data to the appropriate medium, e.g. floppy disk, microfilm, etc.
- *Retrieving data* involves calling it up from the place of storage.
- *Reproducing data* is the process of transferring the same data from one medium to another. At a simple level this could involve photocopying material, or calling up data from one screen to another as with Stock Exchange dealing.
- *Communicating* involves transferring data from one place to another. This can take place at any stage of the data processing cycle. The ultimate aim of information processing is to provide information for the final consumer.

Information technology as an aid to effective communication

The success of a business enterprise depends in large measure on the efficient and accurate production of goods and services that meet customer requirements. We can add to this that the survival of any medium- or large-sized company also depends on the rapid and accurate processing and distribution of information. This process is increasingly being carried out by using new technology, principally computers.

What features of modern business life make computer aided communication so important?

1. The scale of many large organizations makes it impossible for every individual to meet in face-to-face relations.
2. Many organizations are geographically spread out, but require communication links between interrelated plant and offices.
3. Modern business decision making frequently requires up-to-date information drawn from a variety of business functions, e.g. the marketing department may need sales figures from sales, costings from accounts, etc.
4. Competition between firms is more fierce; it is almost impossible for a company to find a market area that is not extremely competitive (this is particularly true with the opening of the single market in 1992).
5. The rate of change of industrial development has increased. Firms must therefore be quicker in responding to factors such as technological change, market forces and better competition.

Case Study—The development of global communication links at Ford

In the late 1980s Ford Motor Company spent 77 million dollars to create a massive database which could be accessed from any of 17 000 terminals worldwide, with a maximum response time of four seconds.

The system, called WERS (Worldwide Engineering Release System), links Ford's hundreds of sites across the world to a database which holds all the engineering information about parts for all cars that the company makes—Thunderbirds, Mustangs, Escorts, Cortinas and many more. Ford believes that this new system will give the company at least a two-year lead over its competitors.

WERS has been set up to replace six formerly separate systems which were difficult to link up.

The new system will link up 20 000 engineers and designers for Ford in Europe, the United States and South America, Australia and East Asia.

The advantage of having all the information centralized and accessible worldwide is that manufacture can be switched to available capacity; and designers need not be in the same factory, site or even country as the engineer or assemblers.

The system is built to be able to handle 500 000 queries daily. One of the key features of the design was speed. This is why the system has been built to respond to queries within four seconds.

Questions

1. Who will benefit from Ford's new Worldwide Engineering Release System? How will they benefit?
2. In what ways will the new system make Ford more competitive?
3. Why is it important to an organization like Ford to use such a high powered communications system?
4. How do you expect other major manufacturers to respond to WERS?
5. How will Ford be able to evaluate the effectiveness of WERS?

The tools of information technology and their applications

Computers have become a very important method of communicating and storing information within a firm. Modern electronic computers are able to process words, numbers, pictures and even sound – any kind of information which needs to be stored, transmitted, analysed or reproduced.

The three main types of computers are:

1. *Personal computers*   The 'desktop', 'personal' or 'home' computer which is seen advertised everywhere. Costing between £100 and several thousand pounds these computers can be used on their own or linked together with other computers to form a network which can exchange information or facilities.
2. *Minicomputers*   These are slightly smaller in both size and cost, and reflect the advantages of modern technology in that they have the latest development built into their design.
3. *Mainframe computers*   These are large units, housed in special rooms with air

conditioning, specially trained staff, etc. They are extremely expensive, and are used or owned mainly by very large companies. They can handle very large and complex tasks very quickly, and are usually connected to the users through local terminals. The system used, for example, in your local electricity-board offices or travel agent is almost certainly of this type.

Personal computers

The work of the personal computer is generally based around a number of standard application packages, which are summarized below. More powerful versions of these programs are also used on minicomputers and on mainframe computers.

Spreadsheets

A spreadsheet program is essentially a very large grid of 'cells', which contain text, numbers or formulae, and are used for numerical problems where a large number of figures are calculated (see Fig. 15.2).

	Jan	Feb	Mar	Apr	May	Jun	Jul	Aug	Sep	Oct	Nov	Dec
REVENUE	200	200	300	400	400	400	500	500	500	500	500	500
COSTS												
Heat	20	20	20	20	20	20	20	20	20	20	20	20
Fuel	20	20	20	20	20	20	20	20	20	20	20	20
Labour	50	50	60	70	70	70	80	80	80	80	80	80
Materials	50	50	60	70	70	70	80	80	80	80	80	80
TOTAL COSTS	140	140	160	180	180	180	200	200	200	200	200	200
PROFIT	60	60	140	220	220	220	300	300	300	300	300	300

TOTAL PROFITS: 2720

Figure 15.2 Layout of a spreadsheet.

The number in any one cell can be calculated from the numbers in any other cell (or combination of cells) using the spreadsheet to perform the calculations. If any one number is changed, the result on all the other cells is seen immediately, saving long calculations. The spreadsheet is usually used as a financial tool, but is also used by engineers, scientists and many others. Most spreadsheet programs have the ability to produce graphs from the data.

Databases

A database is a store of facts that can be called upon to provide up-to-date information. It may be used, for instance, in a bank or building society to store information on the state of all the accounts. Data (information) are fed into the base in a clear form. For instance, a firm could store information about the firms it supplies credit to. For example, it might have a record for the account of Yeaman's Stores. It would store the information in a number of fields, such as address, value of goods bought, payments and balance on the account. If Mrs Yeaman rings up asking for the state of her account the firm can simply order the computer to find the balance on Yeaman's account.

Under the provisions of the Data Protection Act, companies wishing to store personal information on a computer system must register with the (government-appointed) Data Protection Officer, and indicate the type of data they are storing, and the use they make of these data. Any individual has the right to request (on payment of a small fee) details of any information held about them by any firm, and to require any mistakes to be corrected.

Word processing

Word processors are used for manipulating text. Essentially, they simply display on a screen and record in memory the text that a person keys in on the keyboard.

A word processor is made up of:

1.   The keyboard for typing in material and instructions.
2.   A visual display unit which displays the material on a screen.
3.   A disk storage unit.
4.   The printer for finished copy.

The basic features available in all word processing packages are:

- New text can be inserted on screen while existing text moves to create the necessary space.
- Blocks of text can be moved from one place to another.
- Text can be spaced out to fill a whole line.
- A word or phrase can be searched for and replaced by another word or phrase, wherever it occurs.
- A header or footer can be added (a piece of text printed at the top or bottom of the page).

More sophisticated features, available on most expensive word processors used in businesses are:

- Different printing styles (such as italics, underlined text and so on). These can be shown on screen either as different colours or as they would appear when printed.
- Text can be written in more than one column, as in newspapers.
- Graphics can be built into the text.
- A number of similar letters can be produced, with information added, from a database, on each letter. For example, if a company has a database of its suppliers and wishes to contact the local ones, the database can be used to select all suppliers who are situated in the same town. The word processor can then print a

letter to each supplier selected, adding personal information, such as the name and address of the firm, to the letter.

● A spelling checker can be provided. This checks all the text against an inbuilt dictionary facility and points out any words that it does not recognize.

Case Study—Word processing a series of similar letters

A fashion house 'Novelty Fashions' regularly deals with a large number of enquiries from prospective customers. It responds to these enquiries by sending out standard letters, containing a number of set paragraphs. The required text has been entered on to a disk and paragraphs are called up as appropriate. The set paragraphs are listed below, along with the relevant index number used to call the paragraph.

Paragraph of text	*Index no.*
Thank you for your letter expressing an interest in our range of fashion clothes.	e1
Further to our recent telephone conversation in which you expressed an interest in our range of fashion clothes.	e2
Further to our recent meeting at which you expressed an interest in our range of fashion clothes.	e3
We have pleasure in forwarding to you our most recent catalogue and an order form for our goods.	o1
We are able to offer the following terms: 5 per cent 28 days	t1
We are able to offer the following terms: 8 per cent 28 days	t2
Yours sincerely Novelty Fashions	x1
Sales Director	

Questions

1. (a) Load a word processing package into a computer and prepare it to receive text.
    (b) Enter a letter heading for Novelty Fashions, using a fictional address. Enter the complete set of paragraphs. Save on the disk.
    (c) Produce six letters.

(i) To High Street Fashions,
     High Street,
     Grantham. Offering a 5 per cent, 28 days. Responding to a
                telephone call.

(ii) To Black on Black,
      Catlegate,
      Aberdeen. Offering 5 per cent, 28 days. Responding to a
                 personal meeting.

(iii) To Today Fashion,
       High Street,
       Portrush. Offering 8 per cent, 28 days. Responding to a
                 phone call.

(iv) To Shorties,
      Claire Ave,
      Dawlish. Offering 8 per cent, 28 days. Responding to a
               letter.

(v) To Miss Elspeth,
     Donald Road,
     Barnsley. Offering 8 per cent, 28 days. Responding to a
               personal meeting.

(vi) To New Fashion,
      High Street,
      Brighton. Offering 5 per cent, 28 days. Responding to a
                letter.

2. What would be the advantages to Novelty Fashions of word processing
    its letters in this way?
3. What constraints would there be to Novelty Fashions's ability to word
    process its letters?
4. What would be the disadvantages of Novelty Fashions of word process-
    ing letters?
5. What considerations should a firm bear in mind in deciding whether or
    not to word process its letters?

Desk top publishing

Desk top publishing has been an important spin-off from developments in word processing and computer graphics.

Desk top publishing programs make it possible to produce pages of well illustrated
text. No longer do pamphlets and other short publications have to be sent out to the
printers. Large, medium and even some small firms can save a lot of money by developing their own in-house desk top publishing facility.

Desk top packages offer a range of different character designs (typefaces), the freedom to adjust the space between characters and lines, the ability to place a diagram or

picture on a page and a number of other important editing functions. Desk top publishing programs can be used to produce newsletters, training manuals and advertisements. Newspapers can also be produced in this way at a fraction of the cost that would have applied in the early 1980s.

Project planning

Project planning packages can be used to plan and monitor projects consisting of a number of stages, or 'activities'.

Initially the activities will be defined, and an estimation made of the time required for each activity. The interrelationship between activities then needs to be specified.

The computer can then calculate the total time required to undertake the project, and will indicate the way in which activities should be completed, in order to prevent delays.

A simple example could involve the building of a new factory. The activities and times required may be:

1. Prepare the land and build the foundations   30 days
2. Build the walls   30 days
3. Build the roof   15 days
4. Install the machinery and equipment   30 days
5. Equip the offices   20 days

Activity 1 must be carried out first, followed by 2 and 3. Activities 4 and 5 can, however, be carried out simultaneously. The total project can therefore be carried out within 105 days, i.e. $30 + 30 + 15 + 30$ (rather than 125 days if stage 5 had waited for the completion of stage 4).

The program would also inform project planners that stage 5 is not 'critical', i.e. it could start late or take a few days longer than planned without delaying the total project. Such information is a useful aid to decision making because it helps project managers to work out priorities. Most versions of the program can also help to plan the use of resources on activities, record costs and produce a variety of reports.

In a real project many thousands of activities will need to be coordinated, and thus project planning packages can be very useful in cutting down time, costs and waste.

Expert systems

Expert systems (ES) are the first commercial products of research into artificial intelligence. ES are computer programs that embody some of the knowledge of human experts, knowledge which even those human experts have till now found difficult to formulate and communicate.

An ES has two distinct elements, a 'knowledge base' and an 'inference engine'. The 'knowledge base' consists of all the human knowledge that it is possible to collect on a particular subject. The area of knowledge an ES covers may be narrow, but expert systems aspire to quite comprehensive knowledge in those fields. It may be difficult to collect the information from human experts who often think of their expertise as irreducible to rule—though the real difficulty may be that human experts have paid inadequate attention to formulating and communicating their knowledge and the rules according to which their minds work.

But, because they use knowledge gathered from many different human experts, ES may be more knowledgeable than any single human being.

The 'inference engine' is simply a collection of the rules that manipulate the knowledge in the ES. For example, one of the rules might be: If runny nose *then* cold *or* excessive stimulation *or* allergy where 'runny nose', 'cold', 'excessive stimulation' and 'allergy' are all terms that would need to be in the knowledge base.

There are two essentials to an ES functioning properly: the knowledge base should be kept entirely separate from the rules manipulating that knowledge (the inference engine); and the knowledge should be represented uniformly.

These two principles—the representation of knowledge by a uniform means, and the separation of the knowledge base and the inference engine—allow additional pieces of knowledge (new discoveries about medical diagnosis, for example) to be added to an expert system without changing the system itself. When small changes are made, it is not necessary to edit, and recompile relevant parts of a program by human agency as it would be in the case of an ordinary computer-based program. Nor indeed is it necessary to have every full stop and comma in place: ES can operate on the basis of approximate commands or information.

Another thing that differentiates ES from an ordinary computer-based system is that an ES will be able to work out new rules for its own guidance on the basis of its existing knowledge and its inference engine. And, as it gathers new knowledge from the outside world, it can use this to modify its inference engine too.

The only difficulty with an ES, at present, is that of enabling it to keep up with advances in knowledge, especially as some of these may necessitate human intervention to change the rules in the inference engine.

Already, ES can be used by people to get specialist advice on subjects such as where to drill for oil, coal or other natural resources and how to diagnose and treat disease.

Direct communications

Communications between computers takes a variety of forms. The principal link in the communications chain is often the telephone network.

Electronic mail

Instead of writing letters and memos and posting them or delivering them by some sort of internal mail, a business can now use a system of 'electronic mail'.

The 'mail-box' is a computer terminal linked to the telephone network; it can put messages into the system and store messages that have been sent through the system.

Every user has a password to allow him or her to use the system. A message can be sent to several mail-boxes at once, and so the system can be used for internal memos in a company with several branches. The message will be stored in a terminal's memory until the mail-box is 'opened'. There are now a number of subscriber-based electronic mail services such as Telecom Gold. To use such a system, a subscriber sends a message using the telephone line. The advantage over ordinary mail is speed and low cost.

Accessing remote databases

A number of large computer databases have been set up for specialist use, covering rapidly changing areas like the law in relation to business activity, information on companies, international stock exchanges and foreign currency markets.

For a fee, companies can call up and do a search for specific topics. Searches can specify a combination of factors, e.g. an enquiry could be carried out to find out information on 'chemical fertilizer suppliers', 'employing more than 100 workers', 'Birmingham'. Up-to-date information can be readily accessed. Prestel is an example of such a database. Prestel links up an adapted television screen with the telephone service and gives users access to a great range of computer-held information. The information is set out in 'pages'. A page is a screenful of information and the pages are organized into groups.

As well as getting information from the Prestel service, business people can input their own information and use the service for sending messages. Prestel can be used to make hotel reservations and for holiday bookings. Orders can be fed into the system and company personnel can use the system to keep in touch with their office.

While many of the pages of Prestel are accessible to all users it is also possible for a firm to arrange to use private pages only available to members of the firm.

Networking

When a company is using a number of personal computers, it is possible to link the system so that information can be shared. This has been particularly important in the late twentieth century and makes it possible for teams of workers to combine far more frequently and effectively. It also makes it possible for specialists to access information quickly from other company departments.

Rather than continually swopping data using floppy disks, it is possible to connect the machines together using a local area network (LAN). This consists of a mixture of hardware and software which enables data to be transferred between the machines. There are two basic ways of using a local area network:

- Computers use their own programs and their own data, but can exchange data when necessary.
- The program and data are held on one machine, called a 'file server', and the others act as 'terminals', updating the data on the 'file server'.

Homeworking

A number of forecasters have predicted that by the mid-1990s many commuters will be travelling to work only three days a week. It is likely that 'teleworking' will be an important contributory factor to this trend. 'Teleworking' involves working from home with the tools of information technology—mainly a network of personal computers and databases, backed up by fax or other transmission systems.

The availability of information technology is changing the nature of office work. More and more tasks are skill- and knowledge-based 'thinkwork' which, though it is still done from centralized offices, does not need to be. Groups of specialists will still be able to work as a team, but they may be separated by large distances. Employers will be able to tap into the workforce of any part of the country. This will create more employment for skilled women with young families, and for others for whom commuting is an inconvenience.

Minicomputers

Minicomputers can be used for applications which are not possible on personal computers. Generally these will be applications for which personal computers are not powerful enough, such as sophisticated computer aided design programs, or where a lot of information is required to be made available to all users of an integrated system, such as on a production control system. Such systems consist of a central computer and between half a dozen and several hundred terminals. Some of the most frequently used business applications are described below.

Production control

An awareness of the importance of production control systems is essential. MRP is used to describe both materials requirements planning and manufacturing resource planning (sometimes referred to as MRP II)—two activities which stand at the centre of modern manufacturing control philosophy. The functions of MRP are invariably embodied in a sophisticated multi-user computer system which is usually the starting point for the development of computer integrated manufacture (CIM) (see page 281). CIM is a must for all major manufacturers that have any serious intentions of surviving into the twenty-first century.

A materials requirements planning system is one that contains information on all the items that make up a firm's products, all the items currently in stock, and the requirements for finished products. It can calculate the total requirements for all items that the firm uses, work out when they are needed, and tell the production control and purchasing departments to order them. This process would not be possible on a personal computer; even on a minicomputer the calculations are normally carried out overnight.

A manufacturing resource planning sytem extends this process by incorporating items such as cost information, the automatic scheduling of parts on the shop floor, monitoring of purchase orders, etc. The whole company is thus able to use the same set of data. Installing such a program and learning how to use it can take over two years, and they are expensive (tens of thousands of pounds). The benefits to a company in terms of integration of company functions, time saving and cost cutting can be enormous.

For the majority of manufacturing companies, MRP is the central management system. Surveys have shown that at the end of the 1980s over half of manufacturers had an MRP system installed and numbers are increasing. MRP was originally developed in the United States during the 1960s and 1970s around the prevalent technology of the day—the batch mainframe. In the 1970s the original MRP system was developed into a 'closed loop' MRP II manufacturing philosophy consisting of a computerized database of parts, work-in-progress, finished goods and material requirements. Details on production lead time and relationships between parts are also held, so that the computer can calculate the best way to meet the master production schedule (MPS), a plan based on forecasts and orders. Because MRP systems hold details on stock levels at every stage, it is possible to push goods through the manufacturing process according to a carefully drawn up plan. The term 'closed loop' means adjustments can be made when new information arises.

Software and hardware suppliers were quick to jump on the MRP bandwagon and they, as much as anyone else, have been responsible for promoting the MRP philosophy. There are probably more than 100 packages available in the United Kingdom alone, most of these linked closely to accounting systems.

Computer aided design

CAD systems have been described in Chapter 8. Minicomputer-based systems are required where the items are complicated or where a centralized set of data must be used (e.g. in designing an integrated design, such as a car, rather than individual items, e.g. clothes).

Word processing and information distribution

When a minicomputer is used as a word processing system it can also be used as a messaging system. For example, a letter could be word processed before being passed on to several departmental members for their comments. The originator of the document could then quickly amend the original document in the light of suggested changes. The completed document could then be run off and circulated to a wider audience.

In general, the applications of minicomputers are very similar to those of personal computers. However, some of the additional benefits of minicomputers are:

1. The provision of centralized data to all users.
2. Availability of a common set of programs and data.
3. Access to greater power for major projects.

Mainframes

Most large companies will use mainframe computers for many of their data processing requirements.

Mainframes are powerful machines, which occupy the space of a room and require the employment of a team of operators and programmers. The programs that accompany such a system are usually specifically designed for their users.

An example of the application of mainframe computers is that used by mail order firms. Mail order firms rely on mainframes to keep a check on and to re-order stock, to bill customers and to supervise the whole operation. Because mail order products tend to be fairly standard in range and quality, the use of an efficient program is one way of gaining a cost advantage.

Modern information systems in large organizations

Every organization must have some form of system for storing, processing and communicating information. In its simplest form this will consist of filing cabinets, an in and out tray, and a telephone. To have an information system that works effectively it is necessary to organize all the required data in such a manner that it can be readily recorded, stored, processed, retrieved and communicated by a variety of users.

An information system converts raw data into either a finished report or an input for a further stage in the information processing cycle.

The dominant form of information processing in modern organizations is computer based. A computer system, alone, is not an information system. It is a tool that can improve the effectiveness of an information system.

Systems analysis

Before introducing computers to an information system it is necessary to carry out a process of *systems analysis* to investigate the ways in which computers can benefit the system.

Systems development is a procedure used to design and develop an information system. The systems analyst will look at an organizational system as a coordinated whole and will examine the ways in which the parts of the organization need to fit together and support each other. The systems analyst will then attempt to integrate within the organization and its needs a multi-level, cross-functional and timely flow of information. The information system will then hopefully serve the needs of both the management sub-system and the operating sub-system.

A good illustration of a modern computer-based information system is that operated by the commercial banks to handle customer information. A business or private customer may have several accounts with a bank: current accounts, savings accounts, mortgage accounts, loan accounts, etc. Using a customer information system it is possible to cross-reference such accounts easily so that the bank can quickly develop a picture of total customer activity even though the customer may be dealing with several departments. Such information makes it possible for a bank to develop a more detailed picture of its customers, to provide a better service for customers, to provide up-to-the minute information, and to be able to market readily new services to existing customers.

Retailers are able to use computer-based information systems to access and use information related to a variety of functions. This is particularly useful when information related to individual items can be recorded at point of sale. Detailed information can then be accessed and processed in relation to stock levels, prices, turnover, demand and many other important variables.

Designing an information system

Systems design involves the preparation and planning of an information system by using drawings, sketches and plans. It is concerned with deciding how a system should be developed.

The form of the design will depend on a number of factors:

1. The *resources available* to an organization will clearly constrain the type of system planned. The five basic resources of any organization are machines, material, money, methods and men and women. Quite clearly there would be no point in designing an expensive information system for a company with little money to spare.
2. The *information requirements of users* are an important design factor. Systems design clearly needs to be coupled with an understanding of who needs what information, when and in what form.
3. The *user's ability to use information provided and to operate the system*. The designer will have to make a system as user friendly as possible. This will involve the reduction of jargon and technical language to a bare minimum. Other features can be built into a system such as speed of communication to prevent frustration of waiting.
4. The *requirements for the system* are also an important element of design. The designer needs to be clear of what is expected of his or her system, e.g.
    (a)   cost
    (b)   performance
    (c)   reliability
    (d)   flexibility
    (e)   expected life cycle
5. The *use to which data operations will be put* is also an important design feature. As we have seen a number of important operations can be carried out on data: capturing, verifying, classifying, arranging, summarizing, calculating, storing, retrieving, reproducing and communicating. Systems analysis will reveal information such as the order in which these operations need to be carried out in particular operations, e.g. building up a series of personal accounts. This information will need to be carried forward into sytems design.

The designer will then use a number of *design tools* such as flow charts, and decision tables (see Chapter 5) to help with the design of the information system.

Systems evaluation

The systems designer will come up with various alternative plans for implementation. Some of these suggestions will be set out as *imperatives*, i.e. features of design which must be adhered to whatever the final system. In addition, the designer will suggest a number of *desirable features* which are optional.

It will then be necessary to find suppliers who would be willing to provide the required computer equipment to meet the design needs. This might involve finding suppliers who can provide equipment which has the 'best fit' with the desired system in terms of criteria such as cost, reliability, maintainability and other factors. Other considerations will be the ability to extend a system to account for future growth, and the overall level of support from the supplier, e.g. in the form of training and maintenance. These and other factors will need to be weighed up before a final decision is made.

Communications outside the business

As well as the internal communications links that we have just explored, the business also communicates with individuals and groups outside itself. The business communicates externally with its suppliers, its customers and other groups.

The communications network of a country is the means by which goods and people and information are moved around. It will use a wide range of methods including:

1. Postal communications
2. Telecommunications
3. Advertising and the media
4. Transport systems

Postal communications

The Post Office provides a range of services which act as aids to business.

Every working day, nearly 50 million letters are posted and delivered in the United Kingdom. Personal letters, sales letters, invitations, apologies, cheques and bills.

To handle all those letters, more than 100 000 postmen and postwomen work for the Royal Mail. They deliver to all of Britain's 23 million homes and businesses. Moving mail round Britain and overseas is a massive job. Much of it happens at night and involves thousands of trucks, trains and even planes. Many first-class letters are flown across Britain to ensure they get delivered as quickly as possible.

There are more than 21 000 post offices in Britain—the biggest chain of shops in the country. Customers can buy stamps and post mail, collect state pensions and benefits, renew TV licences, pay gas and electricity and telephone bills, or carry out any of 150 other transactions.

Recent developments in Post Office service have been an increase in the number of counter clerks employed and the introduction of new technology, with counter-top computers to help improve service.

The Royal Mail parcels service is an important means of transporting small consignments of goods around the country. In many isolated communities, the post is the only regular link with shops and suppliers many miles away. Over 600 000 parcels are posted every day and mail order companies depend heavily on this service.

Today, there are a number of competitors for post and parcel deliveries. Letters can be delivered by special courier and a number of moves have been made by companies such as TNT to try and remove the legal monopoly of post box delivery currently enjoyed by the Post Office.

Telecommunications

Telecommunications involves communication by means of:

- an electrical current along a wire, e.g. by telephone;
- a laser light signal along a glass optical fibre, e.g. computer links;
- a radio signal (e.g. radio and TV).

Communications in this form can either be *one way* (e.g. when we sit at home watching a television programme) or *interactive* (e.g. when we have a telephone conversation with someone).

Information that is communicated can either be *broadcast* so that many people can receive a message (e.g. a broadcast television service) or sent down a cable or wire to an individual (e.g. a personal telephone call).

Modern business relies on telecommunications services for a wide range of speedy links. Telecommunication links are usually networked through a centralized exchange. Terminals such as telephones, facsimile machines and computer monitors are linked through an exchange.

There are three main types of network:

1. Local area networks (LANs—within a single site organization such as a business, school, building society or hospital).
2. Wide area networks (WANs—connecting various component parts of an organization, e.g. offices and stores of a retailing chain, or the various plants belonging to a manufacturing company).
3. Public and international networks (networks which are open to public subscription such as the telephone network).

The telephone service makes possible direct communications throughout the United

Kingdom and international direct dialling to many parts of the world. Businesses can also make use of the following services:

- Radiophones for communication with moving vehicles.
- Telephone credit cards, whereby telephone calls can be charged to the phone bill when someone is travelling around.
- Phonecards, which can be used in some phone boxes as an alternative to coins.
- Alarm calls.
- Business information services.

Datel is a telecommunications system whereby a computer in a firm can communicate with computers on sites in other parts of the country, and in many overseas countries.

Teletex is a means of communicating a message by means of a word processor or adapted typewriter. The text can automatically be transmitted in seconds over an ordinary telephone line to a receiving word processor or typewriter where the text will appear.

Telex is a commonly used method of communicating between firms although today it is being replaced by more versatile services such as facsimile machines.

The main disadvantage of using a telephone for business purposes is that the message is not presented in a printed form. Sometimes it is essential to have a printed record of a message, particularly when dealing with figures and other detailed pieces of information. The telex system is operated by British Telecom, and subscribers to the service rent a machine called a teleprinter and have their telex number listed in the telex directory which is the equivalent of the phone book. Firms can contact each other simply by dialling the right telex number for national and international calls. The telex operator types the message into the teleprinter and the message is transmitted immediately to the receiving machine. Telex machines can be left unattended and operate 24 hours a day. They are particularly useful for sending international messages which may need translation, and because the telex can be left unattended messages can be sent to other countries where the time is different.

Many paper communications involve diagrams, pictures and documents. These can be sent electronically by using *facsimile* ('fax') machines.

Telemessages allow up to 50-word messages. The firm simply telephones the operator before 8 p.m. (6 p.m. on Sunday) and British Telecom delivers on the next working day. This would only be of general use to a very small firm with no other telecommunications facilities.

Confravision makes it possible for conferences to be arranged in sound and pictures from British Telecom studios in London, Birmingham, Bristol, Glasgow and Manchester. Meetings can take place as if the people involved were in the same room. We are all familiar with this type of situation from seeing television presenters link studios in different parts of the country. Businesses using this service arrange for their staff to visit the nearest Confravision studio. This can save a lot of time and money (hotel bills, air fares, etc.). This service is most frequently used when meetings are arranged for highly paid employees and when large distances are involved.

Satellite communications have made it possible to greatly improve international links in the late twentieth century. Signals can be bounced off satellites which are put into orbit at a fixed point above the earth.

Major users of satellite links include the following:

1. Banks which use an international network for transferring money and making communications about financial transactions.
2. Large businesses which use this link for transferring data between computers in different parts of the world.
3. Governments use satellites for direct links between government officials using voice and picture links, as well as for defence purposes.
4. The media use satellites for the transmission of voice, pictures and textual links.

Advertising and the media

Advertising and public relations through the media can be an important form of communication for business to the outside world. Personal experience informs us that there are some companies that spend large sums on advertising, e.g. those involved in toilet preparations, soap and detergents, pharmaceutical chemicals, cocoa, chocolate and sugar confectionery and soft drinks, British wines, ciders and perry.

The bulk of advertising is undertaken by manufacturers and directed at consumers (over 50 per cent), with other advertising being undertaken by retailers (about 25 per cent), by financial institutions (about 10 per cent) and by industry for trade purposes (under 15 per cent) (1980s figures). Nelson (Advertising as Information) has argued that consumer products can be divided into those with 'search' and those with 'experience' qualities. Products with search qualities can be evaluated prior to purchase (e.g. a suit) and advertising for such products sets out mainly to inform customers of the qualities available. Products with experience qualities, on the other hand, must be purchased before they can be assessed (e.g. a new brand of confectionery), and advertising in this case is mainly to signal the existence and reputaton of the product. Nelson felt that in the former case information would be mainly 'truthful', while in the latter case the advertising would be set out to persuade consumers to make a purchasing decision. Nelson then went on to suggest that advertising intensity would be higher for products with experience qualities and backed this up using evidence from a survey of 40 products.

Transport

Transport is an essential service to business. The success of modern transport has followed from a clever combination of road, rail, sea and air transport. Containerization of loads has made possible the integration of these different forms of transport.

Routes and services have been simplified to cut out wasteful duplications. Special types of vehicles have been designed to carry special loads.

Direct motorway connections between major cities have proved to be of major importance in determining location decisions, coupled with fast intercity rail services, as well as air links. Different methods of transport may prove to be more or less cost effective in different situations depending on the cost of transport relative to the type of good being transported, the price of the good, or the speed with which it is needed. Heavy bulky items may be sent by road, rail or sea depending on the distance involved. Urgent items such as first-class post or important medical suplies may be sent by air. Door-to-door delivery is normally best secured by road links; although with an increasing integration of transport methods a variety of methods can be combined.

Short answer questions

1. What is meant by communication? Give four examples of different types of communication. (Explain, with reference to your work on communication, why different students are likely to give different types of answer to this question.)
2. Outline possible stages involved in the passage of a message from a transmitter to a receiver.
3. Set out a simple memo for members of your class warning them to prepare themselves for a forthcoming examination.
4. Why is it unlikely that information can be transmitted intact from one person to another?
5. Outline the essential features of:
   (a) personal computers;
   (b) minicomputers;
   (c) mainframe computers.
6. For what purposes might a business use spreadsheets? How do spreadsheets facilitate business decision making?
7. What sorts of records may be kept on a bank's database? What fields might records be sorted into?
8. Outline three applications of desk top publishing for a medium-sized furniture wholesaler.
9. How might a project planning package help:
   (a) a building firm constructing a new housing estate;
   (b) a large fashion company producing consignments of shirts, trousers and dresses?
10. What are expert systems?
11. What advantages does electronic mail have over the postal service?
12. Why is homeworking becoming increasingly important?
13. What is the purpose of:
    (a) systems analysis;
    (b) systems design; and
    (c) systems evaluation?

14. What are the key considerations of systems design?
15. What is the difference between one-way and interactive communications? Give three examples of each.
16. Describe (a) telex, (b) teletex.
17. What considerations should be weighed up before using Confravision for a delegate conference?
18. Give three applications of satellite communications.
19. What sorts of firms are most likely to advertise? Explain your answer.
20. Describe six situations in which road transport would be preferable to other forms of transport. Explain your reasons.

Essays

1. Effective communication is vital to the success of any organization. Discuss this statement.
2. Outline the stages that may be involved in preparing a new information system.
3. Discuss the view that, 'Information technology strategies can only be effective if their formulation involves a genuinely two-handed affair with senior management and systems specialists contributing equally'.
4. How important are production control systems to modern industry?
5. Have computer-based information systems removed the need for traditional communication links?
6. Discuss the importance to a modern office of:
   (a) databases;
   (b) word processing facilities;
   (c) spreadsheets.
7. How can information which is required for accounting purposes be gained from raw data?
8. What forms of internal communication are used in an organization with which you are familiar? How could the communications system be improved?
9. How would you set up a database recording the following?
   (a) Hobbies and interests of members of your class.
   (b) Part-time work carried out by members of your class.
10. Select an individual in an organization whose main responsibility is to process data. Observe his or her activities. Take notes on your observations and summarize your findings. Prepare a brief recommendation of possible improvements which could be made in his or her activities.

Data response questions

1   Pirelli slips into total automation on its Welsh industrial kibbutz

Propaganda has become reality on the outskirts of Aberdare. A £20 million factory that at first blush looks utterly boring—it makes household electrical wires—is Britain's best example yet of the twin themes that have been preached for more than 20 years but never realized.

The first theme is routine total automation; the second, multi-skill employment in an industrial version of the kibbutz.

All staff at Pirelli's new wire factory in Mid-Glamorgan are trained in computer literacy and, under a deal with the technical staff union MATSA, they switch jobs to cover holidays and sickness. Thus a shop-floor technician monitoring production may spend a month in the sales office or become an accounts clerk.

Aberdare's significance is clouded by jargon. It uses CIM (computer integrated manufacture) and FMS (flexible manufacturing systems). That means it is not automated piecemeal as are so many UK factories. Office computers and production computers are joined through a network of optical fibre cables, so that managers know what is happening as it happens, rather than catching up too late via a mountain of paper records. Continuous computer monitoring of production and ordering removes the need to hold expensive stocks of components and raw materials.

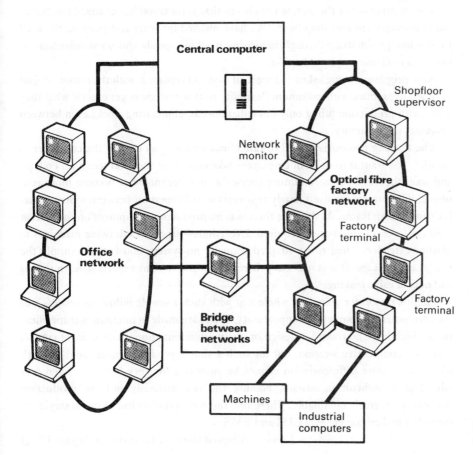

Figure 15.3 Integrated computer systems at the Aberdare plant.

The FMS bit means that production can be switched from one type of wire to another or one colour casing to another within minutes instead of hours.

At the top of Aberdare's computer pyramid is a minicomputer which handles office chores and passes customers' orders to the 100 production microcomputers. They in turn manage the machinery. Overall, that involves about 120 million decisions per second (see Fig. 15.3).

There are three main stages in making electric cables:

- The metallurgy involved in forming the electric conductor.
- The insulating and sheathing of the conductor.
- Combining the components into a finished cable.

At Aberdare these three stages are handled in separate factory zones and each zone is totally automated. The particular triumph is on the first stage, which traditionally has involved labour-intensive skilled work. Only about 20 of the 150 staff are actually in the factory at any one time.

Each massive bobbin of wires, carried from process to process by robot truck, has a radio transmitter so that computers can check it is where it should be.

The chairperson of the company believes that automation has changed the thinking of management and shop floor. 'We have insisted for years and years on the need to improve productivity through increasing machine speeds and on standardization products to favour mass production.'

Now people are being asked to forget all that and replace it with the notion of 'just in time'; to produce with maximum flexibility so that customers get exactly what they want, with production filling only immediate needs, eliminating stocks even between processes in the factory.

The training process is geared towards 'making sure you can get the computer to do what you want it to do'. All employees take courses at the local technical college, and soon they will be on retraining courses as new technologies become more economic. The project involved nearly two years of collaboration between systems analysis and design teams. At the time there was no production equipment on the market with the levels of automation required. Everything—from wire drawing machines to plastics extruders—had to be adapted. Equally no system house could supply the design as a package. It was necessary therefore for the systems experts to learn the ins and outs of cable making.

Pirelli's reason for going the whole hog with such a simple industrial process was the narrowness of competitive opportunity. Wires are made to international specifications which leave no room for design or quality differentiation. Pricing, is, of course, used as a competitive weapon, but for such a simple product, usually sold through wholesalers, price differentiation cannot be sustained for very long. ... Even cost advantage is difficult to sustain, because the raw materials and the production machinery are freely obtainable. Therefore, the concentration had to be on service to the individual customer—via CIM and FMS.

(*Source:* Adapted from the *Guardian*, 4 August 1988.)

(a) What do you understand by the terms:
  (i) total automation;
  (ii) multi-skill employment?
  Briefly explain how these have been applied by Pirelli at Aberdare.
(b) How has Pirelli used a network to combine its information system into a unified whole? What are the advantages of operating in this way?
(c) What are the likely benefits to Pirelli (Aberdare) of its new system of production? Who else is likely to benefit from this development:
  (i) in the short run;
  (ii) in the long run?
(d) In what ways have changes in attitudes been necessary to implement the required changes in production processes and techniques?
(e) What is meant by 'just in time'? What are the benefits of such a scheme? What are the potential pitfalls?
(f) Why did Pirelli carry out the modernization of the Aberdare plant?
(g) What other industries are particularly suitable for the changes carried out at Pirelli (Aberdare)? Why are the industries you have just mentioned suitable for these changes?

2 Study the journal article (Fig. 15.4 overleaf) and answer the questions that follow.
(a) What is the government's data network?
(b) What are the benefits of this network to government departments?
(c) Who else benefits from the network? How do they benefit?
(d) How does this article suggest that the government hopes to improve further its communication links? What will be the additional benefits?
(e) How do such networks enable organizations to develop their activities?
(f) What considerations should be taken into account when developing a new network?
(g) Is the availability of competing suppliers an advantage to consumers of networks? Explain your answer.

State lays plans for all-in-one network

The Government wants telecommunications and network suppliers to start work on a voice and image network that will sit on top of the Government Data Network (GDN), designed to link Whitehall departments with their offices in the rest of the UK.

Prime Minister Margaret Thatcher has indicated her enthusiasm for the GDN, and last week opened the Racal network management centre in Basingstoke with a hint that other network services will be put out to tender.

Departmental IT heads, under pressure to use the GDN service provided by Racal, believe the Government wants to press ahead with an integrated services government network (ISGN) embracing voice and image as well as data.

If adopted, an ISGN will carry electronic mail, electronic data interchange (EDI), fax, video and voice around a backbone network similar to the one Racal has installed for the GDN.

The Department of Social Security (DSS) wants a pilot voice and data facility to link up benefits offices in London with new social security processing centres in Belfast, Wigan and Glasgow.

British Telecom, Mercury and Racal put their proposals to DSS managers on Tuesday for a pilot 20-office system to be ready just as the DSS relocates work and staff away from London.

Government figures show that its overall spending on telecomms is growing at 22% every year.

Martin Davies, IT director at the Department of Employment – which next week formally signs up to join the GDN – says the Kilostream link between the department in London and its DP centre in Runcorn needs replacing within the next couple of years.

The Department has six ICL mainframes and is piloting use of GDN on a range of applications before all its 2,000 local unemployment benefits offices are brought online.

Her Majesty's Stationery Office (HMSO), now run as an executive agency by former CCTA director Paul Freeman, is understood to be ready to follow the department as the next member of the GDN some time within the next two months.

Racal, which beat off BT and Cable & Wireless to win the GDN contract last May, has spent £65m installing the backbone GDN network and

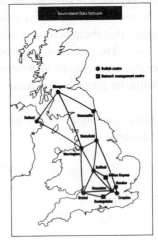

management centre in Basingstoke.

Racal Electronics chairman Ernest Harrison says that by the year 2000 the GDN should carry data from 65% of the 360,000 terminals that will be installed in central governments.

The company claims the government telecomms spending can at worst be held steady, at best trimmed, by departments using GDN, which it says is 45% cheaper than public networks.

"The future for Racal is an integrated services government network that links up faxes, terminals, word processors, telephones – the whole lot – using a common network," says a spokesman.

The concept of a unified network for voice and data was foreshadowed in the confidential requirement for the GDN two years ago, but without timescales.

Four departments, Customs & Excise, DSS, Inland Revenue and the Home Office are users of the GDN.

∎ **Simon Hill**

Figure 15.4 Proposals for an all-in-one network. (*Source: Computer Weekly*, 26 January 1989.)

3 Study the chart (Fig. 15.5).

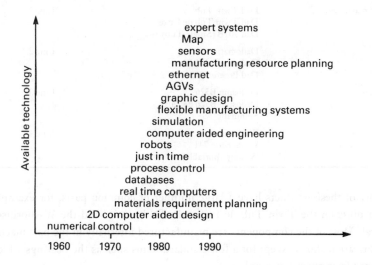

Figure 15.5 CIM technology development.

(a) What is meant by:
    (i)   computer aided design;
    (ii) 'just in time';
    (iii) robots;
    (iv) manufacturing resource planning;
    (v) expert systems?
(b) How can (i) 'just in time', (ii) expert systems help a business to reduce costs and raise productivity?
(c) What factors are likely to constrain the ability and willingness of companies to use the available technology?
(d) Which of the technology developments listed above do you regard to be most important? Explain your reasoning.
(e) Which of the CIM technology developments highlighted in the chart would you regard to be essential to large manufacturing companies wishing to survive into the twentieth century? Explain your answer.
(f) What new developments can be added to the chart?

4 Domestic Appliances Limited

Domestic Appliances Limited makes an almost complete range of the larger electric domestic appliances (washing machines, refrigerators, spin driers, tumble driers, dishwashers, food mixers, cookers) in four widely separated plants. The largest plant which is situated in Scotland manufactures washing machines, spin driers and dishwashers. A full list of products is given on page 482.

Appliance	Model	Production line usually used
Washing machines	Dad Twin Tub Dad Twin Tub de Luxe Dad 707B (Single Tub)	Line 1
	Dadomatic Dadomatic de Luxe Dad Progomatic	Line 2
Spin driers	Dadospin B526 Dadospin B526 de Luxe Spinmatic	Line 3
Dish washers	Washorinse Washorinse 741 Washup (portable)	Line 4

Many of these products have a large number of common parts, for example the heating units on the Twin Tub de Luxe, the Dadomatics and the Washorinses are identical. Most of the components are manufactured internally in the part machining and fabrication shops except for a few standard items such as the bearings which are purchased from specialist suppliers.

Final assembly is done on four lines as indicated above, changeovers are scheduled for the items on a given line in order to obtain the desired product mix, usually at least three shifts are worked on each item before a changeover.

Before final assembly, however, many sub-assemblies are built up (e.g. the heating unit). In general, individual components are manufactured and put into part stores and these are issued against 'kitting lists' to make a batch of sub-assemblies which are again returned to stores and may be issued against a further kitting list to form a 'higher level' assembly which is returned to stores to await final assembly. As many as six levels may be identified for some assemblies and four including raw material is common (see Fig. 15.6).

Although the sub-assemblies which go into the final assembly of an item may not be identical, many of the *components* of the sub-assemblies are common. For example, the heater unit for the Progomatic has identical components (8) to that of the Dadomatic except for the heating coil, the insulator and a switching unit which are all slightly larger and the addition of two other components not used elsewhere.

The component and sub-assembly stores, besides supplying the needs of the assembly lines, also supply spares stores but the requirement is usually for sub-assemb-

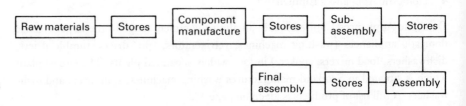

Figure 15.6 (PC short cases) Materials flow in Domestic Appliances Limited.

lies such as the complete heater unit. However, two service centres operate rebuild lines, and these usually place orders for components rather than assemblies.

Orders for components and sub-assemblies are based on a periodic review system with a critical level and re-order quantity rule based on past usage of the particular item.

The management of the company has been very concerned about the amount of capital tied up in inventory and has recently installed a large computer system (run on the company computer adjacent to the washer plant) which records movements, locations and levels of all inventories.

(a) Outline ways in which the new computer system will enable manufacturing and other processes to be carried out more effectively by Domestic Appliances Limited.

(b) Outline further possibilities using computer applications within the company. Explain how these will benefit the company.

(c) How might the company benefit from 'just in time'?

Suggested reading

Gondran, M., *An Introduction to Expert Systems*. McGraw-Hill, 1986.

Gremillion, L. and Pyburn, P., *Computers and Information Systems in Business*. McGraw-Hill, 1988.

Popyk, M., *Word Processing and Information Systems: A Practical Approach to Concepts*. McGraw-Hill, 1986.

Voisinet, D., *An Introduction to CAD*. McGraw-Hill, 1986.

16

The influence of the economy upon organizations

All societies try to provide a system which will efficiently make use of resources. The success of this system will help to determine the standard of living of a country's inhabitants and the well-being of its business structures. As a sub-system of the overall community, the economic system attempts to allocate scarce resources to alternative end uses. At the same time it interacts with monetary, political, social and environmental sub-systems.

Introduction to economics

It is not possible to produce a precise ready-made definition of economics. Economics covers a broad spectrum of areas and ideas.

The media continually make us aware of developments in areas such as the balance of payments, inflation, employment, interest rates, the budget and so on. These are highlighted because they are important and relate to our everyday lives in direct ways.

The word economics is derived from the Greek word which means the management of the household. This infers that economics is concerned with managing the goods and resources that are available to us—as households, firms or nations. Important issues and questions are:

1. How do we earn our money?
2. How do we spend our money?
3. Is money spent wisely?
4. Have we enough to meet our needs?

These questions illustrate that, by its very nature, economics is concerned with people and with human behaviour. They also illustrate that all is not always well.

Though there are some goods which are genuinely free, such as air and seawater, the majority of our needs have to be met by making sacrifices. Limitations upon our incomes force us to make decisions about consumption and this forms the basis of the economic problem of scarcity and choice (see Chapter 1). For example, we would all prefer a higher standard of living. This might involve a better car, a bigger house and so on. The reality is that there are simply not enough of these goods to go around in the quantities that would satisfy everyone's desires.

It is not possible to satisfy these almost *unlimited wants* with the *scarce resources* available. Limited incomes therefore force us to choose between the various scarce items. By having to make a choice we make a sacrifice. Alternatives are forfeited. The next best alternative that is sacrificed is known as the opportunity cost. When you buy good A you give up the opportunity of buying good B. The opportunity cost of buying A is therefore B. In trying to make rational decisions:

1. Consumers will try to gain the maximum benefits or utility from their incomes.
2. Businesses will try to maximize their returns.
3. Government will try to provide a better standard of living for the population.

Economics can be broken down into two distinct areas. *Microeconomics* is derived from the Greek word meaning small and is the study of the individual parts of the economy. It is concerned with the analysis of individual pricing decisions, production decisions an other small-scale issues. *Macroeconomics* is derived from the Greek and refers to large-scale decision making. Macroeconomics deals with totals or aggregates relating to the national economy—e.g. the national employment level, the general level of price rises in the economy, the balance of payments and so on. This chapter concentrates on the macroeconomy and its influence on business activity.

The monetary system

The success of the economic system depends on the monetary system. Money is often likened to the oil that helps the wheels of industry and commerce to run smoothly.

When early man began to develop skills, and to specialize, a limited form of trading using *barter* was developed. Goods and services were exchanged for other goods and services. Though barter enabled surpluses to be traded, it was often difficult to find someone with what you wanted who wanted what you had to offer. There were also problems in deciding upon exchange rates and upon how to give change. What was required was a form of money which would be generally acceptable to all members of society. This money needed to perform the following functions:

1. *A medium of exchange.* So that everyone would accept money as a form of payment.
2. *A unit of account.* The value of items could be measured in money units, e.g. one biro = 10p, one sports car = £20 000, etc.
3. *A store of value.* Wealth could be stored up in the form of money for future use.
4. *A standard for deferred payments.* Debts could be built up in one period and paid off in another. A trader could sell goods on credit, issue an IOU and expect payment at a later date.

Over the centuries in various parts of the world a variety of different commodities have been used as money including: sharks' teeth, cowrie shells, precious stones and many more. Some were more successful than others. As well as being generally acceptable money needs to be scarce enough to be valuable. At the same time it needs to be easily recognizable. Salt is capable of divisibility, but lacks durability. Stones cannot be carried around. Precious metals have many of the properties required of a money form. Gold and silver are easily recognizable, scarce and hence valuable. They have use value as expensive ornaments and jewellery. They can be shaped and divided.

Precious metals came to be used as a form of money in many parts of the world. In this country the goldsmiths played an increasingly prominent part in handling money from the seventeenth century onwards. Gold and silver were increasingly deposited with goldsmiths for safe keeping because of their strongrooms and vaults. Depositors were issued with receipts called promissory notes, so that quantities of gold and silver could be reclaimed on demand. These receipts were often used as a form of payment. Instead of paying for valuable items in gold and silver these receipts could simply change hands. If I wanted to buy an acre of land from Mr Smith I could simply sign on the back of a promissory note to say that it now belonged to Mr Smith.

Goldsmiths soon began to issue bankers' notes for set amounts, e.g. £10, £20 and so on. These were the first bank notes.

As only a fixed proportion of the gold left in the vaults was ever used, goldsmiths started to lend some of the gold that lay idle in their vaults. They had become bankers, and were the forerunners of the *retail banks* which are today one-stop financial supermarkets providing a wide range of services.

The *Bank of England* was founded in 1694 because William III was short of money to finance the war against France. The Bank of England lent him the money in return for a Royal Charter. From this early privileged position the Bank of England went on to play a central part in our financial system. As a result of successive Bank Charter Acts protecting the position of the Bank, it finally became the sole issuer of notes in 1928.

Because the smooth running of the financial system is so vital to the economy it is important for the Bank of England to supervise and monitor closely the operation of financial institutions. Confidence in the financial system is imperative. Since the Banking Act of 1987, the Bank of England now supervises all deposit taking institutions and the name 'Bank' is restricted to authorized institutions with a capital of £5 million or more.

A major role of the Bank of England is to advise the Treasury on the various *monetary policies* necessary to steer the economy in a particular direction and to suggest ways in which this can be undertaken.

Monetary policies are policies designed to influence one or a combination of the following:

- The supply of money
- The demand for money
- The price of money

Money supply is measured by a number of different aggregates or totals. Each of these represents a different level of liquidity (liquidity means the ease with which assets can be converted into money). Many economists believe that there is a direct link between the quantity of money in the economy and the level of spending. In simple terms, the more money in existence the greater the level of spending. If the spending power in the economy increases faster than the quantity of goods available to be bought then prices will be pushed up.

The problem, however, is finding a definition of money which gives an accurate measure of spending power. All of the measures shown in Fig. 16.1 and many more have been used at one time or another as indicators of spending power.

Less liquidity	1.	M0	(a) Notes and coins
			(b) Till money
			(c) Bank operational balances with the Bank of England
	2.	M1	(a) M0
			(b) Private sector *sight* bank deposits which can be withdrawn on demand
	3.	M3	(a) M1
			(b) Private sector *time* deposits where a period of notice has to be given before a withdrawal is made
	4.	M4	(a) M3
			(b) Private sector holding of *building society share and deposit* accounts
			(c) Building societies holding of M3 (to avoid double counting)
	5.	M5	(a) M4
			(b) *Money market instruments* (Treasury bills, local authority deposits, etc.)
			(c) *National Savings* deposits

Figure 16.1 Recent definitions of money.

M0, M3 and M4 are currently regarded by the government as the most useful definitions. However, you should find out for yourself what is currently regarded as being the best measure and why.

The Bank of England uses the following three areas to pursue government monetary policies:

1. *Bank lending* By influencing interest rates, bank lending can be restricted to suit economic conditions. Higher rates lead to a squeeze on credit and a fall in bank lending and lower rates lead to an increase in bank lending.

   In late 1989, for example, the government increased interest rates quite strongly in an attempt to take spending out of the economy to cut back on inflationary pressures.

   In recent years this policy has depended very much on its effects on mortgages and the housing market. It is supposed to work through three channels:

   (a) First, people with mortgages suffer a reduction in their spending power through having to pay more interest.

   (b) Secondly, with house prices no longer rising overall, personal wealth is only rising slowly. People are thus not able to use their rising house price as an asset against which they can increase their borrowing.

(c)   Thirdly, with house prices under pressure, housing sales slump. This depresses spending on household durables such as carpets, curtains, cookers, fridges and so on.

2.   *Funding*   The gilt-edged market provides the bulk of money that government borrows. Gilt-edged stock are fixed-term government securities that pay regular interest. By selling gilt-edged securities to the non-bank private sector the Bank of England reduces the impact of the public sector borrowing requirement (PSBR) on the money supply by soaking up funds in markets.

3.   *Exchange rates*   Exchange rates are the link between the domestic economy and the rest of the world. Exchange rates are important when considering monetary conditions such as inflation and interest rates. The Bank of England supervises exchange rates and carries out government policies by buying pounds if sterling is weak and selling pounds if sterling is too strong.

Discount houses are unique to the British banking system and have a key role to play in helping the Bank of England to exercise monetary controls over the economy. The traditional function of discount houses has been to discount bills of exchange. As a result of trade and communication difficulties, bills of exchange developed as a method of payment in the eighteenth century. Often merchants who accepted these as a form of post-dated payment needed funds more immediately. They took them to brokers who exchanged them for the value of the bill, less a discount for the service. Such brokers became known as discount houses and today they still discount commercial bills of exchange to provide organizations with short-term funds.

Discount houses occupy an important link in the banking system by providing an opportunity for commercial banks to place short-term deposits with them so that they can earn interest for periods which vary between overnight (termed as being 'on call') and up to 14 days. This money is used to underwrite the weekly Treasury bill tender. Discount houses have an arrangement with the government to buy up any Treasury bills which are not purchased by other banks and private investors so that the government can always cover its borrowing requirement. In this way, discount houses engage in the relatively precarious activity of borrowing short and lending long. If discount houses cannot renew loans to balance their books at the end of each day they can approach the Bank of England as lender of last resort or try to sell some of their Treasury bills on the open market. (As lender of last resort, the Bank of England is providing funds to pay for its own Treasury bills!) Because the sale of Treasury bills is underwritten, governments have greater certainty of reducing liquidity and soaking up funds when desired. An important aspect of these open market operations is that they enable the government, through the Bank of England and the discount market, to influence *interest rates*. The discount to the face value of bills bought and sold has an implied interest rate. Interest rates on bills traded have an influence on other market rates such as the London Inter-Bank Offered Rate and these influence bank base rates. One recent change is that since October 1988 the Bank of England has been prepared to deal with institutions other than discount houses if they meet certain requirements.

A large number of other institutions and markets perform the role of bringing together buyers and sellers of money. The *parallel markets* are a recent development and provide short-term funds for a variety of specialized intermediaries and include the lending between banks and between companies, the transaction of fixed-term bank deposits known as Certificates of Deposit (CDs) and the raising of loans by local authorities. Firms needing foreign currency to pay for goods and services as well as individuals going abroad require currency and this is obtainable on the *foreign exchange market*. The *London International Financial Futures Exchange* enables transactions to occur today to purchase finance at a fixed price on a future date. *Merchant banks* are prominent institutions in the City of London. Though their traditional role is that of accepting bills of exchange and providing assurances that they will be paid, today they engage in money markets, provide finance for companies, deal in bullion, arrange shares to be underwritten and so on. London now has around 500 *foreign banks*, British banks with *overseas head offices* and a number of *consortium banks* comprising interests from different banking institutions. The network of financial institutions is larger than it has ever been. Deregulation in the form of the Big Bang has led to more competition in securities in the marketplace and successive privatizations and the subsequent publicity have led to an increasing awareness of the respective roles of life assurance companies, pension funds, unit trusts and building societies.

Case Study—Big Bang in Britain's high street

Deregulation, scatter-gun expansion, devilish competition, skin thin profit margins, job losses. Sounds familiar? Right. Everything that happened during and after Big Bang in London's wholesale securities markets is about to be replayed in Britain's retail financial markets. Banks, building societies and insurance companies are competing keenly in each other's territory. So, too, are mortgage companies, high street stores and credit-card firms. Once again the new world will be painful for many of these firms; but consumers will gain.

Everybody, it seems, wants to be everything to all men. For example, Commercial Union, an insurance company, has bought the private client a bit of Quilter Goodison, a stockbroker; Lloyds Bank now owns a chain of 500 estate agents; Save & Prosper, a unit trust group, has launched its own credit card (charging lower rates of interest than most others). Royal Life, part of the Royal Insurance Group, sells unit trusts and mortgages and owns an 800-branch estate agent.

Under a new law, building societies can do more than simply finance house purchases. Most now sell insurance; several, e.g. the Halifax and the Leeds, provide unsecured personal loans and credit cards; two offer interest-bearing current accounts; the Cheltenham and Gloucester sells shares.

Britain's big high-street retailers are also muscling in. Marks and Spencer, a department-store group which already makes personal loans, unveiled an in-house unit trust this month. Burton, a clothing retailer, offers mortgages and insurance to its 2.5m cardholders; its six share shops, which nestle inside its city-centre stores, have 20,000 regular customers. The retailers apply the same policy to financial products as to clothing; they farm out production to 'manufacturers', concerning themselves with the packaging and marketing. The advantages are both trusted brand names and friendly premises.

(*Source: The Economist.*)

The circular flow of income

In order to achieve macroeconomic objectives, governments constantly influence the economic environment in which organizations operate. Businesses need to be aware of such changes and the ways in which they might affect their levels of performance. The economy of any country comprises a highly sophisticated network of variables and reaching a state of perfection is just not possible. Government policy towards resolving any form of problem or towards any change in the system will depend upon its priorities and this might lead to emphasis being placed upon certain objectives at the expense of others. Economic objectives can be grouped into the following five broad categories:

1. *Economic growth* Governments aim to increase the well-being of their country's inhabitants. By increasing real incomes, living standards improve and this is what is known as economic growth. To obtain economic growth the productive capacity of the economy has to be increased so that more goods and services are produced nationally.

2. *Stable prices* Over recent years the control of inflation has been a government priority. Rising inflation rates destabilize the economy and create an environment of uncertainty for business.

3. *Full employment of resources* Unemployment refers to productive resources such as labour, machines and land which are not being used to produce goods and services. It results in a lower standard of living than would otherwise be obtained. For labour it can become a cause of stress, hardship and worry and can lead to deprivation and political unrest.

4. *Equilibrium in the balance of payments* The balance of payments records a country's trade and capital transactions with the rest of the world. A persistent deficit withdraws income from an economy and drains reserves. Trying to overcome this problem might affect a government's ability to achieve other economic objectives.

5. *An equitable distribution of income* Few of us would like to live in a country of contrasts where incomes are widely distributed and where poverty exists. Governments are concerned about differentials between areas, different types of employment and groups of workers. They aim to eliminate unfair practices and hardships by intervention into the economic system to create greater equity.

National income

The link between consumers and producers is shown in Fig. 16.2. Individuals offer

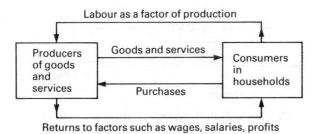

Figure 16.2 A simple economic model.

their services as factors of production and, by working or investing, receive wages or salaries or profits. This income enables goods or services to be purchased from producers. The workings of this simple economic model and the way in which it allocates resources will depend largely upon the type of economic system operating in a country.

National income comprises the total flow of these goods and services produced by factors of production over a given period of time. When national income rises economic growth takes place in the system and this leads to a better standard of living for that country's inhabitants. Not only can figures measuring national income be used to assess living standards, they are also capable of being broken down to show changes in the structure of the economy as well as to provide economic comparisons with other countries.

National income accounting provides three methods of measuring wealth creation:

1. The *income* approach measures the incomes of individuals from employment and self-employment, interest, business profits and incomes from rents.
2. The *output* method assesses the sales or output values of organizations.
3. The *expenditure* approach measures expenditure on goods and services. Final expenditures on goods and services are added together. Intermediate expenditures on raw materials and components are excluded. Thus double counting is avoided.

We refer to all three methods as national income accounting because they each provide the same result, but, by using different techniques. In a small enclosed community, people will sell their output to provide their income. If everything is sold the value of their output equals what has been spent so expenditure equals output. The money received by producers will provide their incomes as well as incomes for their employees and other producers from whom they buy inputs. Incomes will therefore match expenditure.

An *equilibrium* level of income for any country is one which does not change from one time period to another. If all goods and services are bought and all incomes are spent, a country will be in equilibrium (see Fig. 16.3). A disturbance in the equilibrium position would take place if there were a new *withdrawal* from or a new *injection* into the circular flow of income. In order to understand the workings of the more

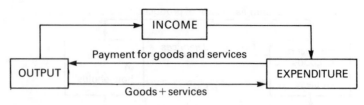

Figure 16.3 The equality of income, expenditure and output.

NATIONAL OUTPUT = NATIONAL INCOME = NATIONAL EXPENDITURE

complex economy and relate our work more closely to reality, these have to be examined.

Injections and withdrawals in the more complex economy

Much of our understanding today of the complicated forces which govern the workings of the UK economy is derived from the work of John Maynard Keynes whose work took place during the high levels of unemployment in the 1920s and 1930s. Keynes argued that demand and supply analysis could be applied to macroeconomic activity and this would determine government jurisdiction. He showed that the level of output and employment resources depended upon the following:

1. Total demand for goods and services in the economy (aggregate demand).
2. Total supply of goods and services in the economy (aggregate supply).

As with microeconomic supply curves, the aggregate supply curve will slope upwards from the bottom left as the economy increases its output towards higher prices, but there will always be a limit to supply and this is where the factors of production are fully employed. At this point the supply curve will be vertical at the current state of technical progress. The aggregate demand curve will slope downwards from the top left because, as prices fall, total demand for goods and services will increase (see Fig. 16.4).

The actual level of national income (Y) is where the aggregate supply and aggre-

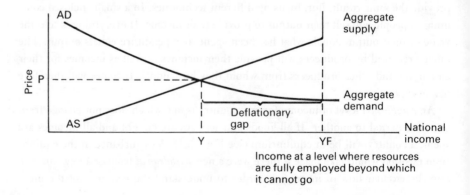

Figure 16.4 The deflationary gap.

gate demand curves intersect. The difference between the equilibrium national income and the full employment position shows the extent to which it is possible to expand national income to minimize the unemployment of resources. This difference between national income and the full employment position is known as the deflationary gap.

Instead of resources being underemployed, there could well be a situation whereby resources are fully employed and increases in aggregate demand put considerable pressure upon prices. Though prices could be at P, aggregate demand is beyond the full employment level and has pushed prices up to P1 and caused an inflationary gap (see Fig. 16.5). High levels of aggregate demand cause price rises but no real change in output. If demand fell, the full employment level might still be achieved but without any form of inflation.

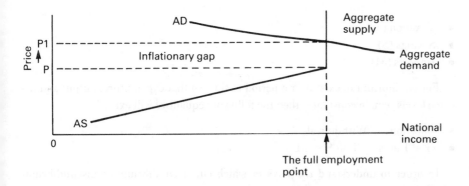

Figure 16.5 The inflationary gap.

Keynesian economists suggest that by manipulating shifts in the aggregate demand curve it is possible to change national income, change price levels and work towards the full employment of resources. Aggregate demand may be shifted upwards to the right by injecting funds into the economy or downwards to the left by withdrawing funds from the economy. If manipulation through this process of demand management causes injections not to equal withdrawals, an economy is being moved in a particular direction and disequilibrium will occur in order to achieve economic objectives. An increase in the level of injections and a decrease in the level of withdrawals will stimulate an economy and increase aggregate demand, whereas a decrease in the level of injections and an increase in the level of withdrawals will deflate an economy and decrease aggregate demand.

Injections into the circular flow of income (see Fig. 16.6) include:

- Government expenditure (G)
- Investment (I)
- Exports (X)

Withdrawals from the circular flow of income include:

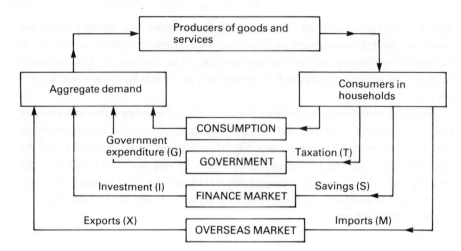

Figure 16.6 Complex circular flow.

- Taxation (T)
- Savings (S)
- Imports (M)

For equilibrium to exist over a period of time so that expenditure, output and income levels remain constant—then the following equalities will exist:

- Injections = Withdrawals
- $G + I + X = T + S + M$

In order to understand the ways in which either equilibrium or disequilibrium takes place, it is necessary to look carefully at the various components of aggregate demand to consider what affects them.

When we looked at the defects of a free-market economy we recognized a need for *governments* to intervene to overcome the defects of that type of system by providing the following:

1. *Public goods and services* These are goods or services where the consumption by one person does not reduce the amount which is available for use by others. They would include the police, defence, streetlighting and so on. As it is almost impossible to exclude anyone from using these goods and services, it would be virtually impossible for them to be provided by the private sector.
2. *Merit goods* These benefit the person who directly consumes them as well as other members of society. By having a well educated population individuals benefit and so does society. A new traffic system will mean that people can get to work more quickly and it also reduces congestion. These benefits are externalities and governments will encourage their consumption by subsidizing them or providing them free of charge.
3. *Monopolies* Governments in the past have been concerned about the provision of certain necessities by the private sector. They were worried about the likeli-

hood of private operators charging high prices and exploiting consumers. By supplying services through a government-owned corporation they were able to set minimum standards, provide a national network, reduce average costs and gain benefits from economies of scale.

4. *Income redistribution*   A vast proportion of government expenditure consists of transferring payments towards low income households. Payments of this kind might include pensions, allowances, social security and unemployment benefits.

Successive privatizations and a movement away from emphasis on the public sector were symbolic of the 1980s as government expenditure gradually decreased as a proportion of the nation's overall spending.

Investment refers to additions to the capital stock of the economy such as new factories, machinery and roads. It will include anything which adds to the physical stock of wealth. Investment or capital goods are not immediately consumed. Their purpose is to facilitate the production of further goods which are for consumption. There is a strong link between the level of savings and investment.

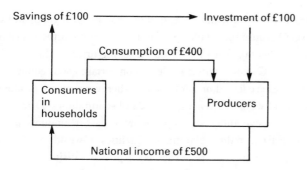

Figure 16.7 The equality of savings and investment.

In the example shown in Fig. 16.7 the injection of £100 as an investment is equal to the leakage of savings of £100 and so national income does not change and equilibrium takes place. If investment were greater than savings national income would rise and this would continue until the increased ability to save would cause the increased savings to equal the increased investment. Conversely, if savings were greater than investment national income would fall; this would cause savings to fall and it would continue until savings matched investment at a lower level of income. Thus savings will always match investment over a period of time. Firms expect to gain through investment and compare their rate of return, known as the marginal efficiency of capital, with the rate of interest their funds would earn.

Exports inject demand from outside our country and provide an injection of money flowing into our economy from other countries. By exporting, British industry has the freedom to specialize and benefit from economies of scale and a bigger marketplace. Often *imported* goods are required by consumers and payments for these goods goes outside the United Kingdom and forms part of the aggregate demand for another country. Money has therefore been leaked out of the circular flow. In an ideal world the amount of money received for exports should match money paid for imports in the long run.

Taxation enables government spending to take place. This relationship between taxes and government expenditure is often expressed as *fiscal policy* and is manipulated by the Chancellor of the Exchequer through use of the budget. Government spending injects into the circular flow of income, and taxes withdraw. The deficit budget whereby the government spent more than it took in taxes has been an important policy instrument. The public sector borrowing requirement is the amount the government must borrow each year when its expenditure exceeds its income. A surplus budget would take in more revenue than it spends and reduce demand in the economy. Direct taxes are levied on income or earnings and are paid to the Department of Inland Revenue. They include:

- taxes on income, such as income tax;
- taxes on profits, such as corporation tax;
- taxes on capital, such as inheritance tax.

Indirect taxes are levied on expenditure as part of a payment for goods and services and are called indirect because the retailer pays to the government the tax charged to the consumer. Value added tax (VAT) is levied on selling prices and is calculated at each stage of production. Customs duties are levied on certain goods coming into the country and excise duties are levied on some goods wherever they are produced. We are affected in a variety of ways by licences, car tax and stamp duties. Direct taxes are more likely to be progressive and take proportionately larger amounts away from people with more in order to reduce extreme inequalities in wealth or income. It is often argued that the progressive nature of such taxes provides disincentives to effort. Indirect taxes are generally said to be regressive as they take a larger percentage of the income of the lower paid. The cost of a television licence will probably take a significantly larger proportion of an old aged pensioner's income than that of an aspiring business executive. The main advantage of indirect taxation is that people are often unaware that they are paying them when they make purchases.

Case Study—A petrol-pump solution

Many economists agree that the easiest way for America to trim its budget deficit is to raise its petrol tax to bring it into line with rates in other countries. It looks so easy that foreigners cannot understand why Congress has not done it already.

The tax on an American gallon of petrol averages 29 cents, of which nine cents goes to the federal government, the rest to state and local governments. This is easily the lowest in the industrial world. On an equivalent quantity, motorists in Japan and most European countries pay taxes of between $1.47 and $3.20.

Each extra cent of tax on a gallon of petrol in the United States would raise roughly $1 billion in government revenue. So a 50 cent increase (phased in over three to four years, say) would reduce the $150 billion budget deficit by $50 billion before taking account of any additional indirect benefits as a result of lower interest rates. American motorists would still pay less than half the tax paid in most other countries and, although an extra 50 cent tax would lift the pump prices to about $1.50, that would still be, in real terms, a fifth lower than in 1981.

(*Source: The Economist*, December 1988.)

Questions

1. What is meant by a budget deficit? Why might it need to be trimmed?
2. To what extent would raising taxation on petrol cut back the US budget deficit?
3. Outline in full the potential economic and political dangers of raising the pump price of petrol.
4. What might be the attitude of the following to the proposed changes? (a) A US oil company. (b) An American motorist. (c) An American manufacturer.

Savings are the levels of income not used for consumption or directed towards another leakage. Over recent years the main savers have been household and business sectors and Treasury figures have suggested a 10 per cent savings ratio. Savings tend to follow interest rates and a rise in interest rates tends to raise savings.

A formula often used for expressing national income is:

National income $= C + I + G + (X - M)$

We have learnt that to move an economy with a deflationary gap towards full employment aggregate demand is expanded by increasing injections and decreasing withdrawals though some increases in prices might occur at full employment levels. On the other hand, if aggregate demand exceeds the full employment position there are inflationary pressures and aggregate demand can be reduced without affecting the output of the economy, by decreasing injections and increasing withdrawals. By looking at Keynesian theory and at the various withdrawals and injections we can understand more about strategies available for governments to pursue their policies.

Fluctuations in activity

The impact of an injection into our economic system will lead to an increase in overall income but the level of this increase might be much greater than that of the initial injection. This is because the initial increase in expenditure will have prompted an increase in other people's incomes. For example, if the government spends £50 million in the North East and workers who receive this income re-spend some of it in the North East, this will help to create further income and jobs in the area. If, in the end, total spending in the area rose by £100 million, the *multiplier* would be 2.

The rate at which consumption increases as income increases is known as the marginal propensity to consume (MPC) and the rate at which withdrawals increase as income increases is known as the marginal propensity to make withdrawals (MPW). If an injection of £200 million is made into an economy, individuals will choose whether to spend it on goods and services, and thus generate further incomes, or whether to withdraw it from the circular flow. The multiplier effect will continue to operate until no further income is generated by another round of consumption. For this £200 million, the marginal propensity to consume is 80 per cent and the marginal propensity to withdraw is 20 per cent. This means that with the initial injection of £200 million, £160 million is spent and £40 million is withdrawn.

The £160 million that is now spent will be received by households as income. Assuming that the householders again spend 80 per cent of their incomes and withdraw the remaining 20 per cent (by buying imports, paying taxes and by saving), then the next round of consumption will be £128 million. This extra spending will again be earned by households. The initial injection thus leads to successive ripple effects of further expenditure, each successive ripple being smaller than the previous one. The final change in income for this £200 million injection can be calculated by the formula:

$$\text{Injection} \times \frac{1}{1 - \text{MPC}} \text{ or Injection} \times \frac{1}{\text{MPW}}$$

The formula results in £200 million $\times \dfrac{1}{0.2}$

The initial injection of £200 million has created an increase in income of £1000 million and so the multiplier is 5. The marginal propensity to withdraw will be the reciprocal of the multiplier. Disturbances to expenditure thus have much wider total effects than the initial change.

The accelerator principle states that where there is a small change in the production of consumer goods, there will be a much larger change in investment in capital goods required to make the consumer goods. Changes in capital goods as a result of this investment will help to speed up the rate of economic growth. For example, a firm makes plastic rulers and has 100 machines in operation. As the lifespan of each machine is 20 years, five machines need to be replaced each year. If during one year, demand for rulers rises by 20 per cent, the firm will now need 120 machines in operation and so will have to buy 20 machines as well as replace five which are worn out. A 20 per cent rise in demand has caused an increase in the number of machines required from five to 25; a 400 per cent increase in demand for capital goods. If the short-term peak demand of 120 machines is not maintained, over-capacity will occur and then the accelerator works in reverse. As a result of over-capacity a decline in demand for consumer goods will result in a sharper decline for capital goods.

Many economists suggest that a combination of multiplier and accelerator theory account for the upswings and downswings of the trade cycle. As a result of multiplier/

accelerator theory large increases or decreases in national incomes occur because of small changes in consumption and investment.

Data provide some confirmation of periodic trade cycles (see Fig. 16.8). The world recession of the 1980s was predicted from the events in economic history. Different researchers over recent years have opted for different periods for trade cycles. As the actions of firms reinforce cyclical trends, by reducing investment and cutting back output at the right time they can avoid a feared depression and, by investing when an economy is picking up, they can make the most of the available opportunities. Business confidence and the anticipation of market trends is therefore a key issue.

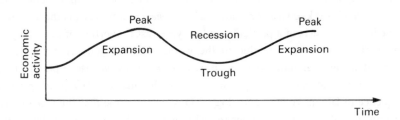

Figure 16.8 The trade cycle.

Unemployment and inflation

Though macroeconomic aims might not seem to contradict each other in theory, in practice governments have found it difficult to balance all of their objectives. The problem is that actions to achieve one objective are often at the expense of another. In particular, a restraint on government ability to control unemployment is the danger of inflation, and policies which attempt to dampen inflation do not promote employment. There are considerable differences between our two major political parties. The Conservatives prioritize inflation as the major economic problem and place emphasis on monetary policies, whereas the Labour Party prioritize unemployment and calls for a return to Keynesian policies and a greater emphasis upon demand management.

Unemployment

Though unemployment refers to the fact that factors of production are not being fully utilized to produce goods and services, we immediately associate it with labour. Unemployment exists where people are willing and able to work but are unable to find work. Figures are obtained from a monthly count of those registered as unemployed and claiming benefit at offices throughout the country and expressed as a percentage of the working population. In Britain during the 1950s and early 1960s the numbers of unemployed were around 300 000, which was less than 2 per cent of the workforce. This era was described as one of full employment as employment figures were at about the lowest which could be achieved, given that some people will be changing jobs, whether voluntarily or not, or waiting for jobs to crop up. Unemployment rose gradually during the 1960s, steadily increased during the 1970s and doubled in the 1980s. From 1979 to 1987 nearly 2 million jobs disappeared from the manufacturing sector as *de-industrialization* set in. Fundamental changes had taken place in our industrial structure. The numbers employed in areas such as mechanical and electrical engineering, textiles and construction fell dramatically while, at the same time, the tertiary sector grew. Industry responded to changes by improving technology and productivity but often by shedding labour. Areas in which certain types of industry were concentrated geographically, and which were therefore dependent upon these industries, felt the harsh realities of unemployment more than any other. This is known as *structural unemployment* as it represents the long-term decline in the products of a particular industry. A vast proportion of unemployment in the 1980s must have been due to the world recession and general deficiency in demand in almost all industries due to *cyclical unemployment* based upon the trough of the 50-year cycle. Some unemployment was undoubtedly *technological* and as a consequence of labour-saving technology. Many would argue that the fear of changing technology led many trade unions to resist change and often new developments were only accepted on the basis that the manning levels were retained. The labour force therefore contained workers who did not contribute to output. This form of *disguised unemployment* holds back efficiency and inhibits growth. Perhaps the most disturbing aspect of unemployment in the 1980s was the number of young people unable to gain employment and many policies have been directed towards this age group.

The causes of unemployment can be divided into demand and supply side factors. A lack of demand for goods and services reduces economic activity and contributes to recession. Whereas increasing spending through injections into the economy would work towards solving any demand deficiency, the Conservative Government of the 1980s used monetary policy with a tight fiscal stance and prioritized inflation at the expense of employment. On the supply side the working population has increased during the 1980s and inevitably unemployment rises and reflects its increasing size.

Case Study—Unemployment age and duration

Study Fig. 16.9 and answer the questions given below.

Questions

1. Explain briefly what Fig. 16.9 measures.
2. Why is it useful to break down the duration of unemployment when looking at statistics?

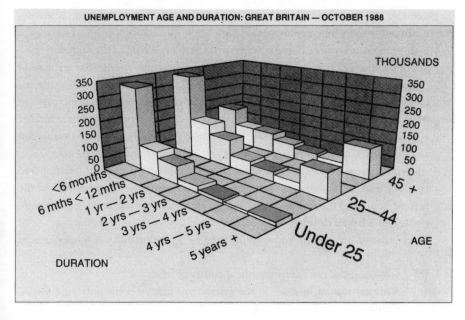

UNEMPLOYMENT AGE AND DURATION: GREAT BRITAIN — OCTOBER 1988

Figure 16.9 Unemployment age and duration. (*Source*: Department of Employment.)

3. Extract the main underlying characteristics shown in Fig. 16.9 and try to provide reasons for the trends being characterized in the way illustrated.

4. What other information would be useful?

Inflation

Inflation occurs where the general price level is persistently moving upwards, though a simple monetarist definition often quoted is 'too much money is chasing too few goods'. *Creeping inflation* is a condition experienced by most developed countries since 1945 whereby continuous but not excessive rises have taken place in average price levels. If people's expectations are based upon the past when inflation rates were low, increases in rates will be *unforeseen* but, then as inflation rates increase they will start to *anticipate* higher increases and will adjust their behaviour accordingly. If inflation then begins to accelerate and dramatic rises in price take place, at hundreds or thousands of per cent, the condition is said to be *galloping* and *hyper-inflation* takes place. In the United Kingdom prior to the 1970s high rates of inflation were linked with low rates of unemployment and vice versa. *Stagflation* developed during the 1970s as this trade-off disappeared and high rates existed side by side with high unemployment. There are three general causes of inflation:

1. *Demand-pull* is a situation whereby aggregate demand persistently exceeds aggregate supply and prices are constantly being pulled upwards. As aggregate

demand only pulls up prices when it exceeds the output capacity of the economy, it can only exist when employment is high.

2. *Cost-push* occurs where rising costs provide better rewards to the factors of production and are then passed on through prices. The *wage–price spriral* is the most dangerous feature of this type of inflation, e.g. increasing prices will cause increases in wage demands from workers and, if these do not match increases in productivity, this will represent a further rise in costs and prices and then further rises in wage demands and so on. Many largely attribute the rises in inflation rates in the 1970s to increasing oil prices and inflationary pay settlements.

3. *Monetarists* argue that increases in the money supply are a cause of inflation and that inflation can be brought under control by reducing the rate of growth of the money supply. Milton Friedman, the most famous advocate of monetarism, points out what he calls five simple truths:

    (a) Inflation arises from a more rapid increase in the quantity of money than in output.

    (b) Governments can determine the quantity of money.

    (c) A slower rate of increase in the quantity of money is the only cure for inflation.

    (d) Inflation develops over years and can only be cured over years.

    (e) Side effects are unavoidable.

Whereas the undesirable effects of unemployment are fairly obvious because it represents a waste of human resources and can lead to severe hardships, the undesirable effects of inflation are much more wide-ranging and require some further examination.

Inflation therefore affects:

*   *The distribution of income*   Inflation influences different types of income groups in different ways. Those who lose tend to have fixed incomes in money terms while those who gain tend to have commission-based incomes related to sales value. Inflation tends to encourage borrowing as loans are repaid in money which is now worthless while those who lend are concerned about whether it is worth their while to do so. Debtors therefore gain and creditors lose. Those whose bargaining power is strong are able to ensure that their salaries keep up or move ahead of inflation while those with weaker bargaining power tend to see their salaries fall behind.

*   *Expectations*   If inflation persists it will distort expectations. A society used to inflation will try to stay ahead of prices by anticipating price rises and this can lead to a wage–price spiral.

*   *Investment*   Inflation can disrupt firms' investment plans as they are put in a situation where it is difficult to predict expenditures, incomes and interest rates. Interest rates will tend to be high as a result of government policies and also so that those who lend can earn a real rate of interest and this discourages invest-

ment. The falling value of money may encourage spending rather than lending and so reduce funds for investment.

- *External effects* If other countries are not experiencing similar high rates of inflation and there is not a compensating adjustment in foreign exchange rates, home produced goods will be more expensive to foreign buyers and this will dampen export trading. At the same time imports will be more competitive with home produced goods and this could lead to balance of payments difficulties.

International trade

No country today can provide all of the resources necessary to develop fully its economic potential and satisfy the needs of its population. By virtue of its location, Britain has historically been a major trading nation. International trade has enabled it to gain from the advantages of specialization by exchanging its surplus goods for surpluses produced by other countries so that its inhabitants can then prosper from lower prices and higher living standards. Though this is of importance, international trade does increase interdependence between nations and can pose a threat to economic stability. This did not matter during the colonial period but today the benefits of international trade must be offset against losses in employment in domestic industries and can lead to arguments for protectionism.

Balance of payments

International trade involves making payments overseas for goods and services received and the receiving of payments for goods and services supplied. At the same time capital movements will have taken place with other countries. The balance of payments is a statistical device used to record both a country's international trade and movements of capital over a particular time period. Balance of payments accounts always balance as they are based upon a double-entry format so that for every plus item there will always be a corresponding minus.

In recent years the method of presenting balance of payments of accounts has changed as there is less of a need to highlight changes in reserves and so today the broad classification of transactions is:

1. *The current account* The current account comprises the visible balance which is sometimes referred to as the 'balance of trade' and the invisible balance. The visible balance is the difference between the sale of exported goods from the United Kingdom and the purchase of imported goods to the United Kingdom. As we depend on raw materials and foodstuffs, the United Kingdom usually runs a deficit on visibles though a surplus developed from 1980 to 1982 because of North Sea oil and gas but soon disappeared because of the glut in the supply of oil and increased import penetration. The invisible balance consists of services. Income earned from selling services abroad is known as invisible exports and

when we buy services from overseas we are creating invisible imports. Invisibles include such areas as interest, profits and dividends earned as a result of investments overseas, the selling of financial services such as banking and insurance overseas, transfers by private individuals, transfers by governments for areas such as overseas aid and embassies as well as tourism.

Visible exports	500	Invisible exports	400	Total exports		=	900
Visible imports	650	Invisible imports	200	Total imports		=	850
Visible balance	− 150	Invisible balance	+ 200	Current balance		=	+ 50

2. *Changes in the United Kingdom's external assets and liabilities* This section is concerned with capital movements by individuals, firms and governments. Assets purchased abroad by UK residents are considered to be an outflow of capital and are given a negative sign and this would include any increases in gold and foreign currency reserves. Investment by foreigners in the United Kingdom are considered to be liabilities and are shown by a positive sign.

Case Study—'When made in Europe' isn't

A small Nissan car factory, built just four years ago in Northern England, is posing two big questions: how much is an argument about the 'local content' of its cars being used to create a Fortress Europe against foreign manufacturers; and can the Japanese help bring manufacturing's next generation to Europe?

Mrs Margaret Thatcher may excoriate the EEC bureaucracy in Brussels, but sometimes she needs its help. Lord Young has asked the European Commission to intervene in a dispute with France over the export of Nissan Bluebird cars from the Japanese carmaker's plant in England. France says it will treat these cars as Japanese until less than 20% of the value of the car comes from components imported from Japan. Britain argues that a car with less than 40% imported components (i.e. 60% 'local content') should be considered European. The outcome of this dispute will shape both Europe's post-1992 trade policy and the type of foreign investment it attracts.

Though Nissan says it will reduce imported components to less than 20% of a Bluebird's value by 1990 the present local content of 70% sits uneasily between the British and French positions. France now counts each Bluebird against 'voluntary' import quotas which allow Japanese cars 3% of France's car market, with Nissan's share just under 1%. For the distributor of Nissan cars in France, Mr Jean-Pierre Richard, delays in delivery from overstretched French carmakers provide a prime opportunity for him to expand—if only the government will let him. There are no hard and fast rules for local content in the EEC because imported goods and components, with duty paid in the country where they first enter the Community, are thereafter supposed to be treated like local products. But recent Community practice in disputes involving local content has tended to use a 60% yardstick for determining when something is European-made.

(Source: The Economist.)

Questions

1. Why are the French expressing concern about the local content of Nissan cars?

2. Comment upon the position of Nissan with regard to:
    (a) visible imports;
    (b) visible exports;
    (c) invisible imports;
    (d) invisible exports.
3. Briefly outline the main arguments to this dispute.
4. Why is resolving it so important?
5. Explain whether your sympathies lie with the British or the French in this particular instance.

Each year countries experience either a deficit or a surplus on their balance of payments. Whereas surpluses provide an injection into the economic system, deficits provide a leakage from the circular flow. Serious problems develop if the balance of payments is in fundamental disequilibrium with persistently large deficits or surpluses over a number of years. Persistent surpluses create inflationary pressures if inflows of reserves are not prevented from raising the money supply, and will mean that the currency is undervalued. A persistent deficit will probably be more serious as it will exhaust official reserves, hinder a country's exchange rate and have serious implications for a country's ability to borrow, cause a downward fall in the exchange rate and have serious implications for a country's stability.

Exchange rates

Whenever international trade takes place there is a need for foreign exchange by at least one of the parties to the transaction. The foreign exchange market is a worldwide market providing the mechanism for the buying and selling of foreign currencies. A country's foreign exchange rate is the price at which its own currency exchanges for that of others. Every currency has many rates to reflect all other traded currencies; the rate of sterling against the dollar, the yen, the Deutschmark and so on. The foreign exchange market is a market whereby buyers and sellers come into contact and set prices according to supply and demand. In theory this provides an automatic mechanism for keeping the balance of payments in equilibrium. For example, with an adverse balance of payments, the exchange rate would fall enabling exports to become cheaper and more competitive and imports to become more expensive. This will change the imbalance and cause the deficit to subside. If the government does not intervene and allows its currency to find its value, it will not be necessary to use up foreign exchange reserves to support its value. In practice, however, this does not tend to work. Falling exchange rates increase the price of imports and, if a country is dependent upon these, this can cause severe inflationary pressures. This would be importing cost-push inflation. The cost of home manufactures would then go up and so the increasing competitiveness as a result of a fall in the exchange rate will have been offset by importing inflation. Governments therefore seldom allow exchange rates to be determined solely by the forces of supply and demand. If currencies threaten to vary too much, authorities intervene to manage the float and ensure that variations do not harm economic objectives. As we will see later, by managing the float governments have to look for alternative measures to overcome balance of payments disequilibrium and using high interest rates or imposing tariffs and quotas can be harmful to economic growth and world trade.

Case Study—Exchange rate stability

The plan to make Europe a fully integrated trading area—a 'single market'—by 1992 has revived the long-running debate about the Community's monetary arrangements. As the Governor of the Bank of England, Mr Robin Leigh-Pemberton, said in a speech this week, this re-examination has been driven by two propositions.

The single market will mean *less exchange-rate stability* in Europe. This is because the reforms are going to abolish capital controls. After 1990 people and companies will be entirely free to switch their assets between different currencies. So the balance of currency demand and supply is sure, other things being equal, to become more volatile. As a result currency prices (exchange rates) will fluctuate more than they do now.

The full benefits of the single market will be realised only if governments can achieve *far greater exchange-rate stability*. This, on Mr Leigh-Pemberton's reckoning, is mainly a matter of uncertainty about future parities. The greater this uncertainty, the greater the risk for companies which invest (in new plant, for instance) with the aim of selling more in international markets. Exchange-rate instability, therefore, is a bar to competition. As the single market emerges, and other barriers are lowered, currency instability will loom larger.

(*Source: The Economist.*)

Questions

1. Why might people and companies switch assets between different currencies?
2. How will currency fluctuations affect trade?
3. Use examples to show why exchange rate instability is likely to be a bar to competition.
4. How might other government objectives be harmed by exchange rate instability?

International cooperation

After the financial crash in the United States in 1929, the European financial crisis that followed and the abolition of the Gold Standard, countries retreated into nationalistic economic policies and erected protectionistic barriers. This just worsened the effects of the depression as economic advantages from specialization were lost. However, during this period views were changing about economic cooperation across international barriers and, though the Second World War hindered development, a conference of the major Western allied nations was held at Bretton Woods in the United States in 1944 with a brief to tackle the problem of international economic relationships. An agreement at this meeting established the *International Monetary Fund* (IMF) with the following broad aims:

1. To provide international monetary cooperation.
2. To encourage the expansion of international trade.
3. To encourage exchange stability.
4. To make resources available from a fund for members needing to correct balance of payments.
5. To lessen the extent of disequilibrium in the balance of payments of members.

The *International Bank for Reconstruction and Development* or *World Bank* was set up as an affiliate organization to the IMF in 1946 to make loans to help war-shattered countries. The *Organization for Economic Cooperation and Development* (OECD) was set up in 1947 also to administer post-war aid. Both have now turned their attention towards helping the poorer countries of the world. A significant effort to control trade was made by the *General Agreement on Tariffs and Trade* (GATT) in 1947 which attempted to limit protectionist restrictions which distorted the pattern of world trade.

In 1957 the Treaty of Rome was signed by France, Germany, Italy, Belgium, the Nertherlands and Luxembourg and the European Economic Community was born. Britain treated the new organization with distrust and continued to favour links with the USA and the Commonwealth. The aims of the EEC were:

1. To eliminate customs duties and quotas between member states.
2. The establishment of common tariffs against goods from outside the market.
3. Free movement of resources.
4. Common policies for agriculture, transport and competition.

In 1973 the United Kingdom became a member together with the Irish Republic and Denmark. In 1981 Greece also joined. Spain and Portugal joined in 1986 and expanded the community to 12 nations with a total population of approximately 320 million. The EEC is a free trade area with a common external tariff. This means that few restrictions exist between member countries but a common external tariff is paid if products enter the area. In this way the EEC is a customs union.

Common Agricultural Policy (CAP) is a prominent and severely criticized feature of the EEC. Its aims have been to increase agricultural productivity, ensure that reasonable prices are charged, provide a fair standard of living for the agricultural community and stabilize markets and supplies. Prices are supported by imposing a levy on imports and by holding up market prices of products and buying them if prices fall too low. These stocks are intended to be released if prices rise beyond certain levels. However, in practice, this has led to the build-up of surpluses and resources being wasted.

By joining the EEC Britain was consolidating its trend towards increasing its share of trade with the European market. Many feel that it is a club comprising rich countries providing each with benefits while disadvantaging others outside the community. The prospect of 1992 and the single market causes concern from many countries outside the Community over the implications of a prosperous and unified Europe.

One of the major objectives of the EEC is European monetary union: 1989 saw the tenth anniversary of the European Monetary System (EMS). This involves a system whereby exchange rates are allowed only limited fluctuations against each other. Britain has been reluctant to join this system because it has been felt that volatile exchange rates have made it disadvantageous to do so. In addition, there has been a reluctance to tie us in with a strong German mark. There is also the fear that joining a monetary system of this type will reduce the power of the British Government to manage its own economy. EMS is based upon a hypothetical unit of account—the European Currency Unit (ECU)—and members' currencies are allowed to fluctuate by plus or minus a rate determined by the value of the ECU. The prospect of a complete monetary union and the abolition of national currencies seems unlikely in the near future. Many feel that such a system poses too many questions to which the answers are not clear.

Case Study—CBI takes the 1992 challenge

Many British companies are unprepared for the Single European Market and will go under come 1992, is the verdict of a Confederation of British Industry survey. Mr John Owens, deputy director general of the CBI, said in January: 'Nearly 10 000 UK companies are sleep-walking towards 1992. Many of them will go out of business in the early 1990s, unless they start preparing now for the complete abolition of trade barriers.' He was announcing results of a sample survey which shows that among the 12 000 firms in Britain with a turnover of more than £10 million:

Only one in five are [*sic*] reviewing their strategy in readiness for the single market.
Only one in five are [*sic*] undertaking market research in Europe.
Only one in 14 are [*sic*] undertaking any language training.
Only one in 25 have [*sic*] sales agents in the European Community, and,
Only one in 100 are [*sic*] opening new manufacturing operations in the rest of the European Community.

As a remedy the CBI and 10 of its member companies have put more than £7 M into a programme to help UK Industry prepare for the coming Eurodawn.

A national 'roadshow' conference tour is taking place which is designed to cover every business aspect affecting planning for 1992. The CBI has already sold 9000 seats nationwide but there are still some available.

(Source: Your Business.)

Questions

1. What are the dangers for companies who are not prepared for 1992?
2. Comment upon the significance of the results from the sample survey.

Managing the economy

Whereas the 1950s and 1960s were periods of economic prosperity and stability, the last 20 years have been characterized by successive economic fluctuations. Unemployment has peaked at levels reminiscent of the 1930s. We have seen: massive deindustrialization; the discovery of North Sea oil; inflation reaching all-time high levels in the 1970s; severe balance-of-payments crises; exchange rate fluctuations; cutbacks in the public sector borrowing requirement as a percentage of gross domestic product. It is difficult to comment on the economy as a whole as certain elements look healthy and others are a cause for concern. We will look at the possible methods to further economic objectives and then briefly mention recent government policies.

Policies designed to influence employment

Our understanding of the circular flow shows us that unemployment takes place when leakages cause national income to settle at a point which is insufficient to provide full employment. Governments could use:

1. *Fiscal policy*   This could try to make the private sector larger so that aggregate demand would grow. A government would aim at a budget deficit by increasing spending and reducing taxation. Firms would respond by producing more to meet the extra demand and, in doing so, would employ more labour. Demand would have increased as a result of the cut in taxes as people would have more to spend and as a result of increased government spending which might have increased benefits and given those receiving them an opportunity to consume more.
2. *Monetary policy*   The price of borrowing and the ease with which loans can be obtained will be determined by restrictions on credit and variations in rates of interest and these will act as a factor determining investment and the creation of employment.
3. *Investment in jobs*   It might be possible to hire more civil servants, provide temporary employment subsidies and job creation schemes.
4. *Reducing the labour supply*   It might be possible to bring down retirement ages and encourage job sharing schemes.
5. *Incentives for industry*   In order to encourage the private sector it might be possible to provide grants, benefits and tax exemptions.

Successive governments' records on both unemployment and inflation were good between 1950 and 1970. Governments used stop–go policies which meant increasing spending to reduce unemployment and reducing spending to decrease inflation. As it was difficult to 'fine tune' the economy it was constantly subject to wide fluctuations of expansion and contraction and this created uncertainty for industry. This theory was backed up by Professor A. W. Phillips who showed that inflation fell when unemployment rose and then rose when unemployment fell (see Fig. 16.10).

The existence of this relationship suggested that governments needed to use

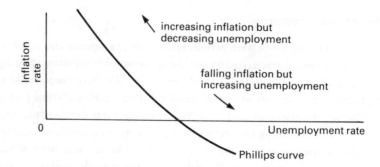

Figure 16.10 The Phillips curve.

demand management policies to achieve some point on the curve which satisfied their objectives. Inflation was therefore due to excess demand and unemployment was due to deficient demand. In the 1970s oil and commodity prices increased causing cost-push inflation with inflation rising as well as unemployment rates. Stagflation meant that the relationship formerly expressed by the Phillips curve now failed to exist. Monetarism meant very little to anyone in 1979 when a Conservative Government led by Margaret Thatcher was voted into office with an intention of introducing new economic policies and a prime objective of controlling inflation. The introduction of such policies at a time of world recession helped to increase unemployment from 1.3 million in 1979 to 3 million by 1983 though rates started to fall during the latter part of the 1980s. Policies during the 1970s and 1980s were directed through a number of government agencies promoting training schemes to provide skills to improve the employment possibilities for the unemployed. At the same time a number of initiatives helped to promote the setting up of small firms and reductions in corporation taxes were used to stimulate growth and create a demand for labour.

Policies designed to influence inflation

Views on what is an appropriate cure for inflation tend to depend upon what is considered to be its prime cause and this is an area where theorists often disagree. Policies might be directed at:

1. *Demand-pull inflation* The standard remedy for this is to pursue deflationary policies by cutting down demand within the economy. This is possible by decreasing injections and increasing withdrawals. It would be possible to do this by cutting back on public expenditure and by increasing taxes to reduce consumption.
2. *Cost-push inflation* If it is thought that inflation is arising from the wage–price spiral, policies could be directed at limiting the size of pay increases. As agreement with trade unions is unlikely to be reached without a commitment to control prices as well, this has usually come in the form of a prices and incomes policy.

3.   *Monetarism*   Monetarists set short-term goals in the form of monetary targets to limit the growth in the money supply. One method is to limit credit by moving interest rates upwards which then has major effects upon investment, savings and the balance of payments. Another method of restricting the growth in the money supply is to fund the public sector borrowing requirement and reduce its impact, by selling gilt-edged securities to the general public. In an economy such as the United Kingdom, which is dependent upon a large import trade, monetary measures to control the exchange rate by buying pounds if sterling is weak are likely to be important to avoid importing inflation.

Case Study—How to spend it

The Treasury has always had an excuse for funking the sensible tax reforms which it would love to go ahead with if only it could: money. Because governments must strive to ensure that there are no taxpaying losers, removing a silly tax exemption here means cutting a tax there, and the usual result is a net fall in revenues. Now this excuse for inaction is getting weaker.

For the moment, fears of spurring inflation still argue against a big cut in taxes next April. But the happy state of the public purse is likely to outlast those worries. With budget surpluses expected as far as the eye can see, tax reform is starting to look affordable.

(Source: The Economist.)

With the breakdown of the Phillips curve and a strongly unionized workforce used to conditions of full employment, prices and incomes policies were introduced in the 1970s both on a voluntary and a compulsory basis. Towards the end of the decade when policies were relaxed, employees tried to catch up on pay rises they felt that they had lost in previous years and this led to an increase in the number of industrial disputes and the 'winter of discontent' in 1978/79. The Conservative Government of 1979 was committed to the use of monetary policy by decreasing the size of the PSBR and through strict control of government expenditure. It believed that supply factors influenced the size of the economy and wished to see a decrease in the size of the public sector and a return to the free market. Privatization stemmed from this aim and, at the same time, brought in considerable revenue for the government. Though successful during the 1980s at controlling inflation, unemployment seems to be the spin-off of its counter-inflationary policies.

Case Study—Second thoughts on Sweden

Sweden, the archetypal corporatist state, has won a standing ovation for its switch to supply-side economics. Polite applause is more in order.

By 1991, says Mr Kjell-Olaf Feldt, the finance minister in Sweden's Social Democratic minority government, central-government income tax will no longer be levied on 90% of the wage-earning population, which will thereafter have to pay only local-government income tax of roughly 30%. The better off will still pay both sorts of income tax, but their top marginal rate will fall from today's confiscatory 72% to a merely penal 60%.

The tax plan is the most striking of Mr Feldt's ideas for reform, but it is only part of his new-found enthusiasm for freer markets. He has promised to remove all controls on foreign exchange by 1991; at present the most restrictive curbs affect foreigners wishing to invest in Swedish bonds and equities. By 1991, too, Mr Feldt promises to scrap all bilateral agreements that restrict imports of clothing and textiles. As part of a GATT settlement, he says, Sweden might scale down its protection against farm imports.

(Source: The Economist.)

Policies to influence the balance of payments

Very few countries can afford to allow a deficit on their balance of payments to continue indefinitely. Though this might be financed in the short term, in the long term a deficit can lead to serious economic repercussions. The various ways in which a deficit can be rectified can be broken down into three areas:

1. *Protectionism*   Direct measures to control the volume of imports might include the introduction of tariffs, an embargo or ban on goods from another country, quotas limiting the number of goods coming in, bureaucratic import restrictions and by making it difficult for importers to obtain foreign currency. Though these are easy to introduce, they endanger the benefits of economic welfare created by international trade. Protection by one nation can provoke retaliation which would reduce the overall volume of world trade, limit the advantages of specialization and ultimately lead to higher prices and recession.

2. *Movements in the exchange rate*   A fall in the exchange rate as a result of an adverse balance of payments would make exports cheaper and therefore more competitive and imports more expensive and this will ultimately move it towards equilibrium. If a country is heavily dependent on imports, this will lead to importing inflation.

3. *Domestic deflation*   It is possible to manipulate demand in a domestic economy with monetary and fiscal policy so that demand for imports falls. Measures such as raising interest rates, cutting government sending and increasing taxation will tackle domestic inflation and also cut back on demand.

During the stop–go period in the 1950s and 1960s periods of expansion sucked in imports and moved the balance of payments into deficit, and periods of contraction slowing growth moved the balance of payments into surplus. Fluctuations were more severe in the 1970s. During the 1980s sterling has become regarded as a 'petro currency' and we have seen balance-of-payments surpluses move to severe balance-of-payments deficits prompting harsh rises in interest rates.

The policies of any government in promoting full employment, reducing inflation and controlling the balance of payments in order to promote economic growth clearly depend upon the extent to which a government is willing to trade off between priorities. The area is complex, policies are entwined and have implications for the distribution of income and wealth and the type of society in which we would like to live.

Short answer questions

1. Why is opportunity cost an important aspect for understanding decision-making processes?
2. Name two differences between an economy geared to the free market and one where central intervention takes place. Comment briefly upon the type of economy you would prefer to live in.
3. What is a monetary policy?
4. Name two functions of discount houses.
5. Why is an 'equitable distribution of income' an objective of government policy?
6. Name two injections and two withdrawals from the circular flow of income.
7. What is meant by an equilibrium level of income?
8. Distinguish between a public good and a merit good.
9. Contrast the workings of a budget deficit and a budget surplus.
10. Name two causes of umemployment.
11. Distinguish between stagflation and creeping inflation.
12. List four undesirable effects of inflation.
13. Explain why countries trade overseas.
14. Provide two examples of a visible and two examples of an invisible.
15. Describe the danger of falling exchange rates on a country dependent upon imports.
16. Give *one* economic argument in favour and *one* economic argument against UK membership of the EEC.   (*Source:* AEB.)
17. Name two policies designed to influence employment.
18. What relationship did the Phillips curve identify?
19. Name two advantages and two disadvantages of privatization.
20. Provide two strategies available to a government to create domestic deflation.

Essays

1. 'Most internationally traded products compete more on quality than on price. Exchange rate fluctuations are relevant only in that they alter an individual importer's and exporter's profit margins.' Comment on this statement and explain the relationship between exchange rates and profit margins.
                                                                    (*Source:* AEB.)
2. Analyse the strategies available to a firm to enable it to survive a period of recession in its home market.   (*Source:* AEB.)
3. Why are some governments of western industrialized countries reconsidering the introduction of Protectionist Trade Policies? What are the main arguments for and against such policies?   (*Source:* Oxford.)

4. There is a major revaluation (+ 20%) of the exchange rate. Discuss:
    (a) the effect on the UK;
    (b) the implications for a manufacturing firm which assembles bought-in components to make its products and exports half its output. Before revaluation profit margins were equal for home and overseas orders.

    (Source: Oxford.)

5. Examine the evidence that Britain has a problem with current industrial performance. Discuss the extent to which industrial management should take the blame. Comment on the methods available to the Government to increase the country's industrial performance.   *(Source:* Oxford.)

6. With reference to at least two criteria, discuss the recent performance of the UK economy.

7. Contrast monetarist strategies with those used for demand management and comment upon their usefulness for dealing with inflation.

8. Assess the respective roles of the Bank of England, discount houses and merchant banks within the financial system.

9. What is meant by cyclical unemployment? With reference to the multiplier and accelerator, examine the role of investment upon the trade cycle.

10. Explain why governments intervene into the economy and comment upon their need to 'trade off' priorities in order to move towards achieving their macro-economic objectives.

Data response questions

1   The following tables make comparisons of employment and inflation between the United Kingdom, the United States and Japan from 1960 to 1986:

Unemployment as a percentage of the workforce

Country	1960–69	1970–79	1980–86
UK	1.9	4.3	10.6
USA	4.8	6.1	7.8
Japan	1.3	1.7	2.5

Consumer price inflation (per cent per annum)

Country	1960–69	1970–79	1980–86
UK	3.6	12.5	5.5
USA	2.3	7.1	3.8
Japan	5.4	8.9	1.9

(a) Comment upon the figures shown in the tables making particular reference to the relationship shown between the UK figures and the US figures.

(b)   Why has Japan been so successful? (Use a library to research the background to its fascinating economic success.)

(c)   What other information would help you to make a better comparison between these countries?

2   Study the following journal article and answer the questions that follow it.

Tax high on lobby list

Many of the small business lobby groups have drawn up their budget proposals to present to the Chancellor in March, in the hope of gaining the best deal for their members. Taxation it seems is the issue causing greatest concern for independent businesses.

The National Federation of Self Employed primary campaign objective is to lobby for tax incentives from the Government to assist the expansion of small businesses.

Tony Miller, chairman of the NFSE tax committee, explains: 'Priority should be given to allowing the self-employed and small business sector to retain more of *its* profits through a revision of pension provision regulations.'

Most radical of the NFSE's proposals is its recommendations that Government introduces a two-tier system of interest rates with a lower rate for commerce and industry. National Westminster Bank's chief economist, David Kern, believes this is unlikely: 'The idea of having a two-tier system is a non-starter. If you think of interest rates as the price of money, it is ludicrous to think that you can charge one group of people one price, and another group another price for the same item.'

NFSE also proposes that Standard Rate Tax should apply in the first £100 000 profits of the self-employed and that 100% Capital Allowance should be reintroduced for the first £50 000 of expenditure.

The Institute of Directors (IOD) has also addressed itself to taxation. Its proposal goes against the tide by suggesting that rather than implement a tighter fiscal policy to combat consumer spending, [the Chancellor] should reduce the overall tax burden and increase the money in our pockets.

Sir John Hoskyns, chairman of the IOD, explains: 'The call for tax increases, or a reversal of tax cuts of March 1988, is particularly inappropriate, not only because the budget is in massive surplus, but also because there were no tax cuts in March 1988 in the sense of reducing the tax burden.'

The IOD's proposals are more realistic according to David Kern, but equally unlikely. 'Though directly in line with Mrs Thatcher's view of the economy, further tax concessions are not likely. This is not to say, they will not happen in the future.'

(Source: Your Business.)

(a)   Why is taxation a major concern for small businesses?

(b)   What are the effects upon the economy of reducing the burden of taxation upon such businesses?

(c)   Why does NFSE wish to see a 'two-tier' system of interest rates with a lower rate for commerce and industry? Is this realistic?

(d)   What might be the result of the IOD suggestion?

(e)   Explain the meaning of the term 'budget surplus'.

Suggested reading

Anderton, A., *Economics: A New Approach*. University Tutorial Press, 1984.
Proctor, N., *The UK Economy*. Checkmate Gold, 1987.
Samuelson, P., *Economics*. McGraw-Hill, 1989.

17

The consequences of business

Society is made up of a large number of individuals, groups and institutions; each with its own aims and views about the way in which scarce resources should be used. Because business activity is such an important part of social relations, it will often be the subject of conflicts of interest. For example, a town wants a company to bring a new factory and its jobs; the trouble is that green fields have to be built on, and lorries add to traffic.

Case Study—Village plan divides rural community

On the southern banks of the River Tweed, among the Scottish border hills, a farmer is planning to create a village. By the time the 18-hole golf course, the 150-bedroom hotel, approximately 200 houses and the village centre are built the cost will exceed £30 million.

The development is likely to stretch over 300 acres of farmland around Cardrona, a small rural community between Peebles and Innerleithen (see Fig. 17.1).

The proposed development is causing bitter controversies in Cardrona and the surrounding communities. The fiercest argument is between those who want to retain rural tranquility and those who believe the project will breathe a new life into the local economy.

William Rae, 65, who retired from the Forestry Commission three years ago, staunchly opposes the project. He said: 'Once the complex is constructed we will just be part of a large housing estate, something we didn't anticipate when we bought this house three years ago. We bought it because it was in the country. We had no ambition to live in a town.' He doubts whether the locals will benefit from the extra jobs the development would bring.

Isabella Chalmers, a pensioner, has lived for 37 years in her end-terrace council house, set back from the Tweed across the river from the Raes. She said: 'Ask the majority of people round about here and they will tell you the same thing. They live here for the privacy and the quietness.'

If the project goes ahead, a road bridge will be built a few hundred yards from her front door. She is worried about the extra traffic the development would generate. 'I just don't seen how the roads are going to cope with it.'

Michael Maher, convener of Tweeddale District Council and also the local councillor for the area, has a different view. He said: 'We have lost quite a lot of employment, and anything that's going to create employment is good for the district.'

Apart from the jobs the development itself would create, Mr Maher believes there would also be a spin-off for the local tourism industry, particularly in Peebles.

Tom Renwick, the farmer behind the project, also believes the local economy would benefit. He said: 'I genuinely feel that Tweeddale needs a shot in the arm with something big. This is one of the reasons I am doing it.'

One of Mr Renwick's three sons lives at Cardrona Mains, which will bear the brunt of the development. He intends to continue living there. Mr Renwick said he understood the feelings of people who lived around Cardrona. But he said the majority in Tweeddale were 'very much in favour' of the development.

Alistair Smith, the Edinburgh-based architect who is drawing up the plans, said: 'It is an attractive area and we are trying to maintain it. It is not in our interests to spoil it.'

(*Source:* Adapted from *The Independent*, January 1989.)

Figure 17.1 The countryside around Cardrona which could be transformed into a small village with 200 houses, a hotel and an 18 hole golf course, if plans by a local farmer are approved. (*Source*: John Voos, *The Independent*.)

Questions

1. Outline at least two perspectives which might be applied to the development at Cardrona. Why do different perspectives exist?
2. What are the likely benefits of the development? Which individuals and groups will benefit?
3. What are the likely costs of the development? Which individuals and groups stand to lose out?
4. Could the issue be resolved so that all parties feel that they have not lost out?
5. What procedures should be established to resolve the issue?
6. How do you think that the project could be evaluated in order to make a decision?

Business activity creates benefits and costs for those directly and indirectly involved with the business. Today it is recognized by many that industrial development can only be socially effective if it takes into consideration community losses as well as profits. Society as a whole has to decide what balance it wants to strike. How much pollution—even destruction—of the environment should we accept? Heavier lorries are more cost effective in moving goods; how heavy is too heavy? More factories and better roads can mean more jobs: but the price can be the loss of more farmland.

We therefore need to look at the social benefits and the social costs of business activity to get a clearer picture of net benefits.

Private benefits are all the benefits to an individual or group resulting from a particular activity, e.g. the *profits* from a business which are earned by the *shareholders*, the *wages* earned by *employees*.

Private costs are all the costs to an individual or group resulting from a particular activity, e.g. the *cost* to a *sole trader* of *building and running* a cinema.

Social benefits are the private benefits, plus all the good effects for other members of the community resulting from a particular activity, e.g. the *entertainment value* received by *cinema goers*, and the *wages* earned by the *projectionist*, *cashier* and *ice cream seller*.

Social costs are the private costs, plus all the bad effects for the other members of the community, e.g. the *extra traffic congestion*, *parking problems* and *litter left in the street* by *cinema goers*.

Wealth creation—the benefits of business activity

Wealth is the sum total of all the ingredients we have come to value as necessary for our material well-being. Comfortable houses, efficient transport, hospitals, health care and education to let us achieve our full potential: all these contribute to well-being—so everyone concerned in providing them is also helping to create our 'wealth'. We all depend on each other to create a wealthy society.

An important distinction is made between *income* and *wealth*. Income is a *flow* which is created by an individual, group or nation in a given period. For example, Citizen Average may earn an income of £15 000 in a year and Somewhereland may have a national income of £10 million in 1990 (national income will be the sum of all the individual incomes).

In contrast, wealth is a *stock*, i.e. a sum of valuables that exist at a given moment in time which are owned by individuals, groups or nations. For example, on 31 March 1990 Citizen Average may own wealth valued at £200 000 which is made up of property, money, stocks and shares, paintings and other valuables. The total wealth of Somewhereland at that date may be calculated at hundreds of millions of pounds and, in addition to personal wealth, will include business wealth in the form of buildings and equipment, and public wealth in the form of public hospitals, schools, parks and other state-owned services. In addition, we should not forget *human wealth* in the form of the skills and aptitudes of people which have been enhanced by education and training.

It is very difficult to measure wealth, because it is often hard to ascribe a monetary value to such items as human capital. In addition, as new wealth is created, some of the old wealth deteriorates in the form of depreciation. Calculations of depreciation values are highly subjective.

Many people involved in business and industry see its fundamental importance as the creation of wealth. Industry provides all the goods and services that we need. Almost everything that we see around us has been produced by industry: our clothes, homes, means of transport, our living environment—even much of our food.

Industry reacts to people's changing wants and produces the products that people are prepared to buy. Sometimes industry creates new demands for products by developing new products and marketing them. For instance, society did not know that it wanted the microwave oven. The product had first to be invented, then tested and researched. Finally, it had to be sold. When the product became popular it was obvious that it would be a commercial success but in the meantime industry had to develop the product.

Product development involves a considerable amount of risk. Many new ideas never get beyond the drawing board, while others flop after being sold for only a few weeks. In recent years a number of new newspaper titles have been launched. Some like the *London Daily News* went under within a few months; others like *Today* managed to survive after significant alterations in strategy; others like *The Independent* went from strength to strength. In May 1989 *The European* was launched with a £10 million promotional budget, and a projected initial circulation of 5–6 million. Readers of this book will be able to gauge whether the product proved to be a success or not. The success of the paper depends in part on whether the people of Europe consider themselves Europeans, and whether advertisers can be convinced to place adverts in the paper.

In modern society, products are often highly complex and may be assembled thousands of miles apart. The modern motor vehicle is an example of a product whose components are built in many different plants before being finally assembled. Workers often have only a very limited knowledge of what they are producing. In a similar way, consumers may have only a sketchy idea of how modern complex products are made and brought to market.

Industry brings together productive resources to produce wealth. In so doing it produces the following major benefits:

1. Industry provides employment. Millions of people are employed in industry and commerce. Some of them are employed in enjoyable, creative work while others work in boring, unimaginative environments where work is a burden rather than a pleasure.
2. Industry creates income. The factors of production that produce goods earn factor incomes. Shareholders receive profits, landlords receive rent, lenders receive interest, workers receive wages, etc.
3. Industry creates products. Value is added at each stage of production. Bringing petrol to the final consumer involves the addition of value at several stages— extracting oil from nature, refining and storing oil, transporting the fuel and the provision of petrol to consumers in an easy to handle form.
4. Industry improves living standards. Figure 17.2 shows that, taken as a group, people became materially better off between 1979 and 1987, and indeed most of us are materially better off today than ever before. However, in this chapter, we shall go on to consider some costs of growth such as pollution of the environment. We might question whether the modern worker in Tokyo, Lagos, New York or London is really better off with more material possessions in situations of noise, smoke and high crime figures.

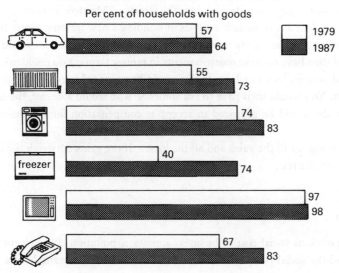

AVAILABILITY OF CERTAIN DURABLE GOODS

Per cent of households with goods

1979 / 1987

57 / 64

55 / 73

74 / 83

freezer 40 / 74

97 / 98

67 / 83

Figure 17.2 Availability of certain durable goods. (*Source*: General Household Survey.)

5. Industry makes it possible for people to enjoy more leisure. Because of industrial growth, people have more free time on their hands. Hospitals, schools, museums and the many welfare functions we have come to expect are all supported from the wealth created by businesses in the public and private sectors of the economy.

The costs of business activity

When a firm produces something it has to bear in mind a number of internal costs:

1. Production costs
2. Marketing costs
3. Financial costs
4. Administration costs

In addition to these, there are external costs, which are costs which go beyond the balance sheet of the firm. These costs are sometimes known as externalities or spill-over costs. Externalities = social costs − private costs.

An individual business will be more interested in weighing up decisions in terms of private profits or losses than in accounting for externalities. However, when a firm applies to the planning authorities or other governmental bodies for permission to put into effect a business decision, the wider social implications will be an important consideration.

At the end of the day, society benefits if resources are used in a socially effective way. It is particularly important for government agencies to employ social criteria in implementing decisions.

Cost–benefit analysis has frequently been used to weigh up government sponsored projects, e.g. to weigh up the building of a new London Underground line, the siting of the third London airport, subsidies to firms in depressed regions, even the building of fences to stop sheep from straying into the streets of Merthyr Tydfil.

In carrying out a cost–benefit analysis of building a new training centre for unemployed workers, it is necessary to find out who would benefit and who would lose out. You would then have to make measurements in money terms. You could ask someone who would benefit, how much he or she would be prepared to pay to see the project carried out. You would then have to ask someone who would lose out, the minimum sum he or she would be prepared to accept as compensation for the project taking place.

We then add up all the gains and all the losses. If the gains outweigh the losses the project passes the test.

Pollution

The most obvious social cost of business activity is pollution. We can compare the private and the social perspectives of pollution by taking the example of a chemical firm which uses a nearby river as a convenient dumping ground for untreated waste products.

If we assume that a firm sets out to maximize profits then it will carry on expanding output so long as the revenue from selling one extra unit is greater than the cost of producing that extra unit. The technical term used to describe an extra unit is the marginal unit. Let us also assume that the firm is faced with the following schedule showing the cost and revenue from producing different levels of output.

Tonnes of chemical produced	Price per tonne (marginal revenue) £	Cost to firm of producing an extra tonne (marginal cost) £
1	40	34
2	40	35
3	40	37
4	40	40
5	40	44

Given the schedule shown in the table, the firm will produce 4 tonnes of chemical in the given period. The surplus of revenue over cost from producing the first tonne would be £6, from the second tonne £5 and the third tonne £3.

However, if we are to take account of social considerations let us assume that the pollution kills a large proportion of the fish population of the river and that this seriously affects the business of a commercial fishery downstream. In order to simplify our example further we will also assume that the only way of reducing the pollution is to cut back on chemical production (bearing in mind that in the real world the firm could invest in pollution control equipment).

We can now draw up a new table which includes the cost of the pollution:

Tonnes of chemical produced	Price per tonne (£)	Cost to firm of producing an extra tonne (£)	Pollution damage to fishery of an extra tonne of production (£)	Social cost of producing an extra tonne (£)
1	40	34	3	37
2	40	35	3	38
3	40	37	3	40
4	40	40	3	43
5	40	44	3	47

The second column shows the price that the firm could get for each tonne given existing market conditions. The third column shows that it is more costly to produce larger outputs than smaller outputs—reflecting the fact that the firm has to bring into use older units of machinery the more it wishes to produce. The fourth column shows the damage to the downstream fishery's business resulting from the dumping of each extra tonne of waste. The last column shows the combined cost to the chemical firm and the fishery of producing extra units of output. If we assume that no one else is affected by the pollution then this final column will represent the marginal cost to society of additional units produced.

If we now look at the table we can see that the most socially efficient output will be 3 tonnes, rather than the 4 tonnes that would have been the case if we only considered the chemical firm. The benefits to society can be measured by the price that consumers of chemicals are prepared to pay for each tonne. These must then be weighed up against the private costs and externalities incurred in chemical production. At the end of the day we still have pollution but society will have traded off the benefits of chemical production against the social costs of chemical production.

Water pollution

It has been standard practice for a long time for industry to locate by canal, river and sea. Industries such as paper production, chemicals and breweries not only use water in the manufacturing process, but also pour out their effluent into rivers and the sea. Perhaps the most notorious example of this type of activity is the dispersal of waste products from the nuclear fuel industry. We have purification and filtration plants where water is treated, but it is difficult to break down the effects of industrial chemicals which destroy water life.

In Hungary, France, West Germany and other European countries firms are charged heavily for causing water pollution. This puts heavy pressure on firms to clean up their water.

Of course, one problem of checking on water pollution levels in order to tax firms that pollute is the cost of administering the system. In the United Kingdom, we tend to prosecute firms that break water safety laws. Fines can be imposed and imprisonment ordered in serious cases.

Air pollution

This has been dramatically illustrated by several events in the mid-1980s. In December 1984, there was a leak of poisonous gas from a Union Carbide plant at Bhopal in India. More than 2000 people died and at least 10 times this number suffered from breathing and eye complaints. The Carbide plant was part of an American multinational producing pesticides to spray on crops. Subsequent investigations have led to a questioning of safety standards at the plant.

Perhaps even more dramatic was the nuclear disaster at Chernobyl in 1986. Here we have an example of a growing centrally planned economy trying to push through the growth of new power sources rapidly. Again, the safety standards of the nuclear reactor were highly questionable. Wide tracts of land have been made uninhabitable and a cloud of nuclear waste was carried airborne across northern Europe. The rein-deer herds of the Laplanders have been declared inedible for several years, threaten-ing the ruin of a whole economy. Livestock of Welsh hill farmers was banned from sale in the marketplace because of heavy contamination.

Emissions from UK factory chimneys and power stations are recognized as major sources of 'acid rain' which results in the destruction of forests and pollution of lakes in Scandinavia and Germany. Acid rain can be described as pollution, both solid and liquid, resulting when emissions of sulphur dioxide, nitrogen oxides and ozones undergo chemical changes in the atmosphere. Reaction of these gases with moisture in the air causes sulphuric and nitric acids to precipitate as well as particles of sul-phur. A special characteristic of acid rain is its ability to travel thousands of miles from the point of emission and the United Kingdom is estimated to export about half of its sulphur dioxide to the rest of Europe. In West Germany, half of the Black Forest has been designated a 'total damage area'. Forests are an essential part of the ecosystem and important for commercial and recreational purposes. They provide employment—1.4 million jobs in the EEC alone—and, converted to wood pulp, help meet a growing demand for paper and packaging.

Dereliction

If we consider the decision to build a new mine, or to drill for oil or natural gas, we can see that this might destroy areas of natural beauty in a non-reversible way. Furthermore, when business pulls out of an area, the effects can be worse, for not only do jobs disappear but the community is also left with derelict land which is un-pleasant to look at and sometimes dangerous. These dangerous remains include dis-used railway tunnels, mine shafts, quarries and old buildings. Generally it has been left to imaginative local councils to redevelop the sites as parks, boating lakes and sites for new industry.

Traffic congestion

The development of the pace of modern business life has put enormous pressures on our road networks. In 1986, the M25 orbital road around London was opened. By the time it was made fully operational it was inadequate to meet the need for a circular road. It has been described as the longest traffic jam in Europe.

Motor vehicles cause accidents, pour out noxious fumes and are noisy. One way of calculating the cost of modern roads is to compare house prices near a large road with those of similar housing which is placed further away from the road in the same loca-lity.

Long-term waste

British Nuclear Fuels PLC reprocesses nuclear waste at its plant in Sellafield. This waste is collected from the United Kingdom's second-generation power stations. A report produced in 1986 shows that if these power stations were shut down immediately, it would take 10 years to reprocess the existing spent fuel.

Highly radioactive spent nuclear fuel is transported by road or rail in nuclear-waste 'flasks'. The resulting waste is then either dumped in the sea or buried in stores underground. It is argued that in this way we are storing up problems for the future.

Noise

This is another external effect of business. Concorde is a great flag-flyer for British airways. It is also a considerable nuisance for those citizens who live close to its take-off and departure points. Noise from road and rail traffic (see Fig. 17.3) can also be a considerable nuisance to householders.

Figure 17.3 Noise pollution and housing. (*Source*: *Grantham Journal.*)

In the United Kingdom, noise nuisance is controlled through by-laws made by local authorities covering a wide range of matters from noisy animals and fireworks to radios and televisions. People can be prosecuted for continually making noise. In the same way, the activities of businesses and construction firms are controlled and certain areas may be designated by the local authority as noise abatement zones.

Food additives

In modern society presentation and value for money are part of the marketing package of many foodstuffs. Artificial colourings and flavourings are used as well as synthetic ingredients. The medical profession has pointed out the dangerous spillover effects particularly in areas such as hyperactivity in children.

Insufficient testing of products

In order to capitalize on market leadership some firms have put products on the market without sufficient background testing. A classic example of this was the production by the Distillers Company of a drug used by women to reduce the effects of morning sickness in pregnancy. The spillover effect was the terrible side-effect of thalidomide children.

Measures to control pollution

Case Study—'Toilets of Shame'

In January 1989, the government of Singapore launched a campaign against the 'truly ugly Singaporean', a public menace whose 'filthy habits' had become 'a terrible embarrassment and a prime complaint by tourists', according to Chia Mia Chiang, head of the Environmental Health Department.

In a series of stories labelled 'Toilets of Shame', the *Straits Times* set out to reveal the extent of the problem. A journalist turned toilet cleaner, found that 80 per cent of his fellow citizens did not flush the toilet.

During the past ten years, Singapore's government has held numerous educational campaigns aimed at improving toilet habits. In the middle of 1988 it announced that anybody caught failing to flush a lavatory or urinal would be fined 200 Singapore dollars (£57). Anybody caught urinating or defecating on 'the floors and sinks' of public toilets would be fined 1000 Singapore dollars.

For those who urinate in the lifts of government-owned apartment blocks, sophisticated detection techniques have been employed. Some lifts have been fitted with urine detectors that jam lifts, at the same time activating a hidden camera to film offenders in the act. Environment officials are considering extending them to all areas where there are 'serious urination problems'.

1. Identify two distinct policies outlined in the article which have been employed by the government of Singapore to deal with 'filthy habits'.
2. What do you see as the major advantages and disadvantages of each method?
3. What alternative methods could you suggest? State your reasons to support particular measures.
4. Why do you think that the government involved itself with this issue?

5. What lessons learnt from this case study can be applied to business practice?

Dirty toilet facilities, and lack of care for other people's property, are all too common a feature of life in the United Kingdom. They are issues over which many people have strong views and areas in which they feel that offenders should be held responsible in some way. But, what about the wider issue of environmental pollution by wealth-creating activities? How should we control the costs of such activities?

Case Study—Many freshwater fish 'in danger of extinction'

More than one-fifth of all species of freshwater fish in Britain face extinction and many others will become threatened unless urgent action is taken, according to a Government-funded survey.

Several species have already died out this century, but the immediate concern should be for those rare and threatened species still in existence, fish biologists Peter Maitland and Alex Lyle said.

Their research, backed by the Government's Nature Conservancy Council, showed that British native freshwater species face a number of problems.

Rivers and lakes have become repositories for enormous amounts of waste, ranging from toxic industrial chemicals to agricultural slurries and herbicides to domestic sewage.

Acid rain has been washed into water courses and as a result fish can no longer survive in many rivers, especially those in the industrial and heavily populated lowland areas. Many rivers were devoid of oxygen and comprised a lethal cocktail of industrial chemicals, the biologists said.

(*Source: The Independent*, January 1989.)

Questions

1. Is the pollution of rivers a problem?
2. Why?
3. For whom is it a problem?
4. Who is responsible for river pollution?
5. What should be done about river pollution?
6. Who should be responsible for dealing with the problem?
7. Who should pay for the implementation of policies for dealing with the problem?

Government intervention to deal with the problem of pollution can take any of five forms: education, provision, regulation, taxation and subsidization.

The purpose of *education* is to make individuals and groups more aware of the real costs of business activity and to bring home the possible long-term effects.

State *provision* would involve the State taking over activities which generate pollution and operating them in such a way as to produce those levels of output which are most socially effective and fair. Such a policy might involve quite an extensive programme of nationalization, and would run against the trend of privatization in the 1980s.

In the real world, *regulation* is the most common form of controlling pollution. Most countries have regulations governing the disposal of waste, restrictions on smoke emissions, and rules about motor vehicle exhaust fumes. Given sufficient information, the government would be in a position to control waste-creating activities effectively. Unfortunately, information to hand is at best imperfect and subject to debate. Powerful producer groups provide convincing statistics and other information to prove that their activities do not need control, while consumer groups provide a strong lobby producing alternative statistics. In such a climate it is difficult for governments to know what types of business activity to regulate and to what extent. This is particularly true in a competitive global economy.

An alternative way of controlling pollution-creating activity is through *taxation*. Taxes can either be levied on the *quantity of a product* produced by a business or on the *quantity of effluent* produced by a firm. Taxation makes it possible to control the output of such firms. However, in order to tax firms according to the social costs they create there needs to be some way of measuring these costs. At best such measures can only be rough and ready, but they create an important principle, i.e. penalizing polluters in proportion to the harm they create.

A final measure is to provide a *subsidy* to businesses in order to reduce the pollution they cause. A firm that causes pollution could be subsidized for each unit of quantity by which it reduces its output. The firm would then consider the loss of the subsidy to be a cost of production for each additional unit of output that it produced. As with taxes, the government would need to be aware of the social cost of each additional unit of output produced.

John Day and David Hodgson have set out a table (see Fig. 17.4) to compare taxes and standards as means of controlling the creation of sulphur dioxide, which as we

Taxes	Standards
High cost of continuous monitoring of total emissions is involved to assess how much tax is to be paid.	Continuous monitoring is not necessary. Standards specify some maximum limit not to be breached and can be monitored by spot checks as sample sites.
Aids law and enforcement by the monitor providing a cumulative record that can be checked. It is less susceptible to coercion.	Enforcement can be lax if it is too informal with firms and enforcement agencies having too 'cosy' a relationship.
Encourages firms to seek new pollution control technologies to cut their tax bills.	Provides little incentive to reduce sulphur emissions at source. Firms may think that they have the right to pollute to the maximum standard set.
Setting the same rate of tax on sulphur emissions irrespective of where they occur is inefficient. Varying the tax rate is more efficient but impractical to administer.	Is administratively easier to use.
Difficult to take account of different meteorological conditions.	Can be used to restrict emissions under certain meteorological conditions or on days when pollution has already built up to danger levels.

Figure 17.4 Sulphur dioxide control: taxes versus standards.

have seen is an important ingredient in acid rain. They point out that currently sulphur dioxide emissions are controlled internationally by pollution enforcement agencies setting standards which polluters ought not to breach. The use of taxes has long been discussed as a possibly more efficient way of controlling pollution.

The authors go on to conclude that, given existing information, there is no single measure which can conclusively be pointed to as the best for dealing with sulphur dioxide emissions, and the same conclusion applies to the general control of pollution.

Case Study—Minimizing the costs of pollution

This case study looks at how decisions could be made as to how many resources should be allocated to pollution control.

Figure 17.5 illustrates three hypothetical cost curves for water pollution. The horizontal axis shows different quantities of pollution control, while the vertical axis represents costs in monetary terms. Curve A shows that the greater the level of control over water pollution the less will be the cost of damage to society caused by water pollution. Curve B shows that the greater the level of pollution control, the greater will be the cost of implementing the control policy. Curve C results from combining curves A and B to give the aggregate cost of damage and control with different levels of pollution control.

Questions

1.   What types of costs might be incorporated in curve A? Give at least six examples.
2.   What types of costs might be incorporated in curve B? Give at least six examples.

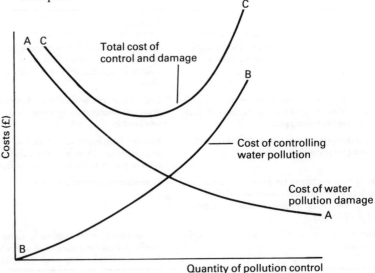

Figure 17.5 The cost of controlling pollution.

3. Explain the shape of curve C. Explain the position of curve C relative to curves A and B.
4. What would be the optimum level of pollution control? Explain your answer.
5. In your opinion, what would be the 'best' level of pollution control?
6. Why might decisions to control water pollution in the real world be more difficult to implement than theory suggests?

Case Study—Pollution control at BP

Public authorities in all parts of the world have become acutely aware of the pollution which may arise from the processing of crude oil. Some countries have already introduced legislation and all are continuously reviewing measures to control liquid or gaseous discharge to their surroundings. It is BP's policy to reduce effluent nuisance to a minimum, not only on the intrinsic merits of such action, but to improve public relations by co-operation with the authorities concerned. The oil industry in particular is able to comply with the regulations because its highly efficient processes keep waste to a minimum. Newly built refineries are equipped with the latest and most sophisticated plant for the purification of waste water and the disposal of waste gases. This plant requires much time, labour and money to develop, apply and evaluate and companies realise that if they are to keep abreast of developments in the pollution field, co-operative action is required. In Western Europe there is a large measure of such co-operation within the oil industry in dealing with pollution problems. This has been done by forming an organisation known as Stichting CONCAWE (Conservation of Clean Air and Water, Western Europe) with offices in the Hague. Stichting CONCAWE, through the activities of its working groups, aims to develop a common and authoritative view of the problems of air and water pollution (and noise) and their abatement, so that the best technical information will be generally available to the oil industry and to the many authorities with whom it has to deal.

In general, new refineries are required to achieve higher standards than those which have been operating over a number of years. These standards have to be taken into account in refinery design at an early stage in consultation with the appropriate authorities on the maximum tolerable limits of contamination.

(Source: Our Industry Petroleum.)

Questions

1. In what ways can the control of pollution be seen as a constraint limiting production decisions.
2. Give two reasons why BP might wish to control the level of pollution it creates. Explain whether these reasons are primarily internal or external constraints.
3. What evidence is given in the extract that pollution control is an increasingly costly business. What will be the implications of rising costs?

4. Would you agree with the statement that efficient industries will be best placed to control pollution? Explain your reasoning.
5. How can firms like BP benefit from collaboration in dealing with pollution?

Pressures on business

Businesses have to operate against a background in which they are faced by many different competing interests.

Internally, the business needs to make a profit for shareholders and the shareholders need to be kept content with the way the business is being run. Externally, the business has more to contend with.

1. Perhaps the biggest pressure is actually to sell its products. Consumers do not *have* to buy a product.
2. The business is faced by the pressure put on it by its competitors. Competition is often a spur to business efficiency.
3. The government and other regulatory bodies also exert pressures on business to produce within certain standards.
4. Businesses also have to respond to the influence put on them by organized 'pressure groups'.

Types of pressure group

Pressure groups do not fall readily into categories. Some groups are highly organized, with paid officials, set subscriptions and planned meetings—these groups may last for many years. Others may be 'three day wonders' being set up on the spur of the moment, lacking any real structure and vanishing as quickly as they arose.

Two main types of pressure groups are commonly recognized:

1. *Protection groups*   These are set up to fight a specific issue such as danger on a local road caused by construction traffic building a local airport. In other words, people or groups are protecting their interests against an outside threat. Other examples would include a parents' protection group set up to fight the threatened closure of their local school, or rail commuters objecting to the closure of a threatened train service. A protest meeting will usually be called at which tactics will be planned. For example, a group of commuters protesting against the threatened cut of an early morning train from Grantham to Kings Cross decided to back up their case by occupying all the toilets on the train, and by pulling emergency communication cords.
2. *Promotional pressure groups*   These are more formal groups which are sometimes highly organized and fight campaigns on a wide range of issues. Examples would include Greenpeace and Friends of the Earth. Such organizations have clearly defined, long-term objectives related to environmental concern. Their sustained

pressure on such issues as the environment has helped to create a radically new perspective to that which existed even 20 years ago. They campaign on a range of topics using measures which vary from madcap adventurist stunts (e.g. climbing up Nelson's Column to hang slogans, colliding with very much larger shipping vessels) to sustained high profile media advertising campaigns.

Promotional pressure groups for environment concern would chart their success in the large number of businesses that have begun to line themselves up behind the green campaign. For example, in November 1988 Varta introduced a 'green' range of batteries. The following week Ever Ready responded claiming that it was taking the green issue 'several steps further'.

In early 1989 Ever Ready marketed a battery in its Silver Seal line (the top selling chloride battery in the United Kingdom) which was mercury and cadmium free, using the colour green in its packaging. The development of a mercury-free battery gave Ever Ready a major advantage over its major UK competitor Duracell.

Businesses also find that from time to time political parties exert strong opposition to some of their activities, e.g. their record of paying low wages, or supplying components to socially undesirable products. For example, in January 1989 two West German firms faced strong criticism from all major political parties in their country, as well as international condemnation, for supplying equipment to a plant producing chemical weapons in Libya.

Consumer pressure groups

A well-known and powerful consumer group is the Consumers' Association, which produces the magazine *Which?* The group is funded by subscriptions from members who buy the magazine. The Consumers' Association uses its funds to test a wide variety of produts on which it then produces reports in its monthly magazine. It also produces books on consumer-related matters.

The influence of the Consumers' Association goes beyond its publication of *Which?* because its reports are frequently reported in the national press. Consumer programmes also get a fair amount of time on national television, the most famous being Esther Rantzen's 'That's Life'. Typical media coverage involves the investigation of complaints, and the comparison of goods and services.

Nationalized industries also have consumers' councils, examples of which are the Post Office Users' National Council for the Post Office and the Central Transport Consultative Committee for British Rail. The government makes provision for the continuation of these groups when industries are privatized.

Consumer boycotts

Consumers are sometimes organized into groups to stop buying certain products. In 1986, Barclays Bank sold off its South African subsidiary. Throughout the 1970s and 1980s opponents of apartheid put pressure on Barclays' customers to use other banks.

It is arguable that this sort of pressure helped finally to influence Barclays' decision.

In a similar way, animal-rights campaigners were encouraging customers to boycott Boots in 1989 because of the way it used mice in drugs testing. The following extract is taken from one of their leaflets:

ANIMAL TESTING OF BOOTS DRUG BRUFEN

Mice were injected with a substance, carrageenan, to induce pain and swelling; Brufen was then given and the effects noted. Not satisfied with this, the unfortunate mice were placed on hot plates, and 'writhing tests' with and without Brufen were conducted. Dogs were addicted to morphine and then deprived of the drug until withdrawal symptoms became apparent. Brufen was then administered to see if the symptoms were eliminated. Standard tests were carried out on dogs, rats, mice and monkeys—the lucky ones at the top dosing levels died quickly—others endured gut damage and ulceration before being put to death.

(*Source: Brufen Clinical and Technical Review*. The Boots Company Limited.)

Please write for further information if you would like to know more about how Boots use many thousands of animals in experiments every year, or how they have used the courts to silence opposition. More about a healthy approach to life which does not involve prescription drugs, cruelty to animals, or human suffering, is available from the address on this leaflet.

TAKE THE FIRST STEP NOW
DON'T CONTRIBUTE TO CRUELTY – DON'T BUY THEIR PRODUCTS

DON'T BOTHER WITH BOOTS

✂ --

Please send me further information about Boots, and how I can help stop animal cruelty

Name_____

Address_____

_____ Donation_____

NOTTINGHAM ANIMAL RIGHTS CONFEDERATION
180 Mansfield Road, Nottingham

Figure 17.6 Part of a leaflet produced by an animal-rights group.

At the same time as trying to draw the public's attention to companies that they believe to be cruel to animals, animal-rights groups also try to publicize businesses which are not cruel. For example, the 'Choose Cruelty-Free' campaign was launched in 1987, in order to highlight the suffering of animals for cosmetics testing and production. Most importantly, it was also aimed at offering consumers a choice in the products that they purchase. A list was drawn up and publicized, showing companies that had not tested their ingredients or finished products on animals in the previous five years.

As an extension of these activities sabotage has been used as an extreme form of protest against some forms of industrial production. For example, just before Christmas 1988, fire bombs were placed in several department stores that sell furs. The bombs were placed by the Animal Liberation Front, and one store in Plymouth was gutted, causing millions of pounds worth of damage, as well as the threat of job losses. Within the area of animal experimentation in the food, chemical and drugs industries, there are several animal-rights protest groups (each with its own way of protesting) including the Animal Liberation Front, and the National Anti-Vivisection Society. Quite clearly this can cause adverse publicity for businesses operating in this area and raise operating costs. Animals have been freed and premises attacked and businesses have had to spend money on the employment of security, such as the specialist security firm Control Risks which specializes in risk assessment and kidnap negotiations.

Local lobbying

There are many reasons why local residents may want to put pressure on a business to change its operations including:

- Traffic danger
- Emission of fumes
- Emission of fluids
- Litter and noise
- Safety hazards such as tips, pits, etc.
- Threats to local employment.

Normally, a pressure group will develop out of protest meetings and letters to the press. The pressure group will then try to encourage the firm to change its policy, or put pressure on local authorities to force the firm to change its policy. The issue may be taken further, with letters to the local Member of Parliament, and attempts to interest national groups in supporting a campaign. At the highest level local issues may come before the notice of Parliament, the national press, and the courts of appeal. For example, disquiet over the safety of nuclear power stations has frequently developed from a local to a national issue.

Enlightened firms will try not to antagonize local feelings, which brings adverse publicity for the business.

Other organized pressure groups

Sometimes groups run themselves in a highly organized way to influence public opinion. They will try to get a wide number of people to accept their views in order to exert pressure on the business community. Trade unions use this method of persuasion quite often. Groups like the teachers, the seamen, and the post office workers have used national advertising to try to win support from the public and from political parties for their cause. Picketing and industrial action are other ways of trying to put pressure on business.

The employers' organization, the CBI, and the unions' organization, the TUC, also exert influence. An example of this was a report published by the TUC in January 1989, circulated to businesses, trying to encourage safe practices at work.

Other promotional groups, such as the campaign for lead-free petrol and the anti-smoking lobby, use similar techniques. Sometimes groups use less peaceful methods to impress their views on the public. Demonstrations, protest marches and sit-ins often lead to publicity on television and in the press.

If a pressure group can gain the support of a political party this will give it greater weight and influence because it will then have the implicit support of a large section of the electorate. It will also have reason to believe that should that party become the government, then its aims will be realized in some measure.

Business responses to pressure groups

There are a number of ways businesses can respond to pressure groups.

1. It can ignore them, using the argument that consumers can choose whether to buy the product, and in the meantime make sure that production takes place within the bounds of legal requirements.
2. It can run a counter-campaign to win public support. This is the policy which has been used by British Nuclear Fuels PLC. 'Come to Sellafield. Look around the place. See for yourself how safe it is.' This, loosely paraphrased, is the message of a multi-million pound advertising campaign which has been commissioned by British Nuclear Fuels. The campaign is appearing on television as well as in newspapers.
3. It can take advice from consumers in order to compromise and win public support in this way.

Case Study—'Are Greens good for you?'

Today 'green consumerism' is being taken seriously. Read the following extract and answer the questions that follow it.

> Retailers have to ascertain the efficiency and cost of new green products, perhaps trading off maximum profits against a good reputation for greenness. For example, organic fruit and vegetables account for under five per cent of Safeway's sales in that area but the company has persisted in giving it valuable shelf space and has given lunch boxes and salad packs of such produce trial periods. In Tesco the number of stores selling organic produce has been upped from an initial eight to roughly thirty. The selected stores tend to be in residential areas where shoppers are more likely to be able to afford an extra ten to 15 pence per pound for organics.
>
> Biodegradable packaging is viewed favourably. Off-licence chain Victoria Wine and Safeway won plaudits at a recent Design Council exhibition for offering recycled paper bags at the checkout in favour of plastic bags.
>
> Tesco (now one of the largest independent petrol retailers in the country) has decided that all its 80 outlets that sell petrol will stock unleaded petrol by the summer of 1989. Currently, however, a store manager can complain that the one

pump provides a much smaller return than a four-star pump—it's a game for the long term, but at least motorists will know one outlet for unleaded.

The supermarkets also have the problem of supply and demand. The market for green products has heretofore not been big enough. It is unlikely that it could cope with a sudden surge in demand. Tesco reckons that if one per cent of its fruit and vegetables were to be organic, demand would outstrip supply. As devotees of BBC Radio's The Archers will know, it takes a farm two years from starting out on organic production before its goods can be labelled as organic by the Soil Association. This process adds a further hiccup in the supply chain. Standards have to be doubly exacting as organic produce can be more susceptible to disease.

There is also a time lag between consumer and manufacturer awareness. The CFC debate crept up on people. Many manufacturers thought that it would remain a fringe issue.

'Increasingly, the greenness of a product will have to be considered within the production, the packaging and the marketing efforts,' says Sheila Moorcroft, a market research analyst looking into future social trends. 'If one product is less environmentally sound than another, then people will choose the better. And, for manufacturers, it will be cheaper in the long run to avoid environmental controversy.

'Companies must think about their vulnerabilities,' Moorcroft adds. 'They may see this as negative but benefits can come out. Companies must ask: what are the risks in our products and/or our production? Where are there alternative possible solutions? If there are no alternatives, how do we respond? And what are our communications strategies as a contingency arrangement?

'Manufacturers must assess their existing product. Is the target audience one that is likely to be concerned about environmental issues? Is it environmentally friendly, and can problems be ironed out or modified?' She warns about a headlong rush into greenness. 'You have got to be sensible and commercial. Do not assume that being green is essential. In some areas it could be irrelevant. In other areas, such as health care or food products, there could be significant competitive advantage to be gained.

'Green consumerism is making an impact on exports to other European countries,' she adds, 'and it will grow to be a major influence. And if European manufacturers already have environmentally friendly products then they may begin to make inroads over here. It is vital that indigenous manufacturers seize on the opportunities in the UK market.'

There are hoops through which any manufacturer must jump before gaining that competitive edge, and they are not just in the adapting of the manufacturing process. There are matters of labelling and legislation. Already phrases such as 'ozone friendly' and 'cruelty free' are appearing on products. The Soil Association has its recognised stamp for approved organic produce. There is a danger that the consumer will simply be blinded and confused by the profusion of claims and symbols.

One of the trickiest aspects is reading and anticipating which issues will be picked up by the consumer.

The CFC battle has been fought—aerosol manufacterers and fast food chains, highlighted as the principal commercial culprits in the depletion of the ozone layer have changed their ways.

The environmental pressure groups are switching their attention. Motor manufacturers Ford and Peugeot have been at the end of stinging attacks over policies relating to cleaner engines. There are also likely to be major changes in the detergents market; phosphates, bleaches and enzymes—ingredients in washing powders and the like—are all under scrutiny.

(*Source: The Director*, January 1989.)

Questions

1. Choose any one environmental issue mentioned in the case study and explain how it might bring pressure to be applied to manufacturing processes.
2. In what ways does environmental concern put pressure on retailers both from a demand and a supply side?
3. What questions might a manufacturer wish to explore before altering production to meet demands from the environmental lobby? Illustrate your answer by exploring the issue of the use of chemical fertilizers in agriculture.
4. What factors might discourage farmers from changing to organic farming?
5. In what type of product areas is 'greenness' most likely to give a competitive edge?
6. What are the costs and benefits to (a) manufacturers, (b) consumers of the reduction in the use of CFC gases?
7. How do pressure groups operate to create an environmental concern? Examine the strategy used by a particular environmental pressure group, e.g. Greenpeace. How effective is it?
8. What is meant in the case study by the statement: 'You have got to be sensible and commercial.' Do you agree with this statement?

Employment and unemployment

Another consequence of business is the creation and destruction of employment. There are more people working in the United Kingdom today than ever before as a consequence of the rise in population. Business has continually to expand to take on extra people. At the same time, the sorts of skills required are constantly changing. Almost 70 per cent of the employed and self-employed in Britain now work in services.

The latest 1987–95 forecasts from the Institute for Employment Research, and other sources, suggest the following employment trends:

- Strong growth in numbers in all professional occupations is expected, particularly between 1987 and 1990; demand for information technology specialists is likely to be very buoyant especially for software and networking skills.
- Managers, engineers, technologists and other professionals are expected to make

up a greater proportion of the workforce in engineering and other production industries.

- Technological change, including use of new materials, components and manufacturing processes points to the importance of keeping engineers and technologists up to date.

- Management jobs are expected to grow, reflecting growth in numbers of small firms.

- In the service sector, an extra 800 000 jobs are forecast in hotels and catering by 1995; 600 000 jobs in business services also by 1995; and 150 000 in distribution by 1992. Growth is expected to be concentrated within small firms; many of these jobs are likely to be part time.

- Engineering craft occupations are likely to contract, reflecting automation. In many manufacturing companies existing engineering craft skills are being upgraded or broadened to support more flexible working and the wider use of new computer controlled equipment.

- Fewer jobs are expected at operative level across manufacturing industry.

- Strong growth is anticipated in demand for construction workers at all levels. There is concern that existing reported shortages at craft level could worsen, particularly as fewer young people will be available for initial training in the 1990s.

At the same time, many jobs have been lost in agriculture and mining. The United Kingdom's manufacturing base has been steadily declining for a long time. In the 1950s, exports of manufactures were three times bigger than imports. Today, we import more manufactured goods than we export. Some of the factors which have been used to account for this deterioration include low quality and an over-concentration on producing low-value products which many other countries now also produce.

Unemployment can be seen as a consequence of the failure of business to keep up to date. In a survey of products developed in the latter half of the twentieth century, Japan's Ministry of International Trade and Industry (MITI) found that Britons were responsible for 52 per cent of what were termed revolutionary ideas. The Americans had come up with 22 per cent, while the Japanese produced only 6 per cent. But when it came to product development this order was reversed. A number of UK commentators have pointed out that industry is not spending enough on research and development to bring new products and processes to the market.

A contrasting view of modern unemployment is that it is a consequence of new technologies. A recent report by the West German Kommerzbank estimated that every robot employed in industry today replaces three workers on average, and that by the early 1990s the second generation of 'intelligent' robots will each replace between five and ten workers in certain assembly jobs. In the service sector too, job losses are being felt, as with CHAPS (a new automated way of clearing cheques in the City of London), which has already made the activities of 8000 messengers unnecessary. Whether information technology will create more jobs than it causes to be lost is subject to debate. If the microchip revolution makes us more competitive we should actually create more jobs than we lose, particularly as we move into the open market of the European Community.

We can thus see that the relationship between business development and unemployment is a complicated one. What is clear, is that in the United Kingdom today a higher level of skill is required in workers.

In the early 1980s, for every 100 unemployed general labourers there was one job vacancy. For every 100 unemployed electronic engineers there were 87 vacancies. As a rule of thumb, higher levels of skill are being required in both factory and office, and people are expected to have a wider range of skills.

A further problem is that regional imbalance is a consequence of the way that business locates in profitable areas and later abandons these areas if locational advantages decline. Firms might choose locations in East Anglia and the South East on the basis of private costs and benefits. However, the greatest benefits to society might be reaped from locating in an unemployment blackspot like Central Scotland, South Wales, the North East, the North West or Northern Ireland. (This argument could be contested by the view that the highest level of net benefit will be achieved by allowing areas with the greatest advantage to expand, while ineffecive labour and other resources are shaken out of less effective areas.)

For much of the 1980s school leavers formed the age group with the highest rate of unemployment, although this trend is being put into reverse by demographic changes. Other groups who have been particularly hard-hit are older workers and those in racial minority groups.

Business and communities

Centres of population develop around work. As these centres become established, a community comes into being. Very strong communites develop where people share similar jobs, working together and experiencing similar lifestyles. Mining communities, farming communities and sea fishing communities, for example, are well known for the strong bonds that tie people together.

In modern society, people tend to move further to get work, change work more frequently, and modern housing estates are characterized by people doing a wide range of different jobs. Inevitably this tends to reduce the bonds that hold people together.

Conservation

Modern business depends on the use of non-renewable resources, particularly in the use of energy. Modern technology is particularly dependent on three main fossil fuels—oil, coal and natural gas. Together they account for over 90 per cent of the world's energy supplies.

A non-renewable resource is one of which only a limited stock exists (not necessarily totally discovered) on the planet of which no new stock is being created.

Some commentators are very worried about the way in which non-renewable resources are being used up. D. H. Meadows and his associates, in their book *The Limits to Growth*, argue that if resources continue to be used up in the way they are today, then within the next 100 years a crisis will occur because certain resources are limited, namely:

- Arable land
- Coal
- Oil
- Aluminium
- Copper
- Iron
- Other minerals

The problem of conservation is both a national and an international one. Businesses are more concerned with relatively short-term profits than with the future of society. Multilateral agreements have been signed between countries limiting whaling and fishing. On a national scale, governments have used subsidies as a means of encouraging farmers to preserve hedgerows and use more traditional methods of farming. Commercial farming has tended to encourage farmers to use chemicals as pesticides and fertilizers to increase yield per acre. Pollution of water by nitrates has increased since the Second World War as farmers have ploughed more and more fertilizers into the land. This is particularly true in areas of heavy cereal production. Rain has then washed the chemicals into the water supply. The Wildlife and Countryside Act has provided scope to compensate farmers to encourage them to consider the environment rather than simply to aim for profit.

In many areas of production and waste disposal there are opportunities to use non-renewable resources sparingly and to recycle renewable and non-renewable resources. For example, there is a strong case for recycling glass on both environmental and financial grounds. Recycled glass melts at a much lower temperature than do the raw materials of new glass. Also, less energy is required to collect, process and deliver the glass from a well-organized recycling scheme than to produce and deliver an equivalent amount of raw materials. To make 1 tonne of new glass requires 12 tonnes of raw materials, or just 1 tonne of broken glass (known as cullet). In all, each tonne of cullet added to the furnace means savings of about 30 gallons of fuel oil.

The procedure of quarrying for sand and limestone uses a lot of land, so substituting cullet for those materials saves countryside. Every tonne of bottles and jars recycled means a tonne less rubbish to be disposed of, so less land is taken up by landfill.

Far from being a drain on local resources, glass recycling schemes can be profitable ventures. The costs of rubbish disposal by landfill in Britain, particularly in cities, are extremely high. While in a rural area the cost may be only £3 per tonne, this rises to £15 per tonne in a large town and up to £23 for some London boroughs, not including the cost of collection.

Over the last few years, report after report has stressed the gravity of world utilization of resources. One of them, Global 2000, concluded that we face a world 'more polluted, less stable ecologically, more vulnerable to disruption than ever before'.

Ethical behaviour of business

Though the media often inform us about highly successful business activities, we are also told about questionable activities. We hear about events such as insider trading, animal rights protesters involved in disputes with cosmetic and pharmaceutical companies who use animals for testing the effect of drugs and cosmetics, protests over tobacco companies sponsoring sporting events, protests about trading with South Africa and so on. As a result of this attention we are becoming increasingly aware of the influence of ethical and moral values upon business decisions. Views about what is or is not ethical vary considerably and this chapter has already covered a number of ethical issues in its analysis of the consequences of business. A recent *Which?* survey found that 63 per cent of respondents to one of their surveys were concerned about the activities of companies they might invest in. Business ethics is clearly becoming an area of growing concern (see Fig. 17.7).

Ethics are moral principles or rules of conduct which are generally accepted by most members of a society. An ethic is a guide to what should be done or what should not be done. It involves what one believes to be right or what is considered to be wrong. From an early age parents, religions and society in general provide us with moral guidelines to help us to learn and form our ethical beliefs. Many ethics are reinforced in our legal system and thus provide a constraint to business activities while others are not. In areas not covered by law, pressure groups often form to put forward their case.

An area of particular concern over recent years has been that of 'insider dealing'. This is where someone who is knowingly in possession of unpublished, confidential, price-sensitive material, which is often acquired illegally, uses it to gain an advantage over others in share dealings. Information might have been passed on by a company employee, by careless tongues or even from directors. The Guinness affair has brought this type of issue into the limelight. Though directors or company employees are privy to confidential information, which is often not of the nature to be made available to large numbers of shareholders as it might lose competitive advantages, they clearly have a duty not to exploit the convenience of their position to their own advantage. The Companies Act of 1980 supports this principle by making it a criminal offence, punishable on conviction with the possibility of imprisonment for up to two years, for individuals to deal in securities if they have 'insider information' which affects the value of these securities.

Another aspect of business ethics concerns the level of dedication to the profit motive. Should the desire of a business for larger profits be moderated by a sense of responsibility to the society in which it exists? Companies such as 3M who introduced the 3P philosophy of 'Pollution Prevention Pays' have had ambitious corporate policies over recent years and recognize that they have a responsibility to the society in which they exist. This issue is really a matter of degree dealing with the extent to which businesses are concerned for the community. For example, should they invest only in areas of high unemployment? Should they forfeit trade with South Africa? To what extent should their products be rigorously tested? How far should they consider the welfare of employees? Do they encourage trade unions? Should they make contributions to political parties? Should they deal with companies involved with producing and selling alcohol and tobacco? The list of these types of issues is almost endless. 3M has a goal to be a good corporate citizen and, in being so, would probaly argue that they try to be socially responsible whilst, at the same time, pursuing profit.

Case Study—Bangers Sausages Limited

Bangers Sausages Limited is a small sausage factory employing 30 people, situated in the heart of an area of high unemployment. The company is doing well and looking to expand, which will probably mean moving away from its existing location.

Express your views on each of the following problems facing the Board of Directors:

Problems

1. Whether to move away from the area of high unemployment in order to obtain cost advantages.
2. Whether to make the sausage more healthy by reducing the fat content and pushing up prices.
3. Whether to purchase an incinerator for waste products which only just meets the necessary health and safety requirements for waste disposal, or whether to consider an alternative form of disposal.
4. Whether to promote the company as an equal opportunity employer.

A frequently debated aspect of business ethics refers to a company's actions where there is no law or where the law is unclear. For example, if there is no law forbidding a particular action, should a company pursue that particular course if it is ethically dubious? There is an example of an American corporation which discovered that it was more cost effective to pay compensation to injured employees than to invest in research to improve safety.

Today business ethics is at the forefront of the industrial debate. We are concerned about living in a better society and if this is to materialize, many people believe that ethics must play an important role.

Case Study—Morality in business

The new morality of business that says 'catch me if you can'

William Rees-Mogg on the significance of the Queen's warning to the City

Even goldfish find it hard to live in a gold-fish bowl; it can be no easier for the Royal Family. The glass bowl of personal publicity in which they live is bathed in the arc lights of television. They are given too little room to breathe freely; in particular the younger members of the Royal Family are allowed little freedom to be young. Those who are trained for this life find it, I suspect, difficult enough. Those who marry into it must find it virtually unbearable. Most of the publicity is trivial, and some of it is malicious.

The tabloid Press is beginning to hint that there is a problem about the Royal Family, but if so it is of their own making. Too much publicity is damaging; drivelling publicity is absolutely damaging. *The Sun*, in particular, is quasi-republican, an attitude which strangely contradicts its fervent nationalism.

This false publicity, which all the members of the Royal Family must resent, is matched by a widespread failure to report the serious business which they conduct so unobtrusively and on the whole so well.

Last Wednesday, for instance, the Queen lunched with the Lord Mayor of London to celebrate the 800th anniversary of the mayoralty. She took the occasion to make a thoughtful and serious speech. Read with any care it contained a serious warning, and to warn is one of the duties of a constitutional monarch. It was only quoted a couple of times in any newspaper; I heard about it by chance, and obtained a copy of the full speech from the Press Secretary.

What the Queen said was this: "The 30,000 people who come to work (in the City) are reaping the benefits of the reputation for honesty, integrity and fair-dealing which has been created by generations of their predecessors. That sort of reputation is beyond price ... Free and open markets may be the key to financial success, but if they are to operate fairly and honestly, someone has to write the rules and to see that they are rigidly enforced ... Rules and structures may be important, but much more important are the unwritten rules and the will to abide by them. In the end it is the loyalty and good sense of the citizens themselves that makes the whole system work."

It is the natural custom of the Queen to couch her warnings in language which will be acceptable to her audience. She is not entitled to be deliberately shocking and aggressive. Not for her the Edwina Currie approach. Perhaps for that reason most of the newspapers missed the significance of what she was saying.

Yet she was taking the occasion to address the issue of City ethics, and was warning the City of the danger that ethical standards might be slipping, or might have slipped. However politely it was put, it was a tough message to a Guildhall audience.

It is a message which has multiple warheads. First, there is the significance that it is the Queen who is saying it. She is not a City journalist, nor is she the Governor of the Bank of England. The Queen would only be raising the question in this way if she had become convinced that the supposed decline in City ethics was not merely a technical question but a national one.

The second warhead is the reminder that the City's business has been built on generations of trust. Trust is slowly won, but quickly lost. The City inherits a vast credit from its ancestors, not only in its business, but in the standards they created. Of course the old City had its rogues, but it was founded on partnership, on unlimited liability and on a code of personal honour. Its credit was earned by good faith.

The third warhead is the statement that regulation must be enforced "rigidly". It is an interesting word. The Queen is not, I think, implying that there ought to be a more bureaucratic type of regulation, of the Securities and Investments Board kind. She is saying that people must not be allowed to bend the rules. That is surely right. When one reads the Companies Acts, one realises that each clause has historically been written to prevent a particular abuse. If the clauses can be bent, the abuses can creep back through the gap — just as the abolition of the old Section 54 has again made it lawful for companies to be bought with their own money.

The biggest warhead came last. What worries people about the City is the suspicion that it will only obey written rules, that it has lost its sense of "unwritten rules and the will to abide by them".

The Queen is attacking a very common view of modern business ethics, that if the law does not forbid an action, it is fair to go ahead. This can be taken to justify all sorts of business malpractice and bad faith, false markets, oppression of the weak, meanness of spirit, dishonouring of assurances. "My word is my bond" becomes "Catch me if you can."

In fact, the City's business cannot be successfully conducted without an ethic which goes wider and deeper than the law can require. The basis of sound finance is not merely keeping inside the statutes, but honesty and honour.

After all, the City's whole existence depends on the acceptance of fiduciary responsibility; that involves an attitude not of bare legality but of the utmost striving to fulfil a trust. Such an attitude is all the more important because no businessman can guarantee always to succeed, or that all his investments will prosper.

The issue, of course, goes much wider than the City. There is a dual basis for every occupation. There is indeed the discipline of the bottom line. Every business has to be profitable if it is to survive and expand. Newspapers must win circulation. Politicians can keep power only if they win votes. Teachers must help their students to pass examinations; doctors must cure their patients when that is possible. The Royal Family must retain the loyalty of the nation.

Yet always there is a moral as well as a practical standard to be met, and the moral standard is also a condition of survival. The City will gradually wither away if it ceases to be seen as a trustworthy manager of other people's funds. Businesses which do not meet their moral commitment to their customers lose them. Newspapers cannot afford to be despised. Politicians who become cynical about the gullibility of the electorate — and electorates can be gullible — lose elections.

The Queen is right about the City — and her warning needs to be taken — but she is also giving a broader warning about national life. That needs to be taken as well.

Figure 17.7 Leader article on business ethics. (*Source: The Independent.*)

Questions

1. Why is the reputation for honesty, integrity and fair dealing in the City beyond price?

2. Consider whether it is fair to go ahead with a particular action if the law does not forbid it.

3. What is the danger of 'my word is my bond' becoming 'catch me if you can'?

4. Present your views of the implications for society if moral and ethical standards begin to wane.

Short answer questions

1. A derelict piece of land in an inner city area of high unemployment can be used:
    (a)   to build a leisure centre;
    (b)   to build a hypermarket;
    (c)   to build an industrial estate.

    The local planning committee decides to allow the land to be used for the development of the leisure centre.
    - List five private costs and five private benefits for the developer.
    - List five further costs and benefits to the local community.

2. Explain the difference between wealth and income. Illustrate your answers with examples of:
    (a)   private and national wealth;
    (b)   private and national income.

3. Explain how value would be added in the production of furniture. How would it be possible to increase the existing levels of value added at each stage?

4. List five major types of pollution. What measures could be taken to (a) prevent, (b) reduce one of these forms of pollution?

5. Explain how taxes could be used as a weapon to control pollution.

6. What are the main types of pressure groups? Outline the main aims of one pressure group.

7. Give an example of nationalized industry consumer council. What is its purpose?

8. What is meant by (a) renewable, (b) non-renewable resources? Give five examples of each.

9. What is meant by conservation? Describe three measures which can be employed by society to conserve a particular resource.

10. What is the purpose of cost–benefit analysis?

11. What are the costs and benefits of installing a new piece of equipment in your school or college?

12. What are the costs and benefits to (a) you personally, (b) society, of your journey into school or college?

13. Make a list of the externalities of some of your social activities.

14. The following table illustrates the costs and revenues of producing additional units of a product. The firm, whose costs and revenues are drawn up, produces chemicals. Some of the effluent is discharged into a local river at a social cost of £2 per tonne. Assuming that the firm is a profit maximizer:

(a) How much output would the firm produce if it did not have to pay for social costs?

(b) How much output would the firm produce if it were made to pay for social costs?

Output (tonnes)	Revenue per additional tonne produced	Cost per additional tonne produced	Pollution damage per additional tonne produced
1	20	10	2
2	20	12	2
3	20	14	2
4	20	16	2
5	20	18	2
6	20	20	2
7	20	22	2
8	20	24	2

15. What problems would be involved in making producers of acid rain responsible for the damage it causes?

16. In what ways can business be seen as being responsible for the creation of unemployment?

17. What are the major benefits of industrial activity for society?

18. What sorts of risks are attached to business activity?

19. Give an example of problems caused by the insufficient testing of products.

20. What is meant by the term 'recycling'? In what circumstances is 'recycling' economically viable?

Essays

1. Suppose that a new urban motorway is to be built around the centre of a large city. This centre contains both commercial development and housing for low- to middle-income families. They will be affected by the motorway.

   (a) List the costs and benefits of such a proposal.

   (b) How will the desirability of this project differ for the following groups:
       (i)   private motorists;
       (ii) commercial vehicle operators;
       (iii) shoppers;
       (iv) local residents?

2. Imagine you live in a semi-rural community which has been worried by the presence of a large chemical factory and its emission of toxic fumes which local farmers have suggested are leading to diseased cattle. Local people are also worried about the possible long-term effects on human health. You have been approached by various residents to help set up a local pressure group and fight a

campaign against the firm in question. What typically are the problems such a group might face and how might you try to overcome them?

3. To what extent should a government legislate to control business activity?

(Source: AEB.)

4. With reference to a local company investigate the costs and benefits of installing a new piece of machinery.

5. Should business be made accountable to the local community?

6. We face a world 'more polluted, less stable ecologically, more vulnerable to disruption than ever before'. What sorts of measures need to be taken to deal with this situation?

7. Compare and contrast the effectiveness of different measures for dealing with the problem of pollution.

8. What is cost–benefit analysis? Examine the strengths and weaknesses of such a method of analysing and evaluating business projects.

9. Is it possible to carry out the process of 'wealth creation' to the benefit of all members of a society?

10. Why is it more difficult to control pollution from several international sources than from a single nation source? What are the implications of this in the case of the destruction of the ozone layer?

Data response questions

1 Dioxin outlawed by manufacturers in search for safer nappies

At the beginning of 1989 the disposable nappy industry launched a clean-up campaign to outlaw dioxins added to the paper wadding filler by traditional chlorine bleaching. It was feared that these substances were being transferred to babies' skins.

The UK nappy maker Peaudouce and its rival Proctor and Gamble both announced that their fillers are being produced without the chlorine bleach process.

The Ministry of Agriculture is investigating dioxin contamination of food from bleached-paper wrappers. In early 1989 the pressure group Women's Environmental Network began lobbying for all sanitary and other soft tissue products to be made without chlorine bleaching.

Peaudouce signalled its change to a lightly bleached filler with harmless hydrogen peroxide as an environmentally friendly gesture to stop water pollution with toxic organochlorides, which is coming under increasingly strict government control, at its Swedish pulp mills. This new process also doubles the number of nappies obtained from each tree felled. A spokesperson for Peaudouce said that the new process reduced dioxins, a by-product of incineration and chemical processing in the pulp, to scarcely detectable levels. The product now contains less dioxin. It is not dioxin free. The company believes that there is no evidence that dioxins in nappy fillings are a danger. They cling tightly to the cellulose and are not likely to be given off by a product designed to absorb.

The Women's Environmental Network have welcomed the modified nappy, but added that dioxins were absorbed by fat and grease, making baby lotions a possible transmitter from the nappy to the skin.

The risk attached to the main dioxin, TCDD, is contentious. The US Environmental Protection Agency called it the most potent cancer-agent in animals it had tested and studies have linked low concentrations—which the chemical industry says are harmless—to human cancers and birth defects.

(*Source: The Independent*, January 1989.)

(a) List three groups mentioned in the extract with different interests in the production of disposable nappies. Outline the particular interest of each group and explain what you think that their perspective is likely to be.

(b) What are the costs and benefits to a disposable nappy producer of outside pressures?

(c) What are the costs and benefits to consumers of disposable nappies of outside pressures?

(d) Is it necessary to have governmental regulation of the production of disposable nappies?

(e) Why do you think that manufacturers have not totally removed dioxins from paper nappies? Is this a desirable state of affairs?

2   A local pollution incident

This question is based on an incident that happened in 1975 and all figures quoted are actual. This exercise can either be used as a written case study or as a role playing exercise; students could then be given only the factual information and arrive at their own verdict.

The Parties Involved:

Regional Water Authority (RWA) prosecutor
Solicitor acting for the firm
Magistrates: Chairman of the Panel and two others
Managing Director of XYZ Cloth Scourers
Day shift Foreman of XYZ Cloth Scourers

NB   Cloth scouring is the process by which dirt and grease that collects on the cloth as it is woven is removed.

Other interested parties are a representative of the local anglers and one could introduce local conservationists and the local government officer responsible for tourism. The latter two did not appear in the original case but the area concerned, in the South Pennines, does now try to market its scenic attractions. These centre around a not unpleasant mix of open countryside and working towns along with close proximity to the Peak National Park.

The Background

The stream involved is classified as Class 1.

Class 1 water has high amenity value, is a potable water supply and will support game fish, e.g. trout. Class 2 is potable after treatment, has moderate amenity value and will support coarse fish. Class 3 is polluted to the extent that fish are absent or only sporadically present. Class 4 waters are grossly polluted and likely to cause a nuisance.

In 1976 the water quality in the RWA area was approximately:

Class 1   82%
Class 2   6%

Class 3   4%
Class 4   8%

The RWA has a policy of maintaining the quality of those watercourses at present in Class 1 and 2 whilst improving those in Class 3 and eliminating all Class 4 watercourses. At the time, the area was subject to drought conditions and this aggravated the effect of the pollutant.

The Incident

Rather than risk damage to an export order worth £10,000 the textile firm deliberately contaminated an adjacent fresh water stream.

The Results

One hundred trout between three and ten inches in length were killed by the waste material which had the approximate strength of untreated sewage. The effluent was discharged for three hours and affected a one and a quarter mile length of the stream. The visual effect of the pollutant was apparent for two to three days afterwards.

The Firm's Decision

The firm normally disposed of this waste into the sewer by means of an electrically driven pump. A fault had developed in the starter for the motor that drove the pump and so had rendered it inoperative. Rather than risk damage to the cloth loaded on the machine the firm turned on a valve to allow the effluent to go directly into the stream. This occurred over the period 7.30 to 10.30 that day. The initial decision was taken by the foreman but was backed by managers at both the senior level and at the top of the firm. The firm normally carried spares for the pump and the motor but it did not have a spare starter in stock.

The solicitor for the firm pointed out that whilst there was no excuse, one could perhaps understand their actions given the nature and value of the order. The firm had from the outset admitted exactly what had happened.

The Firm's Individual Action

Arrangements were being made after the incident:
— to install an alternative pump at a cost of £700
— to restock the water with trout at a cost of £25

The Magistrate's Court Decision

A fine of £500 was imposed on the firm for the two charges of poisoning the water, at that time the maximum fine possible. The Court also awarded costs of £50.

(*Source:* Day and Hodgson, *Economics Journal*, March 1987.)

(a)   Did the firm make the right decision?
(b)   At the end of the day has anybody really suffered?

(c)   Would we have a different view of this incident if seen as:
   (i)   a single incident;
   (ii) part of a wider policy towards the reduction of pollution over the RWA
         catchment area?

Suggested reading

Baumol, W. and Blinder, A., *Economics, Environmental Policy and the Quality of Life*. Prentice-
   Hall, 1979.
Le Grand, J. and Robinson, R., *The Economics of Social Problems*. Macmillan, 1984.

18

Business studies in practice

Business and industrial studies is an area which attempts to link life after school with school and therefore provide a more practical academic experience for students whether they wish to go into higher education, the public sector or the private sector. Though preparation can be immense and provides a real challenge to students, the rewards can be enormous. We have tried to emphasize throughout the text that business studies is a dynamic area, and to make the subject relate to real activities through the persistent use of case studies. By doing so we hope that we have provided:

1. An understanding of the main forces underlying change in the business world.
2. An understanding of many of the problems that businesses face.
3. Opportunities for students to practice basic problem-solving skills.
4. An understanding of factors governing business decision making.

The purpose of this final chapter is firstly to place emphasis upon the interdependent nature of the business world by providing a number of case studies which link in various parts of the subject so that it can be seen as a whole. Looking at case studies covering specific areas of the syllabus is useful but does not show how business problems interrelate. The final part of this book, Linking business studies—Notes for teachers, provides useful suggestions and sources of information which can be used for reference by both student and teacher, together with ideas for activities to enhance courses.

Case Study 1—Micro Tech plc

Micro Tech plc is a progressive and very profitable UK engineering company producing high technology equipment for the aerospace industry. Its biggest customer is the military which takes over 80%, by value, of Micro Tech's products.

An important factor in the firm's success is its ability to modify quickly its standard products and to meet a customer's special needs. It can do this by virtue of a very competent design department well-equipped with up-to-date computer-aided design (CAD) facilities.

The company employs over 500 skilled and well-trained personnel in the manufacturing processes in which it is engaged. Labour turnover is very active and there are plenty of alternative employment opportunities for Micro Tech's employees. Replacement and recruitment are a headache to the company, and the performance of the personnel department is beginning to assume a position of key importance in the company's operations. The company is facing growing competition from a number of American firms and there is evidence of Government support for these companies. At the same time there has been a change of UK Government and the new Chancellor is clearly concerned to make savings and cut back on government expenditure. This is bound to affect the economic environment in which Micro Tech is operating.

Increased overseas competition and the new UK Government's expected austerity measures were the main subjects of Micro Tech's last Board Meeting. The Board decided that the company must diversify its range of products and extend its market opportunities. Such a policy would involve the company in a significant re-equipment programme and there is considerable doubt concerning the company's capacity to finance such an investment programme from within its own resources.

(i)   As Micro Tech's Personnel Manager, how would you set about tackling the company's labour turnover and recruitment problems?

(ii)   Identify the characteristics of the CAD which make the facilities so important for the particular needs of Micro Tech.

(iii)   What are the main mechanisms available to the UK Government to shape the environment within which companies such as Micro Tech operate?

(iv)   What financial alternatives are available to the Board which might facilitate a capital investment programme and allow Micro Tech to diversify its range of products?

On what basis might Micro Tech choose among these alternatives? Make your assumptions clear.

(*Source:* Oxford.)

Case Study 2—The Nowax story

Cross-country ski-ing has been in existence for thousands of years, but it has only been exploited commercially, with any success, for the last fifteen years or so.

The main reason for this boom was the technological breakthrough achieved in 1970 by the founders of a small Scottish company called Nowax. They discovered, patented, and marketed a revolutionary plastic base which did away with the necessity to wax the skis, thereby removing the main consumer resistence to the sport.

But there were other reasons why the 1970s proved to be the right time to promote cross-country ski-ing internationally, and especially in the United States which was, and remains, the largest single market.

Firstly, the sport was environmentally attractive. Downhill ski-ing requires large resorts which are capital intensive, expensive to run, and which are limited by geographical factors. Cross-country ski-ing, on the other hand, is inexpensive, and can be enjoyed almost anywhere.

Secondly, the oil price rises brought about by OPEC in 1972–3, and 1979, increased all the costs associated with downhill ski-ing, from getting to the ski areas to paying for lift tickets.

Thirdly, although leisure time was growing, real disposable incomes were not increasing at a rate sufficient to pay for a sport as expensive as downhill ski-ing. This was especially true as the world moved into recession after 1979. People were looking for a less expensive alternative, and cross country provided the answer.

For all these reasons both the sport, and Nowax, expanded rapidly.

By 1986 50% of Nowax's variable costs were the basic skis which they imported from Austria, at a cost in sterling of £12.50 per pair. At the same time their fixed overheads stood at £200 000 per annum.

In May 1987 the directors of Nowax met to discuss the disappointing profits of the previous year. But before they decided upon action they drew up a list of reasons which might explain the relative failure. These were:

(i)   The technological breakthrough which had formed the basic strength of the company had reached maturity in its life cycle. Competition had entered the market, making it much more price elastic, especially in the U.S., and any increase in the wholesale price of $52 could not be contemplated.

(ii) The price of oil had dropped back to a level which made it cheaper in real terms than it had been ten years before.

(iii) Despite holding back wages below the current rates of inflation administration costs were rising disproportionately.

(iv) The company had become increasingly reliant on the U.S. market, such that 75% of sales were now made there, while the remainder were in Europe.

(v)   Exchange rate fluctuations had made life difficult. Throughout 1986 the pound had exchanged for $1 30 in the United States, and 25 schillings in Austria. However the finance director had been advised that by December 1987 the U.K. government's policy on interest rates would strengthen the pound against the dollar, while the Austrian government were pressing for devaluation to boost their flagging tourist industry. The rates by the end of the year were likely to be £1 : $1 40 and £1 : 30 Sch.

(vi) The world recession had lifted, particularly in the U.S., where major tax cuts had been implemented and people had moved back to downhill ski-ing given their increased purchasing power.

Having set out the problems, it was time for the directors to try to find some answers.

Required

(a)   The text suggest 4 reasons why Nowax were successful in the early years. What do you think were the main elements in the marketing mix which ensured their success?   (10 marks)

(b)   In 1986 Nowax sold 5000 pairs of skis in Europe at an average sales value of £35 in sterling equivalent. Show how you arrive at your answer, calculate the company's profit for the year before Tax and Interest.   (10 marks)

(c)   Suggest some alternative policies which Nowax might employ to improve its trading position.   (10 marks)

(d)   To what extent does the Nowax study demonstrate that a firm's destiny often lies outside its own control?   (10 marks)

(Source: AEB.)

Case Study 3

The organization chart shown below is typical of the organizational approach adopted in many light engineering companies.

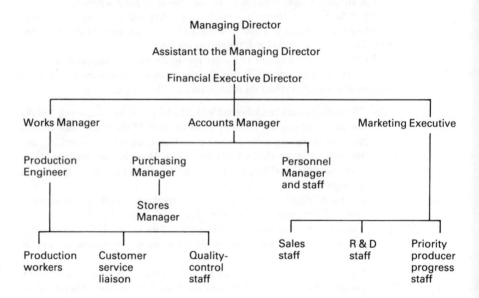

Figure 18.1 Organization chart of an engineering company.

Task 1

Discuss the problems which might arise from such an organizational structure and suggest an alternative, giving reasons for the changes.

Task 2

The Managing Director has been summoned to attend a senior management meeting at the parent company. The meeting will be concerned with evaluating the factors materially affecting the group's long term efficiency. The detailed programme lays great stress on the technique of value engineering. Accordingly the M.D. writes a memo to his Works Manager requesting a reminder to the main points on no more than one side of A4.

Assume that you are the Works Manager and produce the work called for by the Managing Director.

Task 3

The Purchasing Manager is preparing a briefing for the induction of some new members of staff about to join his department. He decides to include in his brief the main objectives of the purchasing department and the major operations with which it is involved. Assume that you are the Purchasing Manager and produce a skeleton draft of the purchasing objectives and operations you would wish to cover in your briefing to the new staff.

Task 4

The Company is going through a major exercise of revising and re-writing its job descriptions. Outline the main responsibilities that you would expect to see covered in the Production Engineer's job description. Base the job description on the alternative structure you devised in Task 1.

(Source: Oxford.)

Case Study 4—High Garth Garden Equipment Limited

High Garth Garden Equipment Limited is a small manufacturing company producing and selling a range of garden tools. It has come to the attention of management that there is a gap in the market relating to hedge clippers. One of the younger employees, Jane Dean, has suggested that there may be an opportunity to exploit the need for a rotary hedge clipper and sell it as a top of the range product.

The Board of Directors finds the idea appealing and is in the process of conducting some market research to assess the viability of the idea. Not only would the survey identify demand, it would also identify physical characteristics and features desired by customers, help with the pricing process and provide a knowledge of distribution channels. Much of this information would help in the drawing up of technical specifications and the installation of the necessary equipment.

In the event of going ahead with this project, the Board is concerned that a prototype should be built and tested as soon as possible. It suspects that similar developments are being looked at by competitors and is also aware that if its company is first to produce a quality product on to the market, current factory capacity may have to be expanded. In addition, the Board is looking at the best means of promoting and advertising the product.

The sales and production team have made an initial estimate of sales for the first year which is independent of the market survey. They suggest a range of between 600 and 1000 units. The Sales Director expects that, if the new product were made, the selling price per unit would be £100 and the variable distribution cost would be £3 per unit. The Production Manager estimates the material cost to be £27 per unit, and that each hedge clipper will require 6 hours' labour. Factory workers receive a basic wage of £5 per hour. New machinery will have to be purchased costing £5000. This is expected to last five years with no scrap value. Fixed factory overheads per annum would be as follows:

	£
Rent and rates	2000
Heat and light	1000
Insurance	100
General expenses	3900

The Company Secretary anticipates that extra paperwork will require a part-time clerical worker at £2000 per annum.

Apart from the variable distribution cost, the only selling cost relating to this product will be advertising. There are two possibilities. One is a local campaign, the total cost of which would be £10 000, and the other is a national and local campaign which would cost £20 000.

Though wary about investing too much too soon on this product, High Garth Garden Equipment Limited is confident of a bright future for rotary hedge clippers.

Questions

1. As High Garth Garden Equipment Limited is only likely to be involved in producing one type of hedge clipper, explain why producing the top of the range model would be an example of concentrated marketing.
2. Briefly advise on the most appropriate and cost-effective strategies for collecting information on this type of product.
3. Explain why quantitative analysis is used to interpret data from market research and suggest two possible methods of presenting consumer data from research conducted in the market for rotary hedge clippers.
4. Comment briefly upon the advisability of expanding factory capacity during a period of rising interest rates.
5. Suggest how an effective advertising campaign capable of reaching the right target group for rotary hedge clippers could be cheap in relation to the extra sales made.
6. Comment upon
    (a) the dangers of putting an insufficiently tested product on the market;
    (b) the social costs and benefits of expanding current factory capacity.
7. Management would like to know the budgeted outcomes of sales of 600 units and 1000 units when the advertising costs are:
    (a) £10 000
    (b) £20 000
    In case the projected figures are not realized management would also like to know the break-even point with regard to sales at each level of advertising. Prepare this information for management use.

Case Study 5—ICI Annual Report

Paints

The paints business achieved record sales and profits in 1987. With manufacturing facilities in 27 countries and direct sales to another 50, ICI is the world's

largest supplier of paints and specialist coatings. In addition, ICI's paint technology is licensed in a further 12 markets. Demand was generally strong in Europe,
North America, Australasia, India and Pakistan and there were encouraging gains
in SE Asia. This wide production and distribution network is dedicated to the
highest level of customer service throughout the world in the key areas of decorative and automotive paints, packaging, and high performance industrial coatings.

The incorporation of the Glidden Company's paint interests into ICI's worldwide paint operations has been accomplished successfully. The addition of a full
year's sales by the Glidden Company in the USA was a major factor in the 66 per
cent rise in paints turnover. Also, the anticipated benefits from the acquisition are
already making a significant contribution to research and development, production and marketing. In the decorative paint sector, there were further advances in
European markets. 'Dulux' maintained its status as the leading brand in the UK
and ICI's innovative solid emulsion is creating a new premium market in France
and West Germany. In North America, the Glidden range of 'Spred' products
for D-I-Y and professionally-applied gloss and emulsion made further market
share advances. In the can coatings markets for food and beverage cans ICI and
Glidden, as the leading international suppliers, offer an unequalled range of technologies. ICI also meets the demanding performance specifications of automotive
companies in Europe, Australasia, Canada, India, Pakistan and the Far East.
'Aquabase', the first water-based basecoat used commercially by automotive
companies, is attracting a growing number of actual and potential users. ICI
Autocolor vehicle refinish coatings made more important advances into new
markets in 1987.

Modern surface finishes have to meet demands for extremely high levels of
resistance to weathering, fading, corrosion and mechanical damage. Increasingly,
powder and coil coatings are being used to satisfy these exacting standards. The
combination of ICI and Glidden formulations and research and development
capability is proving to be an excellent base from which to take advantage of the
rapid growth in the use of these application techniques.

CFCs

The business also manufactures a range of chlorofluorocarbons (CFCs) which in
1987 represented around 7 per cent of General Chemicals' turnover. These
materials have valuable characteristics that include very low toxicity and high
chemical stability which have made them ideal for use in refrigeration and air
conditioning plants, in plastic foams and insulation, as cleaning agents in the electronics industry and as aerosol propellants. Since the early 1970s there have been
concerns that some of these materials, because of their great stability, would
eventually penetrate to the upper atmosphere and lead to the destruction of the
stratospheric ozone layer which performs an important role in protecting the
Earth from ultra-violet radiation. Despite extensive scientific study, to which ICI
has contributed, it has still not proved possible to confirm the exact part the
CFCs play in the ozone layer because of the extreme complexity of the physical
and chemical reactions taking place in the stratosphere. In the absence of definite
conclusions, ICI has supported the need for precautionary measures to be taken
on a global basis to limit the production and use of CFCs. In September 1987, a
Protocol was agreed in Montreal under the auspices of the United Nations Environment Programme and was signed by all major CFC manufacturing nations,

including the UK. ICI welcomes the Protocol agreement, although the effect will be to reduce production and use of the main CFCs by up to 50 per cent over the next decade.

ICI is investing significant sums of money in research into and development of ozone compatibile fluorocarbons intended to replace existing CFCs in most applications. All the necessary resource has been committed to make these alternatives available at the earliest possible opportunity; nevertheless the need for rigorous toxicological testing before product launch will inevitably delay full commercialization by several years.

The US Economy

The US economy produced another year of modest growth, but ended nervously with mixed signals for the future. Reduction of budget and trade deficits has been the major concern, together with the impact any remedial action would have on interest rates, the dollar and inflation. The dollar weakened throughout the year, narrowing real trade deficits. Despite increases in energy costs, inflation rates were contained, partly due to relative stability in interest rates.

Employment in the UK

Employee involvement

Great emphasis continues to be placed on informal consultation at work group level and open management style, with frequent discusson about day-to-day operations and the technical, financial and market factors affecting each business.

In the UK, this is backed by a three-tier system for formal consultation based on workplace representation and led by the senior manager responsible at Works or Department level, the Chief Executive at Business Unit level and the ICI Chairman at meetings held centrally each year with monthly and weekly staff representatives. There are two representative Central Business and Investment Committees, which are chaired by an Executive Director and meet at least twice a year. These groups are supported by similar committees in Business Units. Their aim is to discuss business prospects and plans in greater depth than is possible in larger meetings.

In the UK, the Company has operated a Profit-Sharing Scheme since 1954 and a Savings-Related Share Option Scheme since 1980.

Equal opportunities

The Company's policy and practice require that entry into the Company, and progression within it, will be determined solely by personal merit and the application of criteria which are related to the effective performance of the job and the needs of the business.

ICI in the community

The Group seeks to behave as a responsible member of the many local communities in which it operates, supporting a myriad of activities where a worthwhile contribution can be made. Although these are impossible to list in detail, they include: charitable donations, support for education (particularly the teaching of science and technology), the funding of academic research, initiatives to support small business development, the arts, sport, and the encouragement of Group employees to take on leadership roles in their respective communities.

Extracts from a recent ICI Annual Report.

Questions

1. Identify economies of scale obtained by ICI after the acquisition of Glidden and explain how these will affect
   (a) long run average costs;
   (b) the future of the paint industry.
2. The first extract states that 'This wide production and distribution network is dedicated to the highest level of customer service throughout the world in the key areas of decorative and automotive paints, packaging, and high performance industrial coatings.' Suggest two ways in which ICI could broaden its distribution network.
3. Outline the social costs and benefits of using chlorofluorocarbons. Comment on the progress being made to overcome damage to the ozone layer by the use of CFCs.
4. Read the extract which refers to the US economy. Explain what is meant by:
   (a) 'modest growth';
   (b) 'the dollar weakened throughout the year, narrowing real trade deficits';
   (c) 'inflation rates were contained, partly due to relative stability in interest rates'.
   Why does the extract about the US economy appear in an ICI annual report?
5. Comment upon the ICI techniques of informal management with an open management style. Outline the benefits and pitfalls of such a system.
6. Why do many organizations have an equal opportunities policy? Does such a policy lead to conflict or harmony?
7. What are the benefits to (a) large organizations and (b) communities, of companies investing in their neighbourhood? To what extent does this reflect an acceptance of responsibility to do so?
8. Explain why such a diversity of information appears in an annual report.

Case Study 6—The Business 1000

Study the details on Fig. 18.2 overleaf, and answer the questions that follow it.

THE BUSINESS 1000

RANK	PREV YEAR	COMPANY (ACTIVITY)	SALES £'000s CURRENT YEAR	PREVIOUS YEAR	CHANGE %	PRETAX PROFIT £'000s	RANK
1	1	British Petroleum (Oil & gas exploration & products) ▲	27,578,032	27,171,028	1.5	2,387,004	1
2	2	Electricity Council (Electricity utility)	11,335,445	11,118,600	2.0	511,499	13
3	3	ICI (Chemicals, plastics, paints)	11,123,012	10,136,012	9.7	1,312,001	4
4	4	British Telecom (Telecommunications utility)	10,157,185	9,339,010	8.8	2,285,741	2
5	5	BAT Industries (Conglomerate) ▲	7,522,009	9,006,010	−16.5	1,394,001	3
6	6	British Gas (Gas utility)	7,343,889	7,610,009	−3.5	1,251,573	5
7	15	Hanson (Conglomerate)	6,682,008	4,312,006	55.0	741,001	9
8	9	Grand Metropolitan (Hotels, food, drink, leisure)	5,705,501	5,291,301	7.8	456,100	16
9	10	General Electric Company (Engineering)	5,537,331	5,247,301	5.5	706,066	10
10	8	Unilever (Consumer products, food)▲	5,428,007	5,949,008	−8.8	460,000	15
11	14	Ford Motor Company (Motor manufacture)	5,211,007	4,374,006	19.1	317,000	25
12	11	Dalgety (Food, agriculture)	5,003,001	4,909,801	1.9	92,500	108
13	17	Dee Corporation (Retailing)	4,851,894	4,019,512	20.7	192,728	49
14	12	Shell UK (Oil & gas exploration, oil products)	4,851,006	4,727,006	2.6	1,093,001	6
15	20	J Sainsbury (Retailing)	4,804,665	3,867,697	24.2	309,247	26
16	16	Marks & Spencer (Retailing)	4,565,094	4,220,801	8.2	500,329	14
17	13	British Coal (Mining)	4,387,026	4,513,372	−2.8	−540,481	1,000
18	18	BTR (Consumer, building & industrial products)	4,149,200	3,986,435	4.1	590,300	12
19	21	Tesco (Retailing) ▲	4,130,416	3,534,892	16.8	231,234	36
20	29	British Aerospace (Defence, space equipment, aircraft)	4,075,000	3,137,000	29.9	−159,000	997
21	22	British Steel (Steel)	4,049,434	3,470,512	16.7	412,224	19
22	43	Saatchi & Saatchi (Advertising)	3,954,200	2,087,000	89.5	124,100	86
23	24	Gallaher (Tobacco, optics & office products)	3,886,700	3,404,700	14.2	169,700	61
24	26	British Airways (Air transport) ▲	3,745,742	3,263,004	14.8	227,377	37
25	32	Allied Lyons (Hotels, catering, beverages)	3,596,955	3,020,842	19.1	437,398	17
26	7	Esso UK (Oil & gas exploration, oil products)	3,546,200	6,673,401	−46.9	936,900	7
27	27	The Post Office (Postal services)	3,482,842	3,256,422	7.0	155,125	71
28	25	RTZ Corporation (Mining, metals, engineering)	3,397,100	3,343,900	1.6	594,300	11
29	23	Rover Group (Motor manufacture)	3,096,400	3,412,000	−9.2	−21,600	989
30	31	IBM United Kingdom Holdings (Computer manufacture)	3,077,900	3,042,800	1.2	420,800	18
31	19	S & W Berisford (Sugar, commodities) ▲	3,055,055	3,928,473	−22.2	87,483	113
32	28	Thorn EMI (Electronics)	3,045,656	3,203,200	−4.9	224,684	38
33	66	Hillsdown Holdings (Food, timber, travel)	3,038,600	1,702,600	78.5	110,300	94
34	34	Lonrho (Conglomerate)	3,013,900	2,651,000	13.7	200,200	48
35	48	P & O (Shipping, property, construction)	2,920,200	1,981,700	47.4	274,700	29
36	38	Boots Company (Chemists, retailing)	2,689,731	2,351,700	14.4	266,470	30
37	36	Asda Group (Retailing) ▲	2,674,427	2,475,900	8.0	192,527	50
38	88	Engelhard (Precious metals, refining)	2,654,456	1,323,527	100.6	10,145	456
39	44	Bass (Brewing, betting, hotels, holidays)	2,585,000	2,082,300	24.1	365,000	22
40	37	British Railways Board (Rail services)	2,573,350	2,397,100	7.4	47,171	173
41	33	Beecham Group (Pharmaceuticals, toiletries)	2,473,424	2,769,500	−10.7	405,389	21
42	40	Courtaulds (Textiles, chemicals, paints)	2,414,585	2,261,900	6.8	219,997	40
43	30	Texaco (Oil & gas exploration, oil products)	2,378,143	3,114,629	−23.6	−40,950	995
44	39	Great Universal Stores (Retailing, mail order)	2,366,100	2,290,900	3.3	345,000	24
45	35	Sears (Retailing) ▲	2,359,700	2,480,300	−4.9	245,700	33
46	42	Pilkington Brothers (Glass)	2,326,526	2,103,400	10.6	301,474	27
47	50	BICC (Cables, engineering, construction)	2,250,003	1,968,000	14.3	128,000	85
48	41	Associated British Foods (Food, catering)	2,235,256	2,207,949	1.2	206,997	45
49	54	Rank Xerox (Photocopiers)	2,218,600	1,925,700	15.2	223,000	39
50	56	Woolworth Holdings (Retailing) ▲	2,177,967	1,833,022	18.8	177,486	57

▲See note on page 65

Figure 18.2 Details of top British companies. (*Source: The Business 1000.*)

Questions

1. Comment upon whether ranking by sales is the most appropriate method of assessing company size.

2. Choose *two* companies from the oil industry and *two* from retailing. Make comparisons between companies in each pair and then comment on the differences between each industry.

3. Look at the results of industries privatized over recent years and compare their performance to industries which have remained under public ownership. Is it fair to make such comparisons? Comment upon your findings and refer your arguments to the privatization debate.

4. What is meant by 'conglomerate'? Outline the benefits which exist for companies which develop into this type of organization.

5. List other types of information which could provide a fuller understanding of the comparisons made of companies shown in Fig. 18.2.

6. Choose one company from the top 50. Find out the address of its registered offices and then send a letter asking for a copy of its most recent annual report. Comment upon changes that have taken place since The Business 1000 table (Fig. 18.2) was produced. Write a report outlining the company's most recent developments and future prospects.

7. Survey the present economic climate and comment upon the effect that recent economic indicators might have upon the nation's largest companies.

8. Changes in sales per employee might take place as a result of a number of factors. List the most likely causes.

Case Study 7—Boscom Limited

Two years ago Peter Roberts, a married man of 43 with two children, suddenly found himself faced with the prospect of redundancy. For the last 15 years he had worked for Schultz, a large multinational firm manufacturing electrical components for the 'white goods' industry. Peter had originally been employed as a design draughtsman and was now production manager. Schultz had made the decision to trim its UK operations and to concentrate its main activities on its more profitable operations in Germany where the emphasis was on the manufacture of electrical components for cars.

Schultz was placed in the embarrassing position of letting down long-standing customers, selling off UK assets and dismissing the workforce. It circulated its employees accordingly.

Peter was an enterprising person and saw this as an opportunity to grasp at something he had always wanted to do and start up a business of his own. He made an approach to a number of employees at Shultz whom he trusted and whose skills he respected and they put together a plan to set up in business on their own. They approached Schultz' senior management and presented them with their scheme which involved taking over existing customer contracts and buying the firm's machinery and equipment.

They argued that although Schultz had found this area of its operations unprofitable, a smaller firm with fewer overheads and more efficient use of labour and equipment could be successful. Schultz was delighted at being given a workable solution to its problems, and not only sold the machinery to the men at a reasonable price, but cooperated with them throughout the transfer of ownership.

Boscom Limited was set up as a private limited company in a small factory unit within 300 yards of the old premises. Though on a significantly smaller scale than the previous organization, it employs over half of the previous workforce. During its first year it had difficulty managing its working capital due mainly to an excessive debt collection period but using the payback method all of the formation expenses will have been paid by the end of year 3. The quality of electrical components has been improved and, over recent months, export houses have contacted Boscom and suggested that there is a market for these types of electrical components in the Middle East. Peter and his colleagues anticipate considerable growth in the market over the next few years and with careful planning their future seems bright.

Questions

1. Explain why a large multinational organization such as Schultz might have wished to trim its UK operations and why a smaller organization might be able to make existing UK operations more profitable.
2. Consider the advantages to Boscom Limited of joining the Unlisted Securities Market and critically examine the methods through which the company could achieve growth.
3. Describe the likely objectives Boscom could use to assess its own performance.
4. Consider how growth for Boscom Limited could:
   (a) affect the career prospects of staff;
   (b) affect working conditions.
5. If Boscom Limited decides to diversify in order to expand, outline the sequence of events you could envisage to lead to the successful launching of an alternative product.
6. Discuss the effects of high interest rates and an overvalued pound on Boscom's export competitiveness.
7. Point out the dangers of insufficient working capital. How might Boscom Limited reduce the period of the cash cycle?

8. Explain why the payback method is often criticized as a method of investment appraisal and comment upon the benefits of alternative methods.

9. Explain why quality control is not just a system designed to improve quality but designed to do so at a cost-effective level.

10. As Boscom Limited gets larger, outline the benefits they would achieve from moving from batch to flow production.

Suggested reading

Edge, A. and Coleman, D., *The Guide to Case Analysis and Reporting*. Systems Logistics, 1986.

Linking business studies—Notes for teachers

Perhaps the best form of link for any business studies course is one built up with a local organization which allows *regular student visits* and is also happy to provide *work experience* placements. Both project (e.g. as required by Cambridge) and written case study (e.g. as required by Oxford) requirements of certain examining boards can be met when students establish contacts on work placements and therefore have both the stimulation and close contact with a company so that they can research and develop ideas at first hand. We have deliberately avoided suggesting project titles, because to do so would have taken away the creative element of students choosing titles that: (a) meet their own needs, and (b) are relative to the organization with which they have contact. Creative investigation may be related to something that has recently happened, a problem that needs to be analysed, a change within or external to a business, or it may be based on the future. Comprehensive advice on the preparation of practical projects and their requirements is provided for students by the respective examination boards.

One way in which young people can learn about a particular line of work is through *work shadowing*. This involves a student 'keeping in step' with an employee, observing the tasks performed and learning about the employee's role. In this way the employee acts as a 'work guide' and the student attempts to place himself or herself in the employee's shoes in order to see the world of work through an employee's eyes. Work shadowing is therefore different from work experience in which a student is given a job of his or her own to do. The 'helping-out' a student provides while work shadowing is a way of helping the student to understand the employee's work.

Another area of link and one which is almost as good as first-hand experience is to invite *visiting speakers* into school or college. Though it is always possible to use your contacts or the speaker services of organizations such as the Banking Information Service, it is often better to integrate visits into a comprehensive programme so that it becomes a course covering a spread of areas. Understanding Industry does this by inviting senior speakers from the world of business and industry to visit schools to talk about a variety of carefully identified business areas such as human relations, marketing and management. Visits involve eight sessions and, though it is more common to organize sessions on a weekly basis, a particularly exciting format is to condense all of the UI speakers for a course into a two-day conference. UI therefore aims to:

- Provide 16–19-year-old students staying on in education with a better understanding of industry and commerce.
- Operate in the school/college timetable.
- Work with teachers and lecturers to develop UI as a curriculum resource.
- Involve business people in their local schools and colleges as part of a managed programme.

Through its eight-part courses, Understanding Industry demonstrates to those staying on in education—the future opinion formers and business leaders—how a company operates, and why successful companies are so necessary in the creation of the nation's wealth. As a resource to support a business studies course it is useful to have the opportunity to ask pertinent questions of people who have both specialized and become successful in their particular field.

A particularly popular activity which enables students to appreciate the difficulties involved in integrating the decision-making process as well as the hard work necessary to succeed in business, is to set up some form of *mini-company*. There are a variety of kits on the market and on a number of occasions in recent years there have been sponsored competitions designed to encourage students to produce a business plan and then to go through the motions of setting up a company. Young Enterprise is an organization providing the mechanism by which schools and colleges can set up their own business. Their literature states that:

> Young Enterprise offers a truly exciting opportunity to students aged 15–19. We provide a 'Company Kit' which includes all the paperwork and guidance needed to set up a business. This practical business education helps students to recognise and develop their skills and abilities and helps bridge the gap between school and work. The student can get a better understanding of how a business works and how wealth is created in what amounts to a real business situation. Students will find this opportunity invaluable when it comes to choosing their own career and understanding how work and the business world can be fun. The Young Enterprise company kit involves real money, real products developed by the students and, with the aid of business advisors, will help the students to realise marketing, sales, management and hopefully profit. The results achieved and the business experience gained will be the property of the students alone and relate to their learning needs in school and for life.

The real benefit of Young Enterprise and the setting up of mini-companies is the creation of the ability to put ideas into action to see if they work and to develop practical business skills in real situations.

Another useful form of simulation is that of the *business game*. One of the first of these was, of course, Monopoly in which the combination of dice and strategy determined success. The benefit of business games is that they provide experiments which enable business behaviour to be better understood. Students develop strategies and build up their problem-solving skills, often with an element of competition and tend to enjoy doing so. Business games vary considerably in nature. Some are just macro-economic models, others involve a broad spectrum of interacting business areas such as marketing, purchasing, finance and so on, and many appear as computer models.

Games have several advantages:

- They provide an alternative approach to fulfil learning objectives.
- They provide a vehicle for assessment.
- They provide an opportunity to use alternative resources such as computers.
- They can enable group work to take place.
- They are often surprisingly easy to use.

It is important that with business games teachers carefully brief students before-hand so that they understand the purpose of the exercise and have a good idea of both the principles and the rules involved. It is just as essential that students are de-briefed after the game so that they can identify the principles covered. Games are not a sub-stitute for teaching but do provide a valuable additional technique of putting over principles. It is always useful to try and test a game beforehand to ensure that poten-tial problems are taken into account.

Wherever possible try to bring *written materials* into the classroom. Companies publish a tremendous range of information, much of which is for educational pur-poses. Understanding British Industry produces a directory of teaching materials from industry and commerce which can be used in the classroom. Written materials from companies can add a realistic element to classroom discussion and can often be used as a base for the writing of case studies.

Finally, business studies is an area of constant change. By its very nature it is topi-cal and covers events which appear on a daily basis on both business and headline pages in newspapers, on radio, television and weekly in magazines such as *The Economist*. Keeping up to date with events and using recently published materials enables students to use real world examples in their work and to apply theories to actual situations.

Making this subject practical helps to create realism, generate interest, encourage discussion and ultimately provide a better understanding.

Useful addresses

British Institute of Management (Education liaison)
Management House
Cottingham Road
Corby
Northants
NN17 1TT

Careers Research and Advisory Centre (CRAC)
Bateman Street
Cambridge CB2 1LZ

CRAC provides in-service training resources for teachers, national link conferences, insight into industry activities for pupils and resource materials for learning about jobs, careers, science and technology and the world of work.

Centre for Industrial Studies
1 Church Street
Grantham
Lincolnshire
NG31 6RR

The CIS houses a range of organizations involved in education industry work, produces curriculum development materials and runs INSET activities for teachers.

Confederation of British Industry
Centre Point
103 New Oxford Street
London
WC1A 1DU

Industrial Society
3 Charlton House Terrace
London
SW1Y 5DG

The Industrial Society aims to teach companies how to get their message across to their employees and to the community and to promote closer links between schools and industry.

ORT Trust
ORT House
3 Sumpter Close
Finchley Road
London
NW3 5HR

The ORT Trust is committed to assisting teachers to prepare young people to take their place in a modern technological society.

School Curriculum Industry Partnership (SCIP)
45 Notting Hill Gate
London
W11 3JB

SCIP is a national organization supporting the development of education industry work in schools.

Trades Union Congress
Congress House
Great Russell Street
London
WC1B 3LS

The TUC produces teaching materials and information and encourages school links.

Understanding British Industry
Sun Alliance House
New Inn Hall Street
Oxford
OX1 2QE

As well as providing a free directory of teaching materials UBI provides industry-related in-service training for teachers, secondments to industry and information about work in this field, covering all organizations.

Understanding Industry
91 Waterloo Road
London
SE1 8XP

Young Enterprise
Ewert Place
Summertown
Oxford
OX2 7BZ

Financial information

Banking Information Service
10 Lombard Street
London
EC3V 9AT

Bank of England
Public Liaison Group
Treadneedle Street
London
EC2R 8AH

Bank of Scotland
Public Affairs Department
The Mound
Edinburgh
EH1 1HZ

Barclays Bank PLC
Public Relations Department
54 Lombard Street
London
EC3P 3AH

Building Societies Association
3 Saville Row
London
W1X 1AF

Halifax Building Society
PO Box 60
Trinity Road
Halifax
West Yorkshire
HX1 2RG

Inland Revenue Education Service
PO Box 10
Wetherby
West Yorkshire
LS23 7EH

Lloyds Bank PLC
Enquiry Unit
Corporate Communications Division
Hay's Lane House
1 Hay's Lane
London
SE1 2HN

Midland Bank PLC
Griffin House
41 Silver Street Head
Sheffield
S1 3GG

National Westminster Bank PLC
National House
14 Moorgate
London
EC2R 6BS

TSB England and Wales PLC
PO Box 99
St Mary's Court
100 Lower Thames Street
London
EC3R 6AQ

Statistical information

Central Statistical Office
Great George Street
London
SW1P 3AQ

Department of Trade and Industry
Business Statistics Office Library
Room 1001
Government Buildings
Cardiff Road
Newport
Gwent
NP9 1XG

HMSO
St Crispins
Duke Street
Norwich
NR3 1PD

Office of Population Censuses and Surveys
OPCS Information Branch
St Catherine's House
10 Kingsway
London
WC2B 6JP

Media

Advertising Association
Abford House
15 Wilton Road
London
SW1V 1NJ

Advertising Standards Authority
Brook House
2–16 Torrington Place
London
WC1E 7HN

British Broadcasting Corporation
Broadcasting House
Portland Place
London
WLA 1AA

Independent Broadcasting Authority
70 Brompton Road
London
SW3 1EY

Others

Association of British Insurers
Aldermary House
Queen Street
London
EC4N 1TT

Baltic Exchange
14–20 St Mary Avenue
London
EC3 8BU

British Standards Institution
2 Park Street
London
W1A 2BS

Centre for World Development Education
Regent's College
Inner Circle
Regent's Park
London
NN1 4NS

City Communications Centre
6th Floor
Dunster House
37 Mincing Lane
London
EC3R 7BQ

Council for Environmental Education
School of Education
University of Reading
London Road
Reading
R61 5AQ

Design Council
28 Haymarket
London
SW1Y 4SU

Economic Awareness Teacher Training Programme
Department of Education
University of Manchester
Oxford Road
Manchester
M13 9PL

Lloyds of London
Lime Street
London
EC3M 7HA

Marketing Week
St Giles House
50 Poland Street
London
W1V 4AX

Office of Fair Trading
Field House
15–25 Bream's Buildings
London
EC4A 1PR

Personnel Today
Quadrant House
The Quadrant
Sutton
Surrey
SM2 5AS

Shell Education Service
Shell UK Ltd
Shell Mex House
The Strand
London
WC2R 0DX

Small Firms Service
Department of Employment
Steel House
Tothill Street
London
SW1H 9HF

Stock Exchange
Old Broad Street
London
EC2N 1HP

Index